PHYSICS for Scientists and Engineers 2

Third Edition

W. Bauer
G. D. Westfall
Michigan State University

Boston Burr Ridge, IL Dubuque, IA New York San Francisco St. Louis
Bangkok Bogotá Caracas Lisbon London Madrid
Mexico City Milan New Delhi Seoul Singapore Sydney Taipei Toronto

The McGraw·Hill Companies

Physics for Scientists and Engineers 2
Third Edition

1 2 3 4 5 6 7 8 9 0 DIG DIG 0 9 8 7

ISBN 13: 978-0-07-723150-7
ISBN-10: 0-07-723150-3

Custom Publishing Specialist: James Doepke
Production Editor: Susan Culbertson
Printer/Binder: Digital Impressions

Table of Contents

Chapter 21. Electrostatics

Figure 21.1: Lightning strikes over Seattle.

What we will learn

- Electricity and magnetism together make up electromagnetism, one of the four fundamental forces of nature.
- Electric charge is quantized, meaning that it only comes in integral multiples of a minimum quantity. Electric charge is conserved.
- Most materials around us are electrically neutral.
- The electron is an elementary particle and its charge is the smallest observable quantum of electric charge.

- Like charges repel and unlike charges attract.
- The force between two stationary electric charges is proportional to the product of the charges and varies as the inverse square of the distance between the two charges.
- Electric current is almost always created by the movement of electrons. (Heavy, charged ions can also move and constitute a current.)
- Insulators conduct electricity poorly or not at all.
- Conductors conduct electricity well but not perfectly, as there are energy losses.
- Superconductors conduct electricity perfectly.

21.1. Electromagnetism

In ancient civilizations there was perhaps no greater mystery than that of electricity, primarily associated with lightning strikes, such as the ones depicted in Figure 21.1. The destructive force inherent in this phenomenon, which could set objects on fire and kill people and animals, seemed godlike. The ancient Greeks, for example, believed Zeus, father of the gods, to have the ability to throw lightning bolts. The Germanic tribes believed similar things of the god Thor, and the Romans of the god Jupiter. Characteristically, the ability to cause lightning belonged to the god at the top of the hierarchy.

The ancient Greeks knew that if one rubbed a piece of amber with a piece of fur, one could attract small, light objects with the amber. We now know that the rubbing of amber with a cloth transfers negatively charged particles called electrons from the cloth to the amber. The words electron and electricity derive from the Greek word for amber, which is *ηλεκτρινος*. The early Greeks and others also knew about naturally occurring magnetic objects called lodestones that were found in deposits of magnetite, a mineral consisting of iron oxide. The objects were used to construct compasses as early as 300 BC. Lightning, as depicted in Figure 21.1, consists of a flow of electrons.

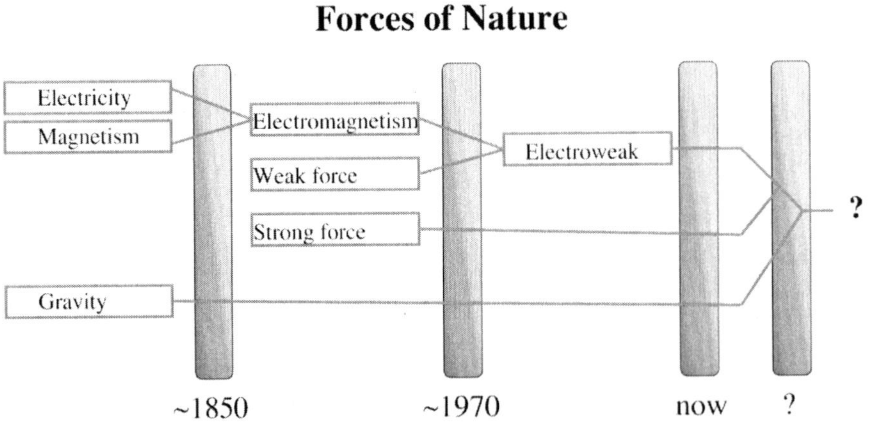

Figure 21.2: The quest for the unification of all fundamental forces.

However, the relationship between electricity and magnetism was not understood until the middle of the 19th century. In the following chapters, we will show how one can unify electricity and magnetism into one common framework called electromagnetism. However, unifying the forces does not stop there. During the early part of the 20th century two more fundamental forces were discovered, the "weak" force that is at play in beta decay (in which an electron and a neutrino are spontaneously emitted from certain types of nuclei), and the "strong" force that acts inside the atomic nucleus. We will study these forces in more detail in chapter 39 on particle physics. Now we would like to point out that in our current understanding, the electromagnetic and weak forces can be understood as two aspects of the "electroweak" force, see Figure 21.2.

For the phenomena that we will discuss in the following chapters this electroweak unification has no influence, but becomes important in the highest energy particle collisions. Because the energy scale for the electroweak unification is so high, many textbooks speak of four fundamental forces: gravitational, electromagnetic, weak, and strong forces.

Today a large number of physicists believe that the electroweak and the strong forces can also be unified, i.e. described in one common framework. There are theories on how to accomplish this task, but until now, any experimental evidence is missing. Interestingly, the force that has been known longer than any of the other forces, gravity, seems to be hardest to shoehorn into a common unified picture with all other forces. Quantum gravity and string theory are two current cutting-edge lines of physics research in which theorists are attempting to construct just this unification. They are mainly guided by symmetry principles and the conviction that nature must be elegant and simple.

We will return to these considerations. They are mentioned here to chart a general course that our investigations will follow for you. Before we can get there, we have to study the basics. In the present chapter, we will consider the electric charge, how materials react to electric charges, static electricity and the forces resulting from electric charges. The chapter is called "electrostatics", because for now we will consider only cases where charges stay in place.

21.2. Electric Charge

When we walk across a carpet on a dry winter day we often notice that we create a spark when we touch a metal doorknob. The process that causes this sparking is called charging. We now know that this charging consists of moving negatively charged particles, electrons, from the atoms and molecules of the material of the carpet to the soles of our shoes. This charge can move relatively easily through our body, including our hands. The built-up electric charge discharges through the metal of the doorknob creating a spark. Normally objects around us do not seem to be charged. They are neutral. Objects around us are composed of positive and negative charges that largely cancel each other. Only when these positive and negative charges are not balanced do we observe the effects of electric charge.

If we rub a glass rod with a cloth, the glass rod will become charged and the cloth acquires a charge of the opposite sign. If we rub a plastic rod with fur, the rod and fur will also become oppositely charged. If we bring together two charged glass rods, they will repel each other. If we bring together two charged plastic rods, they will also repel each other. If we bring together a glass rod and a plastic rod, they will attract each other. This difference arises because the glass rod is positively charged (a deficit of electrons) and the plastic rod is negatively charged (an excess of electrons). This observation leads us to the **law of charges**:

Like charges repel and opposite charges attract.

The unit of charge is the coulomb (C), named after the French physicist Charles-Augustine de Coulomb (1736-1806). The coulomb is defined in terms of the SI unit for current, the ampere (A), named after another French physicist, André-Marie Ampère (1775-1836). Neither the ampere nor the coulomb can be derived in terms of the other basic SI units (m, kg, s). Instead, the ampere is another fundamental SI unit. For this reason, you will sometimes find the expression MKSA (Meter Kilogram Second Ampere) units for the SI unit system. The charge unit is defined as

$$1\ \mathrm{C} = 1\ \mathrm{A} \cdot \mathrm{s}. \qquad (21.1)$$

Obviously, we have not defined yet what an ampere is. This definition must wait until we discuss currents in later chapters. However, until that time we can define the magnitude of the unit coulomb by simply specifying the charge of a single electron

$$q_e = -e \qquad (21.2)$$

where we have used the symbol q for the charge, and the fundamental constant e has the value

$$e = 1.6021892 \cdot 10^{-19}\ \mathrm{C}. \qquad (21.3)$$

(Usually it is enough to carry only the first two to four significant digits of this mantissa. We will use a value of 1.6 or 1.602 in the following, but we should keep in mind that (21.3) gives the full accuracy to which this charge has been measured.)

The charge of the proton is exactly the same magnitude as that of the electron, only the proton's charge is positive

$$q_p = +e. \qquad (21.4)$$

The choice of which charge is positive and which charge is negative is arbitrary. Having $q_e < 0$ and $q_p > 0$ is due to American scientist and inventor Benjamin Franklin (1706-1790).

One coulomb is an extremely large unit of charge. We will see later in this chapter just how big it is when we investigate the magnitude of the forces of charges on each other.

> *In-class exercise:* How many electrons does it take to make up 1.00 C of charge?
>
> a) $1.60 \cdot 10^{19}$
> b) $6.60 \cdot 10^{19}$
> c) $3.20 \cdot 10^{16}$
> d) $6.24 \cdot 10^{18}$
> e) $6.66 \cdot 10^{17}$

Benjamin Franklin also proposed that charge is conserved. When one rubs a plastic rod with fur, electrons are transferred to the plastic rod leaving a net positive charge on the fur. (Protons are not transferred because they are massive and are usually embedded inside a nucleus.) The charge is not created or destroyed.

Law of charge conservation:

The total charge of an isolated system is conserved.

This law is the fourth conservation law that we have encountered so far, after the conservation laws for total energy, momentum, and angular momentum. Conservation laws are a common thread that runs through all of physics and are thus a recurring theme throughout this book as well.

It is important to note that there is a conservation law for charge, but *not* for mass. We will see that mass and energy are not independent of each other. What is sometimes described as mass conservation in introductory chemistry is not an exact conservation law, but only a useful device to keep track of the number of atoms in chemical reactions. The conservation of charge applies to macroscopic systems such as the plastic rod and fur system down to systems of subatomic particles.

Elementary Charge

Electric charge only comes in integral multiples of a minimum size. We thus say that charge is quantized. The smallest observable unit of electric charge is the charge of the electron, which is $-1.602 \cdot 10^{-19}$ C, as stated above.

How do we know this fact? This knowledge is due to an ingenious experiment carried out in 1910 by American physicist Robert A. Millikan (1868-1953). This experiment is known as the Millikan oil drop experiment and is sketched in Figure 21.3. In this experiment, oil drops are sprayed into a chamber where one or more electrons are knocked out of the drops by ionizing radiation. We will come back to a quantitative analysis of this experiment when we introduce electric potentials. However, for now it is enough to learn from this experiment and its subsequent refinements that charge comes only in quantized amounts.

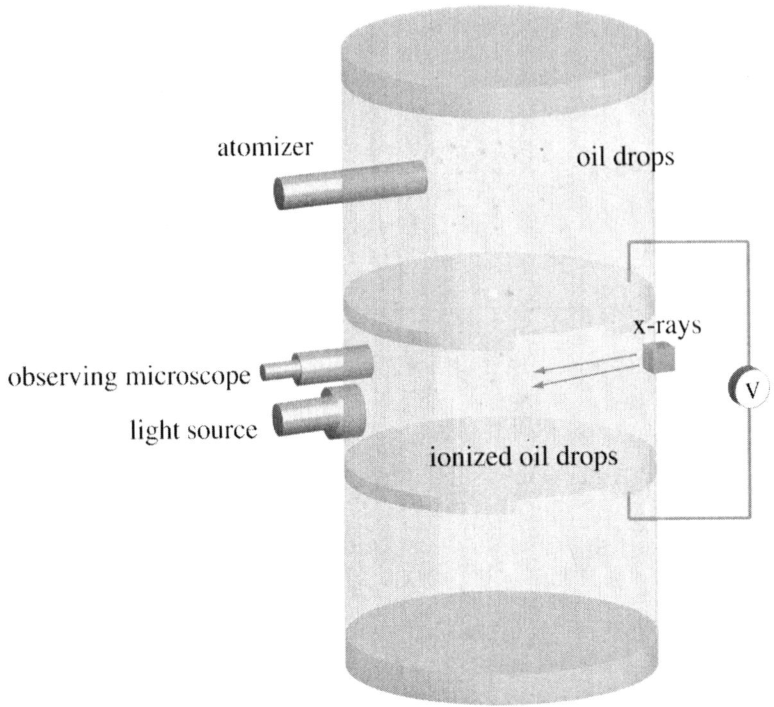

Figure 21.3: Schematic drawing of the Millikan oil drop experiment.

We do not notice that charge is quantized in our everyday experiences with electricity, because most electrical phenomena deal with large numbers of electrons.

The electron is a fundamental particle and has no substructure. The electron is a point particle and its radius is zero. However, using high-energy probes we can look inside the proton and determine the size of a proton. Inside we find that the proton is composed of charged particles called quarks held together by uncharged particles called gluons. These quarks have charges of 1/3 or 2/3 times the charge of the electron. The proton is composed of 2 "up quarks" (each with charge $+\frac{2}{3}e$) and 1 "down quark" (with charge $-\frac{1}{3}e$) giving the proton a charge of $2\cdot(+\frac{2}{3}e)+1\cdot(-\frac{1}{3}e)=+e$. These fractionally charged quarks cannot exist independently and have never been observed directly. Despite numerous extensive searches, objects with charges of a fraction of e have never been observed. The electrically neutral neutron (hence the name!) is composed of an up quark and two down quarks $1\cdot(+\frac{2}{3}e)+2\cdot(-\frac{1}{3}e)=0$

$$q_n = 0\,. \tag{21.5}$$

It is remarkable that the charges of the quarks inside the proton add up to exactly the same magnitude as the charge of the electron. This fact is still a big puzzle pointing to some deeper symmetry in nature and is not yet understood.

Because all objects are made of atoms, which in turn are made of electrons and atomic nuclei consisting of protons and neutrons, we can write down the charge, q, of any object in terms of the sum of the number of protons, N_p, minus the sum of the number of electrons, N_e, that make up the object

$$q = e \cdot \left(N_p - N_e\right). \tag{21.6}$$

Self-Test Opportunity: Give the charge of the following elementary particles or atoms in terms of the elementary charge quantum $e = 1.602 \cdot 10^{-19}$ C.

a) proton
b) neutron
c) helium atom (two protons, two neutron, and two electrons)
d) hydrogen atom (one proton and one electron)
e) up quark
f) down quark
g) electron
h) alpha particle (two protons and two neutrons)

Example

Example 21.1: Net charge

Question:

If we want to put 0.100 C of positive charge on a block of iron metal of mass 3.25 kg, what fraction of the electrons do we have to remove?

Answer:

Iron has the mass number 56. Therefore, we get for the number of iron atoms in the 3.25 kg block

$$N_{atom} = \frac{(3.25\text{ kg}) \cdot (6.022 \cdot 10^{23} \, atoms/mol)}{0.0560 \text{ kg/mol}} = 3.495 \cdot 10^{25} = 3.50 \cdot 10^{25}.$$

In this expression, we have used Avogadro's number, $6.022 \cdot 10^{23}$, and the definition of the mole, which specifies that the mass of a mole of a substance in units of grams is just the mass number of the substance, in this case 56.

Because the element number of iron is 26, which equals the number of protons or electrons in an iron atom, we obtain for the total number of electrons in our 3.25 kg block:

$$N_e = 26 N_{atom} = 26 \cdot (3.495 \cdot 10^{25}) = 9.09 \cdot 10^{26}.$$

Example

We consult (21.6) to find out the number of electrons, $N_{\Delta e}$, that we have to remove. Because the number of electrons equals the number of protons for the original uncharged object, the difference in the number of protons and electrons $N_{\Delta e}$ is the number of electrons we have to remove to put the desired charge on the block

$$q = e \cdot N_{\Delta e} \Rightarrow N_{\Delta e} = \frac{q}{e} = \frac{0.100 \text{ C}}{1.602 \cdot 10^{-19} \text{ C}} = 6.24 \cdot 10^{17}.$$

Finally, we obtain for the fraction of electrons we had to remove

$$\frac{N_{\Delta e}}{N_e} = \frac{6.24 \cdot 10^{17}}{9.09 \cdot 10^{26}} = 6.87 \cdot 10^{-10}.$$

Therefore, we have removed less than one in a billion electrons from the iron metal block in order to put this sizeable positive charge on it.

21.3. Insulators, Conductors, Semiconductors, Superconductors

Materials that conduct electricity are called *conductors*. Materials that do not conduct electricity are called *insulators*. There are materials that are good conductors and materials that are poor conductors as well as materials that are good insulators and materials that are poor insulators. Let us first discuss solid insulators and conductors.

The electronic structure of materials refers to the way in which electrons are bound to nuclei, as we will discuss in later chapters. For now we are interested in the propensity of a material to allow electrons to escape from its atoms or in the tendency of its atoms to acquire extra electrons. For insulators there is no free movement of electrons because there are no loosely bound electrons that can escape the grasp of atoms and thereby move freely throughout the material. Even when external charge is placed on an insulator, this external charge cannot move appreciably. Typical insulators are glass, plastic, or cloth.

On the other hand, conductors have an electronic structure that allows the free movement of some electrons. The positive charges of the atoms of the conductor material do not move since they reside in a heavy nucleus. Typical solid conductors are metals. Copper is a very good and very common conductor and is found in electrical wiring.

Fluids and organic tissue can also serve as conductors. Pure distilled water is not a very good conductor. Dissolving, for example, common household salt in water improves the conductivity of this saltwater tremendously, because the positively charged sodium ions and negatively charged chlorine ions can move inside this liquid and accomplish conduction. In liquids, contrary to solids, positive as well as negative charge carriers are mobile. Organic tissue is not a very good conductor, but it conducts electricity well enough to make high voltages and currents dangerous to our health.

Self-Test Opportunity: Name three common conductors and three common insulators.

Semiconductors

There is also a class of materials called *semiconductors*. A semiconductor can be changed from an insulator to a conductor and back to an insulator again. Semiconductors were discovered only a little more than 50 years ago, but are already the backbone of the entire computer industry. The first widespread use of semiconductors was in transistors (Figure 21.4, left panel), while modern computer semiconductor chips (Figure 21.4, right panel) perform the function of thousands of transistors. Computers and basically all modern consumer electronics products and devices (televisions, cameras, video game players, cell phones, cars, …) would be impossible without semiconductors. Gordon Moore, co-founder of Intel, famously stated that computers' CPU-power doubles every eighteen months, which is an empirical average over the last 5 decades. This doubling phenomenon is now known as "Moore's Law". Physicists have been the driving force behind this process of scientific discovery, invention, and improvement, and will continue to do so in the foreseeable future.

There are intrinsic and extrinsic semiconductors. Intrinsic semiconductors are chemically pure single crystals of gallium arsenide, germanium, or in particular silicon. One can produce extrinsic semiconductors by doping, which is the addition of minute amounts (typically 1 part in a million) of other materials that can act as electron donors or electron receptors. Semiconductors doped with electron donors are called "*n*-type" (*n* stands for negative charge). If the doping acts as an electron receptor, the hole left behind by an electron that chooses to attach itself to a receptor can also travel through the crystal and acts as an effective positive charge carrier. These semiconductors are then consequently called "*p*-type" (*p* stand for positive charge). So, unlike normal solid conductors where only negative charges move, semiconductors give us the ability to have negative and positive charges (which are really electron holes) moving.

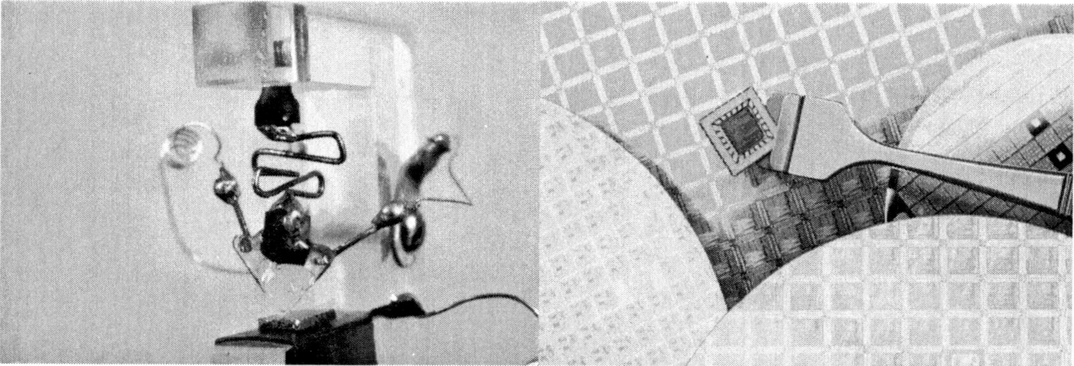

Figure 21.4: Left: Replica of first transistor invented in 1947 by John Bardeen, Walter H. Brattain, and William B. Shockley; right: modern computer chips made from silicon wafers contain many tens of millions of transistors.

Superconductors

Superconductors are materials that have exactly zero resistance to the conduction of electricity as opposed to conductors that conduct electricity well, but not without losses. Materials are superconducting only at very low temperatures. A typical superconductor is a niobium-titanium alloy that must be kept near the temperature of liquid helium (4.3 K) to retain its superconducting properties. During the last 20 years new materials called high-T_c superconductors (T_c stands for "critical temperature," which is the maximum temperature that allows superconductivity) have been developed that are superconducting at liquid nitrogen temperature (77.3 K). Materials that are superconductors at room temperature (300 K) have not been found but would be extremely useful materials. Research on developing such materials and on theoretically explaining what physical phenomena cause high-T_c superconductivity is currently in progress.

We will return to the topics of conductivity, superconductivity, and semiconductors again in more quantitative detail in the following chapters.

21.4. Electrostatic Charging

We will approach the problem of understanding electrostatic charging by starting with the description of a series of simple experiments. We use a power supply to serve as a ready source of positive and negative charge. The battery in our car is a power supply, which uses chemical reactions to create this charge separation. Along with the power supply we use several insulating paddles that we can charge with positive or negative charge using the power supply. In addition, we have a conducting connection to the earth. The earth is conducting and electrically neutral and can take away and neutralize any charge. This taking away of charge is called grounding and an electrical connection to the earth is called a ground.

Figure 21.5: A typical electroscope used in lecture demonstrations.

An electroscope is a device that gives a response when it is charged. The electroscope shown in Figure 21.5 has two conductors that in their nominal position (as in Figure 21.5) are touching and lie along a vertical diagonal. One of the conductors is hinged in its middle so that it will move away from the fixed conductor if a charge exists on the conductors of the electroscope. These two conductors are electrically attached to a conducting ball placed on top of the electrometer to allow us to easily apply charge or remove charge.

First, we use our power supply to negatively charge one of the insulating paddles. When we bring the paddle near the ball of the electroscope, the electrons in the conducting ball of the electroscope are repelled and a net negative charge is produced on the conductors of the electroscope away from the conducting ball. This causes the movable conductor to rotate as the stationary arm having the same sign of charge repels it. Because the paddle did not touch the ball, we say that the charge that is on the movable conductors is induced. If we move the charged paddle away, the induced charge reduces to zero, and the movable conductor returns to its original position. If we carry out the same procedure with a positively charged paddle, the electrons in the conductors will be attracted to the paddle and will flow into the conducting ball. This will leave a net positive charge on the conductors, causing the movable conducting arm to rotate. We note that the net charge of the electroscope is zero in both cases and that the conductor motion only tells us that the paddle is charged. We cannot determine the sign of this charge.

On the other hand if we touch a negatively charged insulating paddle to the ball of the electroscope, the electrons will flow from the paddle to the conductor, producing a net negative charge. When we remove the paddle from ball, the charge remains and the movable arm remains rotated. Similarly, if we touch a positively charged insulating paddle to an uncharged electroscope, the electroscope transfers electrons to the positively charged paddle and becomes positively charged. Again, both a positively charged paddle and a negatively charged paddle have the same effect on the electroscope and we have no way of determining whether the paddles are positively charged or negatively charged. This process is called charging by contact.

We can demonstrate that there are two different kinds of charge if we first touch a negatively charged paddle to the electroscope producing a rotation of the movable arm. If we then touch a positively charged paddle to the electroscope, the movable arm returns to the non-charged position. The net charge will be neutralized (assuming both paddles originally had the same absolute value of charge). Thus, we have shown that there are two kinds of charge. However, we know that these charges are manifestations of mobile negative charges in the form of electrons and that a negative charge is an excess of electrons and a positive charge is a deficit of electrons.

We can also charge the electroscope without touching it with the charged paddle. To carry out this task, we ground the electroscope, bring a negatively charged paddle near the electroscope, and while the charged paddle is still close to but not touching the ball of the electroscope, we remove the ground. Now when the paddle is moved away from the electroscope, we observe that the electroscope is charged. The same process will also work with a positively charged paddle. This process is called charging by induction and yields an electroscope change that has an opposite sign from the charge on the paddle.

21.5. Electric Force – Coulomb's Law

For the electrostatic force due to a charge q_2 on a charge q_1, $\vec{F}_{2\to1}$, one finds that the force on q_1 points toward q_2 for opposite sign charges and away from q_2 for like sign charges as shown in Figure 21.6.

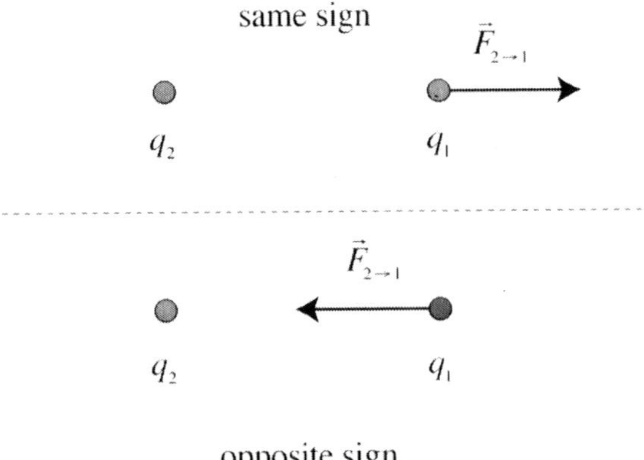

Figure 21.6: The force exerted by charge 2 on charge 1. The top panel depicts two charges with the same sign. The bottom panel shows two charges with opposite signs.

This force on one charge due to one other charge always lies on a line between the two changes. Coulomb's Law gives the magnitude of this force

$$F = k\frac{|q_1 q_2|}{r^2} \tag{21.7}$$

where q_1 and q_2 are electric charges, $r = |\vec{r}_1 - \vec{r}_2|$ is the distance between the two charges, and

$$k = 8.99 \cdot 10^9 \ \frac{\mathrm{N \cdot m^2}}{\mathrm{C^2}} \tag{21.8}$$

is Coulomb's constant. Now we can see that one Coulomb is a *very* large charge. If you place two charges of 1 C each a distance of 1 m apart, the magnitude of the force between them is 8.99 billion N. For comparison, this is the weight of (= gravitational force acting on) 450 fully loaded space shuttles!

One also defines a relationship between Coulomb's constant and a constant ε_0, the electric permittivity of free space

$$k = \frac{1}{4\pi\varepsilon_0}. \tag{21.9}$$

Consequently, we obtain for the value of the constant ε_0

$$\varepsilon_0 = 8.85 \cdot 10^{-12} \frac{\mathrm{C}^2}{\mathrm{N} \cdot \mathrm{m}^2}. \tag{21.10}$$

An alternative way of writing (21.7) is then

$$F = \frac{1}{4\pi\varepsilon_0} \frac{|q_1 q_2|}{r^2}. \tag{21.11}$$

Note that in (21.7) and (21.11) the charges can be positive or negative so that the product of the charges can be positive or negative. We know that opposite charges attract and same charges repel so that a negative value for $q_1 q_2$ signifies attraction and a positive value means repulsion.

Finally, we can also write the Coulomb force law for the force due to charge 2 on charge 1 in vector form

$$\vec{F}_{2\to1} = k\frac{q_1 q_2}{r^3}(\vec{r}_1 - \vec{r}_2) = k\frac{q_1 q_2}{r^2}\hat{r}_{21}. \tag{21.12}$$

In the above equation $\hat{r}_{21}$ is a unit vector pointing from q_2 to q_1.

In-class exercise: You have two charges a distance r apart. You double each charge and double the distance between the charges. How does the force between the two charges change?

a) The new force is twice a large.
b) The new force is half as large.
c) The new force is four times as large.
d) The new force is four times smaller.
e) The new force is the same.

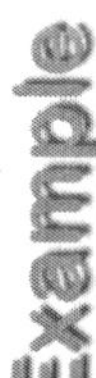

Example 21.2: The electric force inside the nucleus and inside the atom

Question:

What is the magnitude of the electric force between the two protons inside the nucleus of a helium atom?

Answer:

The two protons and two neutrons in the nucleus of the helium atom are held together by the strong force while the electromagnetic force is pushing the protons apart. The charge of the proton is $q_p = +e$. A distance of approximately $r = 2 \cdot 10^{-15}$ m separates the two protons. Using Coulomb's law we can write the force as

$$F = k\frac{|q_p q_p|}{r^2} = \left(8.99\cdot10^9\ \frac{\text{N}\cdot\text{m}^2}{\text{C}^2}\right)\frac{\left(+1.6\cdot10^{-19}\ \text{C}\right)\cdot\left(+1.6\cdot10^{-19}\ \text{C}\right)}{\left(2\cdot10^{-15}\text{m}\right)^2} = 58\ \text{N}.$$

Therefore the two protons in each individual atomic nucleus of helium are being pushed apart with a force of 58 N (= 13 pounds, the weight of a small dog). This force is an astonishingly large force. Why do the atomic nuclei not simply explode? The answer is that an even stronger force, the aptly named "strong force", keeps them together.

Example

Question:
What is the magnitude of the electric force between a gold nucleus and an electron in an orbit with radius $4.88\cdot10^{-12}$ m?

Answer:
The negatively charged electron and the positively charged gold nucleus attract each other with a force whose magnitude is

$$F = k\frac{|q_e q_N|}{r^2}$$

where the charge of the electron is $q_e = -e$ and the charge of the gold nucleus is $q_N = +79e$. The force between the electron and the nucleus is then

$$F = k\frac{|q_e q_N|}{r^2} = \left(8.99\cdot10^9\ \frac{\text{N}\cdot\text{m}^2}{\text{C}^2}\right)\frac{\left(1.60\cdot10^{-19}\ \text{C}\right)\cdot\left(79\cdot1.60\cdot10^{-19}\ \text{C}\right)}{\left(4.88\cdot10^{-12}\text{m}\right)^2} = 7.63\cdot10^{-4}\ \text{N}.$$

Thus, the magnitude of the electric force for an electron in a gold atom is about a million times less that the electric force between protons inside a nucleus.

Because we now have the electric force to consider, we can again ask questions of the kind we have asked in static equilibrium (chapter 11) and in gravitation (chapter 12). Let us solve one sample problem.

Example

Example 21.3: Equilibrium position

Question:
Two charges are placed as shown in Figure 21.7. $q_1 = 0.15\ \mu\text{C}$ is located at the origin, and $q_2 = 0.35\ \mu\text{C}$ is located on the positive x-axis at $x_2 = 0.40$ m. Where do we need to put a third charge for that charge to be at an equilibrium point (the forces sum to zero)?

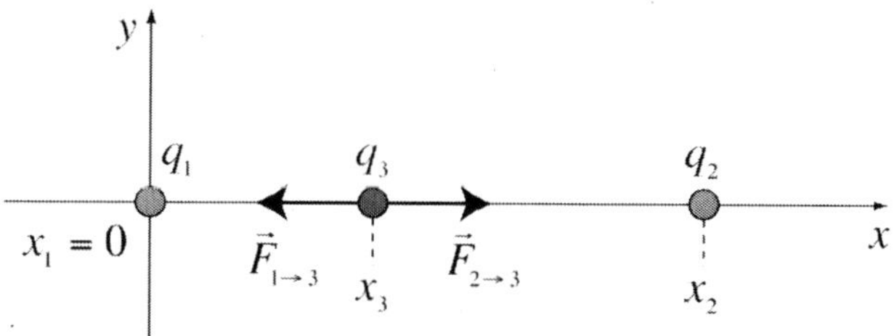

Figure 21.7: Placement of charges in Example 21.4. The case of a third charge with a negative charge is shown.

Example

Answer:
Let us first discuss where *not* to put the third charge. If we put the third charge anywhere off the x-axis, then there will always be a force component pointing towards or away from the x-axis. This argument means that we can only find an equilibrium point (a point where the forces sum to zero) on the x-axis. The x-axis can be divided into three different segments, $x \le x_1 = 0$, $x_1 < x < x_2$, and $x_2 \le x$. For $x \le x_1 = 0$ the force vectors from both charges acting on the third charge will both point in the positive direction if the charge is negative and in the negative direction if the charge is positive. Because we are looking for a location where the two forces cancel, $x \le x_1 = 0$ can be excluded for the location of the equilibrium point. A similar argument excludes $x \ge x_2$.

This analysis leaves $x_1 < x < x_2$. In this interval, the forces from the two charges on a third charge point in opposite directions. We can then look for the location x_3 where the absolute magnitudes of both forces are equal and the forces thus sum to zero. We can express the equality of the two forces as

$$\left|\vec{F}_{1\to3}\right| = \left|\vec{F}_{3\to2}\right|$$

which we can rewrite as

$$k\frac{|q_1 q_3|}{(x_3 - x_1)^2} = k\frac{|q_3 q_2|}{(x_2 - x_3)^2}.$$

We now see that the magnitude and sign of the third charge does not matter, because the third charge cancels out in the calculation. We solve for x_3 and obtain

$$\frac{q_1}{(x_3 - x_1)^2} = \frac{q_2}{(x_2 - x_3)^2} \quad \text{or}$$
$$q_1(x_2 - x_3)^2 = q_2(x_3 - x_1)^2.$$

Taking the square root of both sides we find

$$\sqrt{q_1}(x_2 - x_3) = \sqrt{q_2}(x_3 - x_1) \text{ or}$$

$$x_3 = \frac{\sqrt{q_1}x_2 + \sqrt{q_2}x_1}{\sqrt{q_1} + \sqrt{q_2}}.$$

A remark on taking the square root in the third step of this calculation is in order. Because $x_1 < x_3 < x_2$, both of the roots, $(x_2 - x_3)$ and $(x_3 - x_1)$, are assured to be positive. Therefore it is legitimate to proceed from line two to line three of the above algebraic transformation.

Inserting the numbers given in the problem, we obtain:

$$x_3 = \frac{\sqrt{q_1}x_2 + \sqrt{q_2}x_1}{\sqrt{q_1} + \sqrt{q_2}} = \frac{\sqrt{0.15\ \mu\text{C}} \cdot (0.4\text{ m})}{\sqrt{0.15\ \mu\text{C}} + \sqrt{0.35\ \mu\text{C}}} = 0.16\text{ m}.$$

This result makes sense because we expect the equilibrium point to reside closer to the smaller charge.

Solved Problem 21.1: Charged balls

Question:

Two identical charged balls hang from the ceiling by ropes of equal lengths $\ell = 1.50$ m of insulating material as shown in Figure 21.8. A charge of $q = 25.0\ \mu\text{C}$ is applied to each ball. Then the two balls hang at rest, and each supporting rope has an angle of $25.0°$ with respect to the vertical, as shown in Figure 21.8. What is the mass of the balls?

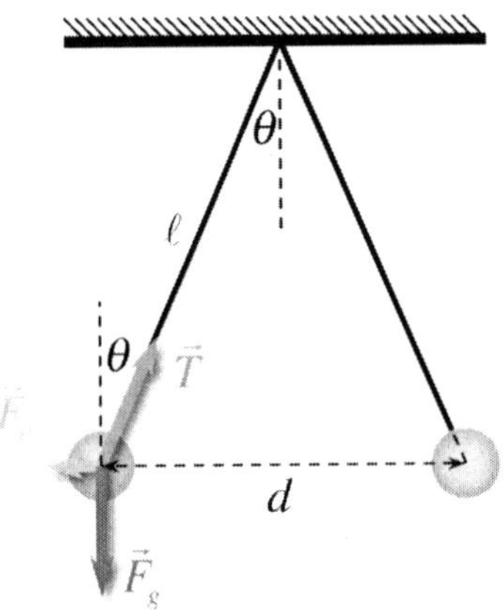

Figure 21.8: Two charged balls hanging from the ceiling in their equilibrium position.

Answer:

THINK:

Each charged ball has three forces acting on it; the force of gravity, the repulsive electric force, and the tension in the supporting string. Using the condition of static equilibrium that we studied in Chapter 11, we know that the sum of all the forces on each ball must be zero. We can then resolve the components of the three forces and set them equal to zero, allowing us to solve for the mass of the charged balls.

SKETCH:

A free-body diagram for the left ball is shown in Figure 21.9.

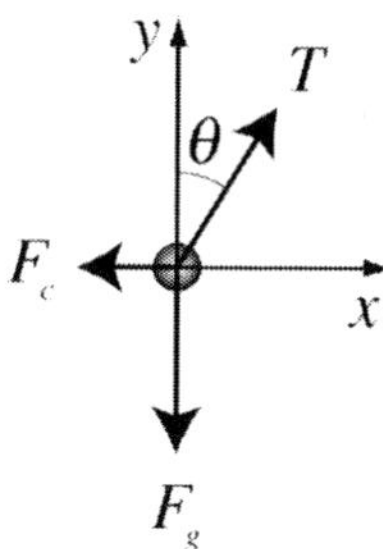

Figure 21.9: Free-body diagram for the left charged ball.

RESEARCH:

The three forces acting on the ball are the force of gravity, F_g, the electric force between the two charged balls, F_c, and the tension on the string, T. The condition of static equilibrium tells us that the sum of the x-components of these forces must equal zero and the sum of y-components of these forces must equal zero. The sum of x-components of the forces is

$$T\sin\theta - F_c = 0. \quad (21.13)$$

The sum of the y-components of the forces is

$$T\cos\theta - F_g = 0. \quad (21.14)$$

The force of gravity is just the weight of the charged ball

$$F_g = mg \quad (21.15)$$

where m is the mass of the charged ball. The electric force between the two balls is given by

$$F_c = k\frac{q^2}{d^2} \quad (21.16)$$

where d is the distance between the two balls. We can express the distance between the two balls in terms of the length of the string ℓ by looking at Figure 21.7. We see that

Solved Problem

$$\sin\theta = \frac{d/2}{\ell}. \tag{21.17}$$

We can then rewrite the electric force in terms of the angle with respect to the vertical and the length of the string

$$F_c = k\frac{q^2}{\left(2\ell\sin\theta\right)^2} = k\frac{q^2}{4\ell^2\sin^2\theta} \tag{21.18}$$

SIMPLIFY:

We rearrange (21.13) and (21.14) and divide the two resulting equations

$$\frac{T\sin\theta = F_c}{T\cos\theta = F_g} \tag{21.19}$$

which gives us

$$\tan\theta = \frac{F_c}{F_g}. \tag{21.20}$$

Putting in our expressions for the force of gravity and the electric force we get

$$\tan\theta = \frac{k\dfrac{q^2}{4\ell^2\sin^2\theta}}{mg} = \frac{kq^2}{4mg\ell^2\sin^2\theta}. \tag{21.21}$$

Solving for the mass of the ball we obtain

$$m = \frac{kq^2}{4g\ell^2\sin^2\theta\tan\theta}. \tag{21.22}$$

CALCULATE:

Putting in our numerical values, we get

$$m = \frac{\left(8.99\cdot10^9\ \text{N}\cdot\text{m}^2/\text{C}^2\right)\left(25.0\ \mu\text{C}\right)^2}{4\cdot\left(9.81\ \text{m/s}^2\right)\left(1.50\ \text{m}\right)^2\sin^2\left(25.0°\right)\tan\left(25.0°\right)} = 0.764116\ \text{kg}.$$

ROUND:

We report our result to three significant figures

$$m = 0.764\ \text{kg}.$$

DOUBLE-CHECK:

To double-check, we make the small angle approximation such that $\sin\theta \approx \tan\theta \approx \theta$ and $\cos\theta \approx 1$. The tension on the string is then $T = mg$ and we can express the x-components of the forces as

Solved Problem

Solved Problem

$$T\sin\theta \approx mg\theta = F_c = k\frac{q^2}{d^2} \approx k\frac{q^2}{\left(2\ell\theta\right)^2}.$$

Solving for the mass of the charged ball we get

$$m = \frac{kq^2}{4g\ell^2\theta^3} = \frac{\left(8.99\cdot 10^9\ \text{N}\cdot\text{m}^2/\text{C}^2\right)\left(25.0\ \mu\text{C}\right)^2}{4\cdot\left(9.81\ \text{m/s}^2\right)\left(1.50\ \text{m}\right)^2\left(0.436\ \text{rad}\right)^3} = 0.768\ \text{kg}$$

which is close to our exact answer.

Self-Test Opportunity: A positive point charge $+q$ is placed at point P right of two charges q_1 and q_2 as shown in the figure. The net force on the positive charge $+q$ is found to be zero. Determine whether the following statements are true or false.

q_1 q_2 P

Two charges q_1 and q_2 and a point P located to the right of the two charges.

a) q_2 must have the opposite sign from q_1 and be less in magnitude.
b) The magnitude of the charge q_1 must be smaller than the magnitude of q_2.
c) q_1 and q_2 must have the same sign.
d) If q_1 is negative, then q_2 must be positive.
e) Either q_1 or q_2 must be positive.

In-class exercise: Consider three charges placed along the x-axis as shown in the figure. The values of the charges are $q_1 = -8.10\ \mu\text{C}$, $q_2 = 2.16\ \mu\text{C}$, and $q_3 = 2.16\ \text{pC}$. The distance between q_1 and q_2 is $d_1 = 1.71\ \text{m}$. The distance between q_1 and q_3 is $d_2 = 2.62\ \text{m}$. What is the magnitude of the electric force on q_3 due to q_1 and q_2?

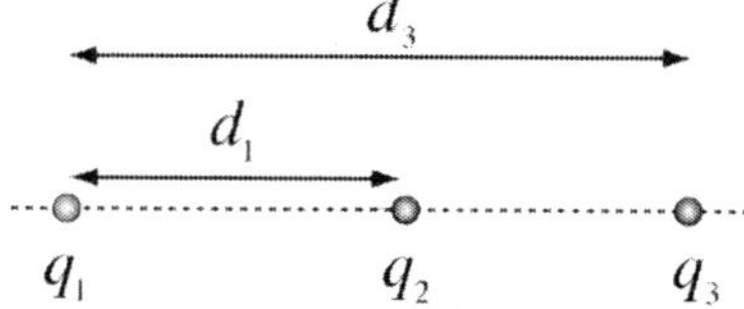

Force on one charge resulting from two other charges.

a) $3.85\cdot 10^{-8}$ N b) $7.92\cdot 10^{-6}$ N c) $1.44\cdot 10^{-5}$ N d) $2.22\cdot 10^{-4}$ N e) $6.71\cdot 10^{-2}$ N

Electrostatic Precipitator

An application of electrostatic charging and electrostatic forces is the cleaning of emissions from coal-fired power plants. A device called an electrostatic precipitator (ESP) is used to remove ash and other particulates resulting from the burning of coal to generate electrical power. The principle of operation is illustrated in Figure 21.10.

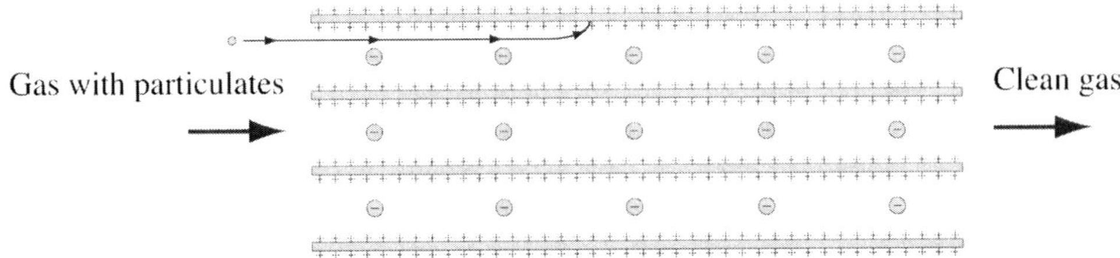

Figure 21.10: Illustration of the principle behind an electrostatic precipitator used to clean the exhaust of a coal-fired power plant. The view is from the top of the device.

The ESP consists of wires held at a high negative voltage that ionize the air between the plates that are held at a positive voltage. In Figure 21.10, the exhaust from the coal burning process enters the ESP from the left. Particulates passing near the wires pick up a negative charge. These particles are then attracted to the positive plate and stick there. The gas continues through the ESP, leaving the ash and other particulates behind. The accumulated material is then shaken off the plates to a hamper below. This waste can be used for many purposes including construction materials and fertilizer. An example of a coal-fired power plant incorporating an ESP is shown in Figure 21.11.

Figure 21.11: Coal-fired power plant at Michigan State University that incorporates an electrostatic precipitator to remove particulates from its emissions.

21.6. Coulomb's Law and Newton's Law of Gravitation

Coulomb's law that describes the force between two electric charges, $F_{electric}$, has a form that is similar to the Newton's law gravitational force between two masses, $F_{gravity}$

$$F_{gravity} = G\frac{m_1 m_2}{r^2} \text{ and } F_{electric} = k\frac{|q_1 q_2|}{r^2} \qquad (21.23)$$

where m_1 and m_2 are the two masses, q_1 and q_2 are the two electric charges, and r is the distance of separation. Both forces vary as the inverse square of the distance. The electric force can be attractive or repulsive because charges can have positive or negative signs. The gravitation force is always attractive because there is only one kind of mass. The strengths of the forces are given by the proportionality constants k and G.

Example

Example 21.4: Forces between electrons

We can obtain an idea of the relative strengths of the two interactions by calculating the ratio of the electric force and the gravitational force between two electrons. This ratio is given by

$$\frac{F_{electric}}{F_{gravity}} = \frac{kq_e^2}{Gm_e^2}.$$

Because the dependence on the distance is the same in both forces, there is no dependence on the distance in the ratio of the two forces – it cancels out. The mass of an electron is $m_e = 9.109 \cdot 10^{-31}$ kg, and we already learned in this chapter that its charge is $q_e = -1.602 \cdot 10^{-19}$ C. Using the value of Coulomb's constant given in (21.8) and the value of the universal gravitational constant $G = 6.67 \cdot 10^{-11}\ \text{N} \cdot \text{m}^2/\text{kg}^2$ we find numerically

$$\frac{F_{electric}}{F_{gravity}} = \frac{(8.99 \cdot 10^9\ \text{N} \cdot \text{m}^2/\text{C}^2)(1.602 \cdot 10^{-19}\ \text{C})^2}{(6.67 \cdot 10^{-11}\ \text{N} \cdot \text{m}^2/\text{kg}^2)(9.109 \cdot 10^{-31}\ \text{kg})^2} = 4.2 \cdot 10^{42}.$$

Therefore, the electrostatic force is more than 42 orders of magnitude stronger than the gravitational force between electrons.

On the contrary, for astronomical length scales gravity is the only force that matters. The reason for this dominance is that all stars and planets and other objects of astronomical relevance carry no net charge. Therefore, there is no electrostatic interaction between them, and gravity dominates.

Coulomb's law in electrostatics applies to large macroscopic systems down to the atom, though subtle effects in atomic and subatomic systems require using a more sophisticated approach called quantum electrodynamics. Newton's law of gravitation fails in subatomic systems and also must be modified in macroscopic systems such as the motion of Mercury around the Sun to reproduce some fine details of the gravitational interaction that are governed by Einstein's general relativity.

What we have learned/Exam Study Guide:

Most Important Points

- Like charges repel and unlike charges attract.
- The elementary quantum of electric charge is $e = 1.602(1892)\cdot 10^{-19}$ C.
- The electron has charge $q_e = -e$ and the proton $q_p = +e$. The neutron has zero charge.
- The net charge of an object is given by e times the number of protons, N_p, minus e times the number of electrons, N_e, that make up the object: $q = e\cdot(N_p - N_e)$.
- Coulomb's law describes the electric force between two stationary charges as $F = k\dfrac{|q_1q_2|}{r^2} = \dfrac{1}{4\pi\varepsilon_0}\dfrac{|q_1q_2|}{r^2}$ and opposite charges attract while like charges repel.
- The constant in Coulomb's law is $k = \dfrac{1}{4\pi\varepsilon_0} = 8.99\cdot 10^9\ \dfrac{\text{N}\cdot\text{m}^2}{\text{C}^2}$.
- The electric permittivity of free space is $\varepsilon_0 = 8.85\cdot 10^{-12}\dfrac{\text{C}^2}{\text{N}\cdot\text{m}^2}$.
- The total charge in an isolated system is always conserved.

New Symbols used in this Chapter

- q is a charge.
- ε_0 is the electric permittivity of free space.
- k is Coulomb's constant.
- e is the elementary charge

Additional Solved Problems

Solved Problem

Solved Problem 21.2: Bead on a Wire

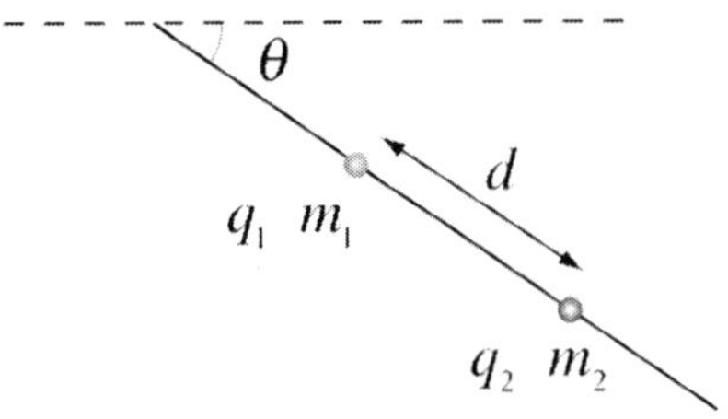

Figure 21.12: Two charged beads on a wire.

Question:
A bead with charge $q_1 = +1.28\ \mu\text{C}$ is fixed in place on an insulating wire that makes an angle of $\theta = 42.3°$ with respect to the horizontal as shown in Figure 21.12. A second

bead with charge $q_2 = -5.06\ \mu\text{C}$ slides without friction on the wire. At a distance $d = 0.380$ m, the net force on the second bead is zero. What is the mass m_2 of the second bead?

Answer:

THINK:

The force of gravity pulling m_2 down the wire is compensated by the attractive electric force between the positive charge on the first bead and the negative charge on the second bead. The second bead can be thought of as sliding on an inclined plane.

SKETCH:

In Figure 21.13 we show a sketch of the forces acting on the second bead. Here we have defined a coordinate system where the positive x-direction is down the wire. We omit the force acting on m_2 due to the wire since this wire force only has a y-component and we can solve the problem by analyzing just the x-components of the forces.

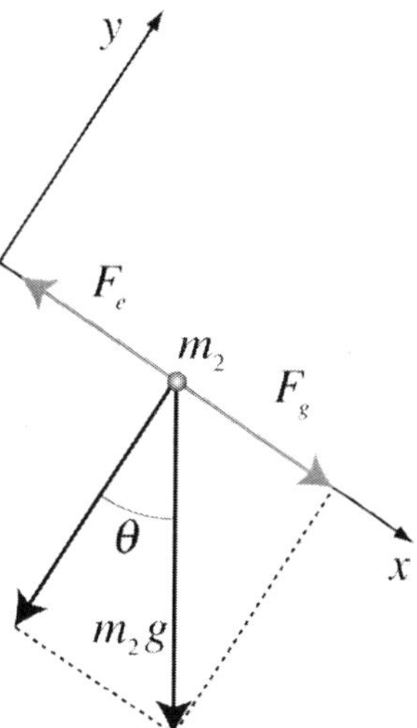

Figure 21.13: Sketch showing the forces acting on the second bead.

RESEARCH:

The attractive electric force between the two beads balances the component of the force of gravity on the second bead acting down the wire. The electric force acts in the negative x direction and its magnitude is given by

$$F_e = k\frac{|q_1q_2|}{d^2}. \tag{21.24}$$

The x-component of the force of gravity on the second bead corresponds to the component of the weight of the second bead parallel to the wire. In Figure 21.13, we can see that the component of the weight of the second bead down the wire is given by

$$F_g = m_2 g \sin\theta . \tag{21.25}$$

SIMPLIFY:

We can equate (21.24) and (21.25) to obtain

$$k\frac{|q_1q_2|}{d^2} = m_2 g \sin\theta . \tag{21.26}$$

Solving for the mass of the second bead gives us

$$m_2 = \frac{k|q_1q_2|}{d^2 g \sin\theta} . \tag{21.27}$$

CALCULATE:

Putting in our numerical values, we get

$$m_2 = \frac{kq_1q_2}{d^2 g \sin\theta} = \frac{\left(8.99\cdot 10^9 \text{ N}\cdot\text{m}^2/\text{C}^2\right)\left(1.28\ \mu\text{C}\right)\left(5.06\ \mu\text{C}\right)}{\left(0.380 \text{ m}\right)^2\left(9.81 \text{ m/s}^2\right)\sin\left(42.3°\right)} = 0.0610745 \text{ kg} .$$

ROUND:

We report our result to three significant figures

$$m_2 = 0.0611 \text{ kg} = 61.2 \text{ g} .$$

DOUBLE-CHECK:

To double-check, let's calculate the mass assuming that the wire is vertical. We can then take $\theta = 90°$ and set the weight of the second bead equal to the electric force between the two beads

$$k\frac{|q_1q_2|}{d^2} = m_2 g .$$

Solving for the mass of the second bead we obtain

$$m_2 = \frac{kq_1q_2}{d^2 g} = \frac{\left(8.99\cdot 10^9 \text{ N}\cdot\text{m}^2/\text{C}^2\right)\left(1.28\ \mu\text{C}\right)\left(5.06\ \mu\text{C}\right)}{\left(0.380 \text{ m}\right)^2\left(9.81 \text{ m/s}^2\right)} = 0.0411 \text{ kg} .$$

As we decrease the angle of the wire relative to the horizontal, the calculated mass of the second bead will increase. Our result of 0.0611 kg is somewhat higher than the mass we calculate taking a vertical wire, so our result seems reasonable.

Solved Problem

Solved Problem

Question:

What are the magnitude and direction of the electric force on q_1 resulting from the electric force from the other three charges?

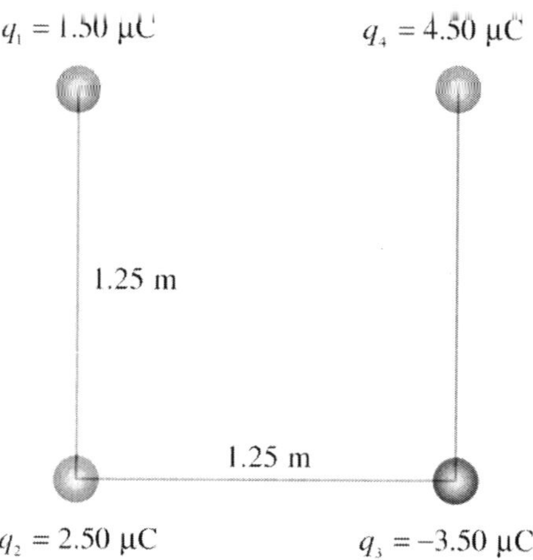

Figure 21.14: Four charges placed at the corners of a square.

Answer:

THINK:

The force on q_4 is the vector sum of the electric forces resulting from interactions with the other three charges.

SKETCH: In Figure 21.15 we show a sketch of the four charges and we define an xy-coordinate system with its origin at the location of q_2.

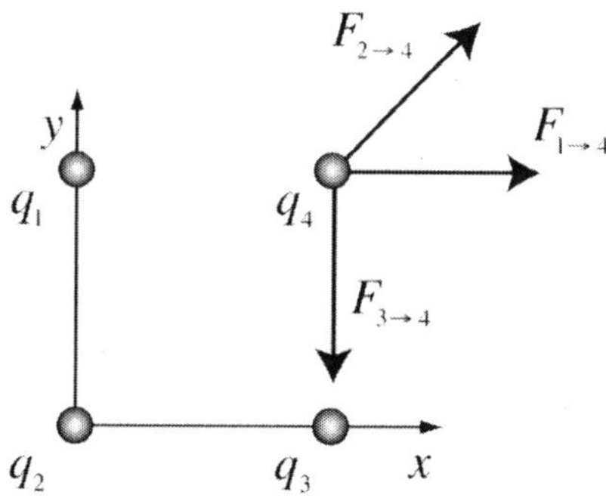

Figure 21.15: The forces acting on q_4 from the other three charges.

RESEARCH:

The force on q_4 will be the vector sum of the forces $\vec{F}_{1\to4}$, $\vec{F}_{2\to4}$, and $\vec{F}_{3\to4}$. The x-component of the summed forces is

$$F_x = k\frac{|q_1q_4|}{d^2} + k\frac{|q_2q_4|}{\left(\sqrt{2}d\right)^2}\cos 45^\circ = \frac{kq_4}{d^2}\left(q_1 + \frac{q_2}{2}\cos 45^\circ\right)$$

where we can see that the x - component of $\vec{F}_{3\to 4}$ is zero. The y -component of the summed forces is

$$F_y = k\frac{|q_2q_4|}{\left(\sqrt{2}d\right)^2}\sin 45^\circ - k\frac{|q_3q_4|}{d^2} = \frac{kq_4}{d^2}\left(\frac{q_2}{2}\sin 45^\circ + q_3\right)$$

where we can see that the y -component of $\vec{F}_{1\to 4}$ is zero. The magnitude of the force is given by

$$F = \sqrt{F_x^2 + F_y^2}$$

and the angle of the force is given by

$$\tan\theta = \frac{F_y}{F_x}.$$

SIMPLIFY:

Simplifying we get

$$F = \sqrt{\left(\frac{kq_4}{d^2}\left(q_1 + \frac{q_2}{2}\cos 45^\circ\right)\right)^2 + \left(\frac{kq_4}{d^2}\left(\frac{q_2}{2}\sin 45^\circ + q_3\right)\right)^2}$$

which we can rewrite as

$$F = \frac{kq_4}{d^2}\sqrt{\left(q_1 + \frac{q_2}{2}\cos 45^\circ\right)^2 + \left(\frac{q_2}{2}\sin 45^\circ + q_3\right)^2}.$$

For the angle of the force we get

$$\theta = \tan^{-1}\left(\frac{F_y}{F_x}\right) = \tan^{-1}\left(\frac{\frac{kq_4}{d^2}\left(\frac{q_2}{2}\sin 45^\circ + q_3\right)}{\frac{kq_4}{d^2}\left(q_1 + \frac{q_2}{2}\cos 45^\circ\right)}\right) = \tan^{-1}\left(\frac{\left(\frac{q_2}{2}\sin 45^\circ + q_3\right)}{\left(q_1 + \frac{q_2}{2}\cos 45^\circ\right)}\right).$$

CALCULATE:

Putting our numerical values in we get

$$\frac{q_2}{2}\sin 45^\circ = \frac{q_2}{2}\cos 45^\circ = \frac{2.50\ \mu\text{C}}{2\cdot\sqrt{2}} = 0.883\ldots$$

Finally, we get the magnitude of the force

$$F = \frac{\left(8.99\cdot 10^9\,\text{N}\cdot\text{m}^2/\text{C}^2\right)\left(4.50\ \mu\text{C}\right)}{\left(1.25\ \text{m}\right)^2}\sqrt{\left(1.50\ \mu\text{C}+0.883883\ \mu\text{C}\right)^2+\left(0.883883\ \mu\text{C}-3.50\ \mu\text{C}\right)^2}$$

$$= 0.0916379\ \text{N}$$

For the direction of the force we get

$$\theta = \tan^{-1}\left(\frac{\left(\frac{q_2}{2}\sin 45^\circ + q_3\right)}{\left(q_1+\frac{q_2}{2}\cos 45^\circ\right)}\right) = \tan^{-1}\left(\frac{\left(0.883883\ \mu\text{C}-3.50\ \mu\text{C}\right)}{\left(1.50\ \mu\text{C}+0.883883\ \mu\text{C}\right)}\right) = \text{-}47.6593^\circ.$$

Solved Problem

ROUND:

We report our result to three significant figures. For the magnitude of the force we get

$$F = 0.0916\ \text{N}.$$

For the direction of the force we get

$$\theta = \text{-}47.7^\circ.$$

DOUBLE-CHECK:

To double-check our result we calculate the magnitude of the three forces acting on q_4. For the force $F_{1\to4}$ we get

$$F_{1\to4} = k\frac{\left|q_1q_4\right|}{r_{14}^2} = \frac{\left(8.89\cdot 10^9\ \text{N}\cdot\text{m}^2/\text{C}^2\right)\left(1.50\ \mu\text{C}\right)\left(4.50\ \mu\text{C}\right)}{\left(1.25\ \text{m}\right)^2} = 0.0384\ \text{N}.$$

For $F_{2\to4}$ we get

$$F_{2\to4} = k\frac{\left|q_2q_4\right|}{r_{24}^2} = \frac{\left(8.89\cdot 10^9\ \text{N}\cdot\text{m}^2/\text{C}^2\right)\left(2.50\ \mu\text{C}\right)\left(4.50\ \mu\text{C}\right)}{\left(\sqrt{2}\cdot 1.25\ \text{m}\right)^2} = 0.0320\ \text{N}.$$

For $F_{3\to4}$ we get

$$F_{3\to4} = k\frac{\left|q_3q_4\right|}{r_{34}^2} = \frac{\left(8.89\cdot 10^9\ \text{N}\cdot\text{m}^2/\text{C}^2\right)\left(3.50\ \mu\text{C}\right)\left(4.50\ \mu\text{C}\right)}{\left(1.25\ \text{m}\right)^2} = 0.0896\ \text{N}.$$

Our result for the vector sum of these three vectors seems reasonable.

The direction we obtain also seems reasonable, because the resulting force is down and to the right, as we could expect from looking at Figure 21.15.

Chapter 22. Electric Field

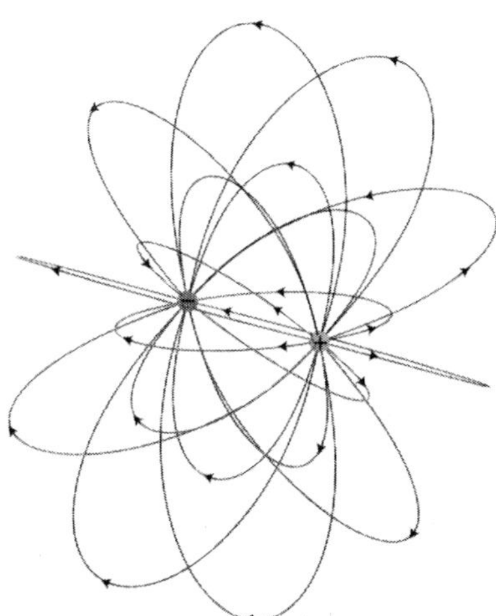

Figure 22.1: Three-dimensional representation of electric field lines from two point charges with opposite signs.

What we will learn

- The electric field is a concept that can be used to determine electric forces.
- Electric field lines represent the force vector exerted on a unit positive electric charge.
- Electric field lines originate on positive charges and terminate on negative charges.
- The electric field from a point electric charge is radial, proportional to the charge, and inversely proportional to the square of the distance from the charge.
- An electric dipole consists of a positive and a negative charge of equal magnitudes.
- The electric flux is the electric field component normal to an area times the area.
- Gauss's Law states that the integral over a closed surface of the electric flux is proportional to the net charge enclosed within the surface.
- The electric field inside a hollow, closed conductor is zero.
- The magnitude of the electric field due to a uniformly charged, infinitely long wire varies as the inverse of the perpendicular distance from the wire.
- The electric field due to an infinite sheet of charge does not depend on the distance from the sheet.

22.1. Definition of Electric Fields

In the previous chapter, we discussed the force between two charges that were not moving. The following questions now arise. How do we treat charges that are not stationary? Because information cannot get from one place to another faster than the speed of light, how can one charge know that another charge has moved so that it can react to the new situation? How does one charge know about the presence of other charges that may affect it?

To deal with this situation, we introduce the concept of a field. A field is a concept that we can use to describe forces. The electric field is defined at any point in space as the force of the electric field on a unit positive point charge. If we place a positive charge of 1 coulomb in an electric field, there will be a vector force (in N units) exerted on the charge in the direction of the electric field that is numerically equal to the electric field (in N/C units) at that point. In this chapter we will discuss a general way to treat the electric force in terms of the electric field, and we will restrict ourselves to fields caused by stationary charges. In later chapters we will see why the field concept is essential when charges are moving.

Rather than using a unit point charge, we can equivalently define the electric field in terms of the force that it exerts on any point charge q. The electric field is then given by

$$\vec{E} = \frac{\vec{F}}{q}. \tag{22.1}$$

The units of the electric field are N/C. We see from (22.1) that, using SI units, when $q = 1$ C we have $\vec{E} = \vec{F}$ (both expressed in SI units), which is our original definition of the electric field. We can also see from (22.1) that the electric field is the force per unit charge.

The electric force is parallel to the electric field and proportional to the charge. The magnitude of the force is given by $F = |q|E$. The direction of the force on a positive charge is along $\vec{E}$, while the direction of the force on a negative charge will be in the direction opposite to $\vec{E}$ with the same magnitude.

If there are several sources of electric field, such as several point charges, the electric field at any given point is given by the superposition of the electric fields from all sources. This superposition follows directly from the superposition of forces that we introduced earlier in our study of mechanics. The superposition principle for the total electric field $\vec{E}_t$ due to n electric field sources can be stated as

$$\vec{E}_t = \vec{E}_1 + \vec{E}_2 + \ldots + \vec{E}_n. \tag{22.2}$$

22.2. Field Lines

Electric field lines graphically represent the vector force exerted on a unit positive test charge. This representation applies separately for each point in space where the test charge might be placed. The direction of the field lines is the same as the direction of the force, while the density of field lines is proportional to the magnitude of the force. Electric field lines originate on positive charges and terminate on negative charges. Electric fields exist in three dimensions as illustrated in Figure 22.1. However, we will often present two-dimensional depictions of the electric field for simplicity.

Electric Field Lines from a Point Charge

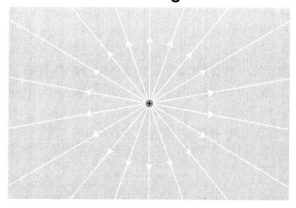

Figure 22.2: Electric field lines from a single positively charged point charge.

The electric field lines from a point charge are shown in Figure 22.2. The field lines emanate in radial direction from the point charge. If the point charge is positive, the field lines point outward and if the point charge is negative, the field lines point in toward the charge. For the case of an isolated positive point charge, the electric field lines originate at the charge and terminate on negative charges at infinity and vice versa for a negative point charge.

Electric Field Lines for Two Opposite Sign Point Charges

We can use the superposition principle to calculate electric field from two point charges. In Figure 22.3 we show the electric field lines for two oppositely charged point charges with the same magnitude. At each point in the plane, the electric field from the positive charge and the electric field from the negative charge are added as vectors to determine the magnitude and the direction of the resulting electric field.

The electric field lines originate on the positive charge and terminate on the negative charge, because when you are close to one charge the field lines are similar to a point charge as the effect of the relatively distant charge is small. Near the charges, the electric lines are close together indicating that the field is stronger near the charges. The fact that the field lines between the two charges connect signifies that there is an attractive force between the two charges.

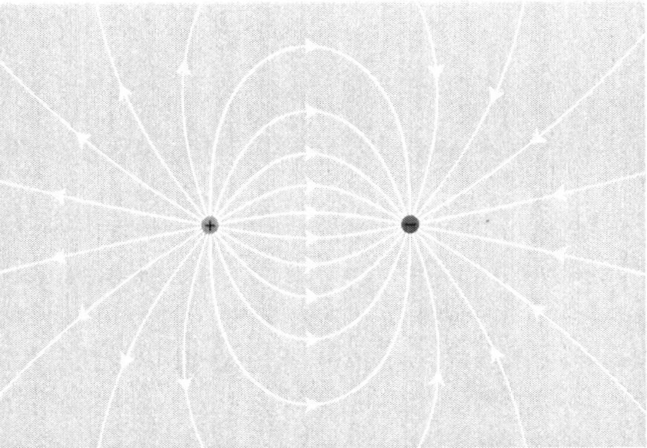

Figure 22.3: Electric field lines from two oppositely charged point charges. Each charge has the same magnitude.

Electric Field Lines for Two Point Charges with the Same Sign

We can also apply the principle of superposition to two charges with the same sign. In Figure 22.4 we show the electric field lines for two point charges with the same sign and same magnitude. If both charges are positive, the electric field lines originate at the charges and terminate at infinity. If both charges are negative, the field lines originate at infinity and terminate at the charges.

For two charges of the same sign, the field lines do not connect the two charges. Rather the field lines terminate on opposite charges at infinity. The fact the field lines never terminate on the other charge signifies that the charges repel each other.

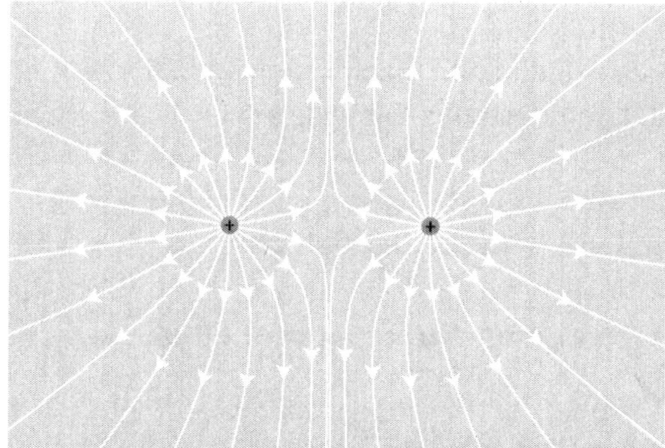

Figure 22.4: Electric field lines from two positively charged point charges with the same magnitude.

General Observations on Electric Field Lines

From the three simplest possible cases that we just examined, one can already see two general rules that all field lines of all charge configurations have to follow. First, we have seen that in all cases, *field lines originate at charges or terminate at charges*, depending on the sign of the charge. Second, we see that *field lines never cross*. This result is a consequence of the fact that the field lines represent the electric field, which in turn is proportional to the force that would act on a charge placed at that particular point. Crossing field lines would imply that the force points simultaneously in two different directions, which is obviously impossible.

22.3. Electric Field from a Point Charge

The magnitude of the electric force on a point charge q_0 due to a charge q is given by

$$F = \frac{1}{4\pi\varepsilon_0}\frac{|qq_0|}{r^2}. \tag{22.3}$$

If we consider q_0 as a test charge, then we can write the magnitude of the electric field due to a single point charge q as

$$E = \left|\frac{F}{q_0}\right| = \frac{1}{4\pi\varepsilon_0}\frac{|q|}{r^2}. \tag{22.4}$$

where r is the distance from the point charge.

The direction of the electric field is radial. The field points outward for a positive point charge and inward for a negative point charge. Figure 22.2 shows representative electric field lines for a point charge. The field lines illustrate the direction of the field at any given point in space. The density of electric field lines represents the strength of the electric field.

The electric field is a vector and to add electric fields we normally add the components separately. Example 22.1 demonstrates the addition of the electric fields caused by three point charges.

Example

Example 22.1: Electric field from three point charges

In Figure 22.5 we show three point charges, $q_1 = +1.50\ \mu\text{C}$, $q_2 = +2.50\ \mu\text{C}$, and $q_3 = -3.50\ \mu\text{C}$. q_1 is located at $(0, a)$, q_2 is located at $(0,0)$, and q_3 is located at $(b,0)$, where $a = 8.00$ m and $b = 6.00$ m.

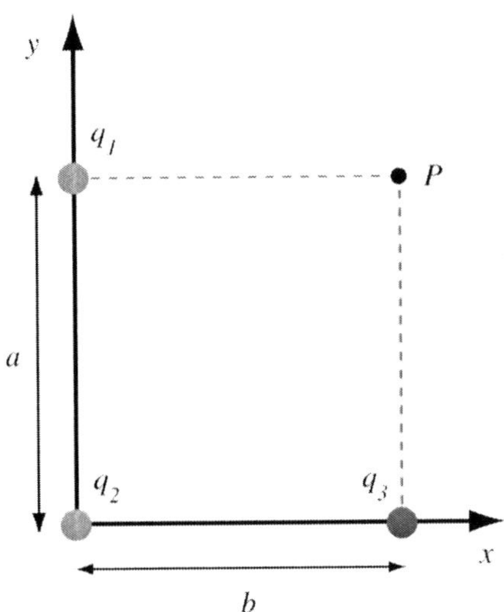

Figure 22.5: Location of three point charges.

Question:
What is the electric field $\vec{E}$ at point $P = (b, a)$ due to these three charges?
Answer:
We must sum the electric fields from the three charges according to (22.2). We will proceed by summing component by component. We start with the field from q_1:

$$\vec{E}_1 = E_{1,x}\hat{x} + E_{1,y}\hat{y}.$$

The field from q_1 acts only in the x-direction at point (b, a), because the location of q_1 is at the same y-coordinate as point P; so $\vec{E}_1 = E_{1,x}\hat{x}$. We can calculate $E_{1,x}$ using (22.4)

$$E_{1,x} = \frac{kq_1}{b^2}.$$

Note that the sign of $E_{1,x}$ is the same as the sign of q_1. Similarly, the field from q_3 acts

Example

only in the y-direction at point (b,a); so $\vec{E}_3 = E_{3,y}\hat{y}$, where

$$E_{3,y} = \frac{kq_3}{a^2}.$$

As shown in Figure 22.6, the electric field from q_2 at P is given by

$$\vec{E}_2 = E_{2,x}\hat{x} + E_{2,y}\hat{y}$$

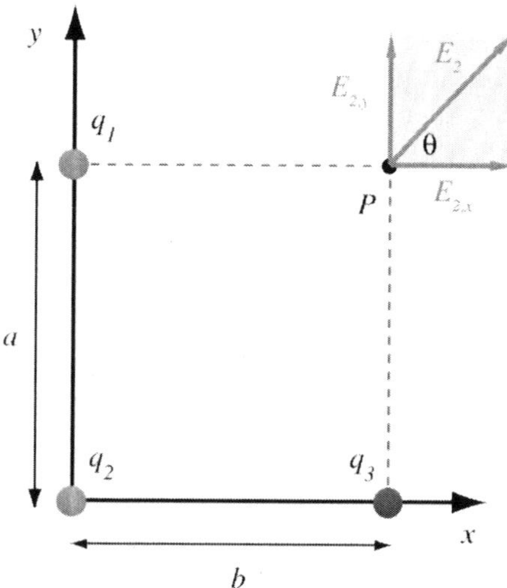

Figure 22.6: Electric field from q_2 and its x- and y- components at point P.

Note that the direction of the electric field due to q_2 at point P points exactly away from the location of q_2. The magnitude of the electric field at point P from q_2 is given by

$$E_2 = \frac{k|q_2|}{a^2+b^2}.$$

Because $q_2 > 0$, $E_{2,x}$ is given by $E_2 \cos\theta$, where $\theta = \arctan(a/b)$, and $E_{2,y}$ is given by $E_2 \sin\theta$. Therefore the total electric field at point P is

$$\begin{aligned}\vec{E} &= \left(E_{1,x} + E_{2,x}\right)\hat{x} + \left(E_{2,y} + E_{3,y}\right)\hat{y} \\ &= \underbrace{\left(\frac{kq_1}{b^2} + \frac{kq_2\cos\theta}{a^2+b^2}\right)}_{E_x}\hat{x} + \underbrace{\left(\frac{kq_2\sin\theta}{a^2+b^2} + \frac{kq_3}{a^2}\right)}_{E_y}\hat{y}.\end{aligned}$$

Example

Putting in the specified values for a and b results in $\theta = \arctan(8/6) = 53.1°$ and $a^2 + b^2 = (8.00 \text{ m})^2 + (6.00 \text{ m})^2 = 100 \text{ m}^2$. We can then calculate the x-component as

$$E_x = \left(8.99 \cdot 10^9 \text{ Nm}^2/\text{C}\right)\left(\frac{1.50 \cdot 10^{-6} \text{ C}}{(6.00 \text{ m})^2} + \frac{\left(2.50 \cdot 10^{-6} \text{ C}\right)\cos(53.1°)}{100 \text{ m}^2}\right) = 509 \text{ N/C}.$$

The y-component is

$$E_y = \left(8.99 \cdot 10^9 \text{ Nm}^2/\text{C}\right)\left(\frac{\left(2.50 \cdot 10^{-6} \text{ C}\right)\sin(53.1°)}{100 \text{ m}^2} + \frac{-3.50 \cdot 10^{-6} \text{ C}}{(8.00 \text{ m})^2}\right) = -311 \text{ N/C}.$$

The magnitude of the field is then

$$E = \sqrt{E_x^2 + E_y^2} = \sqrt{(509 \text{ N/C})^2 + (-311 \text{ N/C})^2} = 597 \text{ N/C}.$$

The direction of the field at point P is

$$\theta = \tan^{-1}\left(\frac{E_y}{E_x}\right) = \tan^{-1}\left(\frac{-311 \text{ N/C}}{509 \text{ N/C}}\right) = -31.5°$$

which means that the electric field point points to the right and downward.

22.4. Electric Field from a Dipole

A system of two equal (in magnitude) but oppositely charged point particles is called an electric dipole. The electric field from an electric dipole is given by the vector sum of the electric fields from the two charges. Figure 22.3 shows the electric field lines in two dimensions for an electric dipole.

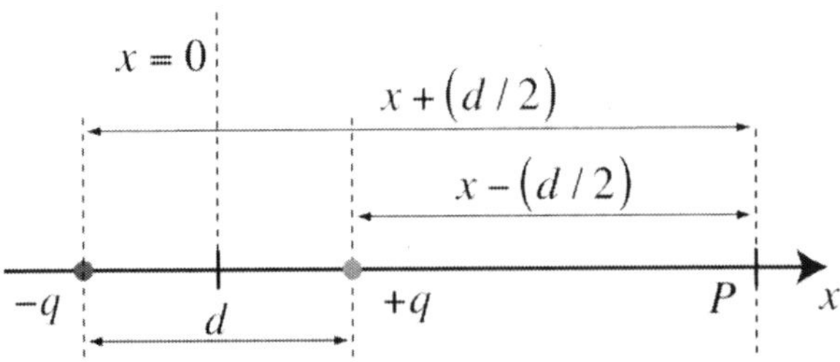

Figure 22.7: Calculation of the electric field from an electric dipole.

The superposition principle tells us that we calculate the electric field of two point charges by adding the vector electric fields from the two charges. Here we calculate the special case of the electric field from a dipole along the x axis, defined by the line going from the negative to the positive charge as illustrated in Figure 22.7.

We first define the electric field, $\vec{E}$, at point P as the sum of the field from $+q$, $\vec{E}_+$, and the electric field from $-q$, $\vec{E}_-$

$$\vec{E} = \vec{E}_+ + \vec{E}_- . \tag{22.5}$$

Using (22.4) we can write the magnitude of the dipole's electric field on the x axis for $x > d/2$ as

$$E = \frac{1}{4\pi\varepsilon_0}\frac{q}{r_+^2} + \frac{1}{4\pi\varepsilon_0}\frac{-q}{r_-^2} \tag{22.6}$$

where r_+ is the distance between p and $+q$ and r_- is the distance between p and $-q$. We do not need absolute value signs in (22.6) because the first term on the right hand side of the equation is positive and is greater than the magnitude of the second (negative) term. The electric field at all points on the x axis except at $x = \pm d/2$ is given by

$$\vec{E} = E_x\hat{x} = \frac{1}{4\pi\varepsilon_0}\frac{q(x-d/2)}{r_+^3}\hat{x} + \frac{1}{4\pi\varepsilon_0}\frac{-q(x+d/2)}{r_-^3}\hat{x} .$$

We continue our analysis by examining the magnitude of $\vec{E}$ and restricting the value of x to $x > d/2$ where $E = E_x > 0$. Then

$$E = \frac{1}{4\pi\varepsilon_0}\frac{q}{\left(x-\frac{1}{2}d\right)^2} - \frac{1}{4\pi\varepsilon_0}\frac{q}{\left(x+\frac{1}{2}d\right)^2} . \tag{22.7}$$

With some rearrangement with the idea that we want to obtain an expression that has the same form as the electric field from a point charge we get

$$E = \frac{q}{4\pi\varepsilon_0 x^2}\left(\left(1-\frac{d}{2x}\right)^{-2} - \left(1+\frac{d}{2x}\right)^{-2}\right). \tag{22.8}$$

If we want an expression for the electric field from the dipole at a large distance, we can make the approximation $x >> d$ and using the binomial expansion we get the expression

$$E \approx \frac{q}{4\pi\varepsilon_0 x^2}\left(\left(1+\frac{d}{x}-...\right)-\left(1-\frac{d}{x}+...\right)\right) \tag{22.9}$$

which can be rewritten as

$$E \approx \frac{q}{4\pi\varepsilon_0 x^2}\left(\frac{2d}{x}\right)=\frac{qd}{2\pi\varepsilon_0 x^3}. \tag{22.10}$$

We can define the vector quantity called the electric dipole $\vec{p}$. The direction of the electric dipole is given by the direction from the negative charge to the positive charge. The magnitude p of the electric dipole is given by

$$p = qd \tag{22.11}$$

where q is the magnitude of one of the charges and d is the distance separating the two charges. Using this definition we get an expression for the magnitude of the dipole electric field on the positive x axis at a distance large compared with the separation between the two charges

$$E = \frac{p}{2\pi\varepsilon_0 |x|^3}. \tag{22.12}$$

Though we do not show this explicitly, (22.12) is also valid for $x << -d/2$. Also an examination of the equation for $\vec{E}$ that is just above (22.7) shows that $E_x > 0$ on either side of the dipole. In contrast to the field due to a point charge, which falls as the distance squared, (22.12) tells us that the dipole field falls as the distance cubed.

Example

Example 22.2: Electric dipole moment of water molecule

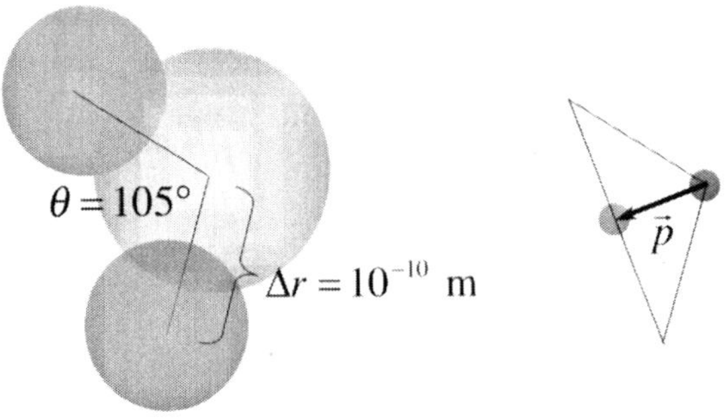

Figure 22.8: Schematic diagram of water molecule, H_2O.

Example

A water molecule, H_2O, consists of two atoms of hydrogen and one atom of oxygen. The charge distributions of each of the individual atoms are approximately spherical, and the atoms are arranged so that the lines connecting the center of the hydrogen atoms with the center of the oxygen atom have an angle of 105° between them (see left side of Figure 22.8).

Question:
Suppose we approximate a water molecule by two positive charges at the location of the two hydrogen nuclei (protons), and two negative charges at the location of the oxygen nucleus. What is the resulting electric dipole moment of water?

Answer:
The center of mass of the two positive charges is located exactly halfway between the centers of the hydrogen atoms, as indicated in the right half of Figure 22.8. If we use the hydrogen-oxygen distance as $10^{-10}\,\text{m}$, as indicated in the figure, then the distance between the positive and negative charge centers is

$$d = (10^{-10}\ \text{m})\cos 52.5° = 0.6 \cdot 10^{-10}\ \text{m}.$$

Multiplication of this distance with $q = 2e$ then results in a dipole moment of water of

$$p = 2ed = (3.2 \cdot 10^{-19}\ \text{C})(0.6 \cdot 10^{-10}\ \text{m}) = 2 \cdot 10^{-29}\ \text{C m}.$$

This result of our extremely oversimplified calculation actually comes close, within a factor of three, to the measured value of $6.2 \cdot 10^{-30}\ \text{C m}$. The fact that the real dipole moment of water is smaller than the result of our very simple model is an indication that the two electrons of the hydrogen atoms do not get pulled over all the way towards the oxygen, but on average only one third of the way.

Electric Field from General Distributions of Charge

We can calculate the electric field from a general distribution of charge as well as from a system of discrete charges using

$$\vec{E}(\vec{r}) = k\int dq \frac{\vec{r} - \vec{r}'}{\left|\vec{r} - \vec{r}'\right|^3} \tag{22.13}$$

where the differential charge dq could be expressed in terms of a linear charge density times a differential length λdx, in terms of a charge per unit area times a differential area σdA, or in terms of a charge per unit volume times a differential volume ρdV.

Example 22.3: Electric field from a finite line charge

We calculate the electric field along a line bisecting a finite length wire with linear charge density λ by directly integrating the electric field due to all the charge in the wire, rather than using Gauss's Law. We take the wire to be along the x axis as shown in Figure 22.9.

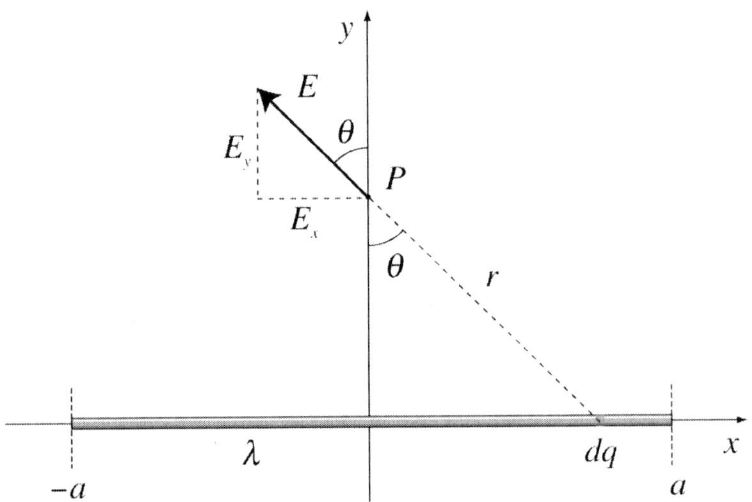

Figure 22.9: Calculation of the electric field from a long wire by integrating the contributions to the electric field from all the charge along the wire.

Example

We assume that the wire is positioned such that its center is located at $x = 0$ and one end is at $x = a$ while the other end is at $x = -a$. We make use of the symmetry of the problem to argue that there cannot be any electric force parallel to the wire (in the x direction) along the line bisecting the wire. Along the line bisecting the wire, the electric field will be in the y direction. We then can calculate the electric field from all the charge with $x > 0$ and multiply the result by two to get the electric field from the whole wire.

We start by assuming a differential charge dq along the x axis as shown in Figure 22.9. The electric field dE at a point $(0, y)$ due to this charge is given by (22.4)

$$dE = k\frac{dq}{r^2} \tag{22.14}$$

where $r = \sqrt{x^2 + y^2}$ is the distance from dq to point P. The component of the electric field perpendicular to the wire (in the y direction) is then given by

$$dE_y = k\frac{dq}{r^2}\cos\theta \tag{22.15}$$

where θ is the angle between the electric field produced by dq and the y axis as shown

Example

in Figure 22.9. We can relate θ to r and y through

$$\cos\theta = \frac{y}{r}. \tag{22.16}$$

We can relate the differential charge to the differential distance along the x axis through the linear charge density λ

$$dq = \lambda dx. \tag{22.17}$$

The electric field at a distance y from the long wire is then

$$E_y = 2\int_0^a dE_y = 2\int_0^a k\frac{dq}{r^2}\cos\theta = 2k\int_0^a \frac{\lambda dx}{r^2}\frac{y}{r} = 2k\lambda y\int_0^a \frac{dx}{\left(x^2+y^2\right)^{3/2}}. \tag{22.18}$$

Evaluating the last integral in (22.18) gives us

$$\int_0^a \frac{dx}{\left(x^2+y^2\right)^{3/2}} = \left[\frac{1}{y^2}\frac{x}{\sqrt{x^2+y^2}}\right]_0^a = \frac{1}{y^2}\frac{a}{\sqrt{y^2+a^2}}. \tag{22.19}$$

Thus the electric field a distance y along a line bisecting the wire is given by

$$E_y = 2k\lambda y\frac{1}{y^2}\frac{a}{\sqrt{y^2+a^2}} = \frac{2k\lambda}{y}\frac{a}{\sqrt{y^2+a^2}}. \tag{22.20}$$

22.5. Force due to Electric Fields

The force $\vec{F}$ exerted by an electric field $\vec{E}$ on a charge q is given by

$$\vec{F} = q\vec{E}. \tag{22.21}$$

Thus, the vector force exerted by the electric field on a positive charge is in the same direction as the electric field. The force is always tangent to the electric field lines and points in the direction of the electric field if $q > 0$.

An example in three dimensions is shown in Figure 22.10 for the case of two oppositely charged particles in three dimensions. We can see that the force on a positive charge is always tangent to the field lines and points in the same direction as the electric field. The force on a negative charge would point in the opposite direction.

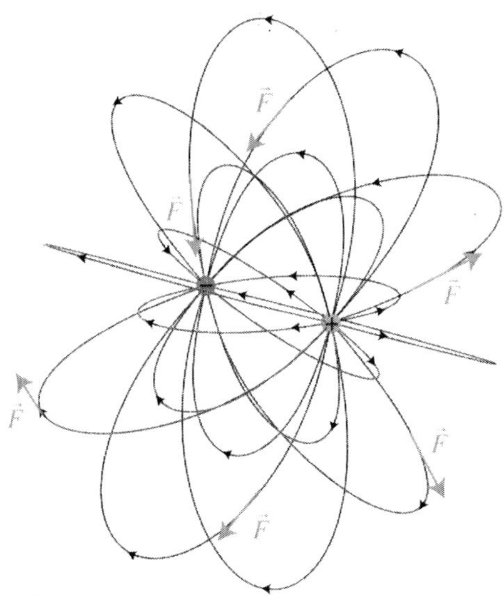

Figure 22.10: Direction of the force exerted on a positive charge by an electric field produced by two oppositely charge point charges at various points in space.

Self-Test Opportunity: The figure shows electric field lines from two opposite charges. What is the direction of the electric field at the five points indicated?

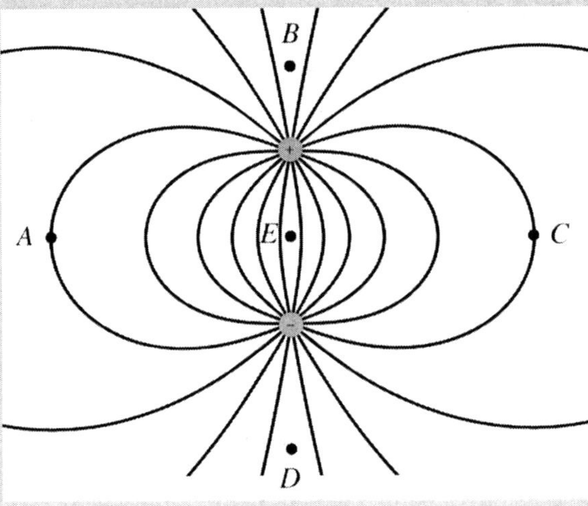

Electric field lines from two opposite charges.

In-class exercise: State whether the following statements about electric field lines are true or false.

a) Electric field lines point inward toward negative charges.
b) Electric field lines make circles around positive charges.
c) Electric field lines may cross.
d) Electric field lines point outward from positive charges.
e) A positive point charge released from rest will initially accelerate along an electric field line.

22.6. Point Charge and Dipole in Electric Fields

Placing a point charge in an electric field produces a force on that charge given by equation (22.1). The electric force will always be tangent to the electric field lines. The effect of an electric field on a dipole can be described in terms of the vector electric field, $\vec{E}$, and the vector electric dipole, $\vec{p}$, without detailed knowledge of the charges making up the electric dipole.

To examine the behavior of an electric dipole let's take two charges, $+q$ and $-q$ separated by a distance d in a constant electric field $\vec{E}$ as shown in Figure 22.11. Note that we are now considering the forces acting on a dipole placed in an external field as opposed to the previous section where we considered the field caused by the dipole.

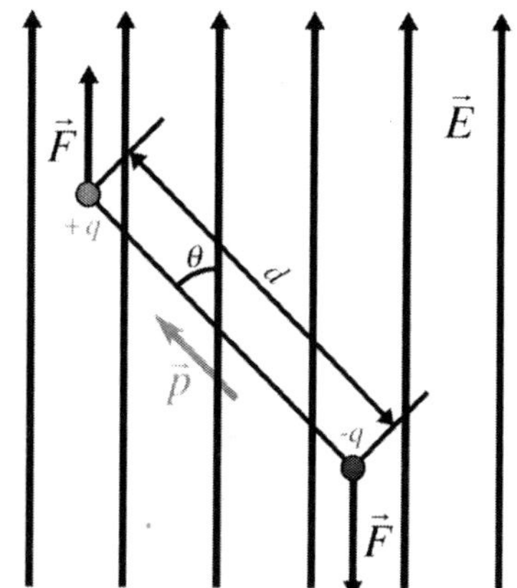

Figure 22.11: Electric dipole in an electric field.

The electric field exerts an upward force on the positive charge and a downward force on the negative charge. Both forces have the magnitude qE. In chapter 10 we learned that a torque $\vec{\tau}$ is given by

$$\vec{\tau} = \vec{r} \times \vec{F} \tag{22.22}$$

where $\vec{r}$ is the moment arm and $\vec{F}$ is the force. If the moment arm and force are perpendicular to each other, the magnitude of the torque can be written as

$$\tau = rF\sin\theta . \tag{22.23}$$

As always, we are free to calculate the torque about any pivot point. For example, we can pick the location of the negative charge. Then only the force on the positive charge contributes to the torque, and the length of the position vector is $r = d$, i.e. the length of the dipole. Since, as already stated, $F = qE$, we arrive at our final expression for the torque on an electric dipole in an external electric field
which can be rewritten as

$$\tau = qEd\sin\theta . \tag{22.24}$$

Remembering that the electric dipole is defined as $p = qd$, we obtain

$$\tau = pE\sin\theta \qquad (22.25)$$

***Self-test opportunity*:**
Use the center of mass of the dipole as the pivot point and show that one obtains the same answer for the torque.

We see that the torque is a vector that is perpendicular to the electric dipole vector and to the electric field and can be expressed by a vector product

$$\vec{\tau} = \vec{p} \times \vec{E}\,. \qquad (22.2$$

As in all cases involving vector products, the direction of the torque is given by the right hand rule. As always, the thumb is aligned with the first term of the vector product, in this case $\vec{p}$, and the index finger is aligned with the second term, $\vec{E}$. The result of the vector product, $\vec{\tau}$, is then aligned with the middle finger and perpendicular to each of the other two fingers, as shown in Figure 22.12.

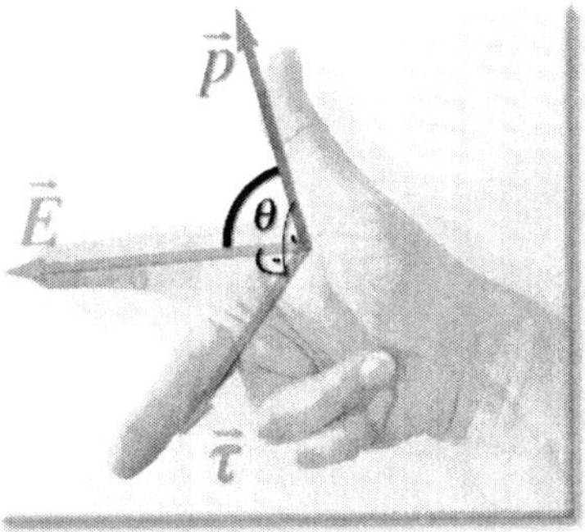

Figure 22.12: Right-hand rule for vector product of the electric dipole and the electric field, producing the torque vector.

Solved Problem

Solved Problem 22.1: Electric dipole in an electric field

Question:

An electric dipole of magnitude $p = 1.40 \cdot 10^{-12}$ C·m is placed in a uniform electric field of strength $E = 498$ N/C as shown in Figure 22.13.

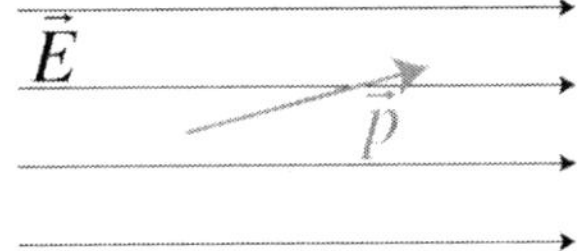

Figure 22.13: An electric dipole in a constant electric field.

The angle between the electric dipole and the electric field is $\theta = 14.5°$. What are the Cartesian components of the torque on the electric dipole?

Answer:

THINK:

The torque on the electric dipole is equal to the vector cross product of the electric field and the electric dipole moment.

SKETCH:

We define the constant electric field to point in the x-direction and electric dipole to be in the $x-y$ plane as shown in Figure 22.14. The z-direction is out of the page.

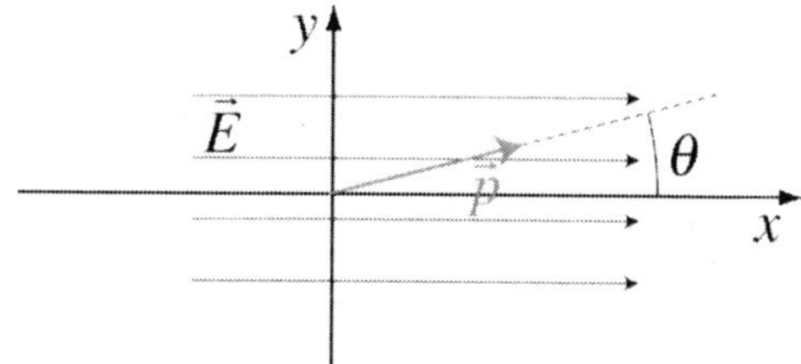

Figure 22.14: Sketch showing an electric field in the x-direction and an electric dipole in the x-y plane.

RESEARCH:

The torque on the electric dipole due to the electric field is given by

$$\vec{\tau} = \vec{p} \times \vec{E}. \tag{22.27}$$

We can write the electric dipole in Cartesian components as

$$\vec{p} = \left(p_x, p_y, 0\right). \tag{22.28}$$

We can write the electric field in Cartesian components as

$$\vec{E} = \left(E_x, 0, 0\right) = \left(E, 0, 0\right). \tag{22.29}$$

From the definition of the vector product we can write the Cartesian components of the torque as

$$\vec{\tau} = \left(p_y E_z - p_z E_y\right)\hat{x} + \left(p_z E_x - p_x E_z\right)\hat{y} + \left(p_x E_y - p_y E_x\right)\hat{z}. \tag{22.30}$$

SIMPLIFY:

For this case we have

$$\vec{\tau} = \left(-p_y E_x\right)\hat{z}. \tag{22.31}$$

The magnitude of the torque is then

Solved Problem

$$\tau = (p\sin\theta)E = pE\sin\theta \qquad (22.32)$$

and the direction of the torque is in the negative z-direction.

CALCULATE:
Putting in our numerical values, we get

$$\tau = pE\sin\theta = (1.40\cdot10^{-12}\ \text{C}\cdot\text{m})(498\ \text{N/C})\sin(14.5°) = 1.74565\cdot10^{-10}\ \text{N}\cdot\text{m}.$$

ROUND:
We report our result to three significant figures

$$\tau = 1.75\cdot10^{-10}\ \text{N}\cdot\text{m}.$$

DOUBLE-CHECK:
From (22.25) we know that the magnitude of the torque is

$$\tau = pE\sin\theta,$$

which is the result we obtained in (22.32) using the explicit vector cross product. Looking at the right-hand rule illustrated in Figure 22.12, we can determine the direction of the torque. If we align our right thumb with the electric dipole and our right index finger with the electric field, our right middle finger points into the page, which agrees with our result using the explicit vector product. Thus our result seems reasonable.

22.7. Electric Flux

Let us imagine that we hold a ring with area A in a stream of water flowing with speed v such that the plane of the ring is perpendicular to the flowing water as shown in Figure 22.15*a*.

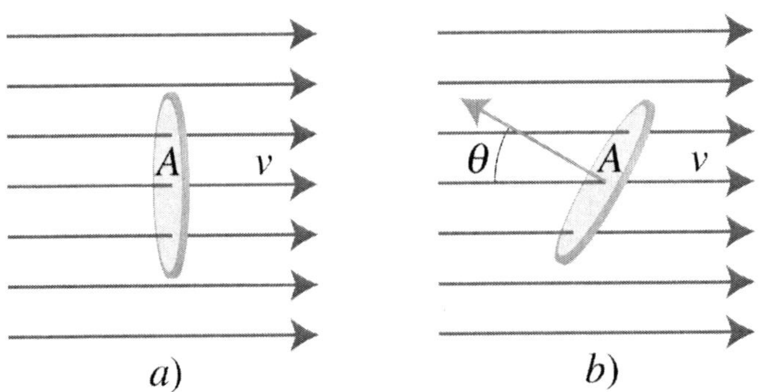

Figure 22.15: Water flowing with a speed v through a ring with area A.

The product Av gives the amount of water passing through the ring per unit time. If we tilt the plane of the ring with respect to the direction of the flowing water as depicted in Figure 22.15*b*, the amount of water flowing through ring is given by $Av\cos\theta$ where θ is the angle between a normal to the plane of the ring and the direction of the flowing water. We can call this amount of water flowing through the ring the flux $\Phi = Av\cos\theta = \vec{A}\cdot\vec{v}$. The units of this quantity are m^3/s, volume per unit time.

Consider a constant electric field of magnitude E passing through a given area A as shown in Figure 22.16.

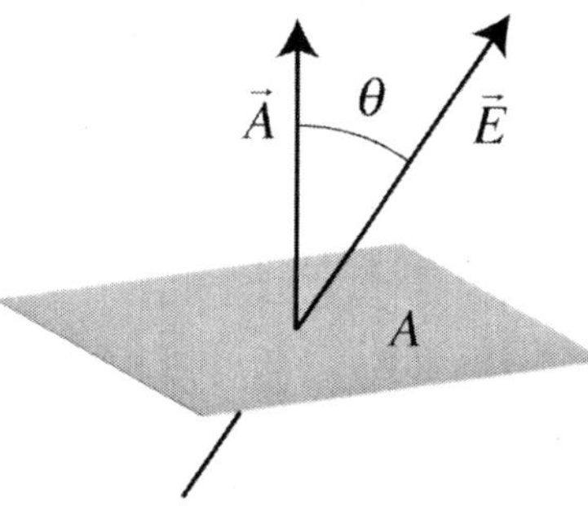

Figure 22.16: A constant magnetic field passing through an area.

We define the vector area $\vec{A}$, which has a direction normal to the surface of the area and a magnitude A. The angle θ is the angle between the vector electric field and the vector area as shown in Figure 22.16. For a constant electric field E, we have a situation analogous to flowing water, where the density of electric field vectors passing through a given area A is called the *electric flux* and is given by $\Phi = EA\cos\theta$. In the following material we will use the case of an electric field given by $\vec{E}(\vec{r})$ and a closed surface rather than the open surface discussed above in terms of a simple ring. In this closed-surface case, the total or net electric flux is given by an integral of the electric field over a closed surface

$$\Phi = \oiint \vec{E}\cdot d\vec{A} \qquad (22.33)$$

where $\vec{E}$ is the electric field at each differential area element $d\vec{A}$ of a closed surface.

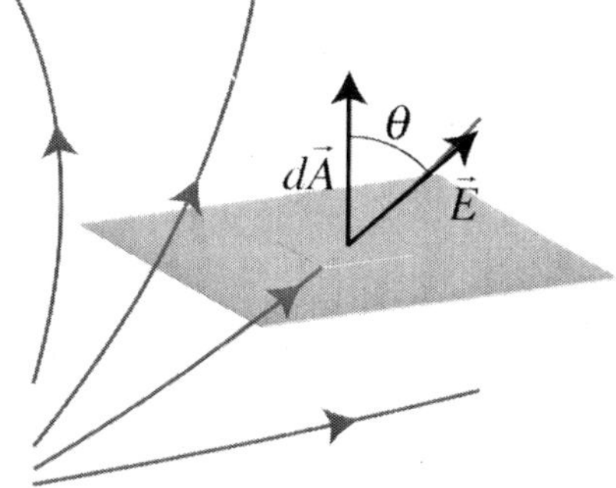

Figure 22.17: A non-uniform electric field passing through a differential area.

In Figure 22.17 we show a non-uniform electric field $\vec{E}$ passing through a differential area element $d\vec{A}$. A portion of the closed surface is also shown. The angle between the electric field and the differential area element is θ.

Self-Test Opportunity: The figure shows a cube with side A in a constant electric field $\vec{E}$ perpendicular to one face of the cube. What is the net electric flux passing though the cube?

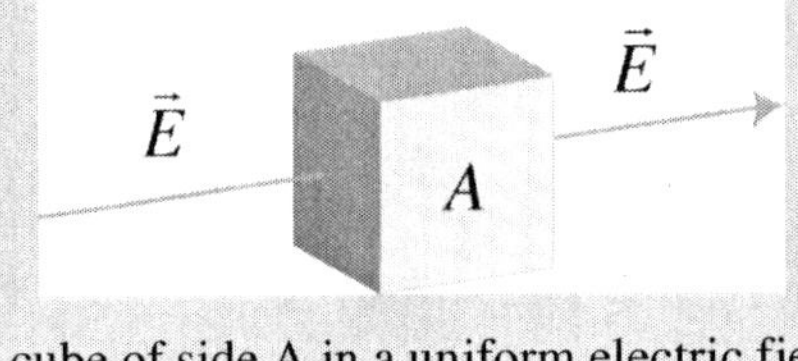

A cube of side A in a uniform electric field.

22.8. Gauss's Law

To help motivate the following discussion of Gauss's Law, let's imagine that we have an imaginary box in the form of a cube as shown in Figure 22.18*a*.

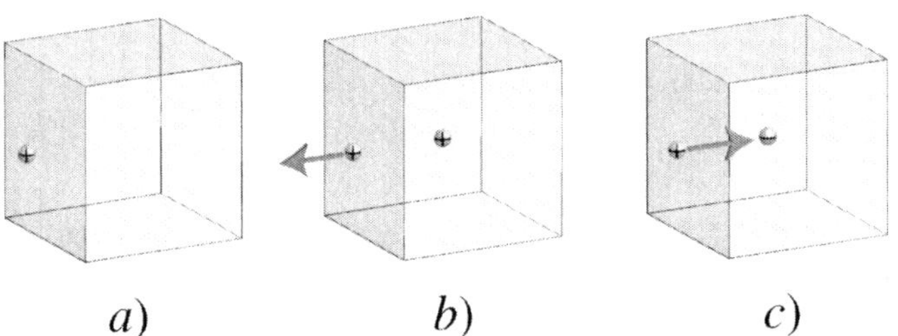

Figure 22.18: Three imaginary boxes constructed of a material that does not affect electric fields. We bring a positive test charge up to the box from the left. *a*) shows an empty box. *b*) depicts a box with a positive charge inside. *c*) represents a box with a negative charge inside.

This box is constructed of a material that does not affect electric fields. If we bring a positive charge test charge up any the surface of the box, it will feel no force.

Now we place a positive charge inside the box and bring the positive test charge up to the surface of the box as shown in Figure 22.18*b*. The positive test charge experiences an outward force due to the positive charge inside the box. If we bring the charge up to any face of the box, the charge will always feel an outward force. If we put twice as much positive charge in the box, we will feel twice the outward force on the positive test charge as we bring it up to any face of the box.

Let's replace the positive charge inside the box with a negative charge as shown in Figure 22.18*c*. When we bring the positive test charge up to one face of the box, the charge will experience an inward force. If we bring the positive test charge up to any of the faces of the box, the test charge will always feel an inward force. If we double the negative charge in the box, we will feel twice the inward force on the positive test charge as we bring it up to the face of the box.

Using the analogy with flowing water, we can say that electric field lines seems to be flowing out of the box containing positive charge and into the box containing negative charge.

Now let's imagine an empty box in a uniform electric field as shown in Figure 22.19.

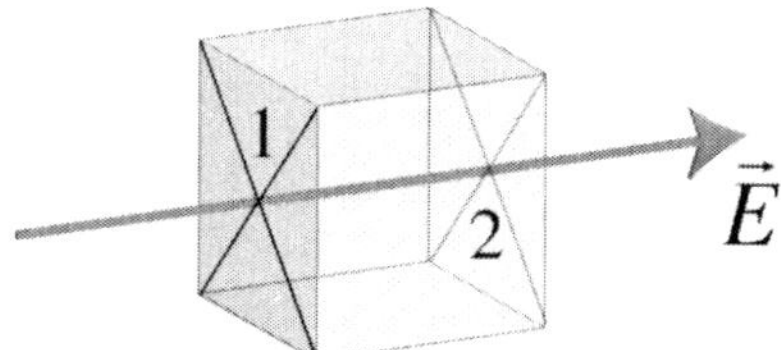

Figure 22.19: Imaginary box in a uniform electric field.

If we bring the positive test charge up to side 1, it will feel an inward force. If we bring the charge up to side 2, it will feel an outward force. The electric field is parallel the other four sides, so we will not feel any inward or outward force on the positive test charge brought up to those sides. Thus, using the analogy with flowing water, the net amount of electric field that seems to be flowing in and out of the box is zero.

Whenever we had a charge inside the box, the electric field lines seemed to be flowing in or out of the box. When there was no charge in the box, the net flow of electric field lines in or out of the box was zero. Using these observations and taking our definition of electric flux to quantify the concept of the flow of the electric field lines, we can formulate *Gauss's Law* as

$$\varepsilon_0 \Phi = q . \qquad (22.34)$$

q is the charge inside a closed surface, which we call a Gaussian surface. The closed surface could be the imaginary box we have been discussing, or could be any closed surface we can imagine. Usually the shape of the Gaussian surface is chosen to incorporate the symmetries of the problem being studied. We can give an alternative formulation of Gauss's Law that uses the definition of the electric flux (22.33)

$$\varepsilon_0 \oiint \vec{E} \cdot d\vec{A} = q . \qquad (22.35)$$

We introduce this law because it allows us to analyze problems which otherwise would be tedious or difficult. From (22.35), we see that Gauss's Law states that the surface integral of the electric field component perpendicular to the area times the area is proportional to the net charge within the closed surface.

Gauss's Law and Coulomb's Law

We can derive Coulomb's Law from Gauss's Law. We start with a point charge q. We assume a spherical Gaussian surface with radius r surrounding the charge with the charge at the center of the sphere.

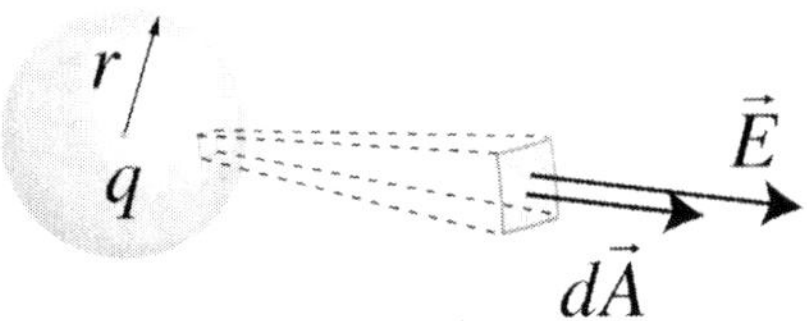

Figure 22.20: A spherical Gaussian surface with radius r surrounding a charge q. A differential surface element with area dA is shown expanded.

From the fact that there is no preferred direction in space (or, space is isotropic) we know that the electric field from a point charge is radial. Thus, the electric field will intersect each differential element of the surface of the Gaussian sphere perpendicularly. Therefore, at each point of this surface the electric field vector and the surface normal vector of the field are parallel. The scalar product between the electric field and the surface area element is then $\vec{E}\cdot d\vec{A} = EdA\cos 0° = EdA$. Thus, we can write in this case

$$\varepsilon_0 \oint\!\!\oint \vec{E}\cdot d\vec{A} = \varepsilon_0 \oint\!\!\oint E dA = q. \tag{22.36}$$

Because the electric field will have the same magnitude anywhere in space at a distance r from the center (because space is isotropic), we can take the electric field out from under the integral sign

$$\varepsilon_0 E \oint\!\!\oint dA = q. \tag{22.37}$$

Now we have the integral over a spherical surface, which is just given by $\oint\!\!\oint dA = 4\pi r^2$. This result means that in the case of a point charge we find from Gauss's Law

$$\varepsilon_0 E\left(4\pi r^2\right) = q \tag{22.38}$$

or

$$E = \frac{q}{4\pi\varepsilon_0 r^2} = \frac{1}{4\pi\varepsilon_0}\frac{q}{r^2}, \tag{22.39}$$

which is the electric field that we found from Coulomb's Law for a point charge.

Shielding

We can immediately state two important consequences of Gauss's Law: The electrostatic field inside any isolated conductor is always zero and cavities inside conductors are shielded from electric fields.

Suppose that there is a net electric field existing at some moment at some point *P* inside an isolated conductor. Let us put a Gaussian surface around this point *P*, such that this entire Gaussian surface is contained within the volume of the conductor. According to Gauss's Law there must then be an accumulation of net charge at some place inside this surface within the conducting body. Because every conductor has free electrons inside it, they can move rapidly due to this field and redistribute the charge. The accumulated charge, therefore, due to mutual repulsion, gets away as far as possible. It will move to the outer surface of the conductor, leaving no net accumulation of charge inside the volume of the conductor. The electric field then becomes zero everywhere inside the conductor.

If a cavity is scooped out of a conducting body, the net charge and thus the electric field inside this cavity is always zero, no matter how strongly the conductor is charged, or no matter in how strong a field it is placed. Proof: Take a closed Gaussian surface surrounding the cavity, completely inside the metal. From the previous paragraph we know that at each point of this surface, the field is zero. Therefore, the net flux over this surface is also zero. Therefore, by Gauss's Law, it follows that this surface encloses zero net charge. If there were equal amounts of positive and negative charge on the cavity surface (and thus no net charge), this charge would not be stationary as the plus and minus charge would be attracted to each other and would be free to move around the cavity surface to cancel each other. Therefore, any cavity inside a conductor is totally shielded from any external electric field.

Figure 22.21: Styrofoam peanuts placed inside a container and placed on top of a Van de Graaff generator that is then charged. Left side: non-conducting plastic container, right side: metal can.

We can demonstrate this shielding impressively by placing a metal and a plastic container filled with Styrofoam peanuts on top of a Van de Graaff generator, which serves as a source of high voltage, as shown in Figure 22.21. Charging up the generator results in a large net charge accumulation on the dome, and thus a strong electric field is produced in the vicinity. Because of this field the charges in the Styrofoam peanuts move slightly and the peanuts acquire a small dipole moment. If the field were uniform there would be no force on these dipoles. However the nonuniform electric field does exert a force even though the peanuts are electrically neutral. The peanuts thus fly away as indicated in the left panel of Figure 22.21. If the same Styrofoam peanuts are placed inside an open metal can (right panel), they do not fly away. For the plastic container the electric field easily penetrates the container walls and reaches the Styrofoam peanuts, whereas the conducting metal can Gauss's Law provides perfect shielding inside and prevents the Styrofoam peanuts from flying away.

The conductor does not have to be a solid piece of metal surrounding the cavity. A wire mesh is sufficient to provide shielding, as in Figure 22.22. Sitting inside a cage and hitting the cage with a lightning-like electric discharge can demonstrate this shielding. The person inside the cage is unhurt, even when touching the metal of the cage *from the inside*. (It is important to realize that severe injuries can result by sticking any body parts out of the cage, as for example when wrapping hands around the bars of the cage!) This cage is called a Faraday cage, after British physicist Michael Faraday (1791-1867), who invented this demonstration.

Figure 22.22: A person inside a Faraday cage with a large voltage applied outside the Faraday cage, producing a huge spark performed at the Deutsches Museum in Munich, Germany.

A Faraday cage has important consequences, probably the most relevant of which is the fact that your car protects you from being hit by lightning while inside it – unless, of course, you drive a convertible. The sheet metal and steel frame that surround the passenger compartment provide the necessary shielding.

22.9. Gauss's Law with Cylindrical, Planar, and Spherical Symmetry

In this section we will calculate the electric field from charged objects with different shapes. We define the charge density differently for different geometries. For a one-dimensional object such as a wire, we use λ as the charge per unit length. For two-dimensional objects such as a sheet of charge, we use σ as the charge per unit area. For three-dimensional objects such as a sphere, we use ρ as the charge per unit volume. Table 22.1 shows a summary of these quantities.

Symbol	Name	Unit
λ	Charge per length	C/m
σ	Charge per area	C/m^2
ρ	Charge per volume	C/m^3

Table 22.1: Symbols used to describe charge distributions.

Cylindrical Symmetry

We can calculate the magnitude of the electric field from a conducting wire with charge per unit length $\lambda > 0$ using Gauss's Law. We start by assuming a Gaussian surface in the form of a right cylinder with radius r and length L placed around the wire such that the wire is along the axis of the cylinder as shown in Figure 22.23.

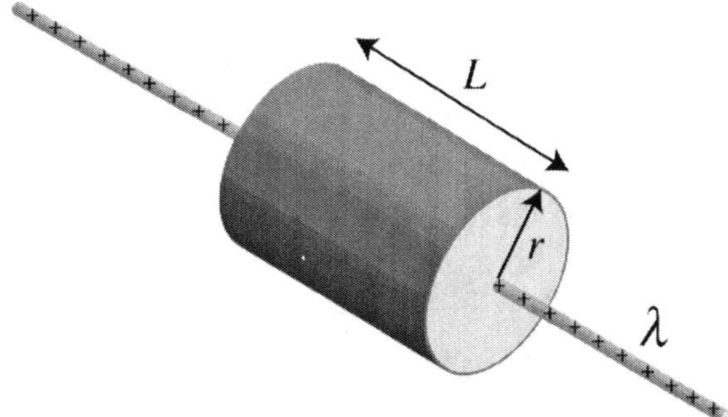

Figure 22.23: Long wire with charge per unit length λ. A Gaussian surface is shown in the form of a right cylinder with radius r and length L.

We can apply Gauss's Law to this Gaussian surface. From symmetry, we know that the electric field from the wire must be radial and perpendicular to the wire. What we mean by invoking symmetry deserves further explanation. In addition, because symmetry arguments of the kind employed here are very common, it is very beneficial to elaborate on this case in detail.

First, we can imagine that we rotate the wire about an axis along the wire. This rotation would also involve all charges on the wire and their electric field. However, the wire would still look the same after a rotation by any angle. The electric field created by the charge on the wire would therefore also look the same. From this argument, we conclude that the electric field cannot depend on the angle around the wire. This argument is rather general: there cannot be a dependence on the rotation angle if an object has rotational symmetry.

Second, if the wire is very long, then we can move up and down the wire, and the wire will still look unchanged. If the wire is unchanged, its electric field is also unchanged. This analysis means that there is no dependence on the coordinate along the wire. This symmetry is called a translational symmetry. We also know from the isotropy of space that there can be no electric field component parallel to the wire.

Returning to our Gaussian surface: The contribution to the integral from the caps is zero because the electric field is parallel to the surface and thus perpendicular to the surface normal vector. The electric field is perpendicular to the wall of the cylinder everywhere so we can write

$$\varepsilon_0 \oiint \vec{E} \cdot d\vec{A} = \varepsilon_0 EA = \varepsilon_0 E\left(2\pi rL\right) = q = \lambda L \tag{22.40}$$

where $2\pi rL$ is the area of the wall of the cylinder. Rewriting this equation, we obtain for the magnitude of the electric field from a wire

$$E = \frac{\lambda}{2\pi\varepsilon_0 r} = \frac{2k\lambda}{r} \tag{22.41}$$

where r is the perpendicular distance to the wire. For $\lambda < 0$, (22.41) still applies and the electric field points in instead of out. Now we begin to see the great computational power contained in Gauss's Law. We can calculate the electric field resulting from all kinds of charge distributions, both discrete and continuous. However it is only practical to use Gauss's Law in situations where one can exploit some symmetry; otherwise it is too difficult to calculate the flux. It is instructive to compare the dependence of the electric field on the distance for the point charge and the long wire. For the point charge, the electric field falls off with the square of the distance and thus much faster than for the wire, for which the electric field only is reduced inversely proportional to the distance.

In-class exercise:

We put a total of $1.45 \cdot 10^6$ electrons on an initially electrically neutral wire of length 1.13 m. What is the magnitude of the electric field a perpendicular distance of 0.401 m away from the center of wire?

a) $9.21 \cdot 10^{-3}$ N/C
b) $2.92 \cdot 10^{-1}$ N/C
c) $6.77 \cdot 10^{1}$ N/C
d) $8.12 \cdot 10^{2}$ N/C
e) $3.31 \cdot 10^{3}$ N/C

In Example 22.3, we derived the electric field for a finite line of charge along a line that bisected that wire (22.13)

$$E_y = \frac{2k\lambda}{y} \frac{a}{\sqrt{y^2 + a^2}}. \tag{22.42}$$

If we now take that result equating y and r, and let the length of the wire become infinite ($a \to \infty$), we obtain

$$E_y = \frac{2k\lambda}{y}\frac{a}{\sqrt{y^2+a^2}} \xrightarrow[a\to\infty]{} \frac{2k\lambda}{y} \tag{22.43}$$

which is the same result we obtained using Gauss's Law for an infinite wire.

Planar Symmetry

Assume that we have a thin infinite non-conducting sheet of positive charge as shown in Figure 22.24. The charge per unit area of this sheet is $\sigma > 0$. Now we find the electric field a distance r from the surface of this infinite plane of charge.

To do this calculation, we choose a Gaussian surface in the form of a closed right cylinder with cross sectional area A and length $2r$ chosen to cut through the plane perpendicularly as shown in Figure 22.24.

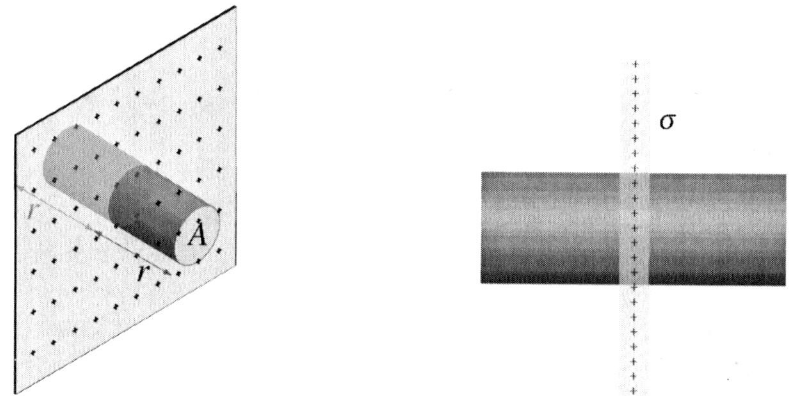

Figure 22.24: Infinite non-conducting sheet with charge density σ. A Gaussian surface in the form of a right cylinder with the end caps of area A parallel to the plane and height r above the plane and r below the plane is used.

Because the plane is infinite and the charge is positive, the electric field must be perpendicular to the caps of the cylinder and parallel to the walls of the cylinder. Using Gauss's Law we obtain

$$\varepsilon_0 \oiint \vec{E} \cdot d\vec{A} = \varepsilon_0 \left(EA + EA \right) = q = \sigma A \tag{22.44}$$

where σA is the charge enclosed in the cylinder. Thus, we get the magnitude of the electric field for an infinite plane of charge to be

$$E = \frac{\sigma}{2\varepsilon_0}. \tag{22.45}$$

If $\sigma < 0$, then (22.45) still holds, and the electric field points toward the plane, instead of away from it. If we consider an infinite conducting sheet with charge density $\sigma > 0$ on each surface instead of a non-conducting sheet with a total charge density σ, we can calculate the electric field by choosing a Gaussian surface in the form of a right cylinder. However, for this case we will embed one end of the cylinder inside the conductor as shown in Figure 22.25.

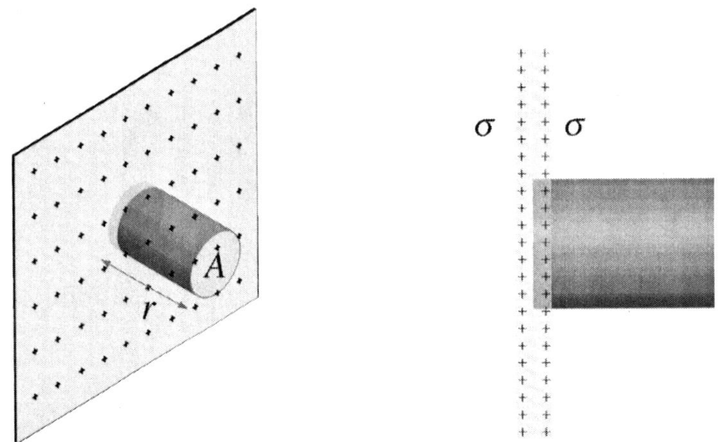

Figure 22.25: Infinite conducting plane with charge density σ on each surface with a Gaussian surface in the form of a right cylinder.

The electric field inside the conductor is zero; therefore, there is no flux through the cap enclosed in the conductor. The electric field outside the conductor must be perpendicular to the surface and therefore parallel to the sides of the cylinder and perpendicular to the cap of the cylinder outside the conductor. Thus the flux through the Gaussian surface is EA. The enclosed charge is given by σA so Gauss's Law becomes

$$\varepsilon_0 \oiint \vec{E} \cdot d\vec{A} = \varepsilon_0 EA = \sigma A. \qquad (22.46)$$

Thus, we get the magnitude of the electric field just outside the surface of a charged conductor to be

$$E = \frac{\sigma}{\varepsilon_0}. \qquad (22.47)$$

Spherical Symmetry

Now we calculate the electric field from a spherically symmetric distribution of charge. Assume that we have a thin spherical shell of charge $q > 0$ and radius r_S as illustrated in Figure 22.26. We assume that we have a spherical Gaussian surface with $r > r_S$ that is concentric with the charged sphere. Applying Gauss's law we get

$$\varepsilon_0 \oiint \vec{E} \cdot d\vec{A} = \varepsilon_0 E\left(4\pi r^2\right) = q \qquad (22.48)$$

which we can solve for the electric field strength E as

$$E = \frac{1}{4\pi\varepsilon_0}\frac{q}{r^2}. \tag{22.49}$$

Figure 22.26: Spherical shell of charge with radius r_s.

If $q < 0$, the field points in radial inward instead of radial outward direction. If we now take another spherical Gaussian surface with $r < r_S$ that is also concentric with the charged spherical shell we obtain

$$\varepsilon_0 \oiint \vec{E} \cdot d\vec{A} = \varepsilon_0 E\left(4\pi r^2\right) = 0 \tag{22.50}$$

What we observe is that the electric field outside a spherical shell of charge behaves as if the charge were a point charge located at the center of the sphere. We also observe that inside the spherical shell of charge the electric field is zero.

Now let's consider a spherical volume of charge that is equally distributed throughout that volume with charge density $\rho > 0$ as shown in Figure 22.27. We will calculate the electric field resulting from this distribution of charge using Gauss's Law.

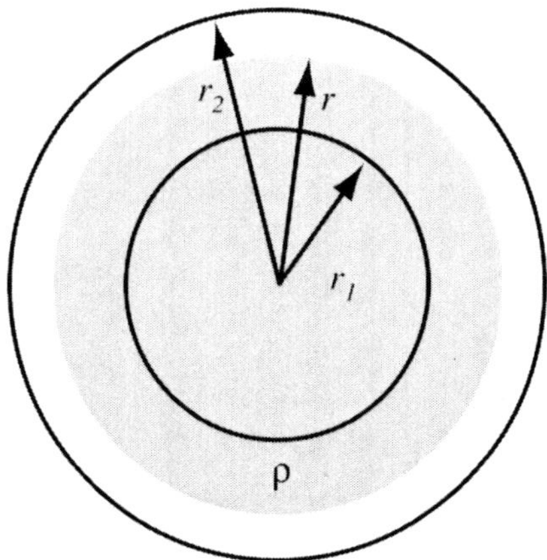

Figure 22.27: Spherical distribution of charge with constant charge per unit volume ρ and radius r. Two spherical Gaussian surfaces are also shown, one with radius $r_1 < r$ and one with $r_2 > r$.

We start by applying Gauss's Law using a Gaussian surface in the form of a sphere with radius $r_1 < r$. From the symmetry of the charge distribution, we know that the electric field resulting from the charge will be perpendicular to the surface of the Gaussian sphere. Thus, we can write

$$\varepsilon_0 \oiint \vec{E} \cdot d\vec{A} = \varepsilon_0 E\left(4\pi r_1^2\right) = q = \rho\left(\frac{4}{3}\pi r_1^3\right) \tag{22.51}$$

where $4\pi r_1^2$ is the area of the spherical Gaussian surface and $\frac{4}{3}\pi r_1^3$ is the volume enclosed by the Gaussian surface. We can rewrite this equation and obtain the result for the electric field at a radius r inside a uniform distribution of charge

$$E = \frac{\rho r_1}{3\varepsilon_0}. \tag{22.52}$$

We can also define the total charge on the sphere to be q_t. We can then relate the total volume of the spherical charge distribution to the charge density by

$$q_t = \rho \frac{4}{3}\pi r^3. \tag{22.53}$$

The charge enclosed by the Gaussian surface then is

$$q = \frac{\text{Volume inside } r_1}{\text{Volume of charge distribution}} q_t = \frac{\frac{4}{3}\pi r_1^3}{\frac{4}{3}\pi r^3} q_t = q_t \frac{r_1^3}{r^3}. \tag{22.54}$$

So we can rewrite (22.51) as

$$\varepsilon_0 \oiint \vec{E} \cdot d\vec{A} = \varepsilon_0 E\left(4\pi r_1^2\right) = q_t \frac{r_1^3}{r^3} \tag{22.55}$$

which gives us

$$E = \frac{q_t r_1}{4\pi\varepsilon_0 r^3} = \frac{k q_t r_1}{r^3}. \tag{22.56}$$

If we consider a Gaussian surface with radius larger than the radius of the charge distribution, $r_2 > r$, we can apply Gauss's Law as

$$\varepsilon_0 \oiint \vec{E} \cdot d\vec{A} = \varepsilon_0 E\left(4\pi r_2^{\,2}\right) = q_t \qquad (22.57)$$

or

$$E = \frac{q_t}{4\pi\varepsilon_0 r_2^{\,2}} = \frac{kq_t}{r_2^{\,2}}. \qquad (22.58)$$

This result tells us that the electric field outside a uniform distribution of charge is the same as a point charge with the same total charge.

In-class exercise: Consider a sphere of radius $R = 6.20$ m in which a charge $q = 12.8$ μC is uniformly distributed throughout the volume of the sphere. What is the magnitude of the electric field at a point half way between the center of the sphere and the surface of the sphere?

a) $2.33 \cdot 10^2$ N/C
b) $1.50 \cdot 10^3$ N/C
c) $4.55 \cdot 10^4$ N/C
d) $2.98 \cdot 10^5$ N/C
e) $5.56 \cdot 10^6$ N/C

Self-Test Opportunity: Consider a sphere of radius R in which a charge q is uniformly distributed throughout the volume of the sphere. What is the magnitude of the electric field at a point $2R$ away from the center of the sphere?

Solved Problem

Solved Problem 22.2: Electric field for a non-uniform spherical charge distribution
A spherically symmetric but non-uniform charge distribution is given by

$$\rho(r) = \rho_0\left(1 - \frac{r}{R}\right) \quad r \le R$$
$$\rho(r) = 0 \quad r > R \qquad (22.59)$$

where $\rho_0 = 10.0$ μC/m^3 and $R = 0.250$ m.

Question:
What is the electric field produced by this charge distribution at $r = 0.125$ m and $r = 0.500$ m?

Answer:

THINK:

We can use Gauss's Law to determine the electric field as a function of radius using a spherical Gaussian surface. The first radius in the problem is located inside the charge distribution. The charge enclosed inside the surface of the spherical charge distribution at $r = r_1$ is given by an integral of the charge density from $r = 0$ to $r = r_1$. Outside the spherical charge distribution, the electric field is the same as a point charge whose magnitude is equal to the total charge of the spherical charge distribution.

SKETCH:

A sketch of the charge density ρ as a function of radius r is shown in Figure 22.28.

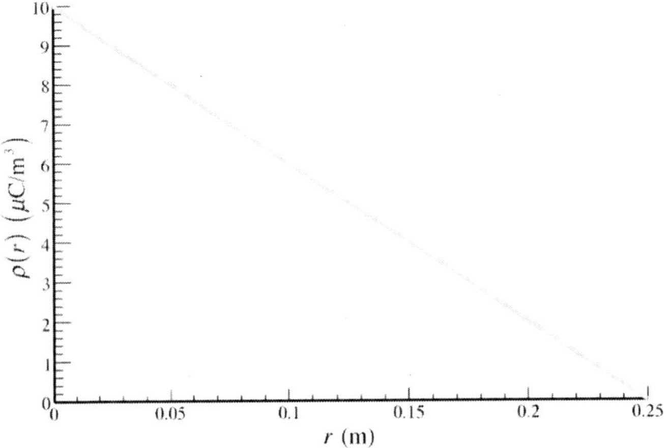

Figure 22.28: The charge density as a function of radius.

RESEARCH:

Gauss's Law (22.35) tells us that $\varepsilon_0 \oiint \vec{E} \cdot d\vec{A} = q$. Inside the non-uniform spherical charge distribution at a radius $r_1 < R$, we can rewrite Gauss's Law as

$$\varepsilon_0 E\left(4\pi r_1^2\right) = \int_0^{V_1} \rho(r)\,dV = \int_0^{r_1} \rho_0\left(1 - \frac{r}{R}\right)\left(4\pi r^2\right)dr. \tag{22.60}$$

Carrying out the integral on the right side of (22.60) we obtain

$$\int_0^{r_1} \rho_0\left(1 - \frac{r}{R}\right)\left(4\pi r^2\right)dr = 4\pi\rho_0 \int_0^{r_1}\left(r^2 - \frac{r^3}{R}\right)dr = 4\pi\rho_0\left(\frac{r_1^3}{3} - \frac{r_1^4}{4R}\right). \tag{22.61}$$

SIMPLIFY:

The electric field for $r_1 \le R$ is then given by

$$E = \frac{4\pi\rho_0\left(\frac{r_1^3}{3} - \frac{r_1^4}{4R}\right)}{\varepsilon_0\left(4\pi r_1^2\right)} = \frac{\rho_0}{\varepsilon_0}\left(\frac{r_1}{3} - \frac{r_1^2}{4R}\right). \tag{22.62}$$

Solved Problem

For $r_1 > R$, we need the total charge contained in the spherical charge distribution. We can obtain the total charge using (22.61) with $r_1 = R$

$$q_t = 4\pi\rho_0\left(\frac{R^3}{3}-\frac{R^4}{4R}\right) = 4\pi\rho_0\left(\frac{R^3}{3}-\frac{R^3}{4}\right) = 4\pi\rho_0\frac{R^3}{12} = \frac{\pi\rho_0 R^3}{3}. \qquad (22.63)$$

The electric field outside the spherical charge distribution ($r_1 > R$) is then

$$E = \frac{1}{4\pi\varepsilon_0}\frac{q_t}{r_1^2} = \frac{1}{4\pi\varepsilon_0}\frac{\frac{\pi\rho_0 R^3}{3}}{r_1^2} = \frac{\rho_0 R^3}{12\varepsilon_0 r_1^2}. \qquad (22.64)$$

CALCULATE:

The electric field at $r_1 = 0.125$ m is

$$E = \frac{\rho_0}{\varepsilon_0}\left(\frac{r_1}{3}-\frac{r_1^2}{4R}\right) = \frac{10.0\ \mu\text{C/m}^3}{8.85\cdot 10^{-12}\ \frac{\text{C}^2}{\text{N}\cdot\text{m}^2}}\left(\frac{0.125\ \text{m}}{3}-\frac{(0.125\ \text{m})^2}{4(0.250\ \text{m})}\right) = 29425.6\ \text{N/C}.$$

The electric field at $r_1 = 0.500$ m is

$$E = \frac{\rho_0 R^3}{12\varepsilon_0 r_1^2} = \frac{(10.0\ \mu\text{C/m}^3)(0.250\ \text{m})^3}{12\left(8.85\cdot 10^{-12}\ \frac{\text{C}^2}{\text{N}\cdot\text{m}^2}\right)(0.500\ \text{m})^2} = 5885.12\ \text{N/C}$$

ROUND:

We report our results to three significant figures. The electric field at $r_1 = 0.125$ m is

$$E = 2.94\cdot 10^4\ \text{N/C}.$$

The electric field at $r_1 = 0.500$ m is

$$E = 5.89\cdot 10^3\ \text{N/C}.$$

DOUBLE-CHECK:

The electric field at $r_1 = R$ can be calculated using (22.62)

$$E = \frac{\rho_0}{\varepsilon_0}\left(\frac{R}{3}-\frac{R^2}{4R}\right) = \frac{\rho_0 R}{12\varepsilon_0} = \frac{(10.0\ \mu\text{C/m}^3)(0.250\ \text{m})}{12\left(8.85\cdot 10^{-12}\ \frac{\text{C}^2}{\text{N}\cdot\text{m}^2}\right)} = 2.35\cdot 10^4\ \text{N/C}.$$

We can also use (22.64) to calculate the electric field outside the spherical charge distribution but very close to the surface, such that $r_1 \approx R$

Solved Problem

$$E = \frac{\rho_0 R^3}{12\varepsilon_0 R^2} = \frac{\rho_0 R}{12\varepsilon_0},$$

which is the same result we obtained using our result for $r_1 \le R$. The calculated electric field at the surface of the charge distribution is lower than the electric field calculated at $r_1 = 0.125$, which seems counter-intuitive. To get can idea of the dependence of the electric field on r_1, we plot the electric field using (22.62) and (22.64) in Figure 22.29.

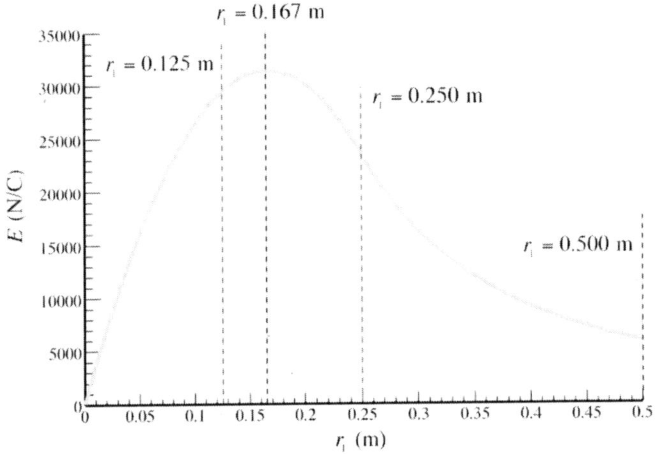

Figure 22.29: The electric field as a function of radius for a non-uniform spherical distribution of charge.

We can see that there is a maximum in the electric field. We also see that our result for $r_1 = 0.125$ m is less than the maximum value of the electric field. We can calculate the radius at which the maximum occurs by differentiating (22.62) with respect to r_1, setting the result equal to zero, and solving for r_1

$$\frac{dE}{dr_1} = \frac{\rho_0}{\varepsilon_0}\left(\frac{1}{3} - \frac{r_1}{2R}\right) = 0$$

$$\frac{1}{3} = \frac{r_1}{2R}$$

$$r_1 = \frac{2}{3}R$$

Thus we expect a maximum in the electric field at $r_1 = (2/3)R = 0.167$ m. Looking at Figure 22.29 we indeed see a maximum at that radius. Thus, our answers seem reasonable.

Sharp Points

We have already established that the electric field is perpendicular to the surface of a conductor. Now consider a sharp point sticking out from a conducting plane. We already calculated that the electric field of a conducting plane is constant, implying uniformly spaced field lines. Near the tip, however, the field should look much more like that of a point charge. This implies that field lines are much closer together near sharp points on conductors, and that the field is much stronger near the sharp tip than on the flat part of the conductor.

Franklin proposed metal rods with sharp points as lightning rods. Franklin reasoned that the sharp points would dissipate the electric charge built up in a storm, and that lightning would be prevented. When Franklin installed his lightning rods, they were struck by lightning. Recent work shows that lightning rods used to protected structures from lightning should have blunt, rounded ends. In addition, lightning rods should be carefully grounded to carry charge from a lightning strike away from the structure on which the lightning rod is mounted.

What we have learned/Exam Study Guide:

Most Important Points

- The electric force $\vec{F}$ on a charge q due to an electric field $\vec{E}$ is given by $\vec{F} = q\vec{E}$.
- The electric field at any point is equal the sum of the electric fields due to all sources, $\vec{E}_t = \vec{E}_1 + \vec{E}_2 + ... + \vec{E}_n$.
- The magnitude of the electric field from a point charge q at a distance r is given by $E = \frac{1}{4\pi\varepsilon_0}\frac{|q|}{r^2} = \frac{k|q|}{r^2}$. The electric field points radially away from positive point charges and radially toward negative charges.
- A system of two equal (in magnitude) oppositely charged point particles is called an electric dipole. The magnitude p of the electric dipole is given by $p = qd$ where q is the magnitude of either one of the charges and d is the distance separating the two charges. The electric dipole is a vector pointing from the negative to the positive charge.
- On the dipole axis the dipole produces an electric field of magnitude $E = \frac{p}{2\pi\varepsilon_0 |x|^3}$ if $|x| >> d$.
- Gauss's Law states that an integral over a closed surface of the electric flux times ε_0 is equal to the enclosed charge, $\varepsilon_0 \oiint \vec{E} \cdot d\vec{A} = q$.
- The magnitude of the electric field a distance r from a charged wire with linear charge density $\lambda > 0$ is given by $E = \frac{\lambda}{2\pi\varepsilon_0 r} = \frac{2k\lambda}{r}$.
- The magnitude of the electric field produced by an infinite non-conducting plane

of charge with charge density $\sigma > 0$ is $E = \dfrac{\sigma}{2\varepsilon_0}$.

- The magnitude of the electric field produced by an infinite conducting plane of charge with charge density $\sigma > 0$ on each side is $E = \dfrac{\sigma}{\varepsilon_0}$.
- The electric field inside a closed conductor is zero.
- The electric field outside a charged spherical conductor is same as that due to a point charge with the same total charge placed at the center of the sphere.

New Symbols used in this Chapter

- p is the electric dipole moment.
- λ is the charge per unit length.
- σ is the charge per unit area.
- ρ is the charge per unit volume

Additional Solved Problems

Solved Problem

Solved Problem 22.3: Electron moving over a charged plate

Question:

An electron with a kinetic energy of 2000.0 eV ($1 \text{ eV} = 1.602 \cdot 10^{-19}$ J) is fired horizontally over a charged conducting plate with surface charge density $+4.00 \cdot 10^{-6}$ C/m^2. Taking the positive direction to be upwards (away from the plate), what is the vertical deflection of the electron after it has traveled a horizontal distance of 4.00 cm?

Answer:

THINK:

The initial velocity of the electron is horizontal. During its flight, the electron experiences a constant attractive force, which causes a constant acceleration downward. We can calculate the time it takes to travel in the horizontal direction and use this time to calculate the vertical deflection of the electron.

SKETCH:

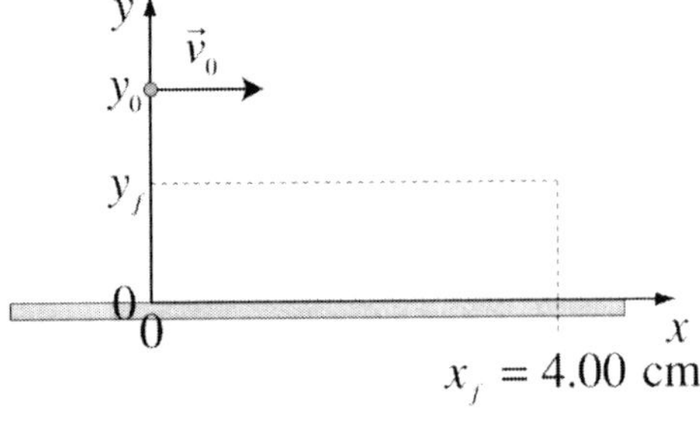

Figure 22.30: Sketch showing an electron moving to the right with over a charge conducting plate.

A sketch of the electron with an initial velocity $\vec{v}_0$ in the horizontal direction is shown in Figure 22.30. The initial position of the electron is taken to be $x_0 = 0$ and $y = y_0$.

RESEARCH:

The time that the electron takes to travel is given by

$$t = \frac{x_f}{v_0} \tag{22.65}$$

where x_f is the final horizontal position and v_0 is the initial speed of the electron. While the electron is in flight, it experiences a force from the charged conducting plate. This force is downward (toward the plate) and the magnitude is given by

$$F = qE = e\frac{\sigma}{\varepsilon_0} \tag{22.66}$$

where σ is the charge density on the conducting plate and e is the magnitude of the charge of an electron. This force causes a constant acceleration in the downward direction given by

$$F = ma \tag{22.67}$$

where m is the mass of the electron. The magnitude of the acceleration can be expressed as

$$a = \frac{F}{m} = \frac{e\sigma}{m\varepsilon_0}. \tag{22.68}$$

The vertical position of the electron as a function of time is given by

$$y_f = y_0 - \frac{1}{2}at^2. \tag{22.69}$$

We can relate the initial kinetic energy of the electron to the initial velocity of the electron through

$$K = \frac{1}{2}mv_0^2. \tag{22.70}$$

SIMPLIFY:

We can combine (22.66), (22.68), and (22.69) to obtain an expression for the vertical deflection

$$y_f - y_0 = -\frac{1}{2}at^2 = -\frac{1}{2}\left(\frac{e\sigma}{m\varepsilon_0}\right)\left(\frac{x_f}{v_0}\right)^2 = -\frac{e\sigma x_f^2}{2m\varepsilon_0 v_0^2} \tag{22.71}$$

Solved Problem

Solved Problem

We can then express the initial speed in terms of the kinetic energy as

$$v_0^2 = \frac{2K}{m}. \qquad (22.72)$$

Combining (22.71) and (22.72) gives us

$$y_f - y_0 = -\frac{e\sigma x_f^2}{2m\varepsilon_0\left(\frac{2K}{m}\right)} = -\frac{e\sigma x_f^2}{4\varepsilon_0 K} \qquad (22.73)$$

CALCULATE:

We first convert the kinetic energy of the electron from eV to J

$$K = (2000.0 \text{ eV})\frac{1.602\cdot 10^{-19}\text{ J}}{\text{eV}} = 3.204\cdot 10^{-16}\text{ J}.$$

Putting in our numerical values, we get

$$y_f - y_0 = -\frac{e\sigma x_f^2}{4\varepsilon_0 K} = -\frac{(1.60\cdot 10^{-19}\text{ C})(4.00\cdot 10^{-6}\text{ C/m}^2)(0.0400\text{ m})^2}{4\cdot(8.85\cdot 10^{-12}\text{ C}^2/(\text{N}\cdot\text{m}^2))(3.204\cdot 10^{-16}\text{ J})} = 0.0902826\text{ m}$$

ROUND:

We report our result to three significant figures

$$y_f - y_0 = -0.0903\text{ m} = -9.03\text{ cm}.$$

DOUBLE-CHECK:

The vertical deflection that we calculate is about twice the distance traveled in the x-direction, which seems to be a reasonable result.

Solved Problem

Solved Problem 22.4: Ring of charge

Question:

Consider a charged ring with radius $R = 0.250$ m as shown in Figure 22.31.

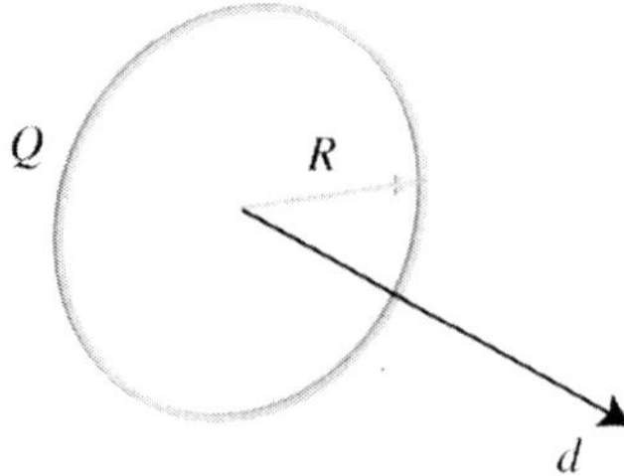

Figure 22.31: Charged ring with radius R and total charge q.

The total charge on the ring is $Q = +5.00\ \mu\text{C}$. What is the electric field a distance of $d = 0.500$ m along the axis of the circle?

Answer:

THINK:

The charge is evenly distributed around the ring. The electric field at position $x = d$ can be calculated by integrating the differential electric field due to a differential electric charge. The components of the electric field perpendicular to the axis of the circle integrate to zero. The resulting electric field is parallel to the axis of the circle.

SKETCH:

A sketch of geometry related to the electric field along the axis of ring of charge is shown in Figure 22.32.

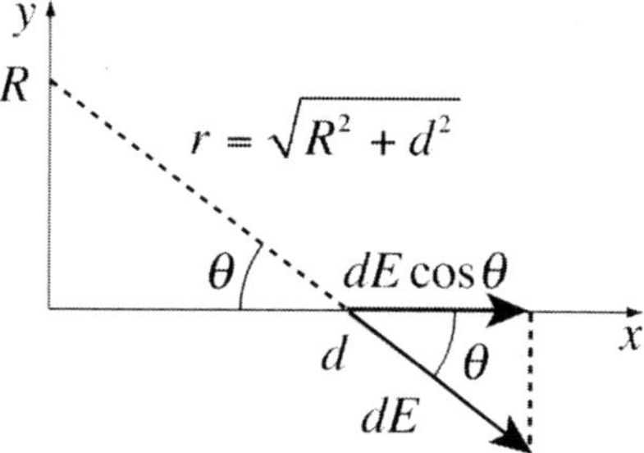

Figure 22.32: The geometry related to the electric field along the axis of a ring of charge.

RESEARCH:

The magnitude of the differential electric field dE at $x = d$ is due to a differential charge dq located at $y = R$ is shown in Figure 22.32. We define the distance from $x = d$ to $y = R$ as

$$r = \sqrt{R^2 + d^2}\ . \tag{22.74}$$

We can write the differential electric field as

$$dE = k\frac{dq}{r^2}\ . \tag{22.75}$$

The component of the differential electric field parallel to the x axis is given by

$$dE_x = dE\cos\theta = dE\frac{d}{r}. \tag{22.76}$$

SIMPLIFY:

We can calculate the electric field by integrating the x-component of the electric field over all the charge on the ring

$$E_x = \int_{\text{ring}} dE_x = \int_{\text{ring}} k\frac{dq}{r^2}\frac{d}{r} \tag{22.77}$$

Solved Problem

Solved Problem

To obtain the electric field, we integrate around the circumference of the ring of charge. We can relate the differential charge to the differential arc length ds as

$$dq = \frac{Q}{2\pi R} ds . \tag{22.78}$$

We can then write the integral over the ring of charge as an integral around the arc length of the circle as

$$E_x = \int_0^{2\pi R} k\left(\frac{Q}{2\pi R} ds\right)\frac{d}{r^3} = \left(\frac{kQd}{2\pi R r^3}\right)\int_0^{2\pi R} ds = kQ\frac{d}{r^3} = \frac{kQd}{\left(R^2+d^2\right)^{3/2}} . \tag{22.79}$$

CALCULATE:

Putting in our numerical values we get

$$E_x = \frac{kQd}{\left(R^2+d^2\right)^{3/2}} = \frac{\left(8.99\cdot 10^9 \text{ N}\cdot\text{m}^2/\text{C}^2\right)\left(5.00\cdot 10^{-6}\text{ C}\right)\left(0.500\text{ m}\right)}{\left(\left(0.250\text{ m}\right)^2+\left(0.500\text{ m}\right)^2\right)^{3/2}} = 128654 \text{ N/C}.$$

ROUND:

We report our result to three significant figures

$$E_x = 1.29\cdot 10^5 \text{ N/C}.$$

DOUBLE-CHECK:

We can check the validity of (22.79) by moving a long distance from the ring of charge such that $d >> R$. We can see that

$$E_x = \frac{kQd}{\left(R^2+d^2\right)^{3/2}} \xrightarrow{d>>R} \frac{kQd}{d^3} = k\frac{Q}{d^2}$$

which is the expression for the electric field from a point charge Q at a distance d. We can also check our result for $d = 0$

$$E_x = \frac{kQd}{\left(R^2+d^2\right)^{3/2}} \xrightarrow{d=0} = 0$$

which what we would expect at the center of a ring of charge. Thus, our results seem reasonable.

Chapter 23. Electric Potential

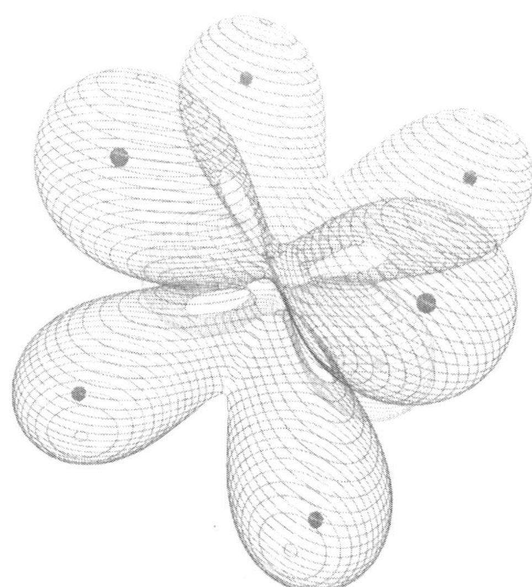

Figure 23.1: Equipotential surface resulting from eight positive point charges placed at the corners of a cube.

What we will learn

- Electric potential energy is analogous to gravitational potential energy.
- The change in electric potential energy is proportional to the work done by the electric field on a charge.
- The electric potential at a given point in space is a scalar.
- The electric potential V at a distance r from a point charge q is given by the form $V = kq/r$.
- The electric potential can be derived from the electric field by integrating the electric field over a distance.
- The electric potential at a given point in space is given by the algebraic sum of the electric potentials from different sources. (Figure 23.1 shows surfaces of equal potential for the case of eight sources.)
- The electric field can be derived from the electric potential by differentiating the electric potential with respect to a distance.

23.1. Electric Potential Energy

The electric field has many similarities with the gravitational field, including its mathematical formulation. The gravitational force is conservative and thus we defined a gravitational potential energy for two objects undergoing gravitational attraction. Because the electric field is also conservative, we can define an electric potential energy U in analogy with the gravitational potential energy.

In chapter 6, we showed that for any conservative force, the change in potential energy due to some spatial rearrangement of a system is equal to the negative of the work done by the conservative force during this spatial rearrangement. For a system of two or more particles, the work done by the electric force, W_e, when the system changes its configuration from some initial state i to final state f, in terms of the change in electric potential energy, ΔU, is given by

$$\Delta U = U_f - U_i = -W_e \tag{23.1}$$

where U_i is the initial electric potential energy and U_f is the final electric potential energy.

As was the case for gravitational potential energy in chapter 6, we must define a reference point for the electric potential energy. To simplify the required equations and calculations, we define the zero point of the electric potential energy as the configuration in which an infinitely large distance separates all the charges. This definition allows us to re-write the change in electric potential energy given in (23.1) when this infinite separation occurs in the initial state i as $\Delta U = U_f - 0 = U$ or

$$U = -W_{e,\infty}. \tag{23.2}$$

The negative sign given in this definition of the work means that when the electric force does negative work on the charges being moved in from infinity, then $U > 0$.

Let's treat the case of a point charge q moving a displacement $\vec{d}$ in a constant electric field $\vec{E}$ as illustrated in Figure 23.2.

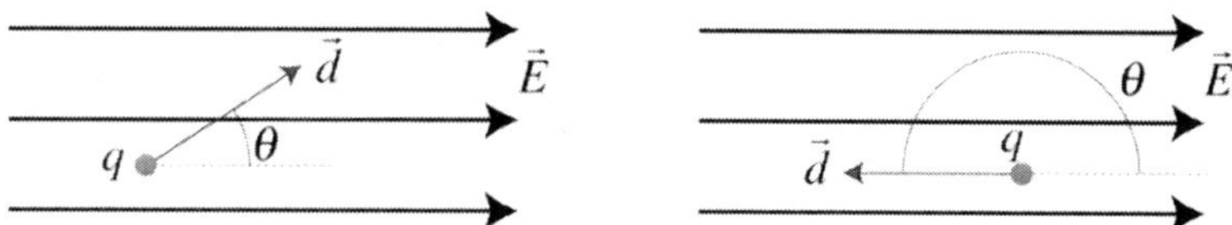

Figure 23.2: Work done by an electric field on a moving charge q.

The definition of the work done by a constant force $\vec{F}$ is

$$W = \vec{F} \bullet \vec{d}. \tag{23.3}$$

For this case, the force is created by the electric field

$$\vec{F} = q\vec{E}. \tag{23.4}$$

Thus, we can write the work done by the field on the charge as

$$W = q\vec{E} \bullet \vec{d} = qEd\cos\theta \tag{23.5}$$

where θ is the angle between the electric force and the displacement. In the case where the displacement is parallel to the electric field ($\theta = 0°$), then the work done by the field on the charge is $W = qEd$ and for the case where the displacement is anti-parallel to the electric field ($\theta = 180°$) the work done by the field is $W = -qEd$. Remembering that the change in electric potential energy is related to the work done on the charge by $\Delta U = -W$, we see that if the charge $q > 0$ the charge loses potential energy when the displacement is in the same direction as the electric field and gains potential energy when the displacement is in a direction opposite to the electric field.

23.2. Definition of the Electric Potential

The potential energy of a charged particle q in an electric field depends on the magnitude of the charge as well as the electric field. To obtain a quantity independent of the charged particle used to probe the field, we define the electric potential V in terms of the electric potential energy

$$V = \frac{U}{q}. \qquad (23.6)$$

Because U is proportional to q, V is independent of q. It is this independence that makes V such a useful variable. V characterizes an electrical property of a point in space even though there is no charge q placed at that point. In contrast with the electric field, which is a vector, the electric potential is a scalar. The electric potential is defined everywhere in space as a value, but has no direction.

The electric potential difference between an initial point i and final point f can be expressed in terms of the electric potential energy at each point

$$\Delta V = V_f - V_i = \frac{U_f}{q} - \frac{U_i}{q} = \frac{\Delta U}{q}. \qquad (23.7)$$

Using Equation (23.2) we obtain an expression relating the change in electric potential to the work done by the electric field on the charge

$$\Delta V = -\frac{W_e}{q}. \qquad (23.8)$$

Taking the electric potential energy to be zero at infinity, we get the definition of the electric potential

$$V = -\frac{W_{e,\infty}}{q} \qquad (23.9)$$

where $W_{e,\infty}$ is the work done by the electric field on the charge when it is brought in from infinity. An electric potential can have a positive, a negative, or a zero value, but it has no direction.

The SI unit for the electric potential is joules/coulomb. The electric potential has been given its own unit, named after Italian physicist Alessandro Volta (1745-1827). It is the volt, abbreviated V, where

$$1\text{ V} = \frac{1\text{ J}}{1\text{ C}}. \qquad (23.10)$$

With this definition for the volt, we can express the units of the electric field as

$$[E] = \frac{[F]}{[q]} = \frac{1\text{ N}}{1\text{ C}} = \left(\frac{1\text{ N}}{1\text{ C}}\right)\frac{1\text{ V}}{\left(\frac{1\text{ J}}{1\text{ C}}\right)}\left(\frac{1\text{ J}}{1\text{ N}\cdot 1\text{ m}}\right) = \frac{1\text{ V}}{1\text{ m}}. \qquad (23.11)$$

For the remainder of this book we will express the electric field in terms of V/m instead of N/C. V/m is the standard convention that is used conventionally.

Example

Example 23.1: Energy gain of a proton

A proton is placed between two parallel conducting plates in a vacuum as illustrated in Figure 23.3. The potential difference between the two plates is 450 V. The proton is released from rest close to the positive plate.

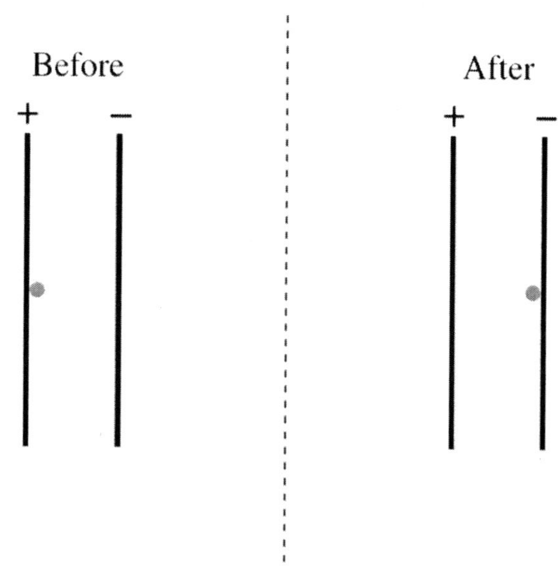

Figure 23.3: Two drawings showing a proton placed between two charged parallel conducting plates in a vacuum. In the left panel, the proton is released from rest. In the right panel, the proton has moved from the positive plate to the negative plate, gaining kinetic energy.

Question:

What is the kinetic energy of the proton when it reaches the negative plate?

Answer:

The potential difference, ΔV, between the two plates is 450 V. We can relate the potential difference across the two plates to the change in electric potential energy, ΔU, of the proton using (23.7)

$$\Delta V = \frac{\Delta U}{q}.$$

Due to the conservation of total energy, all the electric potential energy lost by the proton crossing between the two plates is turned into kinetic energy of motion of the proton. Here we apply the Conservation of Energy, $\Delta K + \Delta U = 0$, where ΔU is the change in the proton's electric potential energy

$$\Delta K = -\Delta U = -q\Delta V.$$

Because the proton started at rest, we can therefore write the final kinetic energy of the proton as $K = -q\Delta V$. Therefore the kinetic of the proton after crossing the gap between the two plates is

$$K = -\left(1.60 \cdot 10^{-19} \text{ C}\right)\left(-450 \text{ V}\right) = 7.20 \cdot 10^{-17} \text{ J}.$$

Because the acceleration of charged particles across a potential difference is used often in the measurement of physical quantities, a common unit for the kinetic energy of a particle is the electron-volt (eV). An eV represents the energy gained by a proton ($q = 1.6022 \cdot 10^{-19}$ C) accelerated across a voltage difference of 1 V. The conversion between eV and J is

$$1 \text{ eV} = 1.6022 \cdot 10^{-19} \text{ J}. \quad (23.12)$$

The proton in the previous example then has a kinetic energy of 450 eV or 0.450 keV, a result we obviously could have obtained just from the definition of the electron-volt without performing any numerical calculations.

The Van de Graaff Generator

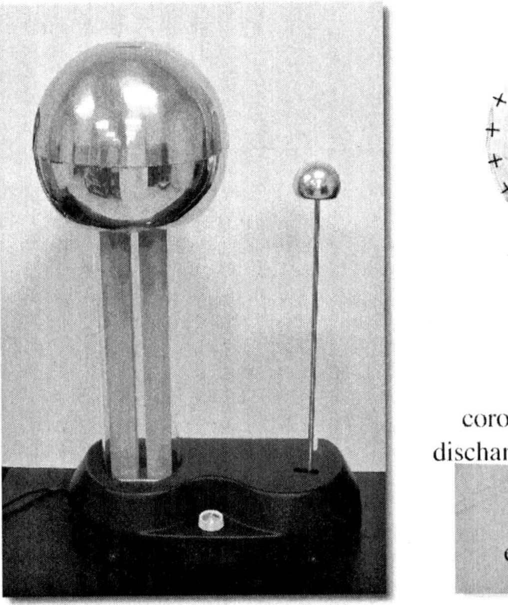

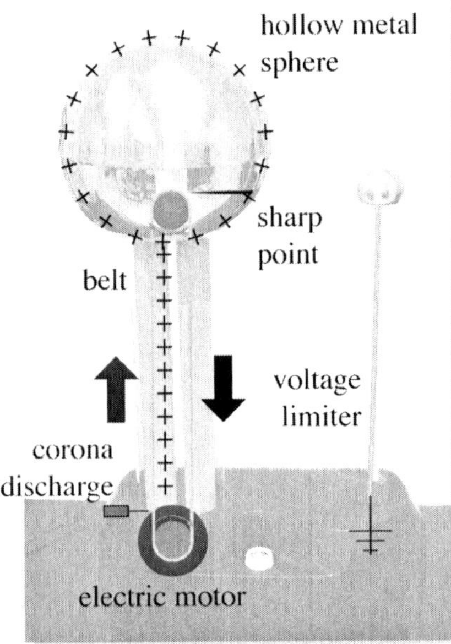

Figure 23.4: A Van de Graaff generator used in physics classrooms. The Van de Graaff generator can produce very high electric potentials by carrying charge from a corona discharge placed on a rubber belt and carried up to a hollow metal sphere, where the charge is extracted from the belt by a sharp piece of metal attached to the hollow sphere.

One way of creating large electric potentials is to use a Van de Graaff generator. The Van de Graaff generator was invented by the American physicist Robert J. Van de Graaff (1901 – 1967). The purpose of a Van de Graaff generator is to produce large electric potentials. Large Van de Graaff generators can produce voltages of millions of volts.

More modest Van de Graaff generators, like the one shown in Figure 23.4, can produce several hundred thousand volts, and are often used in physics classrooms.

The Van de Graaff generator works by applying a positive charge to a non-conducting moving belt using a corona discharge. The moving belt driven by an electric motor carries the charge up into a hollow metal sphere where the charge is taken from the belt by a pointed contact connected to the metal sphere. The charge that builds up on the metal sphere distributes itself uniformly around the outside of the sphere. For this particular Van de Graaff generator, a voltage limiter is used to keep the Van de Graaff generator from producing sparks larger than desired.

Example

Example 23.2: The tandem Van de Graaff accelerator
A Van de Graaff accelerator is a particle accelerator based on high electric potentials. Suppose we have a tandem Van de Graaff accelerator that has a terminal voltage of 10.0 MV (10.0 million volts) as shown in Figure 23.5. This terminal voltage is created using a larger, more sophisticated version of the classroom Van de Graaff generator discussed previously. This voltage is created in the center of the accelerator and is called the terminal. Negative ions are created in the ion source by attaching an electron to the atoms to be accelerated. The negative ions then accelerate toward the positively charged terminal. Inside the terminal the ions pass through a thin foil that strips off electrons, producing positively charged ions that then are accelerated out of the tandem.

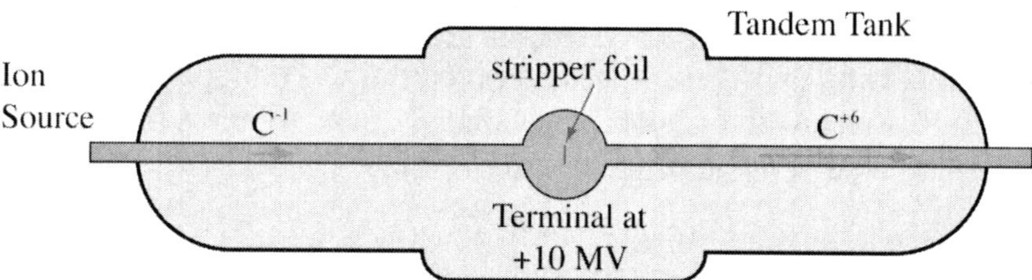

Figure 23.5: A tandem Van de Graaff accelerator.

Question1:
What is the highest kinetic energy we can attain for carbon nuclei using this tandem?

Answer 1:
There are two stages of acceleration in a tandem Van de Graaff accelerator. In the first stage the carbon ions have a net charge of $q_1 = -1e$. After the stripper foil, the maximum charge the carbon ions can have is $q_2 = +6e$. The potential difference over which the ions are accelerated is $\Delta V = 10$ MV. The kinetic energy gained by each carbon ion is

$$\Delta K = |\Delta U| = |q_1 \Delta V| + |q_2 \Delta V| = K .$$

Putting in the numerical values we get

$$K = 1e \cdot V + 6e \cdot V = 7e \cdot V = 7 \cdot 1.602 \cdot 10^{-19} \text{ C} \cdot 10 \cdot 10^{6} \text{ V} = 1.12 \cdot 10^{-11} \text{ J} .$$

Example

Nuclear physicists often use eV instead of J to express the kinetic energy of accelerated nuclei

$$K = 7eV = 7e \cdot 10 \cdot 10^6 \text{ V} = 7 \cdot 10^7 \text{ eV} = 70 \text{ MeV}.$$

Question 2:
What is the highest speed we can attain for carbon nuclei using this tandem?

Answer 2:
To get the speed we use the relationship between kinetic energy and speed

$$K = \frac{1}{2}mv^2$$

where $m = 1.99 \cdot 10^{-26}$ kg is the mass of the carbon nucleus. Solving this equation for the speed we get

$$v = \sqrt{\frac{2K}{m}} = \sqrt{\frac{2 \cdot 1.12 \cdot 10^{-11} \text{ J}}{1.99 \cdot 10^{-26} \text{ kg}}} = 3.36 \cdot 10^7 \text{ m/s}$$

which is 11% of the speed of light.

In-class exercise: A cathode ray tube uses an accelerating voltage of 5.0 kV to produce an electron beam that makes images on a phosphor screen. What is the speed of these electrons in terms of a percentage of the speed of light?

a) 0.025%
b) 0.22%
c) 1.3%
d) 4.5%
e) 14%

23.3. Equipotential Surfaces and Lines

When an electric field is present, the electric potential has a value everywhere in space. Points close together that have the same electric potential form an equipotential surface. Charged particles can move along an equipotential surface without having any work done on them by the electric field. In electrostatics the surface of a conductor is an equipotential. Otherwise, the free electrons on the conductor surface would accelerate. Equipotential surfaces exist in three dimensions - see for example Figure 23.1. However, we will take advantage of symmetries in the electric potential and represent equipotential surfaces in two dimensions as equipotential lines in the plane in which the charges reside. Before we proceed to calculate the shape and location of these equipotential surfaces, let us first have a look at the qualitative features that we encounter in some of the simplest cases. These are cases for which we have already determined the electric field.

In drawing the equipotential lines, we note that charges can move perpendicular to any electric field lines without having any work done on them by the electric field, because according to (23.5) the scalar product of the electric field and the displacement is then zero. If the work done by the electric field is zero, then the potential remains the same, which we can see from (23.8). The equipotential lines and planes are thus always perpendicular to the direction of the electric field.

Constant Electric Field

A constant electric field has straight, equally spaced, and parallel electric field lines. Thus this case produces equipotential surfaces in the form of planes from the condition that the equipotential surfaces or equipotential lines have to be perpendicular to the field lines. These two-dimensional planes are represented as equally spaced equipotential lines as shown in Figure 23.6.

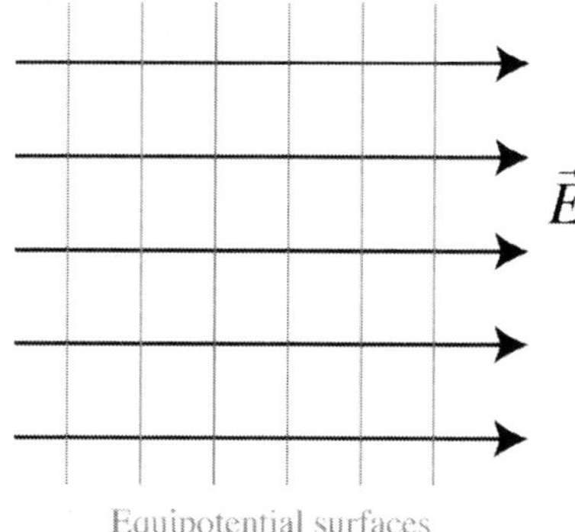

Figure 23.6: Equipotential surfaces (red lines) from a constant electric field.

Electric Field from a Single Point Charge

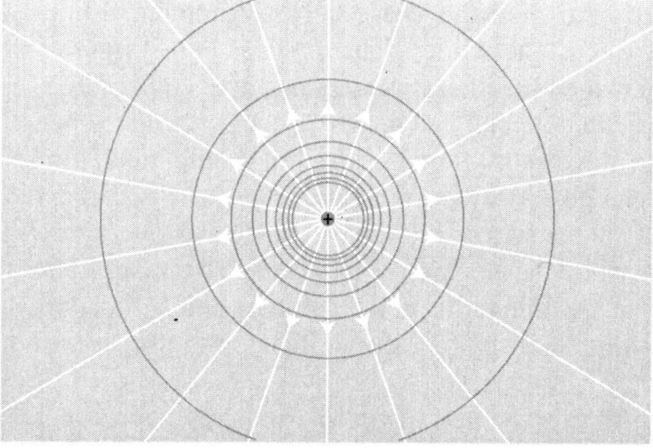

Figure 23.7: Equipotential surfaces (red lines) from a single point charge. The white lines with the arrowheads represent the electric field.

In Figure 23.7 we show the electric field and corresponding equipotential lines from a single point charge. The electric field lines extend radially from the point charge. In the case of a positive charge, the field lines point away from the charge and terminate at infinity. In the case of a negative charge, the field lines originate at infinity and terminate at the charge. The equipotential lines are circles centered on the single charge. The values of the potential difference between neighboring equipotential lines are equal, producing equipotential lines close together near the charge and more widely spaced away from the charge. Note again that the equipotential lines are always perpendicular to the electric field lines.

Electric Field from Two Oppositely Charged Point Charges

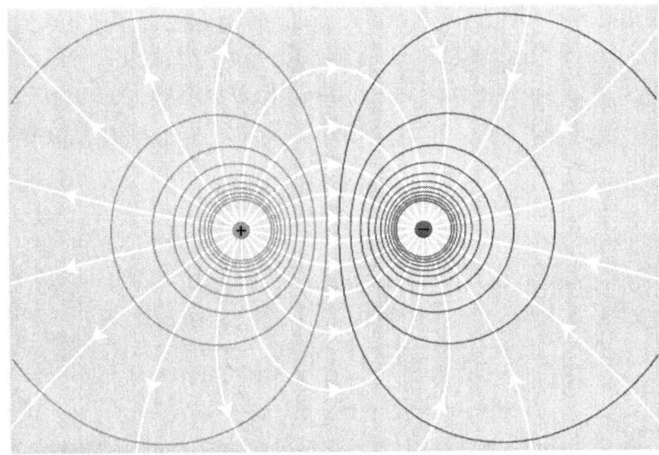

Figure 23.8: Equipotential surfaces created by oppositely charged point charges of the same magnitude. The red lines represent positive potential and blue lines represent negative potential. The white lines with the arrowheads represent the electric field.

In Figure 23.8, the electric field lines from two oppositely charged point charges are shown along with equipotential surfaces depicted as equipotential lines. The Coulomb force attracts these two point charges toward each other, but in this discussion the charges are fixed in space and cannot move. The electric field lines originate at the positive charge and terminate on the negative charge. The equipotential lines again are always perpendicular to the electric field lines. The red lines in this figure represent positive equipotential lines and the blue lines represent negative equipotential lines. Positive charges produce positive potential and negative charges produce negative potential. Close to each charge, the electric field lines and the equipotential lines resemble those from a single point charge. Away from the vicinity of each charge, the electric field and the electric potential are the sum of the electric fields and electric potentials. The electric fields add as vectors while the electric potentials add as scalars. Thus the electric field is defined at all points in space in terms of a magnitude and a direction while the electric potential is defined completely by its value at that point in space with no direction.

Self-Test Opportunity: Suppose the charges in Figure 23.8 were located at $(x,y)=(-10\text{ cm},0)$ and $(x,y)=(+10\text{ cm},0)$. What would the electric potential be along the y-axis ($x=0$)?

Electric Field from Two Identical Point Charges

In Figure 23.9 we present electric field lines and equipotential surfaces resulting from two identical positive point charges. These two charges experience repulsion from the Coulomb force. Because both charges are positive, the equipotential surfaces all represent positive potentials. Again, the electric field and electric potential in this case result from the sum of the electric fields and electric potentials from the two charges.

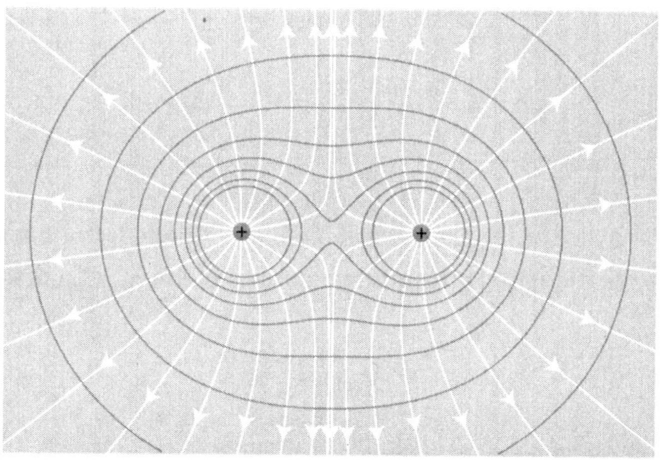

Figure 23.9: Equipotential surfaces (red lines) from two positive point charges with the same charge. The white lines with the arrowheads represent the electric field.

Self-Test Opportunity: Suppose the charges in Figure 23.9 were located at $(x,y)=(-10\text{ cm},0)$ and $(x,y)=(+10\text{ cm},0)$. Would $(x,y)=(0,0)$ correspond to a maximum or a minimum in the electric potential?

23.4. Calculating the Electric Potential from the Electric Field

To calculate the electric potential from the electric field we start with the definition of the work done on a particle with charge q by a force $\vec{F}$ over a displacement $d\vec{s}$

$$dW = \vec{F} \bullet d\vec{s} . \tag{23.13}$$

In this case the force is the electric force given by $\vec{F} = q\vec{E}$; so

$$dW = q\vec{E} \bullet d\vec{s} . \tag{23.14}$$

Integrating the work done by the electric force on the particle as it moves in the electric field from some initial point i to some final point f we obtain

$$W = W_e = \int_i^f q\vec{E} \bullet d\vec{s} . \tag{23.15}$$

Using (23.8) to relate the work done to the change in electric potential, we get

$$\Delta V = V_f - V_i = -\frac{W_e}{q} = -\int_i^f \vec{E} \bullet d\vec{s} \,. \qquad (23.16)$$

Taking the convention that the electric potential is zero at infinity we can express the electric potential in terms of the electric field (letting $f \Rightarrow \infty$) as

$$-\Delta V = V_i - V_f = V_i = V = \int_i^\infty \vec{E} \bullet ds \,. \qquad (23.17)$$

Point Charge

We now use (23.17) to determine the electric potential due to a point charge q. The electric field from a point charge q (for now taken as positive) at a distance r from the charge is given by

$$E = \frac{kq}{r^2} \,. \qquad (23.18)$$

The direction of the electric field from a point charge is radial. Assuming that we integrate from a point a distance R from the point charge along a radial line to infinity such that $\vec{E} \cdot d\vec{s} = Edr$, we can use (23.17) (with $i \Rightarrow R$) to obtain

$$V = \int_R^\infty \vec{E} \bullet d\vec{s} = \int_R^\infty \frac{kq}{r^2} dr = -\left[\frac{kq}{r} \right]_R^\infty = \frac{kq}{R} \,. \qquad (23.19)$$

Thus, the electric potential from a point charge at a distance r from a point charge q is given by

$$V = \frac{kq}{r} \,. \qquad (23.20)$$

This result (23.20) also holds when $q < 0$. Thus, a positive charge will produce a positive potential and a negative charge will produce a negative potential as shown in Figure 23.10. In this figure, the electric potential is calculated for all points in the (x, y) plane. The vertical axis represents the value of the potential at each point on the plane, $V(x, y)$, using $r = \sqrt{x^2 + y^2}$. The potential is not calculated close to $r = 0$ because the potential becomes infinite there.

One can see from Figure 23.10 the origin of the circular equipotential lines shown in Figure 23.7.

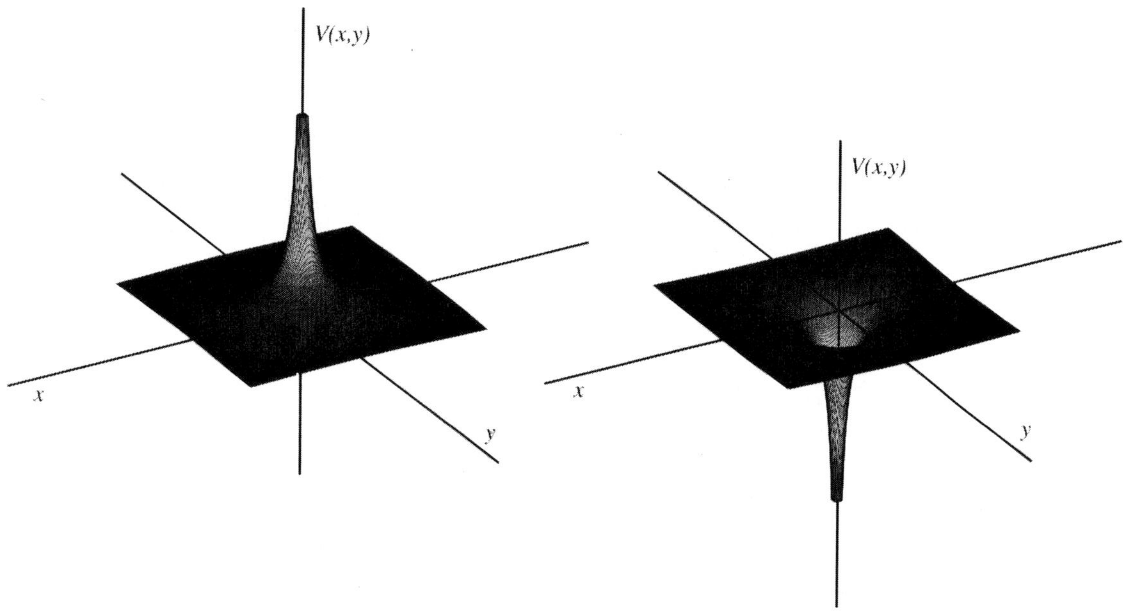

Figure 23.10: Left side: electric potential from a positive charge; right side: electric potential from a negative charge.

Solved Problem

Solved Problem 23.1: Fixed positive charge and moving positive charge

Question:

A positive charge of 4.50 μC is fixed in place. From a distance of 4.20 cm, a particle of mass 6.00 g and charge +3.00 μC is fired with an initial speed of 66.0 m/s directly toward the fixed charge. How close does the moving particle get to the fixed charge before it comes to rest and starts moving away from the fixed charge?

Answer:

THINK:

The moving charge will gain electric potential energy as it nears the fixed charge. The negative of the change of potential energy of the moving particle is equal to the change in kinetic energy of the moving particle because $\Delta K + \Delta U = 0$.

SKETCH:

We define the location of the fixed charge to be $x = 0$ as shown in Figure 23.11.

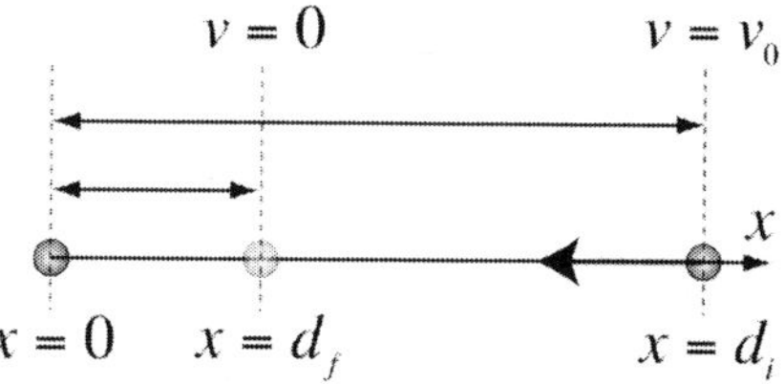

Figure 23.11: Two positive charges. One charge is fixed in place at $x = 0$ and the second charge begins moving at $x = d_i$ and has zero velocity at $x = d_f$.

The moving charge begins moving at $x = d_i$ with $v = v_0$ and comes to rest at $x = d_f$.

RESEARCH:

The moving particle gains electric potential energy as it approaches the fixed charge and loses kinetic energy until it stops. At that point, all the original kinetic energy has been converted to electric potential energy. We can write this relationship as

$$\Delta K = -\Delta U = 0 - \frac{1}{2}mv^2 = -q_{\text{moving}}\Delta V. \tag{23.21}$$

The electric potential seen by the moving charge is due to the fixed charge so we can write the change in potential as

$$\Delta V = V_f - V_i = k\frac{q_{\text{fixed}}}{d_f} - k\frac{q_{\text{fixed}}}{d_i} = kq_{\text{fixed}}\left(\frac{1}{d_f} - \frac{1}{d_i}\right). \tag{23.22}$$

Combining (23.21) and (23.22) we can write

$$\frac{1}{2}mv^2 = q_{\text{moving}}\Delta V = kq_{\text{moving}}q_{\text{fixed}}\left(\frac{1}{d_f} - \frac{1}{d_i}\right). \tag{23.23}$$

SIMPLIFY:

Rearranging (23.23) we get

$$\frac{mv^2}{2kq_{\text{moving}}q_{\text{fixed}}} = \left(\frac{1}{d_f} - \frac{1}{d_i}\right). \tag{23.24}$$

Solving for the final position we get

$$d_f = \frac{1}{\dfrac{1}{d_i} + \dfrac{mv^2}{2kq_{\text{moving}}q_{\text{fixed}}}} = \frac{2d_ikq_{\text{moving}}q_{\text{fixed}}}{2kq_{\text{moving}}q_{\text{fixed}} + d_imv^2}. \tag{23.25}$$

CALCULATE:

Putting in our numerical values, we get

$$d_f = \frac{2(0.0420 \text{ m})(8.99\cdot 10^9 \text{ N}\cdot\text{m}^2/\text{C}^2)(3.00\cdot 10^{-6} \text{ C})(4.50\cdot 10^{-6} \text{ C})}{2(8.99\cdot 10^9 \text{ N}\cdot\text{m}^2/\text{C}^2)(3.00\cdot 10^{-6} \text{ C})(4.50\cdot 10^{-6} \text{ C}) + (0.0420 \text{ m})(0.00600 \text{ kg})(66.0 \text{ m/s})^2}$$
$$= 0.00760545 \text{ m}$$

Solved Problem

Solved Problem

ROUND:

We report our result to three significant figures

$$d_f = 0.00761 \text{ m} = 0.761 \text{ cm}.$$

DOUBLE-CHECK:

The final distance of 0.761 cm is less than the initial distance of 4.20 cm. At the final distance the electric potential energy is

$$U = q_{\text{moving}} V = q_{\text{moving}} \left(k \frac{q_{\text{fixed}}}{d_f} \right) = k \frac{q_{\text{moving}} q_{\text{fixed}}}{d_f}$$

$$U = \left(8.99 \cdot 10^9 \text{ N} \cdot \text{m}^2/\text{C}^2\right) \frac{\left(3.00 \cdot 10^{-6} \text{ C}\right)\left(4.50 \cdot 10^{-6} \text{ C}\right)}{\left(0.00761 \text{ m}\right)}.$$

$$U = 15.95 \text{ J}$$

The electric potential energy at the initial distance is

$$U = q_{\text{moving}} V = q_{\text{moving}} \left(k \frac{q_{\text{fixed}}}{d_i} \right) = k \frac{q_{\text{moving}} q_{\text{fixed}}}{d_i}$$

$$U = \left(8.99 \cdot 10^9 \text{ N} \cdot \text{m}^2/\text{C}^2\right) \frac{\left(3.00 \cdot 10^{-6} \text{ C}\right)\left(4.50 \cdot 10^{-6} \text{ C}\right)}{\left(0.0420 \text{ m}\right)}.$$

$$U = 2.89 \text{ J}$$

The initial kinetic energy is

$$K = \frac{1}{2} m v^2 = \frac{\left(0.00600 \text{ kg}\right)\left(66.0 \text{ m/s}\right)^2}{2} = 13.06 \text{ J}.$$

We can see that (23.21) is satisfied

$$\frac{1}{2} m v^2 = \Delta U$$

$$13.06 \text{ J} = 15.95 \text{ J} - 2.89 \text{ J} = 13.06 \text{ J}.$$

Thus, our result for the final distance seems reasonable.

System of Point Charges

We can calculate the electric potential from a system of n point charges by adding the potential due to each charge,

$$V = \sum_{i=1}^{n} V_i = \sum_{i=1}^{n} \frac{kq_i}{r_i}. \tag{23.26}$$

One can prove (23.26) by inserting the superposition result for the electric field due to n charges ($\vec{E}_t = \vec{E}_1 + \vec{E}_2 + ... + \vec{E}_n$) into (23.17). The summation in (23.26) produces a potential at any point in space that has a value but no direction. Thus, calculating the potential from a group of point charges is usually much simpler than calculating the electric field, which involves adding vectors.

In-class exercise: What is the electric potential 45.5 cm away from a point charge of 12.5 pC?

a) 0.247 V
b) 1.45 V
c) 4.22 V
d) 10.2 V
e) 25.7 V

Example

Example 23.3: Superposition of potentials
As an example, let's calculate the electric potential from a system of point charges at a given point. In Figure 23.12 we show three point charges, $q_1 = +1.50\ \mu\text{C}$, $q_2 = +2.50\ \mu\text{C}$, and $q_3 = -3.50\ \mu\text{C}$. q_1 is located at $(0, a)$, q_2 is located at $(0,0)$, and q_3 is located at $(b,0)$, where $a = 8.00$ m and $b = 6.00$ m.

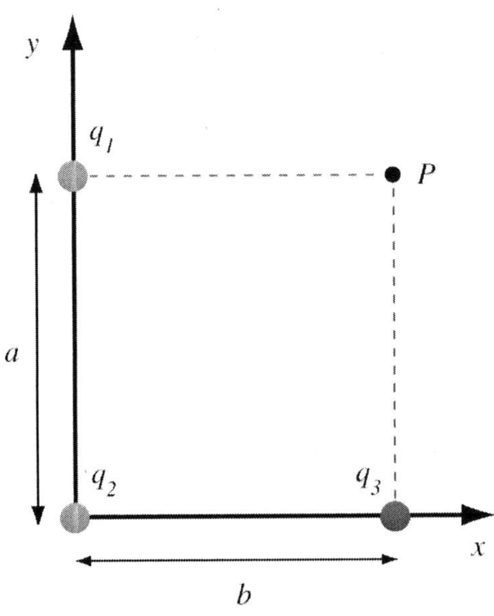

Figure 23.12: Three point charges.

Example

The electric potential at point P is given by the sum of the potential from the three charges

$$V=\sum_{i=1}^{3}\frac{kq_i}{r_i}=k\left(\frac{q_1}{r_1}+\frac{q_2}{r_2}+\frac{q_3}{r_3}\right)=k\left(\frac{q_1}{b}+\frac{q_2}{\sqrt{a^2+b^2}}+\frac{q_3}{a}\right)$$

$$V=\left(8.99\cdot10^9\ \text{N/C}\right)\left(\frac{1.50\cdot10^{-6}\ \text{C}}{6.00\ \text{m}}+\frac{2.50\cdot10^{-6}\ \text{C}}{\sqrt{\left(8.00\ \text{m}\right)^2+\left(6.00\ \text{m}\right)^2}}+\frac{-3.50\cdot10^{-6}\ \text{C}}{8.00\ \text{m}}\right).$$

$$V=562\ \text{V}$$

Note that the potential from q_3 is negative at point P but the resulting sum is positive.

Continuous Distributions of Charge

We can calculate the electric potential from a continuous distribution of charge as well as from a system of discrete charges using

$$V(\vec{r})=k\int\frac{dq}{\left|\vec{r}-\vec{r}'\right|} \quad (23.27)$$

where the differential charge dq could be expressed in terms of a linear charge density times a differential length λdx, in terms of a charge per unit area times a differential area σdA, or in terms of a charge per unit volume times a differential volume ρdV.

Example

Example 23.4: Electric potential from a finite line of charge

As an example of the calculation of the electric potential from a general distribution of charge, we calculate the electric potential at a distance d along the bisecting line of a wire with length $2a$ due to a line of charge with linear charge density λ as shown in Figure 23.13.

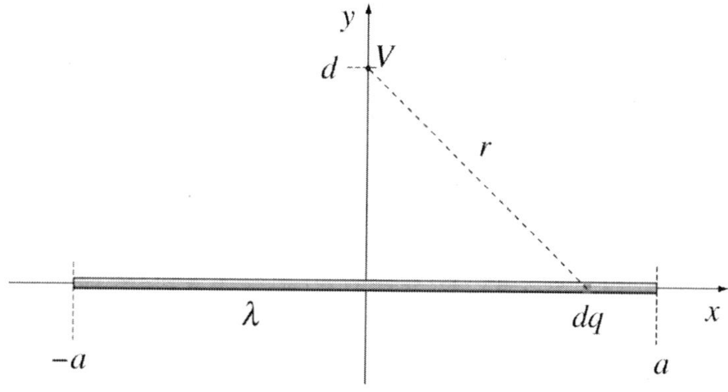

Figure 23.13: Calculating the electric potential due to a line of charge.

Example

The differential electric potential dV at a distance d along the bisecting line of the wire due to a differential charge dq is given by

$$dV = k\frac{dq}{r}. \tag{23.28}$$

The electric potential due to the whole wire is given by the integral over (23.28)

$$V = \int_{-a}^{a} dV = \int_{-a}^{a} k\frac{dq}{r}. \tag{23.29}$$

Taking $dq = \lambda dx$ and $r = \sqrt{x^2 + d^2}$ we can write the electric potential as

$$V = \int_{-a}^{a} k\frac{\lambda dx}{\sqrt{x^2 + d^2}} = k\lambda \int_{-a}^{a} \frac{dx}{\sqrt{x^2 + d^2}}. \tag{23.30}$$

Carrying out the integral gives us

$$\int_{-a}^{a} \frac{dx}{\sqrt{x^2 + d^2}} = \left[\ln\left(x + \sqrt{x^2 + d^2}\right)\right]_{-a}^{a} = \ln\left(\frac{\sqrt{a^2 + d^2} + a}{\sqrt{a^2 + d^2} - a}\right). \tag{23.31}$$

Thus, the electric potential a distance d along the bisecting line of a finite line of charge is given by

$$V = k\lambda \ln\left(\frac{\sqrt{a^2 + d^2} + a}{\sqrt{a^2 + d^2} - a}\right). \tag{23.32}$$

23.5. Calculating the Electric Field from the Electric Potential

We can calculate the electric field starting with the electric potential by making use of equations (23.9) and (23.14)

$$-qdV = q\vec{E} \bullet d\vec{s} \tag{23.33}$$

where $d\vec{s}$ is a vector from an initial point to a final point located a small (infinitesimal) distance away. If we look at the component of the electric field E_S along the direction of $d\vec{s}$, we can write E_S as the partial derivative

$$E_S = -\frac{\partial V}{\partial s}. \tag{23.34}$$

Thus we can calculate any component of the electric field by taking the partial derivative of the potential along the direction of that component. We can then write the components of the electric field in terms of partial derivatives of the potential as

$$E_x = -\frac{\partial V}{\partial x};\ E_y = -\frac{\partial V}{\partial y};\ E_z = -\frac{\partial V}{\partial z}, \tag{23.35}$$

or the equivalent vector calculus formulation $\vec{E} = -\nabla V$, where ∇ is called the gradient operator. Thus, we can determine the electric field either graphically by measuring the negative of the change of the potential per unit distance perpendicular to an equipotential line using (23.34) or analytically by using (23.35).

In-class exercise: Suppose a given electric potential can be described by $V(x,y,z) = 5x^2 + y + z$ V. Which of the following describes the associated electric field in units of V/m?

a) $\vec{E} = 5\hat{x} + 2\hat{y} + 2\hat{z}$

b) $\vec{E} = 10x\hat{x}$

c) $\vec{E} = 5x\hat{x} + 2\hat{y}$

d) $\vec{E} = 10x\hat{x} + \hat{z}$

e) $\vec{E} = 0$

Example

Example 23.5: Graphical extraction of the electric field

Here we present an example of graphically calculating the electric field given the electric potential. We assume a system of three point charges with values $q_1 = -6.00\ \mu\text{C}$, $q_2 = -3.00\ \mu\text{C}$, and $q_3 = +9.00\ \mu\text{C}$ located at positions $(x_1, y_1) = (1.5\text{ cm}, 9.0\text{ cm})$, $(x_2, y_2) = (6.0\text{ cm}, 8.0\text{ cm})$, and $(x_3, y_3) = (5.3\text{ cm}, 2.0\text{ cm})$. In Figure 23.14, the electric potential $V(x,y)$ is shown resulting from these three charges.

We calculate the equipotential lines of the electric potential at potential values from –5000 V to 5000 V in 1000 V steps and show these equipotential lines in Figure 23.15. Now we can calculate the magnitude of the electric field at point P using (23.34) and graphical techniques.

To perform this task, we draw a line through point P perpendicular to the equipotential line reaching from the equipotential line of +0 V to the line of 2000V. As you can see from the figure, the length of this line is 1.5 cm. Therefore, the magnitude of the electric field can be approximated as

$$|E_S| = \left|-\frac{\Delta V}{\Delta s}\right| = \left|\frac{(+2000\text{ V}) - (0\text{ V})}{1.5\text{ cm}}\right| = 1.3 \cdot 10^5\text{ V/m}$$

where Δs is the length of the dotted line drawn through point P.

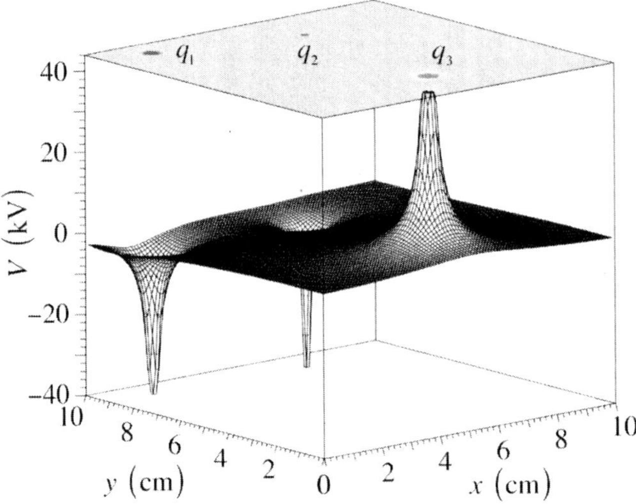

Figure 23.14: Electric potential from three charges. The colors of the top plane represent the strength of the electric potential and are thus an alternative representation of the same information contained in the 3-dimensional drawing.

The minus sign in (23.34) tells us that the direction of the electric field between neighboring equipotentials points from the 2000 V equipotential line to the zero potential line.

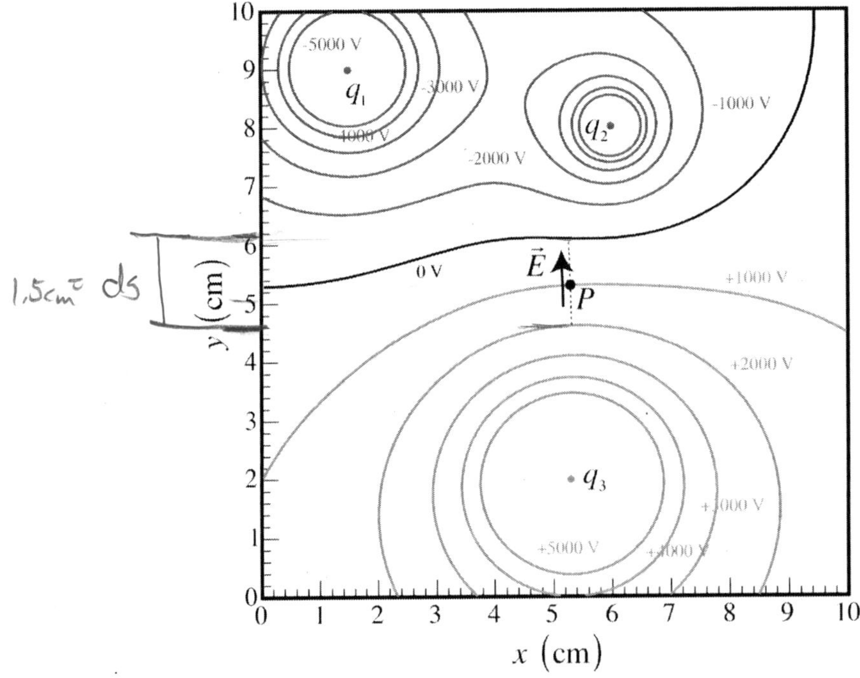

Figure 23.15: Equipotential lines for the electric potential from three point charges.

***Self-Test Opportunity*:**
In Figure 23.15 there is a line of zero electric potential labeled by 0 V. Is the electric field zero along that line?

In Chapter 22 we derived an expression for the electric field along a line bisecting a finite line of charge

$$E_y = \frac{2k\lambda}{y}\frac{a}{\sqrt{y^2+a^2}}. \tag{23.36}$$

In Example 18.4, we derived an expression for the electric potential along a line bisecting a finite line of charge

$$V = k\lambda \ln\left(\frac{\sqrt{y^2+a^2}+a}{\sqrt{y^2+a^2}-a}\right). \tag{23.37}$$

In (23.37) we have replaced the coordinate d with the distance in the y direction. We can calculate the y component of the electric field from the potential using (23.35)

$$E_y = -\frac{\partial V}{\partial y}. \tag{23.38}$$

Putting (23.37) into (23.38) gives us

$$\begin{aligned} E_y &= -\frac{\partial\left(k\lambda \ln\left(\frac{\sqrt{y^2+a^2}+a}{\sqrt{y^2+a^2}-a}\right)\right)}{\partial y} \\ &= -k\lambda\left(\frac{\partial\left(\ln\left(\sqrt{y^2+a^2}+a\right)\right)}{\partial y} - \frac{\partial\left(\ln\left(\sqrt{y^2+a^2}-a\right)\right)}{\partial y}\right) \end{aligned}. \tag{23.39}$$

Taking the partial derivatives, we obtain

$$E_y = -k\lambda\left(\frac{y}{y^2+a^2+a\sqrt{y^2+a^2}} - \frac{y}{y^2+a^2-a\sqrt{y^2+a^2}}\right) = \frac{2k\lambda}{y}\frac{a}{\sqrt{y^2+a^2}}. \tag{23.40}$$

This result is the same as the electric field in the y direction (23.36) derived in Chapter 22 obtained by integrating over a finite line of charge.

23.6. Electric Potential Energy of a System of Point Charges

In section 18.1 we discussed the electric potential energy of a point charge in a fixed electric field. Here we introduce the concept of the electric potential energy of a system of point charges. In the case of a fixed electric field, the point charge did not affect the electric field that did work on the charge. Here we consider a system of point charges that produce the electric potential energy themselves. To study this scenario, we begin with a system of charges that are infinitely far apart. To bring these charges into proximity with each other, we must do work on the charges, which changes the electric potential energy of that system.

We define the electric potential energy of a system of point charges as the work required to bring the charges together from being infinitely far apart.

To illustrate the concept of the electric potential energy of a system of particles we calculate the electric potential energy of a system of two point charges as shown in Figure 23.16.

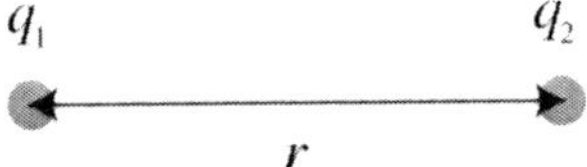

Figure 23.16: Two point charges separated by a distance r.

We start our calculation with the two charges at infinity. We then bring in point charge q_1. Because there is no electric field and no corresponding electric force, this action requires no work to be done on the charge. Keeping this charge stationary, we bring the second point charge q_2 in from infinity to a distance r from q_1. Using (23.6) we can write the electric potential energy of the system as

$$U = q_2 V \tag{23.41}$$

where

$$V = \frac{kq_1}{r}. \tag{23.42}$$

Thus the electric potential energy of this system of two point charges is

$$U = \frac{kq_1 q_2}{r}. \tag{23.43}$$

From the Work-Energy equation, the work W_{NC} that we must do work on the particles to bring them together and keep them stationary is U. If the two charges have the same sign, $W_{NC} = U > 0$ and we do positive work to bring them from infinity and keep them motionless. If the two charges have opposite signs, we must do negative work on the system to bring them together from infinity and hold them motionless. To calculate U

for more than two point charges we assemble them from infinity one charge at a time, in any order.

Example 23.6: Four charges

Let's calculate the electric potential energy of a system of four point charges as shown in Figure 23.17. The four point charges have the values q_1 = +1.0 μC, q_2 = +2.0 μC, q_3 = -3.0 μC, and q_4 = +4.0 μC. The charges are placed such that a = 6.0 m and b = 4.0 m. What is the electric potential energy of this system of four point charges?

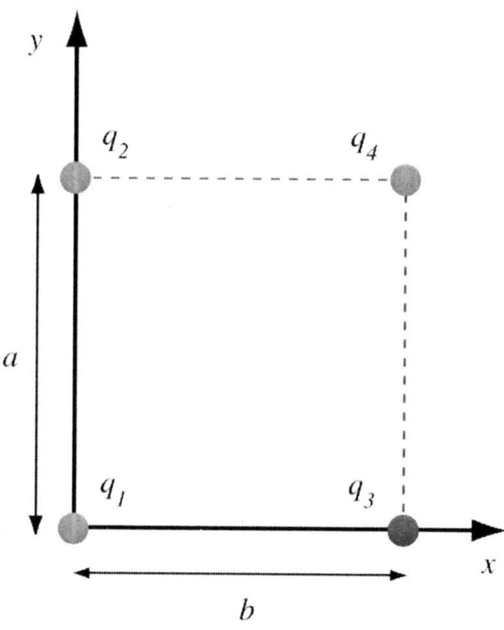

Figure 23.17: Four point charges.

We begin the calculation with all four charges infinitely far apart and assume that the electric potential energy is zero in that configuration. We bring in q_1 and position that charge at $(0,0)$. This action does not change the electric potential energy of the system. Now we bring in q_2 and place that charge at $(0,a)$. The electric potential energy of the system is now

$$U = \frac{kq_1q_2}{a}.$$

Bringing q_3 in from infinity changes the potential energy of the system by the interaction of q_3 with q_1 and the interaction of q_3 with q_2 to

$$U = \frac{kq_1q_2}{a} + \frac{kq_1q_3}{b} + \frac{kq_2q_3}{\sqrt{a^2+b^2}}.$$

Example

Finally bringing in q_4 changes the potential energy of the system by interacting with q_1, q_2, and q_3 bringing the total electric potential of the system to

$$U = \frac{kq_1q_2}{a} + \frac{kq_1q_3}{b} + \frac{kq_2q_3}{\sqrt{a^2+b^2}} + \frac{kq_1q_4}{\sqrt{a^2+b^2}} + \frac{kq_2q_4}{b} + \frac{kq_3q_4}{a}.$$

Note that the order in which the charges are brought from infinity does not change this result. Putting in the numerical values, we obtain

$$U = \left(3.0\cdot 10^{-3}\text{ J}\right) + \left(-6.7\cdot 10^{-3}\text{ J}\right) + \left(-4.2\cdot 10^{-5}\text{ J}\right) + \left(5.0\cdot 10^{-3}\text{ J}\right) + \left(1.8\cdot 10^{-2}\text{ J}\right) + \left(-1.8\cdot 10^{-2}\text{ J}\right) = 1.2\cdot 10^{-3}\text{ J}.$$

From the work done in the above example we can obtain a formula for the electric potential energy of a collection of point charges as

$$U = k \sum_{ij(\,pairings)} \frac{q_iq_j}{r_{ij}}, \tag{23.44}$$

where i and j label the charges and the summation is over each ij pair, and r_{ij} is the distance between the pair.

What We Have Learned/Exam Study Guide

Most Important Points

- The change in the electric potential energy ΔU of a point charge moving in an electric field is equal to the negative of the work done on the point charge by the electric field W_e, $\Delta U = U_f - U_i = -W_e$.
- The change in electric potential energy ΔU is equal to the charge q times the change in electric potential ΔV, $\Delta U = q\Delta V$.
- Equipotential surfaces and equipotential lines represent regions in space that have the same electric potential.
- We can calculate the change in electric potential from the electric field by integrating the field, $\Delta V = -\int_i^f \vec{E}\bullet d\vec{s}$. Taking the potential to be zero at infinity, we can calculate the potential as $V = \int_i^\infty \vec{E}\bullet d\vec{s}$.
- The electric potential from a point charge q at a distance r is given by $V = \dfrac{kq}{r}$.

- The electric potential can be expressed as an algebraic sum of all sources of electric potential, $V = \sum_{i=1}^{n} V_i$.
- We can calculate the electric field from gradients of the electric potential in each component direction, $E_x = -\frac{\partial V}{\partial x}$, $E_y = -\frac{\partial V}{\partial y}$, $E_z = -\frac{\partial V}{\partial z}$.
- The electric potential energy of two point charges is given by $U = \frac{kq_1q_2}{r}$.

New Symbols used in this Chapter

- V is the electric potential.
- ΔV is the electric potential difference.
- eV is the abbreviation for electron volt, a unit of energy.

Additional Solved Problems

Solved Problem

Solved Problem 23.2: Beam of oxygen ions

Question:

Fully stripped (all electrons removed) ^{16}O ions are accelerated in a particle accelerator from rest using a total voltage of $10.0 \text{ MV} = 1.00 \cdot 10^7 \text{ V}$. The nucleus ^{16}O has 8 protons and 8 neutrons. The accelerator produces a beam of $3.13 \cdot 10^{12}$ ions per second. This ion beam is completely stopped in a beam dump. What is the total power the beam dump has to absorb?

Answer:

THINK:

Power is energy per unit time. We can calculate the energy of each ion and then the total energy in the beam per unit time to obtain the power dissipated in the beam dump.

SKETCH:

A beam of fully stripped oxygen ions stopping in a beam dump is illustrated in Figure 23.18.

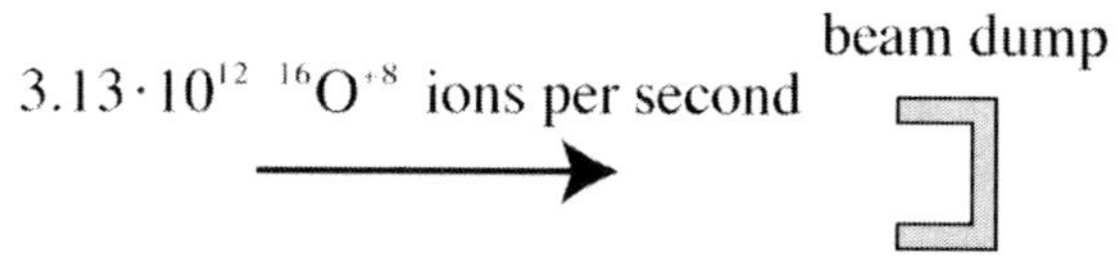

Figure 23.18: A beam of fully stripped oxygen ions stops in a beam dump.

RESEARCH:

The electric potential energy gained by each ion during the acceleration process is given by

Solved Problem

$$U_{\text{ion}} = q\Delta V = ZeV \tag{23.45}$$

where $Z = 8$ is the atomic number of oxygen, $e = 1.602 \cdot 10^{-19}$ C is the charge of a proton, and $V = 1.00 \cdot 10^{7}$ V is the electric potential across which the ions are accelerated.

SIMPLIFY:

The power in the beam that is dissipated in the beam dump is then

$$P = NU_{\text{ion}} = NZeV\,. \tag{23.46}$$

where $N = 3.13 \cdot 10^{12}$ ions/second is the number of ions per second stopping in the beam dump.

CALCULATE:

Putting in our numerical values, we get

$$P = NZeV = \left(3.13 \cdot 10^{12}\ \text{s}^{-1}\right)\left(8\right)\left(1.602 \cdot 10^{-19}\ \text{C}\right)\left(1.00 \cdot 10^{7}\ \text{V}\right).$$

$$P = 40.1141\ \text{W}$$

ROUND:

We report our result to three significant figures

$$P = 40.1\ \text{W}\,.$$

DOUBLE-CHECK:

We can relate the change in kinetic energy for each ion to the change in electric potential energy of each ion

$$\Delta K = \Delta U = \frac{1}{2}mv^2 = U_{\text{ion}} = ZeV$$

The velocity of each ion is then

$$v = \sqrt{\frac{2ZeV}{m}} = \sqrt{\frac{2\left(8\right)\left(1.602 \cdot 10^{-19}\ \text{C}\right)\left(10^{7}\right)}{2.66 \cdot 10^{-26}\ \text{kg}}} = 3.10 \cdot 10^{7}\ \text{m/s}$$

which is about 10% of the speed of light, which seems reasonable for the velocity of the ions. Thus, our formulation of the energy for each ion seems reasonable.

Solved Problem 23.3: Minimum potential

Question:

A charge of $q_1 = 0.811$ nC is placed at $r_1 = 0$ on the x-axis. Another charge of $q_2 = 0.247$ nC is placed at $r_2 = 11.1$ cm on the x-axis. At which point along the x-axis between the two charges does the combined electric potential of these two charges have a minimum?

Answer:

THINK:

We can express the electric potential due to the two charges as the sum of the electric potential from each charge. To obtain the minimum potential, we take the derivative of the potential and set it equal to zero. We can then solve for the distance where the potential is zero.

SKETCH:

A sketch of the location of the two charges is shown in Figure 23.19.

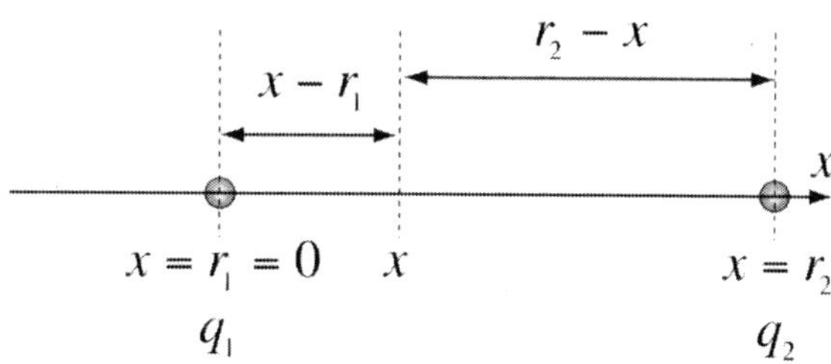

Figure 23.19: Two charges placed along the x-axis.

RESEARCH:

We can express the electric potential along the x-axis resulting from the two charges as

$$V = V_1 + V_2 = k\frac{q_1}{x - r_1} + k\frac{q_2}{r_2 - x} = k\frac{q_1}{x} + k\frac{q_2}{r_2 - x}. \tag{23.47}$$

Note that the quantities x and $r_2 - x$ are always positive for $0 < x < r_2$. We can now take the derivative of the electric potential

$$\frac{dV}{dx} = -k\frac{q_1}{x^2} - k\frac{q_2}{\left(r_2 - x\right)^2}\left(-1\right) = k\frac{q_2}{\left(r_2 - x\right)^2} - k\frac{q_1}{x^2}. \tag{23.48}$$

SIMPLIFY:

Setting the derivative of the electric potential equal to zero and rearranging we obtain

$$k\frac{q_2}{\left(r_2 - x\right)^2} = k\frac{q_1}{x^2}. \tag{23.49}$$

Dividing out k and rearranging we get

$$\frac{x^2}{\left(r_2 - x\right)^2} = \frac{q_1}{q_2}. \tag{23.50}$$

Taking the square root and rearranging we obtain

$$x = \pm\left(r_2 - x\right)\sqrt{\frac{q_1}{q_2}} \tag{23.51}$$

We can choose the correct sign by realizing that $x > 0$ and $\left(r_2 - x\right) > 0$ so that the sign must be positive. Solving for x we get

$$x = \frac{r_2\sqrt{q_1 / q_2}}{1 + \sqrt{q_1 / q_2}} = \frac{r_2}{\sqrt{q_1 / q_2} + 1} \tag{23.52}$$

Solved Problem

CALCULATE:

Putting in our numerical values, we get

$$x = \frac{0.119 \text{ m}}{1 + \sqrt{\dfrac{0.275 \text{ nC}}{0.829 \text{ nC}}}} = 0.0755097 \text{ m}.$$

ROUND:

We report our result to three significant figures

$$x = 0.0755 \text{ m} = 7.55 \text{ cm}.$$

DOUBLE-CHECK:

We double-check our result by plotting the electric potential resulting from the two charges and graphically determining the minimum as shown in Figure 23.20.

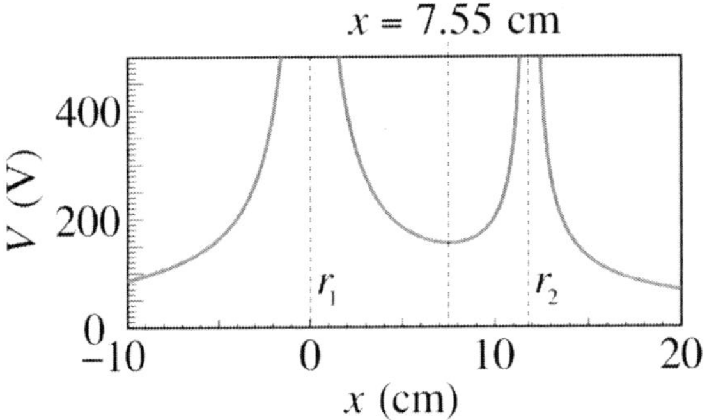

Figure 23.20: Graph of the electric potential resulting from two charges.

The minimum of the electric potential is located at $x = 7.55$ cm, which confirms our numerical result.

Chapter 24. Capacitors

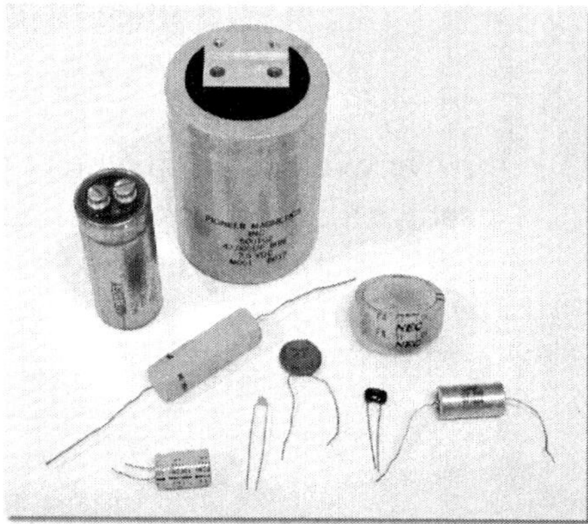

Figure 24.1: Some representative types of capacitors.

What we will learn

- Capacitors are usually composed of two conducting plates.
- A capacitor can store charge on one plate. Normally there is an equal and opposite charge on the other.
- The capacitance of a capacitor is defined as the charge stored on the plates divided by the resulting electric potential difference.
- A capacitor can store electric potential energy.
- A common form of capacitor is the parallel plate capacitor consisting of two flat

parallel conducting plates.

- The capacitance of a given capacitor depends on its geometry.
- Capacitors in circuits wired in parallel or series can be replaced by an equivalent capacitance.
- The capacitance of a given capacitor is increased when a dielectric material is placed between the plates.
- A dielectric material reduces the electric field between the plates of capacitors because of induced electric fields resulting from changes in the atomic and molecular structure of the dielectric material.

Capacitors are used in many every-day applications including heart defibrillators and camera flash units. Capacitors are integral parts of modern electronic devices. Capacitors can be very small devices used in microchips or very large devices used in radio transmitters.

24.1. Capacitance

In Figure 24.1, we show an assortment of capacitors illustrating the fact that capacitors come in a variety of sizes and shapes. In general, a capacitor consists of two separated conductors, which are usually called plates even if these conductors are not simple planes. If we take apart one of these capacitors, we might find two sheets of metal foil separated by an insulating layer of mylar. The metal foil/mylar sandwich can be rolled up with another insulating layer into a compact form that does not resemble two parallel conductors, producing the physical formats shown in Figure 24.1. We will find that the insulating layer between the two metal foils plays a crucial role in the characteristics of the capacitor.

To study the properties of capacitors we will use a convenient geometry and then generalize our results. Figure 24.2 shows a capacitor consisting of two parallel conducting plates each with area A separated by a distance d. We assume that these plates are in a vacuum. We call this device a *parallel plate capacitor.*

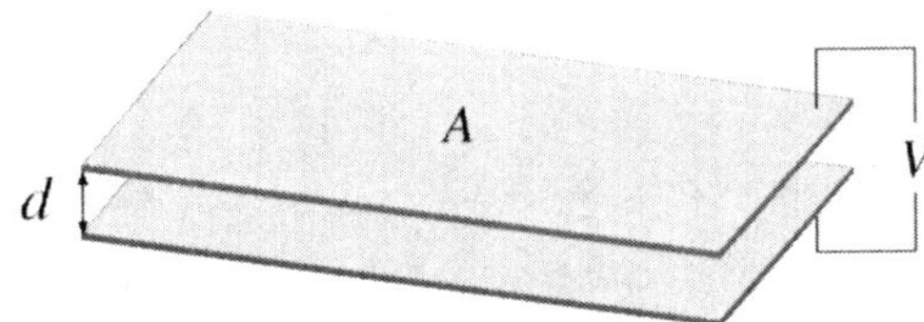

Figure 24.2: Parallel plate capacitor consisting of two conducting plates each having area A separated by a distance d.

We charge the capacitor by placing a charge $+q$ on the top plate and a charge $-q$ on the lower plate. Because the plates are conductors, they are equipotential surfaces so the electrons on the plates will distribute themselves uniformly over the surface of the conducting plates. In Section 24.3 we will see that the potential difference, V, between the two plates is proportional to the amount of charge on the plates. The proportionality constant is the capacitance, C, of the device given by

$$q = CV\,. \tag{24.1}$$

The capacitance of a device depends on the area of the plates and distance between the plates but not on the charge or the potential difference. The capacitance of a device tells us how much charge is required to produce a given voltage across the plates. The larger the capacitance, the more charge is required to reach a given voltage.

From (24.1), we can see that the capacitance is $C = q / V$. Therefore, the units of capacitance are the units of charge divided by the units of potential, coulombs per volt. Capacitance is used often so a new unit named after British physicist Michael Faraday (1791-1867) was assigned to capacitance. This unit is called the farad, which is abbreviated F. The units of F are

$$1\text{ F} = \frac{1\text{ C}}{1\text{ V}}\,. \tag{24.2}$$

One farad represents a very large capacitance. Typically, we will deal with capacitors that have a capacitance in the range from $1\ \mu\text{F} = 1\cdot 10^{-6}\ \text{F}$ to $1\ \text{pF} = 1\cdot 10^{-12}\ \text{F}$.

24.2. Circuits

In the next few chapters we will introduce more and more complex and interesting circuits. So let's first talk in general terms about what a circuit is. A circuit consists of simple wires that connect circuit elements. These circuit elements can be capacitors, as in the present chapter, where we will exclusively deal with this circuit element. But there are other important circuit elements, too. In the next chapter we will introduce a resistor and a galvanometer. In chapter 26 we will introduce additional measurement components in a circuit, the voltmeter and the ammeter. An on-off switch is a very simple component of a circuit that connects and/or disconnects wires in the circuit. In chapter 26 we will learn about a transistor, which can be used as such a switch or as an amplifier. In chapter 29 we will find out about inductors.

Symbol	Element	Symbol	Element
———	Wire	(G)	Galvanometer
⊣⊢	Capacitor	(V)	Voltmeter
—/\/\/—	Resistor	(A)	Ammeter
—ooo—	Inductor	⊣⊢ +	Battery
—• \—	Switch	(~)	AC source

Figure 24.3: Commonly used symbols for circuit elements.

Circuits usually need some kind of power, which can be provided either by a battery or by an AC power source. We have already touched on the concept of a battery in chapter

21, but for the purpose of a circuit we can simply take it as an external source of electrostatic potential difference, something that delivers a fixed voltage. A battery is a device that maintains a voltage across its terminals through chemical reactions. A power supply can produce the same result with a specially designed circuit that maintains a fixed voltage. We will learn about AC power sources in chapters 29 on induction and 30 on electromagnetic oscillations and current. We will be drawing many different circuits in this chapter and the following 7 chapters. Before we start with this, let us introduce the symbols that are used in drawings of circuits. These are listed in Figure 24.3 and will be used throughout this text.

Charging and Discharging a Capacitor

We can charge a capacitor by connecting it to a battery or to a constant voltage power supply and creating a circuit. Charge flows to the capacitor from the battery or power supply until the voltage across the capacitor is the same as the supplied voltage. If we now disconnect the capacitor, it will retain its charge and voltage. A real capacitor would be subject to charge leaking away over time. However, in this chapter we assume that an isolated capacitor retains its charge and voltage indefinitely.

In Figure 24.4, we illustrate this charging process using a circuit diagram. In this circuit, the lines represent conducting wires. The battery or power supply is represented by the symbol ⫧ and is labeled with the plus and minus voltages of the terminals and with the voltage V. The capacitor is represented by the symbol ⫩ and is labeled C.

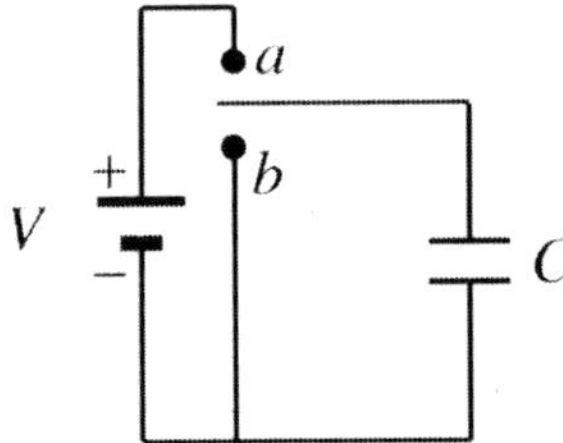

Figure 24.4: Circuit used for charging and discharging a capacitor.

This circuit contains a switch. When the switch is between positions a and b, the battery is not connected and the circuit is open. When the switch is in position a, the circuit is closed; the battery is connected across the capacitor, and the capacitor charges. In position b, the circuit is closed in a different manner. The battery is removed from the circuit, the two plates of the capacitor are connected to each other and, charge can flow between the plates through the external circuit. When the charge has dissipated on the two plates, there is no potential difference between the places and we call the capacitor discharged.

24.3. Parallel Plate Capacitor

Consider a parallel plate capacitor in the form of a pair of parallel conducting plates with charge $+q$ on one plate and charge $-q$ on the other plate as shown in Figure 24.5.

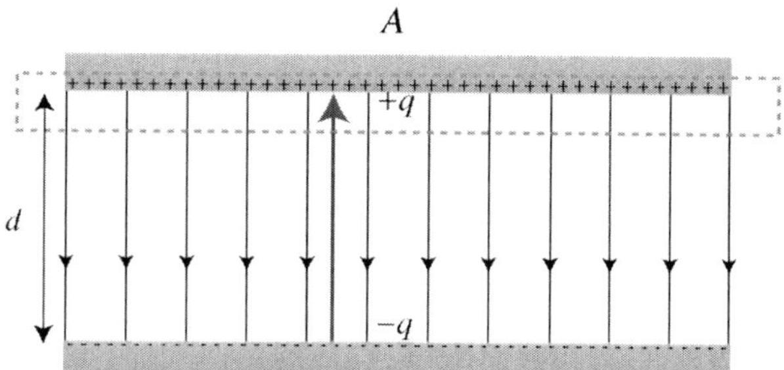

Figure 24.5: Schematic side view of a parallel plate capacitor consisting of two plates with area *A* separated by a distance *d*. Red dashed line: Gaussian surface. The black arrows pointing downward represent the electric field. The blue arrow indicates an integration path.

The plates are charged such that the upper plate has charge $+q$ and the lower plate has charge $-q$. The electric field between the two plates points from the positively charged plate to the negatively charged plate. There is a field near the ends of the plates called the fringe field, but here we will assume that the electric field is constant with magnitude E everywhere between the plates and zero elsewhere. The electric field is always perpendicular to the surface of the two parallel plates.

We can calculate the electric field using Gauss's Law

$$\varepsilon_0 \oiint \vec{E} \bullet d\vec{A} = q . \qquad (24.3)$$

Using our assumptions about the electric field between the plates and taking the Gaussian surface depicted by the dashed red line in Figure 24.5 that encloses the charge on the positive plate we obtain

$$\varepsilon_0 EA = q . \qquad (24.4)$$

where A is the surface area of the positively charged plate and q is the magnitude of the charge on the positively charged plate. Note that the charge on each plate resides entirely on the inside surface due to the presence of the other plate.

Now we can calculate the electric potential difference across the two plates in terms of the electric field using

$$\Delta V = -\int_i^f \vec{E} \bullet d\vec{s} . \qquad (24.5)$$

We can rewrite this equation defining the potential difference across the parallel plate capacitor to be V and integrating from the negatively charged plate to the positively charged plate along the direction shown by the blue arrow in Figure 24.5. Again using our simplifying assumptions about the electric field of the parallel plate capacitor, this integral reduces to

$$V = Ed = \frac{qd}{\varepsilon_0 A}, \tag{24.6}$$

where we used (24.4) to relate the electric field to the charge. Using (24.6) and the definition of capacitance (24.1), we can get an expression for the capacitance of a parallel plate capacitor

$$C = \frac{q}{V} = \frac{\varepsilon_0 A}{d}. \tag{24.7}$$

Note that this expression for the capacitance of a parallel plate capacitor only depends on the area of the plates and the distance between the plates. Just the geometry of the capacitor affects its capacitance. The amount of charge or voltage on the capacitor does not affect the capacitance.

Example

Example 24.1: Area of a parallel plate capacitor
We have a parallel plate capacitor with plates that are separated by a distance of 1.00 mm as shown in Figure 24.6.

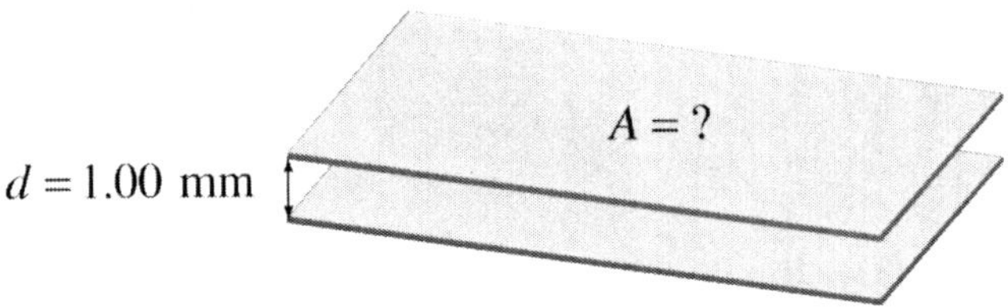

Figure 24.6: A parallel plate capacitor with plates separated by 1.00 mm.

Question:
What is the area required to give this capacitor a capacitance of 1.00 F?

Answer:
The capacitance is given by

$$C = \frac{\varepsilon_0 A}{d}.$$

Solving for the area and putting in $d = 1.00 \cdot 10^{-3}$ m and $C = 1.00$ F, we get

$$A = \frac{dC}{\varepsilon_0} = \frac{\left(1.00 \cdot 10^{-3}\ \text{m}\right)\left(1.00\ \text{F}\right)}{\left(8.85 \cdot 10^{-12}\ \text{F/m}\right)} = 1.13 \cdot 10^{8}\ \text{m}^2.$$

If the plates were square, each plate would be 10.6 km by 10.6 km (6.59 miles by 6.59 miles)! This result emphasizes that a farad is a stunningly large amount of capacitance.

Self-Test Opportunity: We charge a parallel plate capacitor using a battery. We then remove that battery and isolate the capacitor. If we increase the distance between the plates of the capacitor, what will happen to the voltage difference between the plates of the capacitor?

24.4. Cylindrical Capacitor

Consider a capacitor constructed of two conducting collinear cylinders as shown in Figure 24.7. The inner cylinder has a radius r_1 and the outer cylinder has radius r_2. Both cylinders have a charge per unit length λ with the inner cylinder having positive charge and the outer cylinder having negative charge. The electric field between the two cylinders is always radially outward and perpendicular to the surface of both cylinders. Similar to our discussion of the parallel plate capacitor, we assume that the cylinders are long and that there is no fringe field near the ends of the cylinders.

We can apply Gauss's Law to get the electric field between the two cylinders using a Gaussian surface in the form of a cylinder with radius r and length L collinear with the two cylinders forming the capacitor as shown in Figure 24.7

$$\varepsilon_0 \oiint \vec{E} \bullet d\vec{A} = \varepsilon_0 EA = \varepsilon_0 E(2\pi r)L = q = \lambda L \tag{24.8}$$

which we can rewrite to get an expression for the electric field

$$E = \frac{\lambda}{2\pi\varepsilon_0 r}, r_1 < r < r_2 . \tag{24.9}$$

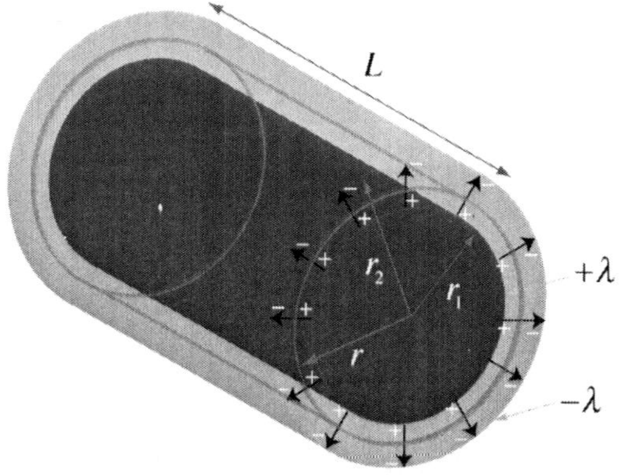

Figure 24.7: Cylindrical capacitor consisting of two long collinear conducting cylinders. The red line shows a Gaussian surface. The black arrows represent the electric field.

As we did with the parallel plate capacitor, we define the voltage difference across the parallel plate capacitor to be $V > 0$. When we integrate along $d\vec{r}$ from the positively charged cylinder at r_1 to the negatively charged cylinder at r_2, $\vec{E} \bullet d\vec{s}$ in (24.5) becomes Edr but we will then be calculating $-V$ because the negatively charged plate is at a lower potential. So to find V, we can remove the minus sign in (24.5) and find

$$V = \int_i^f \vec{E} \bullet d\vec{s} = \int_{r_1}^{r_2} E dr = \int_{r_1}^{r_2} \frac{\lambda}{2\pi\varepsilon_0 r} dr = \frac{\lambda}{2\pi\varepsilon_0} \ln\left(\frac{r_2}{r_1}\right). \tag{24.10}$$

The capacitance can be obtained using this expression and (24.1) as well as the fact that the charge q is given by λL

$$C = \frac{q}{V} = \frac{\lambda L}{\dfrac{\lambda}{2\pi\varepsilon_0} \ln(r_2 / r_1)} = \frac{2\pi\varepsilon_0 L}{\ln(r_2 / r_1)}. \tag{24.11}$$

This expression for the capacitance of a cylindrical capacitor again depends only on the geometry of the capacitor.

24.5. Spherical Capacitor

Now consider a spherical capacitor formed by two concentric conducting spheres with radii r_1 and r_2 as shown in Figure 24.8. The inner sphere has a charge $+q$ while the outer sphere has a charge of $-q$.

The electric field is perpendicular to the surface of both spheres and points radially from the inner, positively charged sphere to the outer, negatively charged sphere as shown by the red arrows in Figure 24.8. To calculate the magnitude of the electric field we employ Gauss's Law using a Gaussian surface consisting of a sphere concentric with the two spherical conductors and having a radius r such that $r_1 < r < r_2$. The electric field is also perpendicular to the Gaussian surface everywhere so we can write

$$\varepsilon_0 \oiint \vec{E} \bullet d\vec{A} = \varepsilon_0 EA = \varepsilon_0 E\left(4\pi r^2\right) = q \tag{24.12}$$

which reduces to

$$E = \frac{q}{4\pi\varepsilon_0 r^2}, r_1 < r < r_2. \tag{24.13}$$

To get the electric potential difference we follow a method similar to the one we used for the cylindrical capacitor and find

$$V = \int_i^f \vec{E} \bullet d\vec{s} = \int_{r_1}^{r_2} E dr = \int_{r_1}^{r_2} \frac{q}{4\pi\varepsilon_0 r^2} dr = \frac{q}{4\pi\varepsilon_0}\left(\frac{1}{r_1} - \frac{1}{r_2}\right) \tag{24.14}$$

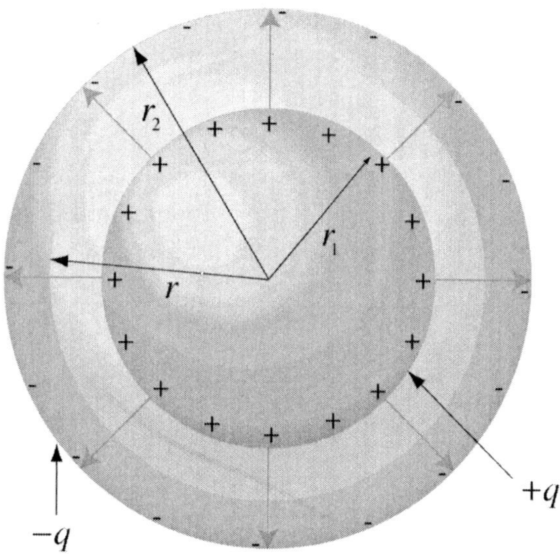

Figure 24.8: Spherical capacitor consisting of two concentric conducting spheres. The Gaussian surface is located at r.

Using (24.1) we can get the capacitance of a spherical capacitor

$$C = \frac{q}{V} = \frac{q}{\frac{q}{4\pi\varepsilon_0}\left(\frac{1}{r_1} - \frac{1}{r_2}\right)} = \frac{4\pi\varepsilon_0}{\left(\frac{1}{r_1} - \frac{1}{r_2}\right)} \tag{24.15}$$

which can be re-written in a more convenient form as

$$C = 4\pi\varepsilon_0 \frac{r_1 r_2}{r_2 - r_1}. \tag{24.16}$$

We can obtain the capacitance of a single conducting sphere by taking our result for a spherical capacitor and moving the outer spherical conductor infinitely far away. Using (24.15) with $r_2 = \infty$ and $r_1 = R$ we get

$$C = 4\pi\varepsilon_0 R \tag{24.17}$$

for the capacitance of an isolated spherical conductor.

24.6. Capacitors in Circuits

A circuit is a set of electrical devices connected with conducting wires. Capacitors can be wired together in circuits in parallel or series. Capacitors in circuits connected by wires such that the positively charged plates are connected together and the negatively charged plates are connected together are connected in parallel. Capacitors wired together such that the positively charge plate of one capacitor is connected to the negatively charged plate of the next capacitor are connected in series.

Capacitors in Parallel

In Figure 24.9 we show a circuit with three capacitors in parallel. Each of three capacitors has one plate wired directly to the positive terminal of a battery with voltage V and one plate wired directly to the negative terminal.

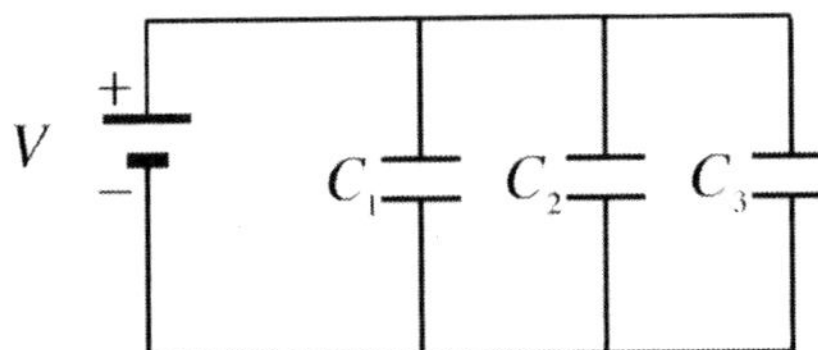

Figure 24.9: Simple circuit with a battery and with three capacitors in parallel.

Thus, the potential difference across each of the three capacitors is the same, V. We can then write for each capacitor in this circuit

$$\begin{aligned} q_1 &= C_1 V \\ q_2 &= C_2 V . \\ q_3 &= C_3 V \end{aligned} \tag{24.18}$$

We can consider the three capacitors as one equivalent capacitor C_{eq} that holds a total charge of q given by

$$q = q_1 + q_2 + q_3 = C_1 V + C_2 V + C_3 V = \left(C_1 + C_2 + C_3\right) V \tag{24.19}$$

where we can now define

$$C_{eq} = C_1 + C_2 + C_3 . \tag{24.20}$$

This result can be extended to any number *n* capacitors connected in parallel,

$$C_{eq} = \sum_{i=1}^{n} C_i . \tag{24.21}$$

In other words, the equivalent capacitance of a system of capacitors in parallel is just the sum of the capacitances. Thus if we can identify several capacitors in parallel in a circuit we can replace those capacitors with an equivalent capacitance given by (24.21) as shown in Figure 24.10.

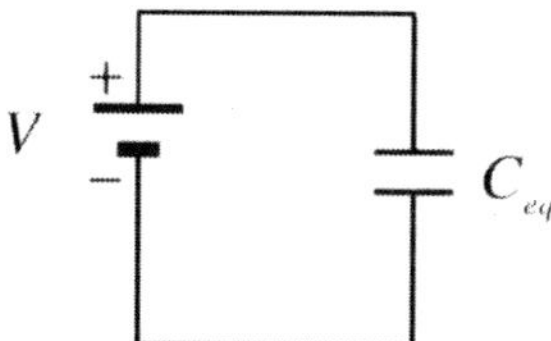

Figure 24.10: The three capacitors in Figure 24.9 are replaced with an equivalent capacitance.

Capacitors in Series

Figure 24.11 shows a circuit with three capacitors wired in series. Here the positively charged plate of C_1 is connected to the positive terminal of the battery, the negatively charged plate of C_1 is connected to the positively charged plate of C_2, the negatively charged plate of C_2 is connected to the positively charged plate of C_3, and the negatively charged plate of C_3 is connected to the negative terminal of the battery.

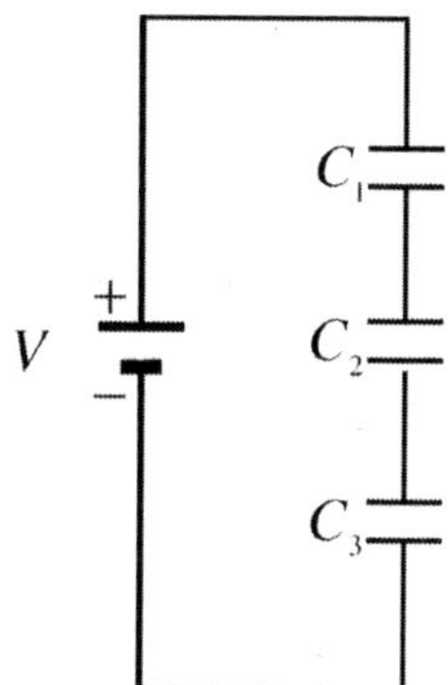

Figure 24.11: Circuit with three capacitors in series.

The battery produces an equal charge q on the top plate of each capacitor and a charge $-q$ on the bottom plate of each capacitor. We can understand this fact by starting with the capacitors initially uncharged. We connect the battery to the three capacitors. The positive plate of C_1 is connected to the positive terminal of the battery and begins to collect positive charge supplied by the battery. This positive charge induces a negative charge of equal magnitude on the other plate of C_1. The negatively charged plate of C_1 is connected to the top plate of C_2 which then becomes positively charged because no net charge can accumulate on the isolated conductor section consisting of the bottom of C_1 and the top of C_2. In turn, the negatively charged plate of C_2 induces a positive charge on the plate of C_3 connected to C_2, which induces a negative charge on the bottom plate of C_3. The negatively charged plate of C_3 is connected to the negative terminal of the battery. Thus, charge flows from the battery, charging the positive plate of C_1 to a charge of value q, and inducing a corresponding charge of $-q$ on the negatively charged plate of C_3. Therefore, we indeed find that each capacitor gains the same charge q.

When the capacitors in the circuit are charged, the sum of the voltage drops across the three capacitors must equal the voltage supplied by the battery so we can write

$$V = V_1 + V_2 + V_3 = \frac{q}{C_1} + \frac{q}{C_2} + \frac{q}{C_3} = q\left(\frac{1}{C_1} + \frac{1}{C_2} + \frac{1}{C_3}\right) \tag{24.22}$$

knowing that each capacitor has the same charge. The equivalent capacitance can be written as

$$V = \frac{q}{C_{eq}} \tag{24.23}$$

where

$$\frac{1}{C_{eq}} = \frac{1}{C_1} + \frac{1}{C_2} + \frac{1}{C_3}. \tag{24.24}$$

Thus, we can replace the three capacitors in series shown in Figure 24.11 with an equivalent capacitance given by (24.24) in the same way as was shown in Figure 24.10.

For a system of n capacitors we can generalize (24.24) to

$$\frac{1}{C_{eq}} = \sum_{i=1}^{n} \frac{1}{C_i} \tag{24.25}$$

We see from (24.25) that the capacitance of a system of capacitors in series is always less than the least capacitance in the system.

Self-Test Opportunity: What is the equivalent capacitance of four 10.0 μF capacitors connected in series? What is the equivalent capacitance of four 10.0 μF capacitors connected in parallel?

Example

Example 24.2: System of capacitors

Question:

Look at the system of capacitors shown in Figure 24.12*a*). This circuit is a complicated looking arrangement of five capacitors with a battery. What is the combined capacitance of this set of five capacitors? If each capacitor has a capacitance of 5 nF, what is the equivalent capacitance of this system? If the voltage of the battery is 12 V, what is the charge on each capacitor?

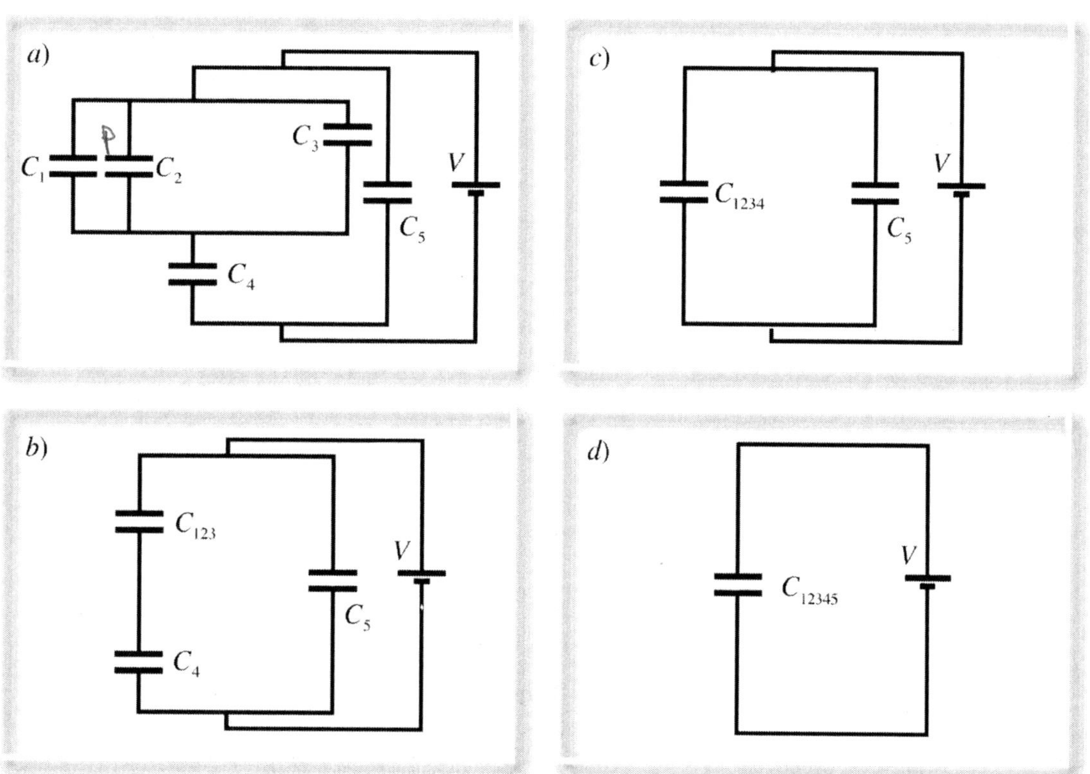

Figure 24.12: System of capacitors.

Example

Question:
Look at the system of capacitors shown in Figure 24.12*a*). This circuit is a complicated looking arrangement of five capacitors with a battery. What is the combined capacitance of this set of five capacitors? If each capacitor has a capacitance of 5 nF, what is the equivalent capacitance of this system? If the voltage of the battery is 12 V, what is the charge on each capacitor?

Answer:
While this task may look complicated at first, we can simplify our work in sequential steps using our rules for equivalent capacitances of capacitors in series and in parallel. We begin with the innermost circuit structures and work outward.

Step 1:
When you look at capacitors 1 and 2, you will perhaps see right away that they are in parallel. Possibly less obvious is that capacitor 3 is also in parallel with 1 and 2. That capacitor 3 is moved some distance away from the other two may obscure this fact. However, if you examine the upper plates of all three capacitors, then you see that they are connected by wires, and are thus at the same potential. The same goes for their lower plates. So they are indeed all in parallel. According to equation (24.21), we have then the equivalent capacity for these three capacitors

Example

$$C_{123} = \sum_{i=1}^{3} C_i = C_1 + C_2 + C_3 .$$

We have performed this replacement in Figure 24.12*b*).

Step 2:
In Figure 24.12*b*), you can observe that now C_{123} and C_4 are in series. Thus, their equivalent capacitance is according to (24.25)

$$\frac{1}{C_{1234}} = \frac{1}{C_{123}} + \frac{1}{C_4} \Rightarrow C_{1234} = \frac{C_{123}C_4}{C_{123} + C_4} .$$

We have performed this replacement in Figure 24.12*c*).

Step 3:
Finally, we realize that C_{1234} and C_5 are again in parallel. Therefore, we can repeat our calculation for two capacitors in parallel and find our desired result of the equivalent capacity of all five capacitors

$$C_{12345} = C_{1234} + C_5 = \frac{C_{123}C_4}{C_{123} + C_4} + C_5 = \frac{(C_1 + C_2 + C_3)C_4}{C_1 + C_2 + C_3 + C_4} + C_5 .$$

This result gives us the simple circuit shown in Figure 24.12*d*).

Step 4: Insert the numbers for the capacitors
We can now find the equivalent capacitance for the case that all capacitors have identical 5 nF capacitances. It is:

$$\left(\frac{(5+5+5)5}{5+5+5+5} + 5 \right) \text{nF} = 8.75 \text{ nF} .$$

As you can see now, more than one half of the total capacitance of this arrangement is provided by capacitor 5 alone. This result makes very clear that one has to be extremely careful how one arranges capacitors in circuits.

Step 5: Calculate the charges on the capacitors
C_{1234} and C_5 are in parallel. Thus, they have the same voltage across them, 12 V. We can then calculate the charge on C_5

$$q_5 = C_5 V = (5 \text{ nF})(12 \text{ V}) = 60 \text{ nC} .$$

C_{1234} is composed of C_{123} and C_4 in series. Thus C_{123} and C_4 must have the same

Example

charge q_4

$$V = V_{123} + V_4 = \frac{q_4}{C_{123}} + \frac{q_4}{C_4} = q_4\left(\frac{1}{C_{123}} + \frac{1}{C_4}\right).$$

The charge on C_4 is then

$$q_4 = V\frac{C_{123}C_4}{C_{123}+C_4} = V\frac{(C_1+C_2+C_3)C_4}{C_1+C_2+C_3+C_4} = (12\text{ V})\frac{(15\text{ nF})(5\text{ nF})}{20\text{ nF}} = 45\text{ nC}.$$

C_{123} consists of three capacitors in parallel. C_{123} also has the same charge as C_4, 45 nC. The three capacitors C_1, C_2, and C_3 have the same capacitance and the sum of the charge on the three capacitors must equal 45 nC. Therefore we can calculate the charges of C_1, C_2, and C_3 to be

$$q_1 = q_2 = q_3 = \frac{45\text{ nC}}{3} = 15\text{ nC}.$$

In-class exercise: Three capacitors are connected to a battery as shown in the figure. If $C_1 = C_2 = C_3 = 10.0\ \mu\text{F}$ and $V = 10.0\text{ V}$, what is the charge on capacitor C_3?

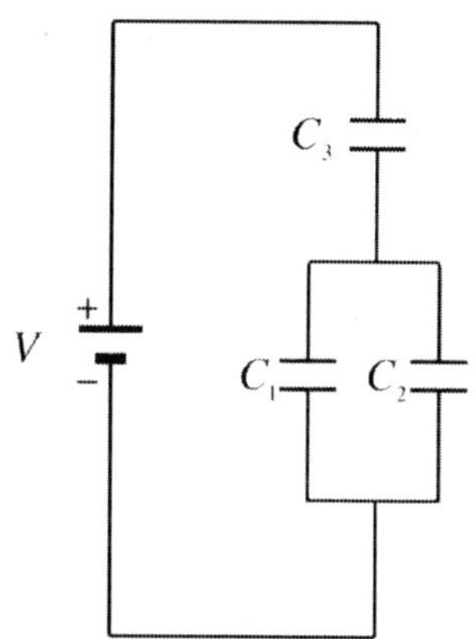

a) 66.7 μC
b) 100. μC
c) 150. μC
d) 300. μC
e) 457 μC

24.7. Energy Stored in Capacitors

A battery must do work to charge a capacitor. We can think of this work as changing the electric potential energy of the capacitor. The differential work dW done by a battery with voltage V to put a differential charge dq on a capacitor with capacitance C is

$$dW = V'dq' = \frac{q'}{C}dq', \tag{24.26}$$

where V' and q' are the instantaneous (increasing) voltage and charge respectively on the capacitor during the charging process. The total work, W_t, required to bring the capacitor to its full charge q is given by

$$W_t = \int dW = \int_0^q \frac{q'}{C}dq' = \frac{1}{2}\frac{q^2}{C} \tag{24.27}$$

This work is stored as electric potential energy

$$U = \frac{1}{2}\frac{q^2}{C} = \frac{1}{2}CV^2 = \frac{1}{2}qV. \tag{24.28}$$

All three of the formulations of the stored electric potential energy expressed in (24.28) are equally valid. One can transform from each one of them to another by using $q = CV$ and eliminating one of the three quantities in favor of the other two.

We can define the energy density, u, as the electric potential energy per unit volume,

$$u = \frac{U}{\text{volume}}. \tag{24.29}$$

(Notation: here we did not use the previously used symbol V to indicate the volume, because it is now reserved for the potential difference!)

Taking the special case of a parallel plate capacitor that has no fringe field, it is easy to calculate the volume enclosed between the two plates of area A that are separated by a perpendicular distance d. The volume between the plates is the area of each plate times the distance between the plates, Ad. Using (24.28) for the electric potential energy we obtain

$$u = \frac{U}{Ad} = \frac{\frac{1}{2}CV^2}{Ad} = \frac{CV^2}{2Ad}. \tag{24.30}$$

Using (24.7) for the capacitance of a parallel plate capacitor we get

$$u = \frac{\left(\dfrac{\varepsilon_0 A}{d}\right)V^2}{2Ad} = \frac{1}{2}\varepsilon_0\left(\frac{V}{d}\right)^2. \tag{24.31}$$

Recognizing that V / d is the magnitude of the electric field, E, we obtain an expression for the electric energy density for parallel plate capacitor

$$u = \frac{1}{2}\varepsilon_0 E^2 . \qquad (24.32)$$

This result, which is specific to the parallel plate capacitor, is in fact much more general. We will not show this generalization at this point, but equation (24.32) holds for all electric fields produced in any way. The electric potential energy stored in an electric field per unit volume occupied by that field can be described using (24.32).

In-class exercise: How much energy is stored in a 1.00 mF capacitor charged with a 300.0 V battery?

a) 1.22 J
b) 15.9 J
c) 45.0 J
d) 115 J
e) 300 J

Example

Example 24.3: Thundercloud
Suppose a thundercloud with a width of 2.0 km and a length of 3.0 km hovers over a flat area, at an altitude of 500 m and carries a charge of 160 C. There is no charge on the ground.

Question 1:
What is the potential difference between the cloud and the ground?

Answer 1:
We can approximate the cloud-ground system as a parallel plate capacitor. Its capacitance is then, according to equation (24.7),

$$C = \frac{\varepsilon_0 A}{d} = \frac{(8.85 \cdot 10^{-12}\text{ F/m})(2000\text{ m})(3000\text{ m})}{500\text{ m}} = 0.11\ \mu\text{F} .$$

Because we know the charge carried by the cloud, 160 C, it is tempting to insert this result into our relationship between charge capacitance and potential difference to extract our desired answer. However, for a parallel plate capacitor we had assumed that there is a charge of $+q$ on one plate, and $-q$ on the other, resulting in a charge difference of $2q$ between the plates. In the present case, this means that $2q = 160\text{ C} \Rightarrow q = 80\text{ C}$. Alternatively, one can think of the cloud as a charged insulator and use the result from the Planar Geometry part of Section 17.9 , $E = \frac{\sigma}{2\varepsilon_0}$, to understand the factor of $\frac{1}{2}$. Now

Example

we can use $q = CV$ and obtain

$$V = \frac{q}{C} = \frac{80\ \text{C}}{0.11\ \mu\text{F}} = 7.2 \cdot 10^8\ \text{V}.$$

The potential difference is more than 700 million volts!

Question 2:
Knowing that lightning strikes require electric field strengths of approximately 2.5 MV/m, are these conditions sufficient for a lightning strike?

Answer 2:
Because we now know the potential difference between cloud and ground, and because we were given the distance between them, we can calculate the electric field from equation (24.6) as

$$E = \frac{V}{d} = \frac{7.2 \cdot 10^8\ \text{V}}{500\ \text{m}} = 1.5\ \text{MV/m}.$$

From this result, we conclude that no lightning will develop in this particular situation. However, as the same cloud drifts over a radio tower, our assumptions about the limits of electric field strengths are no longer valid and we may indeed have a lightning discharge

Question 3:
What is the total electrical energy contained in this thundercloud?

Answer 3:
From equation (24.28), we have learned that the total energy stored in this capacitor system can be written as

$$U = \frac{1}{2}qV = 0.5(80\ \text{C})(7.2 \cdot 10^8\ \text{V}) = 2.9 \cdot 10^{10}\ \text{J}.$$

For comparison, this energy is sufficient to run a typical 1,500 W hair dryer for more than 5,000 hours.

Solved Problem

Solved Problem 24.1: Energy stored in capacitors
Question:
We connect many capacitors each with $C = 90.0\ \mu\text{F}$ in parallel across a battery with a voltage of $V = 160.0\ \text{V}$. How many capacitors do we need to store 95.6 J of energy?

Answer:
THINK:
The effective capacitance of many capacitors connected in parallel is given by the sum of

the capacitances of all the capacitors. The energy stored can be calculated knowing the equivalent capacitance of the capacitors in parallel and the voltage of the battery.

SKETCH:

A sketch of n capacitors connected in parallel across a battery is shown in Figure 24.13.

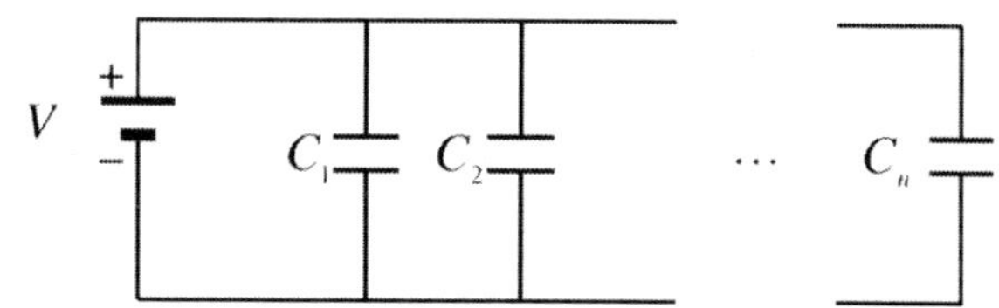

Figure 24.13: n capacitors connected in parallel across a battery.

RESEARCH:

The equivalent capacitance C_{eq} of n capacitors each with capacitance C connected in parallel is

$$C = C_1 + C_2 + \cdots + C_n = nC. \qquad (24.33)$$

The energy stored in the equivalent capacitance is given by

$$U = \frac{1}{2}C_{eq}V^2 = \frac{1}{2}nCV^2. \qquad (24.34)$$

SIMPLIFY:

Solving (24.34) for the required number of capacitors gives us

$$n = \frac{2U}{CV^2}. \qquad (24.35)$$

CALCULATE:

Putting in our numerical values, we get

$$n = \frac{2(95.6 \text{ J})}{(90.0 \cdot 10^{-6} \text{ C})(160.0 \text{ V})^2} = 82.986.$$

ROUND:

We report our result as an integer number of capacitors

$$n = 83 \text{ capacitors}.$$

DOUBLE-CHECK:

The capacitance of 83 capacitors with $C = 90.0\ \mu\text{F}$ is

Solved Problem

$$C_{eq} = 83(90.0\ \mu\text{F}) = 0.00747\ \text{F}.$$

Charging this capacitor with a 160 V battery produces a stored energy of

$$U = \frac{1}{2}CV^2 = \frac{1}{2}(0.00747\ \text{F})(160\ \text{V})^2 = 95.6\ \text{J}.$$

Thus, our answer for the number of capacitors is reasonable.

24.8. Capacitors with Dielectrics

The capacitors we have been discussing so far have air or vacuum between the plates. However, in just about any commercial application, capacitors have an insulating material, called a dielectric, between the two plates. This dielectric serves several purposes. First, the dielectric material provides a convenient way to maintain the mechanical separation between the plates. Second, the dielectric insulates the two plates from each other electrically. Third, the dielectric allows the capacitor to hold a higher voltage than it could with only air between the plates. Thus, the dielectric can increase the capacitance of the capacitor. We will see that this ability to increase the capacity is due to the molecular structure of the dielectric.

Placing a dielectric between the plates of a capacitor increases the capacitance of the capacitor by a numerical factor called the dielectric constant, κ. We can express the capacitance C of a capacitor with a dielectric with dielectric constant κ between the plates as

$$C = \kappa C_{air} \tag{24.36}$$

where C_{air} is the capacitance of the capacitor without the dielectric.

Placing the dielectric between the plates of the capacitor has the effect of lowering the electric field between the plates and allowing more charge to be stored in the capacitor. For example, the electric field between the plates of a parallel plate capacitor given by (24.4) is modified for the case of a parallel plate capacitor with a dielectric to give

$$E = \frac{E_{air}}{\kappa} = \frac{q}{\kappa\varepsilon_0 A} = \frac{q}{\varepsilon A}. \tag{24.37}$$

The constant ε_0 is the electric permeability of free space. We have also replaced the factor $\kappa\varepsilon_0$ with ε, the electric permeability of the dielectric. This result can be generalized to all electric fields in dielectrics.

$$\varepsilon = \kappa \varepsilon_0 . \tag{24.38}$$

The dielectric strength of the material measures the ability of a material to withstand voltage differences. If the voltage across a dielectric exceeds the dielectric strength, the dielectric will break down and begin to conduct charge between the plates. Thus, a useful capacitor must be designed using dielectrics that not only provide a given capacitance but also enable the device to hold the required voltage without breaking down. Capacitors are normally specified by the value of their capacitance and by the maximum voltage that they are designed to handle.

The dielectric constant of vacuum is defined to be one and the dielectric constant of air is close to one. The dielectric constants and dielectric strengths of air and of other common dielectrics are shown in Table 24.1.

Material	Dielectric Constant κ	Dielectric Strength (kV/mm)
Air (1 atm)	1.00059	2.5
Polystyrene	2.6	20
Mylar	3.1	280
Paper	3.0	8
Water	80.4	3.1

Table 24.1: Dielectric constant and dielectric strength for some representative materials.

Self-Test Opportunity: One way to increase the capacitance of a parallel plate capacitor is to decrease the distance between the plates. What is the minimum distance between the plates of a parallel plate capacitor in air if the voltage on the plates is 100.0 V?

Example 24.4: Parallel plate capacitor with dielectric

Question 1:

Consider a parallel plate capacitor with capacitance $C = 2.00\ \mu\text{F}$ connected to a battery with voltage $V = 12.0\ \text{V}$ as shown in Figure 24.14*a*). What is the charge stored in the capacitor?

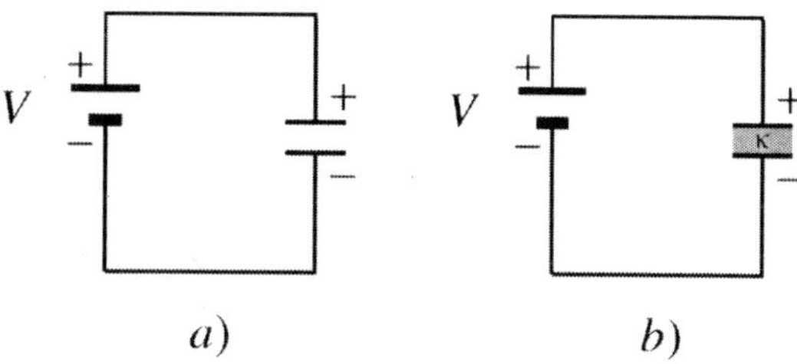

Figure 24.14: Parallel plate capacitor connected to a battery.
In *a*) there is no dielectric. In *b*), a dielectric has been inserted between the plates.

Answer 1:

Using the definition for capacitance (24.1)

$$q = CV = \left(2.00 \cdot 10^{-6}\ \text{F}\right)\left(12.0\ \text{V}\right) = 2.40 \cdot 10^{-5}\ \text{C}.$$

Question 2:
In Figure 24.14*b*), a dielectric with $\kappa = 2.5$ is inserted between the plates of the capacitor. What is the charge on the capacitor?

Answer 2:
The capacitance of the capacitor is increased by the dielectric

$$C = \kappa C_{air}.$$

The charge is

$$q = \kappa C_{air} V = \left(2.50\right)\left(2.00 \cdot 10^{-6}\ \text{F}\right)\left(12.0\ \text{V}\right) = 6.00 \cdot 10^{-5}\ \text{C}.$$

The charge on the capacitor increases when the capacitance increases because the battery maintains a constant voltage across the capacitor. The battery provides the additional charge until the capacitor is fully charged.

Now we disconnect the capacitor from the battery as shown in Figure 24.15*a*).

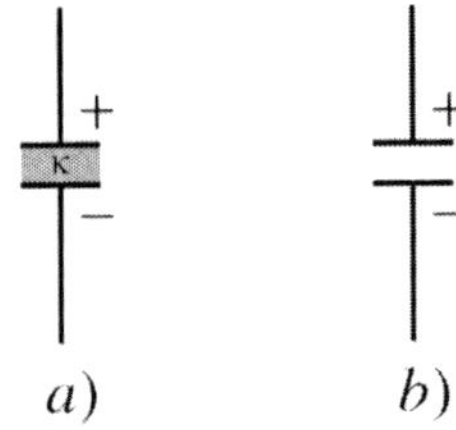

Figure 24.15: Isolated capacitor *a*) with dielectric and *b*) with dielectric removed.

The capacitor, which is now isolated, maintains its charge of $q = 6.00 \cdot 10^{-5}$ C and voltage of $V = 12.0$ V.

Question 3:
What happens to the charge and voltage on the capacitor if we remove the dielectric, keeping the capacitor isolated, as shown in Figure 24.15?

Answer 3:
The charge on the isolated capacitor cannot change because there is nowhere for the charge to flow. Thus the voltage on the capacitor will be

$$V = \frac{q}{C} = \frac{6.00 \cdot 10^{-5}\ \text{C}}{2.00 \cdot 10^{-6}\ \text{F}} = 30.0\ \text{V}.$$

The voltage went up because removing the dielectric increased the electric field and the resulting potential difference between the plates.

Example

Example

Question 4:
Does removing the dielectric change the energy stored in the capacitor?

Answer 4:
The energy stored in a capacitor is given by (24.28). Before the dielectric was removed, the energy in the capacitor was

$$U = \frac{1}{2}CV^2 = \frac{1}{2}\kappa C_{air}V^2 = \frac{1}{2}(2.50)(2.00 \cdot 10^{-6}\text{ F})(12\text{ V})^2 = 3.60 \cdot 10^{-4}\text{ J}.$$

After the dielectric is removed, the energy is

$$U = \frac{1}{2}C_{air}V^2 = \frac{1}{2}(2.00 \cdot 10^{-6}\text{ F})(30\text{ V})^2 = 9.00 \cdot 10^{-4}\text{ J}.$$

The energy increase in the capacitor from $3.60 \cdot 10^{-4}$ J to $9.00 \cdot 10^{-4}$ J when the dielectric is removed occurs because of the work done on the dielectric pulling it out of the electric field between the plates.

Example

Example 24.5: Capacitance of a coaxial cable
Coaxial cables are used to transport TV signals inside your house. Assume that we have a 20.0 m long coaxial cable composed of a conductor and a coaxial conducting shield around the conductor. The space between the conductor and the shield is filled with polystyrene. The radius of the conductor is 0.250 mm and the radius of the shield is 2.00 mm. A cross section of the coaxial cable is shown in Figure 24.16.

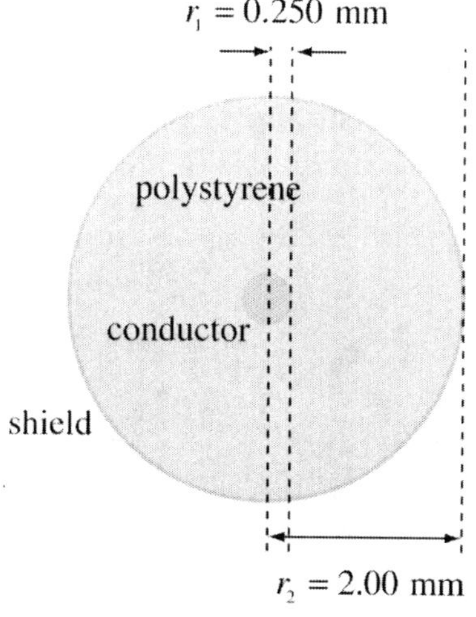

Figure 24.16: Cross section of a coaxial cable.

Question:
What is the capacitance of the coaxial cable?

Example

Answer:

We can think of the conductor of the coaxial cable as a cylinder because all of the charge on the conductor will reside on the surface of the conductor. Looking at Table 24.1, we can see that the dielectric constant for polystyrene is 2.6. We can treat the coaxial cable as a cylindrical capacitor with $r_1 = 0.250$ mm and $r_2 = 2.00$ mm filled with a dielectric with $\kappa = 2.6$. Thus, using (24.11) we can express the capacitance of the coaxial cable as

$$C = \kappa \frac{2\pi\varepsilon_0 L}{\ln(r_2 / r_1)} = \frac{2.6 \cdot 2\pi (8.85 \cdot 10^{-12} \text{ F/m})(20.0 \text{ m})}{\ln(2.00 \cdot 10^{-3} \text{ m} / 2.5 \cdot 10^{-4} \text{ m})} = 1.39 \cdot 10^{-9} \text{ F} = 1.39 \text{ nF}.$$

In-class exercise: Answer whether the following statements are true or false for an isolated parallel plate capacitor.

a) When the distance between the plates of the capacitor is doubled, the energy stored in the capacitor doubles.
b) Increasing the distance between the plates increases the electric field between the plates.
c) When the distance between the plates is halved, the charge on the plates stays the same.
d) Inserting a dielectric between the plates increases the charge on the plates.
e) Inserting a dielectric between the plates decreases the energy stored in the capacitor.

24.9. Microscopic Perspective on Dielectrics

Let's consider what happens at the atomic and molecular level when a dielectric is placed in an electric field. There are two types of dielectric materials. The first type is polar dielectric. This type of material is composed of molecules that have a permanent electric dipole moment due to their molecular structure. A common example of such a molecule is the water molecule. Normally the directions of electric dipoles are randomly distributed as shown in Figure 24.17*a)*.

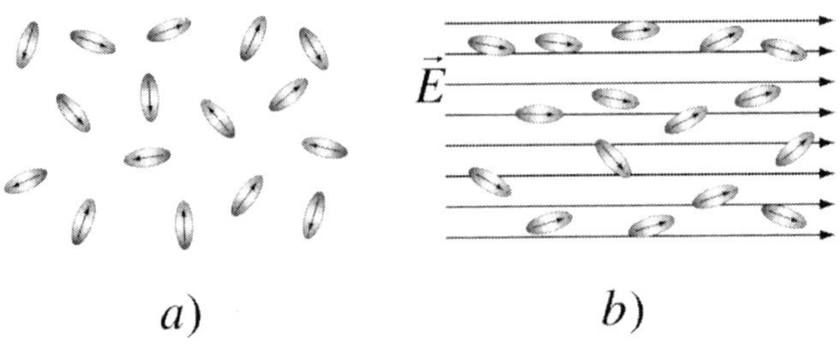

Figure 24.17: Polar molecules *a)* randomly orientated and *b)* oriented by an external electric field.

When an electric field is applied to these polar molecules, they tend to align with the field as shown in Figure 24.17*b)*.

The second type of dielectric is a non-polar dielectric. This type of material is composed of atoms or molecules that have no electric dipole moment as shown in Figure 24.18*a)*.

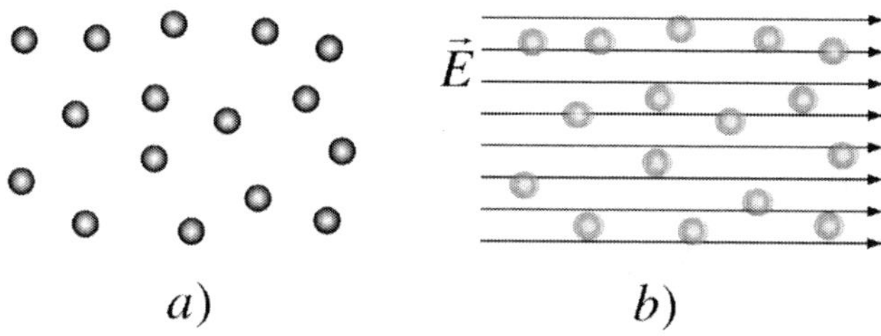

Figure 24.18: Non-polar molecules *a)* with no electric dipole moment and *b)* with an electric dipole moment induced by an external electric field.

These atoms or molecules can be induced to have a dipole moment under the influence of an external electric field. This induction is caused by the opposite direction of the electric force on the negative and positive charges of the atom or molecule, which displaces these two charge distributions and produces an induced electric dipole moment.

In both the case of the polar and non-polar dielectric materials, the resulting aligned electric dipole moments tend to partially cancel the original electric field as shown in Figure 24.19. Taking the electric field originally applied across the capacitor to be $\vec{E}$, the resulting electric field, $\vec{E}_r$, inside a capacitor with a dielectric medium between the plates is just the original field plus the electric field induced in the dielectric material, $\vec{E}_d$ so that

$$\begin{gathered} \vec{E}_r = \vec{E} + \vec{E}_d \text{ , or} \\ E_r = E - E_d \end{gathered} \qquad (24.39)$$

Note that the resulting electric field points in the same direction as the original field and is smaller in magnitude than the original field. The dielectric constant is given by $\kappa = E / E_r$.

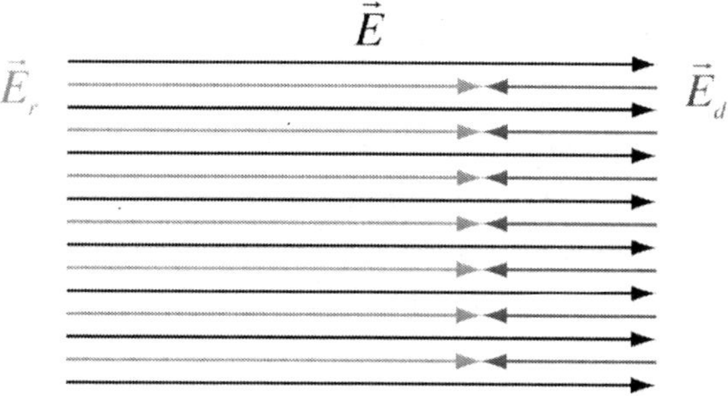

Figure 24.19: Partial cancellation of the applied electric field across a parallel plate capacitor by the electric dipoles of a dielectric material.

Example 24.6: Defibrillator

An important application of capacitors is the portable automatic external defibrillator (AED). The AED is a device designed to shock the heart of a person that is in ventricular fibrillation. A typical AED is shown in Figure 24.20.

When a person's heart is in ventricular fibrillation, the heart is not beating in a regular pattern. Instead, the signals that control the beating of the heart are erratic and confused, preventing the heart from performing its duty to circulate blood in the person's body. This condition must be treated within a few minutes. Having many AED devices located in accessible public places allows quick treatment of this condition.

An AED can be used to run a pulse of electrical current through the heart and possibly to stimulate the heart to beat regularly. Typically, an AED is designed to automatically analyze the heartbeat of the person, determine if the person is in ventricular fibrillation, and administer an electrical pulse if required. The operator of the AED must attach the electrodes of the AED to the chest of the patient and push the start button. The AED will analyze the patient and do nothing if the patient is not in ventricular defibrillation. If the AED determines that the patient is in ventricular fibrillation, the AED will ask the operator to press the button to shock the patient.

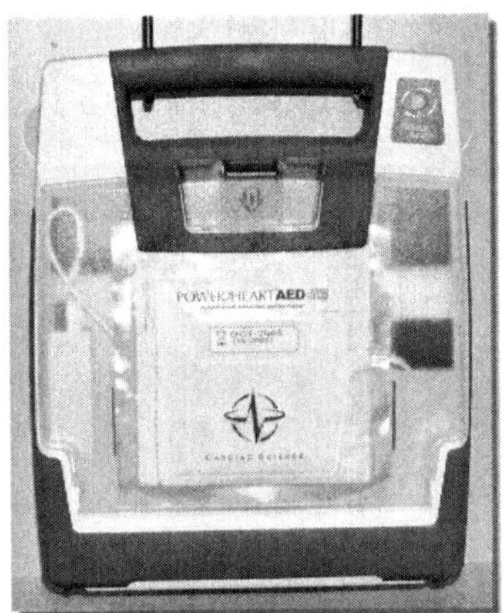

Figure 24.20: An automatic external defibrillator (AED).

Typically, an AED delivers 150 J of electrical energy to the patient. This energy is delivered to the patient by charging a capacitor with a special circuit from a low voltage battery. This capacitor typically has a capacitance of 100 μF and is charged in 10 s. The power used during charging is $P = E / t = 150 \text{ J} / 10 \text{ s} = 15 \text{ W}$, easily within the capacity of a simple battery. The energy of the capacitor is then discharged in 10 ms. The instantaneous power during the discharge is $P = E / t = 150 \text{ J} / 10 \text{ ms} = 15 \text{ kW}$, which is beyond the capability of a small, portable battery, but within the capabilities of a well designed capacitor.

The energy stored in a capacitor is

Example

$$U = \frac{1}{2}CV^2.$$

What is the voltage of the capacitor when it is charged?

$$V = \sqrt{\frac{2U}{C}} = \sqrt{\frac{2(150\text{ J})}{100 \cdot 10^{-6}\text{ F}}} = 1730\text{ V}.$$

When the AED is commanded to deliver a shock, the capacitor is charged from a battery contained in the AED. The capacitor is then discharged through the patient with a specific waveform to stimulate the heart to beat in a regular manner. Most AEDs can perform this shock many times without recharging the battery.

Note that an AED is not designed restart a heart that is not beating. Rather it is designed to restore a regular heartbeat when the heart is beating erratically.

What we have learned/Exam Study Guide:

Most Important Points

- The capacitance of a capacitor is defined in terms of the charge q that can be stored on the capacitor and the voltage V across the plates, $q = CV$.
- The farad is the unit of capacitance given by $1\text{ F} = \frac{1\text{ C}}{1\text{ V}}$.
- The capacitance of a parallel plate capacitor with plates each of area A separated by a distance d is given by $C = \frac{\varepsilon_0 A}{d}$.
- The capacitance of a cylindrical capacitor of length L consisting of two collinear cylinders with radius r_1 and r_2 is given by $C = \frac{2\pi\varepsilon_0 L}{\ln\left(\frac{r_2}{r_1}\right)}$.
- The capacitance of a spherical capacitor consisting of two concentric spheres with radius r_1 and r_2 is given by $C = 4\pi\varepsilon_0 \frac{r_1 r_2}{r_2 - r_1}$.
- The electric potential energy density u between the plates of a parallel plate capacitor is given by $u = \frac{1}{2}\varepsilon_0 E^2$.
- A system of n capacitors in parallel in a circuit can be replaced by an equivalent

capacitance given by the sum of the capacitances of the capacitors in parallel

$$C_{eq} = \sum_{i=1}^{n} C_i .$$

- A system of n capacitors in series in a circuit can be replaced by an equivalent capacitance given by the sum of the capacitances of the capacitors in series

$$\frac{1}{C_{eq}} = \sum_{i=1}^{n} \frac{1}{C_i} .$$

- Placing a dielectric with dielectric constant κ in a capacitor volume increases the capacitance of a capacitor in air to $C = \kappa C_{air}$.

New Symbols used in this Chapter

- C is the capacitance of a capacitor.
- C_{eq} is the equivalent capacitance of a system of capacitors in a circuit.
- F is the abbreviation for farad.
- κ is the dielectric constant
- u is the electric potential energy density.

Additional Solved Problems

Solved Problem

Solved Problem 24.2: Capacitor partially filled with a dielectric

Question:

A parallel plate capacitor is constructed of two square conducting plates with side $L = 10.0$ cm as shown in Figure 24.21. The distance between the plates is $d = 0.250$ cm. A dielectric with dielectric constant $\kappa = 15.0$ and thickness 0.250 cm is inserted between the plates. The dielectric is $L = 10.0$ cm wide and $L/2 = 5.00$ cm long as shown in Figure 24.21. What is the capacitance of this capacitor?

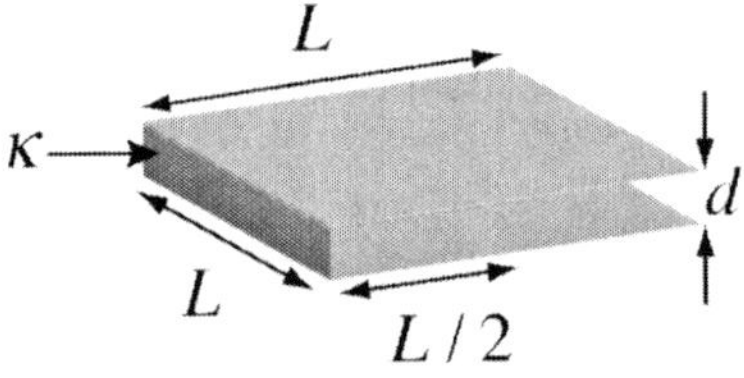

Figure 24.21: A parallel plate capacitor with square plates of side L separated by a distance d. A dielectric with dielectric constant κ is inserted between the plates. The dielectric is L wide and $L/2$ long.

Answer:

THINK:

We have a parallel plate capacitor that is partially filled with a dielectric. We can treat this capacitor as two capacitors in parallel. One capacitor is a parallel plate capacitor with plate area $L(L/2)$ with air between the plates. The second capacitor is a parallel plate capacitor with plate area $L(L/2)$ with a dielectric between the plates.

SKETCH:

A sketch of the partially filled capacitor represented by two capacitors in parallel is shown in Figure 24.22. One half of the capacitor is represented by one capacitor that is filled with a dielectric and the other half of the capacitor is represented by an air-filled capacitor.

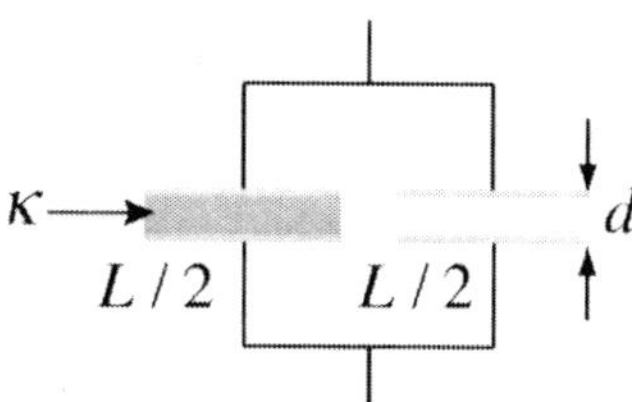

Figure 24.22: The partially filled capacitor represented as two capacitors in parallel. One capacitor has a dielectric between the plates.

RESEARCH:

The capacitance C of a parallel plate capacitor is given by (24.7)

$$C = \frac{\varepsilon_0 A}{d} \tag{24.40}$$

where A is the area of the plates and d is the separation between the plates. If a dielectric is placed between the plates, the capacitance becomes

$$C = \kappa \frac{\varepsilon_0 A}{d} \tag{24.41}$$

where κ is the dielectric constant. For two capacitors C_1 and C_2 in parallel, the effective capacitance C_{12} is given by

$$C_{12} = C_1 + C_2. \tag{24.42}$$

SIMPLIFY:

Substituting (24.40) and (24.41) into (24.42) we get

$$C_{12} = \frac{\varepsilon_0 A}{d} + \kappa \frac{\varepsilon_0 A}{d} = (\kappa + 1)\frac{\varepsilon_0 A}{d}. \tag{24.43}$$

The area of the plates for each capacitor is

$$A = L(L/2) = L^2/2. \tag{24.44}$$

Substituting (24.44) into (24.43) we get the capacitance of the partially filled capacitor to be

Solved Problem

$$C_{12} = (\kappa+1)\frac{\varepsilon_0 (L^2/2)}{d} = \frac{(\kappa+1)\varepsilon_0 L^2}{2d}. \tag{24.45}$$

CALCULATE:

Putting in our numerical values, we get

$$C_{12} = \frac{(15.0+1)(8.85\cdot 10^{-12}\text{ F/m})(0.100\text{ m})^2}{2(0.00250\text{ m})} = 2.832\cdot 10^{-10}\text{ F}.$$

ROUND:

We report our result to three significant figures

$$C_{12} = 2.83\cdot 10^{-10}\text{ F} = 283\text{ pF}.$$

DOUBLE-CHECK:

To double-check our answer, we calculate the capacitance of the capacitor without any dielectric

$$C = \frac{\varepsilon_0 A}{d} = \frac{(8.85\cdot 10^{-12}\text{ F/m})(0.100\text{ m})^2}{0.0025\text{ m}} = 3.54\cdot 10^{-11}\text{ F} = 35.4\text{ pF}.$$

We then calculate the capacitance of the capacitor if it were completely filled with dielectric

$$C = \kappa\frac{\varepsilon_0 A}{d} = (15.0)\frac{(8.85\cdot 10^{-12}\text{ F/m})(0.100\text{ m})^2}{0.0025\text{ m}} = 5.31\cdot 10^{-10}\text{ F} = 531\text{ pF}.$$

Our result for the partially filled capacitor is between these two limits and is approximately half of the filled result, so our answer seems reasonable.

Solved Problem

Solved Problem 24.3: Charge on a cylindrical capacitor

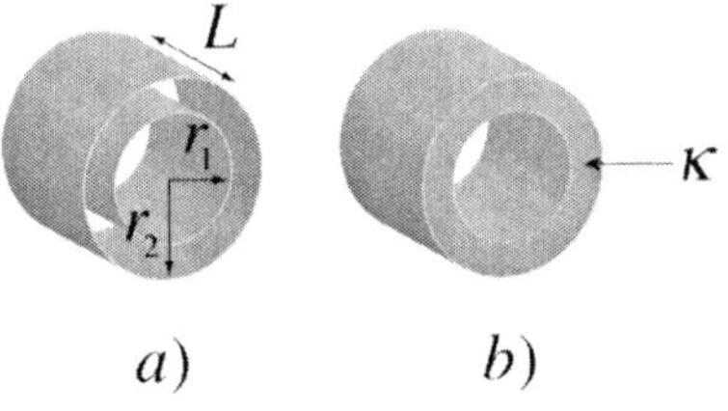

Figure 24.23: A cylindrical capacitor with inner radius r_1 and outer radius r_2 and length L. A dielectric with dielectric constant κ is inserted between the plates.

Question:

Consider a cylindrical capacitor as illustrated in Figure 24.23*a*). The inner radius of the capacitor is $r_1 = 10.0$ cm. The outer radius of the capacitor is $r_2 = 12.0$ cm. The length of the capacitor is $L = 50.0$ cm. A dielectric with dielectric constant $\kappa = 12.5$ fills the volume between the two plates as shown in Figure 24.23*b*). The capacitor is connected to a 100.0 V battery and charged completely. What is the charge on the capacitor?

Answer:

THINK:

We have a cylindrical capacitor filled with a dielectric. When the capacitor is connected to the battery, charge will flow to the capacitor until the capacitor is fully charged. We can then calculate the charge on the capacitor.

SKETCH:

A sketch of the cylindrical capacitor connected to a battery is shown in .

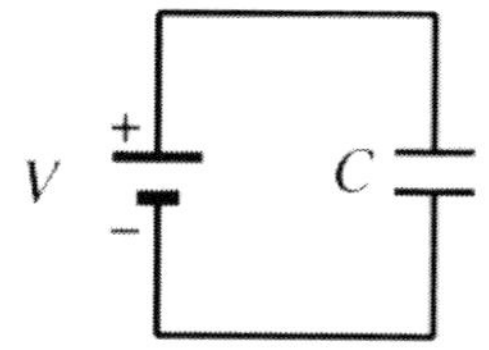

Figure 24.24: A cylindrical capacitor connected to a battery.

RESEARCH:

The capacitance C of a cylindrical capacitor is given by (24.11)

$$C = \frac{2\pi\varepsilon_0 L}{\ln(r_2 / r_1)} \tag{24.46}$$

where r_1 is the inner radius of the capacitor, r_2 is the outer radius of the capacitor, and L is the length of the capacitor. Adding a dielectric between the plates, the capacitance becomes

$$C = \kappa\frac{2\pi\varepsilon_0 L}{\ln(r_2 / r_1)} \tag{24.47}$$

where κ is the dielectric constant. For a capacitor of capacitance C charged to a voltage of V, the charge q is given by (24.1)

$$q = CV. \tag{24.48}$$

SIMPLIFY:

Substituting (24.47) into (24.48) gives us

Solved Problem

$$q = CV = \left(\kappa \frac{2\pi\varepsilon_0 L}{\ln(r_2/r_1)}\right)V = \frac{2\kappa\pi\varepsilon_0 LV}{\ln(r_2/r_1)}. \tag{24.49}$$

CALCULATE:

Putting in our numerical values, we get

$$q = \frac{2\kappa\pi\varepsilon_0 LV}{\ln(r_2/r_1)} = \frac{2(12.5)(8.85\cdot 10^{-12}\text{ F/m})(0.500\text{ m})(100.0\text{ V})}{\ln(0.120\text{ m}/0.100\text{ m})}.$$

$$q = 6.06758\cdot 10^{-8}\text{ C}$$

ROUND:

We report our result to three significant figures

$$q = 6.07\cdot 10^{-8}\text{ C} = 60.7\text{ nC}.$$

DOUBLE-CHECK:

Our result is a very small fraction of a coulomb of charge, so our answer seems reasonable.

Chapter 25. Direct Currents

Figure 25.1: A current flowing through a wire makes this light bulb shine.

What we will learn

- Electric current at a point in a circuit is the rate at which a net charge moves through that point.
- Direct current is current flowing in one direction.
- The direction of current is defined as the direction that positive charge would be moving.
- The current density is the current per cross sectional area passing a given point in a conductor.
- The resistivity of a material characterizes the ability of that material to conduct current.
- The resistance of a device depends on its geometry and on the material from

which it is constructed.

- The resistivity of conductors increases approximately linearly with temperature.
- Ohm's Law states that the voltage across a device is equal to the current flowing through the device times the resistance of that device.
- A simple circuit consists of a source of emf and resistors connected in series or in parallel.
- An equivalent resistance can replace resistors connected in series or in parallel.

In this chapter, we will study charges in motion. Charge moving from one region to another is called current. Current is all around us. Current is flowing through light bulbs (as in Figure 25.1), mp3 players, and lightning strikes. Current usually consists of mobile electrons traveling in conducting materials. Direct current is defined as a current that flows in one direction.

25.1. Electric Current

Quantitatively we define the current i as the net charge passing a given point in a given time divided by that time. Random motion of electrons in conductors or the flowing of electrically neutral atoms are not current in spite of the fact that large amounts of charge are moving past a given point as there is no net charge flow. If net charge dq passes a point during a time dt we define the current at that point to be

$$i = \frac{dq}{dt}. \tag{25.1}$$

The amount of charge passing a given point in time t is the integral of the current with respect to time given by

$$q = \int dq = \int_0^t i dt. \tag{25.2}$$

In this chapter we will use charge conservation, implying that charge flowing in a conductor is never lost. Therefore, the same amount of charge flows into one end of a conductor as emerges from the other end of the conductor.

The unit of current is coulombs per second, which has been given the name ampere, named after French physicist André Ampère, (1775-1836). The ampere is abbreviated as A and is given by

$$1\text{ A} = \frac{1\text{ C}}{1\text{ s}}. \tag{25.3}$$

Some typical currents are: 1 A for a flashlight, 200 A for the starter in your car, $1\text{ mA} = 1\cdot 10^{-3}\text{ A}$ to power your mp3 player, and $100{,}000\text{ A} = 1\cdot 10^{5}\text{ A}$ in a lightning strike (for a short time).

In this chapter we will make extensive use of batteries as devices that provide direct currents in circuits. If you examine a battery, you will find its voltage written on it. This voltage is the potential difference it can provide to a circuit. On modern re-chargeable batteries, you will also find their ratings in units of mAh (milliAmpere-hour). This rating provides information on the total charge that they can deliver when fully charged. The quantity mAh is another unit of charge:

$$1 \text{ mAh} = (10^{-3} \text{ A})(3600 \text{ s}) = 3.6 \text{ As} = 3.6 \text{ C}. \tag{25.4}$$

In this chapter we will depict the direction of the current flowing in a conductor using an arrow. This arrow represents the presumed direction of the net current in a conductor at a given point but does not represent a direction in three dimensions (x, y, z) because the orientation of the conductor is arbitrary. Physically the charge carriers in a conductor are electrons that are negatively charged. However, as is conventionally done, we define positive current to the right (for example) as the sum of the net flow of positive charge to the right plus the net flow of negative charge to the left per unit time.

Self-Test Opportunity: A typical rechargeable AA battery is rated at 700 mAh. How long can this battery provide a current of $100\ \mu\text{A}$?

Example 25.1: Iontophoresis

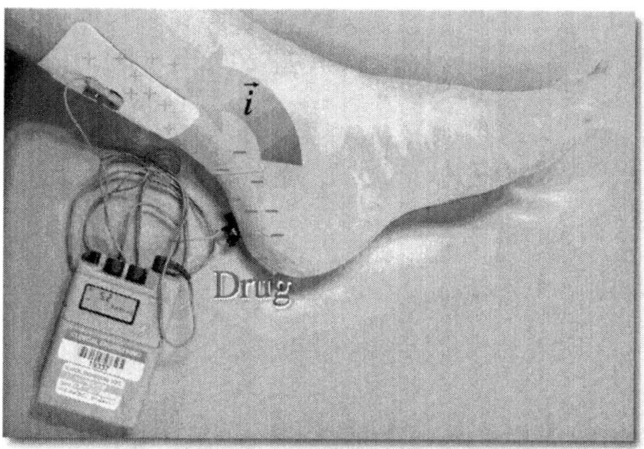

Figure 25.2: Iontophoresis = application of medication under the skin with the aid of electrical current.

If you want to deliver an anti-inflammatory medication to tissue in some well-defined location of your body, you have three alternatives. The painless way is the oral one; you simply swallow the drug. This typically leads to low concentration of dose in the affected tissue, on the order of $1\ \mu\text{g}$. Or you can have the drug injected locally with a needle. This hurts, but can deposit on the order of $10\ \text{mg}$ of the drug where you need it, four orders of magnitude more than the oral method. But since the 1990s there is another way available, which is also painless, and which can deposit on the order of $100\ \mu\text{g}$ of the drug in the area where it is needed. This method is called iontophoresis and works with

Example

the aid of (very week) electrical currents that are sent through the patient's tissue, see Figure 25.2. This method and device basically consists of a battery and two electrodes (plus a minimum amount of electronics that allows the nurse to control the strength of the current applied). The anti-inflammatory drug, usually dexamethasone, is applied to the underside of the negatively charge electrode. A current flows through the patient's skin and deposits the drug in the tissue up to 1.7 cm below the negative electrode.

Question:
The nurse wants to administer $80\ \mu g$ dexamethasone to the heel of a soccer player. If she applies a current of 0.14 mA in the way shown in Figure 25.2, how long does she have to subject her patient to this treatment? Assume that the instrument is rated at an application rate of 650 g/C, and that the current flows at a constant rate.

Answer:
If the drug application rate is 650 g/C, and you want to apply $80\ \mu g$, then you need a total charge of

$$q = \frac{80\ \mu g}{650\ g/C} = 1.23 \cdot 10^{-7} C$$

If the current flows at a constant rate, as stated, then the integral in (25.2) is simply

$$q = \int_0^t i dt = it \tag{25.5}$$

Solving this for the time and inserting the numbers we find

$$q = it \Rightarrow t = \frac{q}{i} = \frac{0.122\ C}{0.14\ mA} = 870\ s$$

This means that the iontophoresis treatment of the athlete will take approximately 15 minutes in this case.

25.2. Current Density

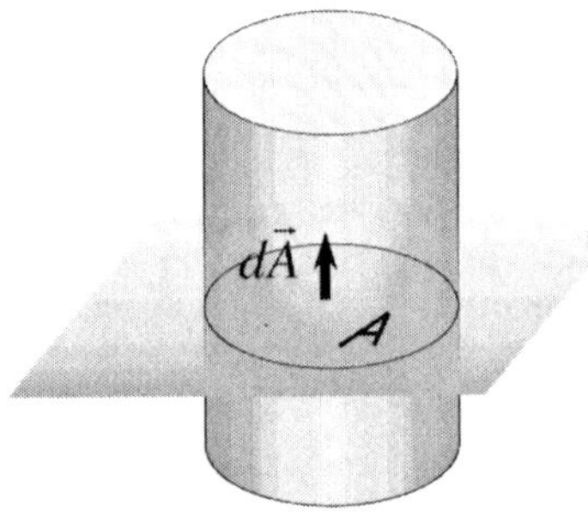

Figure 25.3: Segment of a conductor (wire), with a perpendicular plane intersecting the conductor, and forming a cross-sectional area, *A*.

Consider current flowing in a conductor. Taking a plane through the conductor, we can define the current per unit area flowing through the conductor at that point as the current density, $\vec{J}$. We take the direction of $\vec{J}$ as the direction of the velocity of the positive charges (or opposite to the direction of negative charges) crossing the plane. The current flowing through the surface is

$$i = \int \vec{J} \cdot d\vec{A} \tag{25.6}$$

where $d\vec{A}$ is the differential area element perpendicular to the surface as indicated in Figure 25.3. If the current is constant and perpendicular to the surface, then $i = JA$ and we can write an expression for the magnitude of the current density

$$J = \frac{i}{A}. \tag{25.7}$$

In a conductor that is not carrying current, the conduction electrons move randomly. When current flows through the conductor, the electrons still move randomly but with an added drift velocity. The magnitude of the velocity of random motion is on the order of 10^6 m/s while the magnitude of the drift velocity is on the order of 10^{-4} m/s or even less. With such a slow drift velocity one might ask why lights turn on almost immediately after a switch is thrown. This is because the switch establishes an electric field almost immediately throughout the wire, causing the free electrons in the entire wire (including in the light bulb) to move almost instantly.

We can relate the current density to the drift velocity of the moving electrons. Consider a conductor with cross sectional area A and electric field $\vec{E}$. Suppose that there are n conduction electrons per unit volume. The negatively charged electrons will drift in a direction opposite to the electric field. Here we assume that all electrons have the same drift velocity and that the current density is uniform. In a time interval dt, each electron moves a net distance $v_d dt$. The volume of electrons that passes a cross-section of the conductor is then $Av_d dt$ and the number of electrons in this volume is $nAv_d dt$. Each electron has charge of $-e$ so that the charge dq that flows through the area in time dt is

$$dq = -nev_d Adt \tag{25.8}$$

and the current is

$$i = \frac{dq}{dt} = -nev_d A. \tag{25.9}$$

The resulting current density is

$$J = \frac{i}{A} = -nev_d. \tag{25.10}$$

This equation was derived in one spatial dimension, as is appropriate for wires. However, we can easily generalize our results for arbitrary directions in a three-dimensional space and

$$\vec{J} = -(ne)\vec{v}_d . \qquad (25.11)$$

We see that the drift velocity vector is anti-parallel to the current vector, as stated before. In Figure 25.4, we show a schematic drawing of a wire carrying a current.

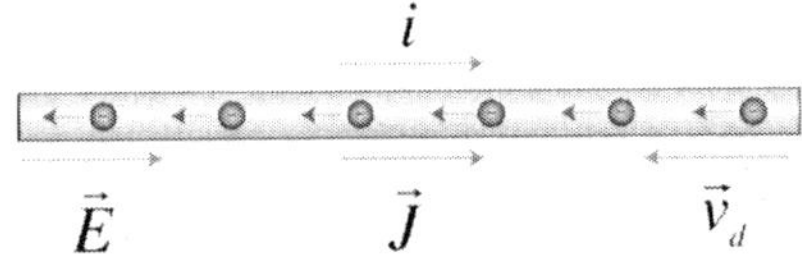

Figure 25.4: Schematic drawing showing electrons moving in a wire.

The physical current carriers are negatively charged electrons. These electrons are moving to the left with their drift velocity, $\vec{v}_d$, in this drawing. However, the electric field, current density, and current are all to the right because of the convention that these quantities refer to positive charges. You may find this convention somewhat confusing. Unfortunately it arises from the historical fact that the convention was established before it was known that the negatively charged electrons are the charges that flow in a conductor and are responsible for the current.

25.3. Resistivity and Resistance

Some materials conduct electricity better than others. If we apply a given voltage across a conductor, we get a relatively large current. If we apply the same voltage across an insulator, we get little current. The property of a material that describes its ability to conduct electric currents is called the *resistivity*, ρ. The property of a particular device or object that describes its ability to conduct electric currents is called the *resistance*, R.

If we apply an electric potential difference V across a conductor and measure the resulting current i in the conductor, we can define the resistance of that conductor as

$$R = \frac{V}{i} . \qquad (25.12)$$

The unit of resistance is volt per ampere. In honor of the German physicist George Simon Ohm (1789-1854), the resistance has been given the unit ohm with symbol Ω, which is the capital Greek letter Omega,

$$1\ \Omega = \frac{1\ \text{V}}{1\ \text{A}} . \qquad (25.13)$$

Sometimes materials are specified in term of their conductance, G, defined as

$$G = \frac{i}{V} = \frac{1}{R} \qquad (25.14)$$

which has the SI derived unit of siemens, S, given by

$$1\text{ S} = \frac{1\text{ A}}{1\text{ V}} = \frac{1}{1\ \Omega}. \tag{25.15}$$

The resistance of a conductor can depend on the direction the current flows in the conductor in some materials. In this chapter we will assume that the resistance of the device is uniform for all directions of the current.

The resistance of a conductor depends on the material from which the conductor is constructed as well as the geometry of the conductor. First we discuss the effects of the material of the conductor and then we will discuss the effects of geometry on resistance.

The conducting properties of a material are characterized in terms of its resistivity. We define the resistivity of a material in terms of the magnitude of the applied electric field, E, and the magnitude of the resulting current density, J, as

$$\rho = \frac{E}{J}. \tag{25.16}$$

The units of resistivity are

$$\frac{\left(\frac{\text{V}}{\text{m}}\right)}{\left(\frac{\text{A}}{\text{m}^2}\right)} = \frac{\text{Vm}}{\text{A}} = \Omega\text{m}. \tag{25.17}$$

The resistivities of some representative conductors at $20\ °\text{C}$ are listed in Table 25.1. As you can see, typical values for the resistivity of conductors used in wires are on the order of $10^{-8}\ \Omega\text{m}$.

Sometimes materials are specified in terms of their *conductivity* σ, rather than ρ, which is defined as

$$\sigma = \frac{1}{\rho}. \tag{25.18}$$

The units of conductivity are $(\Omega\text{m})^{-1}$. Knowing the resistivity of a material, we can then calculate the resistance of a conductor given its geometry. For a homogeneous conductor of length L and constant cross section A, we can use $V = \int \vec{E} \bullet d\vec{s}$ from Chapter 23 to relate the electric field and the electric potential difference V across the conductor as

$$E = \frac{V}{L}. \tag{25.19}$$

Material	Resistivity ρ (Ωm)	Resistivity ρ ($\mu\Omega\cdot$cm)
Silver	$1.59\cdot10^{-8}$	1.59
Copper	$1.72\cdot10^{-8}$	1.72
Gold	$2.44\cdot10^{-8}$	2.44
Aluminum	$2.82\cdot10^{-8}$	2.82
Nickel	$6.84\cdot10^{-8}$	6.84
Mercury	$95.8\cdot10^{-8}$	95.8

Table 25.1: Resistivities of some representative conductors.

Note that in contrast to electrostatics, in which conductors are equipotentials and have no electric field in them and no current flowing through them, here we have $V \neq 0$ and $\vec{E} \neq 0$, causing a current to flow. We can relate the current density and cross sectional area as

$$J = \frac{i}{A}. \tag{25.20}$$

Taking our definition for resistivity (25.16) we obtain

$$\rho = \frac{E}{J} = \frac{\left(\frac{V}{L}\right)}{\left(\frac{i}{A}\right)} = \frac{V}{i}\frac{A}{L}. \tag{25.21}$$

Using the definition for resistance (25.12) and rearranging terms, we get an expression for the resistance of a conductor in terms of the resistivity of its constituent material, length, and cross sectional area

$$R = \rho\frac{L}{A}. \tag{25.22}$$

Wire Size Convention

The American Wire Gauge (AWG) size convention specifies wire cross sectional area on a logarithmic scale. A table of the AWG size convention is shown in Table 25.2.

AWG	d (in)	d (mm)	A (mm^2)
000000	0.5800	14.733	170.49
00000	0.5165	13.120	135.20
0000	0.46	11.684	107.22
000	0.4096	10.405	85.029
00	0.3648	9.2658	67.431
0	0.3249	8.2515	53.475
1	0.2893	7.3481	42.408
2	0.2576	6.5437	33.631
3	0.2294	5.8273	26.670
4	0.2043	5.1894	21.151
5	0.1819	4.6213	16.773
6	0.1620	4.1154	13.302
7	0.1443	3.6649	10.549
8	0.1285	3.2636	8.3656
9	0.1144	2.9064	6.6342
10	0.1019	2.5882	5.2612
11	0.0907	2.3048	4.1723
12	0.0808	2.0525	3.3088
13	0.0720	1.8278	2.6240
14	0.0641	1.6277	2.0809
15	0.0571	1.4495	1.6502
16	0.0508	1.2908	1.3087
17	0.0453	1.1495	1.0378
18	0.0403	1.0237	0.8230
19	0.0359	0.9116	0.6527
20	0.0320	0.8118	0.5176
21	0.0285	0.7229	0.4105
22	0.0253	0.6438	0.3255
23	0.0226	0.5733	0.2582
24	0.0201	0.5106	0.2047
25	0.0179	0.4547	0.1624
26	0.0159	0.4049	0.1288
27	0.0142	0.3606	0.1021
28	0.0126	0.3211	0.0810
29	0.0113	0.2859	0.0642
30	0.0100	0.2546	0.0509
31	0.0089	0.2268	0.0404
32	0.0080	0.2019	0.0320
33	0.0071	0.1798	0.0254
34	0.0063	0.1601	0.0201
35	0.0056	0.1426	0.0160
36	0.005	0.1270	0.0127
37	0.0045	0.1131	0.0100
38	0.0040	0.1007	0.0080
39	0.0035	0.0897	0.0063
40	0.0031	0.0799	0.0050

Table 25.2: Wire diameters as defined by the American Wire Gauge convention.

The wire gauge is related to the diameter. The higher the gauge number is, the thinner is the wire. For large diameter wires, gauge numbers are specified by additional zeros, as shown in Table 25.2. So a 00-gauge is equivalent to a (-1)-gauge, a 000-gauge equivalent to a (-2)-gauge, a 0000-gauge to a (-3)-gauge, and so on. By definition, a 36-gauge wire has a diameter of exactly 0.005 inches, and 0000-gauge has a diameter of exactly 0.46 inches. (These are marked in red in Table 25.2). There are 39 gauge between a 0000-gauge and a 36-gauge, and we want the gauge number to be a logarithmic representation of the wire diameter. Therefore the formula to convert from the AWG size to the wire diameter is by definition:

$$d = 0.005 \cdot 92^{(36-n)/39} \text{ in} \tag{25.23}$$

where n is gauge number.

Typical residential wiring uses 12-gauge to 10-gauge wires. An important rule of thumb to remember: Every reduction by 3 gauges doubles the cross-sectional area. Examining

(25.22) you can see that if you want to cut the resistance of a given length of wire in half, then you have to reduce the gauge number by 3.

Example

Example 25.2: Resistance of a copper wire
Standard wires that electricians put into residential housing have fairly low resistance, as this example shows.

Question:
What is the resistance of a length of 100.0 m of standard 12-gauge copper wire that is typically used in household wiring for electrical outlets?

Answer:
A 12-gauge copper wire has a diameter of 2.053 mm, see Table 25.2. Its cross sectional area is then

$$A = \tfrac{1}{4}\pi d^2 = 3.31 \text{ mm}^2 .$$

Using the value of the resistivity of copper provided in Table 25.1, we then find with the aid of equation (25.22)

$$R = \rho \frac{L}{A} = (1.72 \cdot 10^{-8}\ \Omega\text{m}) \frac{100.0 \text{ m}}{3.31 \cdot 10^{-6} \text{ m}^2} = 0.520\ \Omega .$$

In-class exercise: What is the resistance of a spool of copper wire that has a length $L = 70.0$ m and diameter $d = 2.60$ mm?

a) 0.119 Ω
b) 0.139 Ω
c) 0.163 Ω
d) 0.190 Ω
e) 0.227 Ω

In many electronics applications one needs a range of resistances in various parts of the circuits. For this purpose one can use commercially available resistors such as those shown in the left panel of Figure 25.5.

Resistors are commonly made from carbon inside a plastic cover that looks like a medicine capsule, with two wires sticking out at the two ends for electrical connection. The value of the resistance is indicated by four color-bands on the capsule. The first two bands are numbers for the mantissa, the third is a power of ten, and the fourth is a tolerance for the range of values. The number associated with the colors are: black = 0, brown = 1, red = 2, orange = 3, yellow = 4, green = 5, blue = 6, purple = 7, gray = 8, and white = 9. In the tolerance band, gold means 5%, silver means 10%, and no tolerance band at all means 20%.

Figure 25.5: Left: Selection of resistors with various different resistances; right: Picture of color-coding of a 150 ohm resistor.

For example, the single resistor shown on the right of Figure 25.5 has colors (top to bottom) brown, green, brown and gold. Using our table, we can see that the resistance is $15 \cdot 10^1\ \Omega = 150\ \Omega$, with a tolerance of 5%.

Temperature Dependence, Superconductivity

The values of resistivity and resistance vary with the temperature. For metals, this dependence on temperature is linear over a broad range of temperatures. An empirical relationship for the temperature dependence of the resistivity of metals is given by

$$\rho - \rho_0 = \rho_0 \alpha \left(T - T_0\right) \tag{25.24}$$

where ρ is the resistivity at temperature T, ρ_0 is the resistivity at temperature T_0, and α is the temperature coefficient of electric resistivity for the material under consideration.

In everyday applications we are interested in the temperature dependence of the resistance of various devices. Equation (25.22) states that the resistance of a device depends on the length and the cross sectional area. These quantities depend on temperature. However, because the temperature dependence of linear expansion is much smaller than the temperature dependence of resistivity of a particular conductor, the temperature dependence of the resistance of a conductor can be approximately written as

$$R - R_0 = R_0 \alpha \left(T - T_0\right). \tag{25.25}$$

Note that equations (25.24) and (25.25) deal with temperatures differences, so that one can use °C as well as K for convenience. Values of α for representative conductors are shown in Table 25.3.

Material	Temperature Coefficient of Resistivity, α $\left(\mathrm{K}^{-1}\right)$
Silver	$3.8 \cdot 10^{-3}$
Copper	$3.9 \cdot 10^{-3}$
Aluminum	$3.9 \cdot 10^{-3}$
Tungsten	$4.5 \cdot 10^{-3}$
Iron	$5.0 \cdot 10^{-3}$

Table 25.3: Temperature coefficient of resistivity for various representative conductors.

Looking at (25.24), we see that most materials under ordinary circumstances have a resistivity that varies linearly with the temperature. However, there are materials that do not follow this rule at low temperatures.

At very low temperatures the resistivity of some materials goes to exactly zero. These materials are called superconductors. Superconductors have applications in the construction of magnets for devices such as magnetic resonance imagers (MRI). Magnets constructed with superconductors use less power and can produce higher magnetic fields than magnets constructed with conventional resistive conductors. We will return to a more extensive discussion of superconductivity when we discuss magnetism in chapters 27 and 28.

The resistance of some semiconducting materials actually decreases as the temperature increases. These materials are often found in high-resolution detection devices for optical measurements or particle detectors. These devices must be kept cold to keep their resistance high, by using refrigerators or liquid nitrogen.

25.4. Ohm's Law

To make current flow through a resistor one must establish a potential difference across the resistor. This potential difference is termed an *electromotive force*, emf. A device that maintains a potential difference is called an emf device and does work on the charge carriers. The potential difference created by the emf device is termed V_{emf}. We will assume that emf devices have terminals that we can connect to. The emf device is assumed to maintain V_{emf} between these terminals.

Examples of emf devices are batteries, electric generators, and solar cells. Batteries produce emf through chemical reactions. Electric generators create emf from mechanical motion. Solar cells convert energy from the Sun to electric energy. In this chapter we will assume that the source of emf is a battery.

Electrical components in a circuit can be sources of emf, capacitors, resistors, or other electrical devices. These components are connected with conducting wires that we will assume have no resistance. We will begin with simple circuits that consist of resistors and sources of emf.

Consider a simple circuit of the form shown in Figure 25.6. Here a source of emf provides a voltage V_{emf} across a resistor with resistance R. Ohm's Law gives the relationship between the voltage and the resistance in this circuit,

$$V_{emf} = iR \tag{25.26}$$

where i is the current flowing in the circuit. The current i that flows through the resistor also flows through the source of emf and the wires connecting the components.

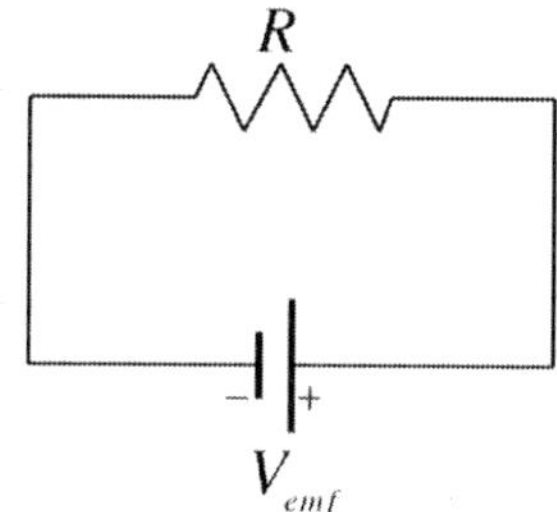

Figure 25.6: Simple circuit containing a source of emf and a resistor.

Understanding the concepts associated with circuits is notoriously difficult for some students. Thus, we would like to visualize the same circuit shown in Figure 25.6 in a different way, making it clearer where the potential drop (which is also called voltage drop) happens and showing what part of the circuit is at which potential. In the top half of Figure 25.7 is Figure 25.6 drawn with a three dimensional perspective. In the bottom part of Figure 25.7 we show the same circuit, but now the vertical dimension represents the voltage drop around the circuit. The voltage is supplied by the source of emf and the entire voltage drop occurs across the single resistor. Ohm's Law applies for the voltage drop across the resistor and we can calculate the current in the circuit using (25.26).

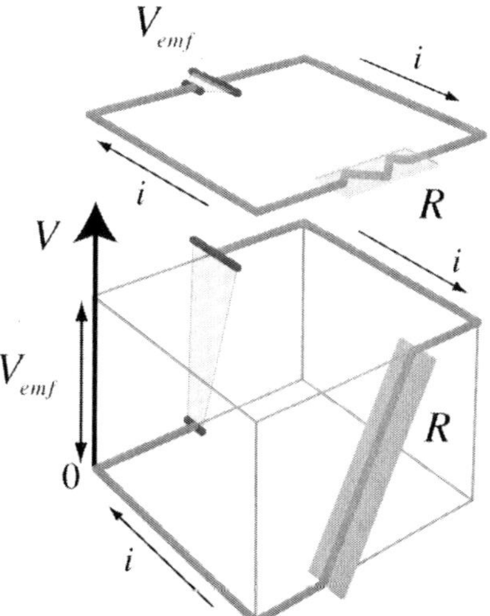

Figure 25.7: Upper part: conventional representation of a simple circuit with a resistance and source of emf. Lower part: Three dimensional drawing showing the same circuit, but with the third dimension used to display the potential at each point in the circuit. The current in the circuit is shown for both views.

A circuit can contain more than one resistor and more than one source of emf. With multiple sources of emf and resistors, the analysis of the circuit requires different techniques to determine the current flowing in various parts of the circuit. We begin with resistors connected in series.

Self-Test Opportunity: A resistor with $R = 10.0\ \Omega$ is connected across a source of emf with voltage $V = 1.50\ \text{V}$. What is the current flowing though the circuit?

25.5. Resistances in Series

Resistors connected such that all the current in a circuit must flow through each of the resistors are connected in series. If we connect two resistors R_1 and R_2 in series with one source of emf with voltage V_{emf}, we have the circuit shown in Figure 25.8.

The voltage drop across resistor R_1 is V_1 and the voltage drop across resistor R_2 is V_2 and the two voltage drops must sum to the voltage supplied by the source of emf

$$V_{emf} = V_1 + V_2 . \tag{25.27}$$

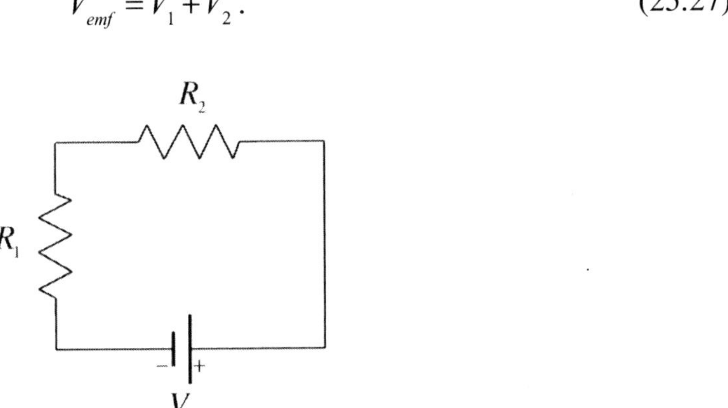

Figure 25.8: Circuit with two resistors in series with one source of emf.

The current must flow through all the elements of the circuit so we can see that the current flowing through each resistor is the same. For each resistor we can apply Ohm's Law and get

$$V_{emf} = iR_1 + iR_2 . \tag{25.28}$$

Now we can rewrite this equation to see that an equivalent resistance R_{eq} can replace the two resistors

$$V_{emf} = iR_1 + iR_2 = iR_{eq} \tag{25.29}$$

where

$$R_{eq} = R_1 + R_2. \tag{25.30}$$

Thus, two resistors in series can be replaced with an equivalent resistance equal to the sum of the two resistances. We can generalize this result for the equivalent resistance of two resistors in series to a circuit with n resistors in series by writing

$$R_{eq} = \sum_{i=1}^{n} R_i. \tag{25.31}$$

To illustrate the voltage drops in this series circuit we again present a three dimensional view of this circuit, which is shown in Figure 25.9.

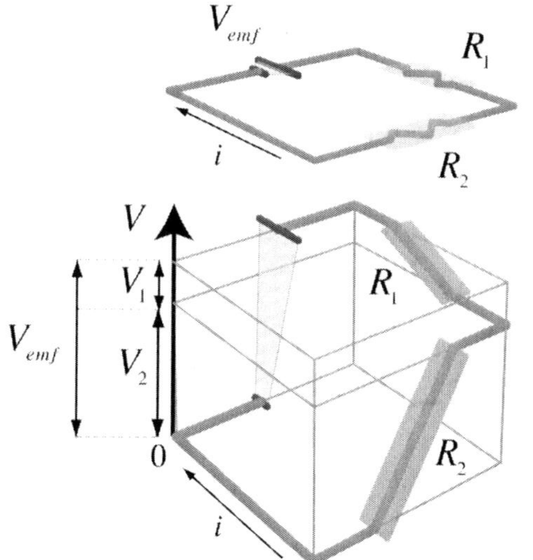

Figure 25.9: Upper part: conventional representation of a simple circuit with two resistances in series and a source of emf. Lower part: Three dimensional drawing showing the same circuit, but with the third dimension used to display the potential at each point in the circuit. The current in the circuit is shown for both views.

Example

Example 25.3: Internal resistance of a battery

When a battery is not connected in a circuit, the voltage across its terminals is V_t. When the battery is connected in series with a resistor with resistance R current i flows through the circuit. When the current is flowing, the voltage, V, across the terminals of the battery is lower than V_t. This drop occurs because the battery has an internal resistance, R_i, that can be thought of as being series with the external resistor. We can express this relationship as

$$V_t = iR_{eq} = i\left(R + R_i\right)$$

as illustrated in Figure 25.10. The battery is depicted by the yellow rectangle. The terminals of the battery are represented by points a and b.

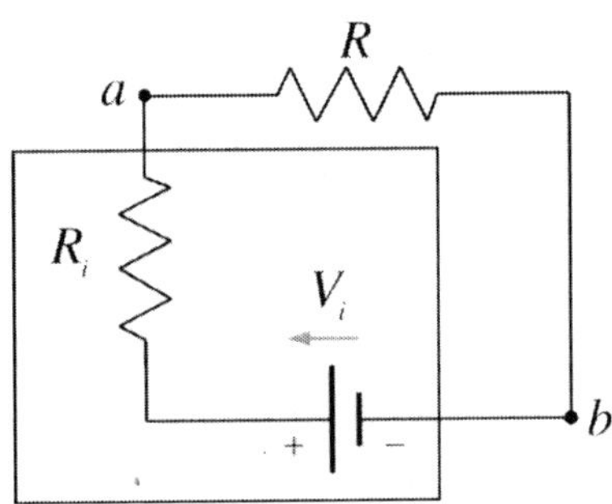

Figure 25.10: Battery (yellow area) with internal resistance R_i connected to an external resistor R.

Example

Consider a battery that has a voltage of 12.0 V when it is not connected to a circuit. When a $10.0\ \Omega$ resistor is connected across the battery, the voltage across the battery terminals drops to $10.9\ \text{V}$. What is the internal resistance of the battery?

The current flowing through the external resistor is given by

$$i = \frac{V}{R} = \frac{10.9\ \text{V}}{10.0\ \Omega} = 1.09\ \text{A}.$$

The current flowing in complete circuit must be the same as the current flowing in the external resistor so we can write

$$V_t = iR_{eq} = i\left(R + R_i\right)$$

$$\left(R + R_i\right) = \frac{V}{i}$$

$$R_i = \frac{V}{i} - R = \frac{12.0\ \text{V}}{1.09\ \text{A}} - 10.0\ \Omega = 1.0\ \Omega$$

The internal resistance of the battery is $1.0\ \Omega$.

Whether a battery can still provide energy cannot be determined by simply measuring the voltage across the terminals of the battery. A load must be placed on the battery and the resulting voltage must be measured. If the battery is no longer functional, it may still provide its rated voltage when it is not connected, while its voltage may drop to zero when connected to an external load. Some brands of batteries now have built-in devices to attach a load to the battery and measure the resulting voltage simply by pressing on a particular spot on the battery and observing an indicator. An assortment of batteries is shown in Figure 25.11.

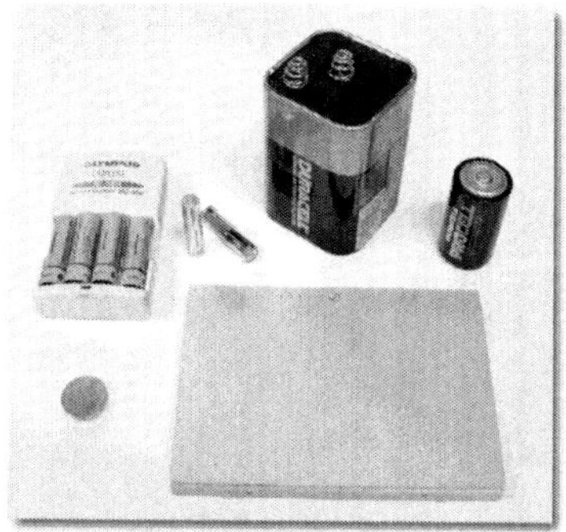

Figure 25.11: Some representative samples of batteries. The batteries are (clockwise from upper left): rechargeable AA Nickel Metal Hydride (NiMH) batteries in their charger, disposable AAA batteries, a 12 V lantern battery, a D-sized battery, a lithium ion laptop battery, and a watch battery.

25.6. Resistances in Parallel

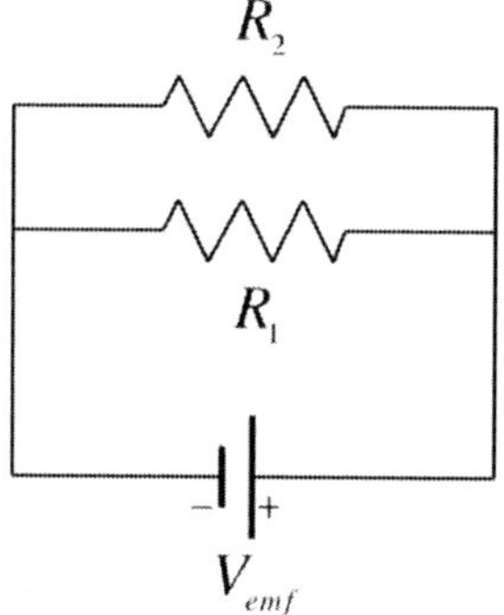

Figure 25.12: Circuit with two resistors connected in parallel connected to a single source of emf.

Instead of connecting resistors in series so that all the current must pass through both resistors, we can connect the resistors in parallel such that the current is divided between the two resistors. This type of circuit is shown in Figure 25.12.

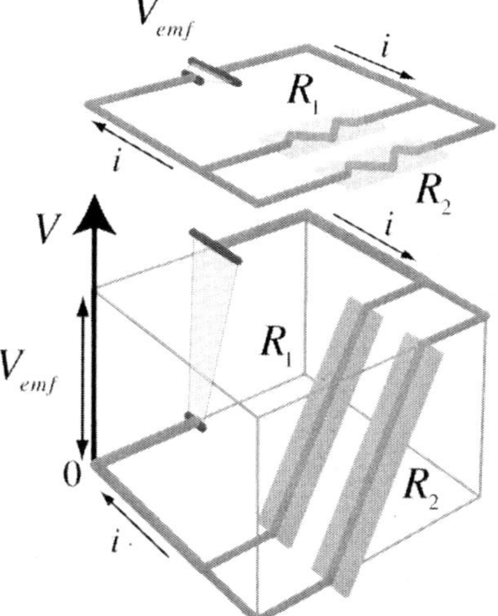

Figure 25.13: Upper part: conventional representation of a simple circuit with two resistances in parallel and a source of emf. Lower part: Three dimensional drawing showing the same circuit, but with the third dimension used to display the potential at each point in the circuit. The current in the circuit is shown for both views.

Again, to better illustrate the voltage drops in this circuit, we present the same circuit in a three dimensional view in Figure 25.13. In this case the voltage drop across each resistor is equal to the voltage provided by the source of emf. Using Ohm's Law (25.26) for the current i_1 in R_1 and i_2 in R_2 we can write

$$i_1 = \frac{V_{emf}}{R_1} \tag{25.32}$$

and

$$i_2 = \frac{V_{emf}}{R_2}. \tag{25.33}$$

The total current in the system i must be

$$i = i_1 + i_2. \tag{25.34}$$

Substituting (25.32) and (25.33) into (25.34) and rearranging we obtain

$$i = i_1 + i_2 = \frac{V_{emf}}{R_1} + \frac{V_{emf}}{R_2} = V_{emf}\left(\frac{1}{R_1} + \frac{1}{R_2}\right). \tag{25.35}$$

Rewriting Ohm's Law (25.26) as

$$i = V_{emf}\frac{1}{R_{eq}}, \tag{25.36}$$

we can see that two resistors connected in parallel can be replaced with an equivalent resistance given by

$$\frac{1}{R_{eq}} = \frac{1}{R_1} + \frac{1}{R_2}. \tag{25.37}$$

We can generalize this result to the equivalent resistance for n resistors connected in parallel to be

$$\frac{1}{R_{eq}} = \sum_{i=1}^{n}\frac{1}{R_i}. \tag{25.38}$$

Clearly, we can now proceed to combine resistors in series and in parallel into equivalent resistances. In this way we can solve for networks of resistances, in a very similar fashion to how we proceeded for networks of capacitors in the previous chapter.

Example 25.4: Network of resistors

In Figure 25.14(a) an arrangement of six resistors with resistance R_1 through R_6 is shown.

Question:
What is the current flowing through resistor R_2 and resistor R_3 in this circuit in terms of V and R_1 through R_6?

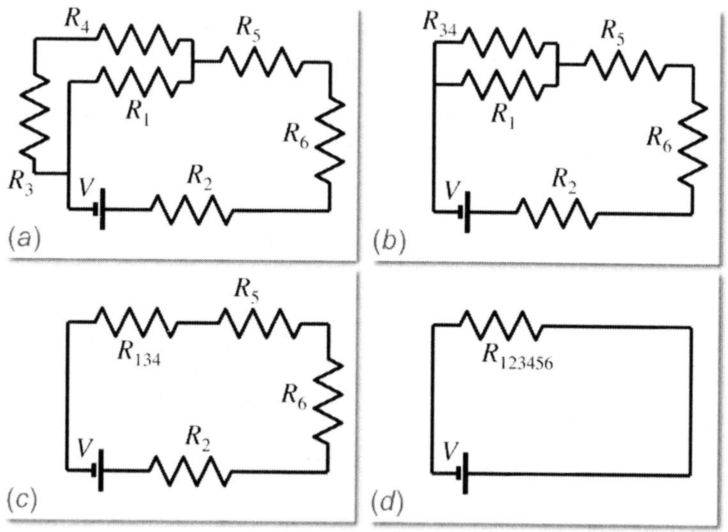

Figure 25.14: Network of resistors (a), and various steps in combining these resistors into equivalent resistances (b-d).

Answer:
We proceed by identifying parts of the circuit that are clearly wired in parallel or in series. The current flowing through R_2 will be the current flowing though the entire circuit. To analyze this circuit, we note that R_3 and R_4 are in series. Thus we can write

$$R_{34} = R_3 + R_4.$$

This substitution is made in Figure 25.14(b). In this figure we can now see that R_{34} and R_1 are in parallel. We can then write

$$\frac{1}{R_{134}} = \frac{1}{R_1} + \frac{1}{R_{34}}$$

or

$$R_{134} = \frac{R_1 R_{34}}{R_1 + R_{34}}.$$

Example

This substitution is depicted in Figure 25.14(c). In this figure we can see that R_2, R_5, R_6, and R_{134} are in series. Thus, we can write

$$R_{123456} = R_2 + R_5 + R_6 + R_{134}.$$

This substitution is shown in Figure 25.14(d). Substituting for R_{134} and R_{34}, we can write

$$R_{123456} = R_2 + R_5 + R_6 + \frac{R_1 R_{34}}{R_1 + R_{34}} = R_2 + R_5 + R_6 + \frac{R_1\left(R_3 + R_4\right)}{R_1 + R_3 + R_4}.$$

Thus we can write the current flowing through R_2, i_2, as

$$i_2 = \frac{V}{R_{123456}}.$$

Example

Now we turn to the determination of the current flowing through R_3. The current i_2 is also flowing through the effective resistor R_{134} that contains resistor R_3. Thus, we can write

$$V_{134} = i_2 R_{134}$$

where V_{134} is the voltage drop across the effective resistor R_{134}. The resistor R_1 and the effective resistor R_{34} are in parallel. Thus, the voltage drop across R_{34}, V_{34}, is the same as the voltage drop across R_{134}, which is V_{134}. The resistors R_3 and R_4 are in series, and thus the current flowing through R_3, i_3, is the same as the current flowing through R_{34}, i_{34}. We can then write

$$V_{34} = V_{134} = i_{34} R_{34} = i_3 R_{34}.$$

Now we can express i_3 in terms of V and R_1 through R_6:

$$i_3 = \frac{V_{134}}{R_{34}} = \frac{i_2 R_{134}}{R_{34}} = \frac{\left(\dfrac{V}{R_{123456}}\right) R_{134}}{R_{34}} = \frac{V R_{134}}{R_{34} R_{123456}} = V \frac{\dfrac{R_1(R_3 + R_4)}{R_1 + R_3 + R_4}}{R_2 + R_3 + R_4 + R_5 + R_6 + \dfrac{R_1(R_3 + R_4)}{R_1 + R_3 + R_4}}.$$

In-class exercise: In the circuit shown, $R_1 = 1.90\ \Omega$, $R_2 = 0.980\ \Omega$, and $R_3 = 1.70\ \Omega$.

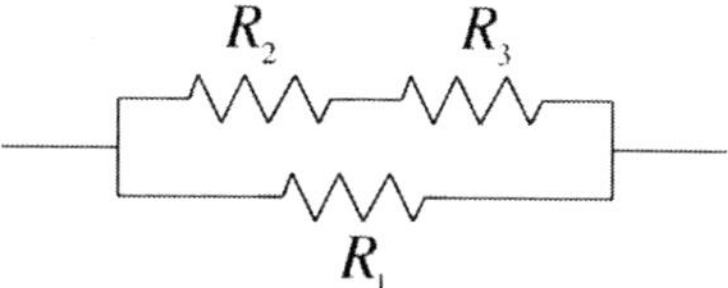

What is the equivalent resistance of this combination of resistor?

a) 0.984 Ω
b) 1.11 Ω
c) 1.26 Ω
d) 1.42 Ω
e) 1.60 Ω

Solved Problem

Solved Problem 25.1: Voltage drop across a series resistor

Question:
The circuit shown in Figure 25.15 has three resistors connected in series across a battery with $V_{emf} = 149$ V. The values of the three resistors are $R_1 = 17.0\ \Omega$, $R_2 = 51.0\ \Omega$, and $R_3 = 114\ \Omega$. What is the magnitude of the voltage drop across R_2?

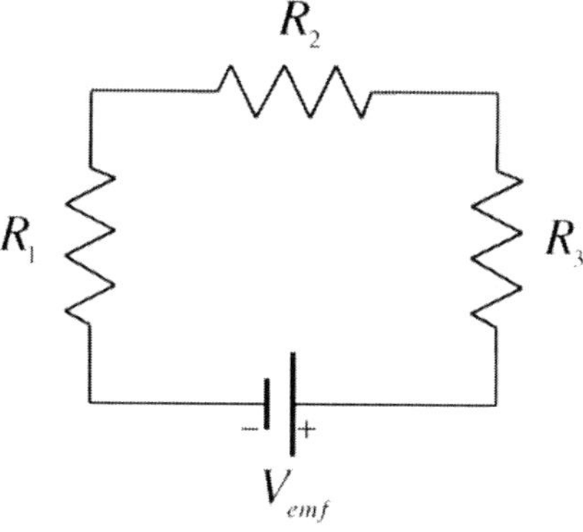

Figure 25.15: A circuit with three resistors in series.

Answer:

THINK:

The current in each of the three resistors is the same because they are in series. We can obtain the current in the circuit by calculating the equivalent resistance of the three resistors and using Ohm's Law. The voltage drop across R_2 is then the current in the circuit times R_2.

SKETCH:

The voltage drop across resistor R_2 is illustrated in Figure 25.16.

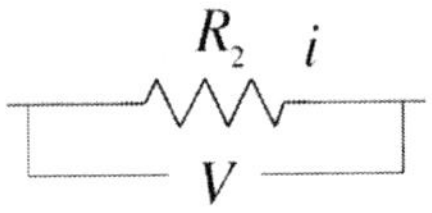

Figure 25.16: Voltage drop across resistor R_2.

RESEARCH:

We can calculate the equivalent resistance of the three resistors in series using (25.31)

$$R_{eq} = \sum_{i=1}^{n} R_i = R_1 + R_2 + R_3. \tag{25.39}$$

We can then calculate the current in the circuit using Ohm's Law

$$V_{emf} = iR_{eq} = i\left(R_1 + R_2 + R_3\right). \tag{25.40}$$

SIMPLIFY:

The voltage drop across R_2 is

$$V = iR_2 = \frac{V_{emf}}{R_1 + R_2 + R_3} R_2 = \frac{R_2 V_{emf}}{R_1 + R_2 + R_3}. \tag{25.41}$$

CALCULATE:

Putting in our numerical values we get

$$V = \frac{R_2 V_{emf}}{R_1 + R_2 + R_3} = \frac{(51.0\ \Omega)(149\ \text{V})}{17.0\ \Omega + 51.0\ \Omega + 114\ \Omega} = 41.7527\ \text{V}.$$

ROUND:

We report our result to three significant figures

$$V = 41.7\ \text{V}.$$

DOUBLE-CHECK:

To double-check our answer, we calculate the voltage drop across the other two resistors and make sure they add up to the voltage of the battery. The voltage drop across R_1 is

$$V_1 = \frac{R_1 V_{emf}}{R_1 + R_2 + R_3} = \frac{(17.0\ \Omega)(149\ \text{V})}{17.0\ \Omega + 51.0\ \Omega + 114\ \Omega} = 13.9\ \text{V}.$$

The voltage drop across R_3 is

Solved Problem

$$V_3 = \frac{R_3 V_{emf}}{R_1 + R_2 + R_3} = \frac{(114\ \Omega)(149\ \text{V})}{17.0\ \Omega + 51.0\ \Omega + 114\ \Omega} = 93.3\ \text{V}.$$

The voltage drop across all three resistors is then

$$V_{\text{total}} = V + V_1 + V_3 = 41.7\ \text{V} + 13.9\ \text{V} + 93.3\ \text{V} = 149\ \text{V},$$

which matches what was given as the voltage of the battery. Thus, our answer seems reasonable.

25.7. Energy and Power in Electric Circuits

Consider a simple circuit in which a source of emf with voltage V causes a current i to flow in a circuit. The work required from the emf source to move a differential amount of charge dq from the negative terminal to the positive terminal is equal to the increase of electric potential energy of that charge dU and is given by

$$dU = dqV. \tag{25.42}$$

Remembering that the definition of current is $i = dq/dt$, we can re-write the differential electric potential energy as

$$dU = idtV. \tag{25.43}$$

Using the definition of the power $P = dU/dt$ and substituting in (25.43) we obtain

$$P = \frac{dU}{dt} = \frac{idtV}{dt} = iV. \tag{25.44}$$

Thus, the product of the current times the voltage gives the power supplied by the source of emf, which, by conservation of energy, is equal to the power dissipated in a circuit consisting of one resister. In a complicated circuit each resister will dissipate power at the rate given by (25.44) provided i and V refer to the current through and voltage across that resister. Using Ohm's Law (25.26), we can write different formulations of the power

$$P = iV = i^2 R = \frac{V^2}{R}. \tag{25.45}$$

The unit of power, as we have previously discussed, (see chapter 5) is the watt (W). Electrical devices, such as light bulbs, are rated by how much power they consume. Your electricity bill depends on how much electrical energy your appliances consume, and this energy is measured in kilowatt-hours (kWh).

Where does this energy go? We will return to this discussion when we talk about alternating currents. For now we can already make some qualitative remarks. Some of the power dissipated in circuits can be converted into mechanical energy by motors. To understand the functioning of electric motors we also need to study magnetism. We will return to this topic later. Much or most of the energy dissipated in resistors is converted into heat. This process of heating a resistor is employed in incandescent lighting, where heating a metal filament to very high temperature causes it to emit light.

Self-Test Opportunity: Consider a battery with internal resistance R_i. What external resistance R should we connect to the battery to produce the maximum heating of the external resistance?

Example

Example 25.5: Temperature dependence of the resistance of a light bulb

A 100 W light bulb is connected in series to a source of emf with $V_{emf} = 100\text{ V}$. When the light bulb is operating, the temperature of its tungsten filament is 2520 °C.

Question:
What is the resistance of the light bulb at room temperature (20 °C)?

Answer:
The resistance of the light bulb when operating can be obtained using (25.45)

$$P = \frac{V^2}{R}.$$

We can rearrange this equation and substitute our values to get the resistance of the light bulb while it is operating

$$R = \frac{V^2}{P} = \frac{(100\text{ V})^2}{100\text{ W}} = 100\ \Omega.$$

The temperature dependence of the resistance of the filament of the light bulb is given by (25.25)

$$R - R_0 = R_0\alpha(T - T_0).$$

We solve for the resistance at room temperature, R_0,

$$R = R_0 + R_0\alpha(T - T_0) = R_0\left(1 + \alpha(T - T_0)\right)$$

$$R_0 = \frac{R}{1 + \alpha(T - T_0)}$$

Using the temperature coefficient of resistivity for tungsten from Table 25.3 we get

$$R_0 = \frac{R}{1+\alpha\left(T-T_0\right)} = \frac{100\ \Omega}{1+\left(4.5\cdot 10^{-3}\ °\text{C}^{-1}\right)\left(2520\ °\text{C}-20\ °\text{C}\right)} = 8.2\ \Omega.$$

In-class exercise: A current of 2.00 A is maintained in a circuit with a total resistance of 5.00 Ω. How much heat is generated in 4.00 s?

a) 55.2 J
b) 80.0 J
c) 116 J
d) 168 J
e) 244 J

What we have learned/Exam Study Guide:

Most Important Points

- The electromotive force is called emf.
- Current, i, is defined as the time rate change of the charge, q, $i=\frac{dq}{dt}$.
- The magnitude of the current density, J, at a given cross sectional area, A, in a conductor is given by $J=\frac{i}{A}$.
- The the current density, J, is related to the drift velocity, v_d, of the current carrying charges, $-e$, by $J=\frac{i}{A}=-nev_d$, where n is the number of charge carriers per unit volume.
- The resistivity, ρ, of a material is defined in terms of the electric field applied across the material, E, and the resulting current density, J, as $\rho=\frac{E}{J}$.
- The resistance R of a specific device having a resistivity ρ, a length L, and a cross sectional area A, is $R=\rho\frac{L}{A}$.
- The temperature dependence of the resistivity of a material is given by $\rho-\rho_0=\rho_0\alpha\left(T-T_0\right)$ where ρ is the final resistivity, ρ_0 is the initial resistivity, α is the temperature coefficient, T is the final temperature, and T_0 is the initial temperature.
- Ohm's Law states that when there is a potential difference V across a resister R,

the current i flowing through the resister is given by $i = \frac{V}{R}$.

- Resistors connected in series can be replaced with an equivalent resistance, R_{eq}, given by the sum of the resistances of the resistors, $R_{eq} = \sum_{i=1}^{n} R_i$.
- Resistors connected in parallel can replaced with an equivalent resistance, R_{eq}, given by $\frac{1}{R_{eq}} = \sum_{i=1}^{n} \frac{1}{R_i}$.
- The power P dissipated by a resistor R through which a current i flows is given by $P = iV = i^2 R = \frac{V^2}{R}$ where V is the voltage drop across the resistor.

New Symbols used in this Chapter

- i is the current.
- $\vec{v}_d$ is the drift velocity of current carrying charges.
- $\vec{J}$ is the current density.
- ρ is the resistivity.
- R is the resistance.
- V_{emf} is the voltage of the source of emf.
- α is the temperature coefficient of resistivity.

Additional Solved Problems

Solved Problem

Solved Problem 25.2: Galvanometer as current-measuring device

Question:

A galvanometer is an instrument for detecting and measuring current. We can use a galvanometer to measure different ranges of current by using a current divider in the form of a shunt resistor connected in parallel with the galvanometer. We have a galvanometer that produces a full-scale reading when a current of $i_{\text{int}} = 5.10$ mA is passed through it. The galvanometer has an internal resistance of $R_i = 16.8\ \Omega$. We want to use this galvanometer to measure a full-scale current of $i_{\text{max}} = 20.2$ A. What shunt resistor R_s should we use in parallel with the galvanometer?

Answer:

THINK:

To make the galvanometer useful for measuring higher currents, we must put a shunt resistor in parallel with the galvanometer. This resistor will have a substantially lower resistance than the internal resistance of the galvanometer. Most of the current then would flow through the shunt resistor rather than the galvanometer.

SKETCH:

A shunt resistor R_s connected in parallel with a galvanometer is shown in Figure 25.17.

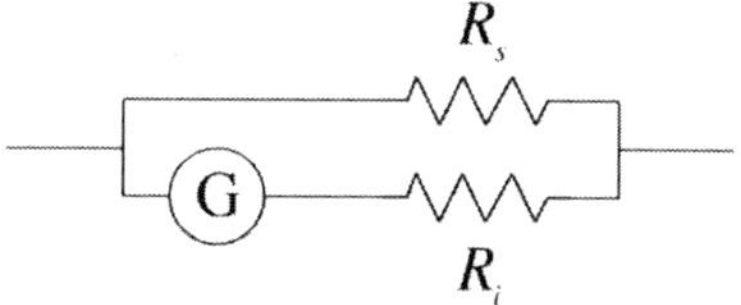

Figure 25.17: A galvanometer with a shunt resistor connected across it in parallel.

RESEARCH:

The two resistors are connected in parallel so the voltage across each resistor will be the same. The voltage that will give a full-scale reading on the galvanometer is

$$V = i_{int} R_i . \qquad (25.46)$$

The equivalent resistance of the two resistors in parallel is given by (25.38)

$$\frac{1}{R_{eq}} = \sum_{i=1}^{n} \frac{1}{R_i} = \frac{1}{R_i} + \frac{1}{R_s} . \qquad (25.47)$$

The voltage drop across the equivalent resistance must equal the maximum voltage drop across the galvanometer when i_{max} is flow through the circuit. Therefore, we can write

$$V = i_{max} R_{eq} . \qquad (25.48)$$

SIMPLIFY:

Combining (25.46) and (25.48) gives us

$$V = i_{int} R_i = i_{max} R_{eq} . \qquad (25.49)$$

We can rearrange (25.49) and substitute in (25.47)

$$\frac{i_{max}}{i_{int} R_i} = \frac{1}{R_{eq}} = \frac{1}{R_i} + \frac{1}{R_s} . \qquad (25.50)$$

We can rearrange (25.50) to get

$$\frac{1}{R_s} = \frac{i_{max}}{i_{int} R_i} - \frac{1}{R_i} = \frac{1}{R_i}\left(\frac{i_{max}}{i_{int}} - 1 \right) = \frac{1}{R_i} \frac{i_{max} - i_{int}}{i_{int}} . \qquad (25.51)$$

Solving for the shunt resistance gives us

$$R_s = R_i \frac{i_{int}}{i_{max} - i_{int}}. \quad (25.52)$$

CALCULATE:

Putting in our numerical values we get

$$R_s = R_i \frac{i_{int}}{i_{max} - i_{int}} = (16.8\ \Omega)\frac{5.10 \cdot 10^{-3}\ \text{A}}{20.2\ \text{A} - 5.10 \cdot 10^{-3}\ \text{A}}.$$

$$R_s = 0.00424266\ \Omega$$

ROUND:

We report our result to three significant figures

$$R_s = 0.00424\ \Omega.$$

DOUBLE-CHECK:

The equivalent resistance of the galvanometer and shunt resistor connected in parallel is given by

$$\frac{1}{R_{eq}} = \frac{1}{R_i} + \frac{1}{R_s}.$$

Solving for the equivalent resistance gives us

$$R_{eq} = \frac{R_i R_s}{R_i + R_s} = \frac{(16.8\ \Omega)(0.00424\ \Omega)}{16.8\ \Omega + 0.00424\ \Omega} = 0.00424\ \Omega.$$

Thus, the equivalent resistance of the galvanometer and shunt resistor connected in parallel is approximately equal to the resistance of the shunt resistor. The low equivalent resistance of the galvanometer and shunt resistance makes the device work well as a current-measuring instrument. A current-measuring device must be placed in series in a circuit to be studied. If the current-measuring device has a high resistance, its presence will disturb the measurement of the current.

Solved Problem

Solved Problem 25.3: Drift velocity of electrons in copper wire

Question:

You play the game "Galactic Destroyer" on your video game console. Your game controller operates at 12 V and is connected to the main box with an 18-gauge copper wire of 1.5 m length. As you fly your spaceship into battle, you hold the joystick in the forward position for 5.3 seconds, sending a current of 0.78 mA to the console. How far have the electrons in the wire moved during those 5.3 seconds that it took your spaceship on the screen to cross half of a star system?

Answer:

THINK:

To find out haw far the electrons move during a given time interval, we need to calculate their drift velocity. To calculate the drift velocity for electrons in a copper wire carrying a current, we need to calculate the density of charge-carrying electrons in copper. Having that result we can apply the definition of the charge density to calculate the drift velocity.

SKETCH:

A sketch of a copper wire with cross sectional area A carrying a current i is shown in Figure 25.18, reminding us that the electrons drift in opposite direction of the conventional definition of the current direction.

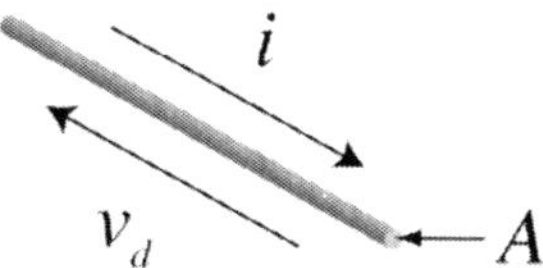

Figure 25.18: A copper wire with cross sectional area *A* carrying a current *i*.

RESEARCH:

We obtain our distance x traveled by the electrons during a time t from

$$x = v_d t$$

where v_d is the drift velocity of the electrons. The drift velocity is related to the current density via (25.10)

$$\frac{i}{A} = nev_d \tag{25.53}$$

where i is the current, A is the cross sectional area (= 0.823 mm^2, according to Table 25.2), n is the density of electrons, e is the charge of an electron, and v_d is the electron drift velocity. The density of electrons is defined as

$$n = \frac{\#\text{ conduction electrons}}{\text{volume}}.$$

We can calculate the density of electrons assuming that there is one conduction electron per copper atom. The density of copper is

$$\rho_{Cu} = 8.96\text{ g/cm}^3 = 8960\text{ kg/m}^3.$$

One mole of copper has a mass of 63.5 g and contains $6.02 \cdot 10^{23}$ atoms. We can then

Solved Problem

Solved Problem

write the density of electrons as

$$n = \frac{1 \text{ electron}}{\text{atom}} \frac{6.02 \cdot 10^{23} \text{ atom}}{63.5 \text{ g}} \frac{8.96 \text{ g}}{\text{cm}^3} \frac{10^6 \text{ cm}^3}{\text{m}^3} = 8.49 \cdot 10^{28} \frac{\text{electrons}}{\text{m}^3}.$$

SIMPLIFY:

We solve (25.53) for the magnitude of the drift velocity

$$v_d = \frac{i}{neA}.$$

and thus the distance

$$x = v_d t = \frac{i}{neA} t$$

CALCULATE:

Putting in our numerical values we get

$$\begin{aligned} x = v_d t = \frac{i}{neA} t &= \frac{0.78 \cdot 10^{-3} \text{ A}}{\left(8.49 \cdot 10^{28} \text{ m}^{-3}\right)\left(1.602 \cdot 10^{-19} \text{ C}\right)\left(0.823 \text{ mm}^2\right)}(5.3 \text{ s}) \\ &= \left(6.96826 \cdot 10^{-8} \text{ m/s}\right)\left(5.3 \text{ s}\right) \\ &= 3.69318 \cdot 10^{-7} \text{ m} \end{aligned}.$$

ROUND:

We report our result to three significant figures

$$\begin{aligned} v_d &= 7.0 \cdot 10^{-8} \text{ m/s} \\ x &= 3.7 \cdot 10^{-7} \text{ m} = 0.37 \ \mu\text{m} \end{aligned}.$$

DOUBLE-CHECK:

Our result for the magnitude of the drift velocity turns out to be a stunningly small number. In section 25.2 we stated that typical drift velocities are on the order of 10^{-4} m/s or smaller. Of course, since the current is proportional to the drift velocity, a relatively small current implies a relatively small drift velocity. 18-gauge wires can carry current of several Amperes. The current specified here is thus less than 1% of the maximum current, and then the fact that our drift velocity is less than 1% of the 10^{-4} m/s, which we stated in section 25.2 as the typical drift velocities for high currents, is reasonable.

The actual drift distance of the electrons that we calculated here is less than 1/1000th of the thickness of a fingernail. Of course this is a very small distance compared to the length of the controller connection cable. Thus this example serves as one more valuable reminder that the electromagnetic field moves with the speed of light inside the cables and causes all conduction electrons to drift basically at the same time, thus making sure that the signal from our game controller arrives almost instantaneously at the console, despite the incredibly slow pace of the individual electrons.

Chapter 26. Circuits

Figure 26.1: A circuit board.

What we will learn

- There are some circuits that cannot be reduced to a single loop circuit.
- Complex circuits can be analyzed using Kirchhoff's Rules.
- Kirchhoff's Junction Rule states that the algebraic sum of the currents at any junction must be zero.
- Kirchhoff's Loop Rule states the algebraic sum of the voltage changes around any closed loop must be zero.
- Single loop circuits can be analyzed using Kirchhoff's Loop Rule.
- Multi-loop circuits must be analyzed using both Kirchhoff's Junction Rule and Kirchhoff's Loop Rule.
- The current in circuits with a resistor and a capacitor varies exponentially with time with a characteristic time constant given by the product of the resistance and the capacitance.

In this chapter we will study circuits that are more complex than we previously encountered. These complex circuits, such as shown in Figure 26.1, can have multiple sources of emf. We will analyze circuits that cannot be broken down into effective resistances. We will also study circuits in which the current changes with time.

26.1. Kirchhoff's Rules

One can create single loop and multi-loop circuits containing sources of emf and resistors that cannot be resolved into simple circuits containing parallel or series resistors. Two examples of such circuits are shown in Figure 26.2.

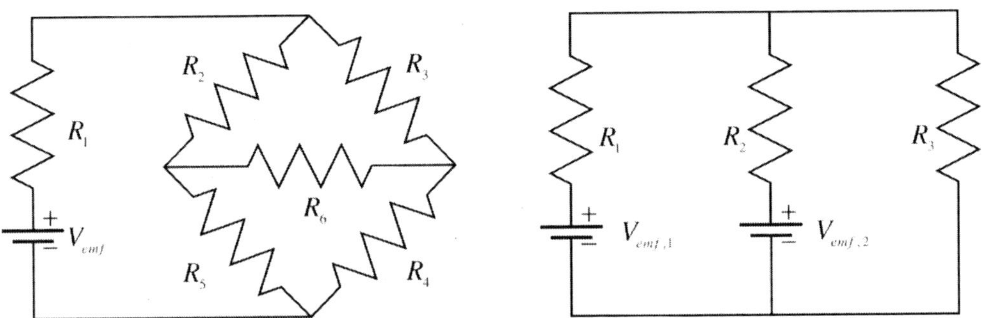

Figure 26.2: Two examples of circuits that cannot be reduced to simple combinations of parallel and series resistors.

To handle these types of circuits, we must apply Kirchhoff's Rules. Kirchhoff's Rules can be stated as

- Kirchhoff's Junction Rule:
  The sum of the currents entering a junction must equal the sum of the current leaving a junction.
- Kirchhoff's Loop Rule:
  The voltage changes around a complete circuit loop must sum to zero.

Kirchhoff's Junction Rule is a direct consequence of the conservation of charge. The amount of the charge residing in a junction remains constant at all times because junctions do not have the capability to store charge. Thus, charge conservation tells us that all charges streaming into a junction must also leave the junction, which is exactly what Kirchhoff's Junction Rule states.

Kirchhoff's Loop Rule is a direct consequence of the fact that the electric potential is single-valued. This means that the electrical potential energy of a conduction electron at a point in the circuit has one specific value. Suppose that this rule were not valid. Then we could analyze the potential changes of a conduction electron in going around a loop and find that the potential energy of the conduction electron has a different potential energy when it returns to its starting point. Thus, the potential energy of this electron at a point in the circuit would change, in obvious contradiction to energy conservation. We can see that Kirchhoff's Loop Rule is equivalent to the law of energy conservation.

26.2. Single Loop Circuits

We begin the study of more complicated circuits by analyzing circuits with several sources of emf and resistors connected in series in a single loop. We will apply Kirchhoff's Loop Rule to these circuits. However, to apply this rule we must establish conventions for determining the voltage drop across each element of the circuit depending on the assumed direction of the current and the direction of the analysis of the circuit.

For emf sources, the rules are straightforward as minus and plus signs (as well as short and long lines) indicate which side of the emf source is at the higher potential. A gravitational analogy is helpful in understanding the conventions for a resister. A ball can start from rest and roll down a steep, heavily wooded hill and reach the bottom with essentially no kinetic energy. The trip down has resulted in a decrease of its potential energy and hence a decrease of its gravitational potential. The ball cannot spontaneously roll up the hill. Likewise a current (like the ball) must flow in a resistor (whose molecules are like trees) from a higher to a lower potential.

Element	Analysis Direction	Current Direction	Voltage Change
R	$\rightarrow$	$\rightarrow$	$-iR$
R	$\leftarrow$	$\rightarrow$	$+iR$
R	$\rightarrow$	$\leftarrow$	$+iR$
R	$\leftarrow$	$\leftarrow$	$-iR$
$-$ $+$ V_{emf}	$\rightarrow$		$+V_{emf}$
$-$ $+$ V_{emf}	$\leftarrow$		$-V_{emf}$
$+$ $-$ V_{emf}	$\rightarrow$		$-V_{emf}$
$+$ $-$ V_{emf}	$\leftarrow$		$+V_{emf}$

Table 26.1: Conventions used to determine the sign of voltage changes around a single loop circuit containing several resistors and sources of emf.

Because we usually do not know the direction of the current in the circuit before we start our analysis, we often must choose the direction of the current arbitrarily. We can determine if our assumption is correct after the analysis is complete. If our assumed current turns out to be negative, then the current is flowing in a direction opposite to the direction we chose. We can also choose the direction in which we analyze the circuit arbitrarily. Any direction that we choose will give us the same information. The conventions used to analyze circuit elements in a loop are summarized in Table 26.1 assuming the magnitude of the current in the loop is i.

If we move around the circuit in the same direction as the current, the voltage changes across resistors will be negative (like the ball rolling downhill). If we move around the circuit in the opposite direction from the current, the voltage changes across the resistors will be positive (again because the ball rolled downhill). If we move around the circuit and encounter a source of emf pointing in the same direction, so that we pass through the emf source from the negative to the positive terminal, this component contributes a positive voltage. If we encounter a source of emf pointing in the opposite direction, we consider that component to contribute a negative voltage.

In Figure 26.3, we show a single loop circuit with two resistors, R_1 and R_2, and two sources of emf, $V_{emf,1}$ and $V_{emf,2}$ wired in series. Note that $V_{emf,1}$ and $V_{emf,2}$ have opposite polarity.

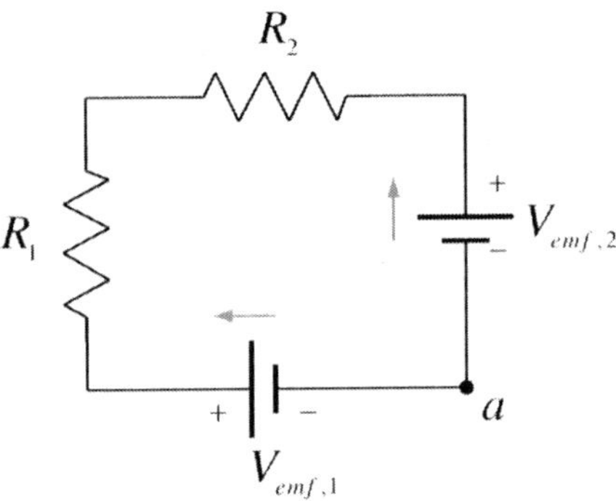

Figure 26.3: A single loop circuit containing two resistors and two sources of emf in series.

To illustrate the voltage changes across the components of this circuit, we re-draw the circuit shown in Figure 26.3 with a three dimensional view in Figure 26.4.

Although we could arbitrarily pick any one point in the circuit to have 0 V, we start at point a with $V = 0$ V and proceed around the circuit in a clockwise direction. Because the components of the circuit are in series, the current i in each component is the same and we assume that the current is in the clockwise direction. The first circuit component is a source of emf $V_{emf,1}$, which produces a positive voltage gain of $V_{emf,1}$. Next we find resistor R_1, which produces a voltage drop V_1 given by $V_1 = iR_1$. Continuing around the circuit, we find resistor R_2, which produces a voltage drop V_2 given by $V_2 = iR_2$. Next, we encounter a second source of emf, $V_{emf,2}$. This source of emf is wired into the circuit with a polarity opposite that of $V_{emf,1}$. Thus, we treat this component as a voltage drop with magnitude of $V_{emf,2}$ rather than a voltage gain. We now have completed the circuit and we are back at $V = 0$ V. We can write the analysis of the voltage changes of this circuit as

$$V_{emf,1} - V_1 - V_2 - V_{emf,2} = V_{emf,1} - iR_1 - iR_2 - V_{emf,2} = 0. \qquad (26.1)$$

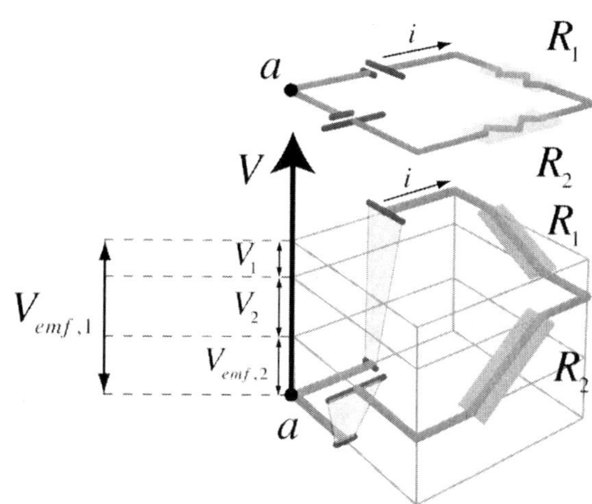

Figure 26.4: Three-dimensional drawing of a circuit containing two resistors and two sources of emf in series.

Now let's analyze the same circuit in the counter-clockwise direction starting at point a. The first circuit element is $V_{emf,2}$, which is a positive voltage gain. The next element is R_2. Because we have assumed that the current is in the clockwise direction and we are analyzing the loop in the counter-clockwise direction, this voltage change is $+iR_2$ according to the conventions listed in Table 26.1. Proceeding to the next element in the loop, R_1, we use a similar argument to designate the voltage change as $+iR_1$. The final element in the circuit is $V_{emf,1}$ which is aligned in a direction opposite to our analysis direction, so the voltage change across this element is $-V_{emf,1}$. Kirchhoff's Loop Rule then gives us

$$+V_{emf,2} + iR_2 + iR_1 - V_{emf,1} = 0. \qquad (26.2)$$

We can see that (26.1) and (26.2) give us the same information, which means that the direction we choose to analyze the circuit does not matter.

Solved Problem 26.1: Charging a battery

A 12.0 V battery with internal resistance $R_i = 0.200\ \Omega$ is being charged by an external battery charger that is capable of delivering a current of $i = 6.00$ A.

Question:
What is the minimum emf required for the battery charger to operate?

Answer:

THINK:

The battery charger, which is an external source of emf, must have enough voltage to overcome the voltage of the battery and the voltage drop across the internal resistance. We can think of the internal resistance as a resistor in a single loop circuit with two sources of emf with opposite polarities.

SKETCH:

A sketch of the circuit consisting of a battery with voltage V and internal resistance R_i connected to an external source of emf V_e is shown in Figure 26.5. The yellow shaded area represents the physical case of the battery.

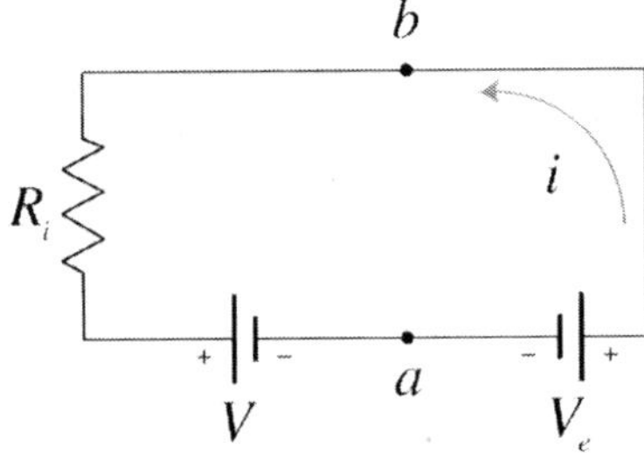

Figure 26.5: Circuit consisting of a battery with internal resistance connected to an external source of emf.

RESEARCH:

We can apply Kirchhoff's Loop Rule to this circuit. We assume a current traveling counter-clockwise around the circuit as shown in Figure 26.5. The voltage changes around the circuit must sum to zero. We can write the voltage changes starting a point b as

$$-iR_i - V + V_e = 0. \tag{26.3}$$

SIMPLIFY:

We can solve (26.3) for the required voltage of the charger

$$V_e = iR_i + V \tag{26.4}$$

where i is the current that the charger supplies.

CALCULATE:

Putting in our numerical values gives us

$$V_e = iR_i + V = (6.00\text{ A})(0.200\ \Omega) + 12.0\text{ V} = 13.20\text{ V}.$$

Solved Problem

Solved Problem

ROUND:

We report our result to three significant figures

$$V_e = 13.2 \text{ V}.$$

DOUBLE-CHECK:

Our result that the battery charge has a higher voltage than the voltage of the battery without load is reasonable. A typical charger for a 12 V battery has a voltage of around 14 V.

26.3. Multi-Loop Circuits

To analyze multi-loop circuits, we must apply both the Loop Rule and the Junction Rule. The procedure to analyze multi-loop circuits consists of identifying complete loops and junction points in the circuit and applying Kirchhoff's Rules to these parts of the circuit separately. At each junction in a multi-loop circuit, the current flowing in to the junction must equal the current flowing out of the junction. As an example, a single junction is shown in Figure 26.6.

In this figure we define a current, i_1, entering the junction a and two currents, i_2 and i_3, leaving the junction a. Kirchhoff's Junction Rule tells us that

$$i_1 = i_2 + i_3. \tag{26.5}$$

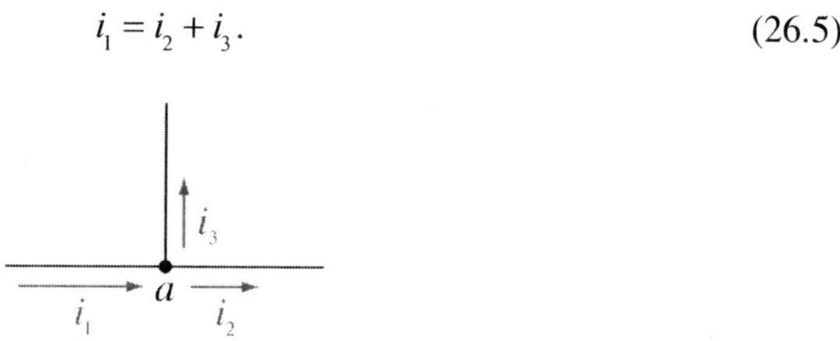

Figure 26.6: A single junction from a multi-loop circuit.

By analyzing the single loops in the multi-loop circuit with Kirchhoff's Loop Rule and the junctions with Kirchhoff's Junction Rule, one can obtain a system of coupled equations in several unknown variables. These equations can be solved for quantities of interest in various ways including direct substitution. An example of the analysis of a multi-loop circuit is given in Example 26.1.

Example 26.1: Multi-loop circuit

Consider the circuit shown in Figure 26.7. This circuit has three resistors, R_1, R_2, and R_3 and two sources of emf, $V_{emf,1}$ and $V_{emf,2}$. This circuit cannot be resolved into simple series or parallel structures.

Example

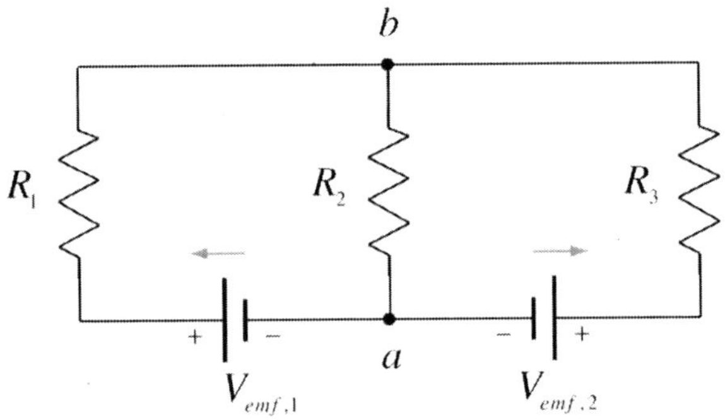

Figure 26.7: Multi-loop circuit with three resistors and two sources of emf.

To analyze this circuit, we need to assign currents flowing through the resistors. We can choose these currents arbitrarily, knowing that if we choose the wrong direction, the resulting current will be negative, indicating that we initially chose the wrong direction.

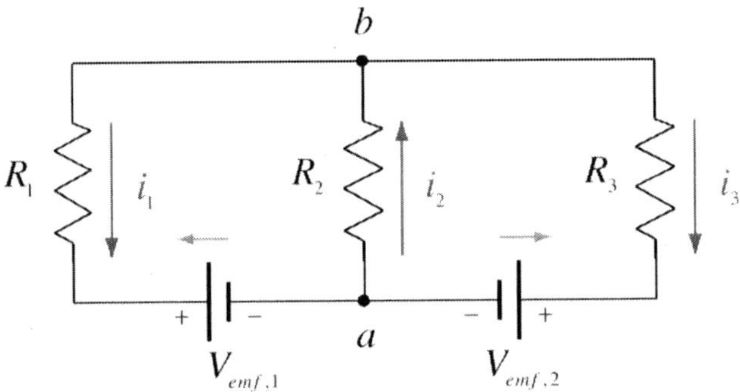

Figure 26.8: Multi-loop circuit with the assumed direction of the current through the resistors indicated.

Consider junction b first. The incoming current must equal the outgoing current so we can write

$$i_2 = i_1 + i_3. \tag{26.6}$$

Looking at junction a and again equate the incoming current and the outgoing current we get

$$i_1 + i_3 = i_2 \tag{26.7}$$

which provides the same information as (26.6) that we obtained by analyzing junction b.

At this point we cannot determine the currents in the circuit because we have three unknown values and only one equation. Therefore, we need two more independent equations to determine the three currents. To get these equations we can apply Kirchhoff's Loop Rule. We can identify three loops in the circuit shown in Figure 26.8,
(1) the left half of the circuit including the circuit elements R_1, R_2, and $V_{emf,1}$,
(2) the right half of the circuit including the circuit elements R_2, R_3, and $V_{emf,2}$,
(3) the outer loop including the elements R_1, R_3, $V_{emf,1}$, and $V_{emf,2}$.
Applying the Loop Rule to the left half of the circuit using the assumed directions for the

currents and analyzing the loop in a counterclockwise direction starting at junction b we obtain

$$-i_1R_1 - V_{emf,1} - i_2R_2 = 0 \Rightarrow$$
$$i_1R_1 + V_{emf,1} + i_2R_2 = 0. \tag{26.8}$$

Applying the Loop Rule to the right half of the circuit again starting at junction b and analyzing the loop in a clockwise direction we get

$$-i_3R_3 - V_{emf,2} - i_2R_2 = 0 \Rightarrow$$
$$i_3R_3 + V_{emf,2} + i_2R_2 = 0. \tag{26.9}$$

Applying the Loop Rule to the outer loop staring a junction b and working in a clockwise direction gives us

$$-i_3R_3 - V_{emf,2} + V_{emf,1} + i_1R_1 = 0. \tag{26.10}$$

This equation provides no new information because we can obtain it by subtracting equation (26.9) from (26.8). For all three loops, we obtain equivalent information if we analyze the circuits in either a counterclockwise direction or a clockwise direction, or if we start at any other point and move around the loops from there.

Having three equations (26.6), (26.8), and (26.9), and three unknowns i_1, i_2, and i_3, we can solve for the currents in several ways. For example, an intrepid student may wish to present the three equations in a matrix format and then solve using Kramer's Method on a calculator. We will proceed by inserting the first equation into the other two, thus eliminating i_2. We then solve one of the two resulting equations for i_1 and insert it into the other. This way we obtain an expression for i_3. Substituting back, we finally find solutions for i_2 and i_1. The solution is

$$i_1 = -\frac{(R_2 + R_3)V_{emf,1} - R_2V_{emf,2}}{R_1R_2 + R_1R_3 + R_2R_3}$$
$$i_2 = -\frac{R_3V_{emf,1} + R_1V_{emf,2}}{R_1R_2 + R_1R_3 + R_2R_3}.$$
$$i_3 = -\frac{-R_2V_{emf,1} + (R_1 + R_2)V_{emf,2}}{R_1R_2 + R_1R_3 + R_2R_3}$$

Note: You do not need to remember the particular solution to this problem, nor the linear algebra needed to get there. However, the general method of approaching all kinds of circuits with the help of Kirchhoff's rules for loops and junctions, as well as the method of assigning currents in arbitrary directions, is illustrated by this exercise.

Example

Solved Problem

Solved Problem 26.2: The Wheatstone bridge

The Wheatstone bridge is used to measure unknown resistances. The circuit diagram of a Wheatstone bridge is shown in Figure 26.9.

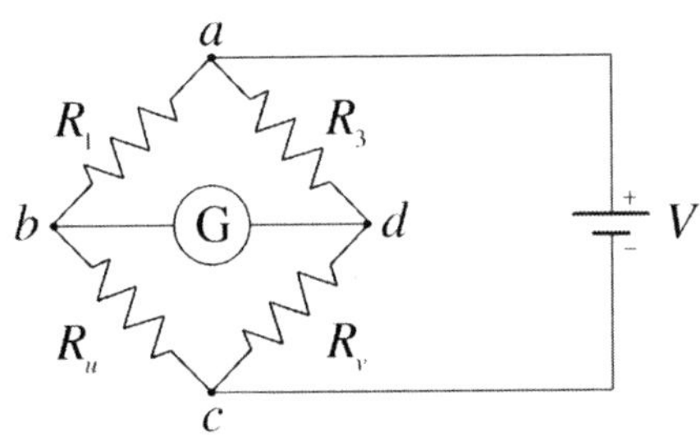

Figure 26.9: Circuit diagram of a Wheatstone bridge.

The Wheatstone bridge consists of three known resistances, R_1, R_3 and a variable resistor R_v, as well as the unknown resistance R_u to be determined. A source of emf V is connected across the points a and c. A sensitive galvanometer is connected between points b and d. The Wheatstone bridge is used to determine R_u by varying resistance R_v until the galvanometer between point b and point d shows no current flowing.

Question:

We use the Wheatstone bridge shown in Figure 26.9 to determine an unknown resistance. The resistances are $R_1 = 100.0\ \Omega$, $R_3 = 110.0\ \Omega$, and $R_v = 15.63\ \Omega$. What is the value of the unknown resistance, R_u?

Answer:

THINK:

We can use Kirchhoff's rules to analyze this circuit. We choose two loops to analyze, adb and cbd. We choose two junctions to analyze, a and c.

SKETCH:

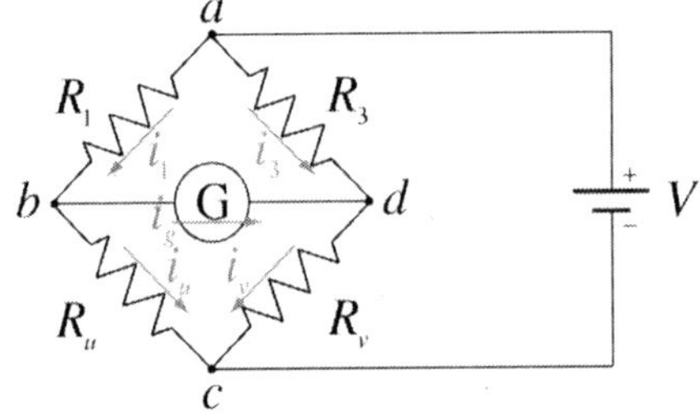

Figure 26.10: Wheatstone bridge with assumed current directions indicated.

A sketch of the Wheatstone bridge with the assumed currents i_1, i_3, i_u, i_v, and i_g, is shown in Figure 26.10.

RESEARCH:

We first apply Kirchhoff's loop rule for loop *adb* clockwise starting at point *a* to obtain

$$-i_3R_3 + i_gR_g + i_1R_1 = 0. \tag{26.11}$$

We apply Kirchhoff's loop rule again for loop *cbd* clockwise starting at point *c* to get

$$+i_uR_u - i_gR_g - i_vR_v = 0. \tag{26.12}$$

Now we can use Kirchhoff's junction rule to junction *b* to obtain

$$i_1 = i_g + i_u. \tag{26.13}$$

Another application of Kirchhoff's junction rule, now to junction *d*, leads to

$$i_3 + i_g = i_v. \tag{26.14}$$

SIMPLIFY:

When the bridge is balanced, the current through the galvanometer is zero ($i_g = 0$), and we can write (26.11) as

$$i_1R_1 = i_3R_3 \tag{26.15}$$

and (26.12) as

$$i_uR_u = i_vR_v. \tag{26.16}$$

We can write (26.13) as

$$i_1 = i_u \tag{26.17}$$

and (26.14) as

$$i_3 = i_v. \tag{26.18}$$

Dividing (26.16) by (26.15) gives us

$$\frac{i_uR_u}{i_1R_1} = \frac{i_vR_v}{i_3R_3} \tag{26.19}$$

which we can rewrite using (26.17) and (26.18) as

$$R_u = \frac{R_1}{R_3}R_v. \tag{26.20}$$

Solved Problem

Solved Problem

CALCULATE:
Putting in our numerical values, we get

$$R_u = \frac{R_1}{R_3} R_v = \frac{100.0\ \Omega}{110.0\ \Omega} 15.63\ \Omega = 14.20901\ \Omega .$$

ROUND:
We report our results to four significant figures

$$R_u = 14.21\ \Omega .$$

DOUBLE-CHECK:
Our result for the unknown resistor is similar to the value of the variable resistor. Thus, our answer seems reasonable.

Self-Test Opportunity: Show that the equivalent resistance of the Wheatstone bridge shown in Figure 26.9 when the current through the galvanometer is zero is given by

$$R_{eq} = \frac{(R_1 + R_u)(R_3 + R_v)}{R_1 + R_u + R_3 + R_v} .$$

In-class exercise: In the multi-loop circuit shown, $V_1 = 6.00\ \text{V}$, $V_2 = 12.0\ \text{V}$, $R_1 = 10.0\ \Omega$, and $R_2 = 12.0\ \text{V}$. What is the current i_2?

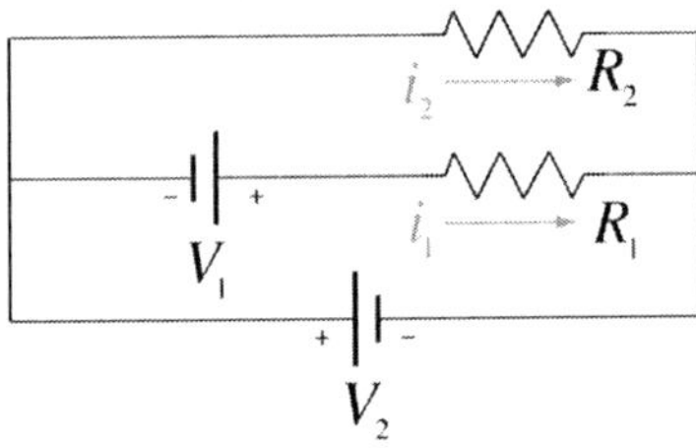

a) 0.500 A
b) 0.750 A
c) 1.00 A
d) 1.25 A
e) 1.50 A

26.4. Ammeters and Voltmeters

A device used to measure current is called an ammeter. A device used to measure voltage is called a voltmeter. To measure the current, the ammeter must be placed in the circuit in series. This placement requires that the circuit be broken and that the ammeter be wired into the circuit. In Figure 26.11, an ammeter is connected in the circuit so that it can measure the current i. To measure the voltage, the voltmeter must be wired in parallel with the component across which the voltage is to be measured. In Figure 26.11, a voltmeter is connected so that it can measure the voltage drop across resistor R_1.

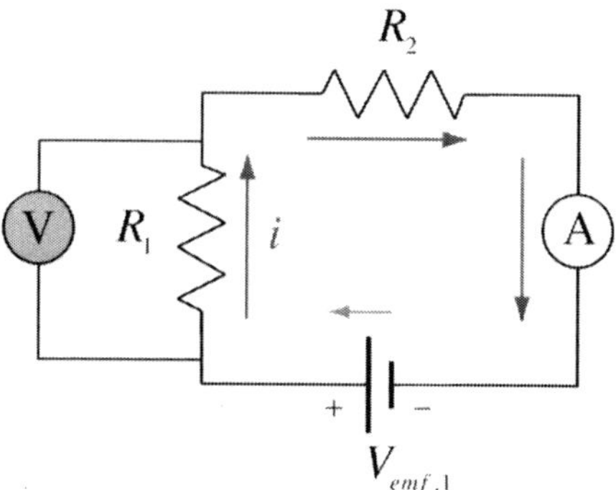

Figure 26.11: Circuit diagram showing the placement of an ammeter and a voltmeter.

Instruments to analyze circuits must be able to make measurements while disturbing the circuit as little as possible. Thus, ammeters are designed to have as low a resistance as possible, usually on the order of 1 Ω, so they do not have an appreciable effect on the current they are intending to measure. Voltmeters are designed to have as high a resistance as possible, usually on the order of 10 MΩ (10^7 Ω), so that they have a negligible effect on the voltage that they will be measuring.

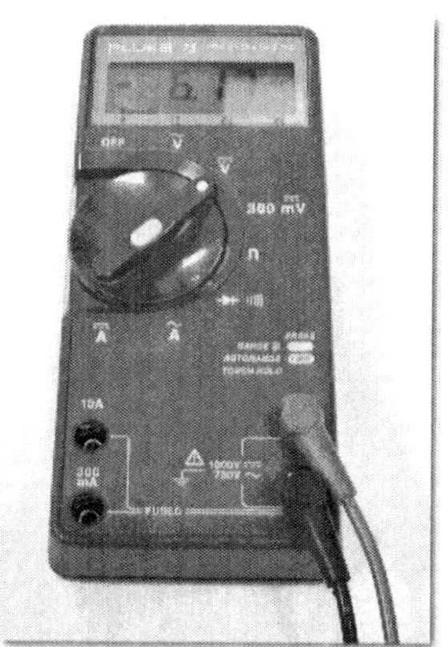

Figure 26.12: A typical digital multimeter.

In practice, these measurements are made with a digital multimeter that is switchable between performing the duties of an ammeter or a voltmeter. It can display the results with an autoranging numerical digital display, which includes the sign of the voltage or the current. Most digital multimeters also include the function of measuring the resistance of a component. This function is called an ohmmeter. The digital multimeter performs this task by applying a known voltage and measuring the resulting current and is very useful for determining circuit continuity and the status of fuses, as well as measuring the resistance of resistors. A typical digital multimeter is shown in Figure 26.12.

Example

Example 26.2: Voltmeter in a simple circuit

Consider a simple circuit consisting of a source of emf with voltage $V = 150.\text{ V}$ and a resistor with resistance $R = 100.\text{ k}\Omega$ as illustrated in Figure 26.13. A voltmeter with resistance $R_V = 10.0\text{ M}\Omega$ is connected across the resistor.

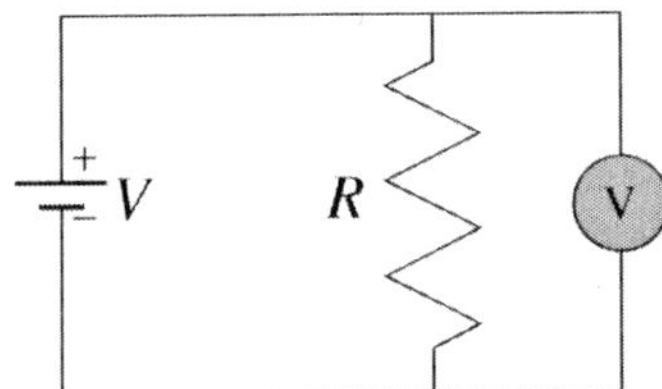

Figure 26.13: A simple circuit with a voltmeter connected in parallel.

Question:
What is the current in the circuit before the voltmeter is connected?

Answer:
Ohm's Law tells us that $V = iR$ so we can find the current in the circuit as

$$i = \frac{V}{R} = \frac{150.\text{ V}}{100.\cdot 10^3\ \Omega} = 1.50\cdot 10^{-3}\text{ A} = 1.50\text{ mA}.$$

Question:
What is the current in the circuit when the voltmeter is connected across the resistor?
Answer:
The equivalent resistance of the resistor and the voltmeter is given by the value of two resistors connected in parallel

$$\frac{1}{R_{eq}} = \frac{1}{R} + \frac{1}{R_V}.$$

Solving for the equivalent resistance and putting in our values we get

$$R_{eq} = \frac{RR_V}{R + R_V} = \frac{\left(100.\cdot 10^3\ \Omega\right)\left(10.0\cdot 10^6\ \Omega\right)}{100.\cdot 10^3\ \Omega + 10.0\cdot 10^6\ \Omega} = 9.90\cdot 10^4\ \Omega = 99.0\text{ k}\Omega.$$

The current is then

$$i = \frac{V}{R_{eq}} = \frac{150.\text{ V}}{9.90\cdot 10^4\ \Omega} = 1.52\cdot 10^{-3}\text{ A} = 1.52\text{ mA}.$$

The current in the circuit goes up by 0.02 mA when the voltmeter is connected because the combination of the resistor and the voltmeter in parallel has a lower resistance than the resistor alone. However, the effect is small, even in this case where the resistor is relatively large ($R = 100.\text{ k}\Omega$).

Self-Test Opportunity: Explain why when the starter of a car is engaged while the headlights are on, the headlights dim.

In-class exercise: Two resistors, $R_1 = 3.00\ \Omega$ and $R_2 = 5.00\ \Omega$, are connected in series with a battery with $V_{emf} = 8.00$ V and an ammeter with $R_A = 1.00\ \Omega$ as shown. What is the current measured by the ammeter?

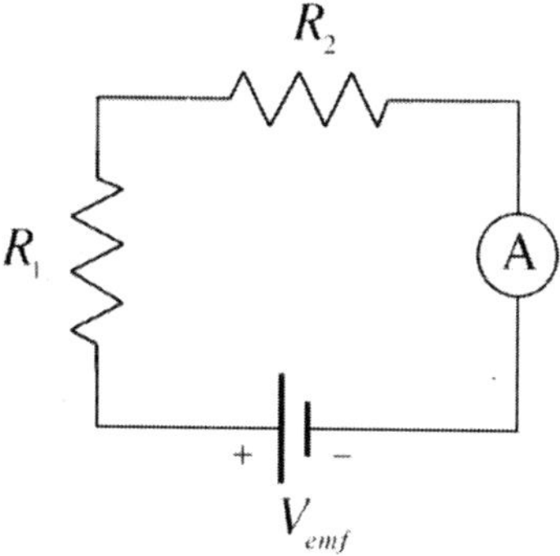

a) 0.500 A
b) 0.750 A
c) 0.889 A
d) 1.00 A
e) 1.50 A

26.5. RC Circuits

So far in this chapter, we have dealt with circuits containing sources of emf and resistors. The currents in these circuits did not vary in time. In this section, we will study circuits that contain capacitors (see chapter 24) as well as sources of emf and resistors. We will find that these circuits have currents that vary with time.

Consider a circuit with a source of emf, V_{emf}, a resistor R, and a capacitor C as shown in Figure 26.14. We start with the switch open and the capacitor initially uncharged, as shown in part (a). We then close the switch (b), and current begins to flow in the circuit, charging the capacitor. The current is provided by the source of emf, which maintains a constant voltage. When the capacitor is fully charged, no more current flows in the circuit. When the capacitor is fully charged, the voltage across the plates will be equal to the voltage provided by the source of emf and the total charge q_{tot} on the capacitor will be $q_{tot} = CV_{emf}$.

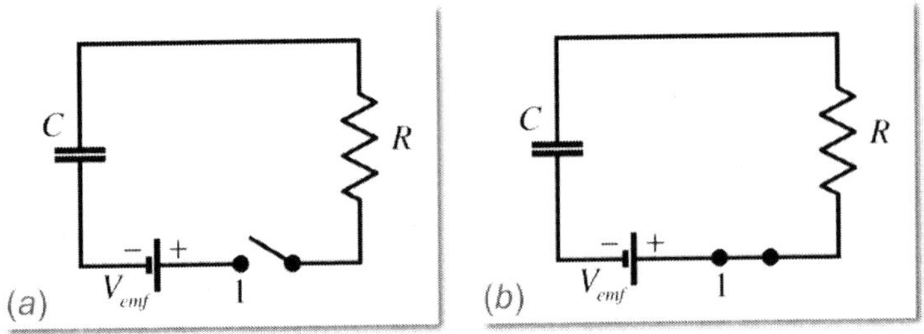

Figure 26.14: The most basic RC circuit containing a source of emf, a resistor, and a capacitor. (a): switch open; (b): switch closed

While the capacitor is charging, we can analyze the current i flowing in the circuit (assumed to flow from the negative to the positive terminal inside the voltage source) using the Loop Rule, taking a loop in the counterclockwise direction in Figure 26.14b):

$$V_{emf} - V_R - V_C = V_{emf} - iR - \frac{q}{C} = 0 \tag{26.21}$$

where V_C is the voltage drop across the capacitor and q is the charge on the capacitor at a given time t. Remembering that the current is defined to be $i = dq/dt$, we can re-write (26.21) as

$$R\frac{dq}{dt} + \frac{q}{C} = V_{emf}$$
$$\frac{dq}{dt} + \frac{q}{RC} = \frac{V_{emf}}{R}. \tag{26.22}$$

This differential equation relates the charge to its time derivative. In the chapter on oscillations, we have already encountered differential equations. In the case of (26.22) we are motivated to try an exponential form for the solution because an exponential is the only function that has the property that when you differentiate the function you get the same function back. Because there is a constant term in (26.22), we need to add a constant term to the trial solution. We therefore try a solution of a constant and an exponential, where we only consider solutions that have $q(0) = 0$:

$$q(t) = q_0\left(1 - e^{-t/\tau}\right) \tag{26.23}$$

with the constants q_0 and τ to be determined. Inserting this trial function back into our differential equation, we obtain:

$$q_0 \frac{1}{\tau} e^{-t/\tau} + \frac{1}{RC} q_0 \left(1 - e^{-t/\tau}\right) = \frac{V_{emf}}{R} \Rightarrow$$

$$q_0 e^{-t/\tau}\left(\frac{1}{\tau}-\frac{1}{RC}\right)=\frac{V_{emf}}{R}-\frac{1}{RC}q_0 . \tag{26.24}$$

In the second line of this equation, we have collected the time dependent terms on the left-hand side and the time-independent terms on the right hand side. This equation can only be true for all times if both sides are zero. From the left-hand side we then find:

$$\tau = RC . \tag{26.25}$$

Thus, the time constant τ is simply the product of the capacitance and the resistance. From the right-hand side we find an expression for the constant q_0:

$$q_0 = CV_{emf} . \tag{26.26}$$

This result means that our differential equation for charging the capacitor has the solution

$$q = CV_{emf}\left(1-e^{-t/RC}\right). \tag{26.27}$$

Note that at $t=0$, $q=0$, which is the condition we started with before the circuit components were connected. At $t=\infty$, $q=q_0=CV_{emf}$, which is the steady state condition in which the capacitor is fully charged. This time dependence is shown on the left side of Figure 26.15 for three different values of the RC time constant τ.

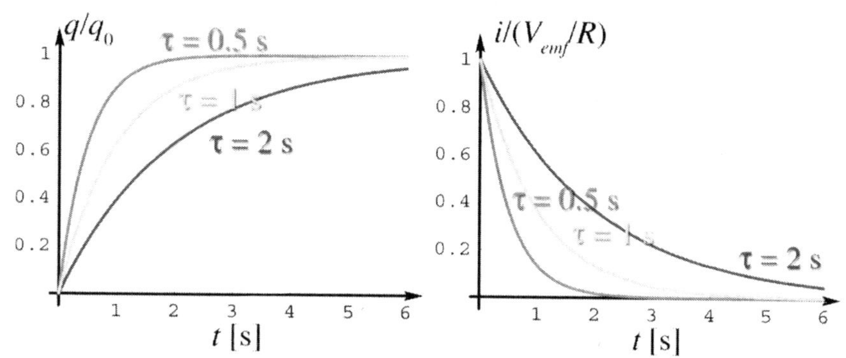

Figure 26.15: Charging a capacitor. Left side: charge on the capacitor as a function of time; right side: current flowing through the resistor as a function of time.

The current flowing in the circuit is given by differentiating (26.27) with respect to time

$$i=\frac{dq}{dt}=\left(\frac{V_{emf}}{R}\right)e^{-t/RC} . \tag{26.28}$$

We can see that at $t = 0$ the current in the circuit is V_{emf}/R, while at $t = \infty$ the current is zero, as indicated in the right side of Figure 26.15.

Now let's take a resistor R and a fully charged capacitor C and connect them together as shown in Figure 26.16 by moving the switch from position 1 to position 2. The charge on the capacitor before it is connected is q_0.

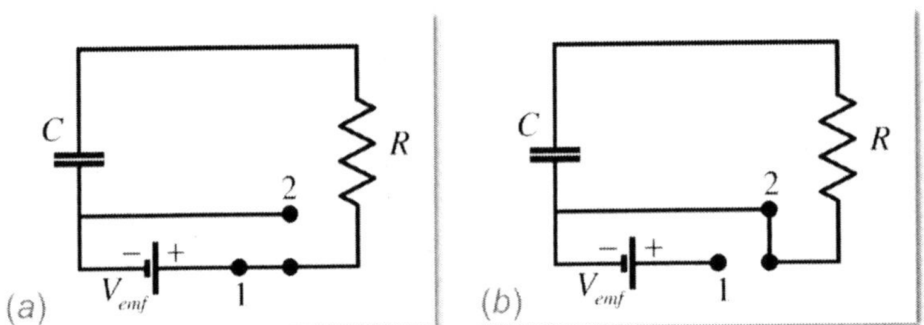

Figure 26.16: RC circuit containing an emf source, a resistor, a capacitor, and a switch.

In this case, current will flow in the circuit until the capacitor is completely discharged. While the capacitor is discharging, we can apply the Loop Rule around the circuit and obtain

$$-iR - V_C = -iR - \frac{q}{C} = 0 \tag{26.29}$$

which we can re-write using the definition of current to get

$$R\frac{dq}{dt} + \frac{q}{C} = 0\,. \tag{26.30}$$

The solution to this differential equation is obtained using the same method shown previously, except that (26.30) has no constant term and now $q(0) > 0$. Thus, we try a solution of the form $q(t) = q_0 e^{-t/\tau}$ and find:

$$q = q_0 e^{-t/RC}\,. \tag{26.31}$$

We can see that at $t = 0$, the charge on the capacitor is q_0. At $t = \infty$, the charge on the capacitor is zero.

We can obtain the current by differentiating (26.31) as a function of time

$$i = \frac{dq}{dt} = \left(\frac{q_0}{RC}\right)e^{-t/RC}\,. \tag{26.32}$$

We can see that at $t = 0$ the current in the circuit is q_{tot}/RC. At $t = \infty$, the current in the circuit is zero.

We could plot the time dependence of charge on the capacitor and current flowing through the resistor for the discharging process, just as we have done in Figure 26.15. However, for the discharging process, both charge and current decrease exponentially, and so we find the same time dependence in both cases as was plotted in the right panel of Figure 26.15.

The equations describing the time dependence of the charging and discharging of capacitors all involve the exponential factor $e^{-t/RC}$. Again, the product of the resistance times the capacitance is defined as the time constant $\tau = RC$ of a RC circuit. From (26.27) we can see that after an amount of time equal to one time constant, the capacitor has charged to 63% of its maximum value. Thus, we can characterize an RC circuit by specifying the time constant of the circuit.

Example

Example 26.3: Time to charge a capacitor

Consider a circuit consisting of a 12.0 V battery, a 50.0 Ω resistor, and a 100.0 μF capacitor wired in series. The capacitor is initially completely discharged.

Question:

How long will it take to charge the capacitor in this circuit to 90% of its maximum charge once the circuit is closed?

Answer:

The charge on the capacitor as a function of time is given by

$$q(t) = q_0\left(1 - e^{-t/RC}\right)$$

where q_0 is the maximum charge of the capacitor. We need to know the time when $q(t)/q_0 = 0.90$, which can be obtained from

$$\left(1 - e^{-t/RC}\right) = \frac{q(t)}{q_0} = 0.90$$

or

$$0.10 = e^{-t/RC}.$$

Rearranging this equation we get

$$\ln(0.10) = -\frac{t}{RC}$$

or

$$t = -RC\ln(0.10) = -(50.0\ \Omega)\left(100\cdot 10^{-6}\ \text{F}\right)(-2.30) = 0.0115\ \text{s} = 11.5\ \text{ms}.$$

lf-Test Opportunity: We have a 1.00 mF capacitor that is fully charged. We connect a 100.0 Ω resistor across the capacitor. How long will it take to remove 99.0% of the charge stored in the capacitor?

In-class exercise: An uncharged capacitor with $C = 14.9\ \mu\text{F}$, a resistor with $R = 24.3\ \text{k}\Omega$, and a battery with $V = 25.7\ \text{V}$ are connected in series as shown. What is the charge on the capacitor at $t = 0.3621\ \text{s}$ after the switch is closed?

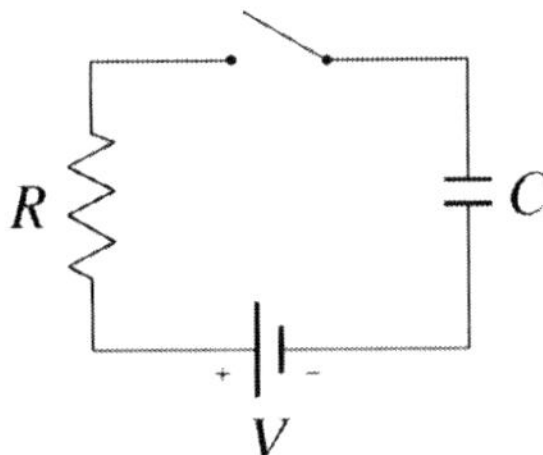

a) $5.48 \cdot 10^{-5}$ C
b) $7.94 \cdot 10^{-5}$ C
c) $1.15 \cdot 10^{-5}$ C
d) $1.66 \cdot 10^{-4}$ C
e) $2.42 \cdot 10^{-4}$ C

What we have learned/Exam Study Guide

Most Important Points

- Kirchhoff's Rules describing complex circuits can be stated as
  - Kirchhoff's Junction Rule:
    The sum of the currents entering a junction must equal the sum of the current leaving a junction.
  - Kirchhoff's Loop Rule:
    The sum of the voltage changes around a complete circuit loop must equal zero.
- When using Kirchhoff's Loop Rule, the sign of the voltage change for each circuit element is determined by the direction of the current and the analysis direction. These conventions can be summarized as follows.
  - Sources of emf in the same direction as the analysis direction are voltage gains while sources opposite to the analysis direction are voltage drops.
  - For resistors the magnitude of the voltage change is $|iR|$ where i is the assumed current and R is the resistance. To get the sign, we must know (or assume) the direction of the current as well as the analysis direction. If the current and analysis direction are the same, the resistor has a voltage

drop. If the current and analysis direction are in opposite directions, the resistor has a voltage gain.

- An RC circuit contains a resistor with resistance R and a capacitor with capacitance C. The time constant, τ, is given by $\tau = RC$.
- In an RC circuit, the charge, q, as a function of time for a charging capacitor with capacitance C is given by $q = CV_{emf}\left(1-e^{-t/RC}\right)$ where V_{emf} is the voltage supplied by the source of emf and R is the resistance of the resistor.
- In an RC circuit, the charge, q, as a function of time for a discharging capacitor with capacitance C is given by $q = q_{tot}e^{-t/RC}$ where q_{tot} is the charge on the capacitor at $t = 0$ and R is the resistance of the resistor.

New Symbols used in this Chapter

- $\tau = RC$ is the time constant of RC circuits.

Additional Solved Problems

Solved Problem

Solved Problem 26.3: Two batteries in parallel across a resistor

Two batteries are connected in parallel across a resistor with $R = 10.0\ \Omega$ as shown in Figure 26.17.

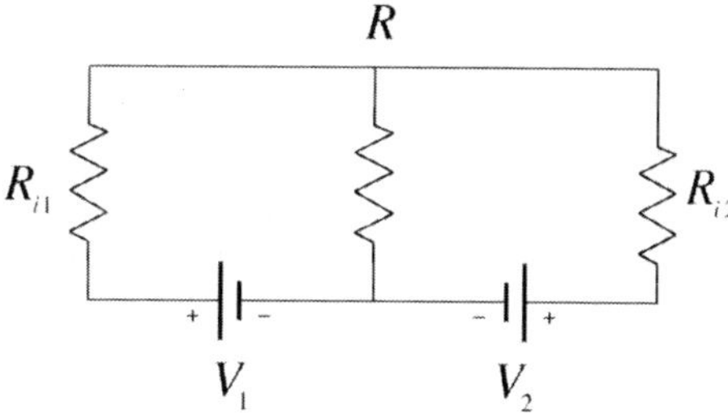

Figure 26.17: Two batteries connected in parallel across a resistor.

The first battery has a voltage $V_1 = 12.0$ V and an internal resistance of $R_{i1} = 1.00\ \Omega$. The second battery has a voltage $V_2 = 6.00$ V and an internal resistance of $R_{i2} = 0.500\ \Omega$.

Question:
What is the current through the external resistor R?

THINK:

We can apply Kirchhoff's Rules to this circuit. We can apply the loop rule to the left loop and right loop. We can apply the junction rule to relate the currents in the two loops.

Solved Problem

SKETCH:

A sketch of the circuit with assumed currents and directions of analysis is shown in Figure 26.18.

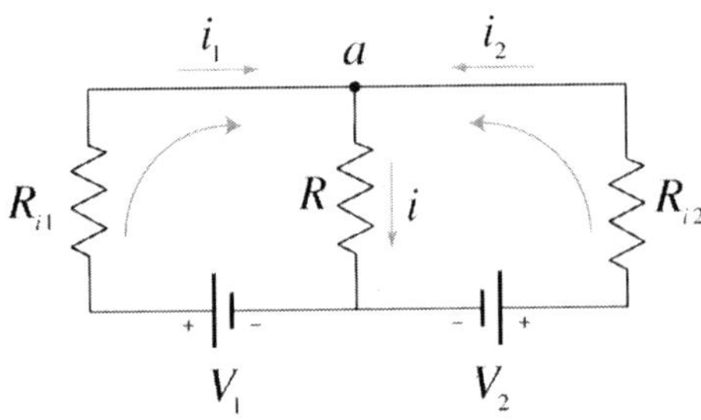

Figure 26.18: Two batteries connected in parallel across a resistor with assumed currents and directions of analysis.

We assume that a current i_1 is flowing in the direction shown in the left loop. We assume that a current i_2 is flowing in the right loop in the direction shown. We assume that a current i is flowing through the external resistor. There is a current junction at point a.

RESEARCH:

We can apply Kirchhoff's Loop rule to the left loop in Figure 26.18 using the analysis direction shown

$$V_1 - i_1 R_{i1} - i_1 R = 0. \tag{26.33}$$

We can apply Kirchhoff's Loop rule to the right loop in Figure 26.18 using the analysis direction shown

$$V_2 - i_2 R_{i2} - i_2 R = 0. \tag{26.34}$$

We can apply Kirchhoff's Junction rule to point a

$$i = i_1 + i_2. \tag{26.35}$$

SIMPLIFY:

We can solve (26.35) for i_1 and substitute that result into (26.33) to get

$$V_1 - \left(i - i_2\right) R_{i1} - \left(i - i_2\right) R = 0. \tag{26.36}$$

We can rearrange (26.36) to give

$$V_1 = iR_{i1} - i_2 R_{i1} + iR - i_2 R. \tag{26.37}$$

We can then isolate i_2 in (26.37) to give

Solved Problem

$$i_2\left(R_{i1}+R\right)=iR_{i1}+iR-V_1. \qquad (26.38)$$

We can then solve (26.34) for i_2 and substitute that result into (26.38) to get

$$\left(\frac{V_2}{R_{i2}+R}\right)\left(R_{i1}+R\right)=iR_{i1}+iR-V_1. \qquad (26.39)$$

Solving (26.39) for i gives us

$$i=\frac{\left(\frac{V_2}{R_{i2}+R}\right)\left(R_{i1}+R\right)+V_1}{R_{i1}+R}=\frac{V_1}{R_{i1}+R}+\frac{V_2}{R_{i2}+R}. \qquad (26.40)$$

CALCULATE:

Putting in our numerical values gives us

$$i=\frac{V_1}{R_{i1}+R}+\frac{V_2}{R_{i2}+R}=\frac{12.0\text{ V}}{1.00\ \Omega+10.0\ \Omega}+\frac{6.00\text{ V}}{0.500\ \Omega+10.0\ \Omega}.$$

$$i=1.66234\text{ A}$$

ROUND:

We report our results to three significant figures

$$i=1.66\text{ A}.$$

DOUBLE-CHECK:

To double-check our result, we look at our result shown in (26.40). We can see that the current flowing through the external resistor is the sum of the currents that would be drawn from each battery if each battery were connected across the external resistor without the other battery being present. Thus, we can increase the current flowing though a load resistor by connecting batteries in parallel across the load.

Solved Problem 26.4: Rate of energy storage in a capacitor

A resistor with $R=2.50\text{ M}\Omega$ and a capacitor with $C=1.25\ \mu\text{F}$ are connected in series with an ideal battery with voltage $V=12.0\text{ V}$. At $t=2.50\text{ s}$ after the circuit is connected, what is the rate at which energy is being stored in the capacitor?

THINK:

Solved Problem

When the circuit components are connected, the capacitor begins to charge. The rate at which energy is stored in the capacitor is given by the time derivative of the energy stored on the capacitor, which is a function of the charge on the capacitor.

SKETCH:

A sketch of the series circuit containing a battery, a resistor, and a capacitor is shown in Figure 26.19.

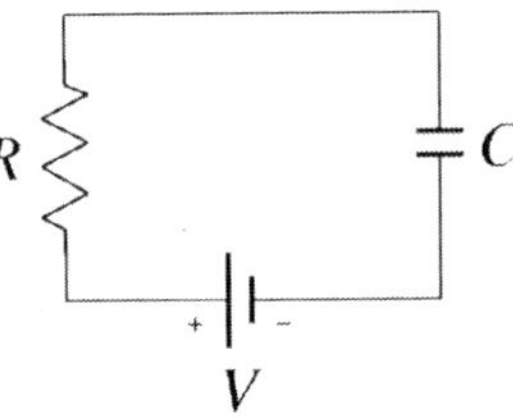

Figure 26.19: Series circuit containing a battery, a capacitor, and a resistor.

RESEARCH:

The charge on the capacitor as a function of time is given by (26.27)

$$q = CV\left(1 - e^{-t/RC}\right). \tag{26.41}$$

The energy stored in a capacitor with charge q is given by (see chapter 24)

$$U = \frac{1}{2}\frac{q^2}{C}. \tag{26.42}$$

The time derivative of the energy stored in the capacitor is then

$$\frac{dU}{dt} = \frac{d}{dt}\left(\frac{1}{2}\frac{q^2}{C}\right) = \frac{q}{C}\frac{dq}{dt}. \tag{26.43}$$

We recognize that the time derivative of the charge is the current i. We can then replace the time derivative of the charge in (26.43) with the expression for the charge as a function of time given in (26.28)

$$i = \frac{dq}{dt} = \left(\frac{V}{R}\right)e^{-t/RC}. \tag{26.44}$$

SIMPLIFY:

We can write the rate of change of the energy in the capacitor by combining (26.41), (26.43), and (26.44)

$$\frac{dU}{dt} = \frac{q}{C}i = \frac{CV\left(1 - e^{-t/RC}\right)}{C}\left(\frac{V}{R}\right)e^{-t/RC} = \frac{V^2}{R}e^{-t/RC}\left(1 - e^{-t/RC}\right). \tag{26.45}$$

Solved Problem

CALCULATE:

We first calculate the value of RC

$$RC = \left(2.50 \cdot 10^6\ \Omega\right)\left(1.25 \cdot 10^{-6}\ \text{F}\right) = 3.125\ \text{s}.$$

We can then calculate the rate of change of the energy of the capacitor

$$\frac{dU}{dt} = \frac{\left(12.0\ \text{V}\right)^2}{2.50 \cdot 10^6\ \Omega} e^{\left(-\frac{2.50\ \text{s}}{3.125\ \text{s}}\right)}\left(1 - e^{-\frac{2.50\ \text{s}}{3.125\ \text{s}}}\right) = 1.42521 \cdot 10^{-5}\ \text{W}$$

ROUND:

We report our result to three significant figures

$$\frac{dU}{dt} = 1.43 \cdot 10^{-5}\ \text{W}. \qquad (26.46)$$

DOUBLE-CHECK:

The current at $t = 2.50\ \text{s}$ is

$$i = \frac{dq}{dt} = \left(\frac{V}{R}\right)e^{-t/RC} = \left(\frac{12.0\ \text{V}}{2.50\ \text{M}\Omega}\right)e^{-\frac{2.50\ \text{s}}{3.125\ \text{s}}} = 2.16 \cdot 10^{-6}\ \text{A}. \qquad (26.47)$$

The rate of energy dissipation in the resistor is

$$P = \frac{dU}{dt} = i^2 R = \left(2.16 \cdot 10^{-6}\ \text{A}\right)^2\left(2.50 \cdot 10^6\ \Omega\right) = 1.16 \cdot 10^{-5}\ \text{W}. \qquad (26.48)$$

The rate at which the battery delivers energy to the circuit is given by

$$P = \frac{dU}{dt} = iV = \left(2.16 \cdot 10^{-6}\ \text{A}\right)\left(12.0\ \text{V}\right) = 2.59 \cdot 10^{-5}\ \text{W}. \qquad (26.49)$$

Energy conservation dictates that the energy supplied by the battery is either dissipated as heat in the resistor or stored in the capacitor. We can see that the power supplied by the battery given in (26.49) is equal to the power dissipated as heat in the resistor (26.48) plus the rate at which energy is stored in the capacitor (26.46). Thus, our answer seems reasonable.

Chapter 27. Magnetism

Figure 27.1: The solenoidal magnet of the STAR Detector at the Relativistic Heavy Ion Collider at Brookhaven National Laboratory.

What we will learn

One can find certain types of naturally occurring minerals that attract and repel each other and attract certain kinds of metal such as iron. These minerals, if floated freely, also line up with the north pole of the Earth. These rocks are various forms of iron oxide and are called magnets. These magnets can be used to create new magnets by touching the mineral to pieces of iron. Running an electric current through a wire can also create magnets, as is done in the STAR detector shown in Figure 27.1. We will learn about the way magnets interact with each other. We will study the magnetic fields produced by magnets and the effect of these magnetic fields on moving charged particles. We will study several applications of the effect of magnetic fields on moving charges.

- Permanent magnets exist in nature.
- Magnets have a north pole and a south pole; a single magnetic north pole or south pole cannot be isolated – they always come in pairs
- Opposite poles attract and same poles repel.
- If you break a bar magnet in half, you will create two new magnets, each with a north and a south pole.
- The unit of the magnetic field is the tesla, abbreviated T.
- The Earth has a magnetic field.
- The magnetic field describes a force exerted on a moving charged particle.
- The magnetic force exerted on a moving charge in a magnetic field is perpendicular to both the magnetic field and the velocity of the particle.
- A current-carrying wire will experience a force in a magnetic field.
- A current-carrying loop will experience a torque in a magnetic field.
- The Hall effect can be used to measure magnetic fields.
- Materials can exhibit three kinds of intrinsic magnetism: ferromagnetism, diamagnetism and paramagnetism.

27.1. Permanent Magnets

Examples of permanent magnets include refrigerator magnets and magnetic door latches. They are all made of compounds of iron, nickel, or cobalt. If you touch an iron bar to a piece of lodestone (magnetic magnetite) the iron bar will be magnetized. If you then float this iron bar in water, the iron bar will align with the north magnetic pole of the Earth. We call the end of the magnet that points north the north pole of the magnet and the other end the south pole of the magnet.

If we bring together two permanent magnets such that the two north poles are together or two south poles are together, the magnets will repel each other as shown in the top two cases of Figure 27.2. If we bring together a north pole and a south pole, the magnets will attract each other as shown in the bottom two cases of Figure 27.2. The north magnetic pole of the Earth is currently a magnetic south pole, which is why it attracts the north pole of magnets.

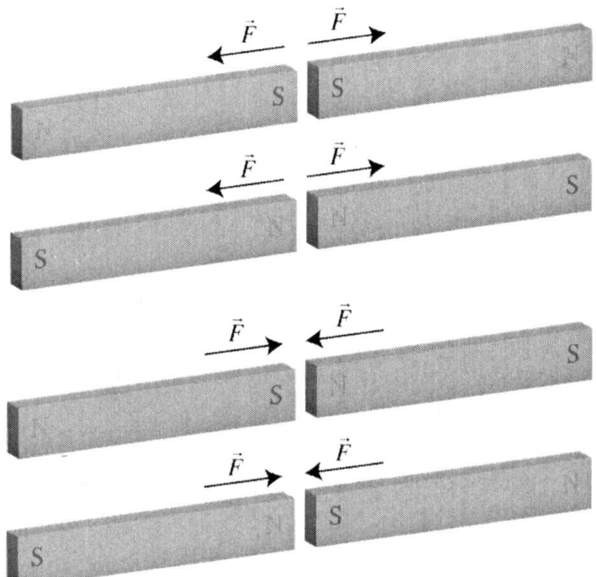

Figure 27.2: Like magnetic poles repel (top two cases), and unlike magnetic poles attract (bottom two cases).

If we break a permanent magnet in half, we do not get a separate north pole and south pole. When we break a bar magnet in half as in Figure 27.3, we always get two new magnets, each with its own north and south pole. Unlike electric charge that exists as positive (proton) and negative (electron) separately, there are no separate magnetic monopoles (an isolated north pole or an isolated south pole). Scientists have carried out extensive searches for magnetic monopoles, the most sensitive being the MACRO experiment performed at the Gran Sasso Laboratory in Italy, and none has been found.

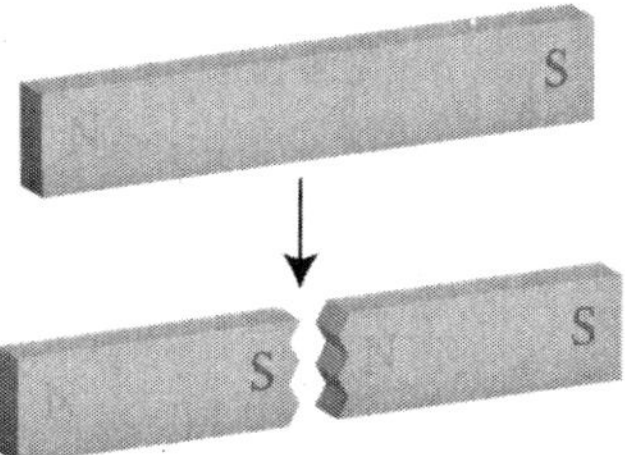

Figure 27.3: Two magnets, each with its own north and south pole, result when we break a bar magnet in half.

Magnetic Field Lines

The permanent magnets just discussed interact with each other at a distance without visibly touching. In analogy with the electric field, we use the concept of a magnetic field to describe the magnetic force. We use the vector $\vec{B}(\vec{r})$ to denote the magnetic field vector at any given point in space.

As we did for the electric field, we can represent the magnetic field using magnetic field lines. The magnetic field is always tangent to the magnetic field lines. The magnetic field lines from a permanent bar magnet are shown in Figure 27.4. For the electric field, the electric force on a positive test charge pointed in the same direction as the electric field. However, because there is no magnetic monopole, we must employ other means to describe the magnetic force.

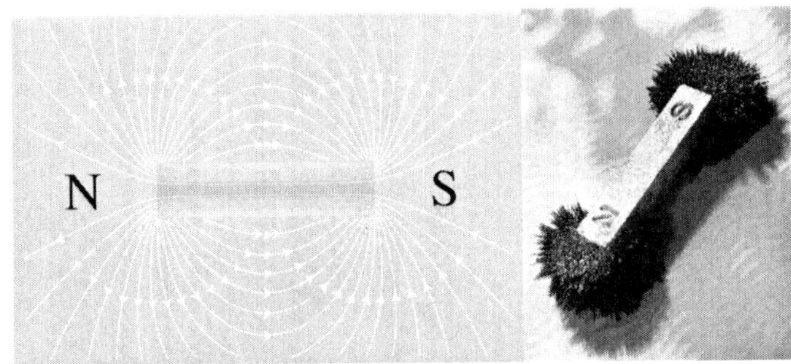

Figure 27.4: Left: Computer-generated magnetic field lines from a permanent bar magnet; right: iron filings align themselves with the magnetic field lines and make them visible.

We can establish the direction of the magnetic field in terms of the direction a compass needle would point. A compass needle, with a north pole and a south pole, will orient itself such that its north pole points in the direction of the magnetic field. Thus, the direction of the field can be measured at any point by moving a compass needle around in a magnetic field and noting the direction that the compass needle points. Externally magnetic field lines appear to originate on north poles and terminate on south poles, but magnetic field lines are actually closed loops that penetrate the magnet itself.

Earth's Magnetic Field

The Earth itself is a magnet. The Earth has a magnetic field similar to the magnetic field of a bar magnet shown in Figure 27.4. This magnetic field is important because it protects us from radiation from space called cosmic rays, as most of these cosmic rays are deflected away from the earth by the earth's magnetic field. The poles of this magnet are not exactly aligned with the geographic poles defined as the endpoints of the axis of the Earth's rotation.

Figure 27.5 shows a sketch of the cross section of Earth's magnetic field lines. The field lines close to form a surface that wraps around the Earth like a doughnut. The Earth's magnetic field is distorted by the so-called Solar Wind, a flow of ionized gas emitted by the Sun moving outward at approximately 400 km/s. There are two bands of captured charged particles around the Earth called the Van Allen Radiation Belts as shown in Figure 27.5. These bands are named after James A. Van Allen (1914-2006), who discovered them in the early days of space flight by putting radiation counters on board of satellites.

Indicated in Figure 27.5 are also the locations of the north and south magnetic poles. They are not exactly at the geographic poles defined by the points where the axis of rotation intersects the Earth surface. The magnetic poles move, presently at the rate of up to 40 km in a single year. Presently, the magnetic north pole (labeled S in Figure 27.5) is located approximately 2800 km away form the geographic south pole, at the edge of Antarctica, in a direction toward Australia. The magnetic south pole is located in the Canadian Arctic and will reach Siberia in 2050, if the present rate of motion continues. The Earth's magnetic field has decreased steadily at the rate of about 7% per century since it was first measured accurately around 1840. At that rate, the Earth's magnetic field will disappear in a few thousand years. There are indications that the magnetic field of Earth has reversed itself approximately 170 times in the past 100 million years. The last reversal occurred about 770,000 years ago.

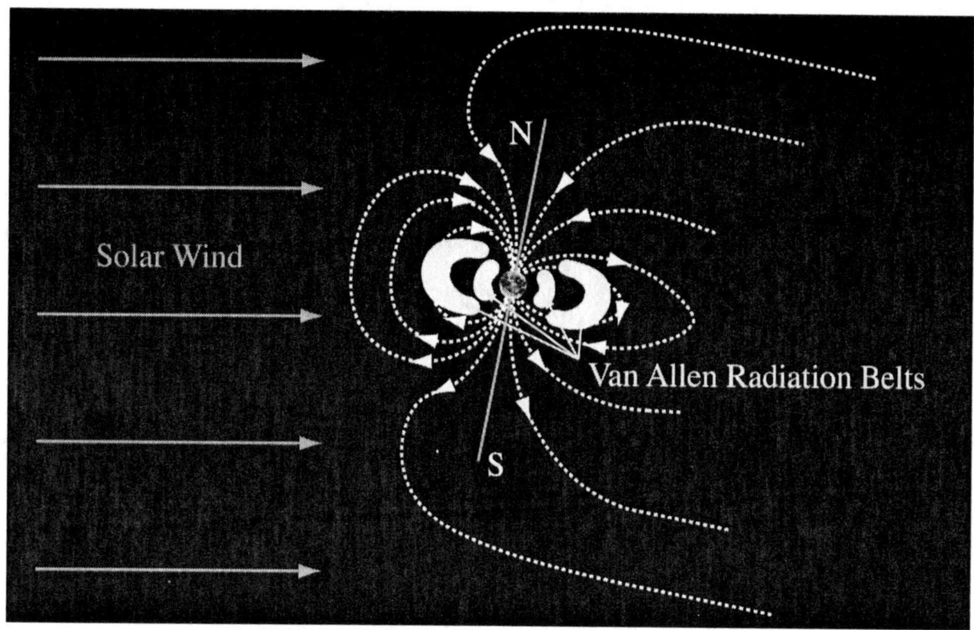

Figure 27.5: Sketch of section through the Earth's magnetic field. The dashed lines represent the magnetic field lines. The axis defined by the magnetic north and south poles (red line) currently forms an angle of approximately 11 degrees with the rotation axis.

What is the cause of the Earth's magnetic field? Surprisingly, the answer to this question is not known exactly yet and is under intense current research. Most likely, it is caused by strong magnetotelluric currents inside the Earth, caused by the spinning liquid iron-nickel core of Earth. This spinning is often referred to as the dynamo effect.

Because the geographic north pole and the north magnetic pole are not in the same location, a compass needle does generally not point exactly to the geographic north pole. This difference is called the magnetic declination. The magnetic declination is taken to be positive when magnetic north is east of true north and negative when magnetic north is west of true north. The north magnetic pole currently resides on a line that passes through central Missouri, Eastern Illinois, Western Iowa, and Eastern Wisconsin. Along this line, the magnetic declination is zero. West of this line the magnetic declination is positive and reaches 18° in Seattle. East of this line the declination is negative, up to -18° in Maine.

Because the positions of the Earth's magnetic poles move with time, the magnetic declinations for all locations on the Earth's surface change with time. For example, the estimated magnetic declination for Lansing, Michigan, is shown for the period 1900 – 2004 in Figure 27.6. Similar graphs can be drawn for any location on earth.

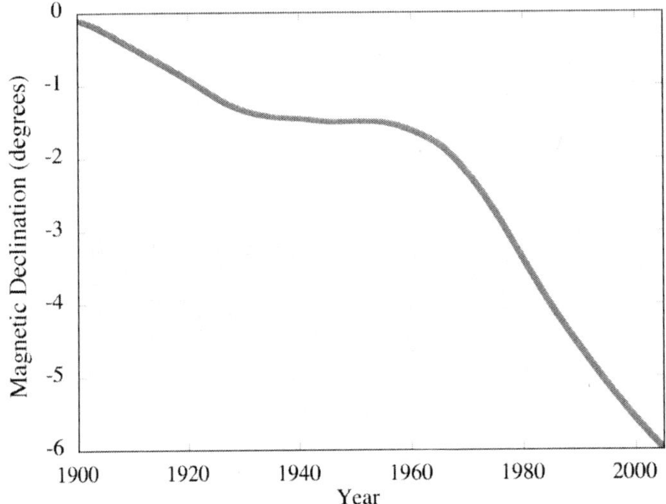

Figure 27.6: History of the magnetic declination at Lansing, Michigan, from 1900 to 2004.

In order to define the magnetic field quantitatively, we define the magnetic field in terms of its effect on a moving charged particle. This definition is done in the following section.

Superposition of Magnetic Fields

If there are several sources of magnetic field, such as several permanent magnets, the magnetic field at any given point in space is given by the superposition of the magnetic fields from all sources. This superposition follows directly from the superposition of forces that we introduced in chapter 4 in our study of mechanics. The superposition principle for the total magnetic field $\vec{B}_{total}(\vec{r})$ due to n magnetic field sources can be stated as

$$\vec{B}_{total}(\vec{r}) = \vec{B}_1(\vec{r}) + \vec{B}_1(\vec{r}) + ... + \vec{B}_n(\vec{r}) \tag{27.1}$$

This superposition principle for magnetic fields is in exact analogy to the superposition principle for electric fields, which we have encountered in chapter 22.

27.2. Magnetic Force

We already found in our qualitative discussion in the previous section that the magnetic field has a direction, along the magnetic field lines. For now, we will start with a constant magnetic field and study its effect on charges. As a reminder, we had found that the electric field exerts a force on a charge, $\vec{F}_E = q\vec{E}$. One finds through experiments such as the one shown in Figure 27.7 that a magnetic field does not exert a force on a charge at rest, but only on a moving charge.

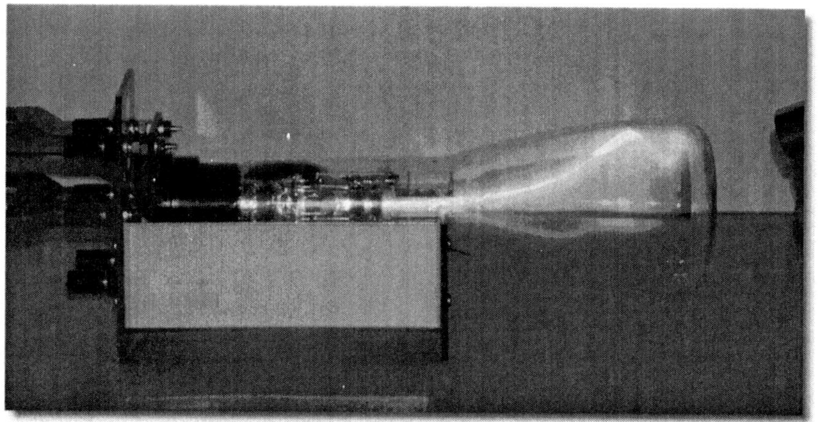

Figure 27.7: A beam of electrons is made visible by a small amount of gas in an evacuated tube (green) and is bent by a magnet (at right edge of picture).

The magnetic field can be defined in terms of the force exerted by the magnetic field on a moving charged particle. The magnetic force exerted by a magnetic field on a moving charged particle with charge q moving with a velocity $\vec{v}$ is given by

$$\vec{F}_B = q\vec{v} \times \vec{B}. \tag{27.2}$$

The direction of the force is perpendicular to both the velocity of the moving charged particle and the magnetic field as shown in Figure 27.8. We will call this right hand rule Right Hand Rule 1.

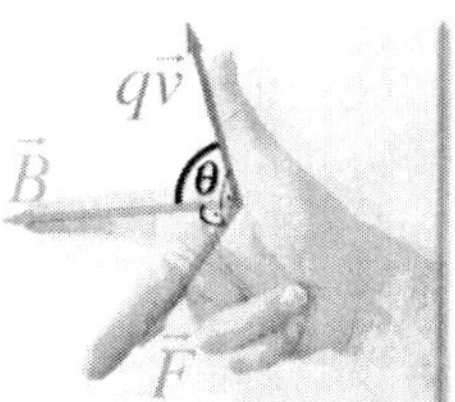

Figure 27.8: Right Hand Rule 1 for the force exerted on a charge q moving with speed v by a magnetic field B. To find the direction of the magnetic force on a moving charge using your right hand, point your thumb in the direction of the velocity of the moving charge, point your index finger in the direction of the magnetic field, and your middle finger will give you the direction of the magnetic force.

The magnitude of the of magnetic force on a moving charged particle is

$$F_B = |q|vB\sin\theta \tag{27.3}$$

where θ is the angle between the velocity of the charged particle and the magnetic field.

One can see that there is no magnetic force on a charged particle moving parallel to the magnetic field because $\theta = 0°$. If a charged particle is moving perpendicular to the magnetic field, $\theta = 90°$ and (for fixed values of v and B), the magnetic force assumes its maximum value of

$$F = |q|vB \tag{27.4}$$

for this special case of $\vec{v} \perp \vec{B}$.

Solved Problem

Solved Problem 27.1: Cathode ray tube

Question:

Consider a cathode ray tube similar to the one shown in Figure 27.8. In this tube, a voltage of $V = 111$ V accelerates electrons horizontally. Beyond the electron gun, there is a constant magnetic field of $B = 3.40 \cdot 10^{-4}$ T. The direction of the magnetic field is upward, perpendicular to the initial velocity of the electrons. What is the magnitude of the acceleration of the electrons due to the magnetic field? (The mass of an electron is $9.11 \cdot 10^{-31}$ kg.)

Answer:

THINK:

The electrons gain energy in the electron gun of the cathode ray tube. The gain in kinetic energy of each electron is equal to the charge of the electron times the potential difference. The velocity of the electrons can be found from the definition of kinetic energy. The magnetic force on the electrons is equal to the mass of the electron times the acceleration of the electron.

SKETCH:

A sketch of the electrons moving with velocity $\vec{v}$ entering a region of constant magnetic field perpendicular to the velocity of the electrons is shown in Figure 27.9.

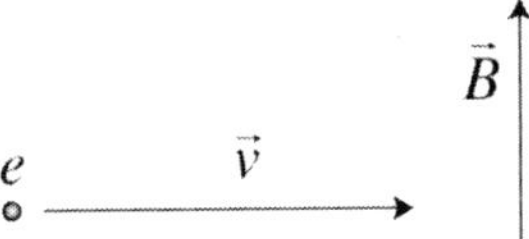

Figure 27.9: Electron moving with velocity v entering a region of constant magnetic field B.

RESEARCH:

The gain in kinetic energy K of the electrons is equal to the gain in electric potential energy

$$K = eV = \frac{1}{2}mv^2. \tag{27.5}$$

where V is the magnitude of the potential difference across which the electrons were accelerated and m is the mass of an electron. We can solve (27.5) for the speed of the electron

$$v = \sqrt{\frac{2eV}{m}}. \tag{27.6}$$

The force exerted by the magnetic field on the electron is given by (27.3)

$$F = evB\sin 90° = evB. \tag{27.7}$$

where $-e$ is the charge of an electron and B is the magnitude of the magnetic field. Newton's second law tells that

$$F = ma = evB \tag{27.8}$$

where a is the magnitude of the acceleration of the electrons.

SIMPLIFY:

We can combine (27.6) and (27.8) and rearrange to obtain the acceleration of the electrons

$$a = \frac{evB}{m} = \frac{eB\sqrt{\frac{2eV}{m}}}{m} = B\sqrt{2V\frac{e^3}{m^3}} \tag{27.9}$$

CALCULATE:

Putting in our numerical values gives us

$$a = B\sqrt{2V\frac{e^3}{m^3}} = \left(3.40 \cdot 10^{-4}\text{ T}\right)\sqrt{2\left(111\text{ V}\right)\frac{\left(1.602 \cdot 10^{-19}\text{ C}\right)^3}{\left(9.11 \cdot 10^{-31}\text{ kg}\right)^3}}.$$

$$a = 3.7357 \cdot 10^{14}\text{ m/s}^2$$

ROUND:

We report our result to three significant figures

$$a = 3.74 \cdot 10^{14}\text{ m/s}.$$

DOUBLE-CHECK:

The calculated acceleration is large compared with our every day experience. To double-check, we first check the speed of the electrons

$$v = \sqrt{\frac{2eV}{m}} = \sqrt{\frac{2\left(1.602 \cdot 10^{-19}\text{ C}\right)\left(111\text{ V}\right)}{9.11 \cdot 10^{-31}\text{ kg}}} = 6.25 \cdot 10^{6}\text{ m/s}.$$

This speed for the electrons is reasonable because it is only 2% of the speed of light. The magnetic force on the electron is then

$$F = evB = \left(1.602\cdot 10^{-19}\ \text{C}\right)\left(6.25\cdot 10^{6}\ \text{m/s}\right)\left(3.40\cdot 10^{-4}\ \text{T}\right) = 3.40\cdot 10^{-16}\ \text{N}.$$

The acceleration is very large because the mass of an electron is very small.

In-class exercise: What is the direction that the electron in Figure 27.9 is bent as it enters the constant magnetic field?

a) into the page
b) out of the page
c) up
d) down
e) not at all

Units for the Magnetic Field Strength

Before we go on in our discussion of the motion of charges in magnetic fields, we need to discuss the units in which the magnetic field strength is measured. This description is easily done by using equation (27.4) and performing a dimensional analysis:

$$[F] = [q][v][B] \Rightarrow [B] = \frac{[F]}{[q][v]} = \frac{\text{Ns}}{\text{Cm}}. \tag{27.10}$$

Because we have introduced the ampere as 1 A = 1 C/s, we could also write $[B] = \text{N/(Am)}$. The magnetic field strength has received its own named unit, the tesla (T), named in honor of Croatian-born American physicist and inventor Nikola Tesla (1856-1943):

$$1\ \text{T} = 1\ \frac{\text{Ns}}{\text{Cm}} = 1\frac{\text{N}}{\text{Am}}. \tag{27.11}$$

A tesla is a rather large unit of the magnetic field strength. Sometimes you will find magnetic field strength stated in units of oersted or gauss (G), 1 oersted = 1 gauss, which are not SI units, where

$$1\ \text{G} = 10^{-4}\ \text{T}. \tag{27.12}$$

For example, the strength of the Earth's magnetic field at the surface of Earth is on the order of 0.5 G ($5\cdot 10^{-5}$ T). It varies between 0.25 G and 0.65 G as illustrated in Figure 27.10.

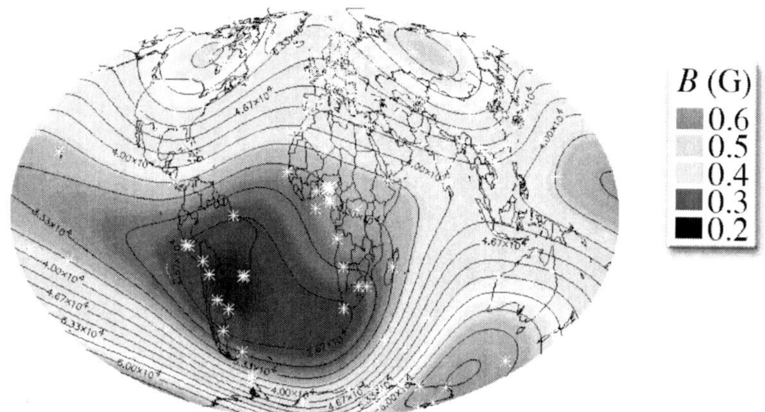

Figure 27.10: Geomagnetic field strength.
(National Geophysical Data Center)

Self-Test Opportunity: Three particles, each with a charge of $q = 6.15\ \mu\text{C}$ and a speed of $v = 465$ m/s, enter a uniform magnetic field with $B = 0.165$ T as shown in the figure. What is the magnitude of the magnetic force on each of the particles?

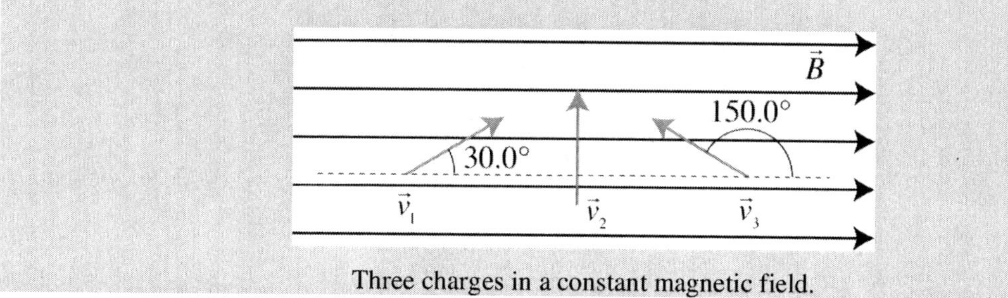

Three charges in a constant magnetic field.

Orbits in a Constant Magnetic Field

Consider the situation in which you tie a string to a rock and twirl it at constant speed in a horizontal circle around your head. The tension of the string provides the centripetal force that keeps the rock moving in a circle. The tension on the string always points to the center of the circle and creates a centripetal acceleration. A similar physical situation occurs when a particle with charge q and mass m moves with velocity $\vec{v}$ perpendicular to a uniform magnetic field $\vec{B}$. In this case, the particle will move in a circle with a constant speed v and the magnetic force of magnitude $F = |q|vB$ will keep the particle moving in a circle. If the velocity of the charged particle is parallel to the magnetic field, the particle will experience no magnetic force and continue to travel in a straight line. If the velocity of the particle is at some angle between 0 and 90 degrees relative to the magnetic field, the charged particle will travel in a helical trajectory.

For the motion perpendicular to the magnetic field as in Figure 27.11, the force required to keep the particle moving in a circle with radius r is the centripetal force

$$F = \frac{mv^2}{r}. \tag{27.13}$$

Setting this centripetal force equal to the magnetic force, we obtain

$$vB|q| = \frac{mv^2}{r}. \tag{27.14}$$

We get an expression for the radius of the circle in which the particle is traveling

$$r = \frac{mv}{|q|B}. \tag{27.15}$$

Figure 27.11: Electron beam bent into a circular orbit by the magnetic field generated by the two coils.

One common application of the motion of charged particles in a magnetic field is a mass spectrometer. In a magnetic spectrometer, the magnetic field is fixed and the radius of curvature of the trajectory of the particles is measured by various means such as a photographic plate. Remembering that the momentum of a particle is $p = mv$ we can rewrite (27.15) as

$$Br = \frac{p}{|q|}. \tag{27.16}$$

The fixed magnetic field combined with (27.16) implies that all particles with the same radius of curvature have the same ratio of momentum to charge. Thus by measuring the charge and the radius of the trajectory of a charged particle moving in a constant magnetic field, one can measure the momentum of the particle. The kinetic energy is usually known from the potential difference used to accelerate the particle as demonstrated in Solved Problems 22.1 and 22.2. Knowing the momentum and the kinetic energy one can determine the mass of the particle.

Example

Example 27.1: Time Projection Chamber

In high-energy nuclear physics, new forms of matter are studied by colliding gold nuclei at very high energies. In particle physics, new elementary particles are created and studied by colliding protons and anti-protons at the highest energies. In these collisions, many particles are created that stream away from the interaction point at high speeds. A simple particle detector is not sufficient to measure and identify these particles. A device that can help physicists study these collisions is the time projection chamber (TPC).

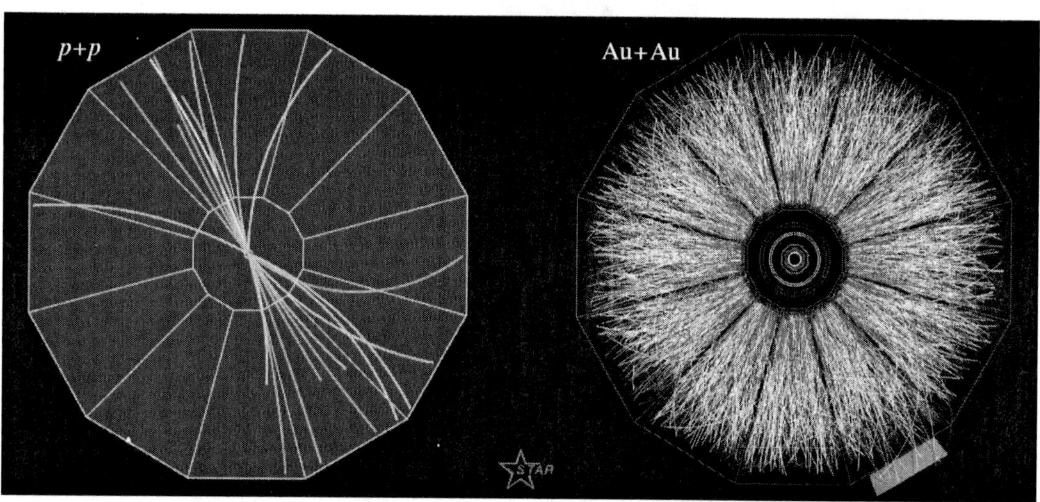

Figure 27.12: Curved tracks left by the motion of charged particles produced in collisions of two protons (left) each with kinetic energy 100 GeV and two gold nuclei (right) each with kinetic energy of 100 GeV per nucleon.

In Figure 27.12 we show a collision of two protons and a collisions of two gold nuclei at a center-of-mass energy of 200 GeV per nucleon pair (100 GeV per nucleon in each direction). (A nucleon is a neutron or a proton.) In the proton-proton collision, dozens of particles are created. In the gold-gold collisions, thousands of particles are created. Each charged particle leaves a track in the TPC. The color of the track represents the ionization density of the track as it passes through the gas of the TPC.

One example of a TPC is the STAR TPC at the Relativistic Heavy Collider at Brookhaven National Laboratory on Long Island, New York. (See Figure 27.1 for a photo of the STAR detector.) The STAR TPC consists of a large cylinder filled with a carefully chosen gas (90% argon, 10% methane) that allows free electrons to drift without recombining. We show a collision of two protons (left) and two gold nuclei (right) that occurred in the center of the STAR TPC. In these collisions, charged particles are created that pass through the gas volume of the TPC. As these charged particles pass through the gas, the particles ionize the atoms of the gas, releasing free electrons. Electric fields are applied between the center of the TPC and the caps of the cylinder that exert an electric force on these freed electrons, making them drift to end-caps of the TPC, where they are recorded electronically. Using the drift time and the recording positions, the computer software reconstructs the trajectories that the produced particles took through the TPC.

The TPC sits inside the giant solenoid magnet shown in Figure 27.1, with the magnetic field pointing into the page. The produced charged particles have a component of their velocity that is perpendicular to the magnetic field and thus have circular trajectories when viewed from this angle. As you can see from the right side of Figure 27.12, a collision of two gold nuclei can produce thousands of particles. From these produced particles nuclear physicists currently are trying to find out if a new state of matter has been created in these nuclear collisions.

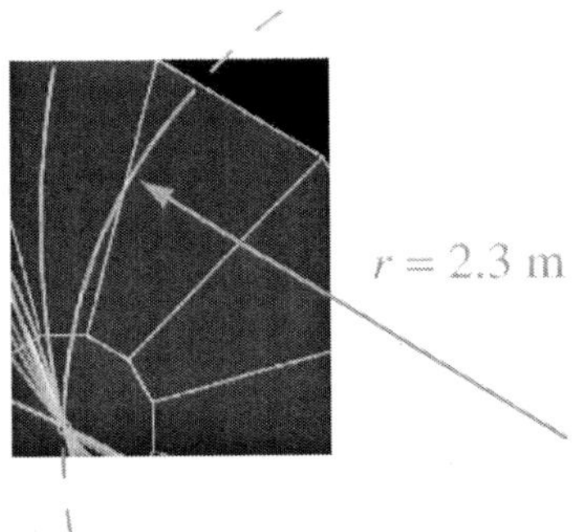

Figure 27.13: Circle fitted to the trajectory of one of the charged particles from the proton+proton collision observed by the STAR TPC shown in Figure 27.12.

Example

As an example, let's calculate the component of the momentum perpendicular to the magnetic field for one particle. We choose a particle track from the proton+proton collision because only a few particles are produced compared with the gold+gold collision and we can easily isolate one track to analyze. We will call this component the transverse momentum of the particle, p_t. We start by fitting a circle to the trajectory of the particle in the view along the magnetic field as shown in Figure 27.13. A dashed red line represents the fitted circle.

The radius of the circular path of the charged particle is $r = 2.3 \text{ m}$. Using the relationship (27.16), with p replaced by p_t because the magnetic force depends only on p_t and not on the component of momentum parallel to $\vec{B}$,

$$Br = \frac{p_t}{|q|},$$

we can get the transverse momentum of the particle in terms of the magnetic field of the STAR magnet ($B = 0.50 \text{ T}$) and the charge of the particle ($|q| = 1.60 \cdot 10^{-19} \text{ C}$)

$$p_t = |q| Br = \left(1.60 \cdot 10^{-19} \text{ C}\right)\left(0.50 \text{ T}\right)\left(2.3 \text{ m}\right) = 1.8 \cdot 10^{-19} \text{ kg} \cdot \text{m/s}.$$

We know that the particle has a charge $|q| = 1 \cdot e$ by measuring the energy loss in the gas of the TPC compared to the radius of the circular path and comparing that result with calculations of the energy loss as a function momentum for a given particle, such as a pion, a kaon, or a proton. (As particles slow down, their energy loss increases due to a

Example

greater ionization of the TPC gas. Using (27.16) we see that if $|q| = 2e$ the momentum would be twice as large and the ionization would be much less than observed. Almost all the particles measured in the STAR TPC have $|q| = 1 \cdot e$.) We use the direction of the magnetic force on the particle and (27.2) to deduce that $q > 0$. We can get the momentum of the particle from the transverse momentum and a measurement of the particle's angle with respect to the magnetic field from another view in the TPC perpendicular to the magnetic field.

These SI units for momentum are not convenient for studying these particles so nuclear physicists usually use the units MeV/c for momentum. Remembering that $1 \text{ MeV} = 1.602 \cdot 10^{-13} \text{ J}$ we can write

$$p_t c = \left(1.8 \cdot 10^{-19} \text{ kg m/s}\right)\left(3.0 \cdot 10^{8} \text{ m/s}\right) = 5.53 \cdot 10^{-11} \text{ J}$$

or

$$p_t = \left(5.53 \cdot 10^{-11} \text{ J}\right)/\text{c} = 345 \text{ MeV/c}.$$

If a particle performs a complete circular orbit inside a magnetic field, as for example the electrons shown in Figure 27.11, then the period of revolution T of the particle is just the circumference of the circle divided by the speed

$$T = \frac{2\pi r}{v} = \frac{2\pi m}{|q|B}. \tag{27.17}$$

The frequency f of the motion of the charged particle is the inverse of the period

$$f = \frac{1}{T} = \frac{|q|B}{2\pi m}. \tag{27.18}$$

The angular frequency ω of the motion is

$$\omega = 2\pi f = \frac{|q|B}{m}. \tag{27.19}$$

Thus, we can see that the frequency and angular frequency of the motion of the particle are independent of the speed of the particle. This fact is used in cyclotrons.

Example 27.2: Energy of a cyclotron

A cyclotron is a particle accelerator (see Figure 27.14 for a computer-generated sketch).

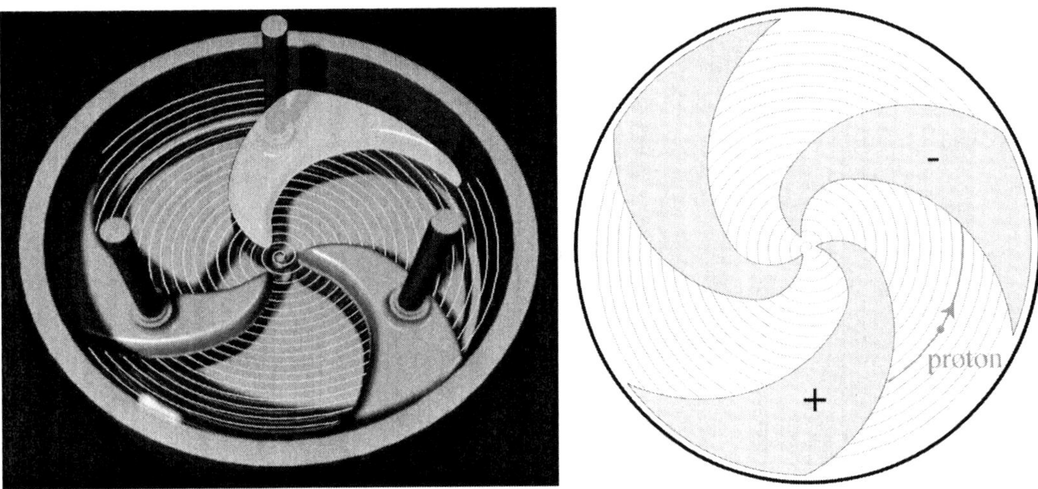

Figure 27.14: The left panel shows a computer-generated drawing of the central section of the K500 superconducting cyclotron at the National Superconducting Cyclotron Laboratory at Michigan State University, with the spiral trajectory of an accelerated particle overlaid. One of the three "dees" of the cyclotron is highlighted in green. The right panel shows a top view of the K500 with proton shown being accelerated between two dees.

The golden D-shaped pieces of metal (descriptively called "dees") have alternating electric potentials applied to them such that a positively charged particle always sees a negatively charged dee ahead when it emerges from under the previous dee, which is now positively charged. The resulting electric field accelerates the particle. Because the cyclotron sits in a strong magnetic field, the trajectory is curved. The radius of the trajectory is proportional to the momentum, see (27.16), so the accelerated particle spirals outward until it reaches the radius of the magnetic field and is extracted (as it is no longer bent by the field). Thanks to (27.19) the angular velocity is independent of the particle's momentum or energy, and thus the frequency with which the polarity of the dees is changed does not have to be adjusted as the particle is accelerated. Of course, these arguments apply only as long as the speed of the accelerated particles does not approach a sizable fraction of the speed of light, as we will see later in chapter 35 on relativity. To compensate for relativistic effects, the magnetic field of a cyclotron increases with the radius of the orbit of the accelerated particles.

Question:

What is the kinetic energy in units of MeV for a proton extracted from a cyclotron with a radius of $r = 1.81$ m if the magnetic field of the cyclotron is uniform and has $B = 0.851$ T ? The mass of a proton is $1.67 \cdot 10^{-27}$ kg .

Answer:

Using (27.15) we can solve for the speed v of the proton

Example

$$v = \frac{rqB}{m}.$$

Remembering that the kinetic energy can be written as $K = (1/2)mv^2$ we can write

$$K = \frac{1}{2}mv^2 = \frac{1}{2}m\left(\frac{rqB}{m}\right)^2 = \frac{r^2q^2B^2}{2m}.$$

Putting in our numbers, we get the kinetic energy in SI units

$$K = \frac{(1.81\ \text{m})^2(1.602 \cdot 10^{-19}\ \text{C})^2(0.851\ \text{T})^2}{2 \cdot 1.67 \cdot 10^{-27}\ \text{kg}} = 1.82 \cdot 10^{-11}\ \text{J}.$$

Remembering that 1 eV = $1.602 \cdot 10^{-19}$ J and that 1 MeV = 10^6 eV we finally find

$$K = 1.82 \cdot 10^{-11}\ \text{J}\frac{1\ \text{eV}}{1.602 \cdot 10^{-19}\ \text{J}}\frac{\text{MeV}}{10^6\ \text{eV}} = 114\ \text{MeV}.$$

Self-Test Opportunity: A uniform magnetic field shown in this figure and is directed out of the page. A charged particle is traveling in the plane of the page as shown by the arrows in the figure.

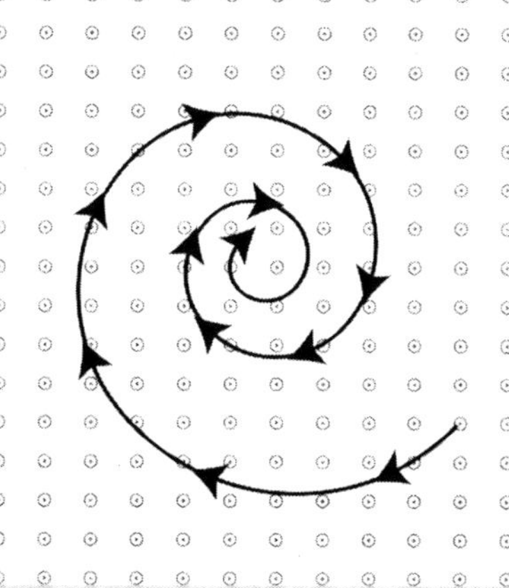

A particle spiraling in a uniform magnetic field.

a) Is the charge of the particle positive or negative?
b) Is the particle slowing down or speeding up, or moving with constant speed?
c) Is the magnetic field is doing work on the particle?

In-class exercise: Protons from the solar wind travel from the Sun and reach Earth's magnetic field with speed of 400 km/s. If the Earth's magnetic field is $5.0 \cdot 10^{-5}$ T and the velocity of protons is perpendicular to the Earth's magnetic field, what is the cyclotron frequency of the solar wind protons in Earth's magnetic field?

a) 122 Hz
b) 233 Hz
c) 321 Hz
d) 432 Hz
e) 763 Hz

Magnetic Levitation

One application of magnetic forces is magnetic levitation, in which a vertical magnetic force on an object balances the downward gravitational force and there is no need for a contact force and thus no need for contact. In Figure 27.15, the principle of magnetic levitation is demonstrated using a commercial toy called the Levitron.

Figure 27.15: The Levitron, a commercial toy demonstrating the magnetic levitation of a spinning magnet above a base magnet.

In this device, a magnetic top is spun on a plate and then lifted to the proper height and released. The top can remain suspended for several minutes.

The stable levitation of a permanent magnetic dipole by a second permanent magnetic dipole requires that the top spin. If the top were not spinning, it would invert and fall. Another method of magnetic levitation involves superconducting materials and permanent magnets, which we will discussed in the next chapter. Magnetic levitation has real-life applications in magnetic levitation (maglev) trains. Magnetic levitation has advantages over normal steel rail trains in that there are no moving parts to wear out, there is less vibration, and reduced friction means that high speeds are possible. Several maglev trains are now in service around the world and more are being planned. One example of a maglev train is the Shanghai Maglev Train shown in Figure 27.16 that operates between the Shanghai Pudong Airport and Shanghai and reaches speeds of up to 120 m/s (268 mph).

Figure 27.16: The Shanghai Maglev Train.

The train was constructed by the Transrapid International company in Germany. The maglev train operates using magnets attached to the train car as shown in Figure 27.17.

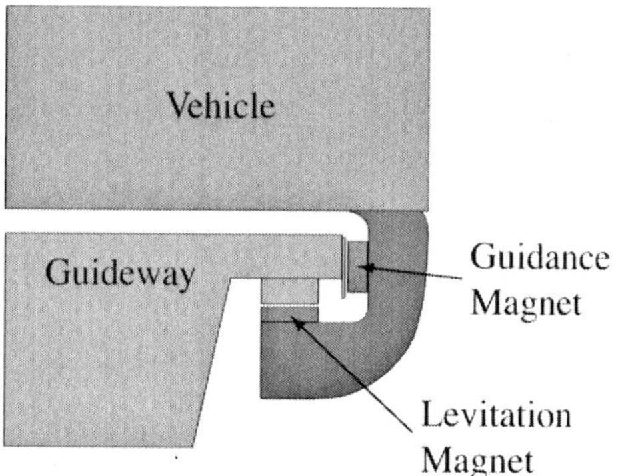

Figure 27.17: Cross section of one side of the Shanghai Maglev Train. The levitation magnets lift the cars 15 cm off the guideway and the guidance magnets keep the cars centered on the guideway. The magnets are all mounted on the traveling vehicle.

The Shanghai Maglev Train uses room-temperature magnetic coils with electronic feedback to produce stable levitation and guidance. The train cars are held 15 cm above the guideway to allow clearance of any objects that may be on the guideway. The levitation and guidance magnets are held at a distance of 10 mm from guideway which is constructed of a magnetic material. The propulsion of the train is provided by magnetic fields built into the guideway. The train propulsion system operates like an electric motor that has been unwrapped from a circular geometry to a linear geometry.

Maglev trains that use superconducting magnets have been tested, although there are technical problems with this type of maglev train including the maintenance of the superconducting coils and the exposure of the passengers to high magnetic fields.

27.3. Magnetic Forces on Current-Carrying Wires

Consider a wire carrying a current i in a constant magnetic field $\vec{B}$ as illustrated in Figure 27.18.

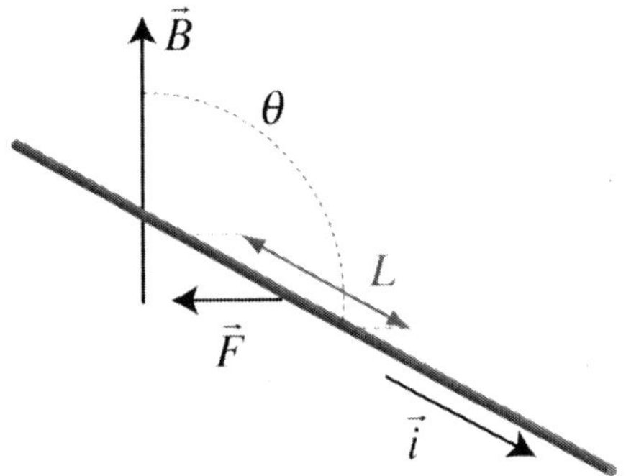

Figure 27.18: Magnetic force on a current-carrying wire.

The magnetic field will exert a force on the moving charges in the wire. The charge q flowing past a point in the wire in a given time t is ti. During this time, the charge will occupy a length L of wire given by $L = vt$ where v is the drift speed of the charge carriers in the wire. Thus, we obtain

$$q = ti = \frac{L}{v}i. \qquad (27.20)$$

The magnitude of the magnetic force is then

$$F = qvB\sin\theta = \left(\frac{L}{v}i\right)vB\sin\theta = iLB\sin\theta. \qquad (27.21)$$

where θ is the angle between the current and the magnetic field. The direction of the force is perpendicular to both the current and the magnetic field and is given by Right Hand Rule 1. Equation (27.21) can be expressed as a vector cross product

$$\vec{F} = i\vec{L} \times \vec{B} \qquad (27.22)$$

where the notation $i\vec{L}$ represent the current in a length of wire. Equation (27.22) is simply a reformulation of the magnetic force law for moving charges for the case in which the moving charges make up a current flowing in a wire.

Self-Test Opportunity: Consider parallel wires carrying the same current in the same direction. What is the force between the two wires? Now consider two parallel wires carrying current in opposite directions. What is the force between the two wires?

In-class exercise: A wire of length $L = 4.50$ m carries a current $i = 35.0$ A at an angle $\theta = 50.3°$ with respect to a constant magnetic field with $B = 6.70 \cdot 10^{-2}$ T as shown in the figure. What is the magnitude of the force on the wire?

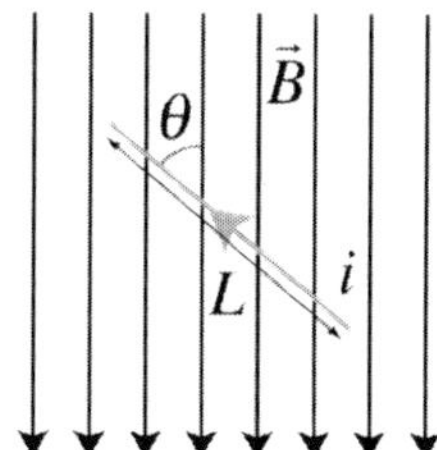

Wire of length L carrying current i in a constant magnetic field B.

a) 2.66 N
b) 3.86 N
c) 5.60 N
d) 8.12 N
e) 11.8 N

27.4. Torque on a Current Loop

Electric motors rely on the magnetic force exerted on a current carrying wire. This force is used to create a torque that turns a shaft. A simple electric motor is depicted in Figure 27.19 consisting of a single square loop carrying current i in a constant magnetic field $\vec{B}$. The two magnetic forces, $\vec{F}$ and $-\vec{F}$, shown in the figure are of equal magnitude and opposite direction. These forces create a torque that tends to rotate the loop around its axis of rotation.

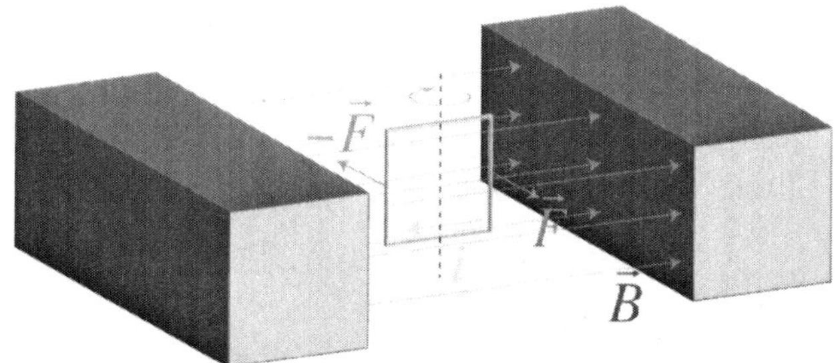

Figure 27.19: A simple electric motor consisting of a current carrying loop in a magnetic field.

These two forces sum to zero. The other two sides of the loop are parallel or anti-parallel to the magnetic field and thus experience no magnetic force. Thus, there are no net forces on the coil.

As the coil turns in the field, the forces on the sides of the loop perpendicular to the magnetic field will not change. The forces on the square loop with sides a are illustrated in Figure 27.20, which shows the top view of the coil.

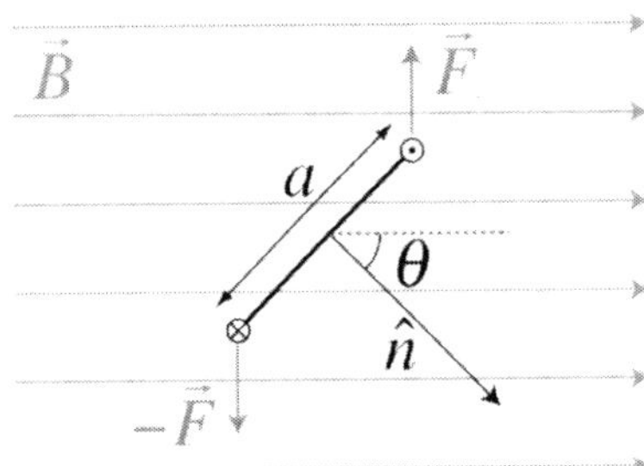

Figure 27.20: Forces on a current carrying loop (top view) in a magnetic field.

In Figure 27.20, θ is the angle between a unit vector normal to the plane of the coil, $\hat{n}$, and the magnetic field, $\vec{B}$. The unit normal vector is perpendicular to the plane of the wire loop and points in a direction given by Right Hand Rule 2 based on the current flowing around the loop, as shown in Figure 27.21. The unit normal vector gives the direction of the magnetic field.

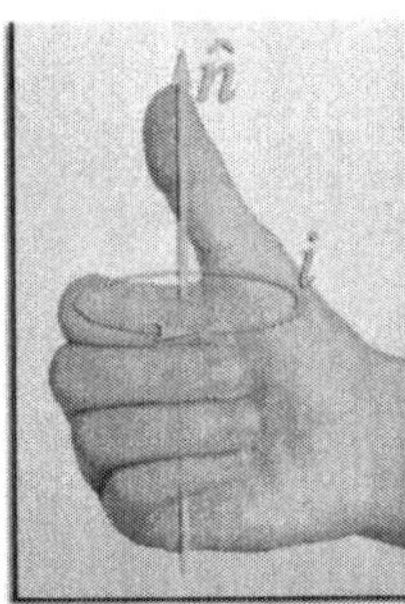

Figure 27.21: Right Hand Rule 2 giving the direction of the unit normal vector for a current-carrying loop. The determine the direction of the unit normal vector for the loop using your right hand, you curl your fingers in the direction of the current in the loop, and your thumb points in the direction of the unit normal vector.

In Figure 27.20 the current is flowing upward (out of the paper) in the top segment and downward (into the paper) in the lower segment as illustrated by the point (representing an arrowhead) and the cross (representing arrow feathers). The force on each of the vertical segments is

$$F = iaB\,. \qquad (27.23)$$

The forces on the other two sides are parallel or anti-parallel to the axis of rotation and do not cause a torque. The sum of the torque on the upper side plus the torque on the lower side gives the torque exerted on the coil about the center of the loop,

$$\tau_1 = \left(iaB\right)\left(\frac{a}{2}\right)\sin\theta + \left(iaB\right)\left(\frac{a}{2}\right)\sin\theta = ia^2 B\sin\theta = iAB\sin\theta\,. \qquad (27.24)$$

where $A = a^2$ is the area of the loop. The reason that the coil continues to rotate and doesn't just stop at $\theta = 0^0$ is that the coil is connected to a device called a commutator, which causes the current to change directions as the coil rotates. If we replace this loop with many loops wound close together, we can write

$$\tau = N\tau_1 = NiAB\sin\theta . \quad (27.25)$$

This expression applies to circular loops as well as square loops as long as the magnetic field is uniform.

In-class exercise: A loop has radius $r = 5.13$ cm and $N = 47$ windings. A current $i = 1.27$ A flows through the loop. This loop is inside a homogeneous magnetic field of strength 0.911 T. What is the maximum torque that the loop can experience due to this magnetic field?

a) 0.148 $\text{N}\cdot\text{m}$
b) 0.211 $\text{N}\cdot\text{m}$
c) 0.350 $\text{N}\cdot\text{m}$
d) 0.450 $\text{N}\cdot\text{m}$
e) 0.622 $\text{N}\cdot\text{m}$

27.5. Hall Effect

Consider a conductor carrying a current i perpendicular to a magnetic field $\vec{B}$ as illustrated in Figure 27.22. The electrons in the conductor will be moving with a velocity $\vec{v}$ in a direction opposite to the current. The moving electrons experience a force perpendicular to their velocity, making the electrons move toward one edge of the conductor.

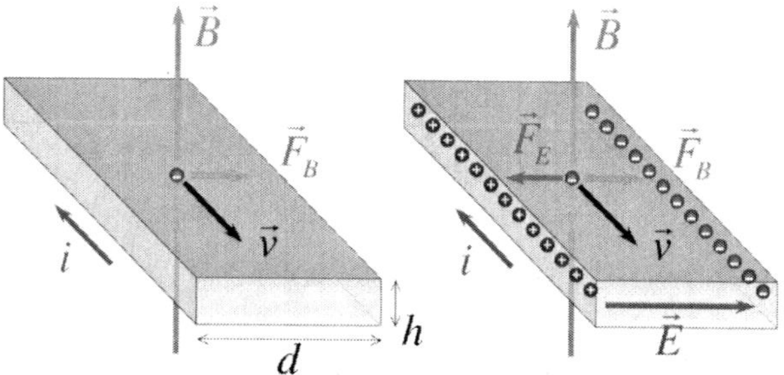

Figure 27.22: A conductor in a magnetic field is carrying a current. The charge carriers are negatively charged electrons. In the right panel, electrons have drifted to one side of the conductor leaving a net positive charge on the opposite side. This distribution of charges creates an electric field. The potential difference across the conductor is the Hall potential difference.

After some time, many electrons move to one edge of the conductor leaving a net positive charge on the opposite edge of the conductor. This charge distribution creates an electric field, $\vec{E}$, that exerts a force on the electrons in a direction opposite to that exerted by the magnetic field. When the magnitude of the force exerted on the electrons by the electric field is equal to the magnitude of the force exerted by the magnetic field, the net number of electrons no longer changes with time. The potential difference V_H between the edges of the conductor in the steady state is termed the Hall potential difference and is given by

$$V_H = Ed \tag{27.26}$$

where d is the width of the conductor and E is the magnitude of the created electric field.

The Hall effect can be used to demonstrate that the charge carriers in metals are negatively charged. If the charge carriers in a metal were positive and moving in the direction of the current shown in Figure 27.22, the positive charges would collect on the same edge of the conductor as the electrons, giving an electric field with an opposite sign. Experimentally we observe that the charge carriers in conductors are negatively charged electrons.

The Hall effect can be used to measure magnetic fields. Knowing the current flowing through the conductor and measuring the resulting electric field across the conductor, one can measure the magnetic field. To obtain this result quantitatively we start by expressing the equal magnitudes of the magnetic and electric forces on an electron

$$F_E = F_B \Rightarrow eE = vBe \Rightarrow B = \frac{E}{v} = \frac{V_H}{dv} \tag{27.27}$$

where we used equation (27.26) in the last step. Earlier we had found that the drift speed v of an electron in a conductor could be related to the current density J in the strip

$$J = \frac{i}{A} = nev \tag{27.28}$$

where A is the cross sectional area of the conductor. Here the area is given by $A = dh$, h is the thickness of the conductor, and n is the number of electrons per unit volume in the conductor. Solving (27.28) for the drift velocity results in

$$v = \frac{i}{Ane} = \frac{i}{dhne}. \tag{27.29}$$

Inserting this result back into (27.27), we find

$$B = \frac{V_H}{dv} = \frac{V_H dhne}{di} = \frac{V_H hne}{i}. \tag{27.30}$$

We can determine the magnetic field strength from measuring the Hall voltage V_H and knowing the height h and density of charge carriers n of the conductor. Equivalently, we can also use (27.30) to solve for the Hall voltage if we know the magnetic field strength:

$$V_H = \frac{iB}{neh}. \tag{27.31}$$

A photo of several different types of Hall probes is shown in Figure 27.23.

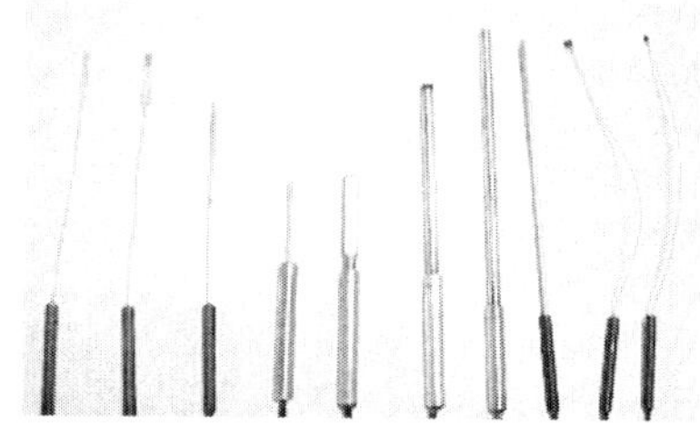

Figure 27.23: Several types of commercial Hall probes.

Example 27.4: Hall Effect

Suppose we put a Hall probe in a constant magnetic field. The Hall probe is constructed of copper and has a width of 2.00 mm. We measure a voltage of 0.250 μV across the probe when we run a current of 1.25 A through the conductor.

Question:

What is the magnitude of the magnetic field?

Answer:

The magnetic field is given by (27.30)

$$B = \frac{V_H}{dv} = \frac{V_H dhne}{di} = \frac{V_H hne}{i}.$$

We are given V_H, h, and i, and we know e. The density of electrons n is defined as the number of electrons per unit volume

$$n = \frac{\text{\# electrons}}{\text{volume}}.$$

The density of copper is $\rho_{\mathrm{Cu}} = 8.96 \text{ g/cm}^3 = 8960 \text{ kg/m}^3$. We know that one mole of copper has a mass of 63.5 g and has $6.02 \cdot 10^{23}$ atoms. We also assume that each copper atom has one free electron. Thus, we get the density of electrons

Example

$$n = \frac{1 \text{ electron}}{\text{atom}} \frac{6.02 \cdot 10^{23} \text{ atom}}{63.5 \text{ g}} \frac{8.96 \text{ g}}{\text{cm}^3} \frac{1.0 \cdot 10^6 \text{ cm}^3}{\text{m}^3} = 8.49 \cdot 10^{28} \frac{\text{electrons}}{\text{m}^3}.$$

We can then calculate the magnetic field to be

$$B = \frac{\left(0.250 \cdot 10^{-6} \text{ V}\right)\left(0.002 \text{ m}\right)\left(8.49 \cdot 10^{28} \frac{\text{electrons}}{\text{m}^3}\right)\left(1.602 \cdot 10^{-19} \text{ C}\right)}{1.25 \text{ A}} = 5.44 \text{ T}.$$

In-class exercise: A copper conductor is carrying a current $i = 1.41$ A perpendicular to a constant magnetic field $B = 4.94$ T as shown in the figure. The conductor is $d = 0.100$ m wide and $h = 2.00$ mm thick. What is the electric potential between points a and b?

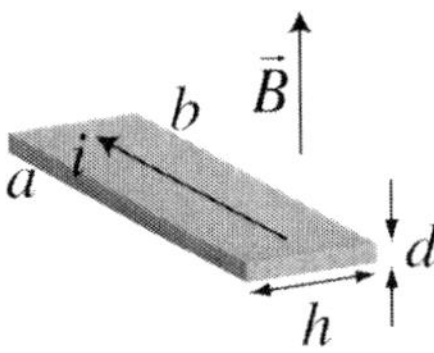

A copper conductor carrying a current in a constant magnetic field.

a) $2.56 \cdot 10^{-9}$ V
b) $5.12 \cdot 10^{-9}$ V
c) $7.50 \cdot 10^{-8}$ V
d) $2.56 \cdot 10^{-7}$ V
e) $9.66 \cdot 10^{-7}$ V

27.6 Ferromagnetism, Diamagnetism, and Paramagnetism

Magnetic materials exhibit three primary types of magnetic phenomena: ferromagnetism, diamagnetism, and paramagnetism. Most materials exhibit one or more of these types of magnetism. If a material dominantly exhibits one type of magnetism, that material is classified in terms of that type of magnetism. For example, iron is ferromagnetic.

Ferromagnetism

The elements iron, nickel, cobalt, gadolinium, and dysprosium and alloys containing these elements exhibit ferromagnetism. Ferromagnetic materials show long-range ordering at the atomic level, which causes the dipole moments of atoms to line up with each other in a limited region called a domain. Within this domain, the magnetic field can be strong. However, in the bulk these domains are randomly oriented leaving no net magnetic field. An external magnetic field can align these domains. A ferromagnetic material will retain all or some of this induced magnetism when the external magnetic field is removed, as the domains stay aligned. In addition, the magnetic field produced by a current in a device like a solenoid or toroid will be larger if a ferromagnetic material is present. This increased magnetic field can be expressed using a relative magnetic permeability instead of μ_0.

Diamagnetism

Most materials exhibit diamagnetism. However diamagnetism is weak compared with the other two types of magnetism and is thus masked by the other forms if they are present in the material. In diamagnetic materials, a weak magnetic dipole moment is induced by an external magnetic field in a direction opposite the direction of the external field. The induced magnetic field disappears when the external field is removed. If the external field is non-uniform, an interaction of the induced dipole moment of the diamagnetic material with the external field creates a force directed from a region of greater magnetic field to a region of lower magnetic field. An example of a live frog exhibiting diamagnetism is shown in Figure 23.1.

In this picture, diamagnetic forces induced by a non-uniform external magnetic field of 16 T are levitating a live frog. (This process apparently did not bother the frog.) The normally negligible diamagnetic force is large enough in this case to overcome gravity.

Figure 23.1: A live frog being levitated by a strong magnetic field at the High Field Magnet Laboratory, Radboud University Nijmegen, The Netherlands.

Paramagnetism

Materials containing certain transition elements, actinides, and rare earths exhibit paramagnetism. Each atom of these elements has a permanent magnetic dipole, but these dipole moments are randomly oriented and produce no net magnetic field. In the presence of an external magnetic field, some of these magnetic dipole moments align in the same direction as the external field. When the external field is removed, the induced magnetic dipole moment disappears. If the external field is non-uniform, this induced magnetic dipole moment interacts with the external field to produce a force directed from a region of lower magnetic field to a region of higher magnetic field.

at we have learned/Exam Study Guide:

v Symbols used in this Chapter

- $\vec{B}$ is the magnetic field.
- $\vec{\mu}$ is the magnetic dipole moment.

Most Important Points

- The magnetic force on a charge q moving with velocity $\vec{v}$ in a magnetic field $\vec{B}$ is given by $\vec{F} = q\vec{v} \times \vec{B}$. Right Hand Rule 1 gives the sign of the force.
- For the special case of a charge q moving with speed v perpendicular to a magnetic field of magnitude B, the magnitude of the magnetic force on the moving charge is $F = |q|vB$.
- The unit of the magnetic field is the tesla abbreviated T.
- The magnitude of the Earth's magnetic field at the surface is approximately $0.5 \cdot 10^{-4}$ T.
- For a particle with mass m and charge q moving with speed v perpendicular to a magnetic field with magnitude B, the particle will move in a circle with radius $r = mv / |q| B$.
- The cyclotron frequency ω of a charged particle with charge q and mass m orbiting in a constant magnetic field is given by $\omega = |q| B / m$.
- The force exerted by a magnetic field $\vec{B}$ on a length of wire $\vec{L}$ carrying a current i is given by $\vec{F} = i\vec{L} \times \vec{B}$. The magnitude of this force is $F = iLB\sin\theta$ where θ is the angle between the current element and the magnetic field.
- The torque on a loop carrying a current i in a magnetic field with magnitude B is $\tau = iAB\sin\theta$ where A is the area of the loop and θ is the angle between a normal to the loop and the magnetic field. Right Hand Rule 2 gives the direction of the unit normal vector of the loop.
- The Hall effect means that a current i flowing through a conductor with thickness h in a magnetic field B will have a voltage produced across the conductor given by $V = (iB)/(neh)$ where n is the density of electrons per unit volume and $-e$ is the charge of an electron.

Additional Solved Problems

Solved Problem 27.2: Velocity filter

Protons are accelerated from rest through an electric potential of $V = 14.0$ kV. The protons enter a velocity filter consisting of a parallel plate capacitor in a constant magnetic field into the paper as shown in Figure 27.24.

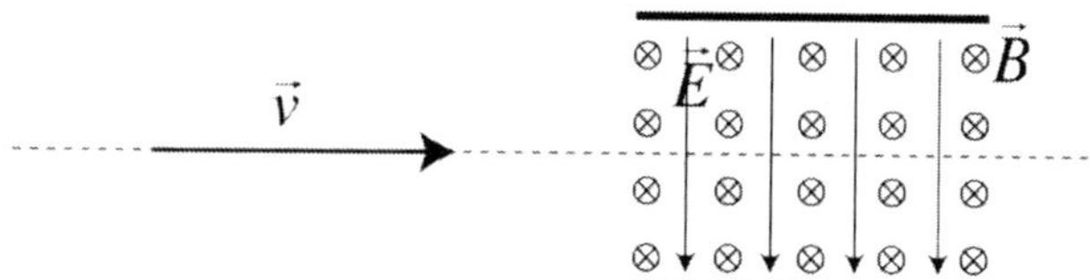

Figure 27.24: Velocity filter consisting of crossed electric and magnetic fields.

The electric field between the plates of the parallel plate capacitor is $\vec{E} = 4.30 \cdot 10^5$ V/m downward.

Question:
What magnetic field is required so that the protons travel without being deflected?

Answer:

THINK:

The change in kinetic energy of the protons is equal to the change in electric potential energy crossing the electric potential difference. The velocity of the protons can be calculated from the definition of kinetic energy. In the velocity filter, the protons will not be deflected if the electric force is equal to the magnetic force.

SKETCH:

A sketch showing the electric and magnetic forces on the protons as they pass through the velocity filter is shown in Figure 27.25.

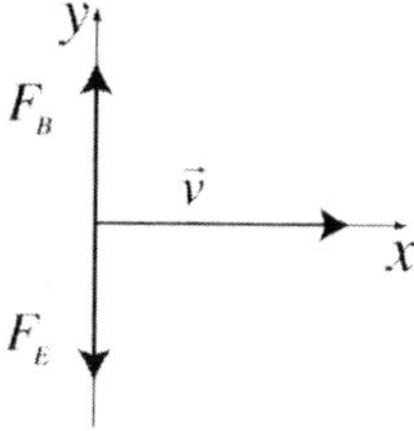

Figure 27.25: Electric and magnetic forces on a proton passing through a velocity filter.

RESEARCH:

The change in kinetic energy of the protons is equal to the change in electric potential energy, which can be expressed as

$$K = U = \frac{1}{2}mv^2 = eV \qquad (27.32)$$

where m is the mass of the proton, v is the speed of the proton after acceleration, e is the charge of the proton, and V is the electric potential across which the protons were accelerated. The velocity of the proton after acceleration is

Solved Problem

$$v = \sqrt{\frac{2eV}{m}}. \qquad (27.33)$$

When the protons enter the velocity filter, the direction of the electric force will be in the direction of the electric field, which is down (negative y-direction). The magnitude of the electric force is

$$F_E = eE \qquad (27.34)$$

where E is the magnitude of the electric field in the velocity filter. Right Hand Rule 1 gives the direction of the magnetic force. Putting our thumb in the direction of the velocity of the protons (positive x-direction), our index finger in the direction of the magnetic field (into the page), our middle finger points up (positive y-direction). Thus, the direction of the magnetic force on the protons is up. The magnitude of the magnetic force is given by

$$F_B = evB \qquad (27.35)$$

where B is the magnitude of the magnetic field in the velocity filter.

Solved Problem

SIMPLIFY:

The condition that allows the protons to pass though the velocity filter without being deflected is that the electric force balances the magnetic force. We can write this condition as

$$F_E = F_B = eE = evB. \qquad (27.36)$$

Solving for the magnetic field and substituting (27.33) we obtain

$$B = \frac{E}{\sqrt{\frac{2eV}{m}}} = E\sqrt{\frac{m}{2eV}}. \qquad (27.37)$$

CALCULATE:

Putting in our numerical values gives us

$$B = E\sqrt{\frac{m}{2eV}} = \left(4.30\cdot 10^5 \text{ V/m}\right)\sqrt{\frac{1.67\cdot 10^{-27}\text{ kg}}{2\left(1.602\cdot 10^{-19}\text{ C}\right)\left(14.0\cdot 10^3\text{ V}\right)}}.$$

$$B = 0.262371 \text{ T}$$

ROUND:

We report our result to three significant figures

$$B = 0.262 \text{ T}.$$

DOUBLE-CHECK:

We double-check that the electric force is equal to the magnetic force. The electric force is

$$F_E = eE = (1.602 \cdot 10^{-19} \text{ C})(4.30 \cdot 10^5 \text{ V/m}) = 6.89 \cdot 10^{-14} \text{ N}.$$

Before we calculate the magnetic force, we check that the velocity is reasonable. The velocity is

$$v = \sqrt{\frac{2eV}{m}} = \sqrt{\frac{2(1.602 \cdot 10^{-19} \text{ C})(14.0 \cdot 10^3 \text{ V})}{1.67 \cdot 10^{-27} \text{ kg}}} = 1.63 \cdot 10^6 \text{ m/s}.$$

This speed is 0.55% of the speed of light; so the velocity seems not totally impossible. The magnetic force is

$$F_B = evB = (1.602 \cdot 10^{-19} \text{ C})(1.63 \cdot 10^6 \text{ m/s})(0.262 \text{ T}) = 6.84 \cdot 10^{-14} \text{ N}$$

which agrees with the value of the electric force within round-off errors. Thus, our results seem reasonable.

Solved Problem 27.3: Torque on a loop

A rectangular loop with height $h = 6.50$ cm and width $w = 4.50$ cm is in a uniform magnetic field $B = 0.250$ T, which points in the negative y direction, as shown Figure 27.26.

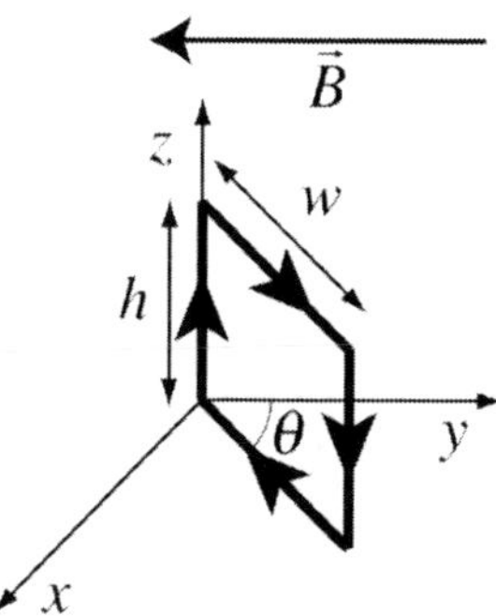

Figure 27.26: A loop carrying a current in a magnetic field.

The loop makes and angle $\theta = 33.0°$ with the y-axis as shown in Figure 27.26. The loop carries a current of $i = 9.00$ A in the direction indicated by the arrows.

Question:
What is the magnitude of the torque on the loop around the z-axis?

Answer:

THINK:

The torque on the loop is equal to the vector cross product of the magnetic dipole moment and the magnetic field. The magnetic dipole moment is perpendicular to the plane of the loop with the direction given by Right Hand Rule 2.

SKETCH:

A sketch of the loop looking down on the $x-y$ axis is shown in Figure 27.27.

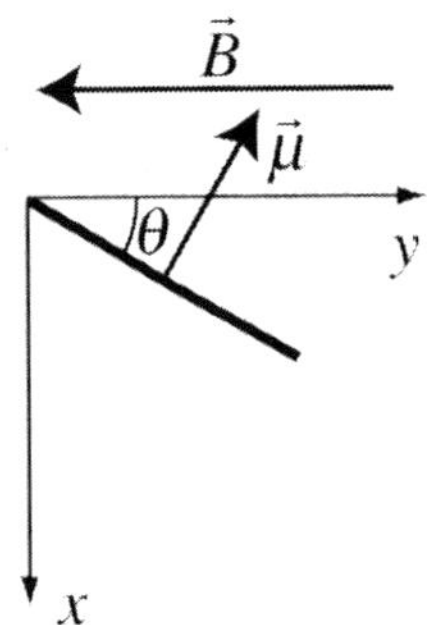

Figure 27.27: The rectangular loop looking down on the *x*-*y* plane. The magnetic moment is perpendicular to the plane of the loop with a direction determined by Right Hand Rule 2.

RESEARCH:

The magnitude of the magnetic dipole moment of the loop is

$$\mu = Nia - iwh . \tag{27.38}$$

The magnitude of the torque on the loop is

$$\tau = \mu B \sin\theta_{\mu B} \tag{27.39}$$

where $\theta_{\mu B}$ is the angle between the magnetic dipole moment and the magnetic field. From Figure 27.27 we can see that

$$\theta_{\mu B} = \theta + 90° . \tag{27.40}$$

SIMPLIFY:

We can combine (27.38), (27.39), and (27.40) to obtain

Solved Problem

$$\tau = iwhB\sin(\theta + 90°). \quad (27.41)$$

CALCULATE:

Putting in our numerical values, we get

$$\tau = (9.00\ \text{A})(4.50 \cdot 10^{-2}\ \text{m})(6.50 \cdot 10^{-2}\ \text{m})(0.250\ \text{T})\sin(33.0° + 90°)$$
$$\tau = 0.0055195\ \text{N} \cdot \text{m}$$

ROUND:

We report of result to three significant figures

$$\tau = 5.52 \cdot 10^{-3}\ \text{N} \cdot \text{m}.$$

DOUBLE-CHECK:

The magnitude of the force on each of the vertical wires is

$$F = ihB = (9.00\ \text{A})(6.50 \cdot 10^{-2}\ \text{m})(0.250\ \text{T}) = 0.146\ \text{N}.$$

The torque is then the force on the vertical wire that is not along the z axis times the moment arm times the sine of the angle between the force and the moment arm

$$\tau = Fw\sin(33.0° + 90°) = 5.52 \cdot 10^{-3}\ \text{N} \cdot \text{m}.$$

Thus, our result is the same.

Chapter 28. Magnetic Fields of Moving Charges

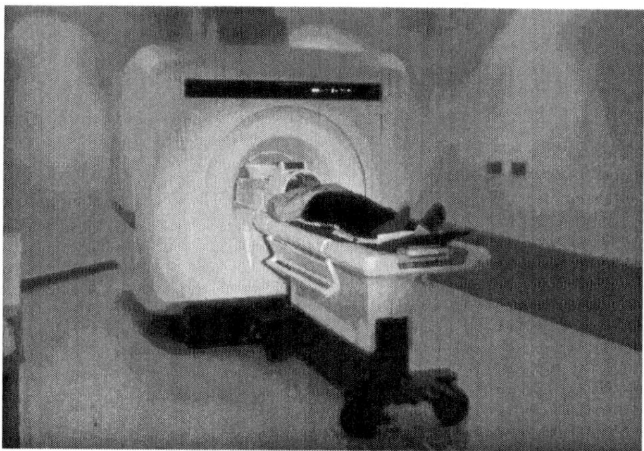

Figure 28.1: A patient receives a magnetic resonance imaging scan.

What we will learn

In the previous chapter we observed that magnetic fields can change the trajectory of moving charges. In the present chapter we will see that moving charged particles create magnetic fields. In particular, currents flowing in wires produce magnetic fields. Various distributions of currents can produce a variety of magnetic fields. For example, a solenoid magnet can produce a large volume of constant magnetic field. We will use Ampere's Law to calculate the magnetic field from the current. We will also discuss applications of magnets, which include medical diagnostics such as in Figure 28.1.

- Charge current creates magnetic fields.

- The magnetic field created by current flowing in a long straight wire varies inversely with the distance from the wire.
- Two parallel wires carrying current in the same direction attract each other. Two parallel wires carrying current in the opposite direction repel each other.
- The torque on a current-carrying loop in a magnetic field can be described in terms of a magnetic dipole moment of the loop and the magnetic field.
- Ampere's Law allows us to calculate the magnetic field caused by certain current configurations having symmetry, much as Gauss's Law was useful in calculating electric fields in situations having symmetry.
- The magnetic field inside a long straight wire varies linearly with the distance from the center of the wire.
- A solenoid magnet can be used to produce a constant magnetic field with a large volume.
- Certain atoms can be thought of as small magnets created by motion of electrons in the atom.
- The interaction of the magnetic dipole moment of protons and molecules with external magnetic fields and time-varying electric fields can be used to produce images of the human body.
- Superconducting magnets can be used to produce very high magnetic fields.

28.1. Fields and Currents

Now we want to address the problem of calculating magnetic fields generated by moving charges. To calculate the electric field in terms of the electric charge we used the form (see chapter 22):

$$dE = \frac{1}{4\pi\varepsilon_0}\frac{|dq|}{r^2} \tag{28.1}$$

where dq is a charge element. The electric field points in radial direction (inward towards or outward from the electric charge, depending on the sign of the charge), so that we can write

$$d\vec{E} = \frac{1}{4\pi\varepsilon_0}\frac{dq}{r^3}\vec{r} = \frac{1}{4\pi\varepsilon_0}\frac{dq}{r^2}\hat{r}\,. \tag{28.2}$$

The situation for the magnetic field is slightly more complicated. This complication arises largely because a current element $id\vec{s}$ producing the magnetic field has a direction, as a opposed to a non-directional scalar charge producing the electric field. As a result of a long series of experiments conducted in the early 19th century by the French scientists Jean-Baptiste Biot (1774-1862) and Felix Savart (1791-1841) established that we can write the magnetic field produced by a current element $id\vec{s}$ as

$$d\vec{B} = \frac{\mu_0}{4\pi}\frac{id\vec{s}\times\vec{r}}{r^3} = \frac{\mu_0}{4\pi}\frac{id\vec{s}\times\hat{r}}{r^2}. \qquad (28.3)$$

Figure 28.2 depicts the elements that appear in this formula, which is called the Biot-Savart Law.

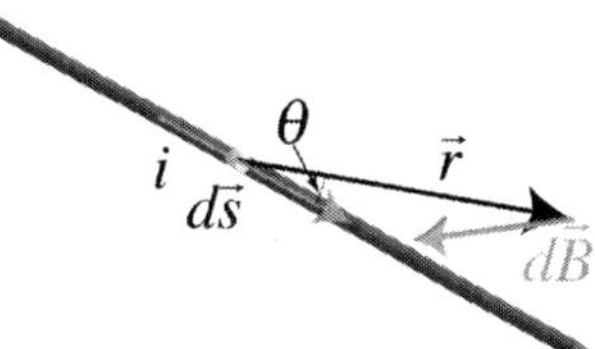

Figure 28.2: Three-dimensional depiction of the terms of the Biot-Savart Law. The differential magnetic field is perpendicular to both the differential current element and the position vector.

μ_0 is the magnetic permeability of free space and has a value of

$$\mu_0 = 4\pi\cdot 10^{-7}\ \frac{\mathrm{Tm}}{\mathrm{A}}. \qquad (28.4)$$

From (28.3) and from Figure 28.2 we see that the direction of the magnetic field produced by the current element is perpendicular to both the radial direction and to the current element $id\vec{s}$. The magnitude of the magnetic field is given by

$$dB = \frac{\mu_0}{4\pi}\frac{ids\sin\theta}{r^2} \qquad (28.5)$$

where θ is the angle between the radial vector and the current element. The direction is given by a variant of Right Hand Rule 1 introduced in chapter 27. To determine the direction of the differential magnetic field using your right hand, point your thumb in the direction of the differential current element, point your index finger in the direction of the radial vector, and your middle finger will point in the direction of the differential magnetic field.

The magnetic field at any point in space is then the sum of the differential magnetic fields, consistent with the superposition principle for magnetic fields, which we addressed in the previous chapter.

Magnetic Field from a Long Straight Wire

For our first application, we will calculate the magnetic field from an infinitely long straight wire. We calculate the magnetic field $d\vec{B}$ at a point P at a distance $r_\perp$ from the wire as illustrated in Figure 28.3.

The magnitude of the field dB at that point due to a current element ids is given by

(28.5) and the direction of the field given by $d\vec{s}\times\vec{r}$, which is out of the page. We will calculate the magnetic field from the right half of the wire and multiply by two to get the magnetic field from the whole wire. Thus, the magnitude of the magnetic field from the whole wire is given by

$$B = 2\int_0^\infty dB = 2\int_0^\infty \frac{\mu_0}{4\pi}\frac{i\,ds\sin\theta}{r^2} = \frac{\mu_0 i}{2\pi}\int_0^\infty \frac{ds\sin\theta}{r^2}. \tag{28.6}$$

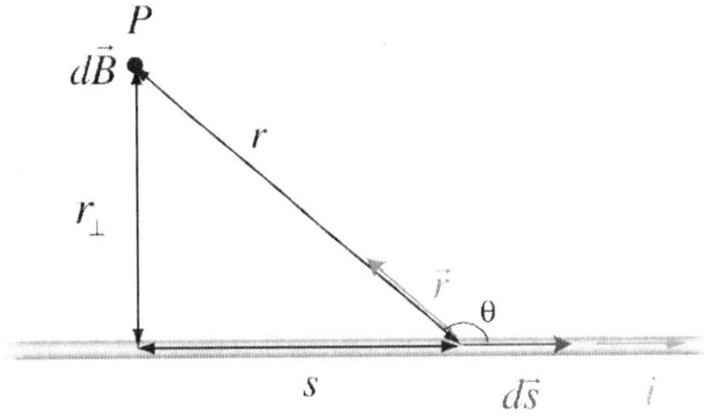

Figure 28.3: Magnetic field from a long straight wire carrying a current.

We can relate r, s, and θ by $r=\sqrt{s^2+r_\perp^2}$ and $\sin\theta = r_\perp/\sqrt{s^2+r_\perp^2}$, where $r_\perp$ is the perpendicular distance from the wire (see Figure 28.3). Substituting we obtain

$$B = \frac{\mu_0 i}{2\pi}\int_0^\infty \frac{r_\perp\,ds}{\left(s^2+r_\perp^2\right)^{3/2}}. \tag{28.7}$$

Carrying out this definite integral we find

$$B = \frac{\mu_0 i}{2\pi}\left[\frac{1}{r_\perp^2}\frac{r_\perp s}{\left(s^2+r_\perp^2\right)^{1/2}}\right]_0^\infty = \frac{\mu_0 i}{2\pi r_\perp}\left(\frac{s}{\left(s^2+r_\perp^2\right)^{1/2}}\right)_{s\to\infty} - 0. \tag{28.8}$$

For $s \gg r_\perp$ the term in the brackets is approximately one. Therefore, our resulting equation for the magnitude of the magnetic field at a perpendicular distance $r_\perp$ from a long straight wire carrying a current i is

$$B(r_\perp) = \frac{\mu_0 i}{2\pi r_\perp}. \tag{28.9}$$

The direction of the magnetic field is given by an application of Right Hand Rule 1 applied to the current element and radius vectors shown in Figure 28.3. We can describe a new right hand rule that can be used to determine the direction of the magnetic field from a current carrying wire, which we call Right Hand Rule 3. If you grab the wire with your right hand such that your thumb points in the direction of the current, your fingers will point in the direction of the magnetic field as shown in Figure 28.4.

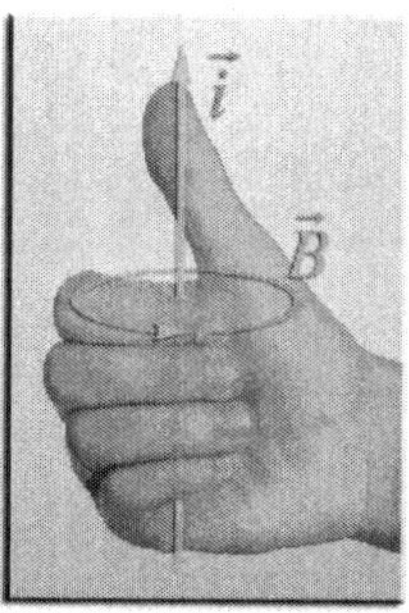

Figure 28.4: Right Hand Rule 3 for the magnetic field from a current flowing in a wire.

Looking down the wire, the magnetic field lines form circles as shown in Figure 28.5.

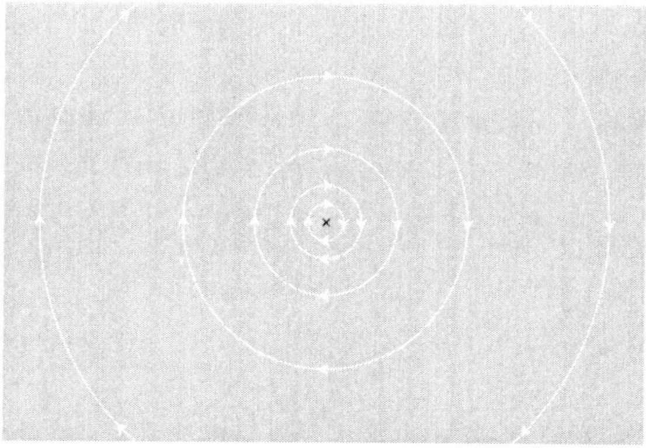

Figure 28.5: Magnetic field lines from a long straight wire, which carries a current perpendicular to the page and points into of the page. The cross signifies the current is into the page.

Self-Test Opportunity: The wire in the figure is carrying a current i in the positive z-direction. What is the direction of the resulting magnetic field at point p_1 ? What is the direction of the resulting magnetic field at point p_2 ?

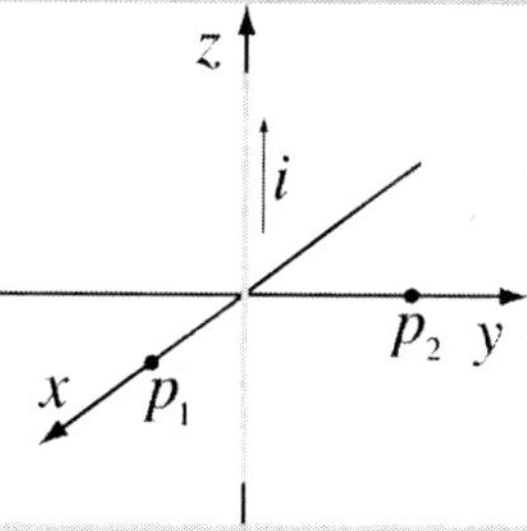

In-class exercise: Assume that a lightning bolt can be represented by a long straight line of current. If 15.0 C of charge passes by in $1.50 \cdot 10^{-3}$ s, what is the magnitude of the magnetic field a distance 26.0 m from the lightning bolt?

a) $7.69 \cdot 10^{-5}$ T
b) $9.22 \cdot 10^{-3}$ T
c) $4.21 \cdot 10^{-2}$ T
d) $1.11 \cdot 10^{-1}$ T
e) $2.22 \cdot 10^{2}$ T

Consider the case in which two parallel wires are carrying current. The two wires will exert a magnetic force on each other because the magnetic field of one wire will exert a force on the moving charges in the second wire. The magnitude of the magnetic field created by a current carrying wire is given by (28.9). This magnetic field is always perpendicular to the wire with a direction given by Right Hand Rule 3 (Figure 28.4).

Let's start with wire one carrying a current i_1 to the right as shown in Figure 28.6*a*). The magnitude of the magnetic field a distance d from wire one is

$$B_1 = \frac{\mu_0 i_1}{2\pi d}. \tag{28.10}$$

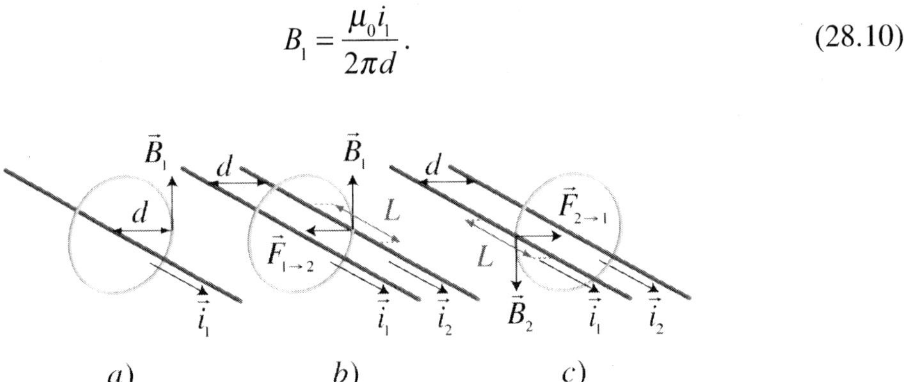

Figure 28.6: a) Magnetic field line from one current carrying wire; b) The magnetic field created by the current in wire one exerting a force on current carrying wire two; c) The magnetic field created by the current in wire 2 creating a force on current carrying wire one.

The direction of $\vec{B}_1$ is given by Right Hand Rule 3 and is shown for a particular point in Figure 28.6*a*).

Now consider wire two carrying a current i_2 in the same direction as i_1 placed a distance d from wire one as shown in Figure 28.6*b*). The magnetic field due to wire one will exert a magnetic force on the moving charges in the current flowing in wire two. In chapter 27, we found that the magnetic force on a current carrying wire is given by

$$\vec{F} = i\vec{L} \times \vec{B}. \tag{28.11}$$

The magnitude of the magnetic force is then

$$F = iLB\sin\theta = i_2 LB_1 \tag{28.12}$$

on a length L of wire two because $\vec{B}_1$ is perpendicular to wire two and thus $\theta = 90^0$. Inserting (28.10) for B_1 we find the magnitude of the force exerted by wire one on wire two

$$F_{1\to2} = i_2 L\left(\frac{\mu_0 i_1}{2\pi d}\right) = \frac{\mu_0 i_1 i_2 L}{2\pi d}. \tag{28.13}$$

Right Hand Rule 1 tells us that $\vec{F}_{1\to2}$ points toward wire one and is perpendicular to both wires. An analogous calculation allows us to deduce that the force of wire two on a length L of wire one has the same magnitude and opposite direction, $\vec{F}_{2\to1} = -\vec{F}_{1\to2}$. This result is shown in Figure 28.6*c*).

Example

Example 28.1: Force on a loop

A long straight wire is carrying a current of $i_1 = 5.00\text{ A}$ to the right as shown in Figure 28.7. A square loop with sides of length 0.250 m is placed a distance 0.100 m from the wire. The square loop carries a counterclockwise current of $i_2 = 2.20\text{ A}$.

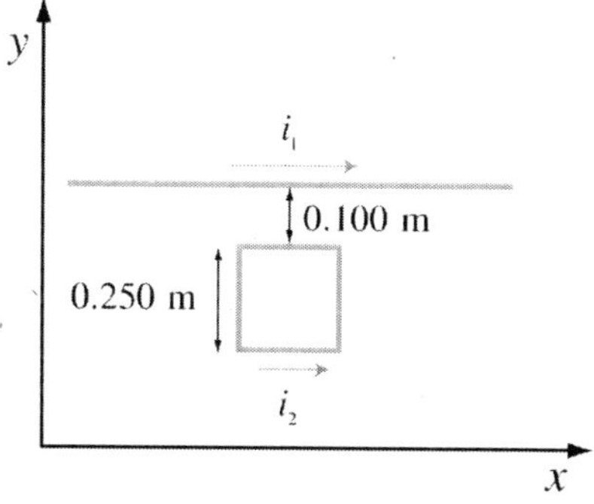

Figure 28.7: A current carrying wire and a current-carrying loop.

Question:

What is the net force on the square loop?

Answer:

The force on the square loop is due to the magnetic field created by the current flowing in the straight wire. Right Hand Rule 3 tells us that the magnetic field from the current flowing in the straight wire is into the page in the region of the loop. (28.11) tells us that the resulting force on the vertical left part of the loop is to the right and the force on the vertical right part of the loop is to the left. These two forces are equal in magnitude and

Example

opposite in direction so they sum to zero.

The force on the upper horizontal part of the loop will be downward and the magnitude is given by

$$F_{down} = \frac{\mu_0 i_1 i_2 L}{2\pi d} = \frac{\mu_0 i_1 i_2 L}{2\pi(0.100 \text{ m})}.$$

The force on the lower horizontal part of the loop will be upward and the magnitude is given by

$$F_{up} = \frac{\mu_0 i_1 i_2 L}{2\pi(0.100 \text{ m} + 0.250 \text{ m})}$$

Taking upward as the positive y direction we can write the net force as

$$\vec{F} = (F_{up} - F_{down})\hat{y} = \frac{(4\pi \cdot 10^{-7} \text{ T}\cdot\text{m/A})(5.00 \text{ A})(2.20 \text{ A})(0.250 \text{ m})}{2\pi}\left(\frac{1}{0.350 \text{ m}} - \frac{1}{0.100 \text{ m}}\right)\hat{y}$$

which results in

$$\vec{F} = -3.93 \cdot 10^{-6} \text{ N}\hat{y}.$$

Magnetic Field Due to a Wire Loop

Now we calculate the magnetic field at the center of a circular loop of wire carrying current i. A cross section of a circular loop with radius R carrying a current i is shown in Figure 28.8.

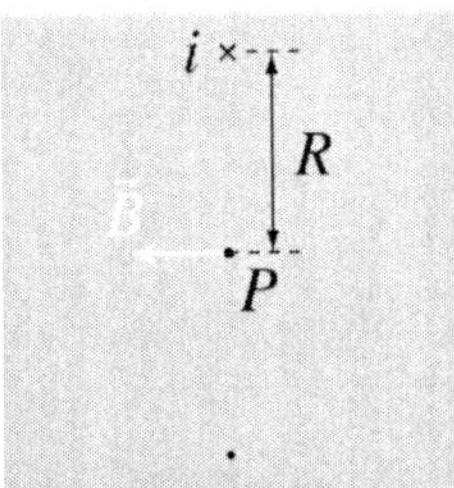

Figure 28.8: A circular loop with radius *R* carrying a current *i*. The cross on the conductor signifies that the current at the top of the loop is into the page and the dot on the conductor signifies that the current at the bottom of the loop is out of the page. Point *P* is located at the center of the loop.

Starting with (28.5) and applying it to this case, we can see that $r = R$ and $\theta = 90°$ for every current element along the loop. For the magnitude of the magnetic field from each current element we get

$$dB = \frac{\mu_0}{4\pi}\frac{ids\sin 90°}{R^2} = \frac{\mu_0}{4\pi}\frac{ids}{R^2}. \quad (28.14)$$

Going around the loop, we can relate the angle ϕ to the current element by $ds = Rd\phi$ allowing us to calculate the magnetic field at the center of the loop to be

$$B = \int dB = \int_0^{2\pi} \frac{\mu_0}{4\pi} \frac{iRd\phi}{R^2} = \frac{\mu_0 i}{2R}. \tag{28.15}$$

Keep in mind that this calculation only gives us information on the value of the magnetic field at the center of the loop, whose magnitude is $B(r=0) = \frac{1}{2}\mu_0 i / R$. To determine the direction of the magnetic field, we again apply a variant of Right Hand Rule 1. Using our right hand, we point our thumb in the direction of the current element (into the page for the top conductor marked with a cross), we point our index finger in the direction of the radial vector from the current element (down), and our middle finger will then point to the left.

Using Right Hand Rule 3 (Figure 28.4), we deduce that the current shown in Figure 28.8 produces a magnetic field $\vec{B}$, which is to the left, which agrees with our analysis using a variant of Right Hand Rule 1.

Now we calculate the magnetic field of the loop not just at the center, but also along the axis of the loop as illustrated in Figure 28.9.

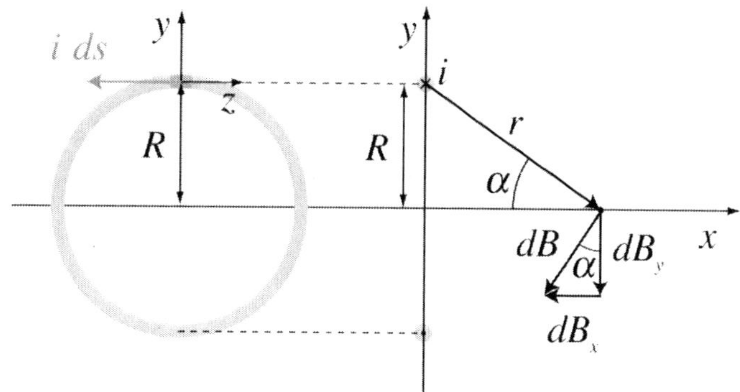

Figure 28.9: Geometry for calculating the magnetic field along the axis of a current-carrying loop.

We place the loop such that the axis of the loop lies along the x axis and the center of the loop is located at $x = 0$, $y = 0$, and $z = 0$. We define the radius $\vec{r}$ from any point along the x axis to a current element $i d\vec{s}$ along the loop. This radius vector will always be perpendicular to any differential current element along the loop. Therefore, we can employ (28.5) with $\theta = 90°$ and obtain an expression the differential magnetic field at any point along the x axis

$$dB = \frac{\mu_0}{4\pi} \frac{ids\sin(90°)}{r^2} = \frac{\mu_0}{4\pi} \frac{ids}{r^2}. \tag{28.16}$$

A variant of Right Hand Rule 1 gives the direction of the differential magnetic field. To determine the direction of the magnetic field using your right hand, point your thumb in the direction of the differential current element (negative z direction). Then point your index finger in the direction of the radial vector (positive x direction and negative y direction). The direction of the differential magnetic field will be given by your middle finger (negative x direction and negative y direction). The resulting differential magnetic field is shown in Figure 28.9. To obtain the magnetic field, we then need to integrate over the differential current element. From the symmetry of the problem, we can see that the y component of the differential magnetic field, dB_y, will integrate to zero. The x component of the differential magnetic field, dB_x, is given by

$$dB_x = dB\sin\alpha = \frac{\mu_0}{4\pi}\frac{ids}{r^2}\sin\alpha \tag{28.17}$$

where α is the angle between $\vec{r}$ and the x axis. We can express the magnitude of $\vec{r}$ in terms of x and R as

$$r = \sqrt{x^2 + R^2}\,. \tag{28.18}$$

We can express $\sin\alpha$ in terms of x and the radius of the loop R

$$\sin\alpha = \frac{R}{\sqrt{x^2 + R^2}}\,. \tag{28.19}$$

We can then rewrite (28.17) as

$$dB_x = \frac{\mu_0}{4\pi}\frac{ids}{x^2 + R^2}\frac{R}{\sqrt{x^2 + R^2}} = \frac{\mu_0 ids}{4\pi}\frac{R}{\left(x^2 + R^2\right)^{3/2}}\,. \tag{28.20}$$

Going around the loop, we can relate the angle ϕ to the current element by $ds = Rd\phi$ allowing us to calculate the magnetic field along the axis of the loop

$$B_x = \int dB_x = \int_0^{2\pi}\frac{\mu_0 iRd\phi}{4\pi}\frac{R}{\left(x^2 + R^2\right)^{3/2}} = \frac{\mu_0 i2\pi}{4\pi}\frac{R^2}{\left(x^2 + R^2\right)^{3/2}} = \frac{\mu_0 i}{2}\frac{R^2}{\left(x^2 + R^2\right)^{3/2}}. \tag{28.21}$$

Our analysis of the direction of the magnetic field after (28.16) tells us that the magnetic field along the axis of the loop is in the negative x direction as shown in Figure 28.9. We can also apply Right Hand Rule 3 to obtain the direction of the magnetic field. We wrap the fingers of our right hand around the loop in the direction of the current, and our thumb points in the direction of the magnetic field. Again, we find that the direction of the magnetic field along the axis of the loop is in the negative x direction.

Self-Test Opportunity: Show that the expression for the magnetic field along the axis of a current carrying loop (28.21) reduces to the expression for the magnetic field at the center of a current carrying loop (28.15).

Using more advanced techniques and the aid of computers, one can also calculate the magnetic field produced by a current carrying loop at other points in space. These magnetic field lines from a wire loop are shown in Figure 28.10. The value for the magnetic field given in (28.15) is only valid at the center point of Figure 28.10. The value for the magnetic field given in (28.21) is valid only along the axis of the loop.

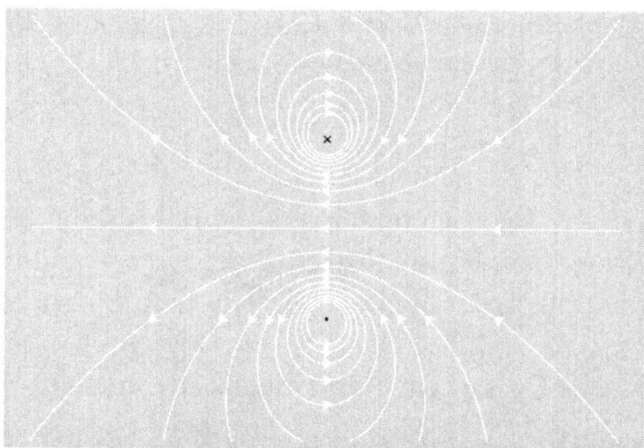

Figure 28.10: Magnetic field lines from a single loop of wire carrying a current looking edge-on at the loop. The wire with an x is carrying current directed into the page and the wire with a dot is carrying current directed out of the page.

Solved Problem

Solved Problem 28.1: Field from loop and wire

A single-coil loop with radius $r = 8.30$ mm is formed in the middle of a long, insulated straight wire carrying a current $i = 26.5$ mA as shown in Figure 28.11.

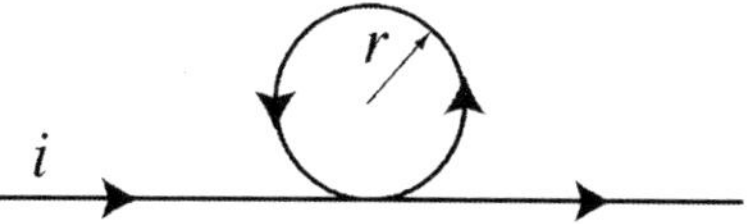

Figure 28.11: A single-coil loop with radius *r* formed in a long insulated wire carrying a current *i*.

Question:

What is the magnitude of the magnetic field at the center of the loop?

Answer:

THINK:

The magnetic field at the center of the loop will be equal to the vector sum of magnetic field from the long wire and the magnetic field from the loop.

SKETCH:

Solved Problem

The magnetic field from the wire, $\vec{B}_{\text{wire}}$, and the magnetic field from the loop, $\vec{B}_{\text{loop}}$, are shown in Figure 28.12

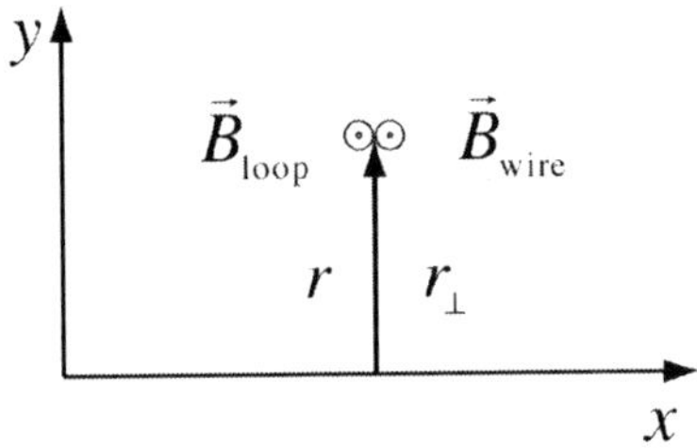

Figure 28.12: The magnetic field from the wire and the magnetic field from the loop. The two magnetic fields are shown displaced from each other for clarity.

RESEARCH:

Using Right Hand Rule 3, we find that both magnetic fields point out of the page at the center of the loop as illustrated in Figure 28.12. Thus, we can add the magnitudes of the magnetic field produced by the wire and the magnetic field produced by the loop.

The magnetic field produced by the wire has a magnitude given by (28.9)

$$B_{\text{wire}} = \frac{\mu_0 i}{2\pi r} \tag{28.22}$$

where r is the perpendicular distance from the wire, which coincides with the center of the loop. The magnitude of the magnetic field produced by the loop at the center of the loop is given by (28.15)

$$B_{\text{loop}} = \frac{\mu_0 i}{2r}. \tag{28.23}$$

SIMPLIFY:

We can add the magnitudes of the two magnetic fields to get

$$B = B_{\text{wire}} + B_{\text{loop}} = \frac{\mu_0 i}{2\pi r} + \frac{\mu_0 i}{2r} = \frac{\mu_0 i}{2r}\left(\frac{1}{\pi}+1\right). \tag{28.24}$$

CALCULATE:

Putting in our numerical values, we get

$$B = \frac{\mu_0 i}{2r}\left(\frac{1}{\pi}+1\right) = \frac{\left(4\pi \cdot 10^{-7}\ \text{T}\cdot\text{m/A}\right)\left(26.5\cdot 10^{-3}\ \text{A}\right)}{2\left(8.30\cdot 10^{-3}\ \text{m}\right)}\left(\frac{1}{\pi}+1\right) = 2.64463\cdot 10^{-6}\ \text{T}$$

ROUND:

We report our result to three significant figures and note the direction to find

Solved Problem

$$\vec{B} = 2.64 \cdot 10^{-6} \text{ T out of the page.}$$

DOUBLE-CHECK:

To double-check our result, we calculate the magnitudes of the magnetic fields from the wire and the loop separately. The magnetic field from the wire is

$$B_{\text{wire}} = \frac{\mu_0 i}{2\pi r} = \frac{\left(4\pi \cdot 10^{-7} \text{ T}\cdot\text{m/A}\right)\left(26.5 \cdot 10^{-3} \text{ A}\right)}{2\pi\left(8.30 \cdot 10^{-3} \text{ m}\right)} = 6.39 \cdot 10^{-7} \text{ T}.$$

The magnetic field from the loop is

$$B_{\text{loop}} = \frac{\mu_0 i}{2r} = \frac{\left(4\pi \cdot 10^{-7} \text{ T}\cdot\text{m/A}\right)\left(26.5 \cdot 10^{-3} \text{ A}\right)}{2\left(8.30 \cdot 10^{-3} \text{ m}\right)} = 2.01 \cdot 10^{-6} \text{ T}.$$

The sum of the two magnetic fields add to our result

$$6.39 \cdot 10^{-7} \text{ T} + 2.01 \cdot 10^{-6} \text{ T} = 2.64 \cdot 10^{-6} \text{ T}.$$

28.2. Magnetic Dipole Moment

We can describe the coil in the previous section with one parameter consisting of information about the coil that tells you how the coil acts in a magnetic field. We define the magnitude of the magnetic dipole moment $\vec{\mu}$ of the coil above to be

$$\mu = NiA \tag{28.25}$$

where N is the number of coils, i is the current through the coils, and A is the area of the coils. The direction of the dipole moment, $\vec{\mu}$, is given by Right Hand Rule 2 and points in the direction of the unit normal vector $\hat{n}$. In chapter 27, we showed that the torque on a current carrying loop is given by

$$\tau = N\tau_1 = NiAB\sin\theta. \tag{28.26}$$

Using (28.25) we can rewrite (28.26) as

$$\tau = \left(NiA\right)B\sin\theta = \mu B\sin\theta. \tag{28.27}$$

We can generalize the expression for the torque on a magnetic dipole as

$$\vec{\tau} = \vec{\mu} \times \vec{B}. \tag{28.28}$$

A magnetic dipole has a potential energy in an external magnetic field. If the magnetic dipole is aligned with the magnetic field, it is in its minimum potential energy condition. If the magnetic dipole oriented in a direction opposite to the external field, the dipole is in its maximum potential energy condition. From Chapter 10 we know that the work done by a torque is

$$W = \int_{\theta_0}^{\theta} \tau(\theta')d\theta'. \tag{28.29}$$

Using (28.27) and setting $\theta_0 = 90^0$ we see that the magnetic potential energy U of a magnetic dipole in an external magnetic field $\vec{B}$ can be written as

$$U = -\vec{\mu} \bullet \vec{B} = -\mu B \cos\theta \tag{28.30}$$

where θ is the angle between the magnetic dipole moment and the external magnetic field.

This potential energy of orientation can be applied to many diverse physical situations concerning magnetic dipoles in external magnetic fields. So far, the only magnetic dipoles we have only discussed are current carrying loops. However, other types of magnetic dipoles exist such as bar magnets and the Earth. In addition, elementary particles such as protons also have intrinsic magnetic dipole moments.

Self-Test Opportunity: What is the maximum magnetic potential energy difference between two orientations of a loop with area $0.100\ \text{m}^2$ carrying a current $2.00\ \text{A}$ in a constant magnetic field of $0.500\ \text{T}$?

28.3. Ampere's Law

Recall that we can calculate the electric field resulting from any distribution of electric charge using (28.2), and if the charge distribution is complicated, we are faced with a difficult integral. However, if the charge distribution has cylindrical, spherical, or planar symmetry, we could apply Gauss' Law and obtain the electric field in an elegant manner.

In a similar way, we can calculate the magnetic field from an arbitrary distribution of current elements using (28.3). However, we again may be faced with a difficult integral. In cases where the distribution of current elements has cylindrical symmetry and in other special situations such as the ideal solenoid, we can apply Ampere's Law to calculate the magnetic field from a distribution of current elements with much less effort than using a direct integration. Ampere's Law is

$$\oint \vec{B} \bullet d\vec{s} = \mu_0 i_{enc}. \tag{28.31}$$

The symbol $\oint$ means that the integrand $\vec{B}\bullet d\vec{s}$ should be integrated over a closed loop called an Amperian loop. This loop is a mathematical loop that is chosen so that the integral in (28.31) is not difficult. (This is similar to the procedure followed in Gauss's Law problems.) The total current enclosed in this loop is i_{enc}.

As an example of Ampere's Law, consider the five currents shown in Figure 28.13. The currents are perpendicular to the plane shown in this figure. We can draw an Amperian loop represented by the red line. This loop encloses currents i_1, i_2, and i_3 and excludes i_4 and i_5.

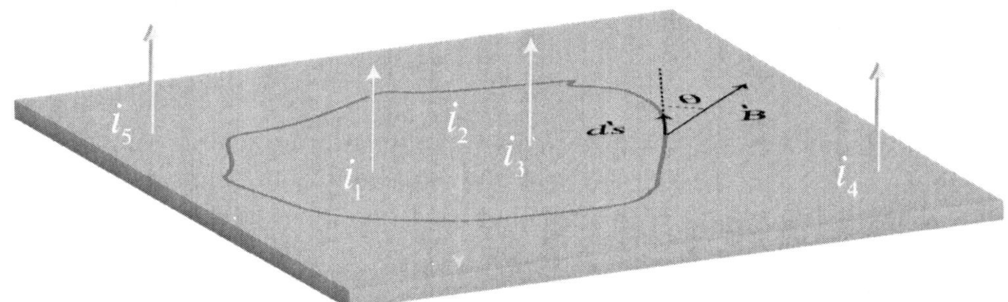

Figure 28.13: Five currents and an Amperian loop.

Thus, the magnetic field resulting from these three currents is given by

$$\oint \vec{B}\bullet d\vec{s} = \oint B\cos\theta ds = \mu_0\left(i_1 - i_2 + i_3\right). \tag{28.32}$$

The integration over the Amperian loop can be done in either direction. In Figure 28.13, a direction of integration is shown along with the resulting magnetic field. The sign of the contributing currents can be determined using a right hand rule as follows. If you point your fingers along the direction of integration and point your palm at the current, your thumb will indicate the positive current direction. Two of the three currents in this example are positive one of the currents is negative.

The three currents on the right hand side of (28.32) are easy to add up but the integral on the left hand side cannot be done easily. However, there are certain cases that we can study that have symmetries that can be exploited to carry out the integral.

Magnetic Field Inside a Long Straight Wire

In Figure 28.14, we show a current i flowing out of the page in a wire with a circular cross section of radius R.

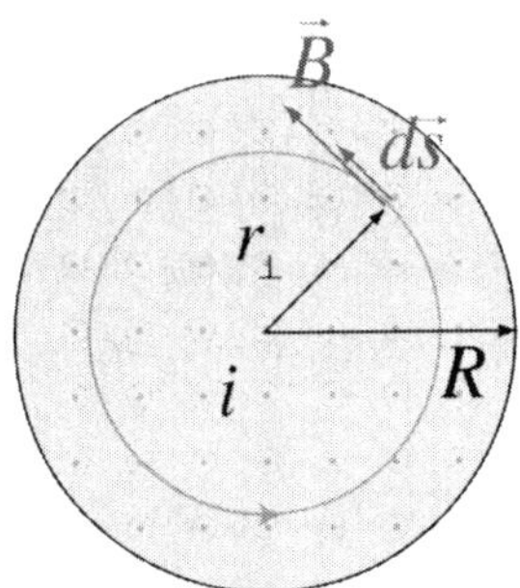

Figure 28.14: Using Ampere's Law to find the magnetic field produced inside a long straight wire.

This current is uniformly distributed over the cross sectional area of the wire. To find the magnetic field, we use an Amperian loop with radius $r_\perp$ represented by the red circle.

$\vec{B}$ is tangential to this Amperian loop; if $\vec{B}$ had an outward (or inward) component, by symmetry it would have an outward (or inward) component at all points around the loop and the corresponding magnetic field line could never be closed. Thus, we can write the left side of Ampere's Law as

$$\oint \vec{B} \bullet d\vec{s} = B\oint d\vec{s} = B2\pi r_\perp \,. \qquad (28.3\text{-})$$

The enclosed current can be calculated from the ratio of the area of the Amperian loop to the cross sectional area of the wire

$$i_{enc} = i\frac{A_{loop}}{A_{wire}} = i\frac{\pi r_\perp^2}{\pi R^2} \,. \qquad (28.34)$$

Thus, we can write

$$2\pi B r_\perp = \mu_0 i \frac{\pi r_\perp^2}{\pi R^2} \qquad (28.35)$$

or

$$B = \left(\frac{\mu_0 i}{2\pi R^2}\right) r_\perp \,. \qquad (28.36)$$

Now that we have obtained expressions for the magnetic field outside and inside the wire, equations (28.9) and (28.36), we can compare them to each other. First, we can insert $r_\perp = R$ into both expressions, and we see that we find the identical result of $B(R) = \mu_0 i / (2\pi R)$ in both cases for the magnetic field strength at the surface of the wire.

This result implies that both solutions merge into the same solution at the wire surface. Inside the wire, we find that the magnetic field strength rises linearly with $r_\perp$ up to the value of $B(R) = \mu_0 i/(2\pi R)$, and from there it falls off with the inverse of $r_\perp$.

In Figure 28.15, this dependence is shown in the lower part. In the upper part we show the cross section through the wire (golden area), the magnetic field lines (black circles, spaced to indicated the strength of the magnetic field), and the magnetic field vector at selected points in space (red arrows).

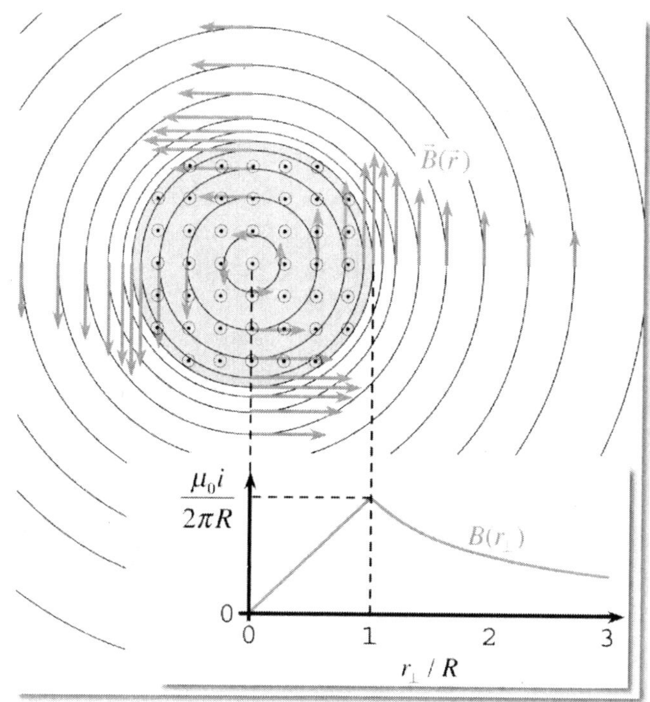

Figure 28.15: Radial dependence of the magnetic field strength for a wire with current flowing out of the page.

28.4. Magnetic Fields of Solenoids and Toroids

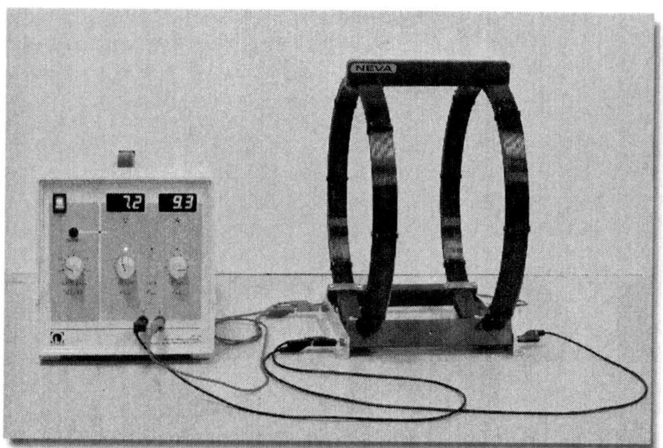

Figure 28.16: A Helmholtz coil used to generate a nearly constant magnetic field in the interior.

Current flowing through a single loop of wire produces a magnetic field that is not uniform, as illustrated in Figure 28.10. Real-world applications often require a uniform magnetic field, however. A common first step toward a uniform magnetic field is the Helmholtz coil. A Helmholtz coil consists of two sets of coaxial wire loops. Each set of coaxial loops consists of multiple turns of a single loop and the set therefore acts magnetically like a single loop. A typical Helmholtz coil used in physics labs is shown in Figure 28.16.

The magnetic field lines from a Helmholtz coil are shown in Figure 28.17. (On the cover of this book, these field lines are overlaid on the picture of the Helmholtz coil). You can see that the region of uniform field (characterized by horizontal parallel segments of the field lines) in the center between the coils is now present, in contrast to the single loop geometry of Figure 28.10. Again, these field lines were calculated with the aid of computers. While we cannot expect to calculate magnetic fields and field lines with the tools presented so far, these field line figures still provide us with an excellent qualitative understanding of the concepts of magnetic field generation.

Figure 28.17: Magnetic field lines for a Helmholtz coil. Each of the wires with an x is carrying current directed into the page and each of the wires with a dot is carrying current directed out of the page.

Carrying the idea of multiple loops one step farther, the magnetic field lines from four loops are shown in Figure 28.18. The region of constant field in the center of the loops is expanded, but near the coils and near the two end coils, the field is not uniform.

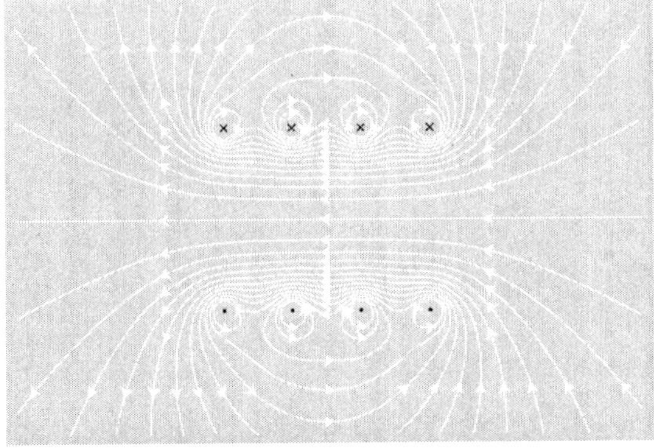

Figure 28.18: Magnetic field lines resulting from four coils. Each of the wires with an x is carrying current directed into the page and each of the wires with a dot is carrying current directed out of the page.

To create a uniform magnetic field, a solenoid consisting of many loops wound close together is used. The magnetic field lines from a solenoid with 600 turns, or loops, are shown in Figure 28.19. You can see from this figure that the magnetic field lines of this solenoid are very close together on the inside of the solenoid, and very far apart on the outside. Compared to the Helmholtz coil (Figure 28.17) the solenoid field is uniform inside the solenoid coil. Because the spacing of the field lines is a measure of the strength of the magnetic field, you can see that the magnetic field is much stronger inside the solenoid than outside.

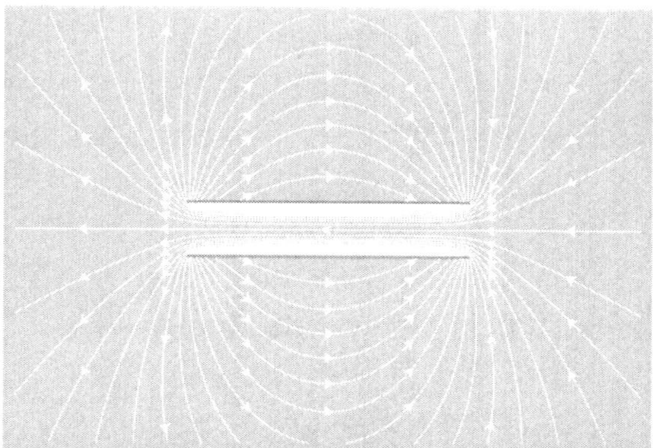

Figure 28.19: Magnetic field lines for a solenoid with 600 turns. The current along the top of the solenoid is directed into the page and the current along the bottom of the solenoid is directed out of the page.

An *ideal* solenoid has a magnetic field of zero outside and a uniform constant finite value of B inside. To calculate the magnetic field inside an ideal solenoid, we can apply Ampere's Law (28.31) to a section of a solenoid far from the ends of the solenoid as shown in Figure 28.20.

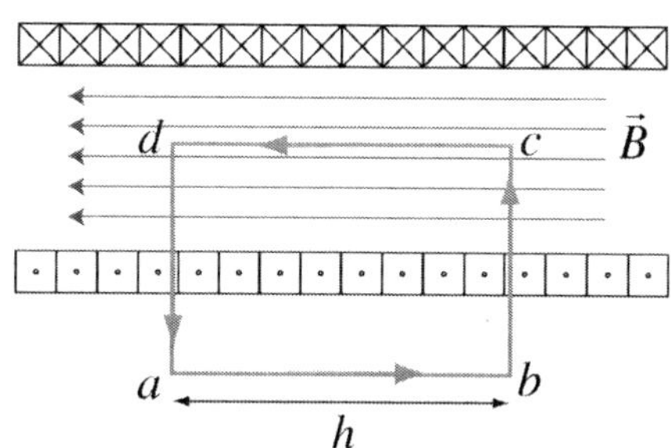

Figure 28.20: Amperian loop applied to calculate the magnetic field of an ideal solenoid.

To apply Ampere's law, we first choose an Amperian loop over which to carry out the integral. A judicious choice, shown by the red lines in Figure 28.20, encloses some current and exploits the symmetry of the solenoid. This choice also simplifies the calculation of the integral

$$\oint \vec{B} \bullet d\vec{s} = \int_a^b \vec{B} \bullet d\vec{s} + \int_b^c \vec{B} \bullet d\vec{s} + \int_c^d \vec{B} \bullet d\vec{s} + \int_d^a \vec{B} \bullet d\vec{s} \,. \tag{28.37}$$

The value of the third integral, between the points c and d in the interior of the solenoid, is Bh. The values of the second and fourth integrals are zero because the magnetic field is perpendicular to the direction of integration. The first integral, between the points a and b in the exterior of the ideal solenoid, is zero because the magnetic field outside of an ideal solenoid is zero. Thus the value of the full integral is Bh.

The enclosed current is the current in the enclosed turns of the solenoid. The current is the same in each turn because the turns are made from one wire and the same current flows through each turn. Thus, the enclosed current is just the number of turns times the current

$$i_{enc} = nhi \tag{28.38}$$

where n is the number of turns per unit length. Therefore, Ampere's Law tells us that

$$Bh = \mu_0 nhi. \tag{28.39}$$

Thus, we find that the magnetic field inside an ideal solenoid is

$$B = \mu_0 in. \tag{28.40}$$

This expression is only valid away from the ends of the solenoid. Note that there is no dependence on position inside the solenoid, so that an ideal solenoid creates a constant and uniform magnetic field inside the solenoid and no field outside the solenoid. A real-world solenoid, like the one shown in Figure 28.19, has fringe fields near the ends of the solenoid and near the coils, but still can produce high quality magnetic fields.

Example

Example 28.2: Solenoid

The solenoid magnet of the STAR detector (Figure 27.1) has a field of 0.50 T when carrying a current of 400 A. The solenoid is 8.0 m long.

Question:

What is the number of turns for the coils of the solenoid assuming a perfect solenoid?

Answer:

We can use (28.40) to calculate the magnetic field of a perfect solenoid

$$B = \mu_0 in.$$

The number of turns per unit length is given by

$$n = \frac{N}{L}$$

where N is the number of turns and L is the length of the solenoid. Substituting we get

$$B = \mu_0 i \frac{N}{L}.$$

Solving for the number of turns we obtain

$$N = \frac{BL}{\mu_0 i} = \frac{(0.50 \text{ T})(8.0 \text{ m})}{\left(4\pi \cdot 10^{-7} \dfrac{\text{Tm}}{\text{A}}\right)(400 \text{ A})} = 8000 \text{ turns}$$

In-class exercise: Two long solenoids have the same length, but solenoid 1 has 15 times the number of turns, 1/9 the radius, and 7 times the current of solenoid 2. Calculate the ratio of the magnetic field inside solenoid 1 to the magnetic field inside solenoid 2.

a) 105
b) 123
c) 144
d) 168
e) 197

One can create a toroidal magnet by "bending" a solenoid magnet such that the two ends meet as illustrated in Figure 28.21. The wire is wound around the doughnut shape forming a series of loops, each with the same current flowing through it.

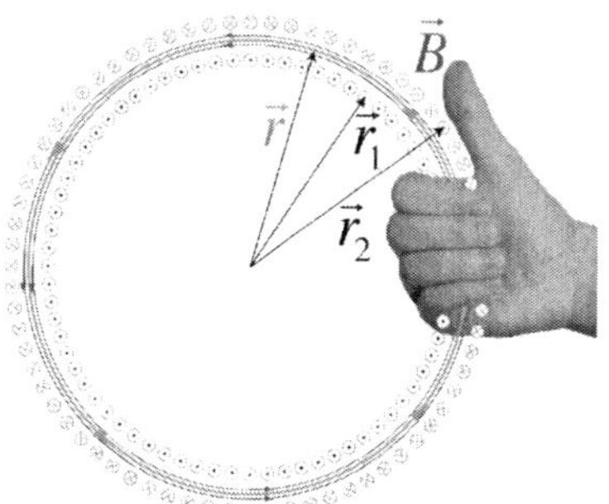

Figure 28.21: Toroidal magnet with Amperian loop (red) in the form of a circle with radius r. Right Hand Rule 4 states that if you place the fingers of the right hand in the direction of the current flow, the thumb will show the direction of the magnetic field inside the toroid.

Just like for the ideal solenoid, the magnetic field outside the coils of the ideal toroidal magnet is zero. The magnetic field inside the toroid coil volume can be calculated by using Ampere's Law and by assuming an Amperian loop in the form of a circle with radius r such that $r_1 < r < r_2$. The magnetic field is always directed tangential to the Amperian loop, so we can write

$$\oint \vec{B} \bullet d\vec{s} = 2\pi r B. \qquad (28.41)$$

The enclosed current is the number of turns N in the toroid times the current i in each loop; so, Ampere's law gives us

$$2\pi rB = \mu_0 Ni . \tag{28.42}$$

Therefore, we find the magnitude of the magnetic field of a toroidal magnet is given by

$$B = \frac{\mu_0 Ni}{2\pi r} . \tag{28.43}$$

Note that, unlike the solenoid, the magnitude of the magnetic field inside a toroid depends on the radius. As the radius increases, the magnitude of the magnetic field decreases. The direction of the magnetic field can be obtained using Right Hand Rule 4 by wrapping your fingers of your right hand around the toroid in the direction of the current as shown in Figure 28.21. Your thumb will then point in the direction of the magnetic field inside the toroid. Like in the case of the ideal solenoid, the field outside the ideal toroid is zero.

Solved Problem

Solved Problem 28.2: Field of a toroidal magnet

We produce a toroidal magnet by wrapping a toroid with 202 m of copper wire that is capable of carrying a current $i = 2.40$ A . The toroid has an average radius $R = 15.0$ cm and a cross-sectional diameter of $d = 1.60$ cm as shown in Figure 28.22.

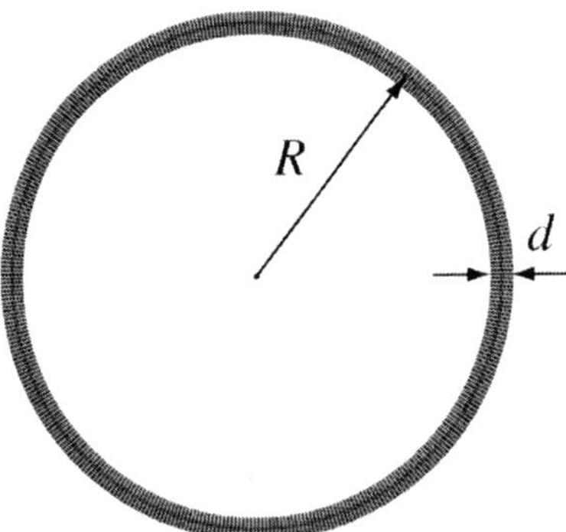

Figure 28.22: A toroidal magnet.

Question:

What is the largest magnetic field you can produce at the average toroidal radius R?

Answer:

THINK:

The inner radius of the toroidal magnet is given by $r_1 = R - (d/2)$ and the outer radius is given by $r_2 = R + (d/2)$. The number of turns in the toroidal magnet is given by the length of the wire divided by the circumference of the cross sectional area of the toroidal magnet. With these parameters, the magnetic field of the toroidal magnet at $r = R$ can be calculated.

SKETCH:

A sketch of a cross-sectional cut of the toroidal magnet is shown in Figure 28.23.

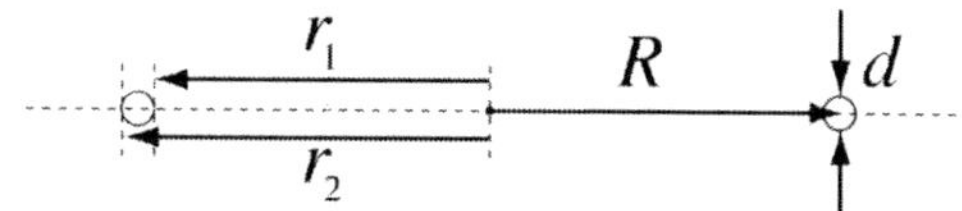

Figure 28.23: Cross-sectional cut of the toroidal magnet.

RESEARCH:

The magnitude of the magnetic field of a toroidal magnet is given by (28.43)

$$B = \frac{\mu_0 Ni}{2\pi R} \qquad (28.44)$$

where N is the number of turns and R is the radius at which the magnetic field is measured, $R = \frac{r_1 + r_2}{2}$. The number of turns N is given by the length L of the wire divided by the circumference of the cross-sectional area

$$N = \frac{L}{\pi d} \qquad (28.45)$$

where d is the diameter of cross-sectional area of the toroidal magnet.

SIMPLIFY:

We can combine (28.44) and (28.45) to obtain an expression for B,

$$B = \frac{\mu_0 \left(\frac{L}{\pi d} \right) i}{2\pi R} = \frac{\mu_0 Li}{2\pi^2 dR}. \qquad (28.46)$$

CALCULATE:

Putting in our numerical values gives us

$$B = \frac{\mu_0 Li}{2\pi^2 dR} = \frac{\left(4\pi \cdot 10^{-7} \text{ T} \cdot \text{m/A}\right)\left(202 \text{ m}\right)\left(2.40 \text{ A}\right)}{2\pi^2 \left(1.60 \cdot 10^{-2} \text{ m}\right)\left(17.0 \cdot 10^{-2} \text{ m}\right)} = 0.0113468 \text{ T}.$$

ROUND:

We report our result to three significant figures: $B = 1.13 \cdot 10^{-2}$ T.

Solved Problem

DOUBLE-CHECK:

As a double-check, we calculate the field inside a solenoid that has the length of the circumference of our toroidal magnet. The number of turns per unit length is

$$n = \frac{\frac{L}{\pi d}}{2\pi R} = \frac{L}{2\pi^2 dR} = \frac{(202 \text{ m})}{2\pi^2 \left(1.60 \cdot 10^{-2} \text{ m}\right)\left(17.0 \cdot 10^{-2} \text{ m}\right)} = 3762 \text{ turns/m}$$

The magnetic field of a solenoid with that number of turns per unit length is

$$B = \mu_0 in = \left(4\pi \cdot 10^{-7} \text{ T} \cdot \text{m/A}\right)\left(2.40 \text{ A}\right)\left(3762 \text{ m}^{-1}\right) = 1.13 \cdot 10^{-2} \text{ T}.$$

Thus our answer for the field inside the toroid seems reasonable.

28.5. Atoms as Magnets

The atoms that make up all matter contain moving electrons that form current loops that produce magnetic fields. In most materials, these current loops are randomly oriented and produce no net magnetic field. Some materials naturally have some fraction of these current loops aligned. These materials produce a net magnetic field and these materials are called magnetic materials. Other materials can have these current loops aligned by an external magnetic field and become magnetized.

Let us construct a much-simplified model of the atom. Consider an electron moving at a constant speed v in a circular orbit with radius r as illustrated in Figure 28.24. We can think of the moving charge of the electron as a current i. Current is defined as the charge per unit time passing a particular point. For this case, the charge is the magnitude of $-e$, the charge of the electron, and the time is related to the period of the orbit. Dealing with magnitudes for now we find

$$i = \frac{e}{T} = \frac{e}{(2\pi r)/v} = \frac{ve}{2\pi r}. \tag{28.47}$$

The magnetic moment of the orbiting electron is given by

$$\mu_{orb} = iA = \frac{ve}{2\pi r}\pi r^2 = \frac{ver}{2}. \tag{28.48}$$

The orbital angular momentum of the electron is

$$L_{orb} = rp = rmv \tag{28.49}$$

where m is the mass of the electron. Solving (28.48) for v and substituting into (28.49) gives us

$$L_{orb} = rm\left(\frac{2\mu_{orb}}{er}\right) = \frac{2m\mu_{orb}}{e}. \tag{28.50}$$

Remembering that the magnetic dipole moment and the angular momentum are vector quantities, we can write

$$\vec{\mu}_{orb} = -\frac{e}{2m}\vec{L}_{orb} \tag{28.51}$$

where the negative sign arises because of the definition of the current as the direction of the flow of positive charge.

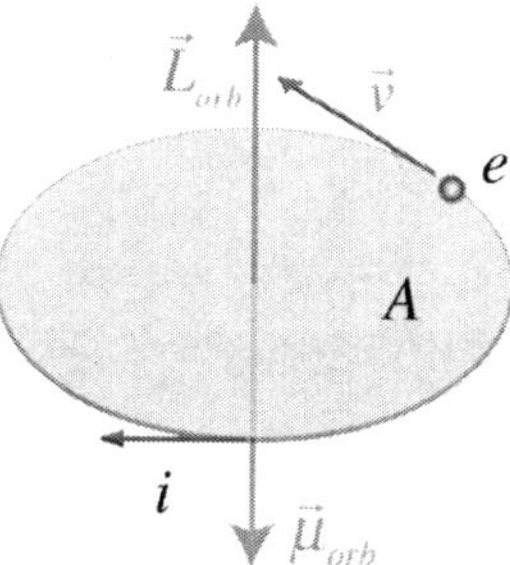

Figure 28.24: An electron moving with constant speed in a circular orbit.

The correct result is obtained when the result of this analysis is applied to the hydrogen atom. However, other predictions of the properties of atoms based on the idea that electrons exist in circular orbits in atoms disagree with experimental observations. Thus, the detailed description of the magnetic properties of atoms must incorporate phenomena described by quantum physics, which will be covered later.

Self-Test Opportunity: Show that the magnitude of the orbital magnetic dipole moment of the hydrogen atom is $\mu_{orb} = 9.27 \cdot 10^{-24}\ \mathrm{A \cdot m^2}$. Assume that the electron orbits the proton with radius $r = 5.29 \cdot 10^{-11}$ m and that the electric force between the electron and proton keeps the electron in orbit around the proton.

28.6. Nuclear Magnetic Resonance

Elementary particles such as protons have an intrinsic magnetic dipole moment. Consider the case in which we place protons in a strong magnetic field. Because of quantum mechanical reasons that will be discussed later, the magnetic dipole moment of a proton can only have two directions, parallel or anti-parallel with the external field. The difference in energy between the two states is given by the difference in magnetic potential energy, which is $2\mu B$ where μ is the component of the proton's magnetic moment along the direction of the external field.

If we now introduce a time-varying electric field at the proper frequency, we can induce some of the protons to flip the direction of their magnetic dipole moments from parallel to anti-parallel to the external field, and the protons thereby gain potential energy. Because the magnetic potential energy can only have two possible values, the energy required to flip the direction is a discrete value depending on the magnitude of the external field. When we study quantum physics we'll see that the energy delivered by the field in proportional to the frequency. Thus, only one given oscillation frequency will cause the dipole moment to flip. If the time-varying electric field is switched off, the protons in the higher energy with dipole moments that are not aligned with the field will flip back to being parallel with the field, emitting electromagnetic energy that can be detected.

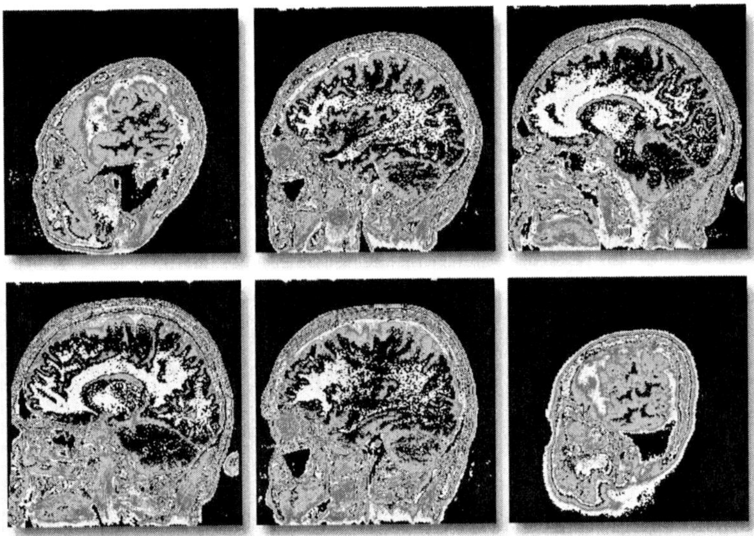

Figure 28.25: MRI brain scan. Displayed are 6 slices through a person's head in equal distances.

A magnetic resonance imaging device uses the physical principle of nuclear magnetic resonance just described. This technique can image the location of the protons in a human body by introducing a time varying electric field, and then varying the magnetic field in a known, precise manner to produce a three dimensional picture of the distribution of tissue containing hydrogen. The quality of this imaging depends on the strength of the external magnetic field.

Self-Test Opportunity: The magnetic moment of the proton is $\mu_p = 1.41 \cdot 10^{-26}$ J/T. What is the maximum difference in magnetic potential energy for the proton in a magnetic field $B = 3.00$ T?

28.7. Magnetism and Superconductivity

Magnets for industrial applications and scientific research can be constructed using ordinary resistive wire with current flowing through the wires. The typical magnet is a large solenoid. The current flowing through the wires of the magnet produces resistive heating. The produced heat is usually taken away by flowing low conductivity water through hollow conductors. Low conductivity water is water that has been purified so that it does not conduct electricity. These room temperature magnets typically can produce magnetic fields up to 1.5 T. Room temperature magnets are usually relatively inexpensive to construct but expensive to operate.

Some applications such as magnetic resonance imaging require the highest possible magnetic field to extract the best signal to noise ratio in the measurements. A magnet can be constructed using superconducting coils rather than resistive coils. Such a magnet can produce a higher field than a room-temperature magnet. The disadvantage of a superconducting magnet is that the conductor must be kept at the temperature of liquid helium, which is approximately 4 K (excluding recent developments described later in this section). Thus, the magnet must be enclosed in a cryostat filled with liquid helium to keep the coils cold. An advantage of superconducting magnets is the fact that once the current is established in the coils of the magnet, the current will continue to flow until it is removed by external means. However, the energy savings realized by having no resistive losses in the coils is offset by the fact that energy must be expended to keep the superconducting coils cold. A superconducting magnet can reach fields up to 10 T or higher. A superconducting magnet typically is more expensive to construct and cheaper to operate than a room temperature magnet.

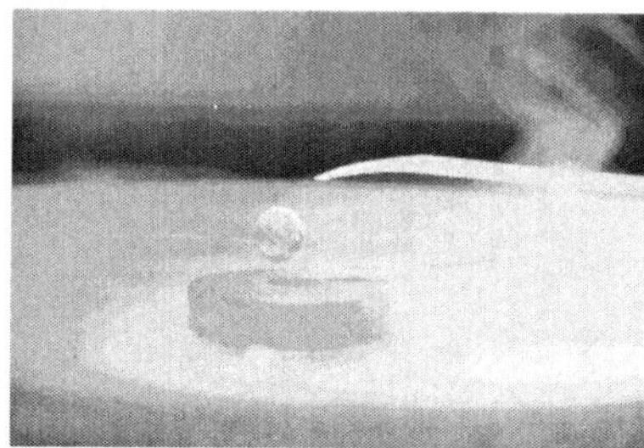

Figure 28.26: High-temperature superconductor cooled to liquid nitrogen temperature expels the magnetic field of a permanent magnet, which thus hovers above it.

The conductor used in a superconducting magnet incorporates a special design to overcome the Meissner effect, in which a superconductor excludes a magnetic field. Materials such as mercury and lead exhibit superconductivity at liquid helium temperatures, while some metals that are good conductors at room temperature such as copper and gold never become superconducting. When current flows through superconducting mercury or lead, the magnetic field is excluded from the superconducting volume and only small current densities can be achieved. Modern superconductors are constructed from filaments of niobium-titanium metals that are embedded in solid copper. The niobium-titanium filaments have microscopic domains in which the magnetic field can exist without being excluded. The copper serves as a mechanical support and can take over the current load should the superconductor become normal conducting. This type of superconductor can support magnetic fields as high as 15 T.

During the last two decades, physicists and engineers have discovered new materials that

: superconducting even at temperatures much above 4 K, such as shown in Figure .26. Temperatures of up to 100 K have been reported in these so-called high-temperature superconductors, which means that they can be made superconducting by cooling them with liquid nitrogen. Many groups around the world are working hard to find materials that are superconducting at room temperature. These materials would revolutionize many parts of industry, in particular transportation.

What we have learned/Exam Study Guide:

New Symbols used in this Chapter

- μ_0 is the magnetic permeability of free space.
- $\vec{s}$ is the vector direction of integration in Ampere's Law.
- i_{enc} is the enclosed current inside an Amperian loop.
- $\vec{\mu}$ is the magnetic dipole moment.
- $\vec{\mu}_{orb}$ is the orbital magnetic dipole moment for an electron in circular orbit.
- $\vec{L}_{orb}$ is the orbital angular momentum for an electron moving in a circular orbit.

Most Important Points

- The magnetic permeability of free space, μ_0, is given by $4\pi \cdot 10^{-7}$ T·m/A .
- The Biot-Savart Law, $d\vec{B} = \frac{\mu_0}{4\pi}\frac{id\vec{s}\times\vec{r}}{r^3} = \frac{\mu_0}{4\pi}\frac{id\vec{s}\times\hat{r}}{r^2}$, describes the field $d\vec{B}$ caused by a current element $id\vec{s}$ at a position $\vec{r}$ relative to the current element.
- The magnetic field at distance $r_\perp$ from a long straight wire carrying a current i is $B = \mu_0 i/(2\pi r_\perp)$.
- The magnetic field at the center of a loop with radius R carrying a current i is $B = \mu_0 i/(2R)$.
- The magnetic dipole moment of a coil with area A carrying a current i is given by $\mu = NiA$ where N is the number of turns. The direction is given by Right Hand Rule 2 and is perpendicular to the cross sectional area of the coil.
- The torque on a current carrying coil with magnetic moment $\vec{\mu}$ in a magnetic field $\vec{B}$ is given by $\vec{\tau} = \vec{\mu}\times\vec{B}$.
- The magnetic potential energy U of a magnetic dipole μ in an external magnetic field B is $U = -\mu B\cos\theta$ where θ is the angle between the dipole and the magnetic field.
- Ampere's Law is given by $\oint \vec{B}\bullet d\vec{s} = \mu_0 i_{enc}$ where $d\vec{s}$ is the integration path and i_{enc} is the current enclosed in a closed loop.
- The magnetic dipole moment of a coil with area A carrying a current i is given

by $\mu = NiA$ where N is the number of turns. The direction is given by the Right Hand Rule 2 and is perpendicular to the cross sectional area of the coil.

- The magnetic field inside a solenoid carrying a current i with n turns per unit length is $B = \mu_0 in$.
- The magnetic field inside a toroid with N turns carrying a current i at a radius r is given by $B = \mu_0 Ni/(2\pi r)$.
- For an electron with charge $-e$ and mass m moving in a circular orbit, the magnetic dipole moment can be related to the orbital angular momentum through $\vec{\mu}_{orb} = -\dfrac{e}{2m}\vec{L}_{orb}$.
- We have defined four right hand rules related to magnetic fields in chapters 27 and 28. In Figure 28.27, we summarize these four right hand rules. Right Hand Rule 1 gives the direction of the magnetic force on a charged particle moving in a magnetic field. Right Hand Rule 2 gives the direction of the unit normal vector of a current-carrying loop. Right Hand Rule 3 gives the direction of the magnetic field of a current-carrying wire. Right Hand Rule 4 gives the direction of the magnetic field inside a toroidal magnet.

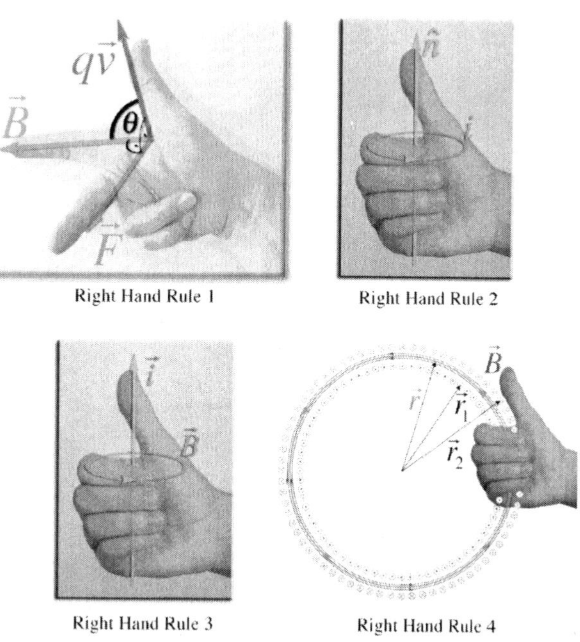

Figure 28.27: Four right hand rules related to magnetic fields.

Additional solved problems

Solved Problem 28.3: Magnetic field from four wires

Four wires are each carrying a current $i = 1.00$ A. The wires are located at the four corners of a square with side $a = 3.70$ cm. Two of the wires are carrying current into the page and two of the wires are carrying current out of the page, as shown in Figure 28.28.

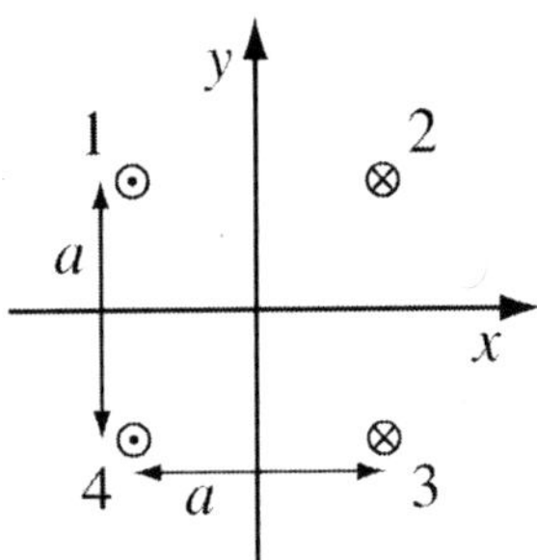

Figure 28.28: Four wires located at the corners of a square. Two of the wires are carrying current into the page and two of the wires are carrying current out of the page.

Question:
What is the y-component of the magnetic field at the center of the square?

Answer:

THINK:

The magnetic field at the center of the square is the vector sum of the magnetic fields from the four current-carrying wires. The magnitude of the magnetic field from all four wires is the same. The direction of the magnetic field from each wire is determined using the Right Hand Rule 3.

SKETCH:

A sketch of the magnetic field from the four wires is shown in Figure 28.29.

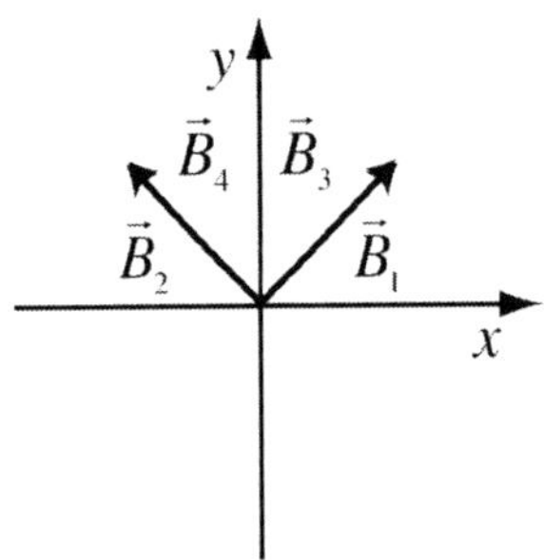

Figure 28.29: The magnetic fields from four current-carrying wires.

$\vec{B}_1$ is the magnetic field from wire 1, $\vec{B}_2$ is the magnetic field from wire 2, $\vec{B}_3$ is the magnetic field from wire 3, and $\vec{B}_4$ is the magnetic field from wire 4. Note that $\vec{B}_2$ and $\vec{B}_4$ are equal and $\vec{B}_1$ and $\vec{B}_3$ are equal.

RESEARCH:

The magnitude of the magnetic field from each of the four wires is given by

$$B = \frac{\mu_0 i}{2\pi r} = \frac{\mu_0 i}{2\pi\left(a/\sqrt{2}\right)} \tag{28.52}$$

where $a/\sqrt{2}$ is the distance from each wire to the center of the square.

Right Hand Rule 3 gives us the directions of the magnetic fields as shown in Figure 28.29. The y-component of each of the magnetic fields is given by

$$B_y = B\sin 45°. \tag{28.53}$$

SIMPLIFY:

The sum of the y-component of the four magnetic fields is

$$B_{y,\text{sum}} = 4B_y = 4B\sin 45° = 4\frac{\mu_0 i}{2\pi\left(a/\sqrt{2}\right)}\left(\frac{1}{\sqrt{2}}\right) = \frac{2\mu_0 i}{\pi a} \tag{28.54}$$

where we have used that $\sin 45° = 1/\sqrt{2}$.

CALCULATE:

Putting in our numerical values gives us

$$B_{y,\text{sum}} = \frac{2\mu_0 i}{\pi a} = \frac{2\left(4\pi\cdot 10^{-7}\text{ T}\cdot\text{m/A}\right)\left(1.00\text{ A}\right)}{\pi\left(3.70\cdot 10^{-2}\text{ m}\right)} = 2.16216\cdot 10^{-5}\text{ T}.$$

ROUND:

We report our result to three significant figures

$$B_{y,\text{sum}} = 2.16\cdot 10^{-5}\text{ T}.$$

DOUBLE-CHECK:

To double-check our result, we calculate the magnitude of the magnetic field from one wire at the center of the square

$$B = \frac{\mu_0 i}{2\pi\left(a/\sqrt{2}\right)} = \frac{\left(4\pi\cdot 10^{-7}\text{ T}\cdot\text{m/A}\right)\left(1.00\text{ A}\right)\sqrt{2}}{2\pi\left(3.70\cdot 10^{-2}\text{ m}\right)} = 7.64\cdot 10^{-6}\text{ T}.$$

The sum of the y-components is then

Solved Problem

$$B_{sum} = \frac{4(7.64 \cdot 10^{-6} \text{ T})}{\sqrt{2}} = 2.16 \cdot 10^{-5} \text{ T}$$

which agrees with our result.

Solved Problem

Solved Problem 28.4: Electron orbit in a solenoid

An ideal solenoid has 200.0 turns/cm. An electron inside the solenoid moves in a circle with radius $r = 3.00$ cm perpendicular to the axis of the solenoid. The electron moves with a speed of $v = 0.0500c$ where c is the speed of light.

Question:

What is the current in the solenoid?

Answer:

THINK:

The solenoid produces a uniform magnetic field and that magnetic field is proportional to the current flowing in the windings of the solenoid. The radius of circular motion of the electron is related to the speed of the electron and the magnetic field inside the solenoid.

SKETCH:

The orbit of electron in the uniform magnetic field of the solenoid is shown in Figure 28.30.

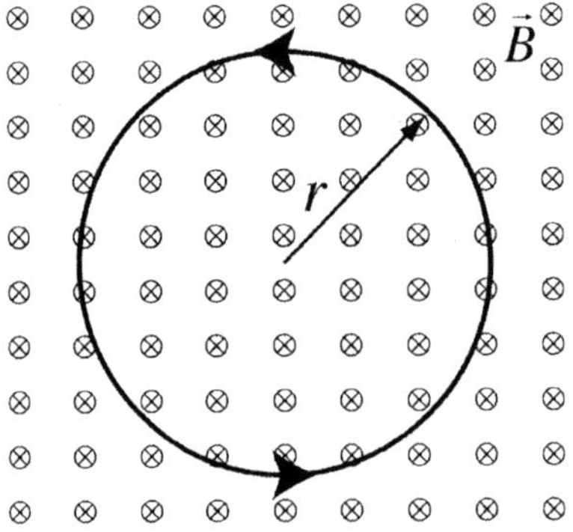

Figure 28.30: Orbiting electron inside a solenoid.

RESEARCH:

The magnitude of the magnetic field inside the solenoid is given by

$$B = \mu_0 in \tag{28.55}$$

where i is the current in the solenoid and n is the number of turns per unit length. The radius of the orbit of the electron can be related to B using

$$r = \frac{mv}{eB} \tag{28.56}$$

where m is the mass of the electron, v is the speed of the electron, and e is the magnitude of the charge of the electron.

SIMPLIFY:

Combining (28.55) and (28.56) we have

$$r = \frac{mv}{e\left(\mu_0 in\right)}.$$

Solving for the current in the solenoid we obtain

$$i = \frac{mv}{er\mu_0 n}.$$

CALCULATE:

The speed of the electron is specified in terms of the speed of light. Thus, we can write

$$v = 0.0500c = 0.0500\left(3.00\cdot 10^{8}\text{ m/s}\right) = 1.50\cdot 10^{7}\text{ m/s}.$$

Putting in our remaining numerical values we get

$$i = \frac{mv}{er\mu_0 n} = \frac{\left(9.11\cdot 10^{-31}\text{ kg}\right)\left(1.50\cdot 10^{7}\text{ m/s}\right)}{\left(1.602\cdot 10^{-19}\text{ C}\right)\left(3.00\cdot 10^{-2}\text{ m}\right)\left(4\pi\cdot 10^{-7}\text{ T}\cdot\text{m/A}\right)\left(200\cdot 10^{2}\text{ m}^{-1}\right)}$$

$$i = 0.113132\text{ A}$$

ROUND:

We report our result to three significant figures

$$i = 0.113\text{ A}.$$

DOUBLE-CHECK:

To double-check out result, we calculate the magnitude of the magnetic field inside the solenoid given the current we obtained

Solved Problem

$$B = \mu_0 in = \left(4\pi \cdot 10^{-7} \text{ T} \cdot \text{m/A}\right)\left(0.113 \text{ A}\right)\left(200 \cdot 10^2 \text{ m}^{-1}\right) = 0.00284 \text{ T}.$$

This magnetic field seems reasonable. Thus, our answer for the current in the solenoid seems reasonable.

Chapter 29. Induction

Figure 29.1: The Grand Coulee Dam on the Columbia River in Washington State is the largest single producer of electricity in the United States.

In chapter 27 we learned that a current carrying loop in a magnetic field experiences a torque, the essence of the electric motor. If we start with a loop with no current in a magnetic field, and force the loop to rotate, we find that a current is induced in the loop. This is an electric generator. Further, if we start with a loop with no current and turn on a magnetic field without moving the coil, again a current is induced in the loop. Faraday's Law of Induction describes these current-creating effects. This law of nature is the basis for electric power generation from mechanical motion. Figure 29.1 shows the power generators at the Grand Coulee Dam.

What we will learn

- A changing magnetic field inside a conducting loop induces a current in the loop.
- A changing current in a loop induces a current in a nearby loop.
- Magnetic flux is the product of the average magnetic field times the perpendicular area that it penetrates.
- Faraday's Law of Induction states that an emf is induced in a loop when there is a change in the magnetic flux through the loop.
- Lenz's Law states that the current induced in a loop by a changing magnetic field produces a magnetic field that opposes this change in magnetic field.
- A changing magnetic field induces an electric field.
- The inductance of a device is a measure of its opposition to changes in current flowing through that device.
- A simple single loop circuit with an inductor and a resistor will have a characteristic time constant given by the inductance divided by the resistance.
- Energy can be stored in a magnetic field.
- Electric motors and electric generators are everyday applications of magnetic induction.

29.1. Faraday's Experiments

Consider the situation in which we have a wire loop connected to an ammeter. We hold a bar magnet some distance from the loop, pointing the north pole of the magnet toward the loop. While the magnet is stationary, there is no current flowing in the loop. If we move the magnet toward the loop as shown in Figure 29.2*a*), a positive current flows in the loop. If we move the magnet toward the loop faster, more current is induced. If we reverse the magnet so that the south pole points toward the loop as shown in Figure 29.2*b*), and move the magnet toward the loop, we observe that current flows in the loop in the opposite direction.

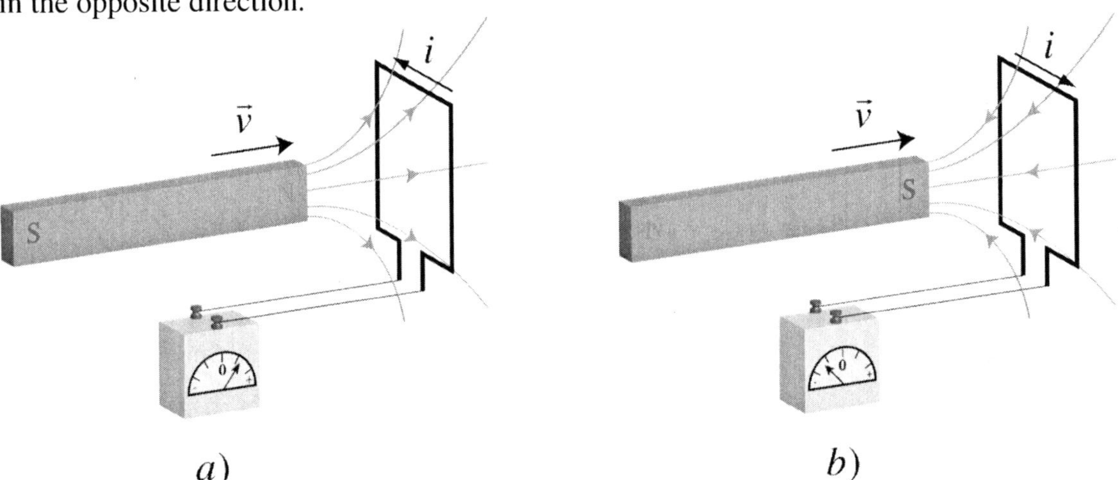

Figure 29.2: Moving a magnet toward a wire loop induces a current to flow in the loop. In the left panel, the north pole of the magnet is pointing toward the loop and induces a positive current. In the right panel, the south pole of the magnet is pointing toward the loop and induces a negative current.

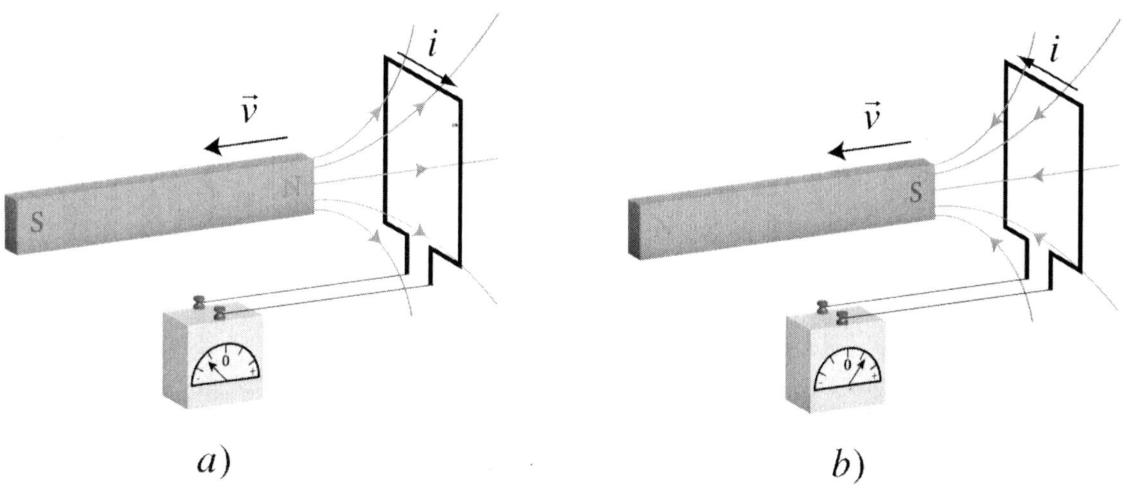

Figure 29.3: Moving a magnet away from a wire loop induces a current to flow in the loop. In the left panel, the north pole of the magnet is pointing toward the loop and induces a negative current. In the right panel, the south pole of the magnet is pointing toward the loop and induces a positive current.

If we point the north pole of the magnet toward the loop, and then move the magnet away from the loop as shown in Figure 29.3*a*), a negative current will be induced. If we point the south pole of the magnet toward the loop, and then move the magnet away from the loop as shown in Figure 29.3*b*), a positive current will be induced.

The four results indicated in Figure 29.2 and Figure 29.3 can be replicated by holding the magnets stationary and moving the coils. For example in Figure 29.2*a*) when one moves the coil towards the fixed magnet a positive current flows in the loop.

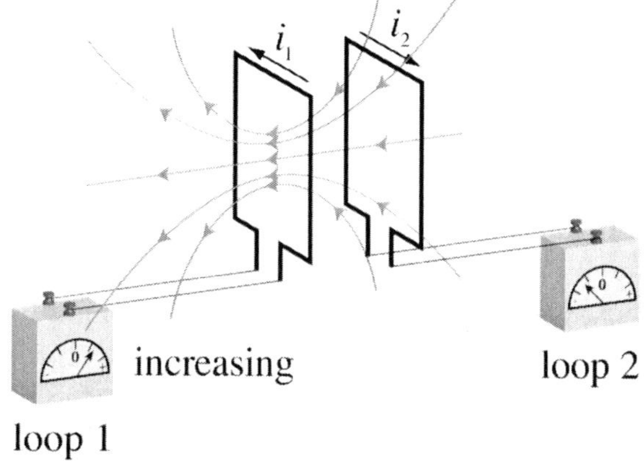

Figure 29.4: An increasing current in loop 1 induces a current in the opposite direction in loop 2.

We can create similar effects by placing a second loop near the first loop but with a quantitative result as shown in Figure 29.4. If a constant current is flowing through loop 1, no current will be induced in loop 2. If we increase the current in the loop 1, we observe that a current is induced in the loop 2 in the opposite direction. Thus, not only does the increasing current in the first loop induce a current in the loop 2, the induced current is in the opposite direction.

Now if we have the current flowing in loop 1 in the same direction as before, and decrease the current as shown in Figure 29.5, we induce a current flowing loop 2 in the same direction as the current in loop 1.

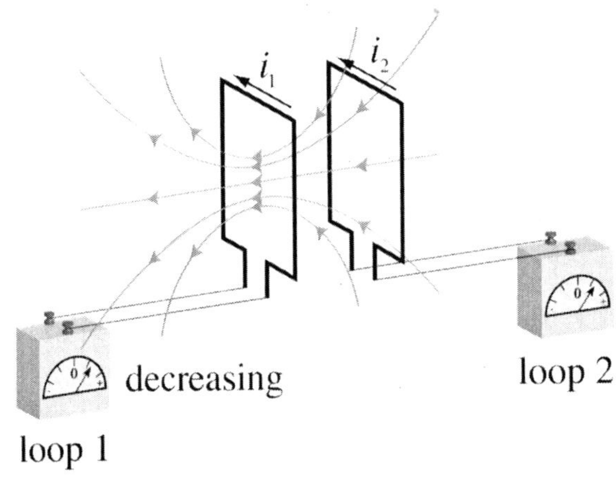

Figure 29.5: A decreasing current in loop 1 induces a current in the same direction in loop 2.

All of the phenomena represented in Figure 29.2, Figure 29.3, Figure 29.4, and Figure 29.5 can be explained by Faraday's Law of Induction, described in the following section, and by Lenz's Law, which we discuss in Section 29.3.

29.2. Law of Induction

From the observations in the previous section, we see that a changing magnetic field through a loop induces a current in the loop. We can visualize the change in magnetic field as a change in the number of magnetic field lines passing through the loop. Faraday's Law of Induction in its qualitative form states that:

> *An emf is induced in a loop when the number of magnetic field lines passing through the loop changes with time.*

The rate of change of magnetic field lines determines the induced emf. The existence of this emf means that the changing magnetic field actually creates an electric field around the loop! Thus there are two ways of producing an electric field, from electric charges and from a changing magnetic field. If the electric field arises from charge, we learned earlier in the book that the corresponding electric force on a test charge is conservative. Conservative forces do no work when they act on an object whose path starts and ends at the same space point. In contrast, electric fields generated by changing magnetic fields give rise to electric forces that are **not** conservative. Thus a test particle that goes once around a circle could have work done on it by this electric field. In fact the amount of this work is just the induced emf times the charge of the test particle.

To quantify the amount of magnetic field lines we define the magnetic flux in analogy to the electric flux. When we introduced Gauss's Law for the electric field, we defined the electric flux as

$$\Phi_E = \int \vec{E} \bullet d\vec{A}. \tag{29.1}$$

For the magnetic field, we can define magnetic flux in analogy as

$$\Phi_B = \int \vec{B} \bullet d\vec{A} \tag{29.2}$$

where $d\vec{A}$ is a vector of magnitude dA, perpendicular to the differential area.

Consider the special case of a flat loop of area A in a constant magnetic field. In this case, we can re-write (29.2) as

$$\Phi_B = BA\cos\theta \tag{29.3}$$

where B is the magnitude of the constant magnetic field, A is the area of the loop, and θ is the angle between the surface normal vector of the plane of the loop and the magnetic field. Thus, if the magnetic field is perpendicular to the plane of the loop, $\theta = 0°$ and $\Phi_B = BA$, and if the magnetic field is parallel to the plane of the loop, $\theta = 90°$ and $\Phi_B = 0$.

The unit of magnetic flux is the weber (Wb). Because $[\Phi_B] = [B][A] = \text{T m}^2$, this result implies:

$$1\ \text{Wb} = 1\ \text{Tm}^2. \tag{29.4}$$

We can then state Faraday's Law of Induction quantitatively in terms of the magnetic flux as

> *The magnitude of the V_{emf} induced in a conducting loop is equal to the time rate of change of the magnetic flux through the loop.*

Faraday's Law of Induction is thus contained in the equation

$$V_{emf} = -\frac{d\Phi_B}{dt}. \tag{29.5}$$

In (29.5) we insert a minus sign because the induced emf tries to establish an induced current whose magnetic field opposes the flux change. In Section 24.3 we discuss this minus sign in detail.

We can change the magnetic flux in several ways including changing the magnitude of the magnetic field, changing the area of the loop or by changing the angle the loop makes with respect to the magnetic field.

Induction in a Flat Loop inside a Magnetic Field

Let us explore equation (29.5) for the special case of a flat loop inside a uniform magnetic field, where uniform means that the field has the same value at all points in space at a given time, but that the field can potentially vary in time. This arrangement is also the simplest case that we can address. According to (29.3), the magnetic flux in this case is given by $\Phi_B = BA\cos\theta$. Using (29.5) the induced potential is then

$$V_{emf} = -\frac{d\Phi_B}{dt} = -\frac{d}{dt}(BA\cos\theta). \tag{29.6}$$

We can now use the calculus product rule to carry out this differentiation and obtain

$$V_{emf} = -A\cos\theta\frac{dB}{dt} - B\cos\theta\frac{dA}{dt} + AB\sin\theta\frac{d\theta}{dt}. \tag{29.7}$$

Because $d\theta / dt = \omega$, we find that the induced potential in the case of a flat loop inside a uniform magnetic field is

$$V_{emf} = -A\cos\theta\frac{dB}{dt} - B\cos\theta\frac{dA}{dt} + \omega AB\sin\theta. \tag{29.8}$$

If we leave two of the three variables (A, B, θ) constant, then we have the following three special cases:

1. We leave the area of the loop and its orientation relative to the magnetic field constant, but vary the magnetic field in time:

$$A,\theta \text{ constant:} \quad V_{emf} = -A\cos\theta\frac{dB}{dt}. \tag{29.9}$$

2. We leave the magnetic field as well as the orientation of the loop relative to the magnetic field constant, but change the area of the loop that is exposed to the magnetic field:

$$B,\theta \text{ constant:} \quad V_{emf} = -B\cos\theta\frac{dA}{dt}. \tag{29.10}$$

3. We leave the magnetic field constant and keep the area of the loop fixed as well, but allow the angle between the two to change as a function of time:

$$A, B \text{ constant:} \quad V_{emf} = \omega AB\sin\theta. \tag{29.11}$$

We now look at a couple of examples for the first two cases and then devote a separate section to the third case, which has the most useful technical applications leading directly to motors and generators.

Self-Test Opportunity: The plane of the circular loop shown in the figure is perpendicular to a magnetic field with magnitude $B = 0.500$ T. The magnetic field goes to zero in 0.250 s. The induced voltage in the loop is 1.24 V during the collapse of the magnetic field. What is the radius of the loop?

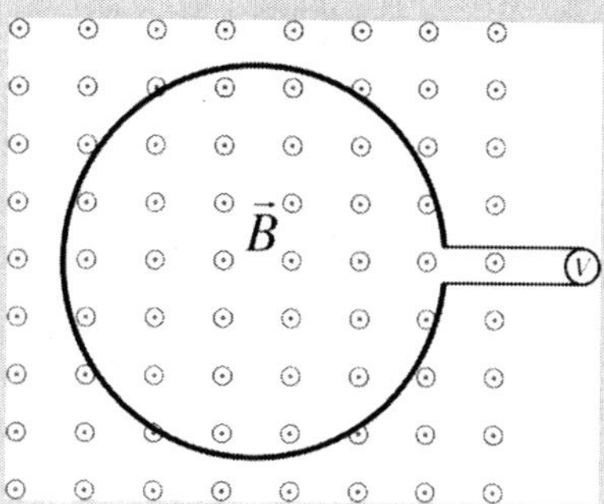

A circular loop in a time-varying magnetic field.

Example

Example 29.1: Changing magnetic field

A direct current of 600 mA is delivered to an ideal solenoid, resulting in a magnetic field of 0.025 T. Then the current increases with time t according to

$$i(t) = i_0(1 + \left(2.4 \text{ seconds}^{-2}\right)t^2).$$

Question:

If a circular loop of radius 3.4 cm with $N = 200$ windings is located inside the solenoid and perpendicular to the magnetic field, what is the induced voltage at $t = 2.0$ s in this loop?

Answer:

First, the area of the loop is easily computed (the number of winding acts as a simple multiplier):

$$A = N\pi R^2 = 200\pi(0.034 \text{ m})^2 = 0.73 \text{ m}^2.$$

From chapter 25 on direct currents, we know that the magnetic field inside an ideal solenoid is $B = \mu_0 in$. Because the magnetic field is linearly proportional to the current, we immediately obtain for the time dependence of the magnetic field in this case

$$B(t) = B_0(1 + \left(2.4 \text{ seconds}^{-2}\right)t^2)$$

Example

with $B_0 = 0.025\text{ T}$, according to the stated problem. Further, in this case the area and angle are kept constant. So the special case of equation (29.9) applies in this example. We then find for the induced voltage:

$$
\begin{aligned}
V_{emf} &= -A\cos\theta\frac{dB}{dt} \\
&= -A\cos\theta\frac{d}{dt}(B_0(1+\left(2.4\text{ seconds}^{-2}\right)t^2)) \\
&= -AB_0\cos\theta(2\left(2.4\text{ seconds}^{-2}\right)t) \\
&= -(0.73\text{ m}^2)(0.025\text{ T})(\cos 90°)\left(4.8\text{ seconds}^{-2}\right)t
\end{aligned}
$$

At time $t = 2.0\text{ s}$ we then obtain for the induced voltage in the loop: $V_{emf} = -0.17\text{ V}$

Example

Example 29.2: Motion voltage

A rectangular loop of width $w = 3.1\text{ cm}$ and depth $d_0 = 4.8\text{ cm}$ is pulled out of the gap between two permanent magnets, with a field of 0.073 T throughout the gap, as shown in Figure 29.6.

Question:

If the loop is removed with a constant velocity of 1.6 cm/s, what is the induced voltage in the loop as a function of time?

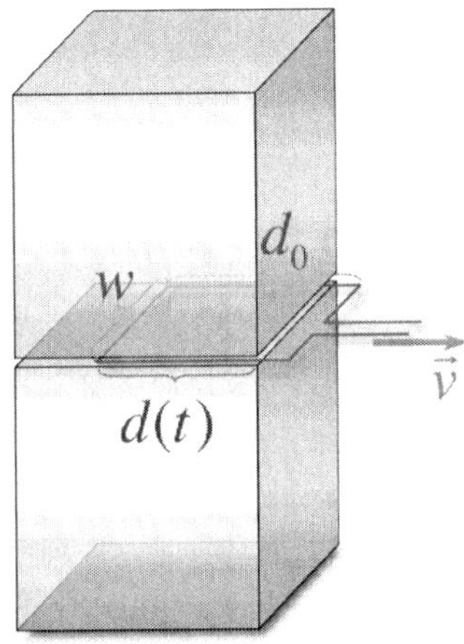

Figure 29.6: Wire loop (blue) is pulled out of the gap between two magnets.

Answer:

This example is constructed as an application of our special case for induction due to an area change. This situation is governed by equation (29.10). The magnetic field as well as the orientation of the loop relative to the field remains constant. What changes is the area of the loop that is exposed to the magnetic field. With the narrow gap shown in Figure 29.6 there will be very little field outside the gap, so the effective area of the loop

Example

exposed to the field is $A(t) = w \cdot d(t)$, where $d(t) = d_0 - vt$ is the depth of the part of the loop inside the magnetic field. While the entire loop is still inside the gap, no voltage is produced. We select the time of arrival of the right edge of the loop at the right edge of the gap at time 0. Then we find

$$A(t) = w \cdot d(t) = w \cdot (d_0 - vt).$$

This formula holds until the left edge of the loop reaches the edge of the gap, after which the area of the loop exposed to a magnetic field is zero. The left edge arrives at $t_f = d / v = 4.8 \text{ cm} / 1.6 \text{ cm/s} = 3.0 \text{ s}$, and $A(t > t_f) = 0$. From equation (29.10) we find then

$$\begin{aligned} V_{emf} &= -B\cos\theta \frac{dA}{dt} \\ &= -B\cos\theta \frac{d}{dt}(w \cdot (d_0 - vt)) \\ &= wvB\cos\theta \\ &= (0.031 \text{ m})(0.016 \text{ m/s})(0.073 \text{ T}) \\ &= 3.6 \cdot 10^{-5} \text{ V} \end{aligned}$$

So our result is that during the time interval between 0 and 3 s, a constant voltage of 36 μV is induced, and no voltage is produced outside this time interval.

29.3. Lenz's Law

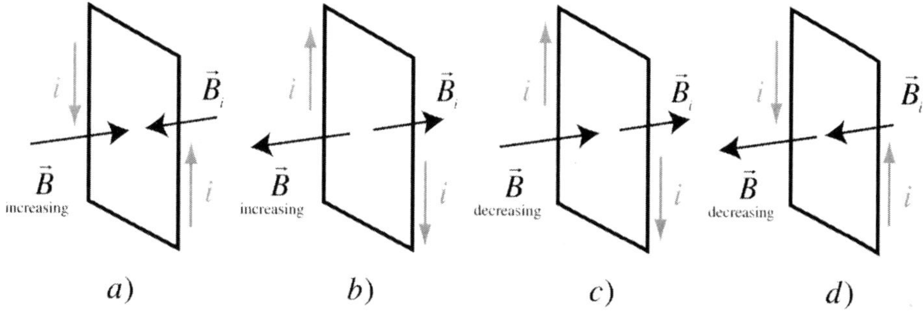

Figure 29.7: *a*) An increasing magnetic field pointing to the right induces a current that creates a magnetic field to the left. *b*) An increasing magnetic field pointing to the left induces a current that creates a magnetic field to the right. *c*) A decreasing magnetic field pointing to the right induces a current that creates a magnetic field to the right. *d*) A decreasing magnetic field pointing to the left induces a current that creates a magnetic field to the left.

Lenz's Law defines a rule for determining the direction of an induced current in a loop. An induced current will have a direction such that the magnetic field due to the induced current opposes the change in the magnetic flux that induces the current. The direction of the induced current corresponds to the direction of the induced emf. We can apply Lenz's Law to the situations described in the first section.

The physical situation shown in Figure 29.2*a*) involves moving a magnet toward a loop with the north pole pointed toward the loop. In this case, the magnetic field lines point away from the north pole of the magnet. As the magnet moves toward the loop, the magnitude of the magnet's field through the loop increases in the direction pointing toward the loop as depicted in Figure 29.7*a*). Lenz's law states that a current is induced in the loop that tends to oppose the change in magnetic flux. This induced magnetic field, $\vec{B}_i$, then points in the opposite direction from the field due to the magnet.
In Figure 29.2*b*), a magnet is moved toward a loop with the south pole pointed toward the loop. In this case the magnetic field lines point toward the south pole of the magnet. As the magnet moves toward the loop, the magnitude of the field increases in the direction pointing toward from the south pole as depicted in Figure 29.7*b*). Lenz's states that the induced current would create a magnetic field that would tend to oppose the increase in magnetic flux. This induced field points in the opposite direction as the field lines from the south pole.

Similarly the drawings in Figure 29.7*c*) and Figure 29.7*d*) represent the physical situations depicted in Figure 29.3*c*) and Figure 29.3*d*) respectively. In these two cases, magnitude of the flux is decreasing, and a current is set up to oppose this decrease. In both cases, a current is induced in the loop that creates a magnetic field in the same direction as the magnetic field from the magnet.

In the case of the two loops with one loop having a changing current, the situation is the same. The increasing current in loop 1 shown in Figure 29.4 will induce a current in loop 2 that creates a magnetic field that opposes the increase in magnetic flux as depicted in Figure 29.7*a*). The decreasing current in loop 1 shown in Figure 29.5 will induce a current in loop 2 that creates a magnetic field that opposes the decrease in magnetic flux as depicted in Figure 29.7*c*).

Self-Test Opportunity: A square conducting loop with no resistance is moved with constant speed from a region with no magnetic field through a region of constant magnetic field and then into a region with no magnetic field as shown in the figure.

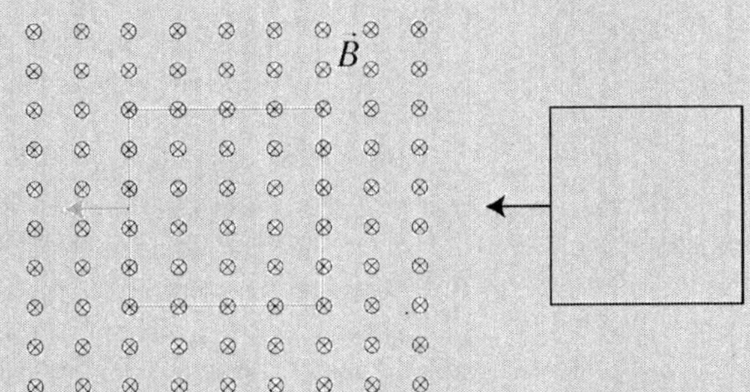

A conducting loop moves with constant speed from a field-free region through constant magnetic field and into a field free region.

As the loop enters the magnetic field, what is the direction of the induced current? As the loop leaves the magnetic field, what is the direction of the induced current?

Eddy Currents

Let's consider two pendulums, each with a non-magnetic conducting metal plate at the end that is designed to pass through the gap of a strong permanent magnet as shown in Figure 29.8. One metal plate is solid and the other has slots cut in it. We pull back both pendulums and release them. We observe that the pendulum with the solid metal sheet stops in the gap of the magnet while the grooved sheet passes through the magnetic field, only slowing slightly.

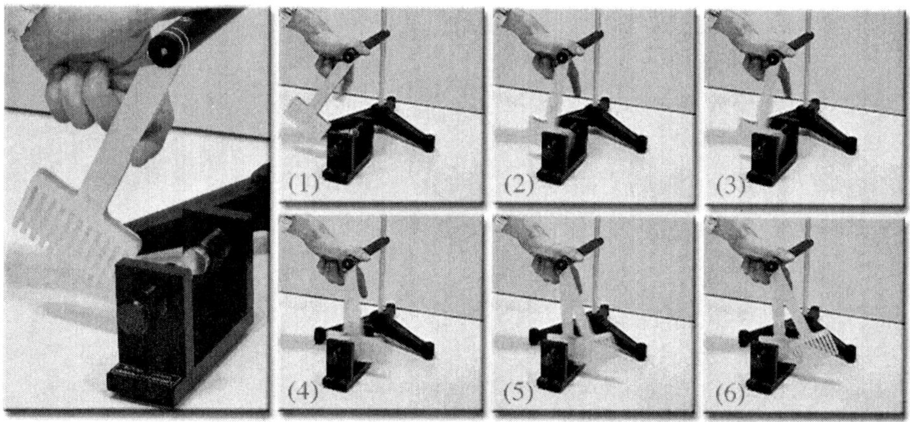

Figure 29.8: Two pendulums, one consisting of an arm and a solid metal plate and a second consisting of an arm and a slotted metal plate. The six numbered frames represent a time sequence, with the two pendulums starting their motion together in frame 1. The pendulum with the solid plate stops while the pendulum with the slotted plate passes through the magnet.

This demonstration illustrates the very important concept of induced eddy currents. As the pendulum with the solid plate enters the magnetic field, Lenz's law tells us that the changing magnetic flux will induce currents that tend to oppose the change in flux. These currents interact with the magnetic field to stop the pendulum. For the slotted plate, the induced eddy currents are blocked by the slots and the slotted plate passes through the magnetic field, only slowing slightly. Eddy currents are not like the current induced in the loop in Example 29.2, but are swirl-like eddy currents like we see in turbulent flowing water.

Eddy currents are often undesirable and steps are taken to minimize them by segmenting or laminating an electrical device that must operate in an environment of changing magnetic fields. Induced eddy currents can also be employed in practical situations such as braking railroad cars.

Induced Voltage on a Moving Wire in a Magnetic Field

Consider a conducting wire of length L moving with constant velocity v perpendicular to a constant magnetic field $\vec{B}$ into the page as shown in Figure 29.9. The wire is oriented such that it is perpendicular to the velocity and to the magnetic field. The magnetic field exerts a force $\vec{F}_B$ on the conducting electrons in the wire, causing them to move downward. This motion of the electrons produces a net negative charge at the bottom of the wire and a net positive charge at the top of the wire. This charge separation produces an electric field $\vec{E}$ that exerts a force $\vec{F}_E$ on the conduction electrons that tends to cancel the magnetic force. After some time the forces on the electrons are in equilibrium and we can write

$$F_B = evB = F_E = eE \,. \tag{29.12}$$

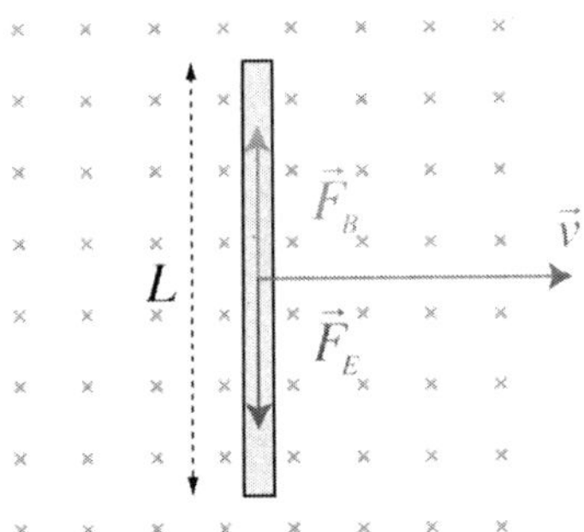

Figure 29.9: A moving conductor in a constant magnetic field. The magnetic and electric forces on conduction electrons are shown.

Thus, we can express the induced electric field as

$$E = vB \,. \tag{29.13}$$

This electric field produces a voltage between the two ends of the wire given by

$$\frac{V}{L} = vB \,. \tag{29.14}$$

We can then write the voltage between the ends of the wire as

$$V = vLB \,. \tag{29.15}$$

Example 29.3: Space shuttle tethered satellite

In 1996, the space shuttle Columbia deployed a tethered satellite on a wire out to a distance of 20 km. The wire was oriented perpendicular to the Earth's magnetic field at that point, $B = 5.1 \cdot 10^{-5}$ T. Columbia was traveling at a speed of 7.6 km/s.

Question:

What was the voltage induced between the ends of the wire?

Answer:

We can use (29.15) to determine the voltage between the ends of the wire. The length of the wire is $L = 20$ km and the speed of the wire moving through the magnetic field of the

Example

Earth ($B = 5.1 \cdot 10^{-5}$ T) is the same as the speed of the space shuttle, $v = 7.6$ km/s. Thus, we can write

$$V = vLB = 7.6 \cdot 10^3 \text{ m} \cdot 20 \cdot 10^3 \text{ m} \cdot 5.1 \cdot 10^{-5} \text{ T} = 7800 \text{ V}.$$

Figure 29.10: The left panel shows an artist's conception of the space shuttle Columbia and the tethered satellite experiment in flight. The right panel shows a photograph of the tethered satellite being deployed from Columbia.

The shuttle astronauts measured a current on the order of 0.5 ampere at a voltage of 3500 V. The circuit consisted of the deployed wire and ionized atoms in space as the return path for the current. The tether broke just as the deployment reached 20 km, but the principle of generating electric current from the motion of a spacecraft had been demonstrated.

Example

Example 29.4: Pulled conducting rod

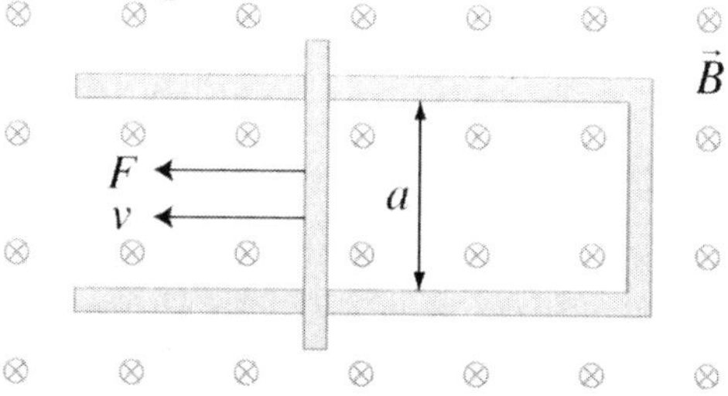

Figure 29.11: A conducting rod is pulled along two conducting rails with a constant velocity in a constant magnetic field directed into the page.

A conducting rod is pulled horizontally with a constant force $F = 5.00$ N along a set of conducting rails separated by a distance $a = 0.500$ m as shown in Figure 29.11. The two rails are electrically connected. A uniform magnetic field with magnitude $B = 0.500$ T is directed into the page. There is no friction between the rod and the rails. The rod moves with a constant speed $v = 5.00$ m/s.

Example

Question:
What is the magnitude of the induced emf around the loop created by the connected rails and the connecting rod?

Answer:
The induced emf is given by (29.10), which is the special case of the induced voltage on a loop in a magnetic field where the angle and magnetic field are held constant, and the area of the loop changes with time

$$V_{emf} = -B\cos\theta\frac{dA}{dt}.$$

In this case, $\theta = 0$ and $B = 0.500$ T. The area of the loop is increasing in time. We can write the area of the loop as an area A_0 before the connecting rod starting moving plus a additional area given by the product of the speed of the loop times the time that the loop has been moving

$$A = A_0 + a(vt) = A_0 + vta.$$

The change of the area as a function of time is then

$$\frac{dA}{dt} = \frac{d}{dt}(A_0 + vta) = va.$$

Thus the magnitude of the induced emf is

$$V_{emf} = \left|-B\cos\theta\frac{dA}{dt}\right| = vaB.$$

Thus, the magnitude of the induced emf is

$$V_{emf} = (5.00 \text{ m/s})(0.500 \text{ m})(0.500 \text{ T}) = 1.25 \text{ V}.$$

Note that our result for the pulled connected rod in a constant magnetic field, $V_{emf} = vaB$, derived using Faraday's Law of Induction, has the same form as (29.15) for the emf induced on a wire moving in a magnetic field derived in the preceding section using the magnetic force on a moving charge.

In-class exercise: Calculate the average induced voltage between the tips of the wings of a Boeing 747-400 with a wingspan of 64.67 m flying at 913 km/hr. Assume that the downward component of the Earth's magnetic field is $B = 5.00 \cdot 10^{-5}$ T.

a) 0.821 V b) 2.95 V c) 10.4 V d) 30.1 V e) 225 V

29.4. Generators and Motors

The third special case of our simple induction processes is by far the most interesting technologically. It is the variation of the angle between the loop and the magnetic field with time, while keeping the area of the loop as well as the magnetic field strength constant in time. In this way we can use equation (29.11), and Faraday's Law of Induction can be applied to the generation and application of electric current. A device that produces electric current from mechanical motion is called a generator. A device that produces mechanical motion from electric current is called a motor.

A simple generator consists of a loop forced to rotate in a fixed magnetic field. The driving force that causes the loop to rotate can be supplied by hot steam running over a turbine, as is the case in nuclear or coal-powered power plants. (Power plants actually use multiple loops in order to increase the power output.) On the other hand, the loop can be made to rotate by water or wind in a completely pollution-free way of generating electrical power. Two types of simple generators are shown in Figure 29.12.

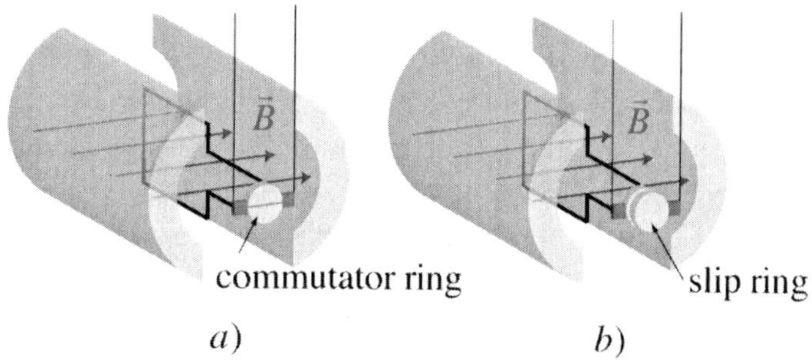

Figure 29.12: *a)* A simple direct current generator/motor. *b)* A simple alternating current generator/motor.

In Figure 29.12*a)* a direct current generator is shown. In this case, the rotating coil is connected to an external circuit using a split commutator ring. As the coil turns, the connection is reversed twice per revolution such that the induced voltage always has the same sign. In Figure 29.12*b)* a similar arrangement can be used to produce an alternating current. Each end of the loop is connected to the external circuit through its own solid slip ring. Thus, this generator produces an induced voltage that varies from positive to negative and back. The voltages produced by these generators are illustrated in Figure 29.13. A generator that produces alternating voltages and the resulting alternating current is called an alternator.

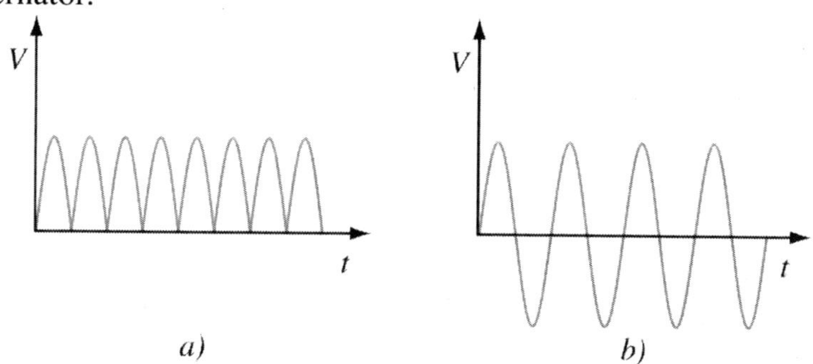

Figure 29.13: Voltage produced as a function of time by
a) a simple direct current generator. *b)* a simple alternating current generator.

These same devices could also be used as motors by supplying current to the loop and using the resulting motion of the coil to do work.

Real-life generators and motors are considerably more sophisticated than these simple generators and motors. For example, current flowing in coils rather than permanent magnets can create the required magnetic field. There can be many loops at closely spaced angles, or phases, to make more efficient use of the rotational motion. These multiple loops also take care of the problem that a simple, one loop motor could stop in a position where running current through the loop produces no torque. The magnetic field may also be changing with time in phase with the rotating coils. In some generators and motors, the coils are fixed and the magnet rotates.

Another fact-of-life concerning electric motors is back emf. An electric motor is essentially the same mechanically as an electric generator. Thus, as the motor runs faster and faster, it begins to generate a voltage called a back emf, which opposes the voltage that is being supplied to create current in the motor. You might have noticed that when a large electric motor such as an air conditioner compressor starts up, the lights dim. The motor drawing a large amount of current causes this effect. As the motor speeds up, the dimming effect disappears. When the motor is running at normal speed, it draws less current because of the back emf. If an electric motor malfunctions and stops, it will draw large amounts of current, because there is no back emf to suppress the current. This could produce enough heat to damage the motor.

Self-Test Opportunity: A generator is constructed by rotating a coil of N turns in a constant magnetic field B at a frequency f. The resistance of the coil is R and the cross-sectional area of the coil is A. Answer whether the following statements are true or false.

a) The average induced emf doubles if the frequency f is doubled.
b) The average induced emf doubles if the resistance R is doubled.
c) The average induced emf doubles if the magnetic field B is doubled.
d) The average induced emf doubles if the area A is doubled.

Regenerative Braking

Hybrid cars use a combination of gasoline power and electrical power to propel the car. One attractive feature of a hybrid vehicle is that it is capable of regenerative braking. When a normal vehicle brakes, the kinetic energy of the vehicle is turned into heat in the brake pads. This heat dissipates into the environment and is lost to the vehicle. When a hybrid vehicle brakes, the brakes are connected to the electric motor of the vehicle which functions as a generator, charging the battery carried by the hybrid car. This energy can later be used to propel the hybrid car. Thus the kinetic energy of the car is partially recovered during braking, contributing to the efficiency of a hybrid car in stop and go driving.

Figure 29.14: Automobile hybrid engine, cut open to show the regenerative brake system. Inset: magnified detail (Image courtesy of Ford Motor Company).

29.5. Induced Electric Field

A changing magnetic field produces an electric field, as we have shown from Faraday's Law of Induction. This section is devoted to exploring the consequences of this effect.

Consider a positive test charge q moving in a circular path with radius r. The work done is equal to the integral of the force times the distance. Considering one revolution of the test charge we obtain the work done on the test charge to be

$$\int \vec{F} \bullet d\vec{s} = (qE)(2\pi r). \tag{29.16}$$

Here we assume that the electric field $\vec{E}$ has field lines that are circular and that the particle moves along one of the lines. Remembering that the work done by an electric field is $V_{emf}q$ we get

$$V_{emf} = 2\pi r E. \tag{29.17}$$

We can generalize this result by considering the work done on a test particle with charge q moving along an arbitrary closed path as

$$W = \oint \vec{F} \bullet d\vec{s} = q\oint \vec{E} \bullet d\vec{s}. \tag{29.18}$$

Again substituting $V_{emf}q$ for the work we obtain

$$V_{emf} = \oint \vec{E} \bullet d\vec{s}. \tag{29.19}$$

Now we can express the induced emf in a different way by combining (29.5) with (29.19)

$$\oint \vec{E} \bullet d\vec{s} = -\frac{d\Phi_B}{dt}. \tag{29.20}$$

This equation states that a changing magnetic field induces an electric field. This equation can be applied to any closed path drawn in a changing magnetic field, even if no conductor exists in the path.

29.6. Inductance

In studying capacitors, we found that independent of the geometry of two conductors, the charge on the plates q is always proportional to the electric potential V between the plates and the proportionality constant is called the capacitance C such that

$$q = CV. \tag{29.21}$$

Consider a long solenoid with N turns carrying a current i. This current creates a magnetic field in the center of the solenoid resulting in a magnetic flux of Φ_B. For this case, we find that the quantity $N\Phi_B$, called the flux linkage, is always proportional to the current with a proportionality constant called the inductance L

$$N\Phi_B = Li. \tag{29.22}$$

Thus, the inductance is a measure of the flux linkage produced by the inductor per unit current. For an inductor to behave in this manner, it must not have any magnetic materials in its core. The unit of inductance is the henry (H) given by

$$[L] = \frac{[\Phi_B]}{[i]} \Rightarrow 1\text{ H} = \frac{1\text{ Tm}^2}{1\text{ A}}. \tag{29.23}$$

Incidentally, we note that the definition of the henry allows us to write the magnetic permeability of vacuum as:

$$\mu_0 = 4\pi \cdot 10^{-7}\text{ H/m}. \tag{29.24}$$

Now let's derive the inductance of a solenoid with cross sectional area A and length l using (29.22). The flux linkage for this solenoid is

$$N\Phi_B = (nl)(BA) \tag{29.25}$$

where n is the number of turns per unit length and B is the magnetic field inside the solenoid. The magnetic field of the solenoid has been calculated in chapter 28 and is given by $B = \mu_0 in$, where $\mu_0 = 4\pi \cdot 10^{-7}$ H/m. Thus, the inductance is given by

$$L = \frac{N\Phi_B}{i} = \frac{(nl)(\mu_0 in)(A)}{i} = \mu_0 n^2 lA. \tag{29.26}$$

This expression for the inductance of a solenoid is good for long solenoids because fringe field effects at the ends of the solenoid are small. You can see from (29.26) that the inductance of a solenoid depends only on the geometry (length, area, and number of turns) of the device. This dependence on geometry alone is true for all inductors in the same way that the capacitance of a capacitor depends only on the geometry of the device.

29.7. Self-Inductance and Mutual Induction

Consider the situation in which two coils, or inductors, are close to each other. A current in the first coil produces magnetic flux in the second coil. The changing current in the first coil also induces an emf in itself. This phenomenon is called self-induction. The resulting emf is termed the self-induced emf. Changing the current in the first coil will also induce an emf in the second coil. This phenomenon is called mutual induction.

Faraday's Law of Induction tells us that the self-induced emf for any inductor is given by

$$V_{emf,L} = -\frac{d(N\Phi_B)}{dt} = -\frac{d(Li)}{dt} = -L\frac{di}{dt} \tag{29.27}$$

where we have used (29.22) for an inductor. Thus in any inductor, a self-induced emf appears when the current changes with time. This self-induced emf depends on the time rate change of the current and the inductance of the device.

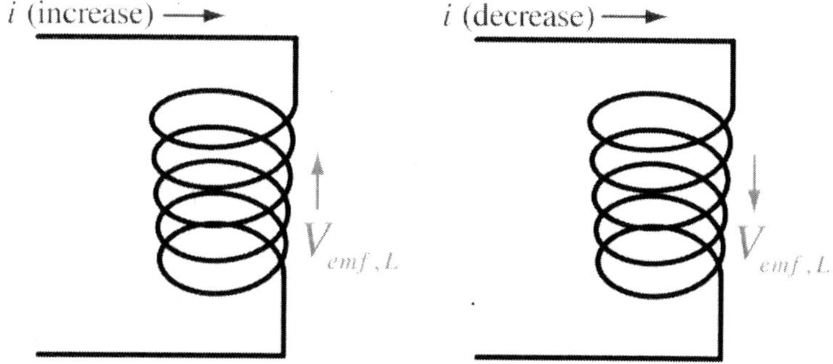

Figure 29.15: Left panel: self-induced emf on an inductor when the current is increasing; right panel: self-induced emf when the current is decreasing.

Lenz's Law provides the direction of the self-induced emf. The minus sign in (29.27) provides the clue that the induced emf always opposes any change in current.

In the left panel of Figure 29.15, the current flowing through an inductor is increasing with time. Thus, a self-induced emf arises to oppose the increase in current. In the right panel of Figure 29.15, the current flowing through an inductor is decreasing with time. Thus, a self-induced emf arises to oppose the decrease in current.

Here we assumed that these inductors are ideal inductors, that is, they have no resistance. All induced emfs manifest themselves across the connections of the inductor. We treat inductors with resistance in the next section.
Now we consider two separate coils as shown in Figure 29.16.

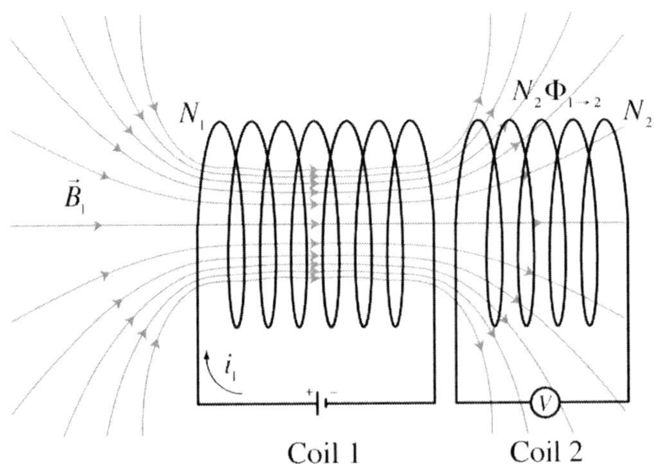

Figure 29.16: Coil 1 has current i_1. Coil 2 has a voltmeter capable of measuring small, induced voltages.

The central axes of these two coils are aligned and the two coils are close together. Coil 1 has N_1 turns and coil 2 has N_2 turns. The current in coil 1 produces a magnetic field $\vec{B}_1$. The quantity $N_2\Phi_{1\to2}$ is the flux linkage in coil 2 resulting from the magnetic field in coil 1. We define the mutual inductance $M_{1\to2}$ of coil 2 with respect to coil 1 as

$$M_{1\to2} = \frac{N_2\Phi_{1-2}}{i_1}. \qquad (29.28)$$

We can rewrite (29.28) as

$$i_1 M_{1\to2} = N_2\Phi_{1-2}. \qquad (29.29)$$

If we now force the current in coil 1 to change with time, we can write

$$M_{1\to2}\frac{di_1}{dt} = N_2\frac{d\Phi_{1-2}}{dt}. \qquad (29.30)$$

We recognize the right-hand side of (29.30) as the right-hand side of Faraday's Law (29.5). Thus, we can write

$$V_{emf,2} = -M_{1\to 2}\frac{di_1}{dt}. \quad (29.31)$$

Now we reverse the roles of the two coils as shown in Figure 29.17.

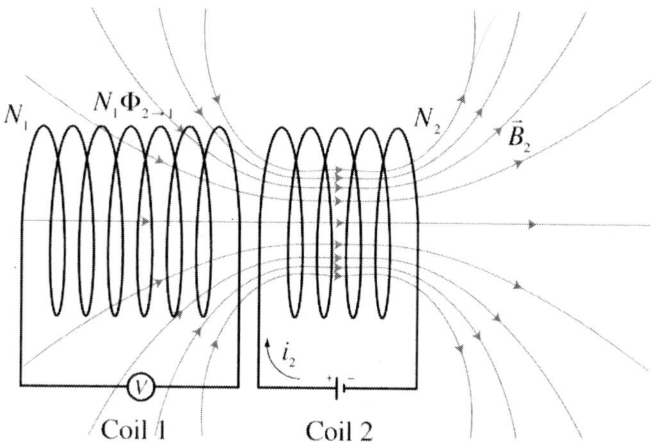

Figure 29.17: Coil 2 has current i_2. Coil 1 has a voltmeter capable of measuring small, induced voltages.

The current i_2 in coil 2 produces a magnetic field $\vec{B}_2$. The quantity $N_1\Phi_{2\to 1}$ is the flux linkage in coil 1 resulting from the magnetic field in coil 2. Using the arguments just presented for the effect of coil 1 on coil 2, we can write

$$V_{emf,1} = -M_{2\to 1}\frac{di_2}{dt} \quad (29.32)$$

where $M_{2\to 1}$ is the mutual inductance of coil 1 with respect to coil 2.

We see that the voltage induced in one coil is proportional to the change of current in the other coil. The proportionality constant is the mutual induction. If we do the previous analysis again, switching the indices 1 and 2, we can show that

$$M_{1\to 2} = M_{2\to 1}. \quad (29.33)$$

We can then rewrite (29.31) and (29.32) as

$$V_{emf,2} = -M\frac{di_1}{dt} \quad (29.34)$$

and

$$V_{emf,1} = -M\frac{di_2}{dt} \quad (29.35)$$

where M is the mutual inductance between the two coils. The SI unit of mutual inductance is the henry. One major application of mutual inductance is the transformer that we will study when we discuss alternating current circuits.

Solved Problem

Solved Problem 29.1: Mutual induction of a solenoid and a coil

A long solenoid with circular cross-section of radius $r_1 = 2.80$ cm with $n = 290$ turns/cm is located inside a short coil with circular cross section of radius $r_2 = 4.90$ cm and $N = 31$ turns as shown in Figure 29.18. The current in the solenoid is ramped up at a constant rate from zero to $i = 2.20$ A over a time interval of 48.0 ms.

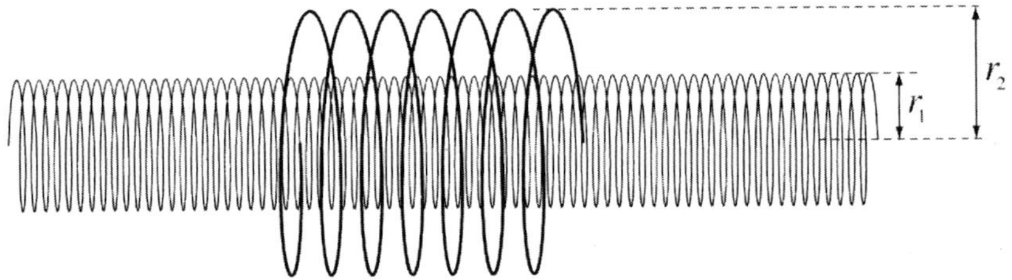

Figure 29.18: A long solenoid of radius r_1 inside a short coil of radius r_2.

Question:

What is the emf induced in the short outer coil while the current is changing?

Answer:

THINK:

The voltage induced in the short outer coil is due to the changing current flowing in the solenoid. From (29.28) we know that the mutual inductance between the two coils is the number of turns in the short coil times the magnetic flux of the solenoid divided by the current flowing in the solenoid. We can then calculate the voltage induced in the short outer coil.

SKETCH:

In Figure 29.19, we show a view of the two coils looking down the central axes of the two coils.

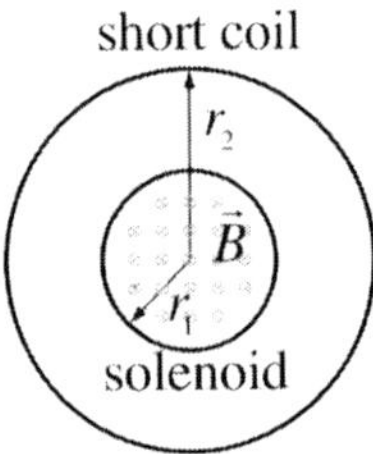

Figure 29.19: Sketch of the two coils looking down the central axes of the two coils.

RESEARCH:

We can formulate the mutual inductance between the two coils as

Solved Problem

$$M = \frac{N\Phi_{\text{solenoid}\to\text{coil}}}{i} \tag{29.36}$$

where N is the number of turns in the short outer coil, $\Phi_{\text{solenoid}\to\text{coil}}$ is the flux linkage of the solenoid with the short outer coil, and i is the current in the solenoid. The flux linkage of the solenoid can be written as

$$\Phi_{\text{solenoid}\to\text{coil}} = BA \tag{29.37}$$

where B is the magnitude of the magnetic field inside the solenoid and A is the cross-sectional area of the solenoid. Remember that for a solenoid we can express the magnetic field as

$$B = \mu_0 in \tag{29.38}$$

where n is the number of turns per unit length. The cross-sectional area of the solenoid is

$$A = \pi r_1^2 . \tag{29.39}$$

The inducted voltage in the short outer coil is then

$$V = -M\frac{di}{dt} . \tag{29.40}$$

SIMPLIFY:

We can combine (29.36), (29.37), and (29.39) to obtain the mutual inductance between the two coils

$$M = \frac{NBA}{i} = \frac{N\left(\mu_0 in\right)\left(\pi r_1^2\right)}{i} = N\pi\mu_0 nr_1^2 . \tag{29.41}$$

The voltage induced in the short outer coil is

$$V = -\left(N\pi\mu_0 nr_1^2\right)\frac{di}{dt} . \tag{29.42}$$

CALCULATE:

The current change is constant so

$$\frac{di}{dt} = \frac{2.20 \text{ A}}{48.0 \cdot 10^{-3} \text{ s}} = 45.8333 \text{ A/s} .$$

Solved Problem

The mutual inductance between the two coils is

$$M = (31)\pi\left(4\pi\cdot 10^{-7}\ \text{T}\cdot\text{m/A}\right)\left(290\cdot 10^{2}\ \text{m}^{-1}\right)\left(2.80\cdot 10^{-2}\ \text{m}\right)^{2} = 0.0027825\ \text{H}.$$

The induced voltage in the short outer coil is then

$$V = -(0.0027825\ \text{H})(45.8333\ \text{A/s}) = -0.127531\ \text{V}.$$

ROUND:

We report our result to three significant figures

$$V = -0.128\ \text{V}.$$

DOUBLE-CHECK:

The magnitude of the voltage induced in the short outer coil is 128 mV, which is a voltage one might obtain using a strong bar magnet moved in and out of a coil. Thus, our result seems reasonable.

In-class exercise: In the Solved Problem 29.1 just preceding, suppose the current in the short outer coil is ramped steadily from zero to $i = 2.80$ A in 18.0 ms. What is the magnitude of the voltage induced in the solenoid while the current in the short outer coil is changing?
a) 0.0991 V
b) 0.128 V
c) 0.233 V
d) 0.433 V
e) 0.750 V

29.8. RL Circuits

While studying electric circuits we found that if we place a source of external voltage, V_{emf}, into a single loop circuit containing a resistor R and a capacitor C, the charge q on the capacitor builds up over time as

$$q = CV_{emf}\left(1 - e^{-t/\tau_C}\right) \tag{29.43}$$

where the time constant of the circuit $\tau_C = RC$ is the product of the resistance and the capacitance. The same time constant governs the decrease of the initial charge q_0 in the circuit if the emf is suddenly removed and the circuit is short-circuited,

$$q = q_0 e^{-t/\tau_C}. \tag{29.44}$$

If we place an emf in a single loop circuit containing a resistance R and an inductor L, a similar phenomenon occurs. In Figure 29.20, we show a circuit in which an emf is connected to a resistor and an inductor in series. If we had connected only the resistor and not the inductor, the current would basically instantaneously rise to the value given by Ohm's Law, V_{emf} / R, as soon as we closed the switch. However in the circuit with both the resistor and the inductor, the increasing current flowing through the inductor creates a self-induced emf that tends to oppose the increase in current. As time passes, the change in current decreases and the opposing self-induced emf decreases. After a long time, the current is steady at the value of V_{emf} / R.

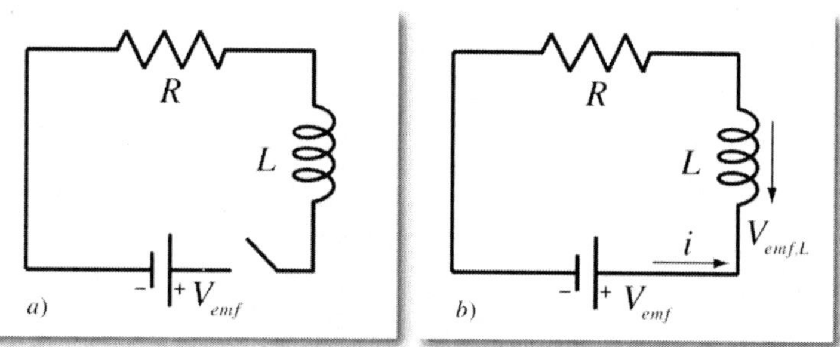

Figure 29.20: Single loop circuit with an emf source, a resistor, and an inductor; *a*) switch open; *b*) switch connected through emf source. When the switch is closed, current increases and flows in the direction shown. An emf is induced across the inductor as shown.

We can use Kirchhoff's loop rule to analyze this circuit assuming that the current i at any given time is flowing through the circuit in a counterclockwise direction. As we go counterclockwise around the circuit the emf source represents a gain in potential, $+V_{emf}$, and the resistor represents a drop in potential, $-iR$. The self-inductance of the inductor represents a drop in potential because it is opposing the increase in current. The drop in potential due to the inductor is proportional to the time rate change of the current and is given by (29.27). Thus, we can write the sum of the potential drops around the circuit as

$$V_{emf} - iR - L\frac{di}{dt} = 0. \tag{29.45}$$

We can re-write this equation as

$$L\frac{di}{dt} + iR = V_{emf}. \tag{29.46}$$

The solution to this differential equation is obtained in exactly the same fashion as was used to solve the differential equation for the RC circuit. You can refer back to chapter 25 on direct currents to see how this result is obtained. Here we simply state the solution, which can be checked by substituting it into (29.46):

$$i(t) = \frac{V_{emf}}{R}\left(1 - e^{-t/(L/R)}\right). \tag{29.47}$$

We can see that the quantity L/R defines the time constant of the circuit defined as

$$\tau_L = \frac{L}{R}. \tag{29.48}$$

This time dependence of the current in an RL circuit is shown on the left side of Figure 29.21 for three different values of the time constant $\tau_L = L/R$.

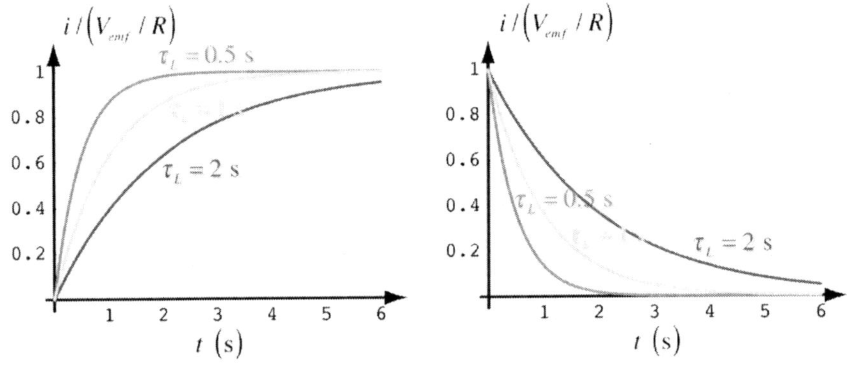

Figure 29.21: The time dependence of the current flowing through an *RL* circuit. The left panel shows the current as a function of time when a resistor, an inductor, and a source of emf are connected in series. The right panel shows the current as a function of time when the source of emf is suddenly removed from an *RL* circuit that has been connected for a long time.

Looking at (29.47) we can see that for $t = 0$ the current is zero. For $t \to \infty$, we can see that $i = \frac{V_{emf}}{R}$. This expression agrees with our expectations.

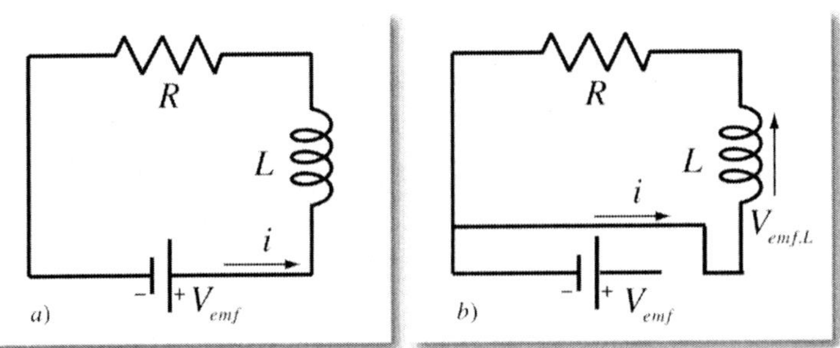

Figure 29.22: Single loop circuit with an emf source, a resistor, and an inductor; *a*) The circuit is in steady state with the source of emf connected. The current is flowing the direction shown. *b*) The source of emf is removed and the resistor and inductor are connected together. Current flows in the same direction as before but is decreasing. An emf is induced across the inductor as shown.

Now consider the case depicted in Figure 29.22, in which an emf source had been connected to the circuit and is suddenly removed. We can use (29.45) with $V_{emf} = 0$ to describe the time dependence of this circuit

$$L\frac{di}{dt} + iR = 0. \tag{29.49}$$

We can see that the resistor causes a potential drop and the inductor has a self-induced emf that tends to oppose the decrease in current. The solution of this differential equation is

$$i(t) = i_0 e^{-t/\tau_L} \tag{29.50}$$

where the initial conditions when the emf was connected can be used to determine the initial current, $i_0 = V_{emf} / R$. This equation describes a single loop circuit with a resistor and an inductor that initially has a current i_0. The current drops with time exponentially with a time constant $\tau_L = L / R$ and after a long time the current in the circuit is zero. The current in this RL circuit as a function of time for three different values of the time constant $\tau_L = L / R$ is shown in the right panel of Figure 29.21.

Solved Problem

Solved Problem 29.2: Work done by a battery

A series circuit containing a battery with $V_{emf} = 40.0\text{ V}$, an inductor with $L = 2.20\text{ H}$, a resistor with $R = 160.\ \Omega$, and a switch is connected as shown in Figure 29.23.

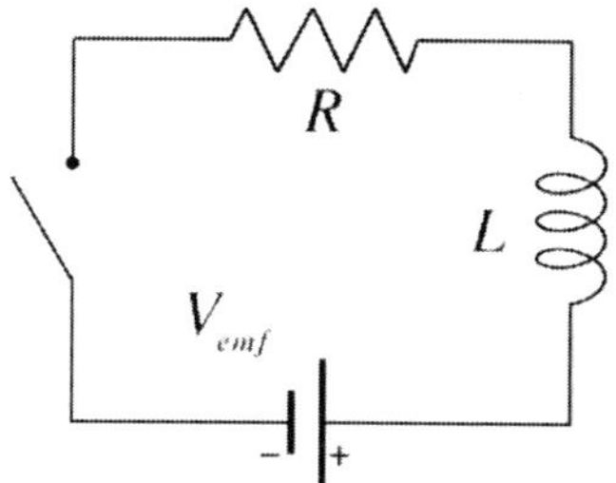

Figure 29.23: An *RL* circuit with a switch.

Question:

The switch is closed at time $t = 0$. How much work by done by the battery from the time the switch is closed until $t = 1.65 \cdot 10^{-2}\text{ s}$?

Answer:

THINK:

When the switch is closed, current will begin to flow and power will be provided by the battery. Power is defined as the voltage times the current at any given time.
Work is the integral of the power over the time the circuit operates.

Solved Problem

SKETCH:

A plot of the current in the RL circuit as a function of time is shown in Figure 29.24.

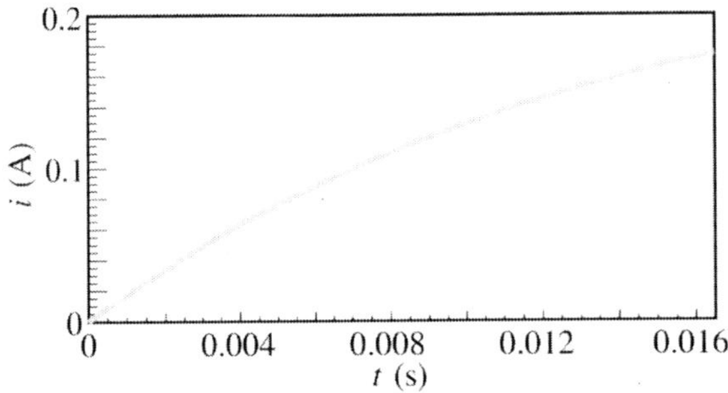

Figure 29.24: Current in the RL circuit as a function of time.

RESEARCH:

The power in the circuit at any time t after the switch is closed is given by

$$P(t) = V_{emf}\, i(t) \tag{29.51}$$

where $i(t)$ is the current in the circuit. The current as a function of time for this circuit is given by (29.47)

$$i(t) = \frac{V_{emf}}{R}\left(1 - e^{-t/\tau}\right) \tag{29.52}$$

where $\tau = L / R$. The work done by the battery is the integral of the power over the time the circuit has been in operation

$$W = \int_0^T P(t)\, dt \tag{29.53}$$

where T is the time after the switch is closed.

SIMPLIFY:

We can combine (29.51), (29.52), and (29.53) to obtain

$$W = \int_0^T \frac{V_{emf}^2}{R}\left(1 - e^{-t/\tau}\right) dt. \tag{29.54}$$

Carrying out the definite integral gives us

$$W = \frac{V_{emf}^2}{R}\left(\left[t + \tau e^{-t/\tau}\right]_0^T\right) = \frac{V_{emf}^2}{R}\left(T + \tau\left(e^{-T/\tau} - 1\right)\right). \tag{29.55}$$

Solved Problem

CALCULATE:

First, we calculate τ

$$\tau = L / R = (2.20\text{ H})/(160.\ \Omega) = 1.375 \cdot 10^{-2}\text{ s}.$$

Putting the remainder of our numerical values gives us

$$W = \frac{(40.0\text{ V})^2}{160.\ \Omega}\left(\left(1.65\cdot 10^{-2}\text{ s}\right) + \left(1.375\cdot 10^{-2}\text{ s}\right)\left(e^{-1.65\cdot 10^{-2}\text{ s}/1.375\cdot 10^{-2}\text{ s}} - 1\right)\right) = 0.0689142\text{ J}.$$

ROUND:

We report our result to three significant figures

$$W = 6.89 \cdot 10^{-2}\text{ J}.$$

DOUBLE-CHECK:

To double-check our result, we assume that the current in the circuit is constant in time. The current we choose for our double-check is half of the final current given by (29.52)

$$i_{ave} = i(T)/2 = \frac{V_{emf}}{R}\left(1 - e^{-T/\tau}\right)/2 = \frac{40.0\text{ V}}{160.\ \Omega}\left(1 - e^{-1.65\cdot 10^{-2}\text{ s}/1.375\cdot 10^{-2}\text{ s}}\right)/2 = 0.0874\text{ A}$$

This current would correspond to the average current if the current increased linearly with time. The work done would then be

$$W = PT = i_{ave}V_{emv}T = (0.0874\text{ A})(40.0\text{ V})\left(1.65\cdot 10^{-2}\text{ s}\right) = 5.77\cdot 10^{-2}\text{ J}.$$

This value is less than, but close to, our calculated result. Thus, our result seems reasonable.

29.9. Energy and Energy Density of a Magnetic Field

We can think of an inductor as a device that can store energy in a magnetic field in a manner similar to the way we think of a capacitor as a device that can store energy in an electric field. The energy stored in the electric field of a capacitor is given by

$$U_E = \frac{1}{2}\frac{q^2}{C}. \qquad (29.56)$$

Consider the situation in which an inductor is connected to a source of emf. The current begins to flow through the inductor producing a self-induced emf opposing the increase in current. The instantaneous power provided by the emf source is the product of the current and voltage of the emf source, V_{emf}. Using (29.45) with $R = 0$ we can thus write

$$P = V_{emf}i = \left(L\frac{di}{dt} \right) i. \tag{29.57}$$

Integrating this power over the time it takes to reach a final current i yields the energy provided by the emf source. Since there are no resistive losses in this circuit, this same energy must be stored in the magnetic field of the inductor and therefore

$$U_B = \int_0^t P dt = \int_0^i L i' di' = \frac{1}{2} L i^2. \tag{29.58}$$

(29.58) has a form similar to the analogous equation for electric fields (29.56) with q related to i and $1/C$ related to L.

Let's consider an ideal solenoid of length l, cross sectional area A, and n turns per unit length carrying current i. The energy stored in the magnetic field of the solenoid is given by

$$U_B = \frac{1}{2} L i^2 = \frac{1}{2} \mu_0 n^2 l A i^2. \tag{29.59}$$

The magnetic field occupies the volume enclosed by the solenoid given by lA. Thus, the energy density of the magnetic field u_B of the solenoid is given by

$$u_B = \frac{\frac{1}{2}\mu_0 n^2 l A i^2}{lA} = \frac{1}{2} \mu_0 n^2 i^2. \tag{29.60}$$

Remembering that for a solenoid

$$B = \mu_0 i n \tag{29.61}$$

we get an expression for the energy density of the magnetic field of a solenoid

$$u_B = \frac{1}{2\mu_0} B^2. \tag{29.62}$$

Although we derived this expression for the special case of a solenoid, it applies to magnetic fields in general.

In-class exercise: Consider a long solenoid with a circular cross-section with radius $r = 8.10$ cm and $n = 2.00 \cdot 10^4$ turns/m. The solenoid is $L = 0.540$ m long and is carrying a current $i = 4.04 \cdot 10^{-3}$ A. How much energy is stored in the solenoid?

a) $2.11 \cdot 10^{-7}$ J
b) $8.91 \cdot 10^{-6}$ J
c) $4.55 \cdot 10^{-5}$ J
d) $6.66 \cdot 10^{-3}$ J
e) $4.55 \cdot 10^{-1}$ J

29.10. Information Technological Applications

Our computers and many of our consumer electronics products use magnetization and induction to store and retrieve information. Examples are computer hard drives, videotapes, audiotapes, and the magnetic strips on credit cards. During the last decade, there has been a tendency to use more storage media based on other technologies, like the optical storage of information on CDs and DVDs, or flash memory cards in digital cameras, but magnetic storage devices are still a technological mainstay and multi-billion dollar industry.

Storage of the information is accomplished by using an electromagnet in the "write-head" of a device such as a computer hard drive. A current that varies in time is sent to the electromagnet and creates a magnetic field that magnetizes the ferromagnetic coding of the storage medium of the hard drive as it passes by the magnet.

Retrieval of the information reverses the process of information storage. As the storage medium passes by the "read head", which is another coil, the magnetization causes a change of the magnetic field inside the coil and thus induces a current in the read head which is then processed by the information technology or consumer electronics device.

Figure 29.25: The read and write heads inside a computer hard drive.

'hat we have learned/Exam Study Guide:

Most Important Points

- The magnetic flux Φ_B is given by $\Phi_B = \int \vec{B} \bullet d\vec{A}$ where $\vec{B}$ is the magnetic field and $d\vec{A}$ is the vector area defined by a vector normal to the surface through which the magnetic field passes.
- For a constant magnetic field $\vec{B}$, the magnetic flux Φ_B passing through an area $\vec{A}$ is given by $\Phi_B = BA\cos\theta$ where θ is the angle between the magnetic field and a normal to the area.
- The induced emf V_{emf} in a loop is given by the negative of the time rate change of magnetic field passing through the loop, $V_{emf} = -\dfrac{d\Phi_B}{dt}$.
- Lenz's Law states that a changing magnetic flux through a loop will induce a current in the loop, which opposes the change in magnetic flux.
- A magnetic field that is changing in time will induce an electric field given by $\oint \vec{E} \bullet d\vec{s} = -\dfrac{d\Phi_B}{dt}$, where the integral is done over any closed path in the magnetic field.
- The inductance L of a device with loops is the flux linkage (the product of the magnetic flux Φ_B times the number of loops N) divided by the current i, $L = \dfrac{N\Phi_B}{i}$.
- The self-induced emf $V_{emf,L}$ for any inductor L is given by $V_{emf,L} = -L\dfrac{di}{dt}$ where $\dfrac{di}{dt}$ is the time rate change of the current flowing through the inductor.
- The inductance of a solenoid is given by $L = \mu_0 n^2 lA$ where n is the number of turns per unit length, l is the length of the solenoid, and A is the cross sectional area of the solenoid.
- The unit of inductance is $1 \text{ henry} = 1 \text{ H} = \dfrac{1 \text{ Tm}^2}{1 \text{ A}}$, which allows us to express the magnetic permeability of free space as $\mu_0 = 4\pi \cdot 10^{-7}$ H/m.
- A single loop circuit with an inductance L and a resistance R has a characteristic time constant of $\tau_L = \dfrac{L}{R}$.
- The energy stored in the magnetic field U_B of an inductor L carrying a current i is given by $U_B = \dfrac{1}{2}Li^2$.

New Symbols used in this Chapter

- Φ_B is the magnetic flux.
- L is the inductance.

Additional Solved Problem

Solved Problem 29.3: Power from rotating rod

Consider a $L = 8.17$ cm long conducting rod, which rotates around one of its ends in a uniform magnetic field $B = 1.53$ T that is parallel to the rotation axis of the rod as shown in Figure 29.26. The other end of the rod slides on a frictionless conducting ring. The rod makes 6.00 revolutions per second.

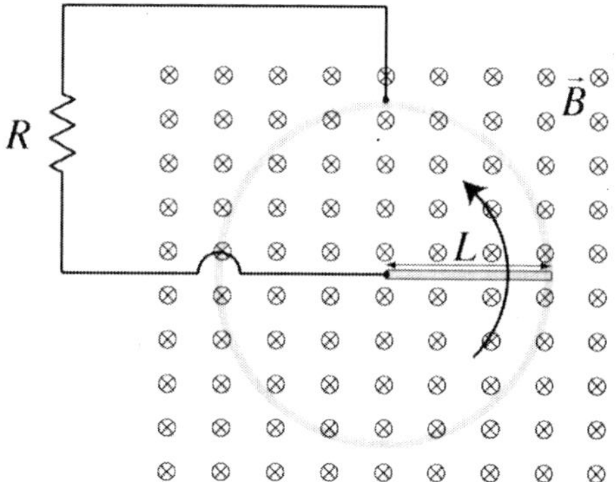

Figure 29.26: Conducting rod rotating in a constant magnetic field directed into the page.

A resistor $R = 1.63$ mΩ is connected between the rotating rod and the conducting ring as shown in Figure 29.26.

Question:

What is the power dissipated in the resistor due to magnetic induction?

Answer:

THINK:

We can calculate the voltage induced on a conductor of length L moving with speed v perpendicular to a magnetic B. However, our conductor has different speeds at different radii $v(r)$. We can calculate the voltage induced on the conductor by integrating $Bv(r)$ over the length of the conducting rod. With the induced voltage, we can calculate the power dissipated in the resistor.

SKETCH:

The velocity as a function of radius for the conducting rod is shown in Figure 29.27.

Solved Problem

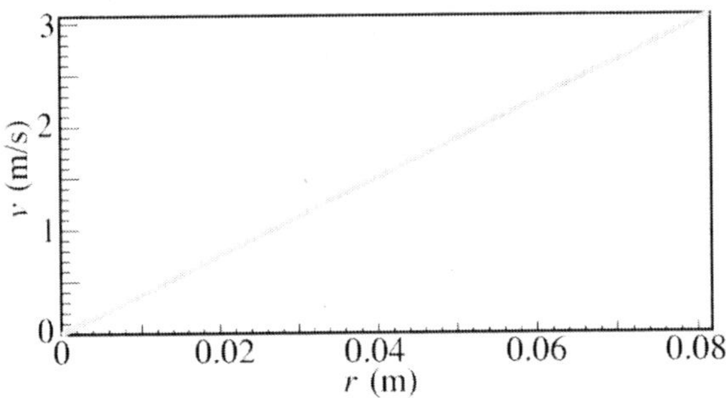

Figure 29.27: Velocity as a function of radius for the conducting rod.

Solved Problem

RESEARCH:

The voltage V induced on a conductor of length L moving with a speed v perpendicular to a magnetic field B is given by (29.15)

$$V = vLB. \tag{29.63}$$

However, in this, different parts of the conducting rod are moving at different speeds. W can express the speed of the different parts of the rod as a function of distance r from the axis of rotation

$$v(r) = \frac{2\pi r}{T} \tag{29.64}$$

where $v(r)$ is the speed of rod at distance r and T is the period of the rotation. We can then calculate the induced voltage on the rotating conducting rod over the length L of the conducting rod

$$V_{emf} = \int_0^L v(r)\,Bdr. \tag{29.65}$$

The power dissipated in the resistor with be

$$P = \frac{V_{emf}^2}{R}. \tag{29.66}$$

SIMPLIFY:

Carrying out the definite integral in (29.65) gives us

$$V_{emf} = \int_0^L \left(\frac{2\pi r}{T}\right) Bdr = \frac{2\pi B}{T}\frac{L^2}{2} = \frac{\pi BL^2}{T}. \tag{29.67}$$

Putting this result into (29.66) leads to our result for the power dissipated in the resistor

$$P = \frac{\left(\frac{\pi BL^2}{T}\right)^2}{R} = \frac{\pi^2 B^2 L^4}{RT^2}. \qquad (29.68)$$

Solved Problem

Calculate:

The period is the inverse of the frequency. The frequency is

$$f = 6.00 \text{ Hz}$$

so the period is

$$T = \frac{1}{f} = \frac{1}{6.00} \text{ s}.$$

Putting in our remaining numerical values gives us

$$P = \frac{\pi^2 B^2 L^4}{RT^2} = \frac{\pi^2 (1.53 \text{ T})^2 (0.0817 \text{ m})^4}{(1.63 \cdot 10^{-3}\ \Omega)\left(\frac{1}{6.00} \text{ s}\right)^2} = 22.7345 \text{ W}.$$

Round:

We report our result to three significant figures

$$P = 22.7 \text{ W}.$$

Double-check:

To double-check our result, we consider a conducting rod of the same length moving perpendicular to the same magnetic field with a speed equal to the speed of the center of the rod. The speed of the center of the rod is

$$v\left(\frac{L}{2}\right) = \frac{2\pi\left(\frac{L}{2}\right)}{T} = \frac{2\pi L}{2T} = \frac{2\pi(0.0817 \text{ m})}{2\left(\frac{1}{6.00} \text{ s}\right)} = 1.54 \text{ m/s}$$

The induced voltage across the conducting rod then would be

$$V = vLB = (1.54 \text{ m/s})(0.0817 \text{ m})(1.53 \text{ T}) = 0.193 \text{ V}.$$

Solved Problem

The power dissipated in the resistor would then be

$$P=\frac{V^2}{R}=\frac{(0.193\text{ V})^2}{1.63\cdot 10^{-3}\ \Omega}=22.9\text{ W}$$

which is close to our original result within round-off errors. Thus, our result seems reasonable.

Finally, let us also point out a possible additional source of potential difference between the two ends of the rod. In this problem we have treated the potential difference on the two ends as exclusively due to the magnetic induction. However, all charge carriers inside the rod are forced on a circular path due to the rotation. This requires a centripetal force, which should in principle reduce the potential difference between the two ends of the rod. However, for the small angular velocities considered here, this effect is negligible.

Chapter 30. Electromagnetic Oscillations and Currents

Figure 30.1: A stereo boom box that uses electromagnetic oscillations to produce music.

In preceding chapters we have studied circuits that have a constant current or a current that increases to a constant current or decreases to a constant current. These currents did not reverse their direction of flow. Here we introduce circuits containing a resistor, an inductor and a capacitor. Such circuits exhibit sinusoidal oscillations in voltage and current. We will study circuits that contain a time-varying source of emf. Although these alternating current (AC) circuits have the same circuit elements (resistors, capacitors, and inductors), which were studied in direct current circuits, alternating current circuits display phenomena not observed in direct current (DC) circuits such as resonances. Alternating currents play a big part of our everyday life, with the boom box (Figure 30.1) being just one example.

What we will learn

- The voltages and currents in single-loop circuits containing an inductor and a capacitor will oscillate with a characteristic frequency.
- The voltages and currents in single-loop circuit containing a resistor, an inductor, and a capacitor will oscillate with a characteristic frequency, but these oscillations will be damped with time.
- A single loop circuit containing a time-varying source of emf and a resistor will have time-varying currents and voltages that are in phase.
- A single loop circuit containing a time-varying source of emf and a capacitor will have time-varying currents and voltages that are $+\pi/2$ rad $(+90°)$ out of phase, with the current leading the voltage. The voltage and the current in this circuit are related by the capacitive reactance.
- A single loop circuit containing a time-varying source of emf and an inductor will have time-varying currents and voltages that are $-\pi/2$ rad $(-90°)$ out of phase, with the voltage leading the current. The voltage and the current in this circuit are related by the inductive reactance.
- A single loop circuit containing a time-varying source of emf and a resistor, a capacitor, and an inductor will have a time-varying current and voltage that have a phase difference that depends on the component values and on the frequency of the emf source.
- A single loop circuit containing a time-varying source of emf and a resistor, a capacitor, and an inductor has a resonant frequency determined by the value of the inductor and the capacitor.
- The impedance of a circuit is similar to the resistance of a direct current circuit but the impedance depends on the frequency of the time-varying source of emf.
- Transformers can raise (or lower) alternating voltages while lowering (or raising) alternating currents.

30.1. Energy in Inductors

In the preceding chapters we have introduced three circuit elements, capacitors, resistors, and inductors. We have studied simple single loop circuits containing resistance and capacitance (RC circuits) and simple single loop circuits containing resistance and inductance (RL circuits). Here we introduce simple single loop circuits containing inductance and capacitance, LC circuits.

We will see that the LC circuits have currents and voltages that vary sinusoidally with time, rather than increasing or decreasing exponentially with time, as we observed for RC and RL circuits. These variations of the voltage and current of LC circuits are called electromagnetic oscillations.

Recall that the energy stored in the electric field of a capacitor C is given by

$$U_E = \frac{1}{2}\frac{q^2}{C} \tag{30.1}$$

where q is the charge on the capacitor. The energy stored in the magnetic field of an inductor L is given by

$$U_B = \frac{1}{2}Li^2. \tag{30.2}$$

where i is the current flowing through the inductor.

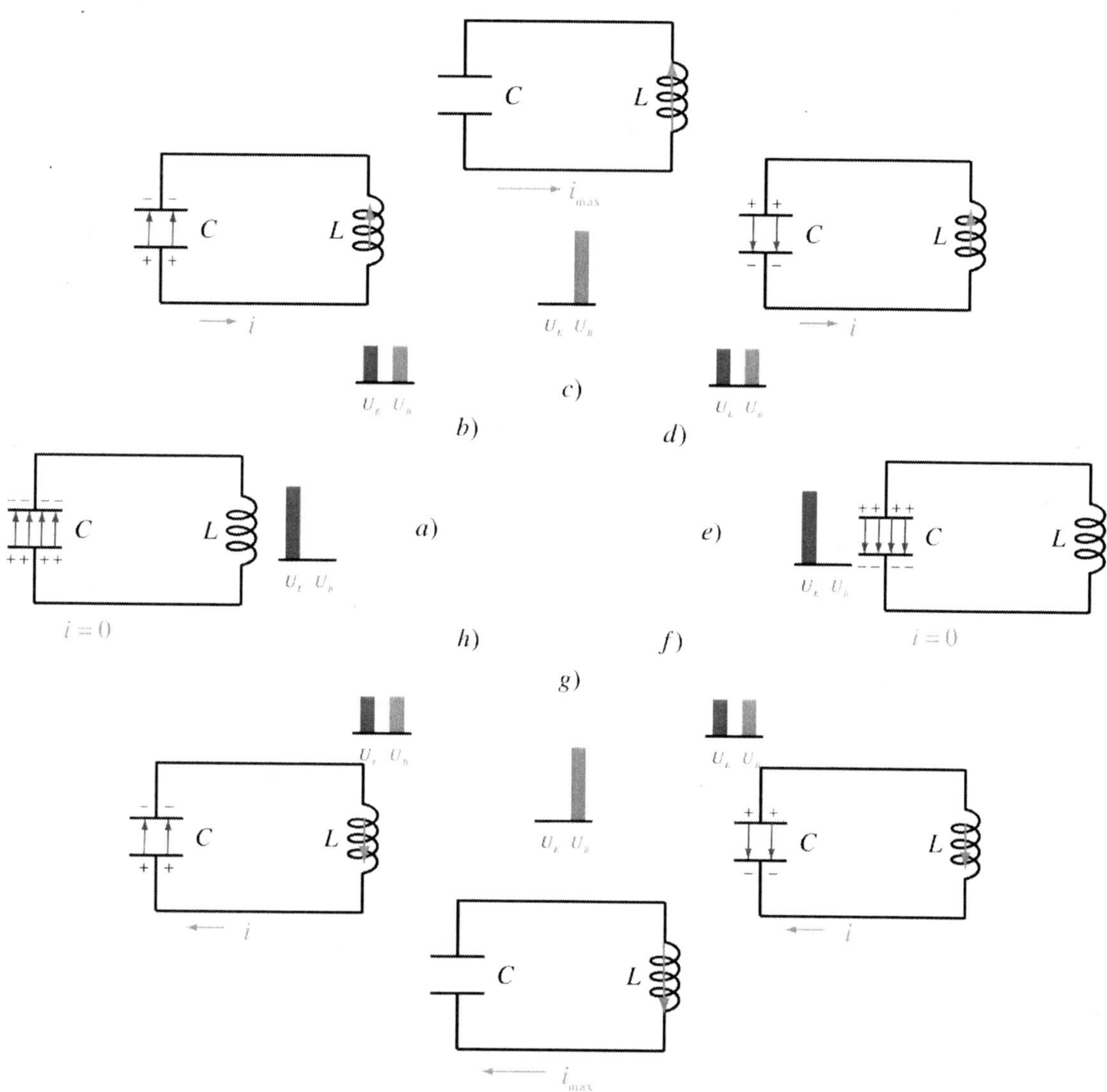

Figure 30.2: A single loop circuit containing a capacitor and an inductor. In part *a*), the capacitor is initially completely charged and then connected to the circuit. The circuit oscillates as illustrated in the remaining parts of the drawing.

To illustrate electromagnetic oscillations, consider a simple single loop circuit consisting of an inductor L and a capacitor C as shown in Figure 30.2.

In part *a*) of this drawing, the capacitor is initially fully charged (with the positive charge on the bottom plate) and then connected to the circuit. At that time, the energy in the circuit resides solely in the electric field of the capacitor. The capacitor begins to discharge through the inductor in *b*). At this point current is flowing through the inductor. (All panels indicate the instantaneous current i direction and magnitude with an arrow at the bottom of the panel.) Now part of the energy of the circuit is stored in the electric field of the capacitor and in the magnetic field of the inductor. In panel *c*) we see that the capacitor is now completely discharged. The maximum current is flowing through the inductor. (When the magnitude of i has its maximum value it is designated as i_{max} in Figure 30.3.) All the energy of the circuit is now stored in the magnetic field of the inductor. In panel *d*) the capacitor now begins to charge with the opposite polarity (positive charge on the top plate). Energy again is stored in the electric field of the capacitor as well as in the magnetic field of the inductor.

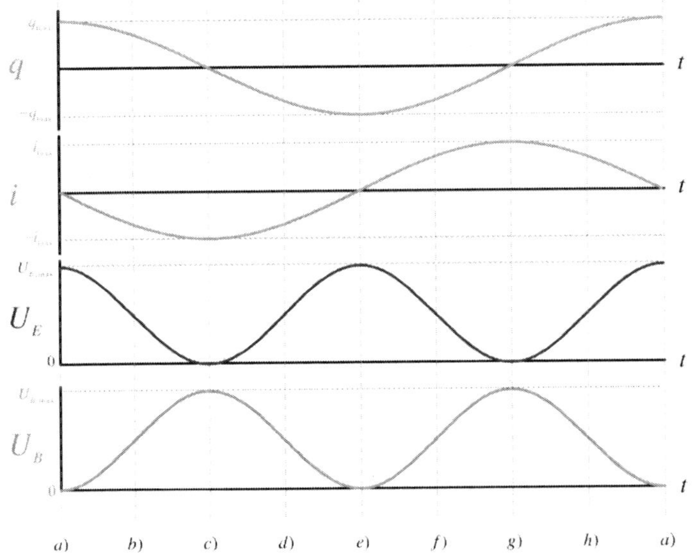

Figure 30.3: Variation of the charge, current, electric energy, and magnetic energy as a function of time. The letters refer to the panels in Figure 30.2.

In panel *e*) the energy in the circuit is again all in the electric field of the capacitor. Note that the electric field is now in the opposite direction from the original field in panel *a*). Here is the current is zero. In panel *f*) the capacitor begins to discharge again, causing a current now in the opposite direction from the previous cases, which in turn creates a magnetic field in the opposite direction in the inductor. Again part of the energy is stored in the electric field and part in the magnetic field. In panel *g*) the energy now is all in the magnetic field of the inductor, but with the magnetic field in the opposite direction from that in *c*) and with maximum current in the opposite direction from that in *c*). In panel h) the capacitor begins to charge again, placing energy in both the electric and magnetic fields. We then return to panel *a*). The circuit will continue to oscillate indefinitely because there is no resistance in the circuit and the electric and magnetic fields together conserve energy. A real-life circuit with a capacitor and an inductor will not oscillate indefinitely but instead the oscillations will die away with time because of small resistances in the circuit.

The charge on the capacitor and the current in the circuit will vary sinusoidally as shown in Figure 30.3. The energy in the electric field depends on the square of the charge on the capacitor and the energy in the magnetic field depends on the square of the current in the inductor. Thus the electric energy U_E and the magnetic energy U_B vary between zero and their respective maximum values as a function of time as shown in Figure 30.3.

30.2. LC Oscillations

Now we derive a quantitative description of the phenomena described in the preceding section. We assume a single loop circuit containing a capacitor C and an inductor L and that there is no resistance in the circuit. We can write the energy in the circuit U as the sum of the electric energy in the capacitor and the magnetic energy in the inductor

$$U = U_E + U_B . \tag{30.3}$$

Using (30.1) and (30.2) for the electric energy and the magnetic energy in terms of the charge and the current we obtain

$$U = U_E + U_B = \frac{1}{2}\frac{q^2}{C} + \frac{1}{2}Li^2 . \tag{30.4}$$

Because we have assumed that there is no resistance so that no energy can be lost to heat, the energy in the circuit will remain constant, because the electric field and magnetic field together conserve energy. Thus, the derivative of the energy in the circuit with respect to time will be zero. We can then write

$$\frac{dU}{dt} = \frac{d}{dt}\left(\frac{1}{2}\frac{q^2}{C} + \frac{1}{2}Li^2\right) = \frac{q}{C}\frac{dq}{dt} + Li\frac{di}{dt} = 0 . \tag{30.5}$$

Realizing that

$$i = \frac{dq}{dt} \tag{30.6}$$

and

$$\frac{di}{dt} = \frac{d}{dt}\left(\frac{dq}{dt}\right) = \frac{d^2q}{dt^2} \tag{30.7}$$

we can write

$$\frac{q}{C}\frac{dq}{dt} + L\frac{dq}{dt}\frac{d^2q}{dt^2} = \frac{dq}{dt}\left(\frac{q}{C} + L\frac{d^2q}{dt^2}\right) = 0 \tag{30.8}$$

which we can rewrite as

$$\frac{d^2q}{dt^2}+\frac{q}{LC}=0. \qquad (30.9)$$

(We discard the solution $\frac{dq}{dt}=0$ because this solution corresponds to an open circuit in which no current flows.) This differential equation has the same form as that of simple harmonic motion describing the position x of an object with mass m connected to a spring with spring constant k

$$\frac{d^2x}{dt^2}+\frac{k}{m}x=0. \qquad (30.10)$$

We previously found in chapter 14 that the solution of (30.10) for the position as a function of time was a sinusoidal function

$$x=x_{max}\cos(\omega_0 t+\phi) \qquad (30.11)$$

where ϕ is a phase angle and the angular frequency ω_0 is given by

$$\omega_0=\sqrt{\frac{k}{m}}. \qquad (30.12)$$

In a similar manner we find that the solution for the charge as a function of time is given by

$$q=q_{max}\cos(\omega_0 t-\phi) \qquad (30.13)$$

where q_{max} is the magnitude of the maximum charge in the circuit. ϕ is the phase, which is determined by initial conditions given in a specific problem. Note that here we employ the most commonly used notation convention for ϕ in electromagnetic oscillations, which uses a negative sign in front of ϕ. The angular frequency is now given by

$$\omega_0=\sqrt{\frac{1}{LC}}=\frac{1}{\sqrt{LC}}. \qquad (30.14)$$

The current is given by

$$i=\frac{dq}{dt}=\frac{d}{dt}\left(q_{max}\cos(\omega_0 t-\phi)\right)=-\omega_0 q_{max}\sin(\omega_0 t-\phi). \qquad (30.15)$$

Realizing from (30.15) that the maximum current in the circuit is given by $i_{max}=\omega_0 q_{max}$ we get

$$i = -i_{max} \sin(\omega_0 t - \phi). \tag{30.16}$$

From (30.13) and (30.16) we now understand the top two curves shown in Figure 30.3. We can write expressions for the electric energy as a function of time as

$$U_E = \frac{1}{2}\frac{q^2}{C} = \frac{1}{2}\frac{\left(q_{max}\cos\left(\omega_0 t - \phi\right)\right)^2}{C} = \frac{q_{max}^2}{2C}\cos^2\left(\omega_0 t - \phi\right) \tag{30.17}$$

and the magnetic energy as a function of time as

$$U_B = \frac{1}{2}Li^2 = \frac{L}{2}\left(-i_{max}\sin(\omega_0 t - \phi)\right)^2 = \frac{L}{2}i_{max}^2\sin^2(\omega_0 t - \phi). \tag{30.18}$$

Remembering that $i_{max} = \omega_0 q_{max}$ and $\omega_0 = \dfrac{1}{\sqrt{LC}}$ we can write

$$\frac{L}{2}i_{max}^2 = \frac{L}{2}\omega_0^2 q_{max}^2 = \frac{q_{max}^2}{2C}. \tag{30.19}$$

Thus, we can write the magnetic energy as a function of time as

$$U_B = \frac{q_{max}^2}{2C}\sin^2(\omega_0 t - \phi). \tag{30.20}$$

Note that both the electric energy and the magnetic energy have a maximum of $\dfrac{q_{max}^2}{2C}$ and a minimum of zero.

We can write an expression for the energy in the circuit U by summing the electric and magnetic energies

$$\begin{aligned} U = U_E + U_B &= \frac{q_{max}^2}{2C}\cos^2\left(\omega_0 t - \phi\right) + \frac{q_{max}^2}{2C}\sin^2(\omega_0 t - \phi) \\ U &= \frac{q_{max}^2}{2C}\left(\sin^2(\omega_0 t - \phi) + \cos^2\left(\omega_0 t - \phi\right)\right) = \frac{q_{max}^2}{2C} \end{aligned} \tag{30.21}$$

where we have used the trigonometric identity $\sin^2\theta + \cos^2\theta = 1$. Thus, the energy in the circuit remains constant with time and is proportional to the square of the original charge put on the capacitor.

Example

Example 30.1: LC circuit

Consider a circuit containing a capacitor C = 1.50 μF and an inductor L = 3.50 mH as shown in Figure 30.4. The capacitor is fully charged using a battery with V_{emf} = 12.0 V and then connected to the circuit.

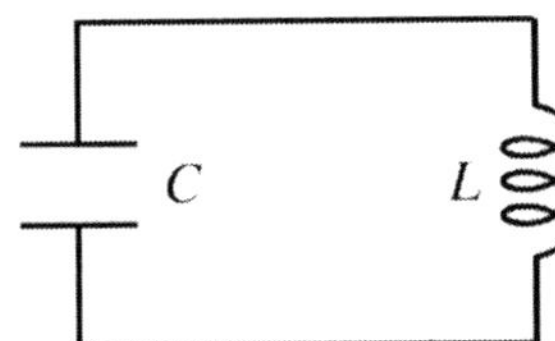

Figure 30.4: Single loop *LC* circuit.

Questions:

What is the oscillation frequency of the circuit?

What is the energy stored in the circuit?

What is the charge on the capacitor after t = 2.50 s?

Answers:

The oscillation frequency of the circuit is given by

$$\omega_0 = \frac{1}{\sqrt{LC}} = \frac{1}{\sqrt{(3.50 \cdot 10^{-3}\text{ H})(1.50 \cdot 10^{-6}\text{ F})}}.$$

$$\omega_0 = 1.38 \cdot 10^5 \text{ rad/s}$$

The energy stored in the circuit is given by

$$U = \frac{q_{max}^2}{2C}.$$

The maximum charge on the capacitor is given by

$$q_{max} = CV_{emf} = (1.50 \cdot 10^{-6}\text{ F})(12.0\text{ V})$$

$$q_{max} = 1.80 \cdot 10^{-5}\text{ C}$$

Thus we can calculate the initial energy stored in the electric field of the capacitor, which is the same as the total energy stored in the circuit, as

$$U = \frac{q_{max}^2}{2C} = \frac{(1.80 \cdot 10^{-5}\text{ C})^2}{2 \cdot 1.50 \cdot 10^{-6}\text{ F}} = 1.08 \cdot 10^{-4}\text{ J}.$$

The charge on the capacitor as a function of time is given by

Example

$$q = q_{max}\cos(\omega_0 t - \phi).$$

To determine the constants q_{max} and ϕ, we remember that at $t = 0$, $q = q_{max}$ so that

$$q = q_{max} = q_{max}\cos(\omega_0 \cdot 0 - \phi) = q_{max}\cos(-\phi) = q_{max}\cos(\phi).$$

Thus we see that $\phi = 0$ and we can write the charge as a function of time as

$$q = q_{max}\cos(\omega_0 t).$$

Putting in our numbers $q_{max} = 1.80 \cdot 10^{-5}$ C and $\omega_0 = 1.38 \cdot 10^5$ rad/s at $t = 2.50$ s, we have

$$q = (1.80 \cdot 10^{-5}\text{ C})\cos([1.38 \cdot 10^5\text{ rad/s}][2.50\text{ s}]) = \text{-}1.21 \cdot 10^{-5}\text{ C}.$$

Self-Test Opportunity: The frequency of oscillation of an LC circuit is 200.0 kHz. At $t = 0$, the capacitor has its maximum positive charge. State whether the following statements are true or false.

a) At $t = 2.50\ \mu\text{s}$, the charge on the capacitor has its maximum negative value.
b) At $t = 5.00\ \mu\text{s}$, the current in the circuit is at its maximum value.
c) At $t = 2.50\ \mu\text{s}$, the energy is stored completely in the inductor.
d) At $t = 1.25\ \mu\text{s}$, half the energy is stored in the capacitor and half the energy is stored in the inductor.

30.3. RLC Circuit, Damped Oscillations

Now let's consider a single loop circuit that has a capacitor and an inductor with an added resistor. We observed that the energy of a circuit with a capacitor and an inductor remains constant and that the energy translated from electric to magnetic and back again with no losses. If there is a resistor in the circuit, the current flow in the circuit will produce ohmic losses, which show up as thermal energy. Thus, the energy of the circuit will decrease because of these losses. The rate of energy loss is given by

$$\frac{dU}{dt} = -i^2 R. \qquad (30.22)$$

We can rewrite the change in the energy in the circuit as a function of time as

$$\frac{dU}{dt} = \frac{q}{C}\frac{dq}{dt} + Li\frac{di}{dt} = -i^2 R. \qquad (30.23)$$

Again remembering $i = dq/dt$ and $di/dt = d^2q/dt^2$ we can write

$$\frac{q}{C}\frac{dq}{dt} + Li\frac{di}{dt} + i^2R = \frac{q}{C}\frac{dq}{dt} + L\frac{dq}{dt}\frac{d^2q}{dt^2} + \left(\frac{dq}{dt}\right)^2 R = 0 \qquad (30.24)$$

or

$$L\frac{d^2q}{dt^2} + \frac{dq}{dt}R + \frac{q}{C} = 0. \qquad (30.25)$$

The solution of this differential equation is

$$q = q_{max} e^{-\frac{Rt}{2L}} \cos(\omega t) \qquad (30.26)$$

where

$$\omega = \sqrt{\omega_0^2 - \left(\frac{R}{2L}\right)^2} \qquad (30.27)$$

and $\omega_0 = 1/\sqrt{LC}$. While we do not show the advanced calculus used in arriving at this solution, the student can verify that the solution satisfies the original equation (30.25) by a straightforward substitution of (30.26) and (30.27) into (30.25).

Now consider a single loop circuit that contains a capacitor, an inductor and a resistor. If we charge the capacitor and then hook it up the circuit, we will observe a charge on the apacitor that varies sinusoidally with time while decreasing in amplitude. This behavior with time is illustrated in Figure 30.5.

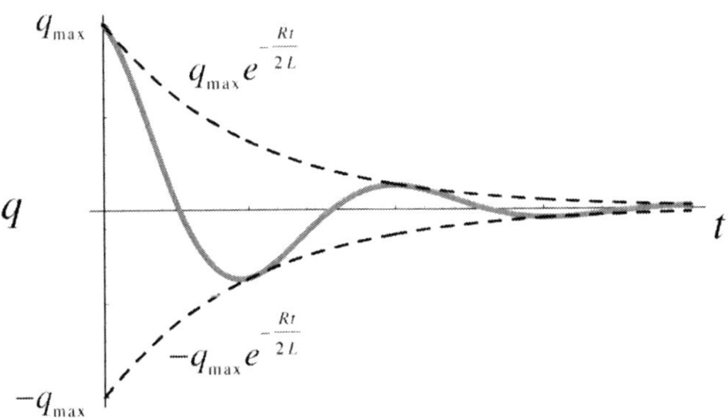

Figure 30.5: Graph of the charge on the capacitor as a function of time in a circuit containing a capacitor, an inductor, and a resistor.

By taking the derivative of (30.26) we would see that the current $i = \frac{dq}{dt}$ has an amplitude that is damped at the same rate that q is damped and that this amplitude varies sinusoidally with time. After some time, no charge remains in the circuit.

We can study the energy in the circuit as a function of time by calculating the energy stored in the electric field of the capacitor

$$U_E = \frac{1}{2}\frac{q^2}{C} = \frac{1}{2}\frac{\left(q_{max} e^{-\frac{Rt}{2L}} \cos\left(\omega t - \phi\right)\right)^2}{C} = \frac{q_{max}^2}{2C} e^{-\frac{Rt}{L}} \cos^2\left(\omega t - \phi\right). \qquad (30.28)$$

Thus U_E and U_B and therefore the total energy in the circuit $U_E + U_B$ all decrease exponentially in time.

30.4. Series RLC Circuit, Impedance

Alternating Current

Now we consider a single loop circuit containing a capacitor, an inductor, a resistor, and a source of emf. This source of emf is capable of producing a time-varying voltage as opposed to the sources of emf we have studied in previous chapters. We will assume that this source of emf provides a sinusoidal voltage as a function of time given by

$$V_{emf} = V_{max} \sin \omega t \qquad (30.29)$$

where ω is that angular frequency of the emf and V_{max} is the amplitude or maximum value of the emf.

The current induced in the circuit will also vary sinusoidally with time. This time-varying current is called alternating current. However, this current may not always remain in phase with the time-varying emf. We can express the current as

$$i = I \sin\left(\omega t - \phi\right) \qquad (30.30)$$

where the angular frequency of the time-varying current is the same as the driving emf but the phase ϕ is not zero. Note that traditionally the phase enters here with a negative sign. Thus the voltage and the current in the circuit are not necessarily in phase.

Circuit with Resistor

To begin our analysis of *RLC* circuits, let's start with a circuit containing only a resistor and a source of time-varying emf as shown in Figure 30.6. Applying Kirchhoff's loop rule to this circuit we obtain

$$V_{emf} - v_R = 0 \qquad (30.31)$$

where v_R is the voltage drop across the resistor. Substituting in (30.29) we get

$$v_R = V_{max} \sin\omega t = V_R \sin\omega t, \tag{30.32}$$

where V_R is the maximum voltage drop across the resistor. Remembering from Ohm's Law that $V = iR$ we can write

$$i_R = \frac{v_R}{R} = \frac{V_R}{R}\sin\omega t = I_R \sin\omega t. \tag{30.33}$$

Thus, we can relate the current amplitude and the voltage amplitude by

$$V_R = I_R R. \tag{30.34}$$

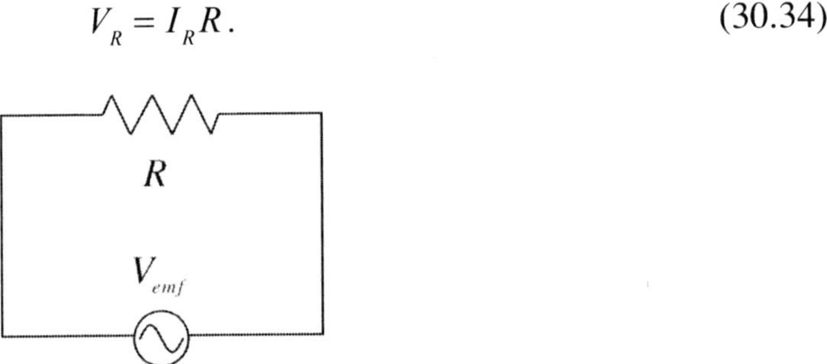

Figure 30.6: Single loop circuit with a resistor and a source of time-varying emf.

Figure 30.7*a*) shows the voltage and current across the resistor as a function of time. We can represent the time-varying current by a phasor I_R and the time-varying voltage by a phasor V_R as shown in Figure 30.7b). A phasor is a counterclockwise rotating vector (with its tail fixed at the origin) whose vertical projection represents a quantity that varies sinusoidally in time. The angular velocity of the phasor in Figure 30.7b) is ω. The current flowing through the resistor and the voltage across the resistor are in phase, which means that the phase difference between the current and the voltage is zero.

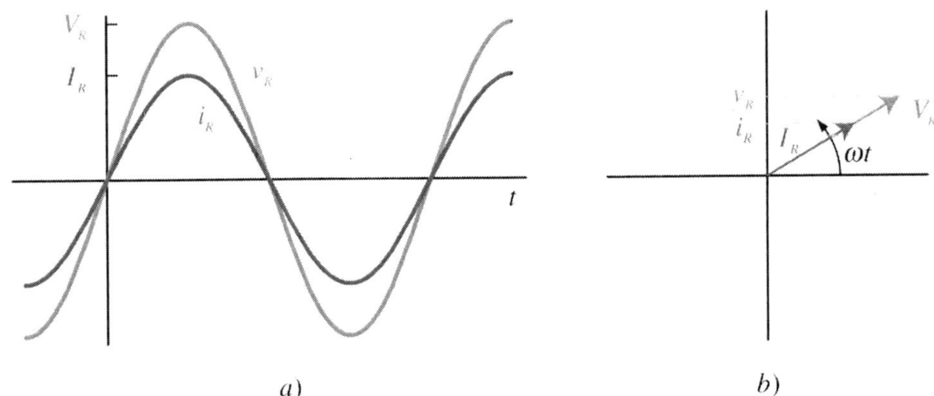

Figure 30.7: Alternating voltage and current for a single loop circuit containing a source of emf and a resistor. *a*) Voltage and current as a function of time. *b*) Phasor representing the voltage and current, showing that the voltage and current are in phase.

Circuit with Capacitor

Now let's address a circuit that contains a capacitor and a time-varying emf as shown in Figure 30.8.

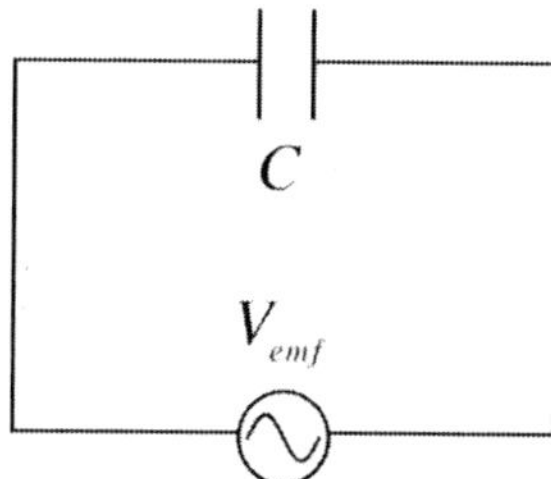

Figure 30.8: Single loop circuit with a capacitor and a source of time-varying emf.

The voltage across the capacitor is given by Kirchhoff's loop rule

$$V_{emf} - v_C = 0$$

where v_C is the voltage drop across the capacitor, Thus

$$v_C = V_{\max} \sin \omega t = V_C \sin \omega t , \tag{30.35}$$

where V_C is the maximum voltage across the capacitor. Remembering that $q = CV$ for a capacitor we can write

$$q = Cv_C = CV_C \sin \omega t . \tag{30.36}$$

However, we would like to know the current (rather than the charge) as a function of time so we can write

$$i_C = \frac{dq}{dt} = \frac{d\left(CV_C \sin \omega t\right)}{dt} = \omega CV_C \cos \omega t . \tag{30.37}$$

We can rewrite this equation in a form that invites a comparison with (30.33) by defining a quantity that is similar to resistance and is called the capacitive reactance

$$X_C = \frac{1}{\omega C} \tag{30.38}$$

which allows us to express (30.37) as

$$i_C = \frac{V_C}{X_C} \cos \omega t . \tag{30.39}$$

We can now express the current in the circuit as

$$i_C = I_C \cos \omega t , \tag{30.40}$$

where $I_C = \frac{V_C}{X_C}$. We can further modify (30.40) to better compare with (30.33) by realizing that $\cos\theta = \sin(\theta + \pi/2)$ to obtain

$$i_C = I_C \sin(\omega t + \pi/2). \quad (30.41)$$

This expression for the current flowing in this circuit with only a capacitor is similar to the expression for the current flowing in a circuit with only a resistor except that it is out of phase by $\pi/2$ rad $(90°)$. Figure 30.9*a*) shows the voltage and current across the capacitor as a function of time.

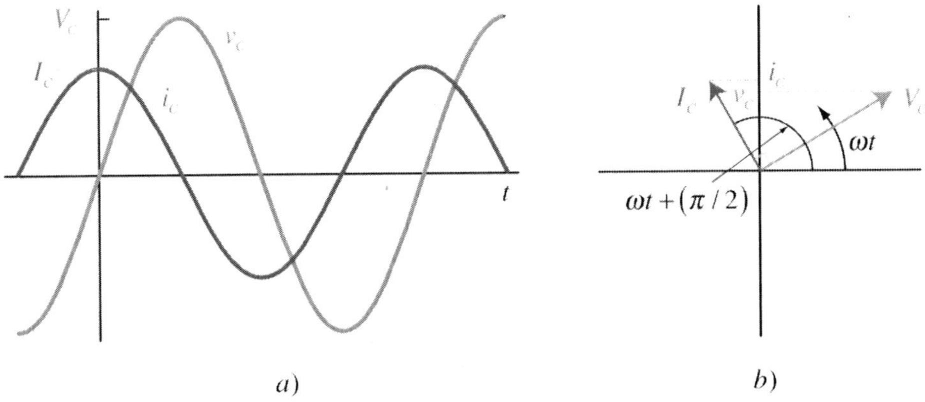

Figure 30.9: Alternating voltage and current for a single loop circuit containing a source of emf and a capacitor. *a*) Voltage and current as a function of time. *b*) Phasor representing the voltage and current showing that the voltage and current are π/2 rad (90°) out of phase.

The corresponding phasors I_C and V_C are shown in Figure 30.9b), and show that the current leads the voltage. We have seen that the amplitude of voltage across the capacitor and the amplitude of current in the capacitor are related by

$$V_C = I_C X_C. \quad (30.42)$$

This equation resembles Ohm's Law with the capacitive reactance replacing the resistance. One major difference between the capacitive reactance and the resistance is that the capacitive reactance depends on the angular frequency of the time-varying emf.

In-class exercise: Consider a circuit with a source of time-varying emf $V_{emf} = 120.0\sin\left(\left(377\ \frac{\text{rad}}{\text{s}}\right)t\right)$ V and a capacitor $C = 5.00\ \mu\text{F}$. What is the current in the circuit at $t = 1.00$ s ?

a) 0.226 A b) 0.451 A c) 0.555 A d) 0.750 A e) 1.25 A

Circuit with Inductor

Now let's consider a circuit with a source of time-varying emf and an inductor as shown in Figure 30.10.

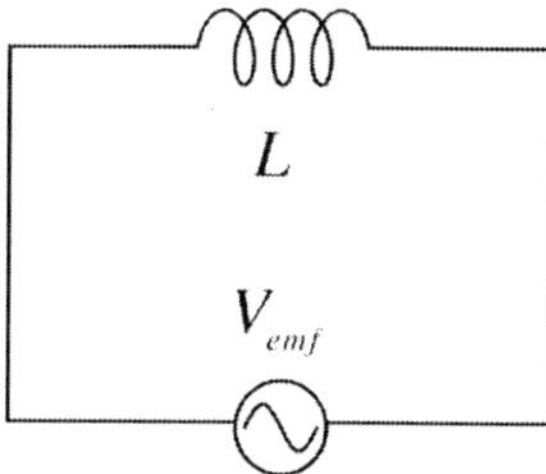

Figure 30.10: Single loop circuit with an inductor and a source of time-varying emf.

We can again apply Kirchhoff's Loop Rule to this circuit to obtain the voltage across the inductor as

$$v_L = V_{\max} \sin \omega t = V_L \sin \omega t \;, \tag{30.43}$$

where V_L is the maximum voltage across the inductance. A changing current in an inductor will induce an emf given by

$$v_L = L\frac{di_L}{dt} \tag{30.44}$$

So we can write

$$L\frac{di_L}{dt} = V_L \sin \omega t \tag{30.45}$$

or

$$\frac{di_L}{dt} = \frac{V_L}{L}\sin \omega t \,. \tag{30.46}$$

We are interested in the current rather than its time derivative so we integrate to get

$$i_L = \int \frac{di_L}{dt}dt = \int \frac{V_L}{L}\sin \omega t dt = -\frac{V_L}{\omega L}\cos \omega t \,. \tag{30.47}$$

In (30.47) we set the constant of integration to zero because we are not interested in solutions that contain both an oscillating and a constant current. We define the quantity inductive reactance as

$$X_L = \omega L \tag{30.48}$$

which, like the capacitive reactance, is similar to a resistance. We can then write

$$i_L = -\frac{V_L}{X_L}\cos \omega t = -I_L \cos \omega t \tag{30.49}$$

where I_L is the maximum current. Thus,

$$V_L = I_L X_L, \tag{30.50}$$

which again resembles Ohm's Law except that the inductive reactance depends on the angular frequency of the time-varying emf.

Because $-\cos\theta = \sin(\theta - \pi/2)$, we can re-write (30.49) as

$$i_L = I_L \sin(\omega t - \pi/2). \tag{30.51}$$

Thus, the current flowing in a circuit with an inductor and a source of time-varying emf will be $-\pi/2$ rad out of phase with the emf. Figure 30.11*a*) shows the voltage and current across the inductor as a function of time. The corresponding phasors I_L and V_L are shown in Figure 30.11*b*), which shows that the voltage leads the current.

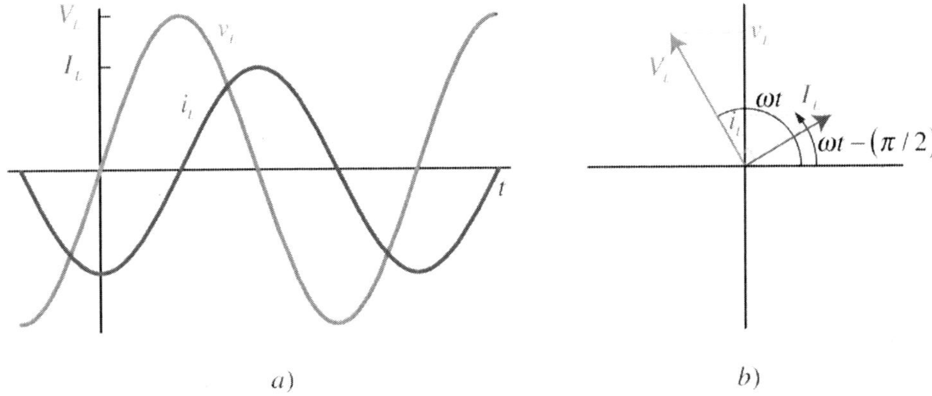

Figure 30.11: Alternating voltage and current for a single loop circuit containing a source of emf and an inductor. *a*) Voltage and current as a function of time. *b*) Phasor representing the voltage and current showing that the voltage and current are $\pi/2$ rad (90°) out of phase.

Series RLC Circuit

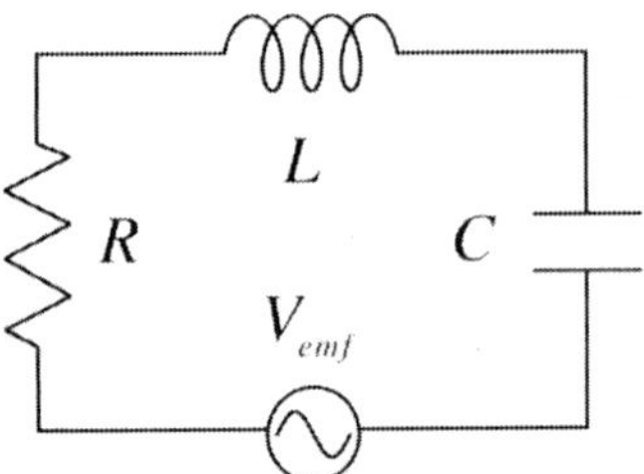

Figure 30.12: A single loop circuit containing a time-varying emf, a resistor, an inductor, and a capacitor.

Now let's consider a single loop circuit that has all three circuit elements in the same circuit along with a source of time-varying emf as shown in Figure 30.12. While we will not show a full mathematical solution of this circuit, we will use phasors to extract the important aspects of the solution. We can describe the time-varying currents and voltages in these circuit elements using a phasor I as shown in Figure 30.13.

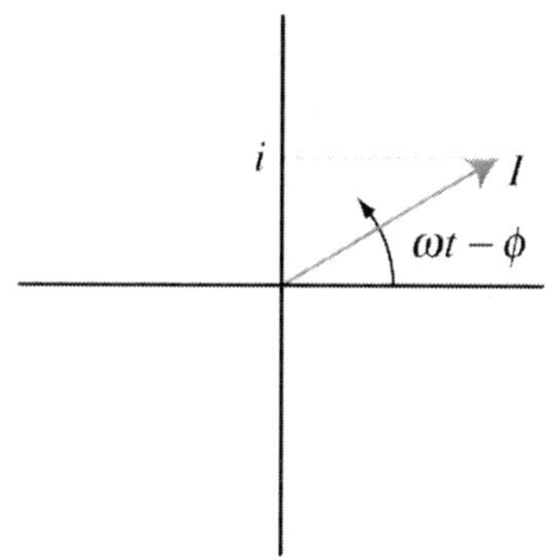

Figure 30.13: Phasor I representing the current i flowing in an RLC circuit.

The projection of I on the vertical axis represents the current i flowing in the circuit as a function of time t, where the angle of the phasor is given by $\omega t - \phi$, such that

$$i = I_{max} \sin(\omega t - \phi). \tag{30.52}$$

The current i and the voltages across the elements of the circuit can have different phases with respect to the emf. For each circuit element the voltage and current have the following relative phases:

- Resistor: The voltage v_R and current i are in phase with each other and the voltage phasor V_R is in phase with I.
- Capacitor: The current i leads the voltage v_C by $\pi/2$ rad $(90°)$ so that the voltage phasor V_C will have an angle $\pi/2$ rad $(90°)$ less than I and V_R.
- Inductor: The current i lags behind the voltage v_L by $\pi/2$ rad $(90°)$ so that voltage phasor V_L will have an angle $\pi/2$ rad $(90°)$ greater than I and V_R.

The voltage phasors for an RLC circuit are shown in Figure 30.14. The instantaneous voltages across each of the components are represented by the projections of the respective phasors on the vertical axis.

We define V as the total voltage drop across all components,

$$V = v_R + v_C + v_L. \tag{30.53}$$

The voltage V can be thought of as the projection on the vertical axis of the phasor V_m representing the time-varying emf in the circuit as illustrated in Figure 30.15. The phasors in Figure 30.14 rotate together, and (30.53) is true at any time.

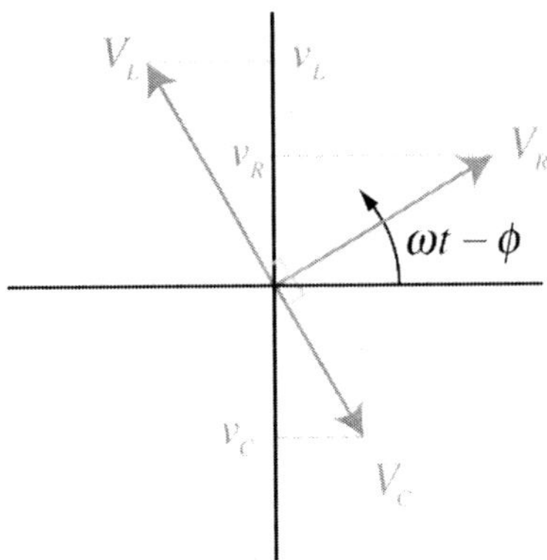

Figure 30.14: Voltage phasors for an RLC series circuit.
The phasor V_R is in phase with the phasor I representing the current in the circuit.

The voltage phasors must sum as vectors to match the phasor V_m in order to satisfy (30.53) at all times. This vector sum is shown in Figure 30.15.

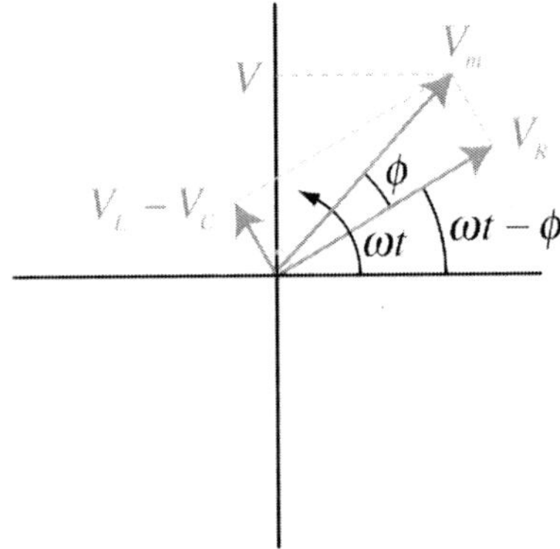

Figure 30.15: Sum of the voltage phasors in an *RLC* series circuit.

In this figure we have replaced the sum of the two phasors V_L and V_C with the phasor V_L-V_C. The vector sum of V_L-V_C and V_R must equal V_m. Thus we can write

$$V_m^2=V_R^2+\left(V_L-V_C\right)^2 \tag{30.54}$$

Now we can apply equations (30.34), (30.42), and (30.54), taking the current in all three components to be I because they are in series

$$V_m^2=\left(IR\right)^2+\left(IX_L-IX_C\right)^2. \tag{30.55}$$

We can then solve for the current in the circuit

$$I = \frac{V_m}{\sqrt{R^2 + \left(X_L - X_C\right)^2}}. \tag{30.56}$$

The denominator of (30.56) is called the impedance

$$Z = \sqrt{R^2 + \left(X_L - X_C\right)^2}. \tag{30.57}$$

The impedance of a circuit depends on the frequency of the time-varying emf. We can express this time dependence explicitly by inserting the definitions of the capacitive reactance and the inductive reactance

$$Z = \sqrt{R^2 + \left(\omega L - \frac{1}{\omega C}\right)^2}. \tag{30.58}$$

The impedance of an alternating current circuit has the units of Ω like the resistance in a direct current circuit. We can then write

$$I = \frac{V_m}{\sqrt{R^2 + \left(\omega L - \frac{1}{\omega C}\right)^2}} = \frac{V_m}{Z}. \tag{30.59}$$

The current flowing in an alternating current circuit depends on the difference between the inductive reactance and the capacitive reactance. We can express the phase constant ϕ in terms of the difference between the inductive reactance and the capacitive reactance. This phase constant is defined as the phase difference between voltage phasors V_R and V_m depicted in Figure 30.15. Thus, we can write the phase constant as

$$\phi = \tan^{-1}\left(\frac{V_L - V_C}{V_R}\right). \tag{30.60}$$

Substituting in (30.34), (30.42), and (30.50) we get

$$\phi = \tan^{-1}\left(\frac{X_L - X_C}{R}\right). \tag{30.61}$$

The current in the circuit can now be written as

$$i = I_{\max} \sin\left(\omega t - \phi\right) \tag{30.62}$$

where I_{max} is the magnitude of the phasor I while the voltage across all the components in the circuit is given by the time-varying source of emf

$$V = V_{emf} = V_{max} \sin(\omega t) \tag{30.63}$$

where V_{max} is the magnitude of the phasor V_m.

Thus, we have three conditions for an alternating current series circuit containing a resistor, a capacitor, and an inductor:

- For $X_L > X_C$, ϕ is positive, and the current in the circuit will lag behind the voltage in the circuit. This circuit will be similar to a circuit with only an inductor, except that the phase constant is not necessarily $\pi/2$ rad $(90°)$, as illustrated in Figure 30.16*a*).
- For $X_L < X_C$, ϕ is negative, and the current in the circuit will lead the voltage in the circuit. This circuit will be similar to a circuit with only a capacitor, except that the phase constant is not necessarily $-\pi/2$ rad $(-90°)$, as illustrated in Figure 30.16*b*).
- For $X_L = X_C$, ϕ is zero, and the current in the circuit will be in phase with the voltage in the circuit. This circuit is similar to a circuit with only a resistance, as illustrated in Figure 30.16*c*). When $\phi = 0$ we say that the circuit is in resonance.

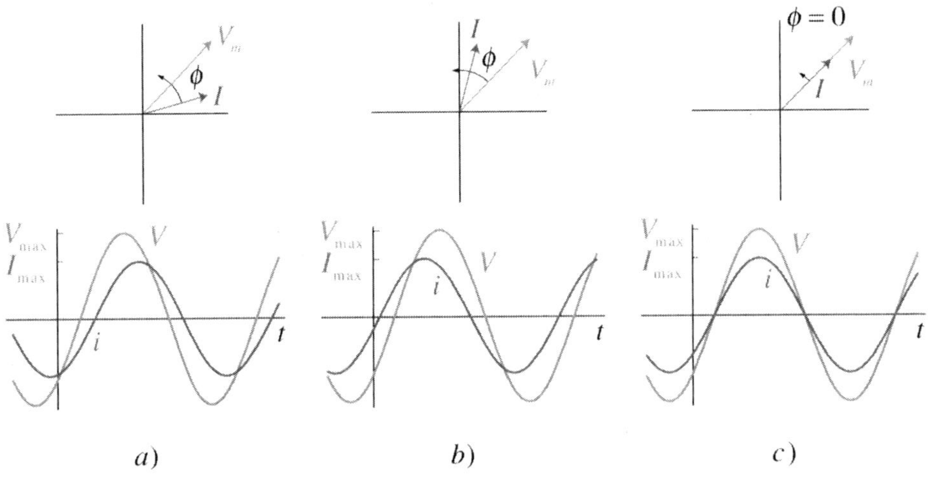

Figure 30.16: Current and voltage as a function of time for an *RLC* circuit with *a)* $X_L > X_C$, *b)* $X_L < X_C$, *c)* $X_L = X_C$.

The current amplitude I_{max} in the circuit depends on the frequency of the time-varying emf as well as on L and C. The maximum current occurs when

$$\omega L - \frac{1}{\omega C} = 0 \tag{30.64}$$

which corresponds to $\phi = 0$ and $X_L = X_C$. The angular frequency ω_0, called the resonant angular frequency, at which the maximum current occurs is

$$\omega_0 = \frac{1}{\sqrt{LC}}. \tag{30.65}$$

Self-Test Opportunity: Consider a series RLC circuit like the one shown in Figure 30.12. The circuit is driven at an angular frequency ω. The resonant angular frequency is ω_0. Answer whether the following statements are true or false.

a) If $\omega = \omega_0$, the voltage and the current are in phase.
b) If $\omega < \omega_0$, the voltage lags behind the current.
c) If $\omega > \omega_0$, then $X_C > X_L$.

Now let's look at a real circuit. The diagram for this circuit is the same as the one shown in Figure 30.12. A physical realization is shown in Figure 30.17.

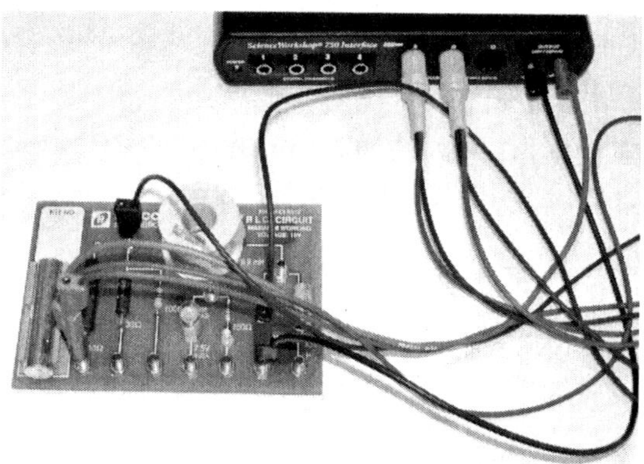

Figure 30.17: Real circuit consisting of a 8.2 mH inductance, 10 Ω resistance, and 100 μF capacitance.

This particular circuit has a source of time-varying emf with $V_{\text{max}} = 7.5\text{ V}$, $L = 8.2\text{ mH}$, $C = 100\ \mu\text{F}$, and $R = 10\ \Omega$. The measured maximum current I_{max} is measured as a function of the ratio of the angular frequency of the time-varying emf divided by the resonant angular frequency, ω/ω_0, is shown in Figure 30.18. Red circles depict the results of the measurement. The maximum value of the current occurs as one expects at the resonant angular frequency, which confirms our knowledge of L and C. However, the expected relationship between I_{max} and ω/ω_0 given by (30.59) using $R = 10\ \Omega$ produces the green curve, which does not reproduce the measured results. To better describe the circuit one must remember that, in a real circuit, the inductor has a resistance, even at the resonant frequency. The black line shown in Figure 30.18 corresponds to (30.59) with $R = 15.4\ \Omega$.

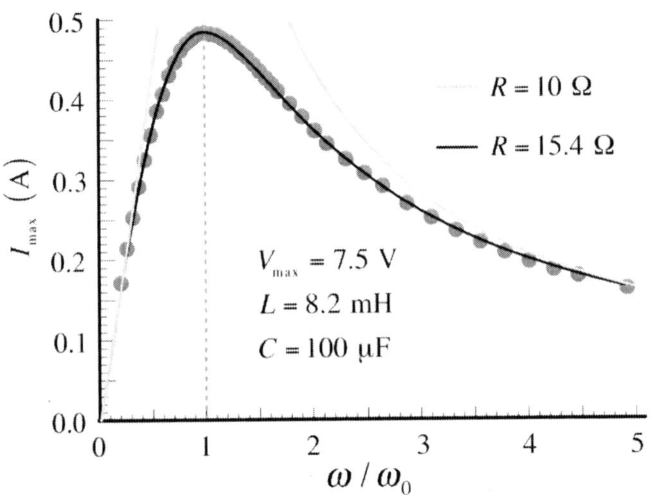

Figure 30.18: Graph of the maximum current I versus the ratio of the angular frequency ω of the time-varying emf divided by the resonance frequency ω_0 for an *RLC* circuit. Red circles represent measurements. See the text for a discussion of the green and black lines.

The resonant behavior of an *RLC* circuit resembles the response of a damped oscillator. In Figure 30.19, the calculated maximum current I_{max} is shown as a function of the ratio of the angular frequency of the time-varying emf divided by the resonant angular frequency, ω / ω_0, for a circuit with $V_{max} = 7.5 \text{ V}$, $L = 8.2 \text{ mH}$, $C = 100\ \mu\text{F}$, and three different resistances.

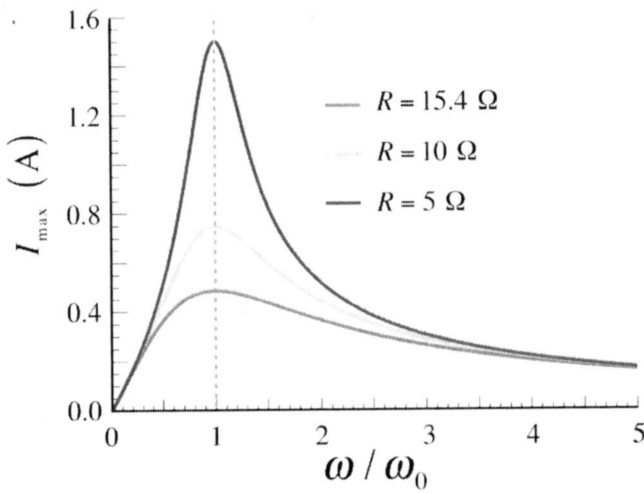

Figure 30.19: Graph of the maximum current I_{max} versus the ratio of the angular frequency ω of the time-varying emf divided by the resonance frequency ω_0 predicted for three *RLC* circuits with L = 8.2 mH, C = 100 μF, and three different resistances.

One can see that as the resistance is lowered, the maximum current at the resonant angular frequency increases and there is a more pronounced resonant peak.

Self-Test Opportunity: Consider a series RLC circuit like the one shown in Figure 30.12. Answer whether following statements are true or false.

a) The current through the resistor is the same as the current through the inductor at all times.
b) Energy is dissipated in the resistor but not in either the capacitor or the inductor.
c) The voltage drop across the resistor is the same as the voltage drop across the inductor at all times.

In-class exercise: A time-varying source of emf supplies $V_{emf} = 115.0 \text{ V}$ at $f = 60.0 \text{ Hz}$ to a series RLC circuit with $R = 374\ \Omega$, $L = 0.310 \text{ H}$, and $C = 5.50\ \mu\text{F}$. What is the impedance of this circuit?

a) $321\ \Omega$
b) $523\ \Omega$
c) $622\ \Omega$
d) $831\ \Omega$
e) $975\ \Omega$

Example

Example 30.2: RLC circuit

Consider an RLC series circuit like the one shown in Figure 30.12. In this circuit $R = 91.0\ \Omega$, $C = 6.00\ \mu\text{F}$, and $L = 60.0 \text{ mH}$. The source of time-varying emf has an angular frequency of $\omega = 64.0 \text{ rad/s}$.

Question 1:
What is the inductive reactance of this circuit?
Answer 1:
The inductive reaction is given by

$$X_L = \omega L = (64.0 \text{ rad/s})(60.0 \cdot 10^{-3} \text{ H}) = 3.84\ \Omega.$$

Question 2:
What is the capacitive reactance of this circuit?
Answer 2:
The capacitive reactance is given by

$$X_C = \frac{1}{\omega C} = \frac{1}{(64.0 \text{ rad/s})(6.00 \cdot 10^{-6} \text{ F})} = 2600\ \Omega.$$

Question 3:
What is the impedance of the circuit?
Answer 3:
The impedance is given by

Example

$$Z=\sqrt{R^2+\left(X_L-X_C\right)^2}=\sqrt{\left(91.0\ \Omega\right)^2+\left(3.84\ \Omega-2600\ \Omega\right)^2}=2600\ \Omega.$$

The impedance is dominated by the capacitive reactance.

Question 4:
What is the resonance frequency for this circuit?
Answer 4:
Resonance occurs at the angular frequency given by

$$\omega_r=\frac{1}{\sqrt{LC}}=\frac{1}{\sqrt{\left(60.0\cdot 10^{-3}\ \text{H}\right)\left(6.00\cdot 10^{-6}\ \text{F}\right)}}=1670\ \text{rad/s}.$$

The angular frequency of the source of time-varying emf is far from the resonance angular frequency. The resonance frequency then

$$f_r=\frac{\omega_r}{2\pi}=\frac{1670\ \text{rad/s}}{2\pi\ \text{rad}}=265\ \text{Hz}.$$

Question 5:
What is the impedance of this circuit at resonance?
Answer 5:

$$Z=\sqrt{R^2+\left(X_L-X_C\right)^2}=\sqrt{\left(91.0\ \Omega\right)^2+0}=91.0\ \Omega$$

Frequency Filters

We have been treating circuits that have a time-varying emf with a single frequency. However, there are many applications in which we must deal with time-varying emfs that contain a superposition of many frequencies. In certain situations, we may want certain frequencies to be filtered out of our circuit. We can use series RLC circuits to produce frequency filters. One example of such frequency filter circuit can be found in DSL (Digital Subscriber Line) Internet connections over a telephone line in a house. A typical DSL filter is shown in Figure 30.20.

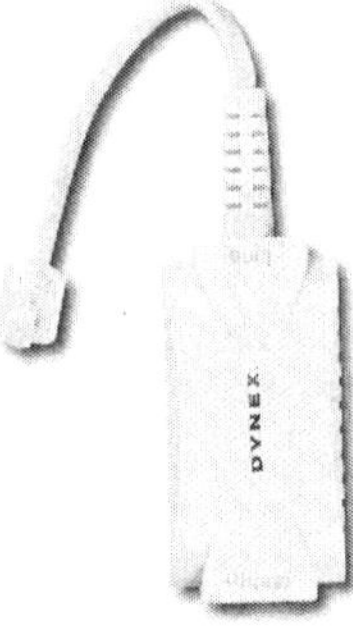

Figure 30.20: A typical band-pass filter for phones that are connected to a house circuit that has a DSL Internet connection.

The DSL Internet connection operates at high frequencies and is connected to the normal audio phone line in the house. The high operating frequency of the DSL connection causes noise on the regular phones in the house. Therefore, a band-pass filter is normally installed on all the phones in the house to filter out the high frequency noise created by the DSL Internet connection. Frequency filters can be designed to pass low frequencies and block high frequencies (low-pass filter) or pass high frequencies and block low frequencies (high-pass filter). A low-pass filter can be combined with a high-pass filter to allow a range of frequencies to pass (band-pass filter) and to block the frequencies outside that range.

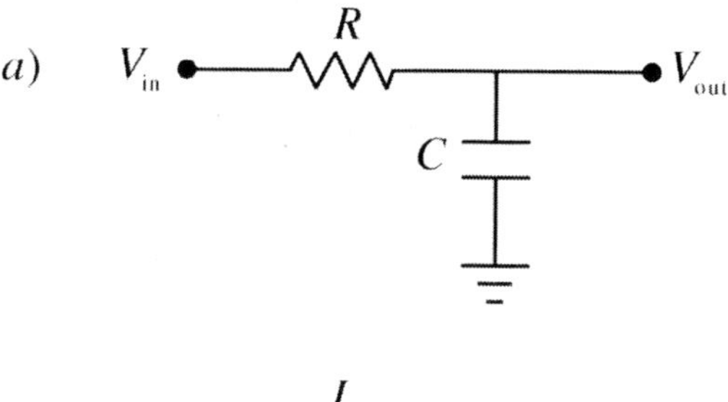

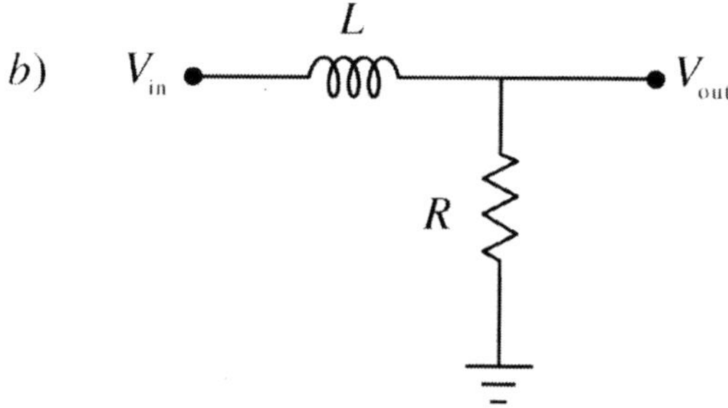

Figure 30.21: Two low-pass filters. In *a*), an *RC* filter is shown. In *b*), an *RL* filter is illustrated.

Two examples of a low-pass filter are shown in Figure 30.21, where we assume that we have a time-varying emf V_{in} with many frequencies. The low-pass filter is essentially a voltage divider. Part of the original emf passes through the circuit while part of the original emf goes to ground. For the RC version of the low-pass filter, low frequencies will essentially see an open circuit to ground, while high frequencies will be preferentially sent to ground. For the RL version shown in Figure 30.21*b*), low frequencies easily pass through the inductor while high frequencies are blocked. To calculate the quantitative performance of the low-pass filter, we start with Figure 30.21*a*). In this figure, we define the input section to be the resistance and the capacitance. The impedance of this section is

$$Z_{\text{in}} = \sqrt{R^2 + X_C^{\ 2}} . \tag{30.66}$$

The impedance of the output section is just $Z_{\text{out}} = X_C$. The ratio of the emf into the circuit element and the emf emerging from the circuit element is

$$\frac{V_{\text{out}}}{V_{\text{in}}} = \frac{Z_{\text{out}}}{Z_{\text{in}}} \tag{30.67}$$

The ratio of emfs can then written as

$$\frac{V_{\text{out}}}{V_{\text{in}}} = \frac{X_C}{\sqrt{R^2 + X_C^2}} = \frac{1}{\sqrt{\left(\frac{R}{X_C}\right)^2 + 1}} = \frac{1}{\sqrt{1 + \omega^2 R^2 C^2}} \tag{30.68}$$

For the RL case, $Z_{\text{in}} = \sqrt{R^2 + X_L^2}$ and $Z_{\text{out}} = R$ allowing us to write

$$\frac{V_{\text{out}}}{V_{\text{in}}} = \frac{R}{\sqrt{R^2 + X_L^2}} = \frac{1}{\sqrt{1 + \left(\omega^2 L^2 / R^2\right)}} \tag{30.69}$$

We define the breakpoint frequency, ω_B, between the response to low and high frequencies as the frequency at which the ratio $V_{\text{out}} / V_{\text{in}}$ is $1/\sqrt{2} = 0.707$. At that frequency for the RC case we have

$$\frac{1}{\sqrt{1 + \omega_B^2 R^2 C^2}} = \frac{1}{\sqrt{2}} \tag{30.70}$$

from which we can solve for the breakpoint frequency

$$\omega_B = \frac{1}{RC}. \tag{30.71}$$

For the RL version of the low-pass filter shown in Figure 30.21*b*), the breakpoint frequency is

$$\omega_B = \frac{R}{L}, \tag{30.72}$$

which can be obtained from (30.69).

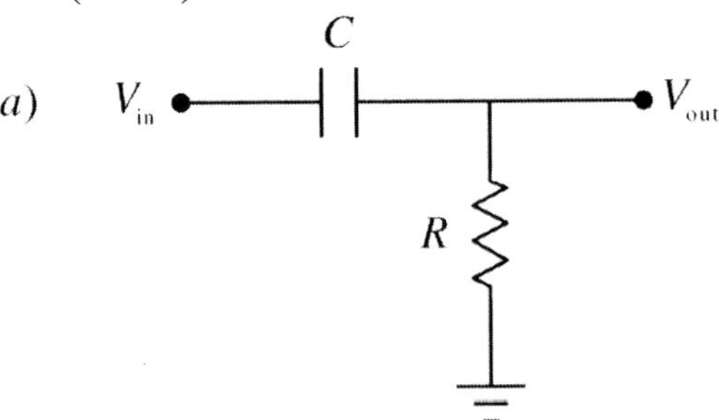

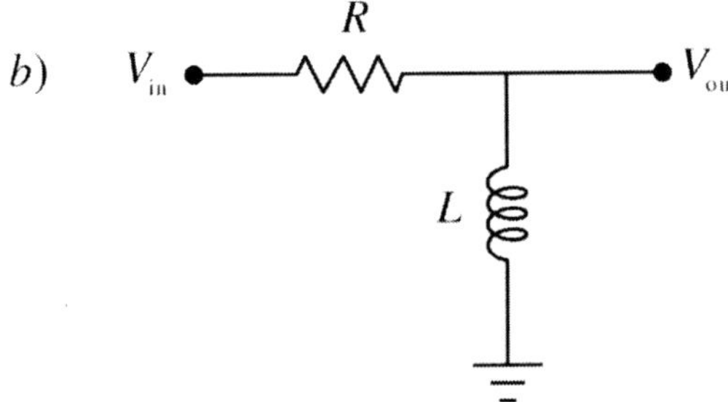

Figure 30.22: Two high-pass filters. In *a*), an *RC* filter is shown. In *b*), an *RL* filter is illustrated.

Two examples of a high-pass filter are shown in Figure 30.22. In Figure 30.22*a*), the RC version of the high-pass filter the impedance of the input section is

$$Z_{\text{in}} = \sqrt{R^2 + X_C^{\ 2}} \tag{30.73}$$

while the impedance of the output section is $Z_{\text{out}} = R$. The ratio of the output emf to the input emf is then

$$\frac{V_{\text{out}}}{V_{\text{in}}} = \frac{R}{\sqrt{R^2 + X_C^2}} = \frac{1}{\sqrt{1 + \dfrac{1}{\omega^2 R^2 C^2}}} \tag{30.74}$$

For the RL high-pass filter shown in Figure 30.22*b*), the ratio of the output emf to the input emf is

$$\frac{V_{\text{out}}}{V_{\text{in}}} = \frac{X_L}{\sqrt{R^2 + X_L^2}} = \frac{1}{\sqrt{\dfrac{R^2}{X_L^2} + 1}} = \frac{1}{\sqrt{1 + \dfrac{R^2}{\omega^2 L^2}}} \tag{30.75}$$

For these high-pass filters, as the frequency increases, the ratio of output to input emf approaches one, while for low frequencies, the ratio of output to input emf goes to zero. The breakpoint frequencies are the same for high-pass filters as the same as those for the low-pass filters, $\omega_B = 1/(RC)$ for the RC high-pass filter and $\omega_B = L/R$ for the RL high-pass filter.

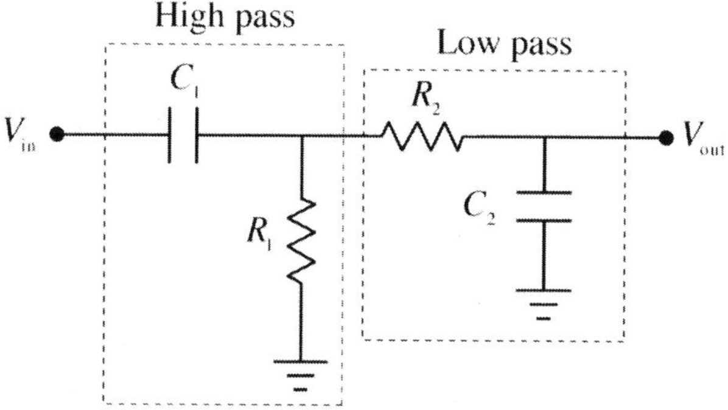

Figure 30.23: A band-pass filter created by a high-pass filter followed by a low-pass filter.

An example of band-pass filter is shown in Figure 30.23. The band-pass filter consists of a high-pass filter in series with a low-pass filter. Thus, both high and low frequencies are suppressed and a band of frequencies are allowed to pass through the band-pass filter.

Examples of a low-pass filter and a high-pass filter with $R = 50\ \Omega$ and $C = 20$ mF are shown in Figure 30.24. For this combination of R and C, the breakpoint frequency is

$$\omega_B = \frac{1}{RC} = \frac{1}{(50\ \Omega)(20 \cdot 10^{-3}\ \text{F})} = 1\ \text{rad/s} . \qquad (30.76)$$

Also shown in Figure 30.24 is an example the frequency response of a band-pass filter with $R_1 = R_2 = 50\ \Omega$ and $C_1 = C_2 = 20$ mF.

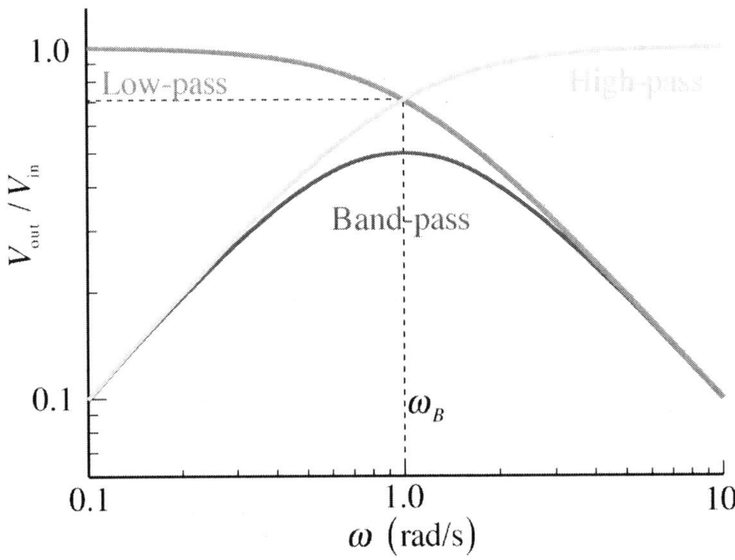

Figure 30.24: The frequency response of a low-pass filter, a high-pass filter, and a band-pass filter. (Note that both axes have logarithmic scales!)

30.5. Energy and Power in AC Circuits

When an RLC circuit is in operation, some of the energy in the circuit is stored in the electric field of the capacitor, some of the energy is stored in the magnetic field of the inductor, and some energy is dissipated in the form of heat in the resistor. We are interested in the steady state behavior of this circuit, behavior that occurs after initial (transient) effects die out. (A full mathematical analysis would have shown the transient effects, which die out exponentially similar to what we found for the solution (30.26) of the RLC with no emf source.) The sum of the energy stored in the capacitor and inductor does not change in the steady state. Therefore the energy transferred from the source of emf to the circuit is transferred to the resistor. The rate at which energy is dissipated in the resistor is the power P given by

$$P = i^2 R = \left(I \sin(\omega t - \phi)\right)^2 R = I^2 R \sin^2(\omega t - \phi) \qquad (30.77)$$

where we have used (30.30) for the alternating current. The average power $\langle P \rangle$ can be obtained by realizing that the average value of $\sin^2(\omega t - \phi)$ is $1/2$. Thus, we can write that the average power is

$$\langle P \rangle = \frac{1}{2} I^2 R = \left(\frac{I}{\sqrt{2}} \right)^2 R. \tag{30.78}$$

It is common to refer to the root-mean-square (rms) current, I_{rms}. In general rms means the square root of the mean of the square of a quantity. From equation (30.77) we have $i^2 = \left(I \sin\left(\omega t - \phi \right) \right)^2$ and the mean (or average) of i^2 is $I^2/2$. Thus $I_{rms} = I/\sqrt{2}$. We can then write the average power as

$$\langle P \rangle = I_{rms}^2 R. \tag{30.79}$$

In a similar way, we can define the rms values of other time-varying quantities such as the voltage

$$V_{rms} = \frac{V_{\max}}{\sqrt{2}}. \tag{30.80}$$

The currents and voltages normally quoted for alternating currents and measured by alternating current ammeters and voltmeters are I_{rms} and V_{rms}. For example, the 110 V wall plugs in the United States provide $V_{rms} = 110 \text{ V}$, which corresponds to a maximum voltage of $\sqrt{2} \cdot 110 \text{ V} \approx 156 \text{ V}$.

We can then re-write (30.59) in terms of rms values by multiplying both sides of the equation by $1/\sqrt{2}$

$$I_{rms} = \frac{V_{rms}}{Z} = \frac{V_{rms}}{\sqrt{R^2 + \left(\omega L - \frac{1}{\omega C} \right)^2}}. \tag{30.81}$$

This form is most often used to describe the characteristics of alternating current circuits.

Now we can describe the average power dissipated in an alternating current circuit in a different way by starting with (30.79)

$$\langle P \rangle = I_{rms}^2 R = \frac{V_{rms}}{Z} I_{rms} R = I_{rms} V_{rms} \frac{R}{Z}. \tag{30.82}$$

Looking at Figure 30.15 we can see that we can relate the phase constant to the ratio of the maximum value of the voltage across the resistor divided by the maximum value of the time-varying emf

$$\cos\phi = \frac{V_R}{V_{\max}} = \frac{IR}{IZ} = \frac{R}{Z}. \quad (30.83)$$

We can re-write (30.82) as

$$\langle P \rangle = I_{rms} V_{rms} \cos\phi . \quad (30.84)$$

This expression gives the average power dissipated in an alternating current circuit where the term $\cos\phi$ is termed the power factor. One can see that for $\phi = 0$, the maximum power is dissipated in the circuit, which means that the maximum power is dissipated in an alternating current circuit when the frequency of the time-varying emf matches the resonant frequency of the circuit.

Solved Problem

Solved Problem 30.1: Unknown inductance

Consider a series RL circuit with a time varying source of emf. In this circuit, $V_{emf} = 33.0$ V with a frequency $f = 7.10$ kHz and $R = 83.0\ \Omega$. A current $I = 0.158$ A flows in the circuit.

Question:

What is the inductance L?

Answer:

THINK:

The specified voltage and current are implicitly rms values. We can relate the voltage and current through the impedance of the circuit. The impedance of this circuit depends on the resistance and the inductance as well as the frequency of the source of emf.

SKETCH:

A sketch of the circuit is shown in Figure 30.25.

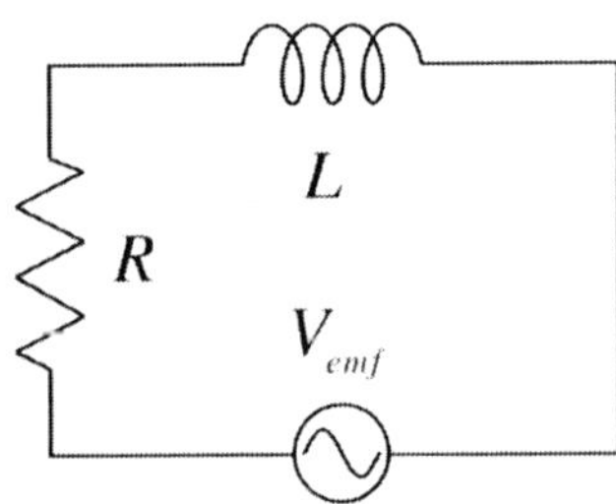

Figure 30.25: A series RL circuit.

RESEARCH:

We can relate the source of time varying emf V_{emf} and the impedance Z in the circuit

$$V_{emf} = IZ . \quad (30.85)$$

The impedance is given by

$$Z=\sqrt{R^2+(X_L-X_C)^2}=\sqrt{R^2+X_L^2} \quad (30.86)$$

where R is the resistance, X_L is the inductive reactance, and the capacitive reactance X_C is zero. The angular frequency ω of the circuit is given by

$$\omega=2\pi f \quad (30.87)$$

where f is the frequency. We can write the inductive reactance as

$$X_L=\omega L. \quad (30.88)$$

SIMPLIFY:

We can combine (30.85), (30.86), and (30.88) to obtain

$$Z^2=R^2+X_L^2=\left(\frac{V_{emf}}{I}\right)^2=R^2+(\omega L)^2. \quad (30.89)$$

We can rearrange (30.89) to get

$$\omega L=\sqrt{\frac{V_{emf}^2}{I^2}-R^2}. \quad (30.90)$$

Solving (30.90) for the unknown inductance gives us

$$L=\frac{1}{2\pi f}\sqrt{\frac{V_{emf}^2}{I^2}-R^2}. \quad (30.91)$$

CALCULATE:

Putting in our numerical values gives us

$$L=\frac{1}{2\pi\left(7.10\cdot 10^3\ \text{s}^{-1}\right)}\sqrt{\frac{(33.0\ \text{V})^2}{(0.158\ \text{A})^2}-(83.0\ \Omega)^2}=0.0042963\ \text{H}.$$

ROUND:

We report our result to three significant figures

$$L=4.30\cdot 10^{-3}\ \text{H}=4.30\ \text{mH}.$$

DOUBLE-CHECK:

To double-check our result for the unknown inductance, we calculate the inductive reactance

Solved Problem

Solved Problem

$$X_L = 2\pi fL = 2\pi\left(7.10\cdot10^3\ \text{s}^{-1}\right)\left(4.30\cdot10^{-3}\ \text{H}\right) = 192\ \Omega.$$

The impedance of the circuit is then

$$Z = \sqrt{R^2 + X_L^2} = \sqrt{\left(83.0\ \Omega\right)^2 + \left(192\ \Omega\right)^2} = 209\ \Omega.$$

The emf would then be

$$V_{emf} = IZ = \left(0.158\ \text{A}\right)\left(209\ \Omega\right) = 33.0\ \text{V}$$

which agrees with the emf specified in the problem. Thus our answer seems reasonable.

In-class exercise: In the series *RL* circuit studied in Solved Problem 25.1, what is the magnitude of the phase difference between the applied voltage and the current in the circuit?

a) 30.0°
b) 45.0°
c) 66.6°
d) 75.0°
e) 90.0°

30.6. Transformers

In the following section we consider all currents and voltages to be rms values rather than maximum values. In addition, we will assume that power is always average power. This practice follows the normal conventions used by scientists, engineers, and electricians in dealing with alternating current circuits.

In an alternating current circuit that has only a resistor, the phase factor is zero and $\cos\phi = 1$. Thus we can write the power as

$$P = IV. \qquad (30.92)$$

For a given power delivered to a circuit, certain situations dictate the choice of high current or high voltage. For example, to provide enough power to operate a computer or a vacuum cleaner, one does not want to use high voltages that might be dangerous. The design of electric generators is complicated by the use of high voltages. Therefore, in these situations, lower voltages and higher currents are advantageous.

However, the transmission of electric power requires the opposite condition. The power dissipated in a transmission line is given by $P = I^2R$. Thus the power lost in the transmission line such as the ones shown in Figure 30.26 is proportional the square of the current in the lines. As an example, consider a power plant that produces 500 MW of power. If the power were transmitted at 350 kV, then the current would be

$$I = \frac{P}{V} = \frac{500 \text{ MW}}{350 \text{ kV}} = \frac{5 \cdot 10^8 \text{ W}}{3.5 \cdot 10^5 \text{ V}} = 1430 \text{ A}. \qquad (30.93)$$

If the total resistance of the power lines were $50\ \Omega$, then the power lost in the transmission lines would be

$$P = I^2 R = \left(1430 \text{ A}\right)^2 \cdot 50\ \Omega = 100 \text{ MW} \qquad (30.94)$$

or 20% of the generated power. From a similar calculation one can see that transmitting the power at 100 kV instead of 350 kV would mean a factor of 3.5 higher loss. Thus 70% of the power generated would be lost in transmission. This is the reason that the transmission of electric power is always done at the highest possible voltages.

Self-test opportunity: You can argue that the power companies should simply reduce the resistance in their wires to avoid these huge losses. Typical wires for these transmission lines are finger-thick. How big would they need to be for a factor of 100 less in resistance, leaving all other parameters (material used, length) the same? (Hint: consult back to chapter 25 for the answer).

Figure 30.26: Left: High voltage power lines; right: transformers for residential power lines.

The ability to raise and lower alternating voltages is useful in everyday life. It allows us to generate and to use electric power at low, safe voltages while transmitting the power at the highest practical voltages. To transform alternating currents and voltages from high to low one uses a transformer. A transformer that takes voltages from lower to higher is called a step-up transformer and a transformer that takes voltages from higher to lower is called a step-down transformer.

A transformer consists of two sets of coils wrapped around an iron core as illustrated in Figure 30.27.

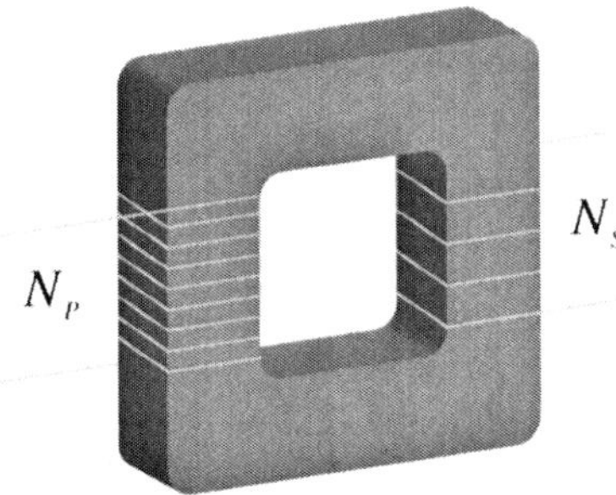

Figure 30.27: Transformer with N_P primary windings and N_S secondary windings.

Consider the primary windings with N_p turns connected to a source of emf described by

$$V_{emf} = V_{\max} \sin \omega t . \tag{30.95}$$

We can assume that the primary windings act as an inductor. This circuit has the current and voltage out of phase by $\pi / 2$ rad $(90°)$ so that the power factor $\cos\phi$ is zero. Thus the source of emf is not delivering any power to the transformer.

Now consider the secondary coil with N_S turns. The time-varying emf in the primary coil induces a time-varying magnetic field in the iron core. This core passes through the secondary coil. Thus a time-varying voltage is induced in the secondary coil described by Faraday's Law

$$V_{emf} = -N \frac{d\Phi_B}{dt} \tag{30.96}$$

where N is the number of turns and Φ_B is the magnetic flux. Because of the iron core both the primary and secondary coils experience the same changing magnetic flux. Thus we have $V_s = -N_s \frac{d\Phi_B}{dt}$ and $V_P = -N_P \frac{d\Phi_B}{dt}$, where V_S and V_P are the voltages across the secondary and primary windings respectively. Dividing these two equations and rearranging slightly we find

$$\frac{V_P}{N_P} = \frac{V_S}{N_S} \tag{30.97}$$

or

$$V_S = V_P \frac{N_S}{N_P} . \tag{30.98}$$

The transformer then changes the voltage of the primary circuit to a secondary voltage given by the ratio of the number turns in the secondary coil divided by the number of turns in the primary coil.

If we now connect a resistor R across the secondary windings, a current I_S will begin to flow through the secondary coil. The power in the secondary circuit is then $P_s = I_S V_S$. This current will induce a time-varying magnetic field that will induce an emf in the primary coil. The emf source then will produce enough current I_P to maintain the original emf. This current I_P will be in phase with the emf because of the resistor R and thus power can be transmitted to the transformer. Energy conservation tells us that the power produced by the emf source in the primary coil will be transferred to the secondary coil so we can write

$$P_P = I_P V_P = P_S = I_S V_S. \tag{30.99}$$

We can write the current in the secondary circuit as

$$I_S = I_P \frac{V_P}{V_S} = I_P \frac{N_P}{N_S} \tag{30.100}$$

using (30.98). The current in the secondary circuit is equal to the current in the primary circuit multiplied by the ratio of the number of primary turns divided by the number of secondary turns.

When the secondary circuit begins to draw current, current must be supplied to the primary circuit. We know that $V_S = I_S R$ in the secondary circuit. Using (30.98) and (30.100) we can therefore write

$$I_P = \frac{N_S}{N_P} I_S = \frac{N_S}{N_P}\frac{V_S}{R} = \frac{N_S}{N_P}\left(V_P \frac{N_S}{N_P}\right)\frac{1}{R} = \left(\frac{N_S}{N_P}\right)^2 \frac{V_P}{R}. \tag{30.101}$$

We can define the effective resistance that the primary circuit in terms of $V_P = I_P R_P$ so the effective resistance seen by the primary circuit is

$$R_P = \frac{V_P}{I_P} = V_P \left(\frac{N_P}{N_S}\right)^2 \frac{R}{V_P} = \left(\frac{N_P}{N_S}\right)^2 R. \tag{30.102}$$

Note that we have assumed no losses in the transformer. We assumed that the primary coil is only an inductive load. We assumed there are no losses in magnetic flux between the primary and secondary coils. We also assumed that the load on the secondary circuit was purely resistive. Real transformers do have some losses. However, modern ansformers can transform voltages with very little loss.

Another application of transformers is impedance matching. The power transfer between a source of emf and a load is at a maximum when the impedance is the same in both. Often sources of emf and the intended devices do not have the same impedance. A common example is a stereo amplifier and its speaker. Usually the amplifier has high impedance and the speakers have low impedance. A transformer placed between the amplifier and the speakers can help match the impedance of the two devices producing a more efficient energy transfer between them.

What we have learned/Exam Study Guide:

Most Important Points

- The energy stored in the electric field of a capacitor C with charge q is given by $U_E = \frac{1}{2}\frac{q^2}{C}$ and the energy stored in the magnetic field of an inductor L carrying current i is given by $U_B = \frac{1}{2}Li^2$.
- A single loop circuit containing an inductor L and a capacitor C will oscillate with a frequency given by $\omega_0 = \frac{1}{\sqrt{LC}}$.
- A single loop circuit containing a resistor R, an inductor L and a capacitor C will oscillate with a frequency given by $\omega = \sqrt{\omega_0^2 - \left(\frac{R}{2L}\right)^2}$ where $\omega_0 = \frac{1}{\sqrt{LC}}$.
- The charge q in a single loop circuit containing a resistor R, an inductor L and a capacitor C will oscillate and decrease exponentially with time as given by $q = q_{\max} e^{-\frac{Rt}{2L}} \cos(\omega t)$ where $q_{\max}$ is the charge originally in the capacitor and ϕ is the phase.
- For a single loop circuit containing a source of time-varying emf and a resistor R we have $V_R = I_R R$ where V_R and I_R are the voltage and current respectively.
- For a single loop circuit containing a source of time-varying emf with frequency ω and a capacitor C we have $V_C = I_C X_C$ where V_C and I_C are the voltage and current respectively and $X_C = \frac{1}{\omega C}$ is the capacitive reactance.
- For a single loop circuit containing a source of time-varying emf with frequency ω and an inductor L we have $V_L = I_L X_L$ where V_L and I_L are the voltage and current respectively and $X_L = \omega L$ is the inductive reactance.
- For a single loop circuit containing a source of time-varying emf with frequency

ω and a resistor R, a capacitor C, and an inductor L we have $V = IZ$ where V and I are the voltage and current respectively and $Z = \sqrt{R^2 + (X_L - X_C)^2}$ is the impedance.

- The phase ϕ between the current and voltage in a single loop circuit containing a source of time-varying emf with frequency ω and a resistor R, a capacitor C, and an inductor L is given by $\phi = \tan^{-1}\left(\frac{X_L - X_C}{R}\right)$.
- The average power in a single loop circuit containing a source of time-varying emf with frequency ω and a resistor R, a capacitor C, and an inductor L is given by $\langle P \rangle = I_{rms} V_{rms} \cos\phi$ where $I_{rms} = \frac{I}{\sqrt{2}}$ and $V_{rms} = \frac{V_{\max}}{\sqrt{2}}$.
- Normally all currents, voltages, and powers are quoted as rms value.
- A transformer with N_p primary windings and N_S secondary windings can convert a primary alternating voltage V_P to a secondary alternating voltage V_S by $V_S = V_P \frac{N_S}{N_P}$ and a primary alternating current I_P to a second alternating current I_S by $I_S = I_P \frac{N_P}{N_S}$.

New Symbols used in this Chapter

- ω_0 is the resonant frequency of LC and RLC circuits.
- X_C is the capacitive reactance.
- X_L is the inductive reactance.
- Z is the impedance of an alternating current circuit.
- $\langle P \rangle$ is the average power dissipated in an alternating current circuit.
- ϕ is the phase constant between the voltage and the current in an alternating current circuit.
- The index *rms* indicates the root-mean-square of a quantity

Additional Solved Problems

Solved Problem

Solved Problem 30.2: Voltage drop across an inductor

A series RLC circuit has a time-varying source of emf $V_{emf} = 170.0$ V rms, a resistor $R = 820.0\ \Omega$, an inductance $L = 30.0$ mH, and a capacitance $C = 0.290$ mF. The circuit is operating at its resonant frequency.

Question:

What is the rms voltage drop across the inductor?

Answer:

THINK:

At the resonant frequency, the impedance of the circuit is equal to the resistance. We can calculate the rms current in the circuit. The voltage drop across the inductor is then the product of the rms current in the circuit and the inductive reactance.

SKETCH:

A drawing of a series RLC circuit is shown in Figure 30.28.

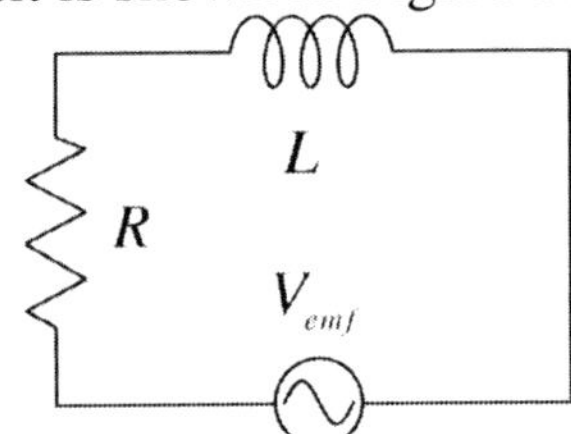

Figure 30.28: A series *RLC* circuit.

RESEARCH:

At resonance, the impedance of the circuit is given by

$$Z = \sqrt{R^2 + (X_L - X_C)^2} = R. \qquad (30.103)$$

At resonance, the rms current i in the circuit is given by

$$V_{emf} = iR. \qquad (30.104)$$

The rms voltage drop across the inductor V_L at resonance is

$$V_L = iX_L. \qquad (30.105)$$

where the inductive reactance X_L is defined as

$$X_L = \omega L \qquad (30.106)$$

where ω is the angular frequency at which the circuit is operating. The resonant frequency ω_0 of the circuit is

$$\omega_0 = \frac{1}{\sqrt{LC}}. \qquad (30.107)$$

SIMPLIFY:

Combining these equations gives us the voltage drop across the inductor at resonance

Solved Problem

$$V_L = \left(\frac{V_{emf}}{R}\right)(\omega_0 L) = \frac{LV_{emf}}{R}\frac{1}{\sqrt{LC}} = \frac{V_{emf}}{R}\sqrt{\frac{L}{C}}. \qquad (30.108)$$

CALCULATE:

Putting in our numerical values gives us

$$V_L = \frac{170.0\ \text{V}}{820.0\ \Omega}\sqrt{\frac{30.0\cdot 10^{-3}\ \text{H}}{0.290\cdot 10^{-3}\ \text{C}}} = 2.10861\ \text{V}.$$

ROUND:

We report our result to three significant figures

$$V_L = 2.11\ \text{V}.$$

DOUBLE-CHECK:

The rms voltage drop across the capacitor is

$$V_L = \left(\frac{V_{emf}}{R}\right)\left(\frac{1}{\omega_0 C}\right) = \frac{V_{emf}}{RC}\sqrt{LC} = \left(\frac{V_{emf}}{R}\right)\sqrt{\frac{L}{C}}$$

which is the same as the rms voltage drop across the inductor. At resonance, the instantaneous voltage drop across the inductor is the negative of the voltage drop across the capacitor. Thus, the rms voltage across the capacitor should be the same as the rms voltage across the inductor. Thus, our result seems reasonable.

Solved Problem 30.3: Power dissipated in an *RLC* circuit

Consider a series RLC circuit that has a source of emf with an rms voltage $V_{emf} = 120.0\ \text{V}$ operating at a frequency $f = 50.0\ \text{Hz}$, an inductor $L = 0.500\ \text{H}$, a capacitor $C = 3.30\ \mu\text{F}$, and a resistor $R = 276\ \Omega$.

Question:

What is the average power dissipated in the circuit?

Answer:

THINK:

The average power dissipated in the circuit depends on the angular frequency of the source of emf. The average power is the rms current times the rms voltage. The current in the circuit can be found using the impedance.

SKETCH:

A series RLC circuit is shown in Figure 30.28.

Solved Problem

RESEARCH:

The angular frequency of the source of emf ω is given by

$$\omega = 2\pi f. \quad (30.109)$$

The impedance Z of the circuit is given by

$$Z = \sqrt{R^2 + (X_L - X_C)^2} \quad (30.110)$$

where the inductive reactance is given by

$$X_L = \omega L \quad (30.111)$$

and the capacitive inductance is given by

$$X_C = \frac{1}{\omega C}. \quad (30.112)$$

We can find the rms current i in the circuit using the following relation

$$V_{emf} = iZ. \quad (30.113)$$

The average power dissipated in the circuit $\langle P \rangle$ is given by

$$\langle P \rangle = iV_{emf} \cos\phi \quad (30.114)$$

where ϕ is the phase angle between the voltage and the current in the circuit

$$\phi = \tan^{-1}\left(\frac{X_L - X_C}{R}\right). \quad (30.115)$$

SIMPLIFY:

We can combine the previous equations to obtain an expression for the average power dissipated in the circuit

$$\langle P \rangle = \frac{V_{emf}}{Z} V_{emf} \cos\phi = \frac{V_{emf}^2}{\sqrt{R^2 + (X_L - X_C)^2}} \cos\phi. \quad (30.116)$$

CALCULATE:

First we calculate the inductive reactance

$$X_L = \omega L = 2\pi fL = 2\pi (50.0 \text{ Hz})(0.500 \text{ H}) = 157.1\ \Omega.$$

Solved Problem

Next we calculate the capacitive reactance

$$X_C = \frac{1}{\omega C} = \frac{1}{2\pi fC} = \frac{1}{2\pi(50.0\text{ Hz})(3.30\cdot 10^{-6}\text{ F})} = 964.6\ \Omega.$$

The phase angle is then

$$\phi = \tan^{-1}\left(\frac{X_L - X_C}{R}\right) = \tan^{-1}\left(\frac{157.1\ \Omega - 964.6\ \Omega}{276\ \Omega}\right) = -1.241\text{ rad} = -71.13°.$$

We now calculate the average power dissipated in circuit

$$\langle P\rangle = \frac{(120.0\text{ V})^2}{\sqrt{(276\ \Omega)^2 + (157.1\ \Omega - 964.6\ \Omega)^2}}\cos(-1.241\text{ rad}) = 5.46477\text{ W}$$

ROUND:

We report our result to three significant figures

$$\langle P\rangle = 5.46\text{ W}.$$

DOUBLE-CHECK:

To double-check our results, we calculate the power that would be dissipated in the circuit if it were operating at the resonant frequency. At the resonant frequency, the maximum power is dissipated in the circuit and the impedance of the circuit is equal to the resistance of the resistor. Thus we can write the maximum average power as

$$\langle P\rangle_{\max} = \frac{V_{emf}^2}{R} = \frac{(120.0\text{ V})^2}{276\ \Omega} = 52.2\text{ W}.$$

Our result for the power dissipated at $f = 50.0$ Hz is lower than the maximum average power, so our result seems reasonable.

Chapter 31. Electromagnetic Waves

Figure 31.1: Very Large Array radio telescope.

What we will learn

- Changing electric fields induce magnetic fields.
- Changing magnetic fields induce electric fields.
- Maxwell's Equations describe electromagnetic phenomena.

- Electromagnetic waves, such as those detected by the Very Large Array shown in Figure 31.1, have electric and magnetic fields.
- Solutions of Maxwell's Equations can be obtained in terms of sinusoidally varying traveling waves.
- For an electromagnetic wave, the electric field is perpendicular to the magnetic field and both fields are perpendicular to the direction in which the wave is traveling.
- The speed of light can be expressed in terms of constants related to electric and magnetic fields.
- Light is an electromagnetic wave.
- The speed of light is the same in all reference frames.
- Electromagnetic waves can transport energy and momentum.
- The intensity of an electromagnetic wave is proportional to the square of the rms electric field of the wave.
- The direction of the electric field of a traveling electromagnetic wave is called the polarization direction.

31.1. Induced Magnetic Fields

In the previous chapter we observed that a changing magnetic field induces an electric field. Faraday's Law of Induction tells us that

$$\oint \vec{E} \bullet d\vec{s} = -\frac{d\Phi_B}{dt} \qquad (31.1)$$

where $\vec{E}$ is the electric field induced around a closed loop by the changing magnetic flux Φ_B through that loop. It is probably no surprise that, in a similar way, a changing electric field induces a magnetic field. Maxwell's Law of Induction describes this phenomenon as

$$\oint \vec{B} \bullet d\vec{s} = \mu_0 \varepsilon_0 \frac{d\Phi_E}{dt} \qquad (31.2)$$

where $\vec{B}$ is the magnetic field induced around a closed loop by a changing electric flux Φ_E through that loop. This equation is similar to (31.1) except that there is an extra constant $\mu_0 \varepsilon_0$ and there is no minus sign. The extra constant appears as a consequence of the SI units of a magnetic field. The positive sign on the right hand side of the equation implies that the induced magnetic field will have an opposite sign relative to an induced electric field when both are induced under similar conditions.

To illustrate induced magnetic fields, we consider the example of a circular capacitor as illustrated in Figure 31.2.

For the capacitor shown in Figure 31.2*a*), the charge is constant and there exists a constant electric field between the plates. There is no magnetic field. For the capacitor shown in Figure 31.2*b*), the charge is increasing with time. Thus, the electric flux between the plates is increasing with time. A magnetic field $\vec{B}$ is induced as indicated by the blue lines, which also indicate the direction of $\vec{B}$. Along each loop the magnetic field vector has the same magnitude and is directed tangent to the loop. When the charge stops increasing, the electric flux remains constant and there is no longer a magnetic field.

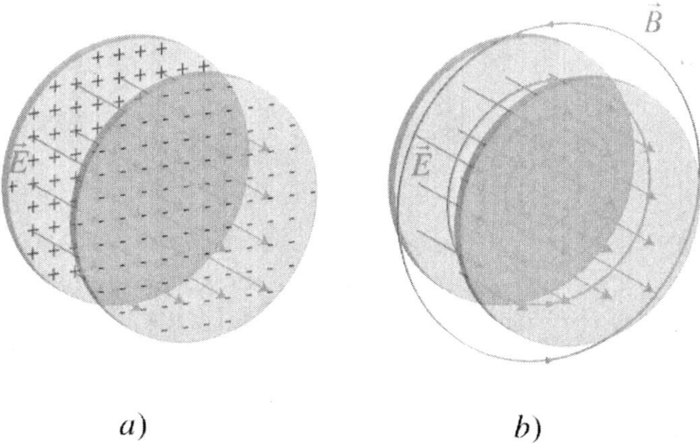

Figure 31.2: *a*) A charged circular capacitor. The red arrows represent the electric field between the plates. *b*) A capacitor with charge increasing with time. The red arrows represent the electric field and the blue lines represent the induced magnetic field.

Now consider a uniform magnetic field as shown in Figure 31.3. In Figure 31.3*a*), a uniform magnetic field that is constant in time is depicted by the blue arrows. In Figure 31.3*b*) the magnetic field is still uniform in space, but is increasing with time, which induces an electric field as shown by the red loops. The electric field vector has constant magnitude along each loop and is directed tangential to the loop as shown. Note that this induced electric field points in the opposite direction from the induced magnetic field resulting from an increasing electric field as shown in Figure 31.2*b*).

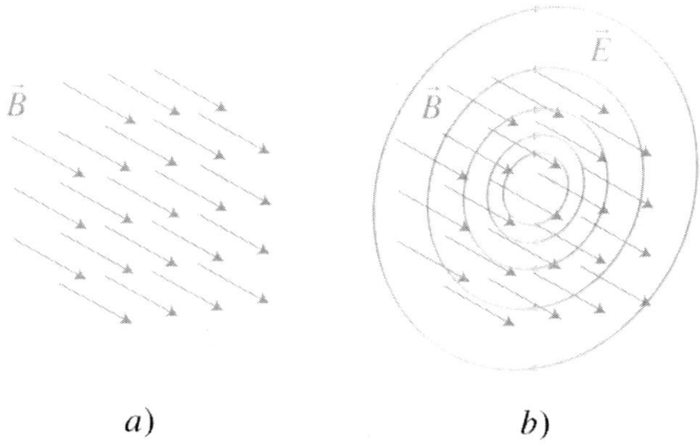

Figure 31.3: *a*) A constant uniform magnetic field. *b*) A uniform magnetic field increasing with time, which induces an electric field illustrated by the red loops.

We now recall Ampere's Law

$$\oint \vec{B} \bullet d\vec{s} = \mu_0 i_{enc} \tag{31.3}$$

relating the integral around a loop of the dot product of the magnetic field and the integration differential, $\vec{B} \bullet d\vec{s}$, to the current flowing through the loop. Comparing (31.2) and (31.3) we see that we can combine the two equations to produce a description of magnetic fields created by moving charges and by changing electric fields

$$\oint \vec{B} \bullet d\vec{s} = \mu_0 \varepsilon_0 \frac{d\Phi_E}{dt} + \mu_0 i_{enc} . \tag{31.4}$$

This equation is called the Maxwell-Ampere Law. You can see that for the case of constant current, such as current flowing in a conductor, this equation reduces to Ampere's Law. For the case of a changing electric field without current flowing, such as the electric field between the plates of a capacitor, this equation reduces to the Maxwell Law of Induction.

31.2. Displacement Current

Looking at the Maxwell-Ampere Law (31.4) one can see that the quantity, $\varepsilon_0 d\Phi_E / dt$, on the right hand side of the equation must have the units of current. This term is called the displacement current

$$i_d = \varepsilon_0 \frac{d\Phi_E}{dt} \tag{31.5}$$

although there is no actual current being displaced. Proceeding with this definition we can re-write (31.4) as

$$\oint \vec{B} \bullet d\vec{s} = \mu_0 (i_d + i_{enc}) . \tag{31.6}$$

Now let's consider a parallel plate capacitor with circular plates as we did earlier in this chapter. We place the capacitor in a circuit in which a current i is flowing while the capacitor is charging as illustrated in Figure 31.4.

For a parallel plate capacitor we can relate the charge q to the electric field as (see equation 24.4):

$$q = \varepsilon_0 AE \tag{31.7}$$

where A is the area of the plates and E is the electric field between the plates. The current i in the circuit can be obtained using the previous equation and taking the time derivative:

$$i = \frac{dq}{dt} = \varepsilon_0 A \frac{dE}{dt} . \tag{31.8}$$

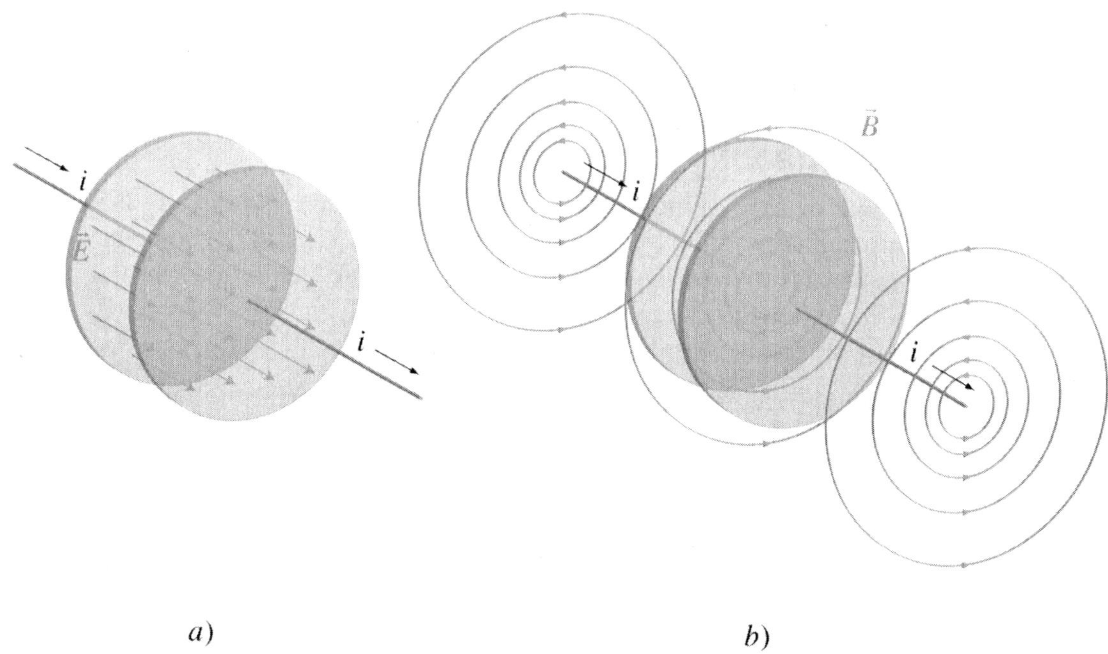

Figure 31.4: Snapshots of a parallel plate capacitor in a circuit being charged by a current *i*;
a) Snapshot of the electric field between the plates.
b) Snapshot of the magnetic field around the wires and between the plates of the capacitor.

Assuming that the electric field between the plates of the capacitor is uniform we can obtain an expression for the displacement current

$$i_d = \varepsilon_0 \frac{d\Phi_E}{dt} = \varepsilon_0 \frac{d(AE)}{dt} = \varepsilon_0 A \frac{dE}{dt}. \tag{31.9}$$

Thus we can see that the current in the circuit i in (31.8) is equal to the displacement current i_d in (31.9). Although there is no actual current flowing between the plates of the capacitor in the sense that no actual charges flow across the capacitor gap from one plate to the other, we can use the concept of displacement current to calculate the induced magnetic field.

To calculate the magnetic field between the two plates of the capacitor, we assume that the volume between the two plates can be replaced with a conductor of radius R carrying current i_d. Thus, from Chapter 27 we know that the magnetic field at a distance r from the center of the capacitor is given by

$$B = \left(\frac{\mu_0 i_d}{2\pi R^2}\right) r,\ r < R. \tag{31.10}$$

Outside the capacitor we can treat the system as a current-carrying wire; so the magnetic field is

$$B = \frac{\mu_0 i_d}{2\pi r},\ r > R. \qquad (31.11)$$

31.3. Maxwell's Equations

The Maxwell-Ampere Law (31.4) completes the explanation of the four equations known as Maxwell's Equations that describe a broad range of electromagnetic phenomena. We have applied these equations to describe electric fields, magnetic fields, and circuits. We now will apply these equations to electromagnetic waves and in chapter 34 to wave optics. A summary of Maxwell's Equations is given in Table 31.1. (Again, as a reminder, the $\oiint d\vec{A}$ symbol represents integration over a closed surface in the top two equations and $\oint d\vec{s}$ indicates integration over a closed line in the second two equations.)

Name	Equation	Description
Gauss's Law for Electric Fields	$\oiint \vec{E} \bullet d\vec{A} = \frac{q_{enc}}{\varepsilon_0}$	Relates the net electric flux to the net enclosed electric charge
Gauss's Law for Magnetic Fields	$\oiint \vec{B} \bullet d\vec{A} = 0$	States that the net magnetic flux is zero (no magnetic charge)
Faraday's Law	$\oint \vec{E} \bullet d\vec{s} = -\frac{d\Phi_B}{dt}$	Relates the induced electric field to the changing magnetic flux
Ampere-Maxwell Law	$\oint \vec{B} \bullet d\vec{s} = \mu_0\varepsilon_0 \frac{d\Phi_E}{dt} + \mu_0 i_{enc}$	Relates the induced magnetic field to the changing electric flux and to the current

Table 31.1: Maxwell's Equations describing electromagnetic phenomena.

If one scrutinizes Maxwell's Equations, one might notice that there is a lack of symmetry between $\vec{E}$ and $\vec{B}$. This difference results from the fact that there exists an electric charge and a corresponding current when this charge moves, but there is apparently no magnetic charge in nature. Particles that have a magnetic charge (such as a North pole or a South pole but not both) are called magnetic monopoles, but empirically we find that magnetic poles always come in dipole pairs, a North pole together with a South pole. There is no fundamental reason for the absence of magnetic monopoles, and many experiments have searched unsuccessfully for them. The most sensitive of these experiments was called MACRO. MACRO consisted of a massive detector that operated for many years in a laboratory, which was located deep under the Gran Sasso mountain in Italy. MACRO searched for magnetic monopoles in cosmic rays, without success.

31.4. Wave Solutions to Maxwell's Equations

It is possible to derive a general wave equation from Maxwell's Equations using advanced calculus. However, here we will assume that electromagnetic waves propagating in vacuum (no moving charges or currents) have a certain form and show that this form satisfies Maxwell's Equations.

Proposed Solution

We will take the following form for the electric and magnetic fields in a particular electromagnetic wave that happens to be traveling in the $+x$-direction:

$$\vec{E}(\vec{r},t) = E_{\max} \sin\left(kx - \omega t\right)\hat{y}$$
$$\vec{B}(\vec{r},t) = B_{\max} \sin\left(kx - \omega t\right)\hat{z} \tag{31.12}$$

where $k = 2\pi / \lambda$ is the angular wave number and $\omega = 2\pi f$ is the angular frequency of a wave with wavelength λ and frequency f. Note that there is no dependence on the y- or z-coordinates, only on the x-coordinate and time. This type of wave in which the electric and magnetic field vectors lie in a plane is called a plane wave. From its mathematical representation, we see that this particular electromagnetic wave is traveling in the $+x$-direction because, as the time t increases, the coordinate x would have to increase to maintain the same value for the fields. The wave described by (31.12) is shown in Figure 31.5.

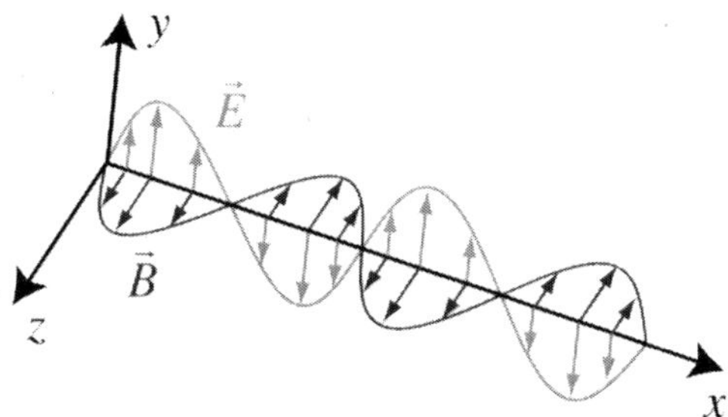

Figure 31.5: Representation of an electromagnetic wave traveling in the +x-direction.

Note that the electric field is in the y-direction and the magnetic field is in the z-direction. It will turn out that the electric field is always perpendicular to the direction the wave is traveling and is always perpendicular to the magnetic field. However, the electric field can point anywhere in the $y-z$ plane for an electromagnetic wave which propagates along the x-axis. It is also easy to see from (31.12) that the electric and magnetic fields are in phase with each other.

The wave shown in Figure 31.5 is a snapshot in time. The vectors shown represent the magnitude and direction for the electric and magnetic fields. However, one must realize that these fields are not solid objects. There is nothing actually moving left and right or up and down as the wave travels. The vectors pointing left and right and up and down represent the electric and magnetic fields.

We now face the task of showing that our proposed wave solution indeed satisfies all of Maxwell's equations. Even this exercise involves quite a bit of vector calculus, but it also uses many of the concepts that we have developed throughout the last few chapters, and so it is worth going through it in some detail.

Gauss's Law for Electric Fields

Let's start with Gauss's Law for electric fields. For an electromagnetic wave, there is no enclosed charge ($q_{enc} = 0$); so we must show that our solution satisfies

$$\oiint \vec{E} \bullet d\vec{A} = 0. \tag{31.13}$$

We can draw a rectangular solid Gaussian surface around a snapshot of the wave as shown in Figure 31.6. For the faces in the $y-z$ plane, $\vec{E} \bullet d\vec{A}$ is zero because the vectors $\vec{E}$ and $d\vec{A}$ are perpendicular to each other. The same is true for the faces in the $x-y$ plane. The faces in the $x-z$ plane will contribute $+EA$ and $-EA$ where A is the area of each of the top and bottom faces. Thus the integral is zero and Gauss's Law for electric fields is satisfied.

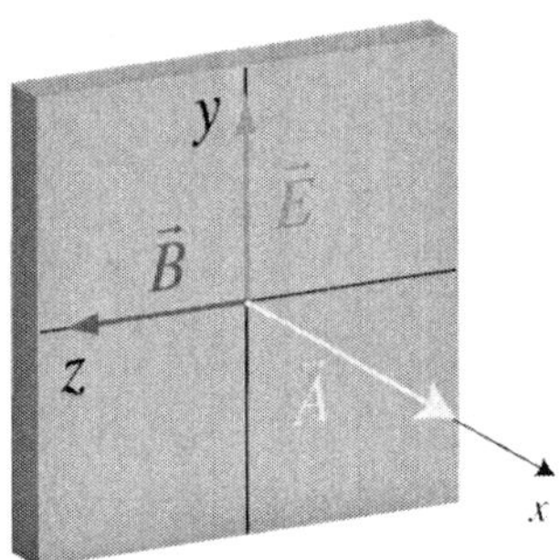

Figure 31.6: Gaussian surface (gray box) drawn around a portion of a snapshot of an electromagnetic wave traveling in the $+x$-direction. The area vector is shown for the front face of the Gaussian surface.

If we analyze snapshots at different times, we will get a different electric field. However, because the electric field is always in the y-direction, the integral will always be zero.

Gauss's Law for Magnetic Fields

For Gauss's Law for magnetic fields, we must show that

$$\oiint \vec{B} \bullet d\vec{A} = 0. \tag{31.14}$$

We again refer to Figure 31.6 and use the same closed integration surface. For the faces in the $y-z$ plane and for the faces in the $x-z$ plane, $\vec{B} \bullet d\vec{A}$ is zero because the vectors $\vec{B}$ and $d\vec{A}$ are perpendicular to each other. The faces in the $x-y$ plane will contribute $+BA$ and $-BA$ where A is the area of each of the top and bottom faces. Thus the integral is zero and Gauss's Law for magnetic fields is satisfied.

Faraday's Law

Now let's address Faraday's Law

$$\oint \vec{E} \bullet d\vec{s} = -\frac{d\Phi_B}{dt}. \tag{31.15}$$

To evaluate the integral on the left hand side of this equation, we assume an integration loop in the $x-y$ plane that has a width dx and height h as depicted by the gray box in Figure 31.7.

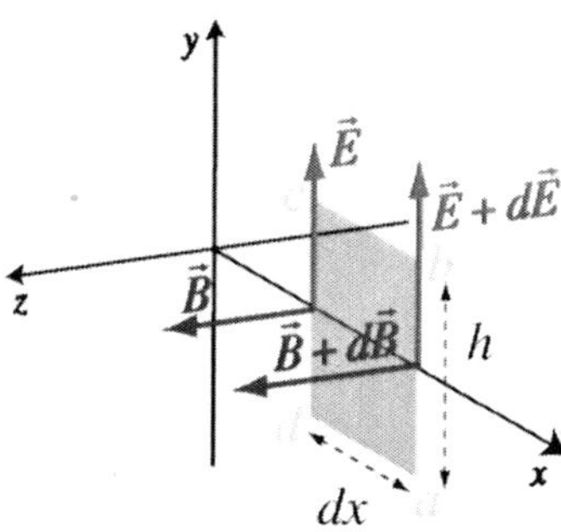

Figure 31.7: Two snapshots of the electric and magnetic fields in an electromagnetic wave. The gray area represents an integration loop for Faraday's Law.

The differential area $d\vec{A} = \hat{n}dA = \hat{n}hdx$ of this rectangle has its unit surface normal vector $\hat{n}$ pointing along the $+z$-direction. Note that the electric and magnetic fields change as we move along the x-direction. So as we move from point x to $x+dx$, the electric field also changes from $\vec{E}(x)$ to $\vec{E}(x+dx) = \vec{E}(x) + d\vec{E}$. The integral around the loop is given by

$$\oint \vec{E} \bullet d\vec{s} = (E + dE)h - Eh = dE \cdot h. \tag{31.16}$$

Why? We can split this integral over a closed loop into four pieces, integrating counterclockwise from ***a*** to ***b***, ***b*** to ***c***, ***c*** to ***d***, and ***d*** to ***a***. The contributions to the integral parallel to the x-axis, integrating from ***b*** to ***c*** and from ***d*** to ***a***, are zero because the electric field is always perpendicular to the integration direction. And for the integrations along the y-direction, ***a*** to ***b*** and ***c*** to ***d***, one has the electric field parallel to the direction of the integration; so the scalar product simply reduces to a conventional product. Because the electric field is independent of the y-coordinate, it can be taken out of the integration. So the integral along each of the segments in $\pm y$-direction is a simple product of the integrand (the magnitude of the electric field at the corresponding x-coordinate) times the length of the integration interval (h) times -1 for the integration along $-y$ because $\vec{E}$ is anti-parallel to the integration direction.

The right hand side of (31.15) is given by

$$-\frac{d\Phi_B}{dt} = -A\frac{dB}{dt} = -hdx\frac{dB}{dt}. \tag{31.17}$$

So we have

$$h(dE) = -hdx\frac{dB}{dt} \tag{31.18}$$

or

$$\frac{dE}{dx} = -\frac{dB}{dt}. \tag{31.19}$$

The derivatives dE/dx and dB/dt are taken with respect a single variable, although both E and B depend on both x and t. Thus, we can more appropriately write (31.19) as

$$\frac{\partial E}{\partial x} = -\frac{\partial B}{\partial t} \tag{31.20}$$

where we now have explicitly specified partial derivatives. Taking our assumed form for the electric and magnetic fields (31.12), we can carry out the derivatives

$$\frac{\partial E}{\partial x} = \frac{\partial}{\partial x}\left(E_{\text{max}}\sin\left(kx-\omega t\right)\right) = kE_{\text{max}}\cos\left(kx-\omega t\right) \tag{31.21}$$

$$\frac{\partial B}{\partial t} = \frac{\partial}{\partial t}\left(B_{\text{max}}\sin\left(kx-\omega t\right)\right) = -\omega B_{\text{max}}\cos\left(kx-\omega t\right). \tag{31.22}$$

Using these derivatives and inserting them into (31.20) we then find:

$$kE_{\text{max}}\cos\left(kx-\omega t\right) = -\left(-\omega B_{\text{max}}\cos\left(kx-\omega t\right)\right). \tag{31.23}$$

The angular frequency and wave number are related via:

$$\frac{\omega}{k} = \frac{2\pi f}{\left(\frac{2\pi}{\lambda}\right)} = f\lambda = c \tag{31.24}$$

where c is the speed of the wave. Thus, we have

$$\frac{E_{\text{max}}}{B_{\text{max}}} = \frac{\omega}{k} = c \tag{31.25}$$

which we can re-write using (31.12) in terms of the ratio of the magnitudes of the fields at a fixed place and time as

$$\frac{E}{B} = c. \tag{31.26}$$

Thus, our assumed form for electromagnetic waves satisfies Faraday's Law if the ratio of the electric and magnetic field magnitudes is c.

Ampere-Maxwell Law

Finally we address the Ampere-Maxwell Law. For electromagnetic waves where there is no current we can write

$$\oint \vec{B} \bullet d\vec{s} = \mu_0 \varepsilon_0 \frac{d\Phi_E}{dt}. \tag{31.27}$$

To evaluate the integral on the left hand side of this equation, we assume an integration loop in the $x - z$ plane that has a width dx and height h as depicted by the gray box in Figure 31.8. The differential area of this rectangle is oriented along the $+y$-direction.

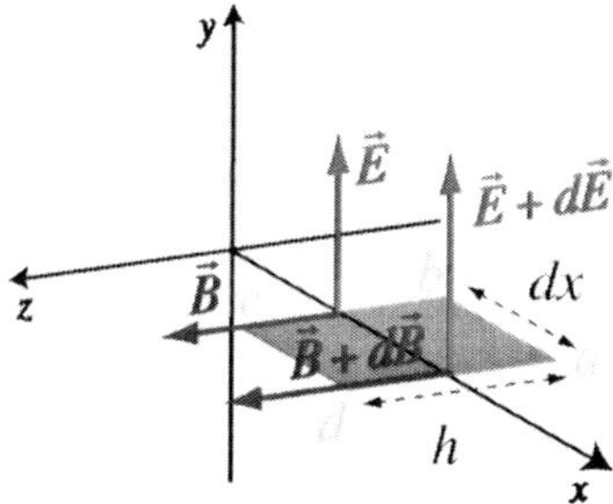

Figure 31.8: Two snapshots of the electric and magnetic fields in an electromagnetic wave. The gray area represents an integration loop for the Ampere-Maxwell Law.

The integral around the loop in a counterclockwise direction (***a*** to ***b*** to ***c*** to ***d*** to ***a***) is given by

$$\oint \vec{B} \bullet d\vec{s} = Bh - \left(B + dB\right)h = -dB \cdot h. \tag{31.28}$$

The parts of the loop that are parallel to the x-axis do not contribute. The right hand side of (31.27) can be written as

$$\mu_0 \varepsilon_0 \frac{d\Phi_E}{dt} = \mu_0 \varepsilon_0 \frac{dE \cdot A}{dt} = \mu_0 \varepsilon_0 \frac{dE \cdot h \cdot dx}{dt}. \tag{31.29}$$

Substituting (31.28) and (31.29) into (31.27) we get

$$-dB \cdot h = \mu_0 \varepsilon_0 \frac{dE \cdot h \cdot dx}{dt}. \tag{31.30}$$

Expressing this equation in terms of partial derivatives as we did before we get

$$-\frac{\partial B}{\partial x} = \mu_0 \varepsilon_0 \frac{\partial E}{\partial t}. \tag{31.31}$$

Now using our assumed solutions (31.12) we get

$$-\left(kB_{max}\cos\left(kx-\omega t\right)\right) = -\mu_0\varepsilon_0\omega E_{max}\cos\left(kx-\omega t\right) \tag{31.32}$$

or

$$\frac{E_{max}}{B_{max}} = \frac{k}{\mu_0\varepsilon_0\omega} = \frac{1}{\mu_0\varepsilon_0 c}. \tag{31.33}$$

We can also express this in terms of the electric and magnetic field magnitudes as before and obtain

$$\frac{E}{B} = \frac{1}{\mu_0\varepsilon_0 c}. \tag{31.34}$$

So our assumed solutions satisfy the Maxwell-Ampere Law if the ratio of the electric and magnetic field magnitudes is given by $\frac{1}{\mu_0\varepsilon_0 c}$.

31.5. The Speed of Light

If we compare (31.26) and (31.34) we can conclude that

$$\frac{E}{B} = \frac{1}{\mu_0\varepsilon_0 c} = c, \tag{31.35}$$

which leads to the result

$$c = \frac{1}{\sqrt{\mu_0\varepsilon_0}}. \tag{31.36}$$

Thus, the speed of an electromagnetic wave can be expressed in terms of two fundamental constants related to electric fields and magnetic fields, the magnetic permeability and the electric permittivity of the vacuum. If we put in the values of these constants that we have been using we get

$$c = \frac{1}{\sqrt{\left(1.26\cdot10^{-6}\text{ H/m}\right)\left(8.85\cdot10^{-12}\text{ F/m}\right)}} = 2.99\cdot10^{8}\text{ m/s}. \tag{31.37}$$

This speed is equal to the measured speed of light. This equality means that all electromagnetic waves travel (in vacuum) at the speed of light. Further this result suggests that light is an electromagnetic wave.

The speed of light plays an important role in the theory of relativity that we will study in chapter 35. The speed of light is always the same in any reference frame. Thus, if you send an electromagnetic wave out in a specific direction, any observer, regardless of whether that observer is moving toward you or away from you or in another direction, will see that wave moving at the speed of light. This amazing result, along with the plausible postulate that the laws of physics are the same for all observers, leads to the theory of relativity. The speed of light can be measured extremely precisely, much more precisely than we can determine the meter from the original reference standard. So now the speed of light is defined as precisely

$$c = 299{,}792{,}458 \text{ m/s}. \tag{31.38}$$

The definition of the meter in modern terms is now simply the distance that light can traverse in vacuum in a time interval of $1/299{,}792{,}458$ s.

In-class exercise: What is the time required for laser light to travel from the Earth to the Moon and back again? The distance between the Earth and the Moon is $3.84 \cdot 10^8$ m.

a) 0.640 s
b) 1.28 s
c) 2.56 s
d) 15.2 s
e) 85.0 s

Self-Test Opportunity: The brightest star in the night sky is Sirius, which is at a distance of $8.30 \cdot 10^{16}$ m from Earth. When we look at this star, how far back in time are we looking? Express the time in years.

31.6. Electromagnetic Spectrum

All electromagnetic waves travel at the speed of light. However, the wavelength and frequency of electromagnetic waves can vary dramatically. The speed of light c, the wavelength λ, and the frequency are related by

$$c = \lambda f. \tag{31.39}$$

Examples of electromagnetic waves include light, radio waves, microwaves, x-rays, and gamma rays. This diverse spectrum is illustrated in Figure 31.9, where we see electromagnetic waves with wavelengths ranging from 1000 m and longer to less than 10^{-12} m and frequencies ranging from 10^6 to 10^{20} Hz. Certain ranges of wavelength and frequency have names that identify the most common application of those electromagnetic waves. Visible light refers to electromagnetic waves that we can see with our eyes, and consists of wavelengths from 400 nm to 700 nm. (The response of the human eye is peaked around 550 nm (green) and drops off quickly away from that wavelength.) Other wavelengths of electromagnetic waves are invisible to the human eye. However, we can still detect the electromagnetic waves by other means. For example, we can feel electromagnetic waves in the infrared (wavelengths just longer than visible up to around 10^{-4} m) as warmth.

FM radio waves have frequencies on the order of 100 MHz. Microwaves that are used to pop popcorn and transmit phone messages have frequencies around 10 GHz. X-rays used to produce medical images have wavelengths on the order of 10^{-10} m. Gamma rays that are emitted in the decay of radioactive nuclei have very short wavelengths on the order of 10^{-12} m and can cause damage to human cells.

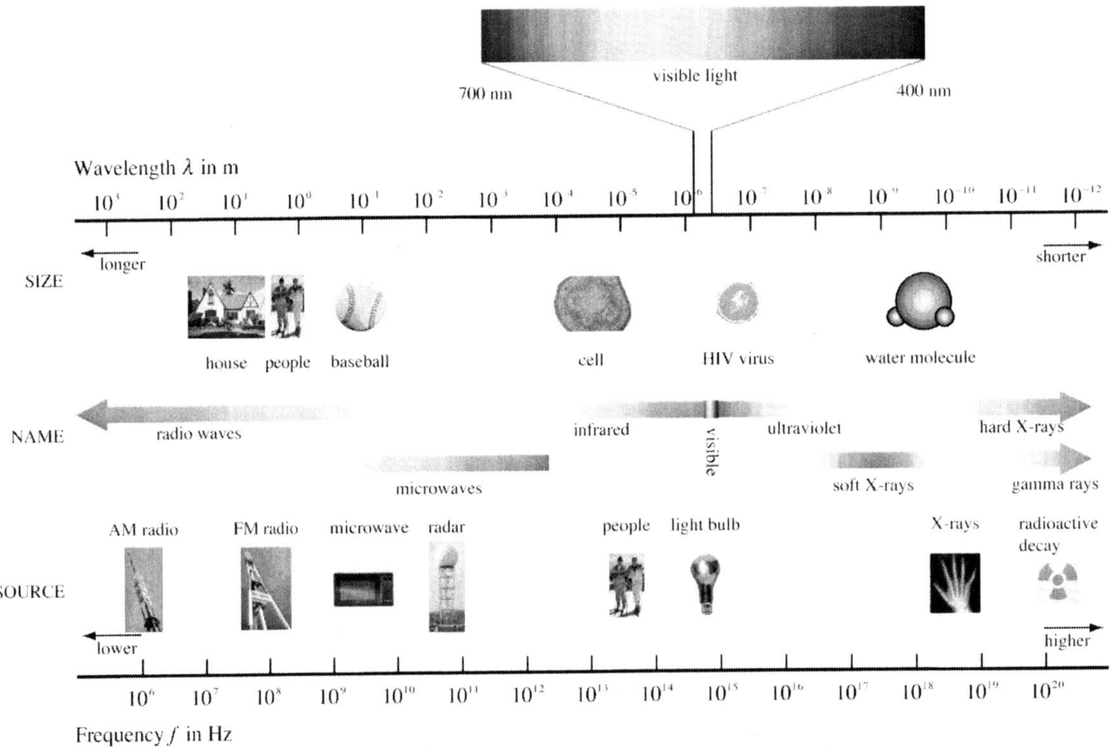

Figure 31.9: The electromagnetic spectrum.

Self-Test Opportunity: An FM radio station broadcasts on 90.5 MHz and an AM radio station broadcasts on 870 kHz. What are the wavelengths of these electromagnetic waves?

Radio and Television Frequency Bands

The frequency ranges assigned to radio and television broadcasts are shown in Figure 31.10. The range of frequencies assigned to AM (amplitude modulation) radio is 535 kHz to 1705 kHz. FM (frequency modulated) radio occupies the frequencies between 88.0 MHz and 108.0 MHz. VHF (very high frequency) television operates in two ranges, 54.0

MHz to 88.0 MHz for channels 2 through 6, and 174.0 MHz to 216.0 MHz for channels 7 through 13. UHF (ultra-high frequency) channels 14 through 83 broadcast in the range 512.0 MHz to 698 MHz. Most high definition television broadcasts use the UHF band and channels 14 through 83.

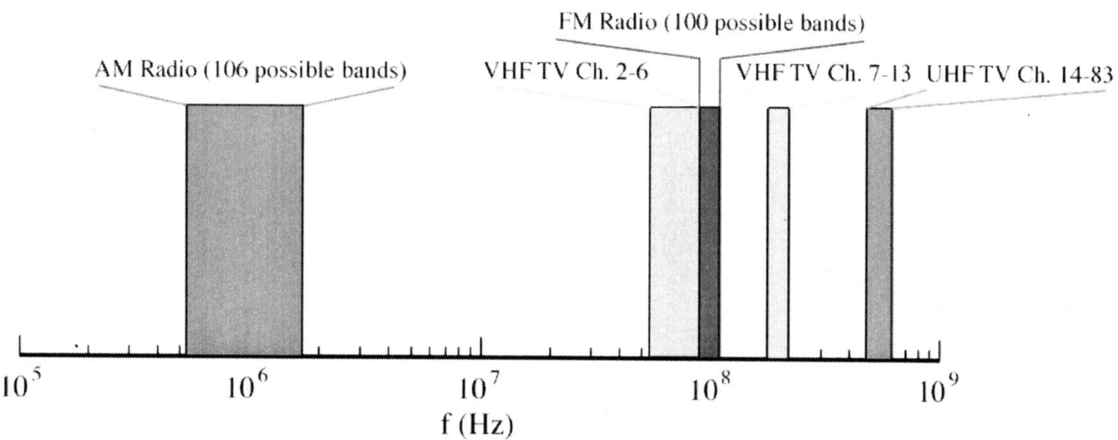

Figure 31.10: The frequency bands assigned to radio and television broadcasts in the United States.

31.7. Traveling Electromagnetic Waves

Sub-atomic processes can produce electromagnetic waves such as gamma rays, X-rays, and light. Electromagnetic waves can also be produced by an RLC oscillator connected to an antenna as shown below in Figure 31.11. The connection between the RLC circuit and the circuit on the right is accomplished using a transformer. A dipole antenna is used to approximate an electric dipole. The voltage and current in the antenna vary sinusoidally with time and cause charge in the antenna to oscillate with the frequency ω_0 of the RLC circuit. These accelerating charges create electromagnetic waves. These waves travel from the antenna with speed c and frequency $f = \omega_0 / (2\pi)$.

We can think of these traveling electromagnetic waves as wave fronts spreading out spherically from the antenna. However, at a large distance from the antenna, the wave fronts will appear to be almost flat, or planar. So we can think of the electromagnetic wave in terms of our assumed form for an electromagnetic wave (31.12). If we now place in the path of these electromagnetic waves, a second RLC circuit tuned to the same frequency ω_0 as the emitting circuit, voltage and current will be induced in this second circuit. These induced oscillations are the basic idea of radio transmission and reception. If the second circuit has $\omega = 1/\sqrt{LC}$ different from ω_0, smaller voltages and currents will be induced, providing selective tuning for different frequencies.

This principle of transmission of electromagnetic waves was discovered by German physicist Heinrich Hertz (1857-1894) in 1888, and then used by Italian physicist Guglielmo Marconi (1874-1937) to transmit wireless signals.

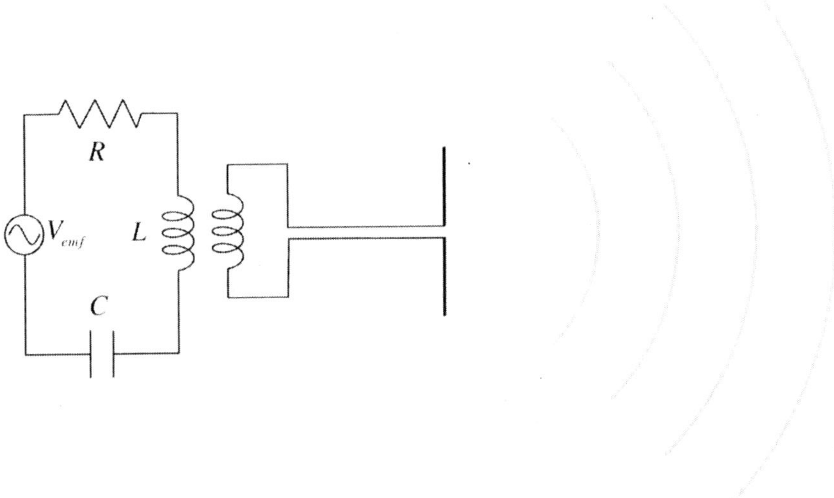

Figure 31.11: An *RLC* circuit coupled to an antenna that emits traveling electromagnetic waves.

31.8. Poynting Vector, Energy Transport

When we walk out into the sunlight, we feel warmth. If we stay out too long in the bright sunshine, we will get sunburned. These phenomena are caused by electromagnetic waves emitted from the Sun. These electromagnetic waves carry energy generated in the nuclear reactions of the Sun to our skin. The rate of energy transported by an electromagnetic wave is usually defined in terms of a vector $\vec{S}$ given by

$$\vec{S} = \frac{1}{\mu_0}\vec{E}\times\vec{B}. \quad (31.40)$$

This quantity is called the Poynting vector after British physicist John Poynting (1852-1914) who first discussed its properties. The magnitude of $\vec{S}$ is related to the instantaneous rate at which energy is transported by an electromagnetic wave over a given area, or more simply, the instantaneous power per unit area

$$S = \left|\vec{S}\right| = \left(\frac{\text{power}}{\text{area}}\right)_{\text{instantaneous}}. \quad (31.41)$$

The units of the Poynting vector are W/m^2. For an electromagnetic wave, where $\vec{E}$ is perpendicular to $\vec{B}$, we can write using (31.40)

$$S = \frac{1}{\mu_0}EB. \quad (31.42)$$

We know from (31.35) that the magnitude of the electric field and the magnetic field are directly related via $E / B = c$. So we can easily express the instantaneous power per unit area of an electromagnetic wave in terms of the magnitude the electric field or the magnetic field. However, usually it is easier to measure an electric field than a magnetic field so we express the instantaneous power per unit area as

$$S = \frac{1}{c\mu_0} E^2. \tag{31.43}$$

We can now substitute a sinusoidal form for the electric field $E = E_{\max} \sin(kx - \omega t)$ and obtain an expression for the transmitted power per unit area. However, the usual method of describing the power per unit area in an electromagnetic wave is the intensity I of the wave given by

$$I = S_{ave} = \left(\frac{\text{power}}{\text{area}} \right)_{ave} = \frac{1}{c\mu_0} \left[E_{\max}^2 \sin^2(kx - \omega t) \right]_{ave}. \tag{31.44}$$

The units of intensity are the same as the units of the Poynting vector, W/m^2. The average of $\sin^2(kx - \omega t)$ over time is $1/2$. So we can express the intensity as

$$I = \frac{1}{c\mu_0} E_{rms}^2 \tag{31.45}$$

where $E_{rms} = E_{\max} / \sqrt{2}$.

Because the magnitude of the electric and magnetic fields of the electromagnetic wave are related by $E = cB$, and c is such a large number, one might conclude that the energy transported by the electric field is much larger than the energy transmitted by the magnetic field. Actually the energy transported by the electric field is the same as the energy transported by the magnetic field. We can understand this fact by remembering from previous chapters that the energy density of an electric field is given by

$$u_E = \frac{1}{2} \varepsilon_0 E^2 \tag{31.46}$$

and the energy density of a magnetic field is

$$u_B = \frac{1}{2\mu_0} B^2. \tag{31.47}$$

If we substitute $E = cB$ and $c = 1 / \sqrt{\mu_0 \varepsilon_0}$ into (31.46) we get

$$u_E = \frac{1}{2}\varepsilon_0 (cB)^2 = \frac{1}{2}\varepsilon_0 \left(\frac{B}{\sqrt{\mu_0 \varepsilon_0}} \right)^2 = \frac{1}{2\mu_0} B^2 = u_B . \tag{31.48}$$

So we obtain the result that the energy density of the electric field is the same as the energy density of the magnetic field everywhere in the electromagnetic wave.

In-class exercise: The average intensity of sunlight at the Earth is approximately 1400 W/m^2, if the Sun is directly overhead. What is the rms electric field of these electromagnetic waves?

a) 0.45 V/m
b) 2.7 V/m
c) 16 V/m
d) 75 V/m
e) 730 V/m

In-class exercise: The average intensity of sunlight at the Earth is approximately 1400 W/m^2, if the Sun is directly overhead. The average distance between the Earth and the Sun is $1.50 \cdot 10^{11}$ m. What is the average power emitted by the Sun?

a) $99.9 \cdot 10^{25}$ W
b) $4.0 \cdot 10^{26}$ W
c) $6.3 \cdot 10^{27}$ W
d) $4.3 \cdot 10^{28}$ W
e) $5.9 \cdot 10^{29}$ W

31.9. Radiation Pressure

When you walk out into the sunlight, you feel warmth, but you do not feel any force from the sunlight. Sunlight is exerting a pressure on you, but that pressure is small enough that you we cannot notice it. Because these electromagnetic waves are radiated from the Sun and travel to you on the Earth, we refer to these electromagnetic waves as radiation. (As we will see in the chapter 40 on nuclear physics this type of radiation is not necessarily the same as radioactive radiation resulting from the decay of unstable nuclei.) Let's calculate the magnitude of the pressure exerted by these radiated electromagnetic waves.

Electromagnetic waves have energy U. Electromagnetic waves also have linear momentum p. This concept is difficult because electromagnetic waves have no mass, and we have learned that momentum is equal to mass multiplied by velocity. To understand the concept of the momentum carried by a wave, we will discuss the effect of an electromagnetic wave on a positively charged particle as illustrated in Figure 31.12.

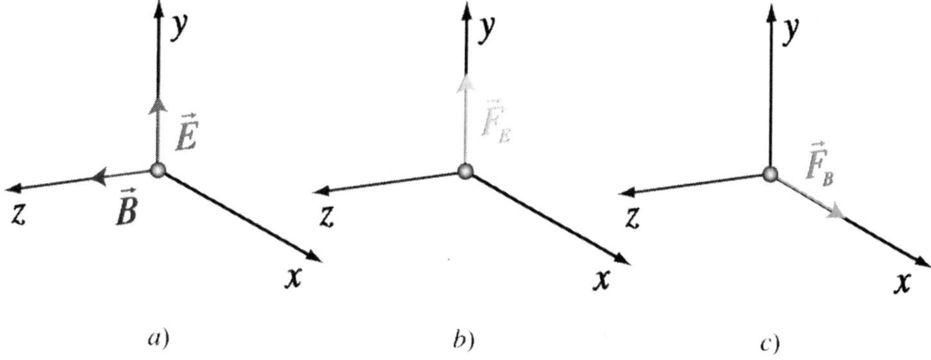

Figure 31.12: An electromagnetic wave traveling in the x-direction interacts with a positively charged particle.

In Figure 31.12*a*), the electric field $\vec{E}$ and magnetic field $\vec{B}$ are shown for a given time and position ($x = y = z = 0$). The electric field will exert a force on the positively charged particle in the positive y-direction as shown in Figure 31.12*b*). This force is given by

$$\vec{F}_E = qE\hat{y} \tag{31.49}$$

where q is the charge of the particle. The magnetic field will not exert a force on the positively charged particle at rest. The positively charged particle will then begin to move in the positive y-direction with a velocity given by

$$\vec{v} = v_y\hat{y}. \tag{31.50}$$

The magnetic field will then exert a force on the positively charged particle in the x-direction

$$\vec{F}_B = q\vec{v} \times \vec{B} = qv_y B\hat{x} \tag{31.51}$$

as shown in Figure 31.12c). The electric force does work on the positively charged particle. The rate of work done on the positively charged particle is given by

$$\frac{dW}{dt} = \vec{F}_E \bullet \vec{v} = qEv_y \tag{31.52}$$

Using (31.26) we can rewrite (31.51) as

$$\vec{F}_B = qv_y \frac{E}{c}\hat{x}. \tag{31.53}$$

Newton's second law tells us that

$$\vec{F} = \frac{d\vec{p}}{dt}. \tag{31.54}$$

We can then write

$$\frac{d\vec{p}}{dt} = qv_y \frac{E}{c}\hat{x}. \tag{31.55}$$

The x-component of the time rate change of momentum is then

$$\frac{dp}{dt} = qv_y \frac{E}{c} \tag{31.56}$$

which can be rewritten as

$$qv_y E = c\frac{dp}{dt}. \tag{31.57}$$

Substituting this result into (31.52) gives us

$$\frac{dW}{dt} = c\frac{dp}{dt} \tag{31.58}$$

which we can rewrite as

$$dW = c(dp). \tag{31.59}$$

The Work Energy Theorem tells us that $dW = dU$, so we can write

$$dp = \frac{dU}{c}. \tag{31.60}$$

If we make the approximation that $dp \approx \Delta p$ and $dU \approx \Delta U$, we can relate the change in momentum of the object Δp to the change in energy of the wave by

$$\Delta p = \frac{\Delta U}{c}. \tag{31.61}$$

The change in momentum of the object will be in the same direction as the incident electromagnetic wave. If the object completely absorbs that electromagnetic wave, the object will have the momentum of the electromagnetic wave.

If instead, the object reflects the electromagnetic wave, the object will gain twice the momentum of the incident wave, because of momentum conservation, in the direction of the incident wave

$$\Delta p = \frac{2\Delta U}{c}. \tag{31.62}$$

We again make us of Newton's second law to write

$$F = \frac{\Delta p}{\Delta t}. \tag{31.63}$$

To get an expression for the pressure exerted when the electromagnetic wave is absorbed in terms of the intensity of the wave, we remember that the intensity is power per unit area, and power is energy per unit time. Therefore we can use (31.61) to relate the intensity of the wave to the momentum transferred to the object when the electromagnetic wave is absorbed by

$$I = \frac{\Delta U / \Delta t}{A} = \frac{c\Delta p}{A\Delta t} \tag{31.64}$$

which gives us an expression for the force exerted by the radiation on the object

$$F = \frac{\Delta p}{\Delta t} = \frac{IA}{c}. \tag{31.65}$$

The pressure is defined as force per unit area so we can write the radiation pressure p_r due to a totally absorbed electromagnetic wave as

$$p_r = \frac{I}{c}. \tag{31.66}$$

If the electromagnetic wave is reflected the radiation pressure is

$$p_r = \frac{2I}{c}. \tag{31.67}$$

The radiation pressure from sunlight is small. The intensity of sunlight is at most 1400 W/m^2. Thus the maximum radiation pressure for sunlight that is totally absorbed is

$$p_r = \frac{I}{c} = \frac{1400 \text{ W/m}^2}{3 \cdot 10^8 \text{ m/s}} = 4.67 \cdot 10^{-6} \text{ N/m}^2. \tag{31.68}$$

Self-Test Opportunity: Suppose that the particle shown in Figure 31.12 is a negatively charged particle rather than a positively charged particle. Show that the resulting force on the negatively charged particle is also in the positive x-direction.

Example

Example 31.1: Radiation pressure from a laser pointer

A green laser point has a power of 1.00 mW. We shine the laser pointer perpendicularly on a white sheet of paper, which reflects the light. The spot of the laser pointer is 2.00 mm in diameter.

Question:
What force does the light from the laser pointer exert on the paper?

Example

Answer:
The intensity of the light is given by

$$I = \frac{\text{power}}{\text{area}} = \frac{1.00 \cdot 10^{-3}\ \text{W}}{\pi\left(1.00 \cdot 10^{-3}\ \text{m}\right)^2} = 318\ \text{W/m}^2 .$$

The radiation pressure is equal to the force exerted by the light divided by the area over which it acts

$$p_r = \frac{\text{force}}{\text{area}} = \frac{2I}{c} .$$

Thus the force exerted on the paper is

$$\text{force} = \text{area} \cdot \frac{2I}{c} = \pi\left(1.0 \cdot 10^{-3}\ \text{m}\right)^2 \cdot \frac{2 \cdot 318\ \text{W/m}^3}{3.00 \cdot 10^8\ \text{m/s}} = 6.66 \cdot 10^{-12}\ \text{N} .$$

As shown in the example above, the force exerted on an object by light is on the order of 10^{-12} N (= pico-Newton). This force is too small to affect macroscopic objects. However, physicists using very intense lasers focused to a small area can exert forces to manipulate objects as small as a single atom. These forces are large enough to move and contain these objects. These devices are called optical traps or "laser tweezers".

Laser tweezers are constructed by focusing an intense laser beam to a point using the objective lens of a microscope. We will discuss the focusing properties of lenses in the next chapter on geometric optics and the properties of microscopes in chapter 33 on optical instruments. The force exerted by a laser pointer on a piece of paper produces a force in the direction of the original laser beam. In the physical realization of laser tweezers, the laser beam is focused such that the light is more intense in the middle of the light distribution. In addition, the focusing produces light rays that converge on a point.

We will discuss the effect of the focused laser light in terms of a spherical, optically transparent object. This object could be a small plastic sphere or a living cell that is approximately spherical. We define the original direction of the laser light as the z-direction. We then have the $x-y$ plane perpendicular to the incident direction. In Figure 31.13*a*) we show the object in the $y-z$ plane. The object is displaced slightly in the negative y-direction. Light coming from center of the distribution of light is more intense and also (as we will see in the next chapter) is refracted (or bent) downward. Light coming from the edge of the distribution is less intense and is refracted upward. The resultant change in momentum of the incident light rays in the y-direction is downward. To conserve momentum, the object must then acquire a resultant change in momentum in the positive y-direction. Thus, the intense focused light of the laser produces a restoring force on the object if it is not positioned at $y = 0$ and the object is trapped in the y -direction.

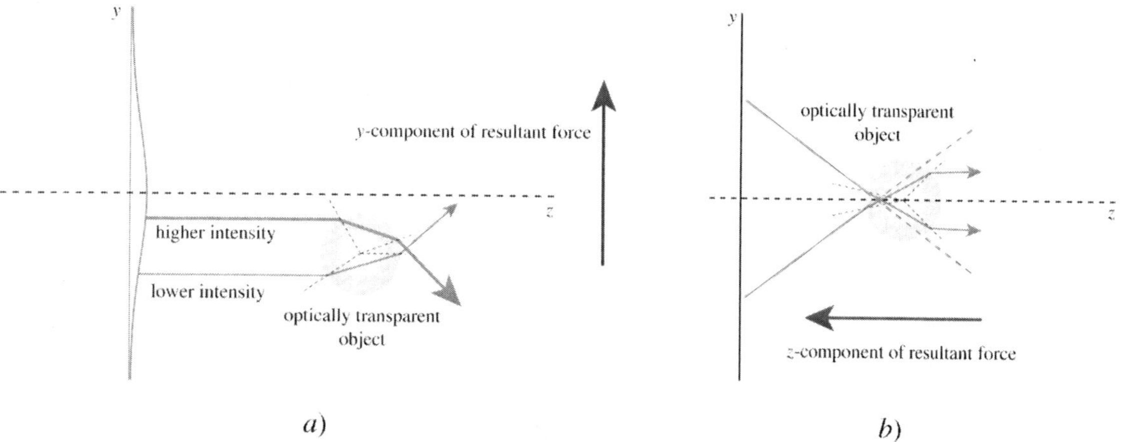

Figure 31.13: Drawing representing the effect of focused laser light on a small, spherical, optically transparent object. In panel *a*), the curved red line on the left represents the varying intensity of the wave. In addition the restoring force in the *y*-direction is shown. In panel *b*), the restoring force in the *z*-direction is shown.

In the z -direction, which is the direction of the incident laser light, trapping also occurs because of the converging rays produced by the focusing of the light by the objective lens. The converging rays incident on the transparent object are shown in Figure 31.13*b*). In this case, the object is just to the right of the focus point. The incident rays are refracted such that they are more parallel to the incident direction than before. Thus the component of the momentum of the light in the z -direction has been increased and the transparent object must experience a force in the opposite direction to conserve momentum. If the object were to the left of the focus point, it would experience a force to the right. Thus the object is trapped in the direction parallel to the light as well as the direction perpendicular to the incident laser light.

This technique relies on the transmission of the incident light. If this technique is applied to an object that is not transparent, the incident light will be reflected and will produce a force pushing the object in the general direction of the incident light.

Laser tweezers have been used to trap cells, bacteria, viruses, and small polystyrene beads. Laser tweezers have been used to manipulate DNA strands and to study molecular motors.

Self-Test Opportunity: Suppose you have a satellite in orbit around the Sun as shown in the figure. The orbit is in the clock-wise direction looking down on the north pole of the Sun. You deploy a solar sail consisting of a large, totally reflecting mirror. You can deploy the solar sail such that it is perpendicular to the light coming from the Sun or at an angle with respect to the light coming from the Sun. Describe the effect on the orbit of your satellite for the three deployment angles shown in the figure!

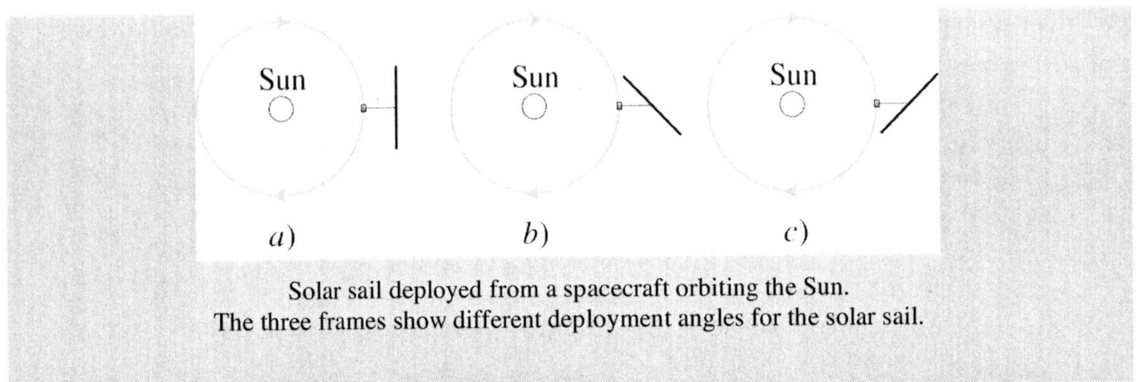

Solar sail deployed from a spacecraft orbiting the Sun.
The three frames show different deployment angles for the solar sail.

Solved Problem

Solved Problem 31.1: Solar stationary satellite

We want to place a satellite above the north pole of the Sun, which is stationary with respect to the sun in order to study the long-term rotational characteristics of the Sun. We accomplish this goal by placing a satellite with a totally reflecting solar sail at a distance of $1.50 \cdot 10^{11}$ m from the center of the Sun. The intensity of sunlight at that distance is 1400 W/m^2. The plane of the solar sail is perpendicular to a line connecting the satellite and the center of the Sun. The mass of the satellite and sail is 100.0 kg.

Question:
What is the necessary area of the solar sail?

Answer:

THINK:

The area of the solar sail times the radiation pressure from the Sun produces a force that is balanced by the gravitational force between the satellite and the Sun. We can equate these two forces and solve for the area of the solar sail.

SKETCH:

A drawing of the satellite with a solar sail near the Sun is shown in Figure 31.14.

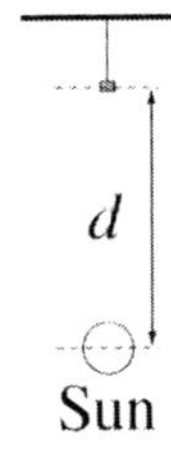

Figure 31.14: A satellite with a solar sail near the Sun.

RESEARCH:

The satellite will be stationary if the force of gravity F_g is balanced by the force from the radiation pressure of sunlight F_{rp}

$$F_g = F_{rp}. \tag{31.69}$$

The force corresponding to the radiation pressure from sunlight is equal to the radiation pressure p_r times the area of the solar sail A

$$F_{rp} = p_r A. \tag{31.70}$$

The radiation pressure can be expressed in terms of the intensity of sunlight I incident on the reflecting solar sail

$$p_r = \left(\frac{2I}{c}\right) \tag{31.71}$$

where we have assumed that the light is totally reflected. The force of gravity between the satellite and the Sun is given by

$$F_g = G\frac{mm_{\text{Sun}}}{d^2} \tag{31.72}$$

where G is the universal gravitational constant, m is the mass of the satellite and sail, m_{Sun} is the mass of the Sun, and d is the distance between the satellite and the Sun.

Solved Problem

SIMPLIFY:

We can combine the previous equations to obtain

$$\left(\frac{2I}{c}\right)A = G\frac{mm_{\text{Sun}}}{d^2}. \tag{31.73}$$

Solving for the area of the solar sail gives us

$$A = G\frac{cmm_{\text{Sun}}}{2Id^2}. \tag{31.74}$$

CALCULATE:

Putting in our numerical values, we get

$$A = \left(6.67\cdot 10^{-11}\ \text{m}^3\cdot\text{kg}^{-1}\cdot\text{s}^{-2}\right)\frac{\left(3.00\cdot 10^8\ \text{m/s}\right)\left(100.0\ \text{kg}\right)\left(1.99\cdot 10^{30}\ \text{kg}\right)}{2\left(1400\ \text{W/m}^2\right)\left(1.50\cdot 10^{11}\ \text{M}\right)^2} = 63206.2\ \text{m}^2.$$

ROUND:

We report our result to three significant figures

$$A = 6.32\cdot 10^4\ \text{m}^2.$$

Solved Problem

DOUBLE-CHECK:

If the solar sail were circular, the radius of the sail would be

$$R=\sqrt{\frac{A}{\pi}}=\sqrt{\frac{6.32\cdot 10^{4}\ \text{m}^{2}}{\pi}}=141\ \text{m}$$

which is a reasonably achievable size. We can relate the thickness of the sail t to the density ρ of the material from which the sail is constructed to the mass per unit area of the sail

$$t\rho=\frac{m}{A}.$$

If the sail were composed of a sturdy material such as kapton ($\rho=1420\ \text{kg/m}^{3}$) and the sail had a mass 75 kg, the thickness of the kapton would be given by

$$t=\frac{75\ \text{kg}}{\left(1420\ \text{kg/m}^{3}\right)\left(6.32\cdot 10^{4}\ \text{m}^{2}\right)}=8.36\cdot 10^{-7}\ \text{m}=0.836\ \mu\text{m}.$$

That thickness is too thin for current production techniques for making kapton. The required areal mass density may be realizable using other materials in the future.

31.10. Polarization

Consider the electromagnetic wave shown in Figure 31.5. The electric field for this electromagnetic wave always points along the y-axis. Taking the x-axis as the direction in which that the wave is traveling, we see the plane of oscillation for the electric field of the electromagnetic wave as shown in Figure 31.15.

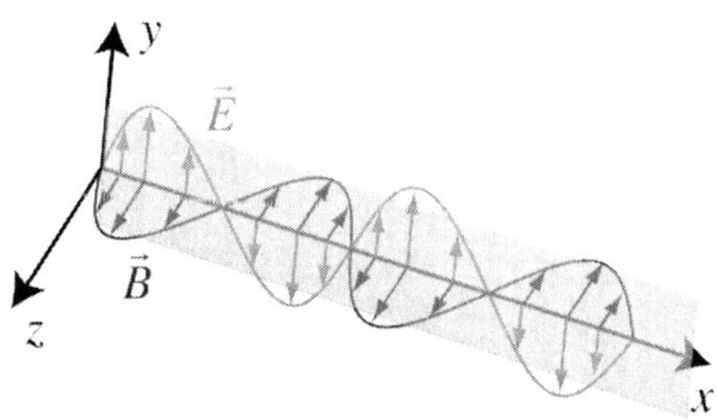

Figure 31.15: An electromagnetic wave with the plane of polarization shown as a pink rectangle.

We can represent the polarization of an electromagnetic wave by looking at the electric field vector of the wave in the $y-z$ plane, which is perpendicular to the direction the wave is traveling as shown in Figure 31.16*a*), where the electric field vector changes from positive y-direction to the negative y-direction and back again as the wave travels. The electric field part of the wave oscillates in the y-direction. This type of wave is called a plane-polarized wave in the y-direction.

The electromagnetic waves making up the light emitted by most common light sources such as an incandescent light bulb have random polarizations. Each wave has its electric field vector oscillating in a different plane. This light is called unpolarized light. We can represent the light from an unpolarized source by drawing many waves like the one shown in Figure 31.16*a*) but with random orientations as shown in Figure 31.16*b*).

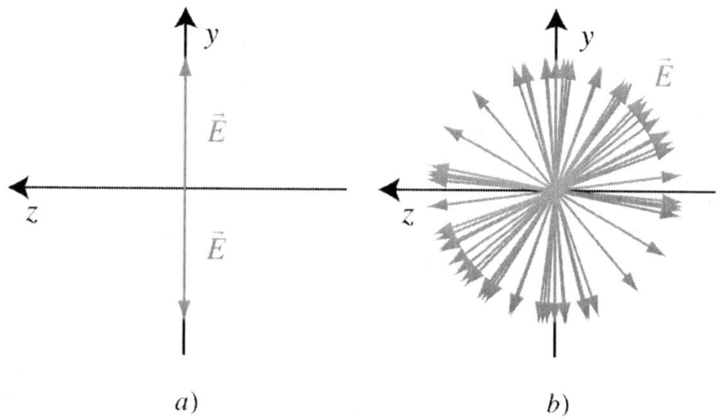

Figure 31.16: *a*) Electric field vectors in the *y*-*z* plane defining the plane of polarization to be the *x*-*y* plane. *b*) Electric field vectors oriented at random angles.

We can represent light with many polarizations by summing the y-components and summing the z-components to produce the net y- and z-components. For unpolarized light, we obtain equal components in the y- and z-directions as shown in Figure 31.17*a*). If there is less net polarization in the y-direction than in the z-direction, then we say that the light is partially polarized in the z-direction as shown in Figure 31.17*b*).

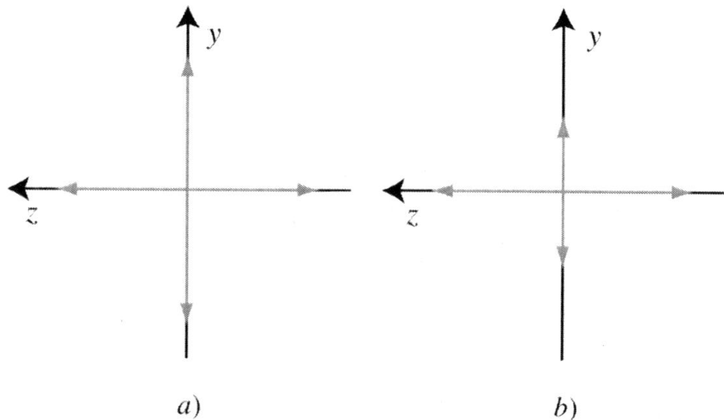

Figure 31.17: *a*) Net components of the electric field for unpolarized light. *b*) Net components of the electric field for partially polarized light.

We can change unpolarized light to polarized light by passing the unpolarized light through a polarizer. A polarizer allows only one component of the polarization of the light to pass through. One way to make a polarizer is to produce a material that consists of long parallel chains of molecules that effectively let components of the light pass with one polarization and block light with components perpendicular to that direction.

We will discuss polarizers without taking into account the details of the molecular structure. Instead we will characterize each polarizer with a polarizing direction. Unpolarized light passing through a polarizer will emerge polarized in the polarizing direction as illustrated in Figure 31.18.

The components of the light that have same polarization as the polarizer are transmitted but the components of the light that are perpendicular to the polarizer are absorbed. Now let's consider the intensity of the light that passes through a polarizer. We begin with unpolarized light with intensity I_0. Unpolarized light has equal components of polarization in the y- and z-directions. After passing through a vertical polarizer only the y (or vertical) component of the polarization remains. The intensity I of the light passing through the polarizer is given by

$$I = \frac{1}{2} I_0 \tag{31.75}$$

because the unpolarized light had equal contribution from the y- and z-components and only the y-components are transmitted by the polarizer. This factor of one half only applies to the case of unpolarized light passing through a polarizer.

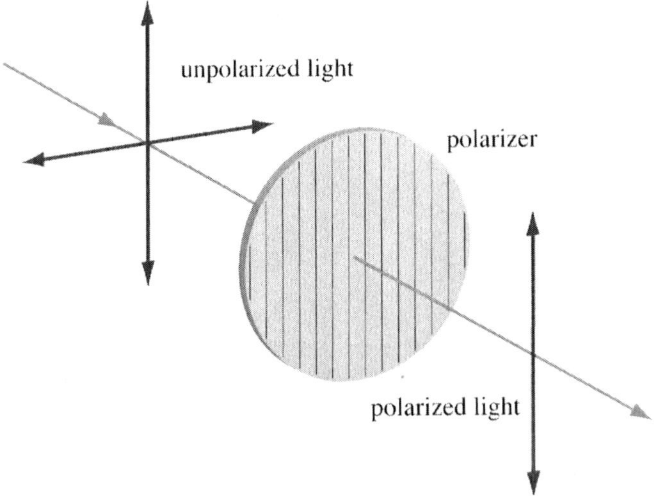

Figure 31.18: Unpolarized light passing through a vertical polarizer.
After the light passes through the polarizer, the light is vertically polarized.

Let's assume that polarized light passes through a polarizer as shown in Figure 31.19.

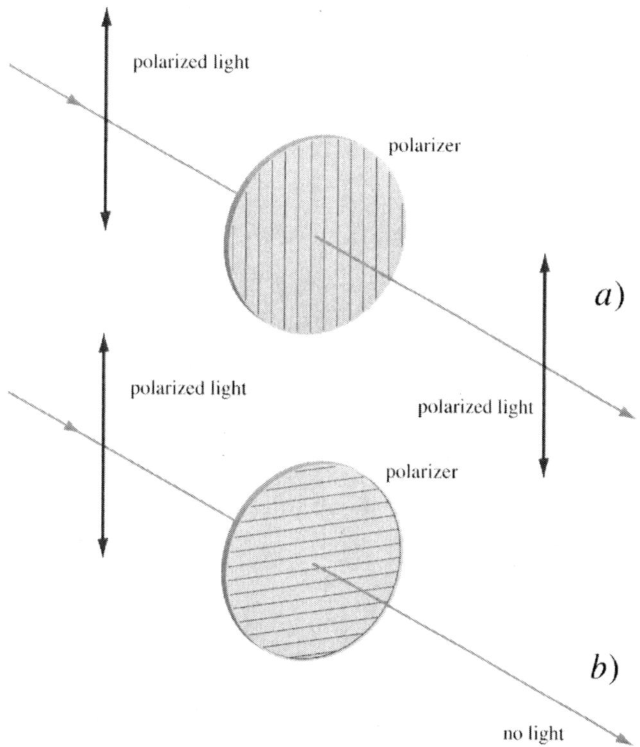

Figure 31.19: a) Vertically polarized light incident on a vertical polarizer.
b) Vertically polarized light incident on a horizontal polarizer.

If the polarizer axis is parallel to the polarization direction of the incident polarized light, all the light will be transmitted with the original polarization as depicted in Figure 31.19*a*). If the polarizing angle of the polarizer is perpendicular to the polarization of polarized light, no light will be transmitted as shown in Figure 31.19*b*).

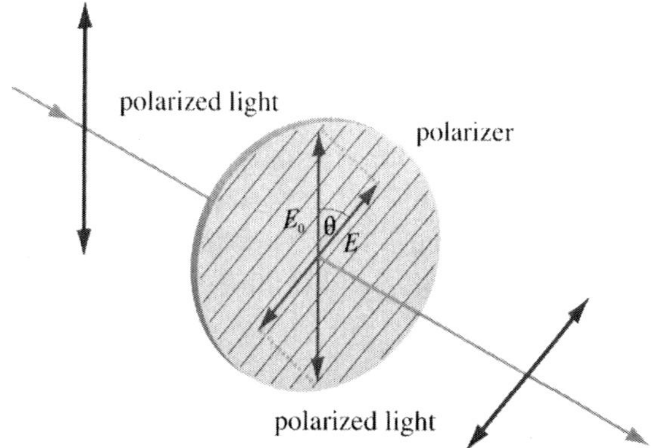

Figure 31.20: Polarized light passing through a polarizer whose polarizing angle is not parallel or perpendicular to the polarization of the incident light.

Now we consider the case where polarized light is incident on a polarizer and the polarization of the light is not parallel or perpendicular to the polarizing angle of the polarizer as shown in Figure 31.20. The angle between the incident polarization and polarizing angle is θ.

The magnitude of the transmitted electric field, E, is given by

$$E = E_0 \cos\theta \tag{31.76}$$

where E_0 is the magnitude of the electric field of the incident polarized light. Using (31.45) we can see that the intensity of the light I_0 before the polarizer is given by

$$I_0 = \frac{1}{c\mu_0} E_{rms}^2 = \frac{1}{2c\mu_0} E_0^2 . \tag{31.77}$$

After the light passes through the polarizer the intensity I is given by

$$I = \frac{1}{2c\mu_0} E^2 \tag{31.78}$$

so we write the transmitted intensity in terms of the initial intensity as

$$I = \frac{1}{2c\mu_0} E^2 = \frac{1}{2c\mu_0} \left(E_0 \cos\theta \right)^2 = I_0 \cos^2\theta . \tag{31.79}$$

This result is called the Law of Malus. This equation only applies to the case of polarized light incident on a polarizer.

Example

Example 31.2: Three polarizers

Consider the case of unpolarized light with intensity I_0 incident on three polarizers. The first polarizer has a polarizing direction that is vertical. The second polarizer has a polarizing angle of 45° with respect to the vertical. The third polarizer has a polarizing angle of 90° with respect to the vertical. What is the intensity of the light passing through all the polarizers in terms of the initial intensity?

We illustrate the result of passing unpolarized light through the three polarizers in this example in Figure 31.21.

The intensity of the unpolarized light is I_0. The intensity of the light passing through the first polarizer is

$$I_1 = \frac{1}{2} I_0 .$$

The intensity of the light passing the second polarizer is

Example

$$I_2 = I_1 \cos^2\left(45° - 0°\right) = I_1 \cos^2\left(45°\right) = \frac{1}{2} I_0 \cos^2\left(45°\right)$$

The intensity of the light passing the third polarizer is

$$I_3 = I_2 \cos^2\left(90° - 45°\right) = I_2 \cos^2\left(45°\right) = \frac{1}{2} I_0 \cos^4\left(45°\right) = I_0 / 8 .$$

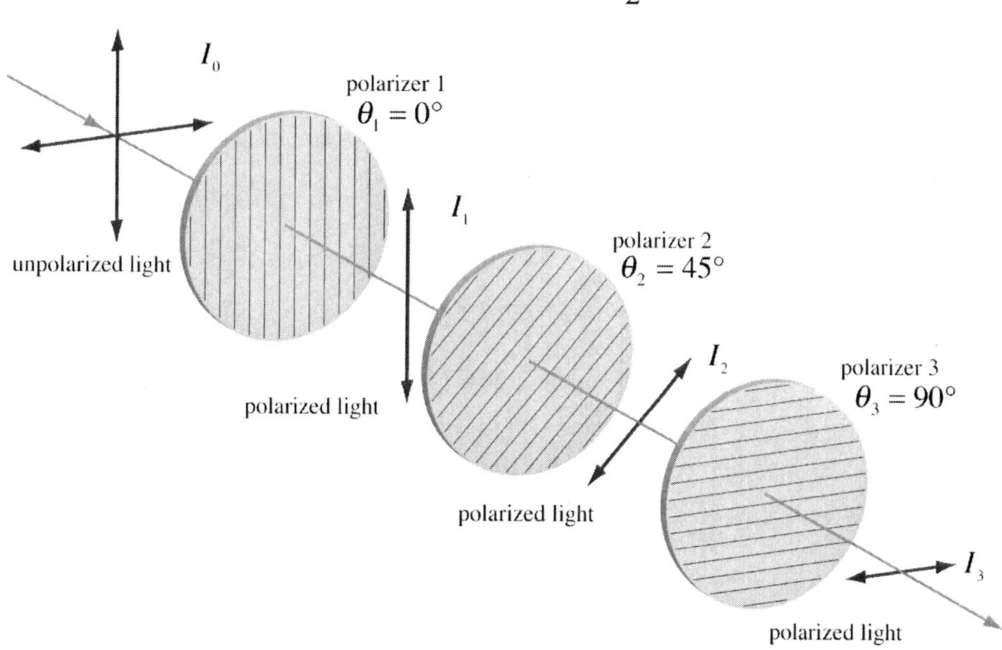

Figure 31.21: Unpolarized light passing through three polarizers.

The fact that $1/8$ of the intensity of the light is transmitted is somewhat surprising because polarizers 1 and 3 have polarizing angles that are perpendicular to each other. Acting by themselves, polarizers 1 and 3 would block all of the light. Yet by adding an additional obstacle (polarizer 2) between these two polarizers, $1/8$ of the original light intensity gets through! One can imagine that a series of polarizers with small differences in their polarizing angles could be used to rotate the polarization of light with small losses in intensity.

In-class exercise: Unpolarized light with intensity $I_{\text{in}} = 1.87 \text{ W/m}^2$ enters a set of two polarizers. The emerging polarized light has intensity $I_{\text{out}} = 0.383 \text{ W/m}^2$. What is the angle between the two polarizers?

a) 23.9°
b) 34.6°
c) 50.2°
d) 72.7°
e) 88.9°

Applications of Polarization

There are many practical applications of polarization. Sunglasses often have a polarized coating that blocks reflected light that is usually polarized. A liquid crystal display for a computer works by sandwiching an array of liquid crystals between two polarizers whose polarizing angle are rotated 90° with respect to each other. Normally the liquid crystal rotates the polarization of the light between the two polarizers so that light passes through. An array of addressable electrodes can put a varying voltage across each of the liquid crystal, causing the liquid crystal rotate the polarization less, darkening the area covered by the electrode. An LCD television or computer monitor can then display a large number of picture elements, or pixels, that can produce a high-resolution image.

Figure 31.22: An LCD computer monitor.

A portion of an LCD screen is illustrated in Figure 31.23.

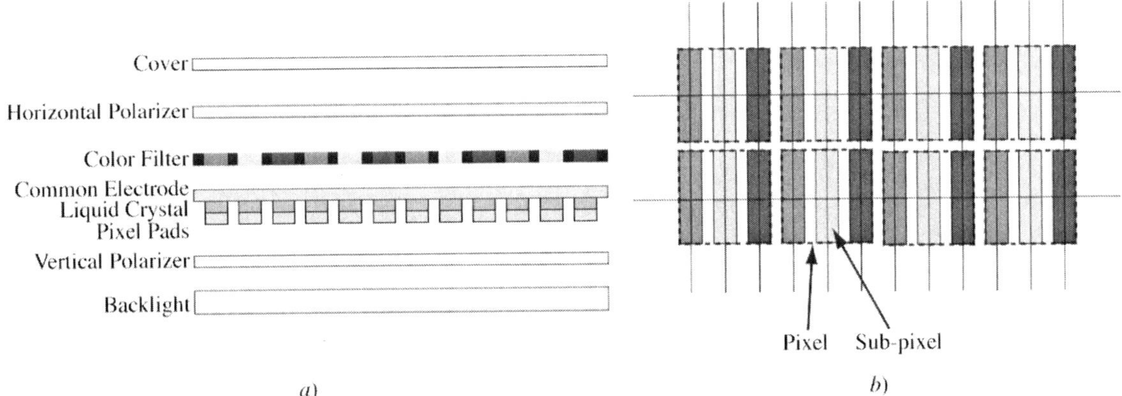

Figure 31.23: *a*) Top view of the layers making up an LCD screen.
b) Front view of a subset of the pixels and sub-pixels of an LCD screen.

Figure 31.23*a*) shows a top view of the layers of an LCD screen. Unpolarized light is emitted by a backlight. This light passes through a vertical polarizer. The now polarized light then passed through a transparent layer of conducting pixel pads. These pads are designed to put varying amounts of voltage across the next layer, which is a a liquid crystal, with respect to the transparent common electrode. If there is no voltage applied across the liquid crystal, the liquid crystal rotates the polarization of the incident light by 90°. This light with rotated polarization can then pass through the transparent common electrode, the color filter, the horizontal polarizer, and the screen cover. When voltage is applied to the pixel pad in varying magnitude, the liquid crystal rotates the polarization of the incident light by a varying amount. When the full voltage is applied to the pixel pad, the polarization of the incident light is not rotated and the subsequent horizontal polarizer blocks any light transmitted through the transparent common electrode and the color filter.

Figure 31.23*b*) shows a front view of the LCD screen illustrating how the screen produces an image. The image is created by an array of pixels. Each pixel is subdivided into three sub-pixels; one red pixel, one green pixel, and one blue pixel. By varying the voltage across each sub-pixel, a superposition of red, green, and blue light is created, producing a color for the pixel. It is difficult to connect a single wire to each sub-pixel. For example, a high definition 1080p LCD screen would have $1920 \cdot 3 = 5760$ sub-pixels in the horizontal direction and $1080 \cdot 3 = 3240$ sub-pixels in the vertical direction, giving a total of 18,662,400 sub-pixels. To address this large number of sub-pixels, the sub-pixels are connected in columns and rows as shown in Figure 31.23*b*). To turn on a sub-pixel, a voltage from both a column and a row must be applied. Thus, all the pixels cannot be addressed individually at the same time. The sub-pixels are addressed one row at a time. With the voltage for one row on, the voltages for sub-pixels in the desired columns are turned on. A small capacitor holds the voltage until the row is addressed again. A high definition 1080p LCD screen is scanned 60 times a second, producing a complete image in each scan. A high definition 1080i screen scans every-other row of the image 60 times a second and then interlaces the two images. Another high definition standard is 720p that scans 720 rows 60 times a second with a horizontal resolution of 1280 pixels. The 720p and 1080i are in common use in television broadcasting. The standard resolution television image is designated 480p with 480 rows being updated 60 times a second and producing 640 columns of pixels.

What we have learned/Exam Study Guide:

Most Important Points

- When a capacitor is being charged, one can think of a current called the displacement current existing between the plates given by $i_d = \varepsilon_0 d\Phi_E / dt$ where Φ_E is the electric flux.
- Maxwell's Equations are stated below.
  - Gauss's Law for electric fields given by $\oiint \vec{E} \bullet d\vec{A} = \frac{q_{enc}}{\varepsilon_0}$ relates the net electric flux to the net enclosed electric charge.
  - Gauss's Law for magnetic fields given by $\oiint \vec{B} \bullet d\vec{A} = 0$ states that the net magnetic flux is zero.
  - Faraday's Law given by $\oint \vec{E} \bullet d\vec{s} = -\frac{d\Phi_B}{dt}$ relates the induced electric field to the changing magnetic flux.

- The Ampere-Maxwell Law given by $\oint \vec{B} \bullet d\vec{s} = \mu_0 \varepsilon_0 \frac{d\Phi_E}{dt} + \mu_0 i_{enc}$ relates the induced magnetic field to the changing electric flux and to the current.

- For a traveling electromagnetic wave, we can describe the electric and magnetic fields as $\vec{E}(\vec{r},t) = E_{\max} \sin(kx - \omega t)\hat{y}$ and $\vec{B}(\vec{r},t) = B_{\max} \sin(kx - \omega t)\hat{z}$ where $k = 2\pi / \lambda$ is the wave number and $\omega = 2\pi f$ is the angular frequency.
- The magnitude of the electric and magnetic fields of an electromagnetic wave are related by the speed of light $E = cB$.
- The speed of light can be related to the two basic electromagnetic constants $c = 1/\sqrt{\mu_0 \varepsilon_0}$.
- The speed of light is always constant for any observer.
- For an electromagnetic wave, the energy density carried by the electric field is $u_E = \frac{1}{2}\varepsilon_0 E^2$ and the energy density carried by the magnetic field is $u_B = \frac{1}{2} B^2 / \mu_0$ and $u_E = u_B$.
- The instantaneous power carried by an electromagnetic wave is $S = E^2 / c\mu_0$ where E is the magnitude of the electric field.
- The intensity of an electromagnetic wave is defined as the average power carried by the wave given by $I = S_{ave} = E_{rms}^2 / c\mu_0$ where E_{rms} is the root mean square of the electric field.
- The radiation pressure exerted by electromagnetic waves of intensity I is given by $p_r = I / c$ if the electromagnetic waves are absorbed and $p_r = 2I / c$ if the waves are reflected.
- The polarization of an electromagnetic wave is given by the direction of the electric field.
- The intensity of unpolarized light passing through a polarizer is $I = I_0 / 2$ where I_0 is the intensity of unpolarized light incident on the polarizer.
- The intensity of polarized light passing through a polarizer is $I = I_0 \cos^2\theta$ where I_0 is the intensity of polarized light incident on the polarizer and θ is the angle between the polarization of the incident polarized light and the polarizing angle of the polarizer.

New Symbols used in this Chapter

- i_d is the displacement current.
- k is the wave number.
- S is the magnitude of the Poynting vector representing the instantaneous power carried by an electromagnetic wave.
- I is the average power carried by an electromagnetic wave.
- c is the speed of light

Additional Solved Problem

Solved Problem 31.2: Multiple polarizers

Suppose that we have polarized light that is polarized in the vertical direction. We want to rotate the polarization to the horizontal direction ($\theta = 90.0°$). If we pass the vertically polarized light through a polarizer whose polarization angle is horizontal, all the light will be blocked. If instead we use a succession of ten polarizers, each of whom have polarizing angles $\theta = 9.00°$ more that the preceding polarizer starting with $\theta = 9.00°$, we can rotate the polarization by $90.0°$ and still have light passing through.

Question:

What fraction of the incident intensity is transmitted through the ten polarizers?

Answer:

THINK:

Each polarizer is rotated nine degrees from the preceding polarizer. Thus each polarizer will transmit a fraction of the intensity equal to $f = \cos^2(9°)$. The fraction transmitted is then f^{10}.

SKETCH:

A sketch of the direction of the initial polarization and the orientation of the ten polarizers is shown in Figure 31.24.

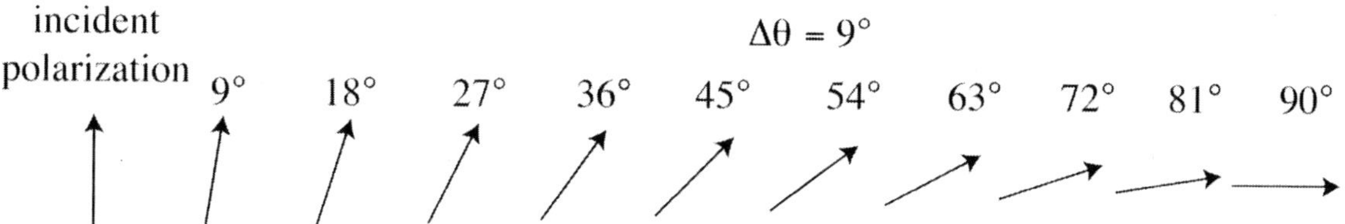

Figure 31.24: The direction of incident polarization and the direction of the polarizing angles of ten polarizers.

RESEARCH:

The intensity I of polarized light passing through a polarizer whose polarizing direction makes an angle θ with the polarization of the incident light is given by

$$I = I_0 \cos^2 \theta \tag{31.80}$$

where I_0 is the intensity of the incident polarized light. In this case, the polarizing direction of each successive polarizer is $\Delta\theta = 9°$ larger than the preceding polarizer. Thus, each polarizer reduces the intensity by the factor

Solved Problem

$$\frac{I}{I_0} = \cos^2(\Delta\theta). \tag{31.81}$$

SIMPLIFY:

The intensity reduction after passing through ten polarizers each with its polarization direction different than the polarization direction of the preceding polarizer by $\Delta\theta$ is given by

$$\frac{I_{10}}{I_0} = \left(\cos^2(\Delta\theta)\right)^{10}. \tag{31.82}$$

CALCULATE:

Putting in our numerical values we get

$$\frac{I_{10}}{I_0} = \left(\cos^2(9°)\right)^{10} = 0.780546$$

ROUND:

We report our result to three significant figures

$$\frac{I_{10}}{I_0} = 0.781 = 78.1\%.$$

DOUBLE-CHECK:

Using ten polarizers each rotated by $9°$, the polarization of the incident polarized light was rotated by $90°$ and 78.1% of the light was transmitted as opposed to using one polarizer rotated by $90°$ that would have blocked the entire incident light intensity. To see if our answer is reasonable, let's assume that instead of ten polarizers, we use n polarizers each rotated by an angle $\Delta\theta = \theta_{max}/n$ where $\theta_{max} = 90°$. For each polarizer, the angle between that polarizer and the preceding polarizer is small, and we can use the small angle approximation for $\cos\Delta\theta$ to write

$$\frac{I_1}{I_0} \approx \left(1 - \frac{(\Delta\theta)^2}{2}\right)^2.$$

The intensity passing through the n polarizers is then

$$\frac{I_n}{I_0} \approx \left(1 - \frac{(\theta_{max}/n)^2}{2}\right)^{2n} = \left(1 - \frac{\theta_{max}^2}{2n^2}\right)^{2n}.$$

For large n

Solved Problem

$$\frac{I_n}{I_0} \approx 1 = 100\% .$$

Thus, our use of ten polarizers to rotate the polarization of the incident polarized light allowed 78.1 % of the light to pass. If we had used more polarizers with smaller steps, we would have approached 100% transmission. Thus our result seems reasonable.

Solved Problem

Solved Problem 31.3: Laser powered sailing

One idea for long-range spacecraft involves using a high-powered laser focused on a spacecraft with a large totally reflecting sail rather than using sunlight. The spacecraft could then be propelled from Earth. Suppose we have a 10.0 GW laser that can be focused at long distances. The spacecraft has a mass of 200.0 kg and a totaling reflecting sail that is large enough to intercept all of the light emitted by the laser.

Question:

Neglecting gravity, how long would it take for the spacecraft to reach a speed of 30.0% of the speed of light starting from rest?

Answer:

THINK:

The radiation pressure from the laser produces a constant force on the spacecraft resulting in a constant acceleration. Using a constant acceleration, we can calculate the time to reach the final speed starting from rest.

SKETCH:

A sketch showing a laser focusing light on a spacecraft with a totally reflecting sail is shown in Figure 31.25.

Figure 31.25: A laser focusing its light on a spacecraft with a totally reflecting sail.

RESEARCH:

The radiation pressure p_r from the light with intensity I produced by the laser is given by

$$p_r = \left(\frac{2I}{c}\right). \tag{31.83}$$

Pressure is defined as force F per unit area A of the beam spot, so we can write

$$\frac{2I}{c} = \frac{F}{A}. \tag{31.84}$$

The intensity of the laser is given by the power P of the laser divided by the area A. Assuming that the sail of the spacecraft can intercept the entire laser beam spot, we can write

$$\frac{F}{A} = \frac{2(P/A)}{c}. \tag{31.85}$$

Solving for the force exerted by the laser beam on the spacecraft and using Newton's Second Law we can write

$$F = \frac{2P}{c} = ma. \tag{31.86}$$

SIMPLIFY:

We can solve (31.86) for the acceleration to obtain

$$a = \frac{2P}{mc}. \tag{31.87}$$

Assuming that the laser can keep all of its power focused on the sail of the spacecraft, the spacecraft will experience a constant acceleration. We then relate the final speed v of the spacecraft to the time it takes to reach that speed through

$$v = at = 0.300c. \tag{31.88}$$

Solving for the time gives us

$$t = \frac{0.300c}{\frac{2P}{mc}} = \frac{0.300mc^2}{2P}. \tag{31.89}$$

CALCULATE:

Putting in our numerical values gives us

$$t = \frac{0.300mc^2}{2P} = \frac{0.300(200.0\text{ kg})(3.00\cdot 10^8\text{ m/s})^2}{2(10.0\cdot 10^9\text{ W})} = 270000000\text{ s}.$$

ROUND:

We report our result to three significant figures

$$t = 270000000\text{ s} = 8.56\text{ years}.$$

Solved Problem

Solved Problem

DOUBLE-CHECK:

To double-check our result, we calculate the acceleration of the spacecraft

$$a = \frac{2P}{mc} = \frac{2\left(10.0 \cdot 10^{9}\ \mathrm{W}\right)}{\left(200\ \mathrm{kg}\right)\left(3.00 \cdot 10^{8}\ \mathrm{m/s}\right)} = 0.333\ \mathrm{m/s}^2 .$$

This acceleration is 3% of the acceleration of gravity on the surface of the Earth. This acceleration is produced by a laser with 10 times the power of a typical power station, which must run continuously for 8.56 years. The distance the spacecraft has traveled during that time is

$$x = \frac{1}{2}at^2 = \frac{1}{2}\left(0.333\ \mathrm{m/s}^2\right)\left(2.70 \cdot 10^{8}\ \mathrm{s}\right)^2 = 1.21 \cdot 10^{16}\ \mathrm{m}$$

which is 32% of the distance light travels in a year. The laser must remain focused on the spacecraft at this distance. Thus, although our calculations seem reasonable, the requirements for a laser-driven space sailor seem difficult to achieve. Finally we note that when we study Relativity in chapter 35 we will see that we must modify this calculation because the speed involved is so close to the speed of light.

Chapter 32. Geometrical Optics

Figure 32.1: Rainbow formed by refraction and reflection of light in raindrops over Ka'anapali Beach on Maui, Hawaii.

What we will learn

- Light is a wave, which, in many situations, can be approximated by straight-line trajectories representing the direction of a propagating plane wave.
- The law of reflection states that the angle of incidence is equal to the angle of reflection.
- Mirrors can focus light and produce images governed by the mirror equation, which states that the inverse of the object distance plus the inverse of the image

distance equals the inverse of the focal length of the mirror.

- Light is refracted (or bent) when it is incident on a boundary between two optically transparent media. Figure 32.1 shows light, which has been refracted and reflected by raindrops. Snell's Law states that the product of the index of refraction of the first medium times the sine of the angle of incidence on the boundary is equal to the product of the index of refraction of the second medium times the sine of the angle of the transmitted light.
- When light crosses the boundary between two media and the index of refraction of the second medium is less than the index of refraction of the first medium, there is a critical angle of incidence above which refraction cannot take place, but instead the light is reflected.
- Lenses can focus light and produce images governed by the lens equation that states that the inverse of the object distance plus the inverse of the image distance equals the inverse of the focal length of the lens.

32.1. Light Rays and Shadows

The study of light divides itself into three fields, geometric optics, wave optics and quantum optics. In the previous chapter, we learned that light is an electromagnetic wave, and in chapter 34, we will deal with the wave properties of light. In the present chapter, we will deal with geometric optics in which we will characterize light as light rays, described in the next paragraph. Quantum optics makes use of the fact that light is quantized, whereby the light energy is localized in point particles called photons.

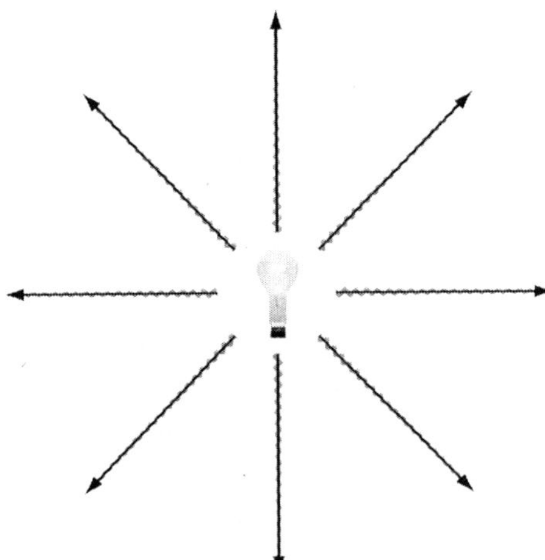

Figure 32.2: Yellow: spherical wave fronts, red: oscillating electric field, black: rays.

As we remarked in the previous chapter, electromagnetic waves spread spherically from a source. The concentric yellow spheres in Figure 32.2 represent the spreading of spherical wave fronts of the light emitted from the light bulb. (A front is a locus of points, which have the same magnitude for the electric field.) The black arrows are the light rays, which are perpendicular to the wave fronts at every point in space and point in the direction of propagation of the light. The undulating red line represents the electric field.

We can treat light waves from sources that are far away as plane waves whose wave fronts are traveling in a straight line as illustrated in Figure 32.3. We can further represent these traveling planes by vectors or arrows perpendicular to the surface of these planes. These planes can be represented by a series of parallel rays or just one ray. In this chapter, we will treat light as a ray traveling in a straight line while in one homogeneous medium. Using rays, we can solve many problems both geometrically and by various constructions. Thus, for the remainder of this chapter we will we will use rays to attack a broad range of practical problems.

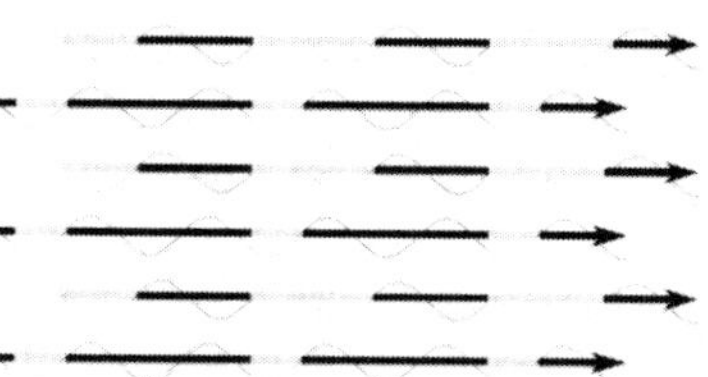

Figure 32.3: Planes representing wave fronts of a traveling light wave. The red sinusoidal oscillations represent the oscillating electric or magnetic field. The black arrows are the corresponding light rays that are always perpendicular to the plane of the wave.

Our everyday experience tells us that light travels in a straight line. We cannot easily see that light has a wave structure or a quantum structure. If we are standing outside in the bright sunshine, we see shadows cast by objects in the sunlight. The edges of the shadow appear sharp. Thus, we theorize that light travels in a straight line and the objects block the light rays from the Sun when they strike the object and otherwise continue in a straight line to the ground. A shadow is created where light is intercepted, while bright areas are created where the un-intercepted light strikes the ground or other surface. The shadow is not completely black because light scatters from other sources and partially illuminates the shadowed area.

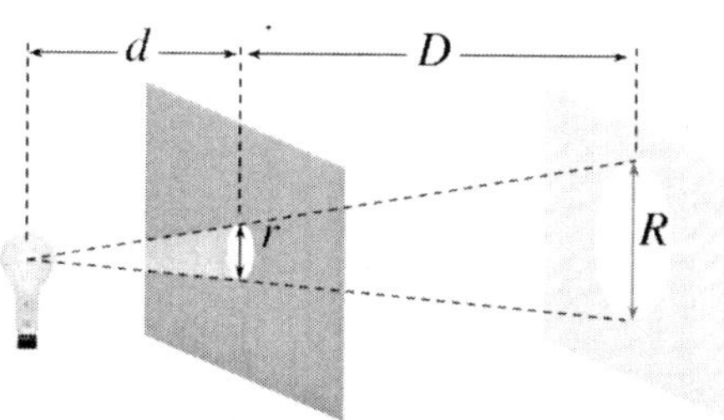

Figure 32.4: Light shining through an opening onto a screen.

Let's carry out this observation in a more controlled manner. Starting with a bright projector light, we put a piece of cardboard containing a small hole in front of the projector as in Figure 32.4. We will get a round bright spot on the screen. If we make the hole smaller, the spot on the screen gets smaller. If we make the hole larger, the spot projected on the screen gets larger.

If the size of the light source is small enough ("point-like"), then we can use the similar triangles in Figure 32.4 to find the relationship between the size of the hole (r), the size of the image (R), the distance between light source and the hole (d), and the distance between the hole and the screen (D):

$$\frac{r}{d} = \frac{R}{d+D}. \tag{32.1}$$

This equation is sometimes also referred to as the law of rays.

Solved Problem 32.1: Shadow of a ball

A small light bulb emits light that creates a shadow of a ball on a wall. The diameter of the ball is 14.3 cm and the diameter of the shadow of the ball on the wall is 27.5 cm. The ball is 1.99 m away from the wall.

Question:
How far is the light bulb from the wall?

Answer:

THINK:

The triangle formed by the light bulb and the ball is similar to the triangle formed by the light bulb and the shadow. The distance from the ball to the wall is given, so we can solve for the distance from the light bulb to the ball, add that distance to the distance of the ball from the wall, and obtain the distance of the light bulb from the wall.

SKETCH:

A sketch of a light bulb casting a shadow of a ball on a wall is shown in Figure 32.5.

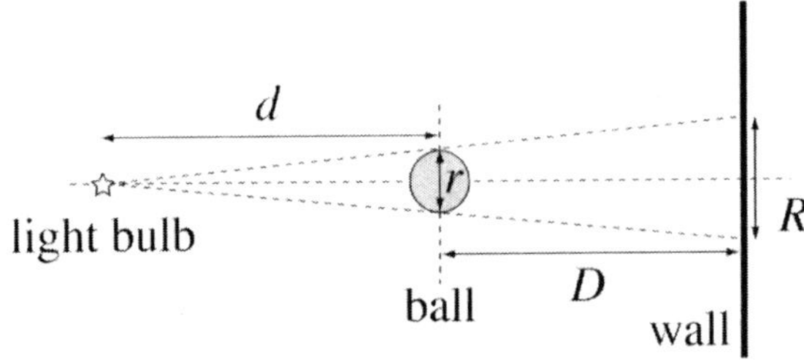

Figure 32.5: A light bulb casts a shadow of a ball on a wall.

RESEARCH:

The triangle formed by the light bulb and the ball is similar to the triangle formed by the light bulb and the shadow. Using (32.1) we can write

Solved Problem

Solved Problem

$$\frac{r}{d}=\frac{R}{d+D} \qquad (32.2)$$

where r is the diameter of the ball, R is the diameter of the shadow cast on the wall, d is the distance of the light bulb from the ball, and D is the distance of the ball from the wall.

SIMPLIFY:
We can rearrange (32.2) to obtain

$$d+D=\frac{dR}{r}. \qquad (32.3)$$

Gathering the common factors of the distance from the light bulb to the ball gives us

$$d\left(1-\frac{R}{r}\right)=-D. \qquad (32.4)$$

Solving for the distance from the light bulb to the ball leads to

$$d=\frac{D}{\frac{R}{r}-1}=\frac{Dr}{R-r}. \qquad (32.5)$$

The distance of the light bulb from the wall $d_{\text{lightbulb}}$ is then

$$d_{\text{lightbulb}}=d+D=\frac{Dr}{R-r}+D. \qquad (32.6)$$

CALCULATE:
Putting in our numerical gives us

$$d_{\text{lightbulb}}=\frac{Dr}{R-r}+D=\frac{(1.99 \text{ m})(0.143 \text{ m})}{(0.275 \text{ m})-(0.143 \text{ m})}+1.99 \text{ m}=4.14583 \text{ m}$$

ROUND:
We report our result to three significant figures

$$d=4.15 \text{ m}.$$

DOUBLE-CHECK:
To double-check our result, we calculate the ratio of r/d and compare that result with the ratio $R/(d+D)$. The first ratio is

Solved Problem

$$\frac{r}{d} = \frac{0.143 \text{ m}}{1.99 \text{ m}} = 0.0663.$$

The second ratio is

$$\frac{R}{d+D} = \frac{0.275 \text{ m}}{4.15 \text{ m}} = 0.0663.$$

Our ratios agree; so our answer seems reasonable.

32.2 Reflection and Plane Mirrors

A mirror is a surface that reflects light. A plane mirror is a flat mirror. For reflection from plane mirrors we have a simple rule for light rays incident on the surface of the mirror. This rule states that the angle of incidence θ_i is equal to the angle of reflection θ_r. These angles are always measured from the normal, which is defined to be a line perpendicular to the surface of the plane mirror. In addition, the incident ray, the normal, and the reflected ray all lie in a plane. This geometry is shown in Figure 32.6.

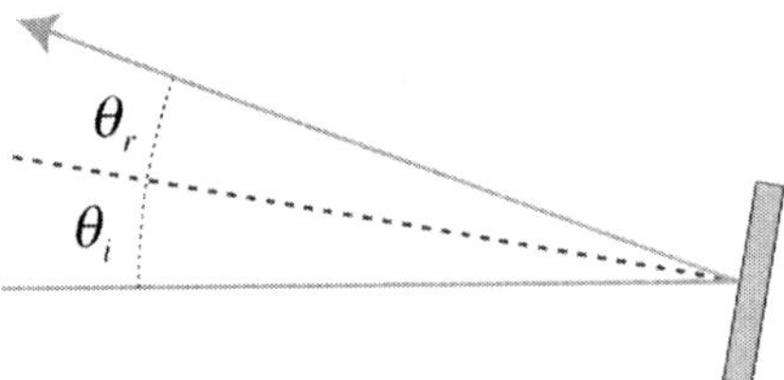

Figure 32.6: The angle of incidence equals the angle of reflection for reflection of light off a mirror. The dashed line is normal (perpendicular) to the mirror.

Figure 32.7: In the top panel, parallel light rays reflect off a mirror. In the bottom panel, arrows are superimposed on the light rays.

The law of reflection is given by

$$\theta_r = \theta_i . \tag{32.7}$$

Parallel rays incident on a plane mirror will be reflected such that the reflected rays are also parallel, as shown in Figure 32.7, because every normal to the surface (dashed line in Figure 32.6) is parallel to the other normals.

Image Formed by a Plane Mirror

Images can be formed by light reflected from plane mirrors. For example, when you stand in front of a mirror, you see an image of yourself that appears to be behind the mirror. This perception occurs because the brain assumes that light rays reaching the eyes have traveled in straight lines with no bending. Thus if light rays appear to originate at a point (say behind the mirror), the brain sees a source of light at that point whether or not there is an actual light source there. This type of image from which the light does not emanate is referred to as a virtual image. By their nature, virtual images cannot be displayed on a screen. In contrast, real images have light that actually goes through the image. Images formed by plane mirrors appear to be reversed because the light rays incident on the surface of the mirror are reflected back on the other side of the normal. Thus, we have the term "mirror image".

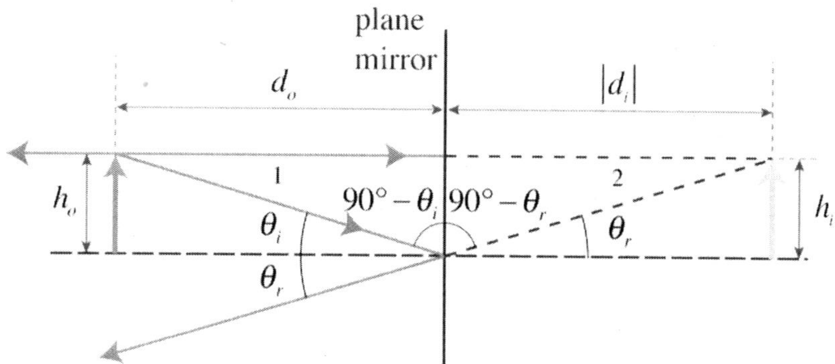

Figure 32.8: Image formed by a plane mirror.

Now let us talk about forming actual images with a plane mirror such as the mirror in Figure 32.8. For this explanation, we choose the case where an object with height h_o is placed a distance d_o from the mirror. As is traditional, we will represent the object with an arrow, which tells us the height and orientation of the object. We orient the object so that the tail of the arrow is on the optical axis, which is defined as a normal to the plane of the mirror. We use three light rays to determine where the image is formed. The first light ray emanates from the bottom of the arrow along the optical axis. This ray is reflected directly back on itself. The extrapolation of this reflected ray along the optical axis to the right of the mirror tells us that the bottom of the image will be located on the optical axis. The second light ray starts from the top of the arrow parallel to the optical axis and is reflected directly back on itself. The extrapolation of this ray past the mirror is shown in Figure 32.8 as a dashed line. The third ray begins with the top of the arrow, strikes the mirror when the optical axis intersects the mirror, and is reflected with an angle equal to its angle of incidence. The extrapolation of the reflected ray is shown as a dashed line in Figure 32.8. The extrapolations of these last two rays intersect at the point where the image of the top of the object is formed. This reconstruction is shown in Figure 32.8. It turns out that all rays from the arrow tip that hit the mirror will extrapolate such that they intersect at the image – not just the two rays shown here. Thus, the mirror produces a virtual image on the opposite side of the mirror. This image has a height h_i and is located a distance d_i to the right of the mirror.

We can see in Figure 32.8 that the yellow triangle 1 is congruent with the blue triangle 2. Thus, we can see that

$$h_i = h_o \tag{32.8}$$

and

$$|d_i| = d_o \,. \tag{32.9}$$

By convention, the sign of the image distance for a virtual image produced by a mirror is negative. Thus, we use the absolute value of the image distance in (32.9). The image produced by a plane mirror appears to be the same distance behind the mirror as the object is in front of the mirror. In addition, the image appears upright and the same size as the object.

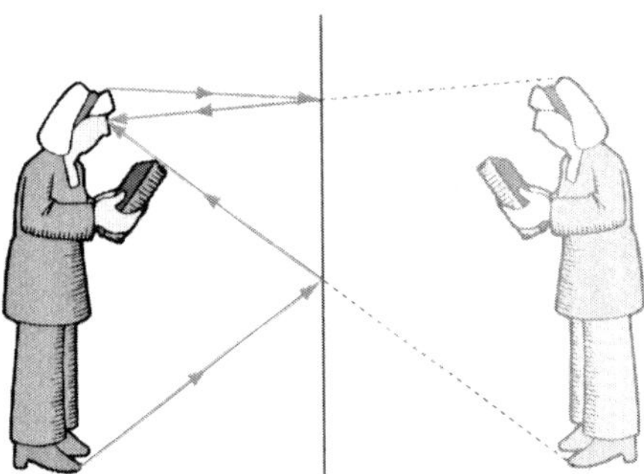

Figure 32.9: A person standing in front of a mirror sees a virtual image of herself.

Incidentally, have you thought about why mirror images seem to be left-right reversed but not up-down reversed? Let us take as an example a person standing in front of a plane mirror. The person standing in front of the mirror sees an image of herself standing at the same distance behind the mirror as she is standing in front of the mirror as shown in Figure 32.9. The image seen by the person can be constructed with two light rays as shown but of course light rays are coming from every visible point of the person. The image is upright (meaning that it has the same orientation as the object, not "upside-down") and virtual (implying that the image is formed behind the surface of the mirror).

Now let us discuss the left-right question for the mirror image, as shown in Figure 32.10. Again, we construct the virtual image with two rays, but all rays behave the same way. The figure shows that the mirror actually does a front-to-back reversal. There is no left-right or top-bottom reversal. If one holds an arrow pointing to the right and looks in the mirror, the arrow still points to the right! One can see that the real live person has his watch on his left hand. He perceives that his virtual self has his watch on his right hand only because the brain imagines that the image was formed by a 180° rotation through a vertical axis and not by a front-back reversal. If you find this too complicated, perhaps the following visualization works for you: Suppose you paint the letters of your university on your forehead to get yourself ready for the big game. Then you take a length of clear packaging tape and tape it over the letters on your forehead. As you pull the tape off, some of the paint sticks to it. If you pull the tape straight away from you, you see the backside of the tape that contacted the paint, and the letters are on it mirror-reversed. Looking at your image in the mirror is just like looking at the backside of the tape.

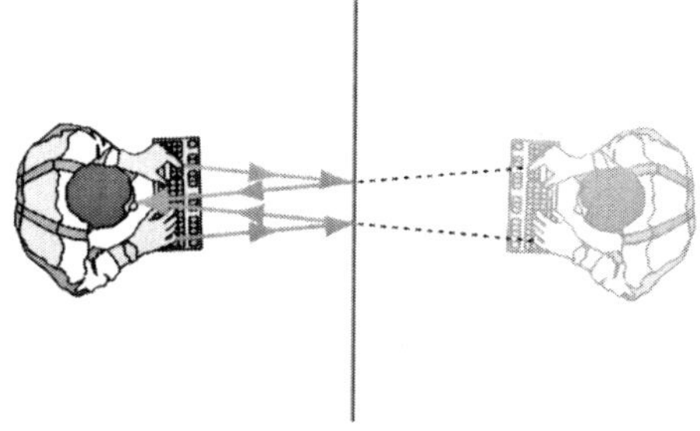

Figure 32.10: A person sitting in front of a mirror sees a mirror image of himself.

If you look at an image of yourself using a web cam on your computer, you see yourself as other people see you. Thus, the image from the web cam is not reversed back-to-front. This image of yourself is confusing after your long experience with seeing yourself in a mirror. Every movement you make seems to go in the opposite direction in the image from what you expect. Thus, clever videoconferencing software presents a reversed image that represents the back-to-front reversal inherent in a mirror image, which makes for a more natural experience for local user of the videoconferencing software.

Example

Example 32.1: Full-length mirror

Question:

A 184 cm (6 ft 1/2 inch) tall person wants to buy a mirror such that he can see the full length of himself in the mirror. His eyes are 8 cm from the top of his head. What is the minimum height of the mirror?

Answer:

For the purposes of this example, let us represent the person as a 184 cm tall pole with eyes 8 cm from the top of the pole (this number does not matter, as the discussion below will show) as shown in Figure 32.11.

First, we discuss where the light from the feet of the person must travel to reach the eyes of the person. The light leaving the feet of the person is represented by a red arrow in Figure 32.11. The angle of incidence on the mirror, θ_i, is equal to the angle of reflection from the mirror, θ_r. Thus we can form two triangles a) and b) as shown in Figure 32.12.

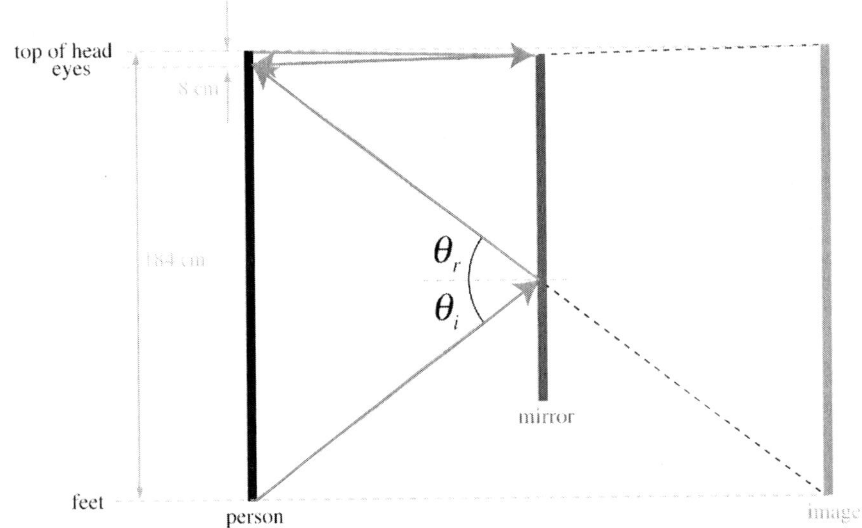

Figure 32.11: Distances for person standing in front of a mirror, which is the blue line.

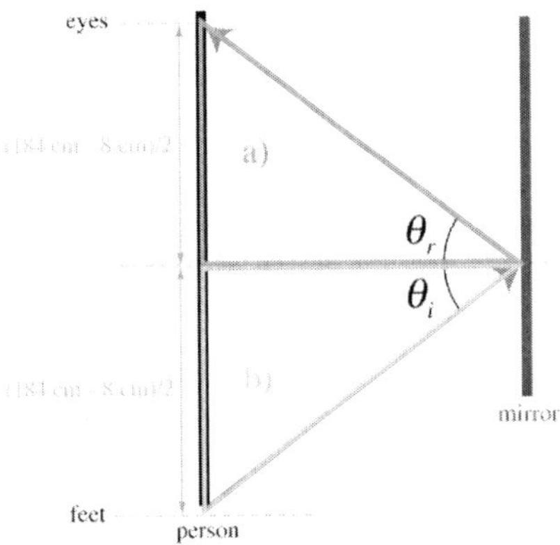

Figure 32.12: Two congruent triangles formed by the light from the feet of person.

Example

These two triangles are congruent because $\theta_i = \theta_r$, they each have a right angle, and they share a common side. Thus, the vertical sides of each triangle must have the same length. The sum of these two sides is equal to the height of the person minus the distance from the top of the person's head to the eyes of the person. Therefore, the vertical side of each triangle has the length (184 cm -8 cm)/2 as indicated in Figure 32.12.

We can see then that the bottom of the only needs to extend to a height of (184 cm – 8 cm)/2 = 88 cm above the floor. A similar analysis of two congruent triangles gives us the top edge of the mirror. The top edge of the mirror needs to be (8 cm)/2 = 4 cm below the top of the head of the person. Therefore, the minimum height of the mirror is 184 cm – 4 cm – 88 cm = 92 cm. This mirror then is exactly half the 184 cm height of the person. Thus, a mirror that is half the height of the person will afford the person a full-length view. This result does not depend on the distance of the eyes from the top of the head of the person. This result also does not depend on how close to the mirror the person stands.

32.3. Curved Mirrors

When light is reflected from the surface of a curved mirror, the light rays follow the law of reflection at each point on the surface. However, unlike the plane mirror, the surface of a curved mirror is not flat. Thus, light rays that are parallel before they strike the mirror are reflected in different directions depending on the part of the mirror that they strike. Depending of the shape of the mirror, the light rays can be made to converge or diverge.

Focusing Spherical Mirrors

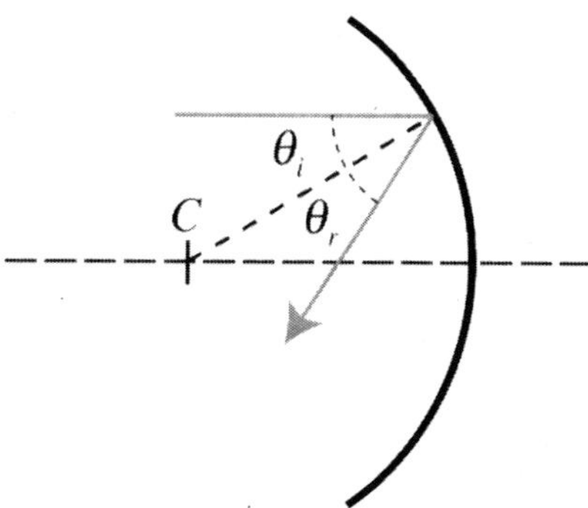

Figure 32.13: A horizontal light ray reflected through the focal point of the mirror.

Suppose that we have a spherical mirror which has a reflecting surface on its inside. Thus, we have a concave reflecting surface. In Figure 32.13, we have represented this sphere as a semicircle. The optical axis of the mirror is a line through the center of the sphere, marked as C in Figure 32.13. The optical axis is represented in this drawing by a horizontal dashed line. Imagine that a horizontal light ray above the optical axis is incident on the surface of the mirror parallel to the optical axis. The law of reflection applies at the point where the light ray strikes the mirror. The normal to the surface at this point, a dashed line in Figure 32.13, is a radial line that goes through the center of the sphere. Using the isosceles triangle in Figure 32.13, you can see that each short side of the triangle is about half the length of the long side provided that θ_r is small. (In Derivation 32.2, we will show this result in detail.) Thus, the reflected ray crosses the optical axis approximately half way between the mirror and point C.

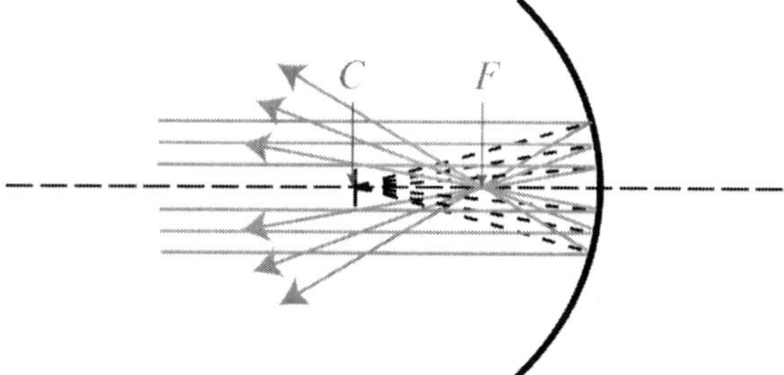

Figure 32.14: Many parallel light rays reflected through the focal point of the lens.

Now let us suppose that we have many horizontal light rays incident on this spherical mirror as shown in Figure 32.14. Each light ray obeys the law of reflection at each point.

Each ray will cross the optical axis half way between the mirror and point C. This crossing point F is called the focal point.
Thus F is half way between point C and the surface of the mirror. C is located at the center of the sphere so the distance of C from the surface of the mirror is just the radius of the mirror, R. Therefore the focal length f of a converging spherical mirror is

$$f = \frac{R}{2} \text{ (converging mirror)} \tag{32.10}$$

Light rays incident on an actual converging mirror are shown in Figure 32.15.

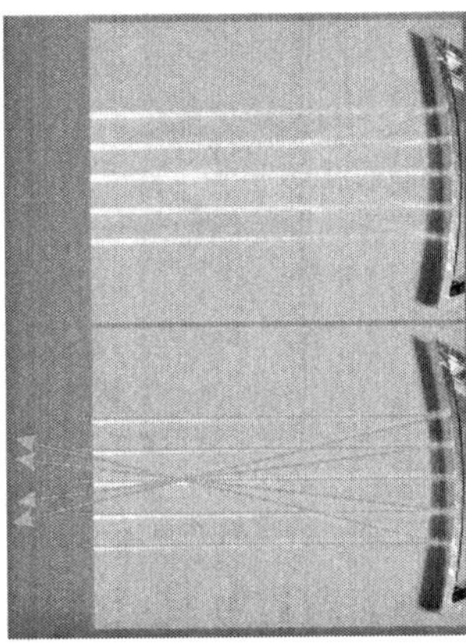

Figure 32.15: Top frame focusing of parallel light rays to the focal point by a converging mirror. Bottom frame same image with arrows superimposed.

Now let us talk about forming actual images with a converging mirror such as the one in Figure 32.16. For this explanation we choose the case where an object with height h_o is placed a distance d_o from the mirror, where $d_o > f$. As is traditional, we represent the object with an arrow, which tells us the height and orientation of the object. We orient the object so that the tail of the arrow is on the optical axis. The optical axis is a normal to the surface of the spherical mirror along a line passing through the center C of the sphere. We use three light rays to determine where the image is formed. The first light ray emanates from the bottom of the arrow along the optical axis. This ray just tells us that the bottom of the image will be located on the optical axis. The second light ray starts from the top of the arrow parallel to the optical axis and is reflected through the focal point of the mirror. The third ray begins with the top of the arrow, passes through the center of the sphere, and is reflected back on itself. The last two rays intersect at the point where the image of the top of the object is formed. This reconstruction is shown in Figure 32.16. It turns out that all rays from the arrow tip that hit the mirror will intersect at the image – not just the two shown here. Thus, we say that the mirror focuses the rays to form the image.

The reconstruction of the special case shown in Figure 32.16 shows a real image (on the same side of the image as the object, not behind the mirror) with height h_i a distance d_i from the surface of the mirror on the same side of the mirror as the object. This image has a height h_i, which will be assigned a negative value to denote that the image is inverted, and is a distance d_i from the mirror. By convention, we define this image distance to be positive because the image is on the same side of the mirror as the object. The image is inverted and reduced in size relative to the object that produced the image. The image is called real when you are able to place a screen at the image location and obtain a sharp projection of the image on the screen at that point. For a virtual image, the light rays do not go through the image and thus no light reaches a screen that is placed at the location of the image.

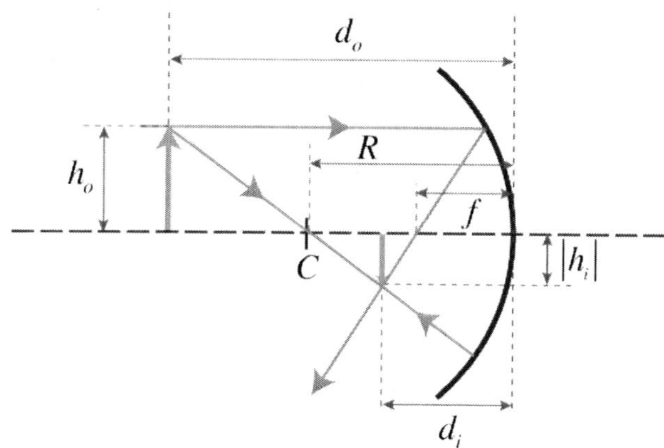

Figure 32.16: Image produced by converging mirror of an object with object distance greater than the focal length of the mirror.

Now let's reconstruct another case for a converging mirror, where $d_o < f$ as in Figure 32.17. We place the object on the optical axis. We again use three light rays. The first just establishes that the tail of the image will lie on the optical axis. The second ray starts from the top of the object parallel to the optical axis and is reflected through the focal point. The third ray leaves the top of the object along a radius and is reflected back on itself through the center of the sphere. The reflected rays are clearly diverging. To determine the location of the image, we must extrapolate the reflected rays to the other side of the mirror. These two rays intersect a distance d_i from the surface of the mirror producing an image with height h_i.

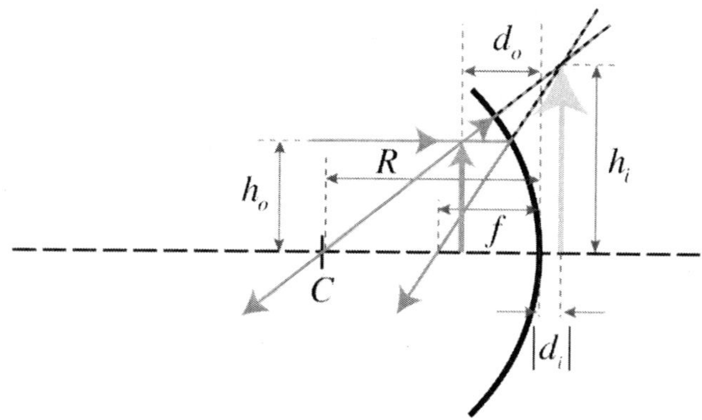

Figure 32.17: Image produced by converging mirror of an object with object distance less than the focal length of the mirror.

In this case, we have the image formed on the opposite side of the mirror from the object, a virtual image. (By convention, the quantity d_i will be assigned a negative value to denote that the image is virtual.) To an observer, the image appears to be behind the mirror, as was the case for the plane mirror. The image is upright and larger than the object. These results for $d_o < f$ are quite different from those for $d_o > f$.

Before treating diverging mirrors, we will formalize the sign conventions for distances and heights. We define all distances on the same side of the mirror as the object to be positive and all distances on the opposite side of the mirror from the object to be negative. Thus f and d_o are positive for converging mirrors. In the case of real images, d_i is positive. In cases where the image is virtual, d_i is negative. If the image is upright then h_i is positive, while if the image is inverted h_i is negative.

We can derive the mirror equation (32.11), which relates the object distance d_o, the image distance d_i, and the focal length of the mirror f:

$$\frac{1}{d_o}+\frac{1}{d_i}=\frac{1}{f} \qquad (32.11)$$

The signs of the terms in this equation are based on the convention that we defined in the preceding paragraph.

Derivation 32.1: Spherical mirror equation
We can derive the spherical mirror equation by starting with a converging mirror that has a focal length f. We place an object h_o tall at a distance d_o from the surface of the mirror as shown in Figure 32.18.

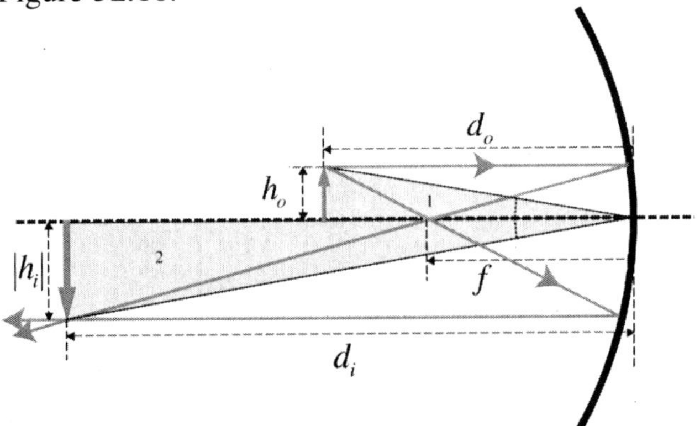

Figure 32.18: The two similar triangles 1 and 2.

Let us now trace a ray from the top of the object parallel to the optical axis and reflect it through the focal point. Let us trace a second ray from the top of the object through the focal point that is reflected parallel to the optical axis. The image is formed with height h_i as distance d_i from the mirror. We can see that these quantities form a right triangle with h_o as the height and d_o as the length (green triangle 1 in the Figure 32.18). We can form a second right triangle with $-h_i > 0$ as the height and d_i as the length (green triangle 2 in Figure 32.18). Using the law of reflection for a ray hitting the mirror on the optical axis, we know that the indicated angles in the two triangles are the same and thus the two triangles are similar. Thus, we know that

$$\frac{h_o}{d_o} = \frac{-h_i}{d_i} \text{ or } \frac{-h_i}{h_o} = \frac{d_i}{d_o}.$$

Now let us look at the same geometry but two different triangles. One right triangle (yellow triangle 4 in Figure 32.19) is defined by the height $-h_i$ and the length d_i - f. The second triangle (yellow triangle 3 in Figure 32.19) is defined by the height h_o and the length f. The two triangles are similar and we can write

$$\frac{h_o}{f} = \frac{-h_i}{d_i - f} \text{ or } \frac{-h_i}{h_o} = \frac{d_i - f}{f}.$$

We can substitute our expression for the ratio of the heights derived above, and we obtain

$$\frac{d_i}{d_o} = \frac{d_i - f}{f}.$$

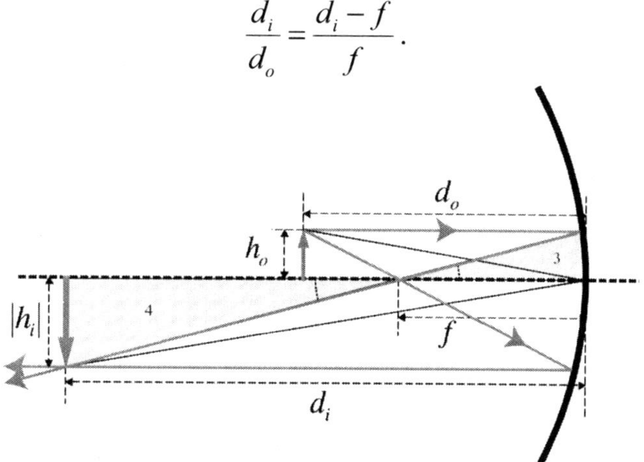

Figure 32.19: The two similar triangles 3 and 4.

At this point some algebra leads us to

$$\frac{fd_i}{d_o} = d_i - f \Rightarrow \frac{fd_i}{d_o} + f = d_i,$$

and finally dividing both sides of this equation by the product fd_i leads to the spherical mirror equation

$$\frac{1}{d_o} + \frac{1}{d_i} = \frac{1}{f}.$$

Derivation

Case	Type	Direction	Magnification
$d_o < f$	Virtual	Upright	Enlarged
$d = f$	Real	Upright	Image at infinity
$f < d_o < 2f$	Real	Inverted	Enlarged
$d_o = 2f$	Real	Inverted	Same size
$d_o > 2f$	Real	Inverted	Reduced

Table 32.1: Image characteristics for converging mirrors.

The magnification m of the mirror is defined to be

$$m = \frac{h_i}{h_o} = -\frac{d_i}{d_o} \tag{32.12}$$

Note that the magnification m is negative for the situation in the example used in the derivation. Algebraically this is because $h_i < 0$. The significance of a negative m is that $m < 0$ tells us that the image is inverted. In Table 32.1 we summarize the characteristics of images formed by a converging mirror for five different classes of object distances.

Diverging Spherical Mirrors

Suppose we have a spherical mirror, which has the reflecting surface on the outside of the sphere as shown in Figure 32.20.

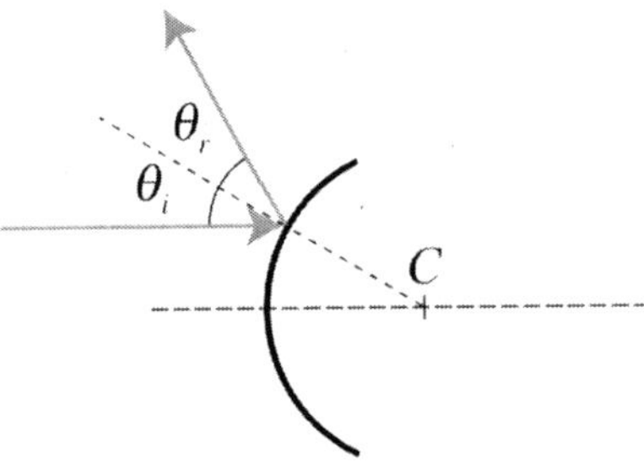

Figure 32.20: Reflection of a horizontal light ray from a diverging spherical mirror.

Thus, we have a convex reflecting surface and the reflected rays will diverge. In Figure 32.20, we have indicated this sphere by a semicircle. The optical axis of the mirror is a line through the center of the sphere, represented in this drawing by a horizontal dashed line. Imagine that a horizontal light ray above the optical axis is incident on the surface of the mirror. At the point where the light ray strikes the mirror the law of reflection applies.

In contrast to the converging mirror, the normal points away from the center of the sphere. When we extrapolate the normal through the surface of the sphere, it intersects the optical axis of the sphere at the center of the sphere marked C in Figure 32.20. When we observe the reflected ray, it seems to be coming from inside the sphere.

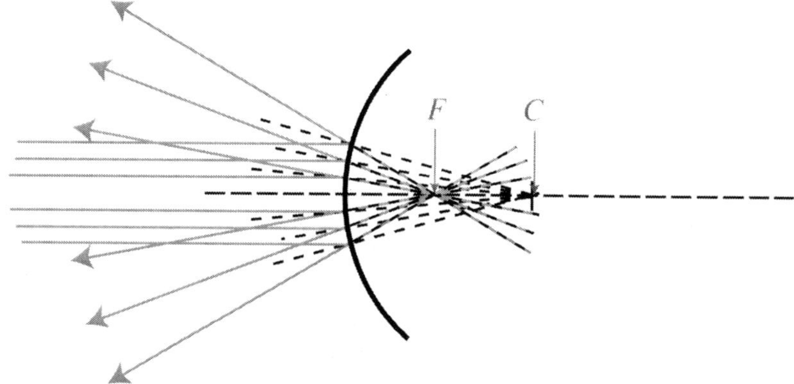

Figure 32.21: The reflection of parallel light rays from the surface of a diverging mirror.

Now let us suppose that we have many horizontal light rays incident on this spherical mirror as shown in Figure 32.21. Each light ray obeys the law of reflection. You can see that the rays diverge and do not seem to form any kind of image. However, if we extrapolate the reflected rays through the surface of the mirror they all intersect the optical axis at one point. This point called the focal point of this diverging mirror. In Figure 32.22, five parallel light rays are incident on an actual diverging spherical mirror. The dashed lines represent the extrapolated direction of the reflected rays.

Figure 32.22: The top frame shows parallel light rays reflected from a diverging spherical mirror. The bottom frame shows the arrows corresponding to the light rays, with the dashed lines representing the extrapolated light rays.

Now let us discuss images formed by diverging mirrors as illustrated in Figure 32.23. Again we use three rays. The first ray establishes that the tail of the arrow lies on the optical axis. The second ray starts from the top of the object traveling parallel to the optical axis and is reflected from the surface of the mirror such that its extrapolation crosses the optical axis a distance from the surface of the mirror equal to the focal length of the mirror. The third ray begins at the top of the object and is directed so that its extrapolation would intersect the center of the sphere. This ray is reflected back on itself. The reflected rays diverge but the extrapolated rays converge a distance d_i from the surface of the mirror on the side of the mirror opposite the object. The rays converge a distance h_i above the optical axis.

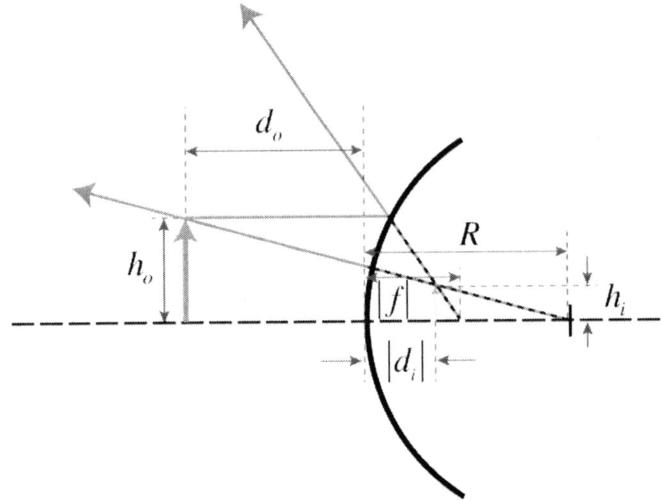

Figure 32.23: Image formed by an object placed in front of a diverging spherical mirror.

Thus, we form an upright, reduced image on the side of the mirror opposite the object. This image is virtual because the light rays do not actually go through it. These characteristics (upright, reduced, virtual image) are valid for all object distances for a diverging mirror. In the case of a diverging mirror, the focal length f is negative because the focal point of the mirror is on the opposite side of the object. We also assign a negative value to the radius of a diverging mirror. Thus, we have

$$f = \frac{R}{2} \text{(with } R < 0 \text{ for a diverging mirror)}$$

We always take the object distance d_o to be positive. If we rearrange the mirror equation (32.11), which is also valid for a diverging mirror, we get

$$d_i = \frac{d_o f}{d_o - f}. \quad (32.13)$$

If d_o is always positive and f is always negative, we can see that d_i will always be negative. Applying the equation for the magnification we find that m is always positive. Looking at the diagram of the ray construction for the diverging mirror will also convince you that the image will always be reduced in size. Thus for a diverging mirror (even if $d_o < |f|$), we always will obtain a virtual, upright, and reduced image.

Self-Test Opportunity: You are standing 2.50 m from a diverging mirror with focal length $f = -0.500$ m. What do you see in the mirror?

Spherical Aberration

The equations we have derived for spherical mirrors ($\frac{1}{d_o}+\frac{1}{d_i}=\frac{1}{f}$ and $m=\frac{h_i}{h_o}=-\frac{d_i}{d_o}$) apply only to light rays that are close to the optical axis. If the light rays are far from the optical axis, they will not be focused through the focal point of the mirror. Then we will see a distorted image. In Figure 32.24, several light rays are incident on a spherical converging mirror.

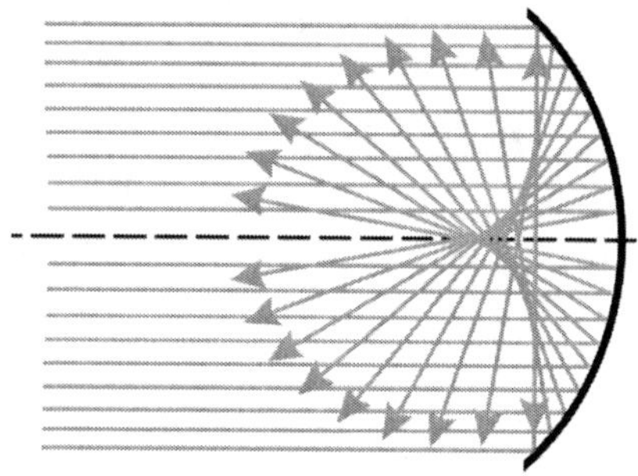

Figure 32.24: Parallel light rays incident on a spherical converging mirror demonstrating spherical aberration.

You can see that the rays farther from the optical axis are reflected such that they cross the optical axis closer to the mirror than rays that strike the mirror closer to the optical axis. As the rays approach the optical axis, they are reflected through points closer and closer to the focal point.

Derivation 32.2: Spherical aberration for spherical mirrors
Light rays parallel to the optical axis that are close to the optical axis will be reflected such that they cross the optical axis at the focal point of the mirror. The focal point is defined as half the radius of curvature of the mirror. However, light rays that are far from the optical axis will not be reflected through the focal point. To derive an expression for the point at which rays that are parallel to the optical axis while also being far from the optical axis cross the optical axis, we draw the geometry in Figure 32.25.

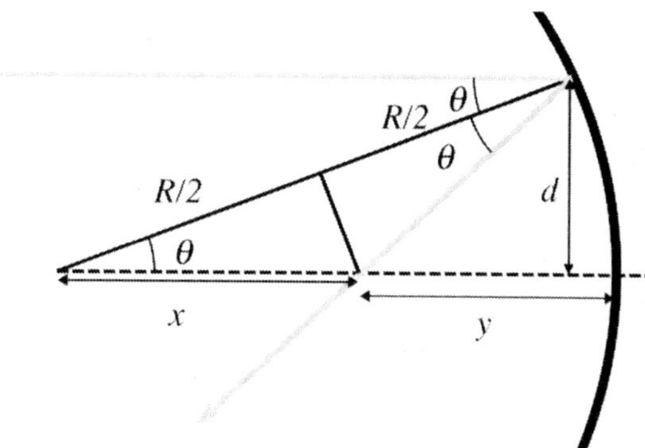

Figure 32.25: Geometry of the spherical aberration of a converging spherical mirror.

We start with a light ray parallel to the optical axis a distance d from the optical axis. The ray reflects and crosses the optical axis a distance y from the mirror. The ray makes

Derivation

Derivation

an angle θ with respect to the normal to the mirror surface, which is a radius R of the spherical mirror. The law of reflection tells us that angle of incidence of the ray on the surface of the mirror is equal to the angle of reflection.

We define the distance from the center of the spherical mirror to the point at which the reflected ray crosses the optical axis as x. We draw a line from the point where the ray crosses the optical axis perpendicular to the normal. We thus form two congruent right triangles with angle θ, hypotenuse x, and adjacent side $R/2$ such that

$$\cos\theta = \frac{R/2}{x} \Rightarrow x = \frac{R}{2\cos\theta}$$

We can also express θ in terms of d as

$$\sin\theta = \frac{d}{R} \Rightarrow \theta = \sin^{-1}\left(\frac{d}{R}\right)$$

The distance y is given by

$$y = R - x = R - \frac{R}{2\cos\theta} = R\left(1 - \frac{1}{2\cos\theta}\right) = R\left(1 - \frac{1}{2\cos\left(\sin^{-1}\left(\frac{d}{R}\right)\right)}\right)$$

We can see that for $d << R$, $\sin^{-1}\left(\frac{d}{R}\right) \approx 0$ and $y \approx R/2$, which agrees with (32.10).

The amount of spherical aberration is given by the next leading term, $y \approx \left[\frac{R}{2} - \frac{d^2}{4R}\right]$.

Self-Test Opportunity: Consider a converging spherical mirror with $R = 7.20$ m without assuming that the incident light rays are close to the optical axis of the mirror. However the incident light rays are parallel to the optical axis. Calculate the position at which the reflected light rays intersect the optical axis if the incoming ray is

a) 0.720 cm away from the optical axis
b) 0.800 cm away from the optical axis
c) 1.80 cm away from the optical axis
d) 3.60 cm away from the optical axis

Parabolic Mirrors

Parabolic mirrors have a surface that reflects light from a distant source to the focal point from anywhere on the mirror. Thus, the full size of the mirror can be used to collect light and form images. In Figure 32.26, horizontal light rays are incident on a parabolic mirror. All rays are reflected through the focal point of the mirror.

Parabolic mirrors are more difficult to produce than spherical mirrors and are accordingly more expensive. Most large reflecting telescopes use parabolic mirrors in order to avoid spherical aberration.

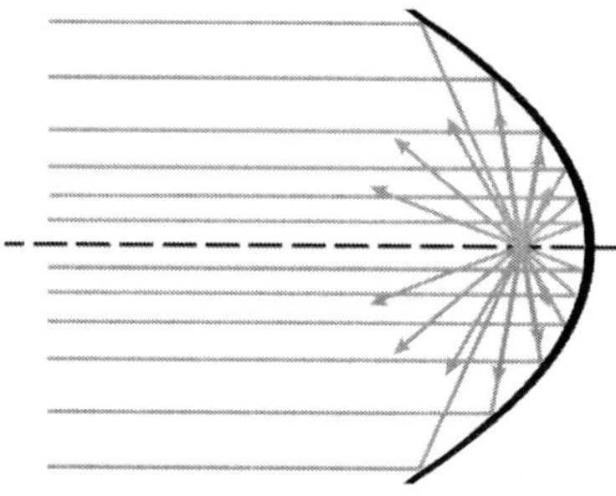

Figure 32.26: Light rays reflected by a parabolic mirror.

Example

Example 32.2: Image formed by a converging mirror
Consider an object 5.00 cm tall placed 55.0 cm from a converging mirror with focal length 20.0 cm as shown in Figure 32.27.

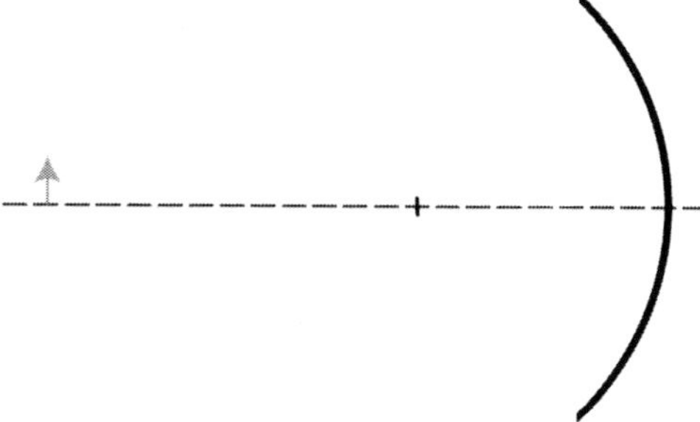

Figure 32.27: An object (green arrow), which forms an image using a converging mirror.

Question 1:
Where is the image produced?
Answer 1:
We can use the mirror equation to find the image distance d_i

$$\frac{1}{d_o} + \frac{1}{d_i} = \frac{1}{f}$$

in terms of the object distance d_o and the focal length of the mirror f. The mirror is specified as converging so we know that the focal length is positive. The image distance is

$$d_i = \frac{d_o f}{d_o - f} = \frac{(55.0 \text{ cm})(20.0 \text{ cm})}{55.0 \text{ cm} - 20.0 \text{ cm}} = 31.4 \text{ cm}.$$

Question 2:
What is the size and orientation of the produced image?

Example

Answer 2:
The magnification m is given by

$$m = \frac{h_i}{h_o} = -\frac{d_i}{d_o}$$

where h_o is the height of the object and h_i is the height of the produced image. The image height is then

$$h_i = -h_o \frac{d_i}{d_o} = -(5.00 \text{ cm}) \frac{31.4 \text{ cm}}{55.0 \text{ cm}} = -2.85 \text{ cm}.$$

The magnification is then

$$m = \frac{h_i}{h_o} = \frac{-2.85 \text{ cm}}{5.00 \text{ cm}} = -0.570.$$

Thus the produced image is inverted and reduced.

In-class exercise: A small object is placed in front of a converging mirror with radius $R = 7.50$ cm such that the image distance equals the object distance. How far is this small object from the mirror?

a) 2.50 cm
b) 5.00 cm
c) 7.50 cm
d) 10.0 cm
e) 15.0 cm

32.4 Refraction and Snell's Law

Light travels at different speeds in different optically transparent materials. The ratio of the speed of light in vacuum divided by the speed of light in a material is called the index of refraction of the material. The index of refraction n is given by

$$n = \frac{c}{v} \tag{32.14}$$

where c is the speed of light in a vacuum and v is the speed of light in the medium. The speed of light in a physical medium such as glass is always less that the speed of light in a vacuum. Thus the index of refraction of a material is always greater than or equal to one, and by definition the index of refraction of vacuum is one. Below is a table of the index of refraction for common materials.

Material	Index of Refraction
Air	1.00029
Water	1.333
Ice	1.310
Ethyl alcohol	1.362
Quartz glass	1.459
Typical lucite	1.5
Typical glass	1.5
Typical oil	1.5
Diamond	2.417

Table 32.2: Indices of refraction for common materials for light with wavelength 589.3 nm.

When light crosses the boundary between two transparent materials, most of it is refracted although there is usually a little reflection as well. Refraction means that the light rays do not travel in a straight line across the boundary. When light crosses a boundary from a medium with a lower index of refraction n_1 to a medium with a higher index of refraction n_2, the light rays change their direction and bend toward the normal as shown in Figure 32.28.

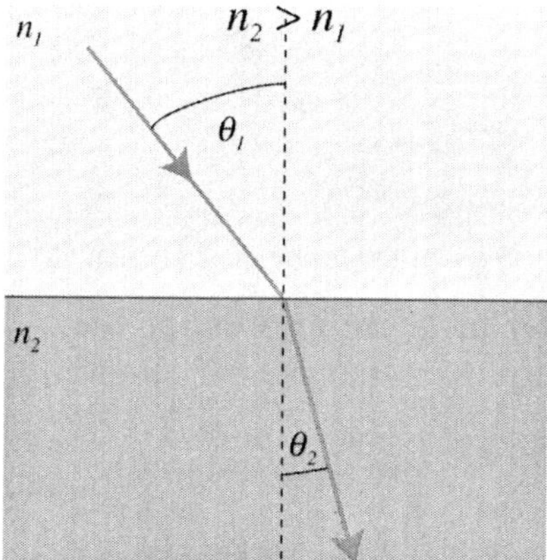

Figure 32.28: Light rays refracted at the boundary between two optical media with $n_1 < n_2$.

Figure 32.29: Top frame: light rays refracted when crossing the boundary between air and glass. Bottom frame: arrows superimposed on the light rays. The dashed lines are normal to the surface.

In Figure 32.29 actual light rays in air are incident on the boundary between air and glass. The light rays are refracted toward the normal. (The reflected light is also observable.) Changing direction toward the normal means that the angle of refraction $\theta_2 < \theta_1$, the angle of incidence.

When light crosses a boundary from a medium with a higher index of refraction n_1 to a medium with a lower index of refraction n_2 the light rays are bent away from the normal as shown in Figure 32.30.

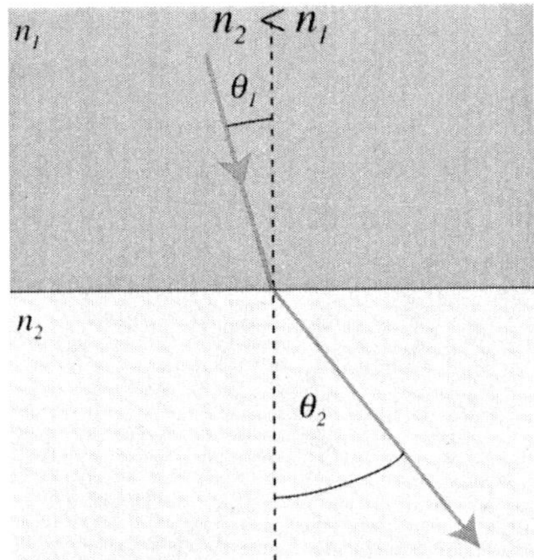

Figure 32.30: Light rays refracted at the boundary between two optical media with $n_1 > n_2$.

In Figure 32.21 actual light rays in air are incident on the boundary between glass and air. The light rays are refracted away from the normal. Bending away from the normal means $\theta_2 > \theta_1$.

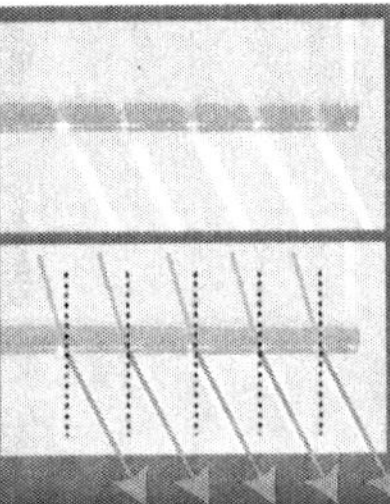

Figure 32.31: Top frame: light rays refracted when crossing the boundary between glass and air. Bottom frame: arrows superimposed on the light rays. The dashed lines are normal to the surface.

From measurements of the angles of incident and refracted rays in media with different indexes of refraction, one can experimentally construct a law of refraction. This law of refraction can be expressed as

$$n_1 \sin\theta_1 = n_2 \sin\theta_2 \qquad (32.15)$$

where n_1 and θ_1 are the index of refraction and angle from the normal in the first medium and n_2 and θ_2 are the index of refraction and angle from the normal in the second medium. This law of refraction is also called Snell's Law. It cannot be proven by using ray optics concepts alone. In chapter 34, we will derive this law using wave optics.

The index of refraction of air is very close to one as shown in Table 32.2. For the purposes of this book, we will always assume the index of refraction of air $n_{air} = 1$. The situation of light incident on various media from air is common so we will write the formulas for refraction of light incident on a surface with index of refraction n_{medium}

$$n_{medium} = \frac{\sin\theta_{air}}{\sin\theta_{medium}} \tag{32.16}$$

where θ_{air} is the angle from the normal for the light in air and θ_{medium} is the angle from the normal for the light in the medium. Note that θ_{air} is always greater than θ_{medium}. If we have the case of light coming out of a medium into air then we have the same formula.

Now let's consider light traveling in an optical medium with index of refraction n_1 that crosses a boundary with another optical medium with a lower index of refraction n_2 such that $n_2 < n_1$. In this case, the light is bent away from the normal. As one increases the angle of incidence θ_1 one can see that the angle of the transmitted light θ_2 can approach $90°$. When θ_2 reaches $90°$, total internal reflection takes place instead of refraction; all of the light is reflected internally. The critical angle θ_c at which total internal reflection takes place is given by

$$\frac{n_2}{n_1} = \frac{\sin\theta_1}{\sin\theta_2} = \frac{\sin\theta_c}{\sin 90°}$$

or

$$\sin\theta_c = \frac{n_2}{n_1} \quad (n_2 \le n_1) \tag{32.17}$$

because $\sin 90° = 1$. One can see from this equation that total internal reflection can only occur for light traveling from a medium with a higher index of refraction to one with a lower index of refraction because the sine of an angle cannot be greater than one. At angles less than θ_c, some light is reflected and some is transmitted. At angles greater than θ_c, all the light is reflected and none is transmitted.

If the second medium is air, then we can take n_2 equal to one and we obtain an expression for the critical angle for total internal reflection for light leaving a medium with index of refraction n and entering air

$$\sin\theta_c = \frac{1}{n}. \tag{32.18}$$

Solved Problem 32.2: Displacement of light rays in transparent material

A light ray in air is incident on a $t = 5.90$ cm thick sheet of transparent material with index of refraction $n = 1.50$ with an incident angle of $\theta_{air} = 38.5°$ as shown Figure 32.32.

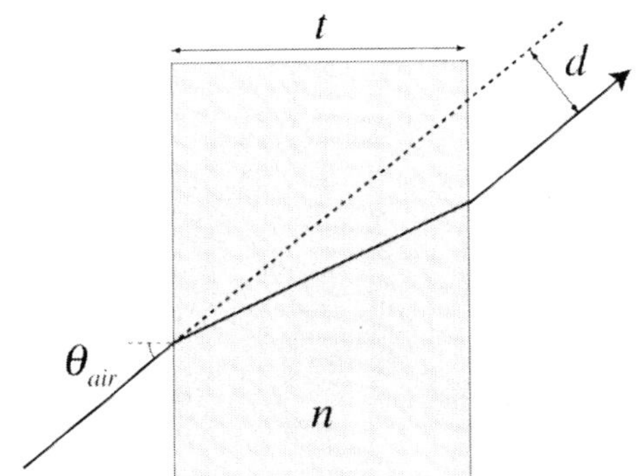

Figure 32.32: Light ray incident on a sheet of transparent material with thickness *t* and index of refraction *n*.

Solved Problem

Question:

What is the distance d that the light ray is displaced after it passes through the sheet?

Answer:

THINK:

The light ray will refract toward the normal as it enters the transparent sheet and will refract away from the normal as it exits the transparent sheet. After passing through the transparent sheet the light ray is parallel to the incident light ray but is displaced. Using Snell's Law, the angle from the normal in the transparent sheet can be calculated. Having that angle, we can use geometry to calculate the displacement of the light ray passing through the transparent sheet.

SKETCH:

A sketch of the light ray passing through a transparent sheet is shown in Figure 32.33.

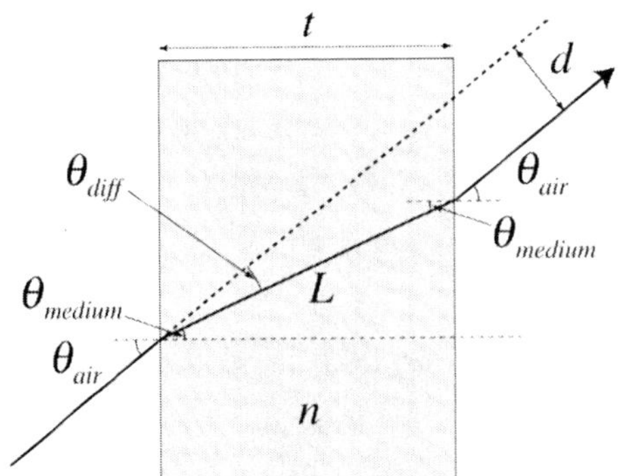

Figure 32.33: A light ray passes through a sheet of transparent material

RESEARCH:

Solved Problem

The light ray is incident on the sheet with an angle θ_{air}. Snell's law relates the incident angle with the refracted angle θ_{medium} through the index of refraction of the transparent material n

$$n = \frac{\sin\theta_{air}}{\sin\theta_{medium}}. \quad (32.19)$$

We can solve (32.19) for the refracted angle

$$\theta_{medium} = \sin^{-1}\left(\frac{\sin\theta_{air}}{n}\right). \quad (32.20)$$

We call L the distance that the light ray travels in the transparent sheet. Using Figure 32.33, we can relate the thickness of the sheet t to the transmitted angle

$$\cos\theta_{medium} = \frac{t}{L}. \quad (32.21)$$

If θ_{diff} is the difference between the incident angle and the refracted angle as shown in Figure 32.33 then

$$\theta_{diff} = \theta_{air} - \theta_{medium}. \quad (32.22)$$

We can see in Figure 32.33 that the displacement of the light ray d can be related to the distance the light ray travels in the sheet and the difference between the incident angle and the refracted angle

$$\sin\theta_{diff} = \frac{d}{L}. \quad (32.23)$$

SIMPLIFY:

We can combine the preceding equations to obtain

$$d = L\sin\theta_{diff} = \frac{t}{\cos\theta_{medium}}\sin\left(\theta_{air} - \theta_{medium}\right) \quad (32.24)$$

where

$$\theta_{medium} = \sin^{-1}\left(\frac{\sin\theta_{air}}{n}\right).$$

CALCULATE:

We first calculate the refracted angle

$$\theta_{medium} = \sin^{-1}\left(\frac{\sin(38.5°)}{1.50}\right) = 24.5199°.$$

Solved Problem

Now we calculate the displacement of the light ray

$$d = \frac{5.90 \text{ cm}}{\cos(24.5199°)}\sin(38.5° - 24.5199°) = 1.56663 \text{ cm}.$$

ROUND:

We report our result to three significant figures

$$d = 1.57 \text{ cm}.$$

DOUBLE-CHECK:

If the light ray were incident perpendicularly on the sheet ($\theta_{air} = 0°$), the displacement of the ray would be zero. To calculate what the displacement would be of the incident angle were $\theta_{air} = 90°$, we can rewrite (32.24) as

$$d = \frac{t\sin(\theta_{air} - \theta_{medium})}{\cos\theta_{medium}} = t\frac{\sin\theta_{air}\cos\theta_{medium} - \cos\theta_{air}\sin\theta_{medium}}{\cos\theta_{medium}}$$

using the trigonometric identity $\sin(\alpha - \beta) = \sin\alpha\cos\beta - \cos\alpha\sin\beta$. Taking $\theta_{air} = 90°$, we get

$$d = t\frac{1\cdot\cos\theta_{medium} - 0\cdot\sin\theta_{medium}}{\cos\theta_{medium}} = t.$$

Thus, our result must be between zero and the thickness of the sheet. Our result is $d = 1.57$ cm compared with $d = 5.90$ cm for $\theta_{air} = 90°$, so our result seems reasonable.

Optical Fibers

An important application of total internal reflection is the optical fiber. Light is injected into a fiber so that the reflection angle at the curved surface of the fiber is greater than the critical angle for total internal reflection. The light will then be transported the length of the fiber as it bounces repeatedly from the fiber surface. Thus, optical fibers can be used to transport light from a source to a destination as shown in Figure 32.34. In this picture, a bundle of optical fibers is shown with the end of the fibers open to the camera. The other end of the fiber is optically connected to a light source. Note that optical fibers can transport light in directions other than a straight line. The fiber may be bent as long as the radius of curvature of the bend is not small enough to allow the light traveling in the optical fiber to have angles of incidence θ_i less than θ_c. If $\theta_i < \theta_c$, the light will be absorbed by the cladding around the surface of the fiber. These arguments are applicable to optical fibers with core diameters greater than 10 μm.

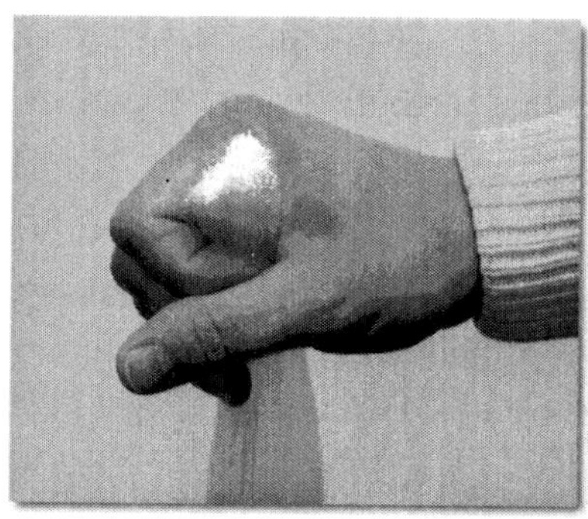

Figure 32.34: Light transported from a light source by fiber optics.

One type of optical fiber used for digital communications consists of a glass core surrounded by cladding composed of glass with lower index refraction than the core. The cladding is then coated to prevent damage. A schematic drawing of the structure of an optical fiber is shown Figure 32.35.

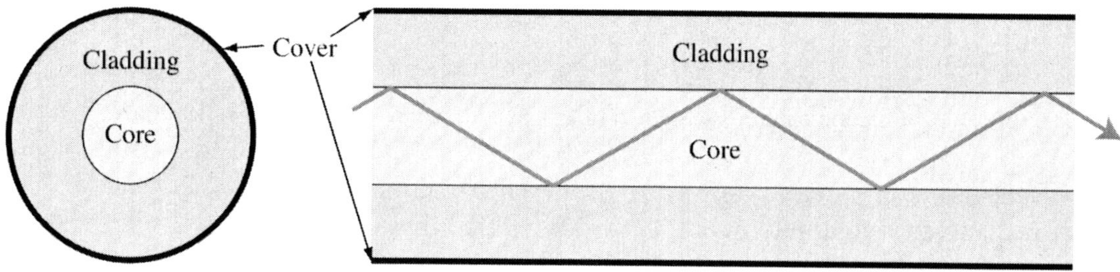

Figure 32.35: The structure of optical fibers incorporating total internal reflection.

For a typical commercial optical fiber, the core material is SiO_2 doped with Ge to increase its index of refraction. The typical commercial fiber can transmit light 500 m with small losses. The light is generated using light-emitting diodes (LEDs) that produce light with a long wavelength. The light is generated as digital pulses. Small light losses do not affect digital signals because digital signals are transmitted as binary bits rather than as analog signals. As long as the bits are registered correctly, the information is transmitted flawlessly as opposed to analog signals that would be directly degraded by any signal loss. Every 500 m the signals are received, boosted, and re-transmitted. Thus, very high data rates that are immune to interference can be transmitted long distances. This scenario explains the physics behind the fiber-optics backbone of the modern Internet.

Solved Problem

Solved Problem 32.3: Optical fiber

Consider a long glass optical fiber with index of refraction $n = 1.265$ that is surrounded by air. (There is no cladding.) The end of the fiber is polished to be flat and is perpendicular to the length of the fiber. A light ray from a laser is incident from air onto the center of the circular face of the optical fiber.

Question:

What is the maximum angle of incidence for this light ray such that it will be confined and transported by the optical fiber? (Neglect any reflection as the light ray enters the fiber.)

THINK:

The light ray will refract as it enters the optical fiber. Once inside the fiber, if the angle of incident on the surface of the optical fiber is greater than the critical angle for total internal reflection, then the light will be transmitted without loss.

SKETCH:

A sketch of the light ray entering the fiber and reflecting off the inner surface of the optical fiber is shown in Figure 32.36.

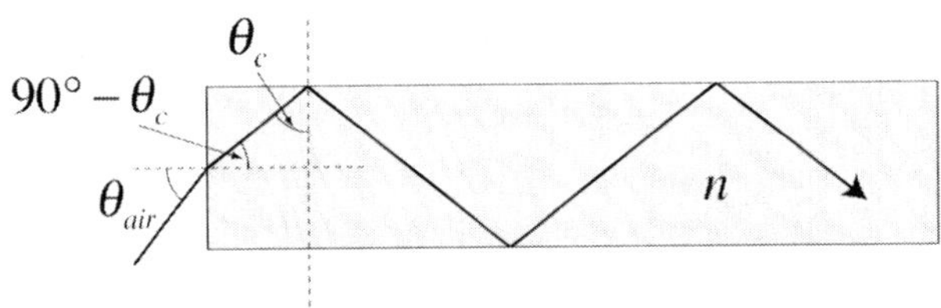

Figure 32.36: Light entering an optical fiber and undergoing total internal reflection.

RESEARCH:

The critical angle for total internal reflection θ_c in the fiber is given by

$$\sin\theta_c = \frac{1}{n} \qquad (32.25)$$

where n is the index of refraction of the optical fiber. For the light entering the optical fiber, Snell's Law tells us that since $n_{air} = 1$

$$\sin\theta_{air} = n\sin\theta_{medium} \qquad (32.26)$$

where θ_{medium} is the angle of the light ray in the fiber. From Figure 32.36 we can see that

$$\theta_{medium} = 90° - \theta_c . \qquad (32.27)$$

SIMPLIFY:

We can solve (32.26) to obtain the maximum angle of incidence

$$\theta_{air} = \sin^{-1}\left(n\sin\theta_{medium}\right). \qquad (32.28)$$

Using (32.27) we can write

Solved Problem

Solved Problem

$$\theta_{air} = \sin^{-1}\left(n\sin\left(90° - \theta_c\right)\right) = \sin^{-1}\left(n\cos\theta_c\right) \quad (32.29)$$

where we have used the trigonometric identity $\sin\left(90° - \alpha\right) = \cos\alpha$. We can then use (32.25) to obtain

$$\theta_{air} = \sin^{-1}\left(n\cos\left(\sin^{-1}\left(\frac{1}{n}\right)\right)\right). \quad (32.30)$$

CALCULATE:

Putting in our numerical values, we get

$$\theta_{air} = \sin^{-1}\left(\left(1.265\right)\cos\left(\sin^{-1}\left(\frac{1}{1.265}\right)\right)\right) = 50.7816°. \quad (32.31)$$

ROUND:

We report our result to four significant figures

$$\theta_{air} = 50.78°.$$

DOUBLE-CHECK:

The critical angle of total internal reflection for the optical fiber is

$$\theta_c = \sin^{-1}\left(\frac{1}{1.265}\right) = 52.23°.$$

Snell's Law at the entrance of the optical fiber gives us

$$\theta_{medium} = \sin^{-1}\left(\frac{\sin\left(50.78°\right)}{1.265}\right) = 37.77°.$$

Thus

$$\theta_{medium} = 37.77° = 90° - \theta_c = 90° - 52.23° = 37.77°,$$

and our result appears reasonable.

Chromatic Dispersion

The index of refraction of an optical medium depends on the wavelength of the light traveling in that medium. This dependence of the index of refraction on the wavelength of the light means that light of different colors will be refracted differently at the boundary between two optical media. This effect is call chromatic dispersion.

In general, the index of refraction for a given optical medium is greater for shorter wavelengths than for longer wavelengths. Therefore, blue light will be refracted more than red light as depicted in Figure 32.37. We can see that $\theta_b < \theta_r$ in this figure.

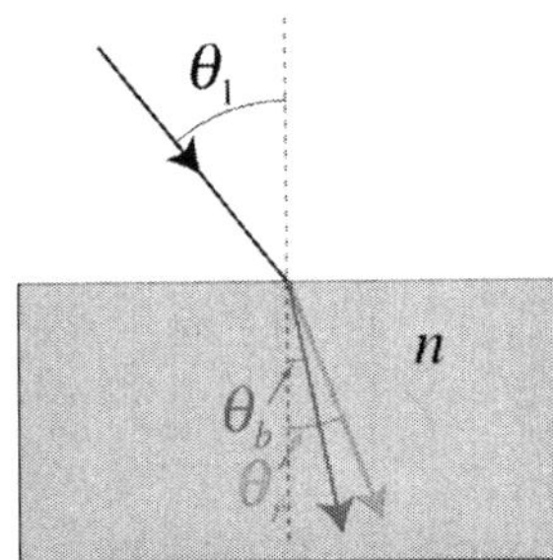

Figure 32.37: Chromatic dispersion for light refracted across the boundary of two optical media.

White light consists of a superposition of all visible wavelengths. If we send a beam of white light onto a glass prism as shown in Figure 32.38, we can separate the incident white light into the various visible wavelengths because different wavelengths are refracted to different angles.

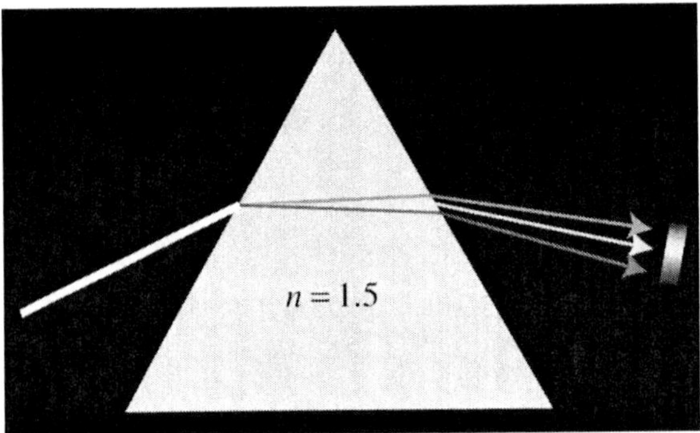

Figure 32.38: White light incident on a glass prism.

In Figure 32.38, we draw three refracted light rays for red, green, and blue light, but of course white light contains a continuum of wavelengths such as you see in a rainbow.

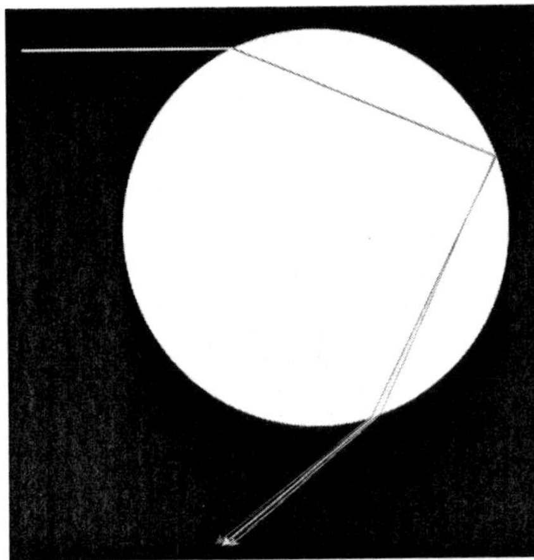

Figure 32.39: Chromatic dispersion in a spherical drop of water that produces a rainbow.

A rainbow is a common example of chromatic dispersion. Spherical drops of water refract and reflect sunlight and thereby create a rainbow as shown in Figure 32.39. A rainbow is created when water drops are suspended in the air and you observe these water drops with the sun at your back. The white light from the Sun enters the drops, refracts at the surface of the drop, is transmitted through the water to the far side where it is reflected, is transmitted again to the surface of the drop where it exits the drop and is refracted again. In the two refraction steps, the index of refraction is different for different wavelengths. The index of refraction for green light in water is 1.333, while the index of refraction for blue light is 1.337, and for red light it is 1.331. Of course, there is a continuum of indices of refraction for all the colors. These different indices of refraction result in an apparent spreading of light according to color. The rainbow will appear at an angle of $42°$ with respect to the direction of the sunlight.

A typical rainbow is shown in Figure 32.1. You can see the blue light in the inner part of the rainbow and the red light on the outside of the rainbow. The arc of the rainbow represents the $42°$ angle from the direction of the sunlight.

However, there are several other features of rainbows evident in this photograph. One can see that the region inside the arc of the rainbow appears to be brighter than the region outside the arc of the rainbow. One can understand this phenomenon by looking at the path light rays take that are refracted and reflected in the raindrops as illustrated in Figure 32.40.

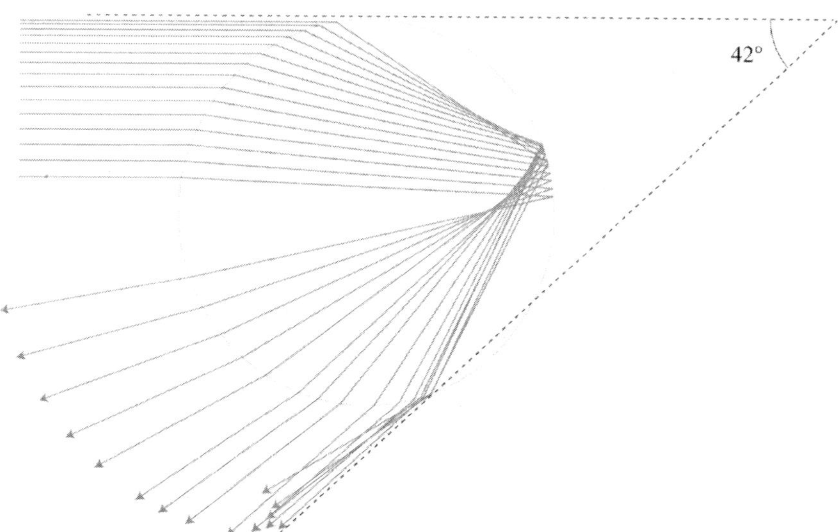

Figure 32.40: The path taken by parallel light rays in a spherical drop of water.

One can see from this figure that most of the light that is refracted and reflected back to the observer has an angle less than $42°$. At angles smaller than $42°$, most of the light is refracted and reflected back to the observer although no separation of the different wavelengths is observed because dispersed colors from one ray merge with those from another ray and form white light. At larger angles, no light is sent back to observer by this process, thus outside the arc of the rainbow there is much less light. There is still some light there because it is scattered from other sources.

Another feature that is apparent in Figure 32.1 is a secondary rainbow. The secondary rainbow appears at a larger angle than the primary rainbow and the order of the colors is reversed. The secondary rainbow is created by light that reflects twice inside the raindrop as shown in Figure 32.41. In contrast to the situation shown in Figure 32.39, when the ray in Figure 32.41 strikes the drop surface the third time (after one refraction and one reflection) the angle of incidence is greater than the critical angle and the ray reflects once more.

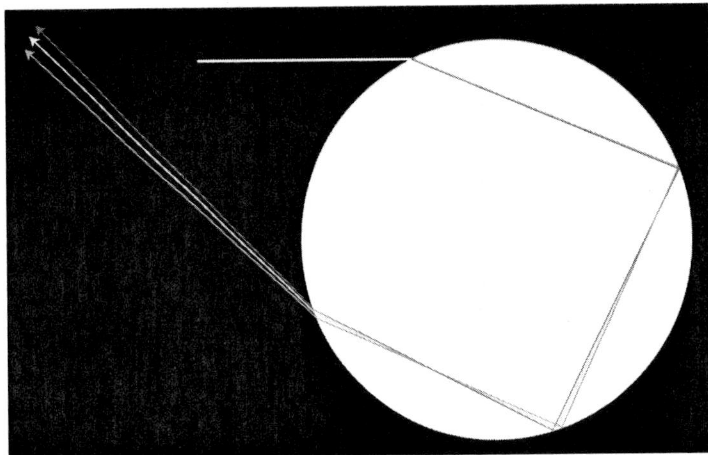

Figure 32.41: Chromatic dispersion in a raindrop that produces a secondary rainbow.

In this figure you can see that the angle of the emerging blue and red light is reversed compared to the blue and red light shown in Figure 32.39 for the primary rainbow.

> *In-class exercise*: Sunlight strikes a piece of glass at an angle of incidence of $\theta_i = 33.4°$. What is the difference in the angle of refraction between a red light ray ($\lambda = 660.0$) and a violet light ray ($\lambda = 410.0$ nm) inside the glass? The index of refraction for red light is $n = 1.520$ and the index of refraction for violet light is $n = 1.538$.
>
> a) 0.03°
> b) 0.12°
> c) 0.19°
> d) 0.26°
> e) 0.82°

32.5. Lenses

When light is refracted while crossing a curved boundary between two different media, the light rays follow the law of refraction at each point on the boundary. The angle at which the light rays cross the boundary (with respect to the local normal to the boundary) is different along the boundary, so the refracted angle is different at different points along the boundary. A spherical curved boundary between two optically transparent media is called a spherical surface. If the light enters a medium through a spherical surface and then returns to the original medium through another spherical surface, the device that has the spherical surfaces is called a lens. Light rays that are initially parallel before they strike the lens are refracted in different directions depending on the part of the lens they strike. Depending of the shape of the lens, the light rays can be focused or can be caused to diverge.

If the front surface of a lens with index of refraction n is part of the surface of a sphere with radius R_1 and the back surface of the lens is part of the surface of a sphere with radius R_2, then we can calculate the focal length f for a thin lens using the lens-makers formula

$$\frac{1}{f}=(n-1)\left(\frac{1}{R_1}-\frac{1}{R_2}\right). \qquad (32.32)$$

We will derive this equation, which applies to thin lenses in air, in Derivation 32.3. There we will learn a sign convention for the radii, because they can be positive or negative.

Derivation 32.3: Lens-makers formula and the lens equation for thin lenses

We start the derivation of the Lens-Makers Formula by assuming that we have light traveling in air incident on a spherical surface of an optical medium with index of refraction n and radius R as shown in Figure 32.42. We draw the optical axis of the optical medium as a line perpendicular to the spherical face of the medium drawn through the center of the spherical face. We assume a light ray originating a distance d_o from the lens at an angle α with respect to the optical axis. This ray makes an angle θ_1 with respect to a normal to the surface of the optical medium. Using the law of refraction (32.15) and taking $n_1=1$ and $n_2=n$ we get

$$\sin\theta_1 = n\sin\theta_2$$

where θ_2 is the angle the refracted light ray makes with respect to the normal to the surface. If α is a small angle, then the angles θ_1 and θ_2 will be small and we can write the relation

$$\theta_1 = n\theta_2 .$$

Looking at Figure 32.42 we can see the relationship between the angles $\theta_1=\alpha+\beta$ and $\beta=\theta_2+\gamma$. We can rewrite these equations as $n\theta_2=\alpha+\beta$ and $\theta_2=\beta-\gamma$. We insert the second of them into the first to eliminate θ_2 and obtain

$$\frac{\alpha+\beta}{n}=\beta-\gamma ,$$

which we can rearrange to get

Derivation

$$\alpha + n\gamma = \beta(n-1).$$

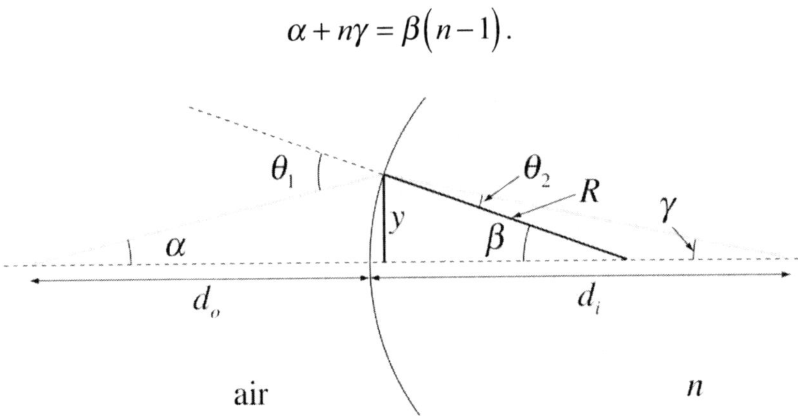

Figure 32.42: Light traveling in air incident on a spherical surface of an optical medium with index of refraction n.

Looking at Figure 32.42 and making the small angle approximation, we can write

$$\alpha \approx \tan\alpha \approx \frac{y}{d_o},\ \beta \approx \tan\beta \approx \frac{y}{R},\ \gamma \approx \tan\beta \approx \frac{y}{d_i}.$$

Now we can write

$$\frac{y}{d_o} + \frac{ny}{d_i} = \frac{(n-1)y}{R}$$

or

$$\frac{1}{d_o} + \frac{n}{d_i} = \frac{(n-1)}{R}.$$

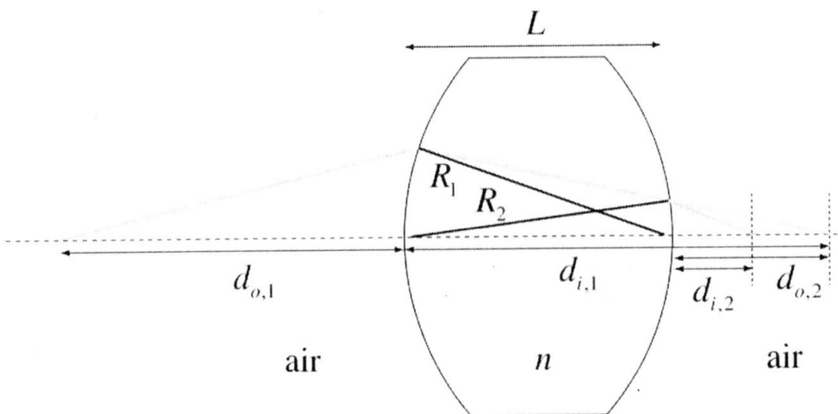

Figure 32.43: A lens of thickness L composed of an optical medium with index of refraction n in air. The left face of the lens has radius R_1 and the right face of the lens has radius R_2.

We have now derived an expression for the image formed by one surface. Since d_i is independent of α, all of the light from the source goes through the same point and therefore the light is focused. Now let's put two surfaces together to make a lens as shown in Figure 32.43.

The light ray originating from the left of the lens can be described by our result for the image distance and object distance derived above (with an added subscript 1 to denote the first surface)

$$\frac{1}{d_{o,1}}+\frac{n}{d_{i,1}}=\frac{(n-1)}{R_1}.$$

The relationship between image distance and object distance for the second surface is described by

$$\frac{n}{d_{o,2}}+\frac{1}{d_{i,2}}=\frac{(1-n)}{R_2}.$$

From Figure 32.43 we can see that

$$\left|d_{i,1}\right|=L+\left|d_{0,2}\right|.$$

If we assume a thin lens, then L will be much smaller than any other object or image distances and we can safely neglect the thickness of lens and write

$$\left|d_{i,1}\right|\approx\left|d_{0,2}\right|.$$

Next, we will choose a sign convention for distances. Agreeing that the light goes from left to right, object distances will be positive for objects on the left of the lens and negative for objects on the right of the lens. Image distances will be positive for objects on the right of the lens and negative for images on the left of the lens. Just as for mirrors, image distances are positive for images formed where the light eventually goes. Because the object for the second surface of the lens is to the right of the lens, we then have

$$-d_{o,2}=d_{i,1}.$$

Substituting this equation into our equation for the second surface we get

$$-\frac{n}{d_{i,1}}+\frac{1}{d_{i,2}}=\frac{(1-n)}{R_2}$$

or

$$\frac{n}{d_{i,1}}=\frac{1}{d_{i,2}}-\frac{(1-n)}{R_2}.$$

Substituting this equation into our expression for the first surface we get

$$\frac{1}{d_{o,1}}+\frac{1}{d_{i,2}}-\frac{(1-n)}{R_2}=\frac{(n-1)}{R_1}.$$

The object distance of the lens as a whole is the same as the object distance for the first surface of the lens, $d_o = d_{o,1}$. The image distance of the lens as a whole is the same as the image distance for the second surface of the lens, $d_i = d_{i,2}$. We then obtain

$$\frac{1}{d_o}+\frac{1}{d_i}=(n-1)\left(\frac{1}{R_1}-\frac{1}{R_2}\right).$$

The focal length is defined as the image distance when the object is at infinity, which gives us

$$\frac{1}{\infty}+\frac{1}{f}=\frac{1}{f}=(n-1)\left(\frac{1}{R_1}-\frac{1}{R_2}\right).$$

This result is the Lens Makers Formula.

We can take this expression together with our expression relating the image and object distances of the lens and get the Thin Lens Equation

$$\frac{1}{d_o}+\frac{1}{d_i}=\frac{1}{f}.$$

In the above derivations, we have tacitly assumed that the light would strike a convex surface as seen by the light. If the surface happens to be concave as seen by the light then our results are still valid provided that we use a negative value for the radius of curvature. When we observe the second surface of a lens we see it from the opposite perspective from that seen by the light, so much care is needed to assign the proper signs to the radii. What we would call a double convex lens would have $R_1 > 0$ and $R_2 < 0$ because the light would perceive the second surface as being concave.

In order to avoid the complicated discussion in the paragraph above, we adopt the commonly used convention: If the focal length of a lens is positive, we say that the lens is converging, while if the focal length is negative we say that the lens is diverging.

In-class exercise: A single lens with two convex surfaces made of sapphire with index of refraction $n = 1.77$ has surfaces with radii of curvature $R_1 = 27.0$ cm and $R_2 = -27.0$ cm. What is the focal length of this lens in air?

a) 17.5 cm b) 20.0 cm c) 27.0 cm d) 54.0 cm e) 60.0 cm

Converging Lenses

A converging lens, which has $f > 0$, is shaped such that parallel rays will be focused by refraction at the focal distance f from the center of the lens. In Figure 32.44, a light ray is incident on a converging glass lens. At the surface of the lens, the light ray is refracted toward the normal. When the ray leaves the lens, it is refracted away from the normal. The resulting refracted ray will pass through the focal point of the lens on the opposite side of the lens from the incident ray.

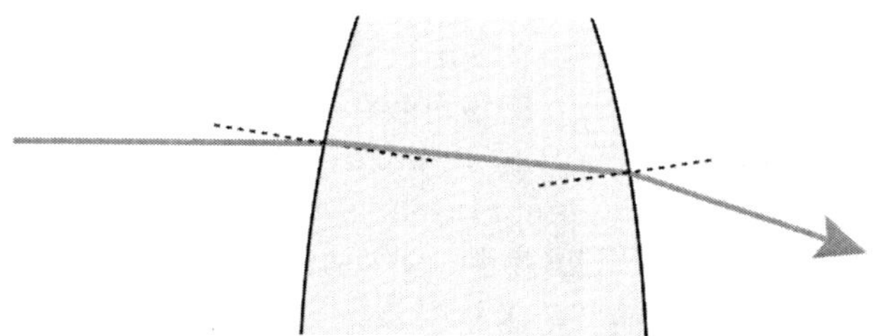

Figure 32.44: Refraction of a horizontal light through a converging lens.

Let us now study the case of several horizontal light rays incident on a converging lens. These rays will be focused to a point a distance f from the center of the lens on the opposite side of the lens from the incident rays. A photograph of a converging lens with five parallel lines of light incident in the surface from the left is shown in Figure 32.45.

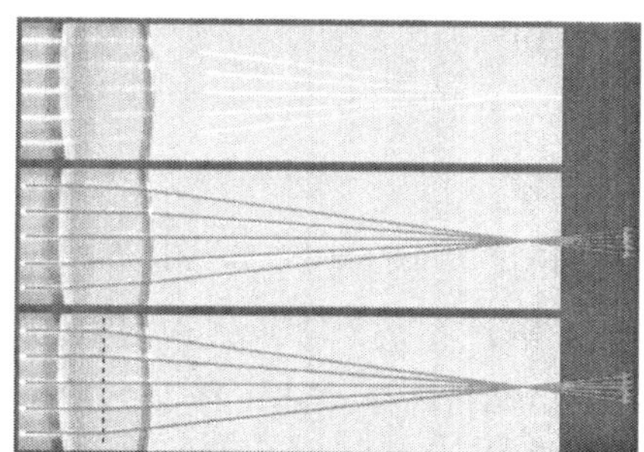

Figure 32.45: Top frame: parallel light rays are incident in a converging lens.
Middle frame: arrows are superimposed on the light rays.
Bottom frame: the optical center of the lens is indicated by a dashed line.

In the top frame of Figure 32.45, we can see that the parallel lines of light are focused to one point on the right of the lens. In the second frame, we superimpose red lines to represent the light rays. We can see the rays enter the lens, refract at the surface, traverse the lens in a straight line, and refract when they exit the lens. In the third frame, we draw a black dotted line at the center of the lens. In this panel, we draw the rays using the thin lens approximation whereby the incident rays refract just once at the center of the lens. Instead of following the detailed trajectory of the light rays inside a thin lens, we draw the incident rays to the centerline and then on to the focal point. Our real life lens (Figure 32.45) is a thick lens and there is displacement between the refraction at the entrance and exit surfaces. In this book, we will only consider thin lenses and we will treat the lens as a line at which refraction takes place.

Converging lenses can be used to form images. In Figure 32.47, we show the geometric construction of the formation of an image using a converging lens. We place an object represented by the green arrow on the optical axis. This object has a height h_o and is located a distance d_o from the center of the lens such that $d_o > f$. We start with a ray from the bottom of the object that goes that passes straight through the lens along the optical axis. This ray will go through the bottom of the image. A second ray is then drawn from the top of the object parallel to the optical axis. This ray goes through the focal point on the other side of the lens. A third ray is drawn through the center of the lens that has no net refraction in the thin lens approximation. (It goes through surfaces that are approximately parallel as in Solved Problem 32.2.) A fourth ray is drawn from the top of the object through the focal point on the same side of the lens that is then directed parallel to the optical axis. The three rays starting at the top of the object intersect, locating the top of the image formed. Any two of these three rays from the top of the object can be used to locate the top of the image.

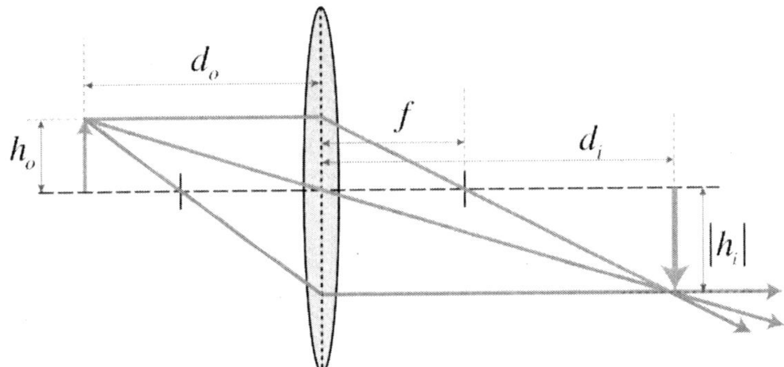

Figure 32.46: Real image produced by a converging lens.

In this case a real, inverted, and enlarged image with height $h_i < 0$ is formed a distance $d_i > 0$ from the center of the lens.

Now let us consider the image formed by an object with height h_o placed a distance d_o from the center of the lens such that $d_o < f$ as shown Figure 32.47. The first ray again is drawn from the bottom of the object along the optical axis. The second ray is drawn from the top of the object parallel to the optical axis and is refracted through the focal point on the opposite side of the lens. A third ray is drawn straight through the center of the lens. A fourth line is drawn such that it appears to have originated from the focal point on the same side of the lens and is then refracted parallel to the optical axis. One can see that these three rays are diverging. A virtual image is formed on the same side of the lens as the object by extrapolating the three rays back until they intersect. Red and black dashed lines represent the extrapolated rays.

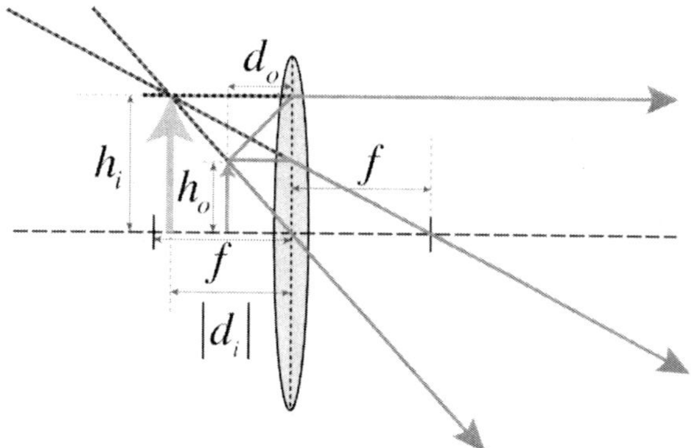

Figure 32.47: Virtual image produced by a converging lens.

In this case we see that we form a virtual, upright, and enlarged image with $h_i > 0$ and $d_i < 0$.

Diverging Lenses

A diverging lens, which has $f < 0$, is shaped such that parallel rays will be caused to diverge by refraction such that their extrapolation would intersect at a focal distance from the center of the lens on the same side of the lens as the object. In Figure 32.48, a light ray parallel to the optical axis is incident on a diverging glass lens. At the surface of the lens, the light rays are refracted toward the normal. When the rays leave the lens, they are refracted away from the normal as shown below. The extrapolated line is shown as a red and black dashed line and points to the focal point on the same side of the lens as the incident ray.

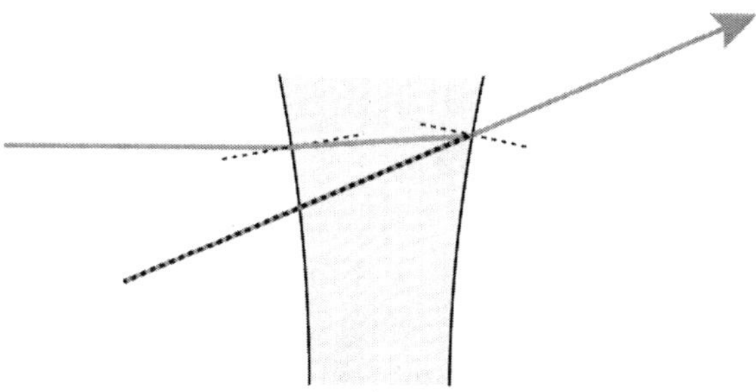

Figure 32.48: Horizontal light ray refracted by a diverging lens.

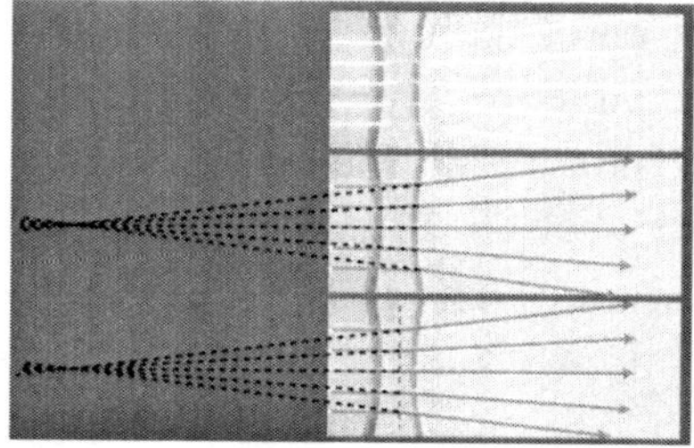

Figure 32.49: Top frame: parallel light rays are incident on a diverging lens; middle frame: arrows are superimposed on the light rays; bottom frame: the optical center of the lens is indicated by a dashed line.

Let us now study the case of several horizontal light rays incident on a diverging lens. After passing through the lens, the rays will diverge such that their extrapolations intersect at a point a distance f from the center of the lens on the same side of the lens as the incident rays. The top panel of Figure 32.49 is a photograph of a diverging lens with five parallel lines of light incident in the surface of a diverging lens from the left.

In the second panel of Figure 32.49, we have drawn red lines representing light rays. We can see that the light rays diverge after passing through the lens. We have drawn red and black dashed lines to show the extrapolation of the diverging rays. The extrapolated rays intersect at a distance equal to one focal length away from the center of the lens. In the third panel, we draw the diverging rays using the thin lens approximation whereby the incident rays refract just once at the center of the lens. The diverging rays are drawn so that their extrapolations intersect at the focal point.

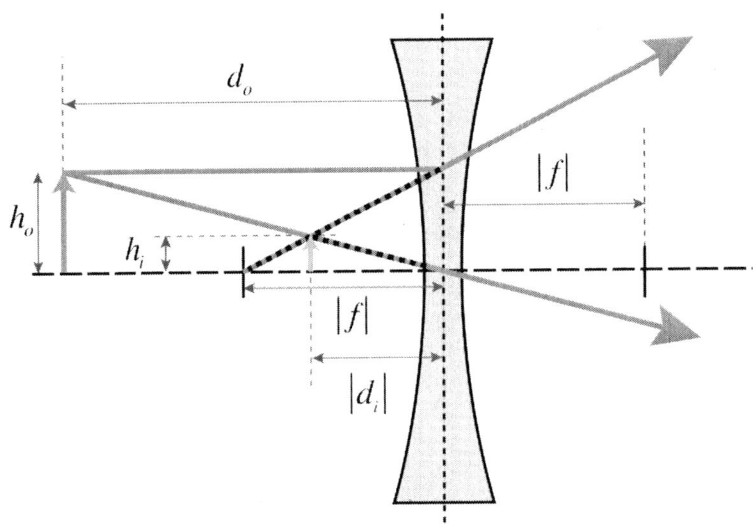

Figure 32.50: Image produced by a diverging lens of object placed a distance from the lens larger than the focal length of the lens.

Diverging lenses can be used to form images. In Figure 32.50, we show the geometric construction of the formation of an image using a diverging lens. We consider an object represented by the taller green arrow standing on the optical axis. This object has a height h_o and is located a distance d_o from the center of the lens such that $d_o > |f|$. We again start with a ray along the optical axis of the lens that passes straight through the lens and which defines the bottom of the image. A second ray is then drawn from the top of the object parallel to the optical axis. This ray is refracted such that its extrapolation of the diverging ray passes through the focal point on the left side of the lens. A third ray drawn through the center of the lens is not refracted in the thin lens approximation. This ray is extrapolated back along its original path. The two extrapolated rays intersect at the top of the produced image. The image formed is virtual, upright, and reduced in size.

The images that we have formed by ray tracing can all be described algebraically with the lens equation (derived above)

$$\frac{1}{d_o}+\frac{1}{d_i}=\frac{1}{f}. \tag{32.33}$$

Note that this is the same relationship between focal length, image distance and object distance that we had found for mirrors.

We now introduce and/or review our sign conventions. We earlier defined the focal length of a converging lens to be positive and the focal length of a diverging lens to be negative. The object distance d_0 and height h_0 for a single lens are both positive. (With multi-lens systems, one can encounter negative object distances and heights.) If the image is on the opposite side of the lens from the object, the image distance d_i is positive and the image is real. If the image is on the same side of the lens as the object, the image distance is negative and the image is virtual. The magnification formula for lenses is the same as for mirrors,

$$m=\frac{h_i}{h_o}=-\frac{d_i}{d_o}.$$

If the image is upright, then h_i and the magnification m are positive, while if the image is inverted, h_i and m are negative.

For a converging lens, we find that for $d_o > f$ we always get a real, inverted image formed on the opposite side of the lens. If $d_o = f$, then $1/d_i = 0$ and the image is located at infinity. For a converging lens and $d_o < f$, we always get a virtual, upright, and enlarged image on the same side of the lens as the object. The results for all values of d_0 are summarized in Table 32.3.

Case	Type	Direction	Magnification
$f < d_o < 2f$	Real	Inverted	Enlarged
$d_o = 2f$	Real	Inverted	Same size
$d_o > 2f$	Real	Inverted	Reduced
$d_o = f$			Infinity
$d_o < f$	Virtual	Upright	Enlarged

Table 32.3: Image characteristics for converging lenses.

For diverging lenses, we always get an image that is virtual, upright, and reduced in size.

The power of a lens is often quoted rather than its focal length. The power of a lens D, in diopters, a dimensionless number, is given by the equation

$$D = \frac{1 \text{ m}}{f} \quad . \tag{32.34}$$

Eyeglass lenses and camera lenses are typically characterized in terms of diopters.

Self-Test Opportunity: In the four diagrams shown in this figure the solid arrow represents the object and the dashed arrow represents the image. The dashed rectangle represents a single optical element. The possible optical elements include a plane mirror, a converging mirror, a diverging mirror, a diverging lens, and a converging lens. Match each diagram with the corresponding optical element.

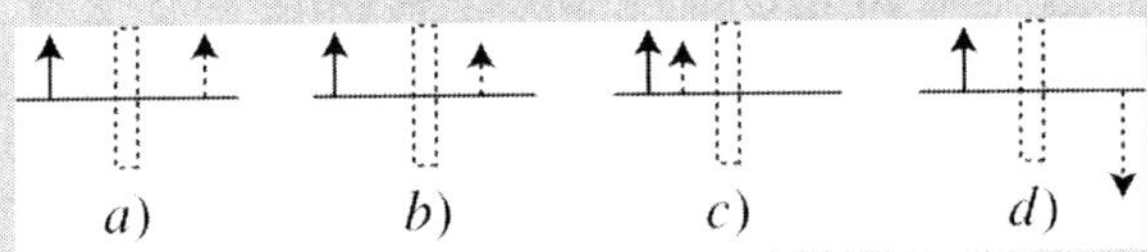

In-class exercise: An object is placed 15.0 cm to the left of a converging lens with focal length $f = 5.00$ cm as shown in the figure. Where is the image formed?

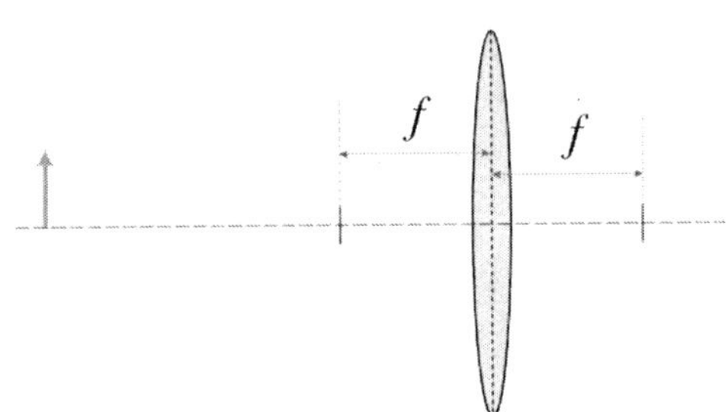

a) 1.25 cm to the right of the lens
b) 2.75 cm to the left of the lens
c) 3.75 cm to the right of the lens
d) 5.00 cm to the left of the lens
e) 7.50 cm to the right of the lens

Example 32.3: Image formed by a thin lens

We place an object with height $h_o = 5.00$ cm a distance $d_o = 16.0$ cm from a thin converging lens with focal length $f = 4.00$ cm as shown in Figure 32.51.

Question:
What is the image distance? What is the magnification of the image? What is the image height?

Answer:
The image distance can be calculated using the lens equation (32.33)

$$\frac{1}{d_o} + \frac{1}{d_i} = \frac{1}{f}.$$

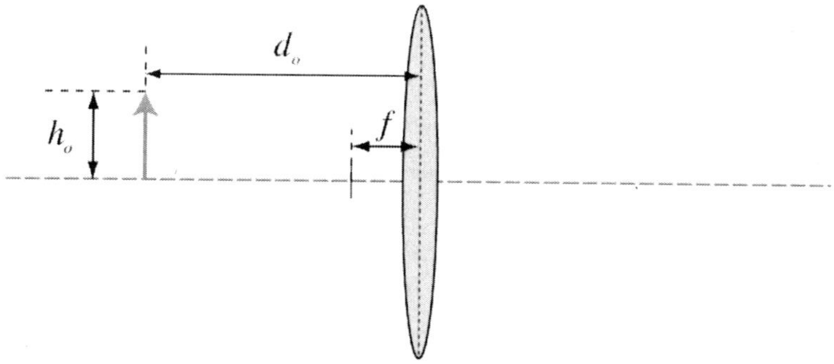

Figure 32.51: An object placed in front of a thin converging lens.

Solving for the image distance we get

$$d_i = \frac{d_o f}{d_o - f} = \frac{(16.0 \text{ cm})(5.00 \text{ cm})}{16.0 \text{ cm} - 5.00 \text{ cm}} = 7.27 \text{ cm}.$$

The image distance is positive. Therefore, the image is real and will be produced on the opposite side of the lens from the object. The magnification formula for lenses is given by

$$m = \frac{h_i}{h_o} = -\frac{d_i}{d_o}.$$

Thus, we can calculate the magnification using the given object distance and the calculated image distance

$$m = -\frac{d_i}{d_o} = -\frac{7.27 \text{ cm}}{16.0 \text{ cm}} = -0.454.$$

The magnification is negative. Thus, the image is inverted. The magnitude of the magnification is less than one. Therefore, the image is reduced. The image height can then be calculated

$$h_i = mh_o = (-0.454)(5.00 \text{ cm}) = -2.27 \text{ cm}.$$

We see that the image height is negative, so the image is inverted, as we expected from the negative magnification.

The resulting image is illustrated in Figure 32.52.

Example

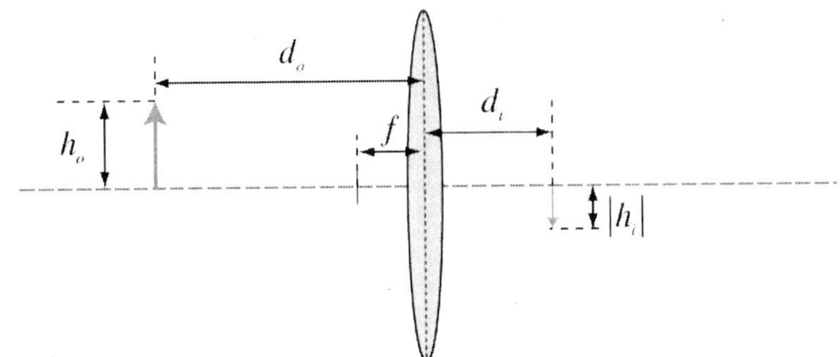

Figure 32.52: Image formed by converging thin lens.

What we have learned/Exam Study Guide:

New Symbols used in this Chapter

- θ_i Angle of incidence
- θ_r Angle of reflection
- θ_c Critical angle of total reflection
- d_o Object distance
- d_i Image distance
- f Focal length
- h_o Object height
- h_i Image height
- n Index of refraction
- m Magnification
- D Diopter

Most Important Points

- The angle of incidence equals the angle of reflection, $\theta_i = \theta_r$.
- The focal length of a spherical mirror is equal to half its radius, $f = \frac{R}{2}$. R is positive for converging (concave) mirrors and negative for diverging (convex) mirrors.
- For images formed with spherical mirrors, the object distance, the image distance, and the focal length of the mirror are related by the mirror equation, $\frac{1}{d_o} + \frac{1}{d_i} = \frac{1}{f}$. d_o is always positive, d_i is positive if the image is on the same side of the mirror as the object and negative if the image is on the other side. f is positive for converging (concave) mirrors and negative for convex (diverging) mirrors.
- Light is refracted (bent) as it crosses the boundary between two media with different indices of refraction. This refraction is governed by Snell's Law:

$n_1 \sin\theta_1 = n_2 \sin\theta_2$.

- The critical angle for total reflection at the boundary between two media with different indices of refraction is given by $\sin\theta_c = \frac{n_2}{n_1}$ $(n_2 \leq n_1)$.
- For images formed by lenses, the object distance, the image distance, and the focal length of the mirror are related by the lens equation, $\frac{1}{d_o} + \frac{1}{d_i} = \frac{1}{f}$. d_o is always positive, d_i is positive on the opposite side of the lens as the object and negative if on the same side, f is positive for converging lenses and negative for diverging lenses.
- The diopter is defined as the inverse of the focal length in m.

Additional Solved Problem

Solved Problem 32.4: Two positions of a converging lens

Consider a light bulb a distance $d = 1.45$ m away from a screen. A converging lens with focal length $f = 15.3$ cm will form an image of the light bulb on the screen for two lens positions.

Question:

What is the distance between these two positions?

Answer:

THINK:

The sum of object distance of the lens plus the image distance of the lens is equal to the distance of the light bulb from the screen. Using the lens equation, we can solve for the possible image distances using the quadratic equation. The distance between the two image positions is the distance between the two lens positions.

SKETCH:

A sketch of the lens placed between the light bulb and the screen is shown in Figure 32.53.

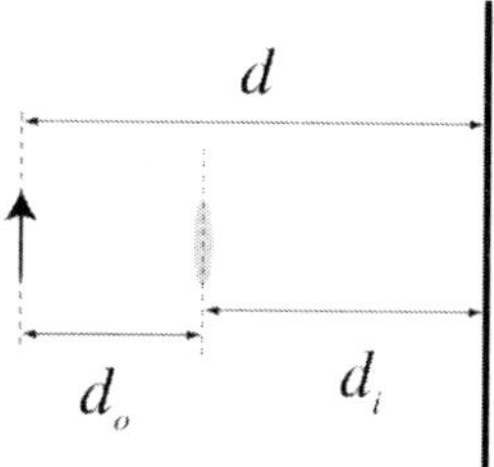

Figure 32.53: A lens is placed between a light bulb and a screen.

Solved Problem

Solved Problem

RESEARCH:

The lens equation is

$$\frac{1}{d_o}+\frac{1}{d_i}=\frac{1}{f} \quad (32.35)$$

where d_o is the object distance, d_i is the image distance, and f is the focal length. We can express the object distance in terms of the image distance and the distance of the light bulb from the screen d

$$d_o = d - d_i. \quad (32.36)$$

Substituting (32.36) into (32.35) gives us

$$\frac{1}{d-d_i}+\frac{1}{d_i}=\frac{1}{f}. \quad (32.37)$$

We can rearrange this equation to get

$$d_i+\left(d-d_i\right)=\frac{d_i\left(d-d_i\right)}{f}. \quad (32.38)$$

Collecting terms and multiplying by f gives us

$$df = d_i d - d_i^2. \quad (32.39)$$

SIMPLIFY:

We can rewrite (32.39) so that we can recognize it as a quadratic equation for which we know the solutions

$$d_i^2 - d_i d + df = 0. \quad (32.40)$$

The solutions of this equation are

$$x=\frac{d\pm\sqrt{d^2-4df}}{2} \quad (32.41)$$

where one solution corresponds to the $+$ sign and the other solution corresponds to the $-$ sign.

CALCULATE:

The solution corresponding to the $+$ sign is

Solved Problem

$$x_+ = \frac{(1.45 \text{ m}) + \sqrt{(1.45 \text{ m})^2 - 4(1.45 \text{ m})(0.153 \text{ m})}}{2} = 1.27616 \text{ m}.$$

The solution corresponding to the $-$sign is

$$x_- = \frac{(1.45 \text{ m}) - \sqrt{(1.45 \text{ m})^2 - 4(1.45 \text{ m})(0.153 \text{ m})}}{2} = 0.173842 \text{ m}.$$

The difference between the two positions is

$$\Delta x = 1.10232 \text{ m}.$$

ROUND:

We report our result to three significant figures

$$\Delta x = 1.10 \text{ m}.$$

DOUBLE-CHECK:

To double-check our answer, we substitute our solutions for the image distance into the Thin Lens Equation and show that they work. For the first solution, $d_i = 1.28$ m, so the corresponding object distance would be $d_o = d - d_i = 0.17$ m. The lens equation then tells us

$$\frac{1}{0.174} + \frac{1}{1.28} = \frac{1}{0.153 \text{ m}}$$

which agrees within round-off errors. For the second solution, we simply reverse the role of the image distance and object distance in the Thin Lens Equation, and we get the same answer. Thus our result seems reasonable.

Chapter 33. Optical Instruments

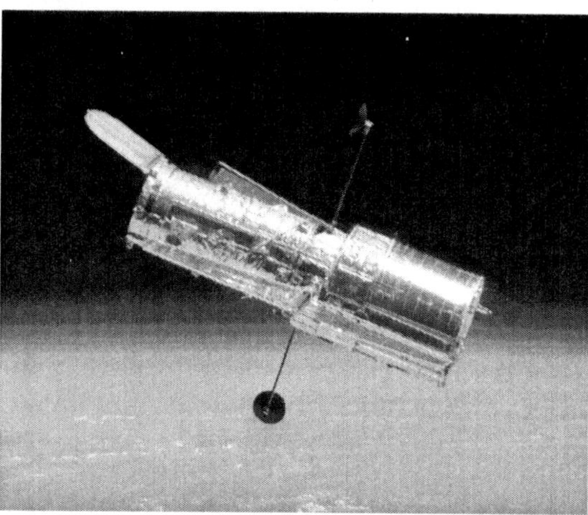

Figure 33.1: The Hubble Space Telescope is arguable the world's most famous optical instrument and has changed our understanding of the universe. A replacement for the Hubble Space Telescope, the James Webb Space Telescope, will explore the universe using infrared light.

What we will learn

Optical instruments are combinations of mirrors and lenses.

- A single converging lens can be used as a magnifier.
- Two lens systems can by used in optical instruments.

- Placing a converging lens close to a diverging lens can produce a zoom lens.
- The human eye is an optical instrument governed by the Lens Equation. Various lenses can be used to correct vision.
- Microscopes are systems of lenses designed to magnify the image of close but very small objects.
- Telescopes are systems of lenses or mirrors designed to magnify the image of distant but very large objects.

33.1. Magnifier

One way to make an object appear larger is to bring it closer. However, if you bring the object too close to your eye, the object will appear fuzzy. The minimum distance for which the human eye can focus is called the near point, as discussed in detail below. Another way to make an object appear larger is to use a magnifier or magnifying glass. . A typical magnifying glass is shown in Figure 33.2.

Figure 33.2: A magnifying glass.

A magnifier consists of a converging lens that is used to produce an enlarged virtual image of an object. This image appears at a distance that is at or beyond the near point of the eye so that the observer can clearly see the image. The angular magnification of the magnifier is defined as the apparent angle subtended by the image created by the magnifier compared with the angle subtended by the object when located at the near point.

In Figure 33.3, we show the geometry of a magnifier. We assume an object with height h_o. Without a magnifier, the largest angle θ_1 that one can attain and still see the object clearly occurs when one places the object at the near point d_{near} of the observer. One can get a magnified image of the object by placing the object just inside the focal length of a converging lens. The observer then looks through the lens at the image, which is intentionally located at least as far away as his near point. Therefore the observer can see the enlarged, upright, virtual image. The angle subtended by the image is θ_2.

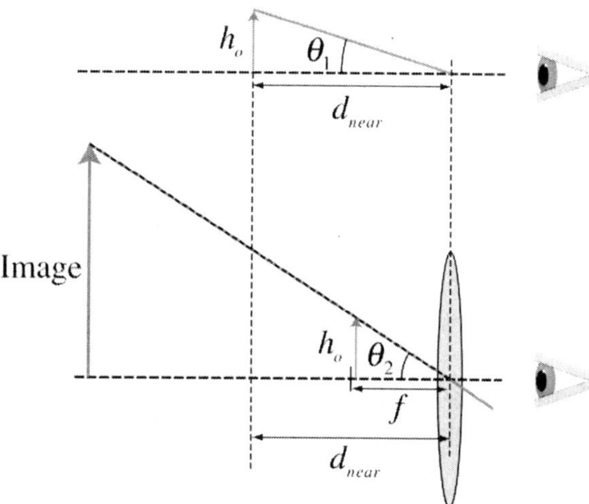

Figure 33.3: The geometry of a magnifier.

The angular magnification of the magnifier is defined as

$$m_\theta = \frac{\theta_2}{\theta_1}. \tag{33.1}$$

From Figure 33.3 (top panel) we can see that the angle subtended by the object without the magnifier is given by

$$\tan\theta_1 = \frac{h_o}{d_{near}}. \tag{33.2}$$

We can also see in Figure 33.3 (bottom panel) that the angle subtended by the image of the object is given by

$$\tan\theta_2 = \frac{h_o}{f} \tag{33.3}$$

where f is the focal length of the lens and we assume that the object is placed at the focal length of the lens so the image is at minus infinity. (Recall from Chapter 32 that a ray through the center of the lens is not bent. It is this ray that forms the hypotenuse of the right triangle used for (33.3)). We then make a small angle approximation to get $\tan\theta_1 \approx \theta_1$ and $\tan\theta_2 \approx \theta_2$. Thus we can write the angular magnification of a magnifier as

$$m_\theta = \frac{\theta_2}{\theta_1} \approx \frac{h_o / f}{h_o / d_{near}} = \frac{d_{near}}{f}. \tag{33.4}$$

Assuming a typical value for the near point of 25 cm we can write the angular magnification as

$$m_\theta \approx \frac{d_{near}}{f} \approx \frac{0.25 \text{ m}}{f}. \tag{33.5}$$

Alternatively the final image can be placed at the near point. Using the lens equation with $d_i = -d_{near}$ to find d_o and then using $\theta_2 = \frac{h_o}{d_o}$, one finds $m_\theta = \frac{0.25 \text{ m}}{f} + 1$.

Henceforth, unless otherwise stated, we will assume that the image is at infinity and use (33.5).

In-class exercise: What is the focal length (in meters) of a magnifying glass that gives a magnification of 6?

a) 0.010 m
b) 0.021 m
c) 0.035 m
d) 0.042 m
e) 0.055 m

33.2. Systems of Two or More Optical Elements

A lens or a mirror can be used to produce an image of an object. This image can then in turn be used as the object for a second lens or mirror. The recurring theme for all two-lens systems is that the image of the first lens becomes the object of the second lens. Let's start our study of multi-lens systems by considering a two-lens system consisting of two converging lenses placed as shown in Figure 33.4.

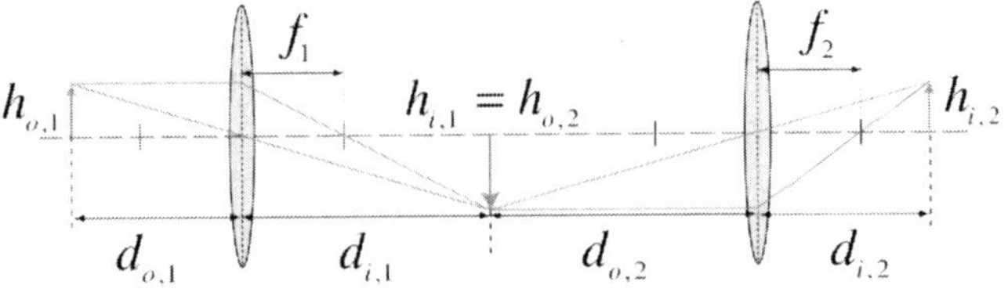

Figure 33.4: A system of two converging lenses.

An object with height $h_{o,1}$ is placed a distance $d_{o,1}$ from the first lens, which has a focal length f_1. An image is produced at a distance $d_{i,1}$ given by the Lens Equation

$$\frac{1}{d_{o,1}} + \frac{1}{d_{i,1}} = \frac{1}{f_1}. \tag{33.6}$$

Because of the value of $d_{o,1}$ that we have chosen, this produced image is real, inverted, and enlarged. This image then becomes the object for the second lens. The height of this object is same as the height of the image produced by the first lens. The object is located a distance $d_{o,2}$ from the second lens, which has a focal length f_2. An image is formed at a distance $d_{i,2}$ governed by the Lens Equation

$$\frac{1}{d_{o,2}}+\frac{1}{d_{i,2}}=\frac{1}{f_2}. \tag{33.7}$$

With the parameters that we have chosen for the system depicted in Figure 33.4, the final image of the second lens is real, inverted, and reduced in size. The magnification of the first lens is given by $m_1 = h_{i,1} / h_{o,1}$ and the magnification of the second lens is given by $m_2 = h_{i,2} / h_{o,2}$. The product of the magnifications of the two lenses gives the magnification of the two-lens system

$$m_{12} = m_1 m_2 = \left(\frac{h_{i,1}}{h_{o,1}}\right)\left(\frac{h_{i,2}}{h_{o,2}}\right) = \frac{h_{i,2}}{h_{o,1}}. \tag{33.8}$$

We can see that the image produced by this two-lens system is real and upright. Thus this system of lenses can be used to produce real images that are not inverted. This cannot be done with a single converging lens.

Now let's consider a two-lens system with one converging lens and one diverging lens as shown in Figure 33.5.

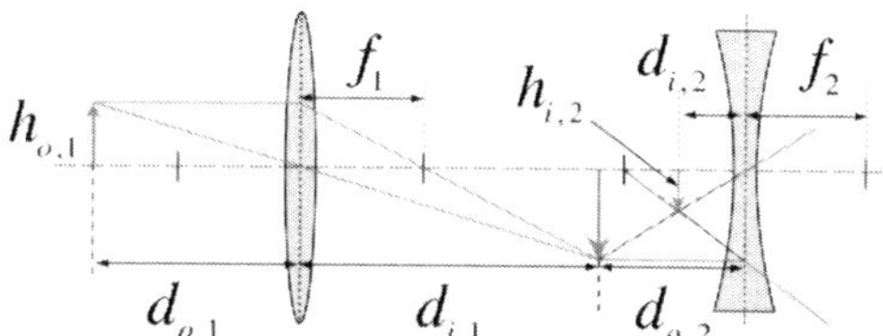

Figure 33.5: A two-lens system consisting of a converging lens and a diverging lens.

An object with height $h_{o,1}$ is placed a distance $d_{o,1}$ from the first lens, which has a focal length f_1. An image is produced at a distance $d_{i,1}$ given by the Lens Equation

$$\frac{1}{d_{o,1}}+\frac{1}{d_{i,1}}=\frac{1}{f_1}. \tag{33.9}$$

This particular image is real, inverted, and enlarged. This image then becomes the object for the second lens. The height of this object is same as the image produced by the first lens. The object is located a distance $d_{o,2}$ from the second lens, which has a focal length f_2. An image is formed at a distance $d_{i,2}$ governed by the lens equation

$$\frac{1}{d_{o,2}}+\frac{1}{d_{i,2}}=\frac{1}{f_2}. \quad (33.10)$$

This image is virtual, upright, and reduced. The magnification of the first lens is given by $m_1 = h_{i,1} / h_{o,1}$. The magnification of the second lens is given by $m_2 = h_{i,2} / h_{o,2}$. The product of the magnifications of the two lenses gives the magnification of the two-lens system

$$m_{12} = m_1 m_2 = \left(\frac{h_{i,1}}{h_{o,1}}\right)\left(\frac{h_{i,2}}{h_{o,2}}\right) = \frac{h_{i,2}}{h_{o,1}}. \quad (33.11)$$

We can see that the image produced by this two-lens system is virtual and inverted.

Now let's take this same two-lens system consisting of a converging lens followed by a diverging lens and put the two lenses close together. We will place the two lenses a distance x apart as shown in Figure 33.6. This two-lens system acts as a converging lens. By varying the distance x we can vary the effective focal length of the converging lens system. This arrangement is called a zoom lens.

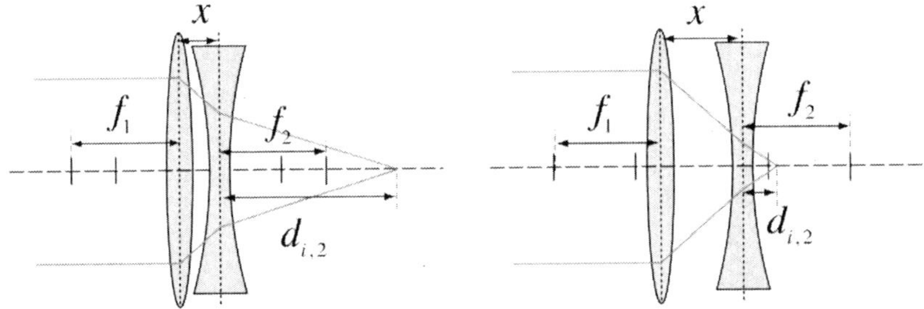

Figure 33.6: A zoom lens system consisting of a converging lens followed by a diverging lens. Two different distances between the two lenses are shown.

We define the effective focal length of this two-lens system as the distance from the center of the first lens to the position of the final image for an object originally located at infinity. The first lens has a focal length f_1, which means that objects placed at a large distance will produce an image at an image distance of $d_{i,1} = f_1$. We can understand this result using the lens equation

$$\frac{1}{d_{o,1}}+\frac{1}{d_{i,1}}=\frac{1}{\infty}+\frac{1}{d_{i,1}}=0+\frac{1}{d_{i,1}}=\frac{1}{d_{i,1}}=\frac{1}{f_1}. \quad (33.12)$$

Assuming $f_1 > x$, the image produced by the first lens is generated on the right side of the second lens. This means that the object distance for the second lens must be negative in this case, because we have defined positive object distances to be to the left of a lens. The object distance for the second lens is given by

$$d_{o,2} = -\left(d_{i,1} - x\right) = x - d_{i,1} = x - f_1. \tag{33.13}$$

Using this image as the object for the second lens we get

$$\frac{1}{d_{o,2}} + \frac{1}{d_{i,2}} = \frac{1}{x - f_1} + \frac{1}{d_{i,2}} = \frac{1}{f_2}. \tag{33.14}$$

We can solve this equation and get the effective focal length of the zoom lens system

$$f_{eff} = x + d_{i,2} = x + \frac{f_2\left(x - f_1\right)}{x - \left(f_2 + f_1\right)}. \tag{33.15}$$

We can see from (33.15) and from Figure 33.6 that when the lenses are close together, the effective focal length is longer and when they are farther apart, the effective focal length is shorter. Thus by adjusting the distance between the converging lens and the diverging lens, we can produce an effective lens with varying focal lengths as is done in cameras. Note that for cameras this result is useful only for $f_{eff} > x$ because objects at infinity must produce a real image on the film or on the charged-coupled device (for a digital camera).

Self-Test Opportunity: Use (33.15) to show that the effective focal length f_{eff} of two thin lenses with focal lengths f_1 and f_2 close together is given by

$$\frac{1}{f_{eff}} = \frac{1}{f_1} + \frac{1}{f_2}.$$

Self-Test Opportunity: A normal 35 mm camera has a lens with a focal length of 50 mm. Suppose you replace the normal lens with a zoom lens whose focal length can be varied from 50 mm to 200 mm. and use the camera to photograph an object at infinity. Compared to a 50 mm lens, what magnification of the image would be achieved using the 200 mm focal length?

Solved Problem

Solved Problem 33.1: Image produced by two lenses

Consider a system of two lenses. The first lens is a converging lens with a focal length $f_1 = 21.4$ cm. The second lens is a diverging lens with focal length $f_2 = -34.4$ cm. The center of the second lens is $d = 80.0$ cm to the right of the center of the first lens. An object is placed a distance $d_{o,1} = 63.5$ cm to the left of the first lens. These lenses produce an image of the object.

Question:

Where is the image produced by the second lens located with respect to the center of the second lens? What are the characteristics of the image? What is the magnification of the final image with respect to the original object?

Answer:

THINK:

The thin lens equation (which we will call the lens equation) tells us where the first lens produces an image of the object placed to the left of the first lens. The image produced by the first lens becomes the object for the second lens. We again use the lens equation to locate the image produced by the second lens.

SKETCH:

A sketch of the object, the first lens, and the second lens is shown in Figure 33.7.

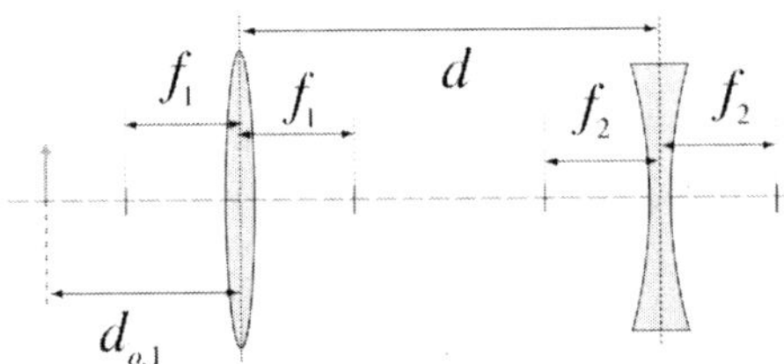

Figure 33.7: A system of two lenses.

RESEARCH:

The lens equation applied to the first lens gives us

$$\frac{1}{d_{o,1}} + \frac{1}{d_{i,1}} = \frac{1}{f_1} \tag{33.16}$$

where $d_{i,1}$ is the image distance for the first lens. We can solve (33.16) for the image distance of the first lens

$$d_{i,1} = \frac{d_{o,1} f_1}{d_{o,1} - f_1}. \tag{33.17}$$

The lens equation applied to the second lens tells us

$$\frac{1}{d_{o,2}} + \frac{1}{d_{i,2}} = \frac{1}{f_2} \tag{33.18}$$

where $d_{o,2}$ is the object distance for the second lens and $d_{i,2}$ is the image distance for second lens. We can solve (33.18) for the image distance for second lens

$$d_{i,2} = \frac{d_{o,2} f_2}{d_{o,2} - f_2}. \tag{33.19}$$

The object for the second lens is the image produced by the first lens. The object distance for the second lens can be related to the image distance of the first lens and the distance between the two lenses

$$d_{o,2} = d - d_{i,1}. \tag{33.20}$$

SIMPLIFY:

We can substitute (33.20) into (33.19) to obtain

$$d_{i,2} = \frac{\left(d - d_{i,1}\right) f_2}{\left(d - d_{i,1}\right) - f_2}. \tag{33.21}$$

We can then substitute (33.17) into (33.21) to obtain an expression for the image distance of the second lens in terms of the quantities given in the problem

$$d_{i,2} = \frac{\left(d - \left(\frac{d_{o,1} f_1}{d_{o,1} - f_1}\right)\right) f_2}{\left(d - \left(\frac{d_{o,1} f_1}{d_{o,1} - f_1}\right)\right) - f_2}. \tag{33.22}$$

CALCULATE:

Putting in our numerical values gives us

$$d_{i,2} = \frac{\left((80.0\text{ cm}) - \left(\frac{(63.5\text{ cm})(21.4\text{ cm})}{(63.5\text{ cm}) - (21.4\text{ cm})}\right)\right)(-34.4\text{ cm})}{\left((80.0\text{ cm}) - \left(\frac{(63.5\text{ cm})(21.4\text{ cm})}{(63.5\text{ cm}) - (21.4\text{ cm})}\right)\right) - (-34.4\text{ cm})} = \text{-}19.9902\text{ cm}$$

ROUND:

We report our result for the location of the image to three significant figures

Solved Problem

$$d_{i,2} = -20.0 \text{ cm}.$$

DOUBLE-CHECK:

To double-check our result and calculate quantities need to answer the remaining parts of the problem, we calculate the position of the image produced by the first lens

$$d_{i,1} = \frac{d_{o,1}f_1}{d_{o,1} - f_1} = \left(\frac{(63.5 \text{ cm})(21.4 \text{ cm})}{(63.5 \text{ cm}) - (21.4 \text{ cm})} \right) = 32.3 \text{ cm}.$$

The image distance for the first lens is positive so the image will be formed 32.3 cm to the right of the first lens. The object distance for the second lens is then

$$d_{o,2} = d - d_{i,1} = 47.7 \text{ cm}.$$

The image formed by the first lens is 47.7 cm to the left of the second lens, which seems reasonable. We can then calculate the image distance for the second lens

$$d_{i,2} = \frac{d_{o,2}f_2}{d_{o,2} - f_2} = \left(\frac{(47.7 \text{ cm})(-34.4 \text{ cm})}{(47.7 \text{ cm}) - (-34.4 \text{ cm})} \right) = -20.0 \text{ cm}$$

which agrees with our result. Thus, our answer for the distance of the image from the center of lens 2 seems reasonable.

The image is virtual because it is on the same side of lens 2 as the object for lens 2, which we know because the image distance for lens 2 is negative. The magnification for the final image compared with the original object is

$$m = m_1 m_2 = \left(-\frac{d_{i,1}}{d_{o,1}} \right) \left(-\frac{d_{i,2}}{d_{o,2}} \right) = \left(\frac{32.3 \text{ cm}}{63.5 \text{ cm}} \right) \left(\frac{-20.0 \text{ cm}}{47.7 \text{ cm}} \right) = -0.213.$$

The image is reduced because $|m| < 1$. The image is inverted because $m < 0$.

Solved Problem

33.3. The Human Eye

The human eye can be considered an optical instrument. The eye is nearly spherical in shape and is about 2.5 cm in diameter. The front part of the eye is more sharply curved than the rest of the eye and is covered with the cornea. Behind the cornea is a fluid called the aqueous humor. Next is the lens composed of a fibrous jelly. The lens is held in place by ligaments that connect it to the ciliary muscle that allows the lens to change shape and thus change the focus of the lens. Behind the lens is the vitreous humor. The index of refraction of the two fluids in the eye is 1.34, close to that of water (1.33). The index of refraction of the material making up the lens is about 1.40. Thus, most of the refraction occurs at the air/cornea boundary, which has the largest difference in indices of refraction. A drawing of the human eye is shown in Figure 33.8.

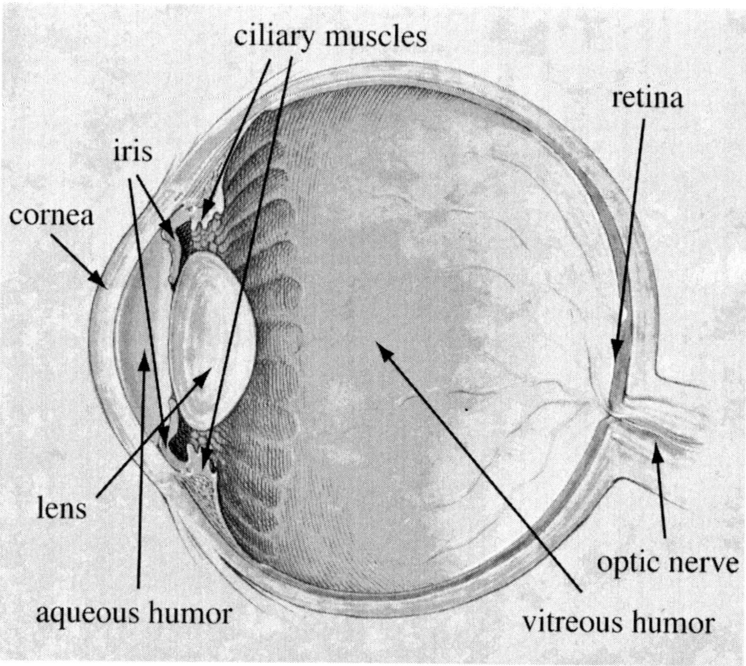

Figure 33.8: Drawing of the human eye showing its major features.

Refraction at the cornea and lens surfaces produces a real, inverted image on the retina of the eye. The image is converted from light to electrical impulses by rods and cones in the retina. The impulses are sent to the brain through the optic nerve. The brain inverts the inverted image so that we see it upright. In front of the lens is the iris, which opens and closes to regulate the amount of light that is incident on the retina.

For an object to be seen clearly, the image must be formed at the location of the retina as shown in Figure 33.9*a*). The shape of the eye cannot be changed; so shaping the lens must control the distance of the image. For a distant object, relaxing the lens focuses the image. For close objects, the ciliary muscle increases the curvature of the lens to focus the image on the retina. This process is called accommodation.

The extremes over which distinct vision is possible are called the far point and near point. The far point of a normal eye is infinity. The near point of a normal eye depends on the ability of the eye to focus. This ability changes with age. A young child can focus on objects as near as 7 cm. As a person ages, the near point increases. Typically, a 50 year-old person has a near point of 40 cm.

Several common vision defects result from incorrect focal distances. In the case of myopia (near-sightedness), the image is produced in front of the retina as is shown in Figure 33.9*b*). In the case of hypermetropia (far-sightedness), the image would be produced behind the retina as is shown in Figure 33.9*c*) if it could, but the light gets absorbed by the retina before an image can be formed. Myopia can be corrected using diverging lenses while hypermetropia can be corrected using converging lenses.

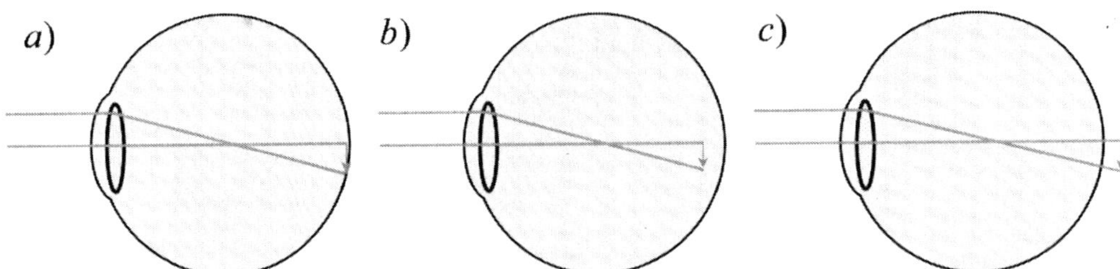

Figure 33.9: *a)* Image produced by the lens of a normal sighted person; *b)* Image produced by the lens of a near-sighted person; *c)* Image produced by a the lens of far-sighted person.

Example 33.1: Corrective lenses

Question:

The power of a lens is often quoted rather than its focal length. The power of a lens, D, in diopter, is given by

$$D = \frac{1\text{ m}}{f}. \tag{33.23}$$

where f is the focal length of the lens. What is the power of the corrective lens for a myopic (near-sighted) person whose uncorrected far point is 15 cm? The

Answer:

The corrective lens must form a virtual, upright image 15 cm in front of the lens of an object located at infinity as shown in Figure 33.10.

Object at large distance — Virtual image at uncorrected far point

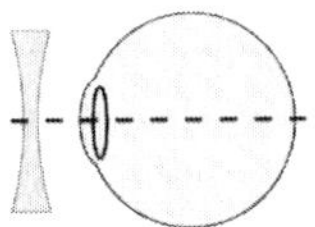

Figure 33.10: Geometry of a corrective lens for near-sightedness.

Thus, the object distance d_o will be ∞ and the image distance d_i will be –15 cm. Because

$$\frac{1}{d_o} + \frac{1}{d_i} = \frac{1}{f}$$

we have

$$\frac{1}{\infty} + \frac{1}{-0.15\text{ m}} = \frac{1}{f} = -6.7\text{ diopter}.$$

The required lens is a diverging lens with a power of –6.7 diopter and a focal length

Example

of -0.15 m.

Question:
A hypermetropic (far-sighted) person whose uncorrected near point is 75 cm wishes to read a newspaper at a distance of 25 cm. What is the power of the corrective lens needed for this person to read the paper?

Answer:
The corrective lens must produce a virtual, upright image of the newspaper at the uncorrected near point of the person's vision as shown in Figure 33.11.

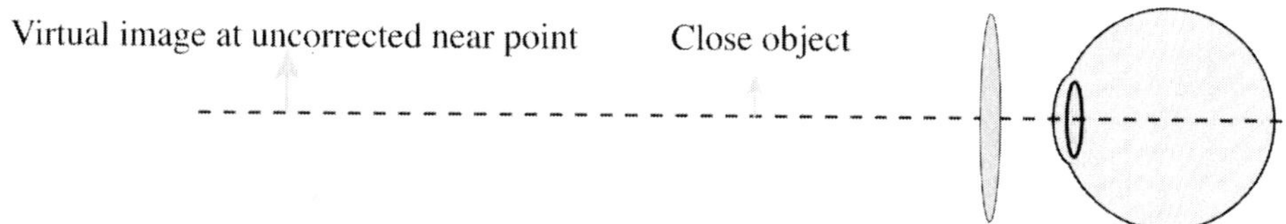

Figure 33.11: Geometry of a corrective lens for far-sightedness.

The object and image are on the same side of the lens so the image distance is negative. Thus the object distance is 25 cm and image distance is -75 cm

$$\frac{1}{0.25\text{ m}}+\frac{1}{-0.75\text{ m}}=\frac{1}{f}=+2.7\text{ diopter}.$$

The required lens is a converging lens with a power of +2.7 diopter corresponding to a focal length of +0.37 m.

In-class exercise: A hypermetropic (far-sighted) person can read a newspaper at a distance of $d = 125$ cm, but no closer. What power lens should this person use for reading?

a) -3.5 diopter
b) -1.25 diopter
c) +0.50 diopter
d) +2.5 diopter
e) +3.2 diopter

Contact Lenses

The corrective lenses described above consist of converging and diverging lenses. The converging lenses are convex on both surfaces and the diverging lenses are concave on both surfaces. These lenses correct vision well, but can be inconvenient. A more convenient type of corrective lens is the contact lens. A contact lens is placed directly on the cornea of the eye, relieving the person from wearing external glasses. These lenses are convex on the entrance surface and concave on the exit surface. The concave exit surface is placed directly on the eye. It is possible to produce contact lenses that are converging and diverging as shown in Figure 33.12.

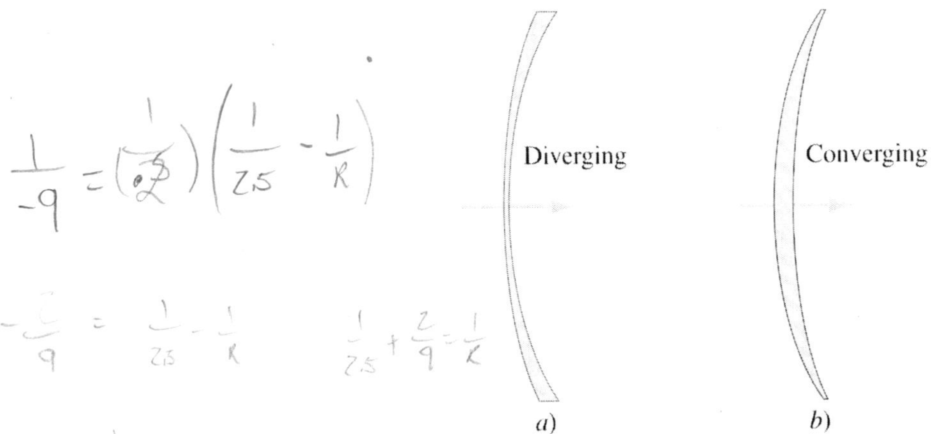

Figure 33.12: *a*) A diverging contact lens. *b*) A converging contact lens. The green arrows represent the direction of the light traveling through the lenses.

The Lens-Maker Formula from chapter 32 p407-410

$$\frac{1}{f}=(n-1)\left(\frac{1}{R_1}-\frac{1}{R_2}\right) \tag{33.24}$$

can be used to calculate the focal length of the contact lens where R_1 is the radius of curvature of the entrance surface and R_2 is the radius of curvature of the exit surface. Because the light entering the contact lens sees a convex surface, $R_1 > 0$. The light exiting the contact lens sees a convex surface also, so that $R_2 > 0$ as well.

The contact lens shown in Figure 33.12*a*) has $R_1 > R_2$ and thus has a negative focal length corresponding to a diverging lens. The contact lens shown in Figure 33.12*b*) has $R_1 < R_2$, which gives a positive focal length and a converging lens.

In-class exercise: The radius of curvature of the cornea of a myopic person is 8.0 mm. Thus, the exit surface of a contact lens would be designed to have a radius of curvature of 8.0 mm to fit on the surface of the cornea. What radius of curvature should a contact lens constructed from a material with $n = 1.5$ have on the entrance surface to produce a lens with a power of -1.5 diopter?

a) 7.6 mm
b) 7.8 mm
c) 8.0 mm
d) 8.2 mm
e) 8.4 mm

LASIK Surgery

An alternative to corrective lenses has been developed in which the cornea of the eye is altered to produce the desired optical response of the human eye. One such method, Laser-Assisted in Situ Keratomileusis (LASIK) surgery uses a laser to modify the curvature of the cornea.

An example of LASIK surgery used to correct myopia is shown in Figure 33.13.

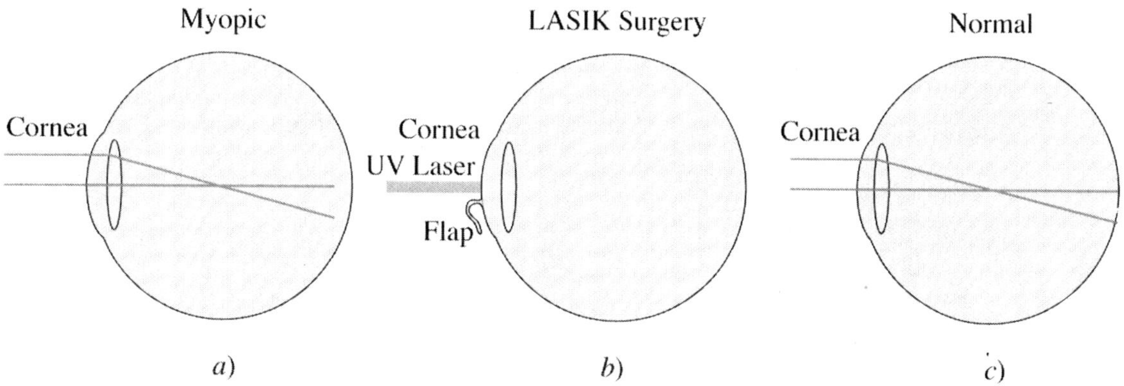

Figure 33.13: *a*) A myopic (near-sighted) human eye where the image is formed in front of the retina. *b*) LASIK surgery where a flap is cut from the surface of the cornea and part of the stroma is removed using a UV laser. The flap is then folded back and the cornea heals. *c*) Normal vision is produced by focusing the image on the retina.

In Figure 33.13*a*), a myopic human eye is shown with the image being produced in front of the retina. The effective focal length of this eye is too short. The LASIK procedure begins with the cutting of a flap off the surface of the cornea and folding it back as shown in Figure 33.13*b*), exposing the inner part of the cornea called the stroma. An ultraviolet (UV) laser is used to remove material in the stroma to produce a flatter surface. This flatter surface corresponds to a larger radius of curvature for the cornea. The laser operates with ultraviolet light that breaks down the molecular structure of the cornea without heating the surface. The flap is then folded back and the cornea heals. The Lens-Maker Formula (33.24) tells us that increasing the front radius R_1 will increase the effective focal length f of the eye. Thus, the surgery allows the image to be produced on retina as illustrated in Figure 33.13*c*).

33.4. The Microscope

The simplest microscope is a system of two lenses. In our example, the microscope is constructed of two thin lenses as shown in Figure 33.14. The first lens is a converging lens of short focal length, f_o, called the objective lens. The second lens is another converging lens of greater focal length, f_e, called the eyepiece.

The object to be magnified is placed just outside the focal length of the objective lens. This arrangement allows the objective lens to form a real, inverted, and enlarged image of the object some distance from the objective lens. This image then becomes the object for the eyepiece lens. This intermediate image is placed just inside the focal length of the eyepiece lens so that the eyepiece lens can produce a virtual, upright, and enlarged image of the intermediate image. The resulting magnification of the microscope is just the product of the magnifications from each lens. Let L be the distance between the two lenses and assume $L >> f_2$. Using the notation of Section 33.2, this means that $d_{i,1} \approx L$. Thus, the magnification of the microscope is given by

$$m = \frac{d_{i,1}d_{i,2}}{d_{o,1}d_{o,2}} = -\frac{(0.25 \text{ m})L}{f_o f_e} \tag{33.25}$$

where we have used $d_{i,2} = -0.25$ m because we assume that the final image is produced at a comfortable viewing distance of 0.25 m.

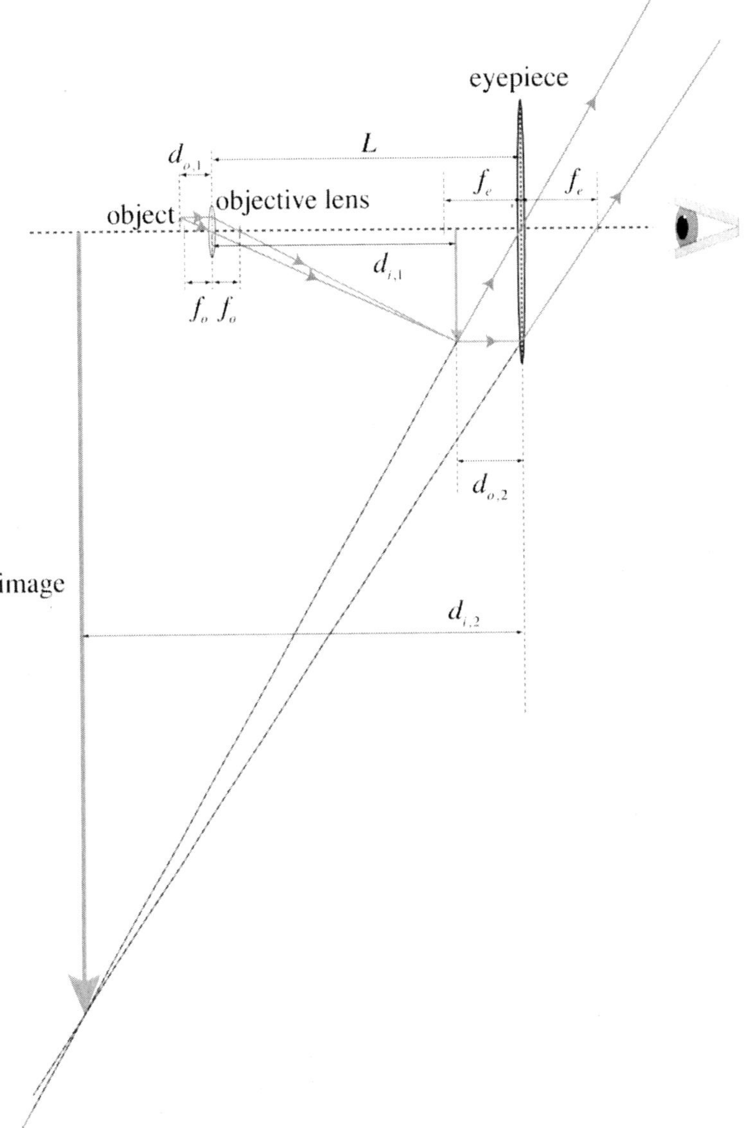

Figure 33.14: Geometry of the image formed by a microscope.

Example

Example 33.2: Magnification of a microscope
We have a microscope consisting of an objective lens and an eyepiece lens separated by 30 cm. The focal length of the objective lens is 20 mm and the focal length of the eyepiece lens is 20 mm.

Question:
What is the magnitude of the magnification of this microscope?

Answer:
Taking our expression for the magnification of a microscope (33.25) we have

$$|m| = \frac{(0.25\ \text{m})L}{f_o f_e} = -\frac{0.25\ \text{m} \cdot 0.30\ \text{m}}{(0.020\ \text{m})(0.020\ \text{m})} = 188.$$

In-class exercise: A microscope is intended to have a magnification whose magnitude is 330. If the objective lens has a power of 350 diopter and the eyepiece lens has a power of 10.0 diopter, how long must the microscope be?
a) 37.7 cm
b) 40.0 cm
c) 51.3 cm
d) 65.0 cm
e) 75.0 cm

33.5. The Telescope

Telescopes come in many forms. First we will discuss the refracting telescope and then we will delve into the reflecting telescope. In this chapter we study the magnification of the telescope, which is a measure of our ability to use the telescope to see large but distant objects. The resolution of a telescope, the capability to resolve two nearby objects, is equally important and will be covered in the next chapter.

The Refracting Telescope

The refracting telescope consists of two converging lenses, the objective and the eyepiece. An historic refracting telescope is shown in Figure 33.15.

Figure 33.15: The Fraunhofer 23 cm diameter refracting telescope used to discover Neptune in 1846.

In our following examples, we represent the telescope using two thin lenses. However, an actual refracting telescope will use more sophisticated lenses. Because the object to be viewed is at a large distance, the incoming light rays can be thought of as being parallel. Thus the objective lens forms a real image of the distant object at distance f_o. The eyepiece is placed so that the image formed by the objective is a distance f_e from the eyepiece. The eyepiece forms a virtual, magnified image of the image formed by the objective. The eyepiece forms a virtual image at infinity again producing parallel rays.

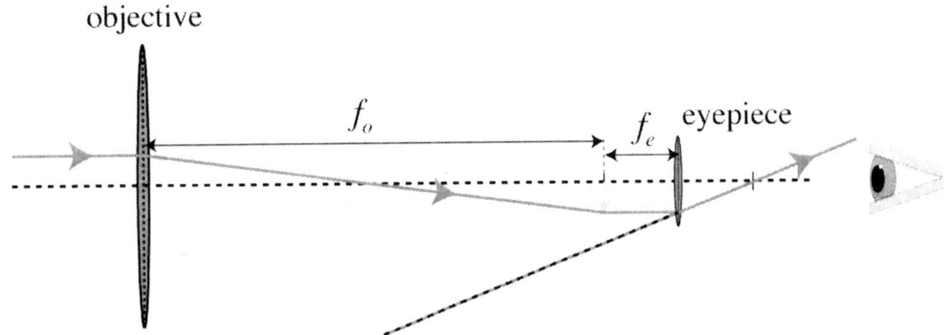

Figure 33.16: Geometry of an image formed by a refracting telescope.

In Figure 33.16 the parallel light rays from the object are depicted by a single ray. A red-black dashed line depicts the parallel light rays forming the virtual image.

Because the telescope deals with objects at large distances, it is not enlightening to determine the magnification of the telescope using the lens equation. Therefore we define the magnification of the telescope as -1 times the angle observed in the eyepiece θ_o divided by the angle subtended by the object being viewed θ_e,

$$m_\theta = -\frac{\theta_e}{\theta_o} = -\frac{f_o}{f_e}. \tag{33.26}$$

We derive (33.26) using the quantities shown in Figure 33.17.

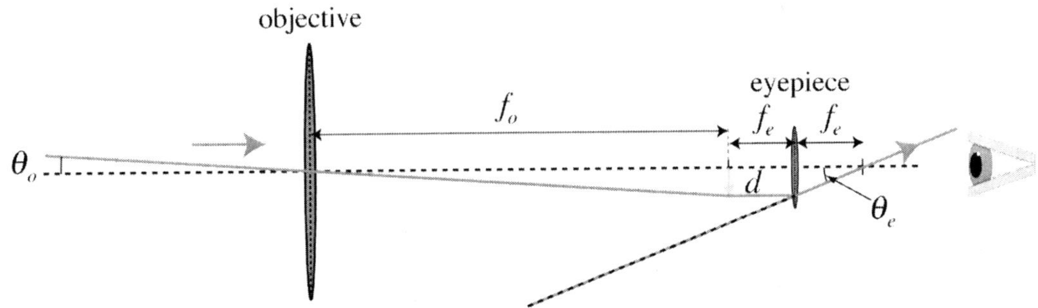

Figure 33.17: Geometry used to determine the angular magnification of a refracting telescope.

The angle θ_o is the angle subtended by a distant object. The height of the image produced by the objective lens is d. This image is produced at the focal length of the objective lens, f_o. Because the focal length of the objective lens is large compared with the image size we can write

$$\theta_o \approx \tan\theta_o = \frac{d}{f_o}. \tag{33.27}$$

The image is placed at the focal point of the eyepiece lens. The apparent angle in the eyepiece, θ_e, can be written as

$$\theta_e \approx \tan\theta_e = \frac{d}{f_e} \tag{33.28}$$

again assuming that the image size is small compared with the focal length of the eyepiece. The ratio of the apparent eyepiece angle to the objective angle gives the angular magnification

$$\frac{\theta_e}{\theta_o} = \frac{d/f_e}{d/f_o} = \frac{f_o}{f_e}. \tag{33.29}$$

Thus the angular magnification of a refracting telescope is

$$m_\theta = -\frac{f_o}{f_e} \tag{33.30}$$

where the minus signs means that the image is inverted.

Example

Example 33.2: Magnification of a refracting telescope

The world's largest refracting telescope was completed in 1897 and installed in Williams Bay, Wisconsin (between Chicago and Milwaukee). It had an objective lens of diameter 40 inches (1.0 m) with a focal length of 62 feet (19 m).

Question:

What should the focal length of the eyepiece be to give a magnification of magnitude 250?

Answer:

The focal length of the objective lens is $f_o = 19$ m. The absolute value of the magnification is to be $|m| = 250$. The magnification is given by $|m| = f_o/f_e$, which gives us the focal length of the eyepiece lens

$$f_e = \frac{f_o}{|m|} = \frac{19 \text{ m}}{250} = 0.076 \text{ m} = 7.6 \text{ cm}.$$

The Reflecting Telescope

Most large astronomical telescopes are reflecting telescopes with the objective lens being replaced with a concave mirror. Large mirrors are easier to fabricate and position than large lenses. Also mirrors don't have chromatic aberration and they work for a larger range of wavelengths. Finally the size of refracting telescopes is limited because large lenses tend to sag because of their own weight. However the eyepiece of a reflecting telescope is still a lens. Various types of reflecting telescopes have been developed. Three simple examples are shown below.

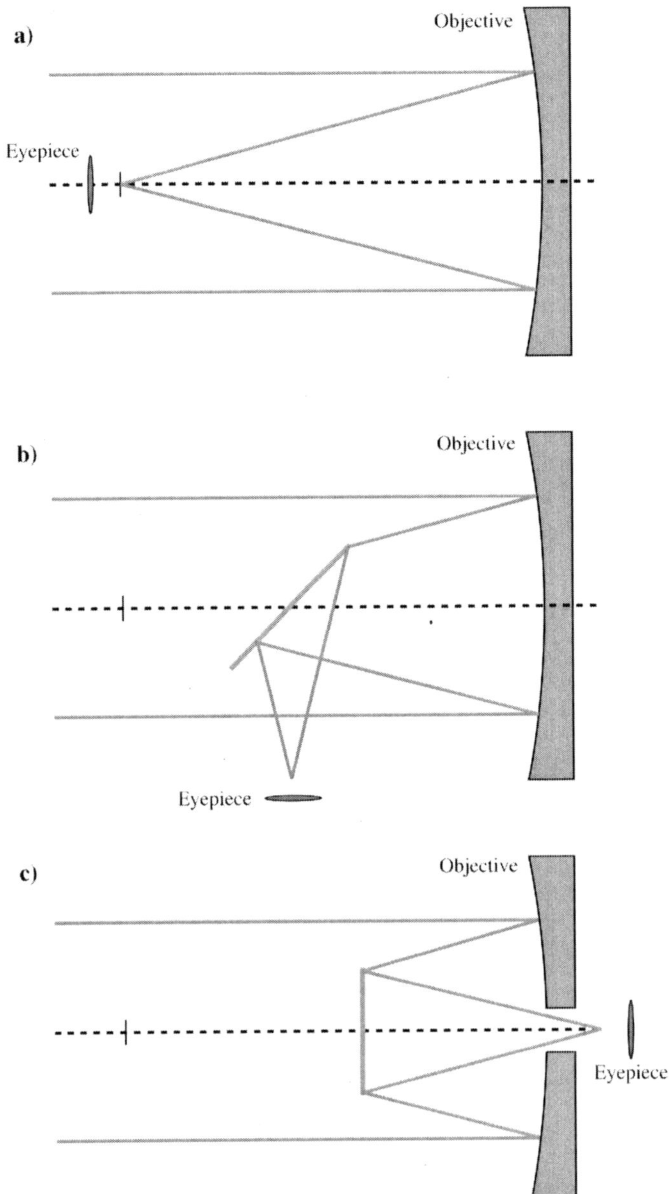

Figure 33.18: *a*) Geometry of standard reflecting telescope. *b*) Geometry of a Newtonian reflecting telescope with the eyepiece to the side. *c*) Geometry of a Cassegrain reflecting telescope with a secondary mirror and an eyepiece in the rear.

In Figure 33.18*a*), the simplest form of a reflecting telescope is shown incorporating a parabolic mirror and an eyepiece. This geometry is impractical because the observer must be placed in the direction that the light comes from. In Figure 33.18*b*), the Newtonian solution to a reflecting telescope is shown where a mirror at an angle of 45° reflects the light outside the structure of the telescope to an eyepiece. In Figure 33.18*c*), the Cassegrain geometry is shown where a secondary mirror, placed perpendicular to the optical axis of the mirror, reflects the light through a hole in the center of the mirror. In the last two cases the secondary mirror is small enough so that it absorbs a negligible fraction of the incoming light. In all three cases, an eyepiece is used to magnify the image produced by the objective mirror.

Self-Test Opportunity: A refracting telescope using two converging lenses is often called a Keplerian telescope. The eyepiece lens is placed a distance $d = f_o + f_e$ from the objective lens. Another type of refracting telescope uses a converging lens for the objective lens and a diverging lens for the eyepiece lens as illustrated in the figure.

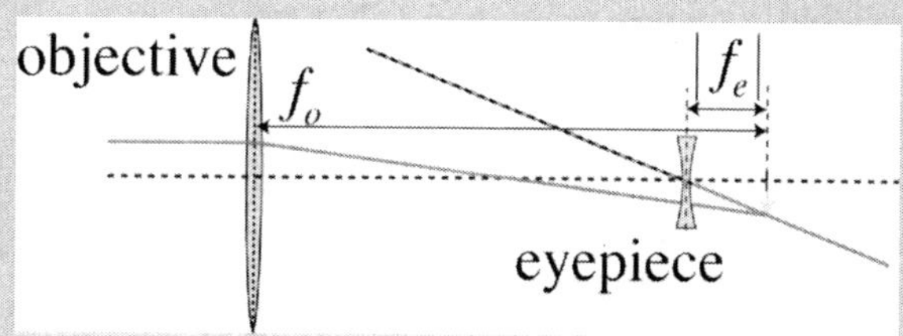

The geometry of a Galilean telescope.

The eyepiece lens in this telescope is placed at a distance $d = f_o + f_e$ where $f_e < 0$. This type of telescope is often called a Galilean telescope. Discuss some advantages of a Galilean telescope versus a Keplerian telescope.

In-class exercise: A reflecting telescope consisting of a convex mirror with a radius of curvature $R = 17.0$ m and an eyepiece lens of focal length $f_e = 29.0$ cm. What is the magnitude of the magnification of this telescope?

a) 29.3
b) 45.0
c) 58.6
d) 66.1
e) 78.9

The Hubble Space Telescope

The Hubble Space Telescope (HST) was deployed April 25, 1990 from the Space Shuttle mission STS-31. The HST orbits the Earth 590 km above the surface of the Earth, far above the atmosphere that disturbs the images gathered by ground based telescopes. The HST is a Ritchey-Chrétien reflecting telescope arranged in Cassegrain geometry. This type of telescope uses a concave hyperbolic objective mirror rather than a spherical mirror and a convex hyperbolic secondary mirror. This arrangement gives the HST a wide field of view and eliminates spherical aberration. The objective mirror is 2.40 m in diameter and has an effective focal length of 57.6 m. The secondary mirror is 0.267 m in diameter and is located 4.91 m from the objective mirror. The secondary mirror can be moved under ground control to produce the best focus. The eyepiece is replaced by a set of electronic instruments specialized for various astronomical tasks.

The original HST objective mirror was produced with a flaw caused by a defective testing instrument. In December 1993, Space Shuttle Service Mission 1 (STS-61) deployed the COSTAR package that corrected the flaw in the objective mirror and allowed the HST to begin revolutionizing our understanding of the universe. The two images of the galaxy M100 shown in Figure 33.19 demonstrate the image quality of the HST before and after the installation of COSTAR.

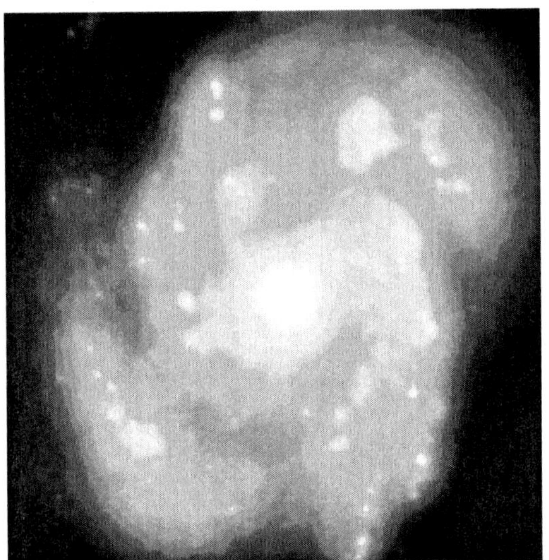
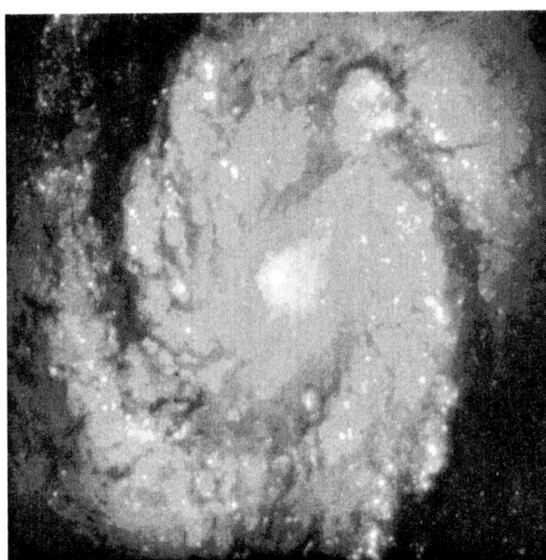

Figure 33.19: Two images of the galaxy M100. The left panel shows an image produced by the Hubble Space Telescope just after it was launched. The right panel shows the same object photographed after the optics were corrected.

In February 1997, two new instrument packages were installed in the HST on Shuttle Servicing Mission 2. These instruments contained their own optical corrections. In December 1997, the Shuttle Servicing Mission 3A was launched to correct a serious problem with the HST's stabilizing gyroscopes. In March 2002, the Shuttle Servicing Mission 3B added several new instruments. Servicing Mission 4 will finally replace all instruments that require COSTAR. NASA plans a service mission for the HST in 2008.

The James Webb Space Telescope

The planned replacement for the HST is the James Webb Space Telescope (JWST). This project is planned for launch in the year 2013. The objective mirror for the JWST will be 6.5 m in diameter and will be composed of 36 mirror segments. An artist's conception of the JWST is shown in Figure 33.20.

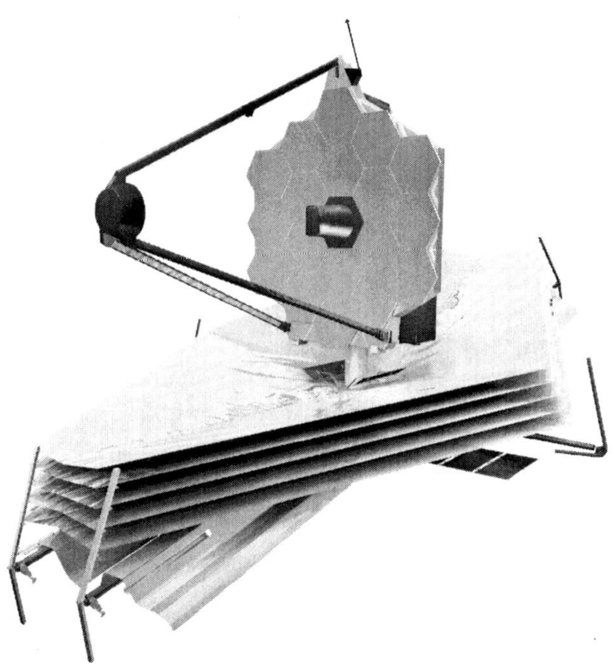

Figure 33.20: The planned James Webb Space Telescope.
(Drawing from the Space Telescope Science Institute)

The JWST will use infrared light to study the universe. Using infrared light instead of visible light allows the penetration of the dust clouds that exist in the universe that block visible light. The JWST will orbit the Earth at a distance of 1.5 million km (about four times the earth-moon distance) such that the Earth will always be between the Sun and the JWST. Having the Sun always blocked by the Earth will allow continuous viewing and shield the cryogenic infrared detectors aboard the JWST from changes in sunlight. The JWST is also equipped with a multiple layer sunshield as shown in Figure 33.20.

What we have learned/Exam Study Guide:

Most Important Points

- The angular magnification of a simple magnifier with an image at infinity is given by $m_\theta \approx \dfrac{0.25\text{ m}}{f}$.
- The magnification of a microscope is given by $m = -\dfrac{0.25L}{f_o f_e}$ where L is the distance between the two lenses. f_o is the focal length of the objective lens and f_e is the focal length of the eyepiece lens.
- The magnification of a telescope is given by $m_\theta = -\dfrac{\theta_e}{\theta_o} = -\dfrac{f_o}{f_e}$. f_o is the focal length of the objective lens and f_e is the focal length of the eyepiece lens.

New Symbols used in this Chapter

f_o Focal length of the objective lens or mirror

f_e Focal length of the eyepiece

Additional Solved Problems

Solved Problem

Solved Problem 33.2: Image of the Moon

An image of the Moon is focused onto a screen using a converging lens of focal length $f = 50.0$ cm. The radius of the Moon is $R = 1.737 \cdot 10^6$ m and the mean distance between the Earth and the Moon is $d = 3.844 \cdot 10^8$ m. What is the radius of the image of the Moon on the screen?

THINK:

The magnification of the image produced by the lens can be expressed in terms of the ratio of the image size to the object size and in terms of the ratio of image distance to the object distance.

SKETCH:

A sketch showing the image of the Moon produced by a converging lens is shown in Figure 33.21. A blue arrow represents the image of the Moon.

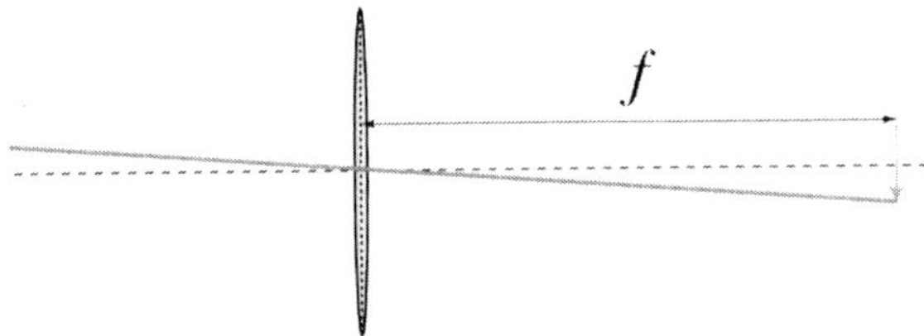

Figure 33.21: Image of the Moon produced by a converging lens.

RESEARCH:

The relationship between the object distance d_o and the image distance d_i for a lens with focal length f is given by the lens equation

$$\frac{1}{d_o} + \frac{1}{d_i} = \frac{1}{f}. \qquad (33.31)$$

We can solve this equation for the image distance

$$d_i = \frac{d_o f}{d_o - f}. \qquad (33.32)$$

In this case, the object distance is the distance from the Earth to the Moon. Because the object distance is much greater than the focal length of the lens, we can write

$$d_i \approx \frac{d_o f}{d_o} = f. \tag{33.33}$$

The magnitude of the magnification m for a lens can be written as

$$m = -\frac{d_i}{d_o} = \frac{h_i}{h_o} \tag{33.34}$$

where h_i is the height (radius) of the image and h_o is the height of the object, which in this case is the radius of the Moon.

SIMPLIFY:

We can solve (33.34) for the image height

$$h_i = -h_o \frac{d_i}{d_o}. \tag{33.35}$$

Taking the object height to be the radius of the Moon R, the object distance to be the distance from the Earth to the Moon d, and the image distance to the be the focal length of the lens f, we can write

$$h_i = -R\frac{f}{d}. \tag{33.36}$$

CALCULATE:

Putting in our numerical values we have

$$h_i = -R\frac{f}{d} = \left(1.737 \cdot 10^6 \text{ m}\right)\frac{0.500 \text{ m}}{3.844 \cdot 10^8 \text{ m}} = -0.00225937 \text{ m}.$$

ROUND:

We report our result for the radius of the image of the moon on the screen to three significant figures

$$h_i = -2.26 \cdot 10^{-3} \text{ m} = -2.26 \text{ mm}.$$

DOUBLE-CHECK:

The Moon is relatively close to Earth and we can see the Moon as a disk easily with the naked eye. Thus it seems reasonable that we could produce an image of the Moon with radius 2.26 mm on a screen with a lens of focal length 50.0 cm. The negative sign for the image height means that our image of the Moon is inverted.

Solved Problem

Solved Problem

Solved Problem 33.3: Image produced by a lens and a mirror

An object is placed a distance $d_{o,1} = 25.6$ cm to the left of a converging lens with focal length $f_1 = 20.6$ cm. A converging mirror with focal length $f_2 = 10.3$ cm is placed a distance $d = 120.77$ cm to the right of the lens.

Question:
What is the magnification of the image that is produced by the lens and mirror combination?

Answer:

THINK:

The lens will produce a real, inverted image of the object. This image becomes the object for the converging mirror. The object distance for the mirror is the distance between the lens and the mirror minus the image distance of the lens. The overall magnification is the magnification of the lens times the magnification of the mirror.

SKETCH:

A sketch of the object, the lens, and the mirror is shown in Figure 33.22.

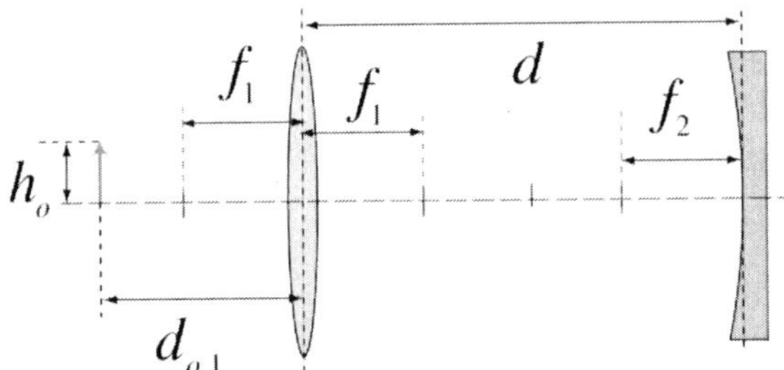

Figure 33.22: An object being imaged by a lens and a mirror.

RESEARCH:

The lens equation tells us that the image distance $d_{i,1}$ for the lens is given by

$$d_{i,1} = \frac{d_{o,1} f_1}{d_{o,1} - f_1}. \quad (33.37)$$

The mirror equation tells us that image distance for the mirror

$$d_{i,2} = \frac{d_{o,2} f_2}{d_{o,2} - f_2} \quad (33.38)$$

where the object distance for the mirror is given by

Solved Problem

$$d_{o,2} = d - d_{i,1}. \quad (33.39)$$

The magnification m of the lens and mirror system is given by

$$m = m_1 m_2 \quad (33.40)$$

where m_1 is the magnification of the lens and m_2 is the magnification of the mirror. The magnification of the lens is

$$m_1 = -\frac{d_{i,1}}{d_{o,1}} = -\frac{\left(\dfrac{d_{o,1}f_1}{d_{o,1}-f_1}\right)}{d_{o,1}} = -\frac{f_1}{d_{o,1}-f_1} = \frac{f_1}{f_1-d_{o,1}}. \quad (33.41)$$

Similarly, the magnification of the mirror is given by

$$m_2 = -\frac{d_{i,2}}{d_{o,2}} = -\frac{\left(\dfrac{d_{o,2}f_2}{d_{o,2}-f_2}\right)}{d_{o,2}} = -\frac{f_2}{d_{o,2}-f_2} = \frac{f_2}{f_2-d_{o,2}} \quad (33.42)$$

SIMPLIFY:

We can then write

$$m = \left(\frac{f_1}{f_1-d_{o,1}}\right)\left(\frac{f_2}{f_2-d_{o,2}}\right) = \left(\frac{f_1}{f_1-d_{o,1}}\right)\left(\frac{f_2}{f_2-\left(d-d_{i,1}\right)}\right). \quad (33.43)$$

Substituting in (33.37) for the image distance for the lens gives us

$$m = \left(\frac{f_1}{f_1-d_{o,1}}\right)\left(\frac{f_2}{f_2-\left(d-\dfrac{d_{o,1}f_1}{d_{o,1}-f_1}\right)}\right) \quad (33.44)$$

CALCULATE:

Putting in our numerical values gives us

$$m = \left(\frac{(20.6 \text{ cm})}{(20.6 \text{ cm})-(25.6 \text{ cm})}\right)\left(\frac{(10.3 \text{ cm})}{(10.3 \text{ cm})-\left((120.77 \text{ cm})-\dfrac{(25.6 \text{ cm})(20.6 \text{ cm})}{(25.6 \text{ cm})-(20.6 \text{ cm})}\right)}\right)$$

$m = 8.490596$

Solved Problem

ROUND:

We report our result to three significant figures

$$m = 8.49 .$$

DOUBLE-CHECK:

To double-check our result, we first calculate the image distance for the lens

$$d_{i,1} = \frac{d_{o,1} f_1}{d_{o,1} - f_1} = \frac{(25.6 \text{ cm})(20.6 \text{ cm})}{(25.6 \text{ cm}) - (20.6 \text{ cm})} = 105.5 \text{ cm} .$$

The object distance for the mirror is then

$$d_{o,2} = d - d_{i,1} = 120.77 \text{ cm} - 105.47 \text{ cm} = 15.3 \text{ cm} .$$

The image distance for the mirror is then

$$d_{i,2} = \frac{d_{o,2} f_2}{d_{o,2} - f_2} = \frac{(15.3 \text{ cm})(10.3 \text{ cm})}{(15.3 \text{ cm}) - (10.3 \text{ cm})} = 31.52 \text{ cm}$$

The distance of the final image from the center of the lens is

$$d_{\text{final}} = 120.77 \text{ cm} - 31.52 \text{ cm} = 89.25 \text{ cm}$$

The magnification of the image is then

$$m = \frac{d_{i,1}}{d_{o,1}} \frac{d_{i,2}}{d_{o,2}} = \frac{105 \text{ cm}}{25.6 \text{ cm}} \frac{31.52 \text{ cm}}{15.3 \text{ cm}} = 8.45$$

which agrees with our result within round-off errors.

Chapter 34. Wave Optics

Figure 34.1: Different colors resulting from constructive interference from sunlight striking a blank DVD.

What we will learn

- The wave nature of light leads to phenomena that cannot be explained using geometric optics.
- Superimposed light waves that are in phase interfere constructively.
- Superimposed light waves that are 180° out of phase interfere destructively.
- Light waves that have the same phase and frequency are called coherent light waves.
- Superimposed light that has traveled different distances can interfere constructively or destructively depending on the path length difference. An example of this is shown in Figure 34.1.
- Coherent light incident on two narrow slits produces an interference pattern.

- Light waves spread out after passing through a narrow slit or after encountering an obstacle. This spreading out is called diffraction.
- Coherent light incident on one narrow slit produces a diffraction pattern.
- Interference can occur in light that is partially reflected from each of the two surfaces (front and back) of a thin optical film.
- An interferometer is a device designed to measure lengths or changes in length using interference of light.
- Diffraction can limit the ability of a telescope or camera to resolve distant objects.
- A diffraction grating consists of many narrow slits or rulings that can be used to produce an intensity pattern that consists of narrow bright fringes separated by wide dark areas.
- X-ray diffraction can be used to study the atomic structure of materials.

34.1. Light Waves

In Chapter 32, we discussed light as rays. These rays traveled in a straight line except when they were reflected off a mirror or were refracted at the boundary between two optical media. Here we will discuss the wave nature of light. We know that light is an electromagnetic wave. However, normally we do not think of light as a wave, because its wavelength is so short that we usually do not notice this wave behavior.

One way to reconcile the wave nature of light with the geometric optical properties of light is to use Huygens's principle developed by Christian Huygens. Huygens was a Dutch physicist who proposed a wave theory of light in 1678. This theory was put forward before Maxwell developed his theories of light. Huygens's principle states that every point on a propagating wave front serves as a source of spherical secondary wavelets. Later, the envelope of these secondary waves becomes a wave front. If the original wave has frequency f and speed v, the secondary wavelets have the same f and v.

Diagrams of phenomena based on Huygens's principle are called Huygens constructions. A Huygens construction for a plane wave is shown in Figure 34.2.

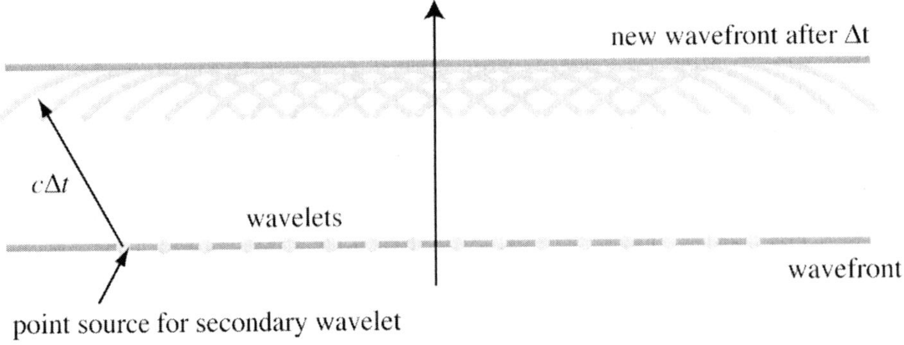

Figure 34.2: Huygens construction for a traveling light wave.

We start with a plane wave traveling at the speed of light c. We assume point sources of spherical wavelets along the wave front as shown. These wavelets also travel at c so at a time Δt the wavelets have traveled a distance of $c\Delta t$. If we assume many point sources along the wave front, we can see in Figure 34.2 that the envelope of these wavelets forms a new wave front parallel to the original wave front. Thus, the wave continues to travel in a straight line with the original frequency and speed.

Now let's use a Huygens construction to derive Snell's Law for refraction between two optical media with different indices of refraction. Assume that we have a wave with wave fronts separated by a wavelength λ_1 traveling with speed v_1 in an optically clear medium incident on the boundary with a second optically clear medium as shown in Figure 34.3.

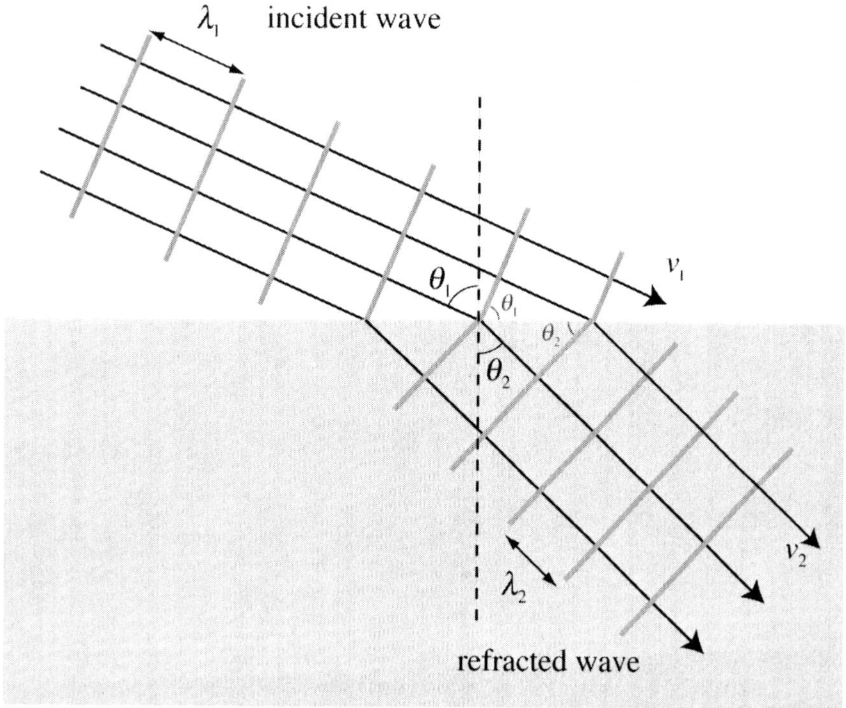

Figure 34.3: A Huygens construction of a traveling wave in an optical medium incident on the boundary with a second optical medium. The green lines represent wave fronts while the black arrows denote rays.

The angle of the incident wave front (green line in medium 1) with respect to the boundary is θ_1, which is also the angle the light ray (black arrow) makes with respect to a normal to the boundary. When the wave enters the second medium, it travels with speed v_2. According to Huygens's principle, the wave fronts are the result of wavelet propagation at the speed of the original wave so we can write the separation of the wave fronts in the second medium in terms of the wavelength in the second medium λ_2. Thus, the time interval between wave fronts for the first medium is λ_1 / v_1 and the time interval for the second medium is λ_2 / v_2. (If these intervals were not equal, fronts would be mysteriously appearing or disappearing!) This time interval is the same at the boundary so we can write

$$\frac{\lambda_1}{v_1} = \frac{\lambda_2}{v_2} \tag{34.1}$$

or

$$\frac{\lambda_1}{\lambda_2} = \frac{v_1}{v_2}. \tag{34.2}$$

Thus, the wavelengths of the light in the two media are proportional to the speed of the light in those media.

We can get a relation between the angle of the incident wave fronts θ_1 with the boundary and the angle of the transmitted wave fronts θ_2 with the boundary by analyzing the yellow shaded region of Figure 34.3 as shown in Figure 34.4.

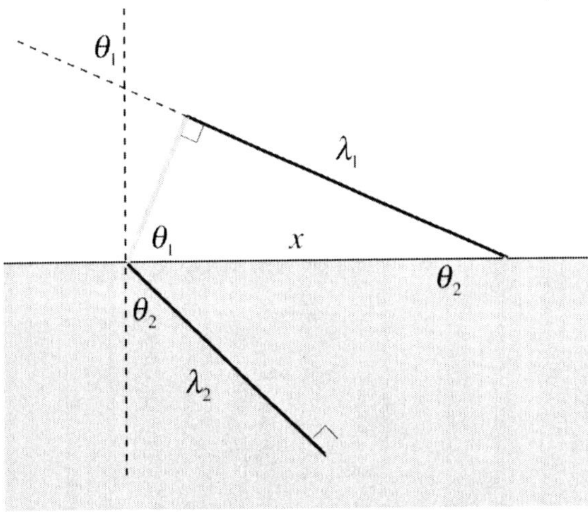

Figure 34.4: Expanded section of Figure 34.3 showing the incident wave front and direction as well as the transmitted wave front and direction.

We can see that

$$\sin\theta_1 = \frac{\lambda_1}{x} \tag{34.3}$$

and

$$\sin\theta_2 = \frac{\lambda_2}{x}. \tag{34.4}$$

Dividing (34.3) by (34.4) we get

$$\frac{\sin\theta_1}{\sin\theta_2} = \frac{\lambda_1}{\lambda_2} = \frac{v_1}{v_2}. \tag{34.5}$$

Remembering the definition of the index of refraction n of an optical medium is

$$n = \frac{c}{v} \tag{34.6}$$

where c is the speed of light and v is the velocity of light in the optical medium, we get

$$\frac{\sin\theta_1}{\sin\theta_2} = \frac{v_1}{v_2} = \frac{c/n_1}{c/n_2} = \frac{n_2}{n_1} \tag{34.7}$$

or

$$n_1 \sin\theta_1 = n_2 \sin\theta_2 \tag{34.8}$$

which is Snell's Law.

We have seen that the wavelength of light changes when going from vacuum to an optical medium with index of refraction greater than one. Taking (34.1) with medium one being a vacuum while medium two has an index of refraction n we can write

$$\lambda_n = \lambda \frac{v}{c} = \frac{\lambda}{n}. \tag{34.9}$$

Thus, the wavelength of light is shorter in a medium with index of refraction greater than one than it is in vacuum. The frequency f of this light can be calculated remembering

$$v = \lambda f. \tag{34.10}$$

The frequency f_n of light traveling in the medium is then given by

$$f_n = \frac{v}{\lambda_n} = \frac{c/n}{\lambda/n} = \frac{c}{\lambda} = f. \tag{34.11}$$

Thus, the frequency of light traveling in an optical medium with $n > 1$ is the same as the frequency of that light traveling in a vacuum. (Equation (34.11) is equivalent to our earlier statement that the time interval between wave fronts for the first medium equals the time interval between fronts for the second medium.) We perceive color by the frequency of light that strikes the retina. Thus placing an object under water, which changes its wavelength, does not change our perception of the color of the object because the frequency of the light does not change.

In-class exercise: A light ray with wavelength $\lambda = 560.0$ nm enters from air into a block of plastic at an incident angle of $\theta_i = 36.1°$ with respect to the normal. The angle of refraction is $\theta_r = 21.7°$. What is the speed of the light ray inside the plastic?

a) $1.16 \cdot 10^8$ m/s b) $1.31 \cdot 10^8$ m/s c) $1.67 \cdot 10^8$ m/s d) $1.88 \cdot 10^8$ m/s e) $3.00 \cdot 10^8$ m/s

34.2. Interference

Sunlight is composed of light containing a broad range of frequencies and corresponding wavelengths. We often see different colors separated out of sunlight after the sunlight refracts and reflects in raindrops, thereby forming a rainbow. We also sometimes see various colors from sunlight due to constructive and destructive interference phenomena in thin transparent layers of materials such as soap bubbles or small amounts of oil floating on water. In contrast to rainbows, this thin film effect is due to interference.

The geometric optics of the previous chapters cannot be used to explain interference. To understand these interference phenomena, we must take into account the wave nature of light. In this section, we will consider light waves that have the same wavelength in vacuum. Interference takes place when such light waves are superimposed. If the light waves are in phase, they interfere constructively, as illustrated in Figure 34.5.

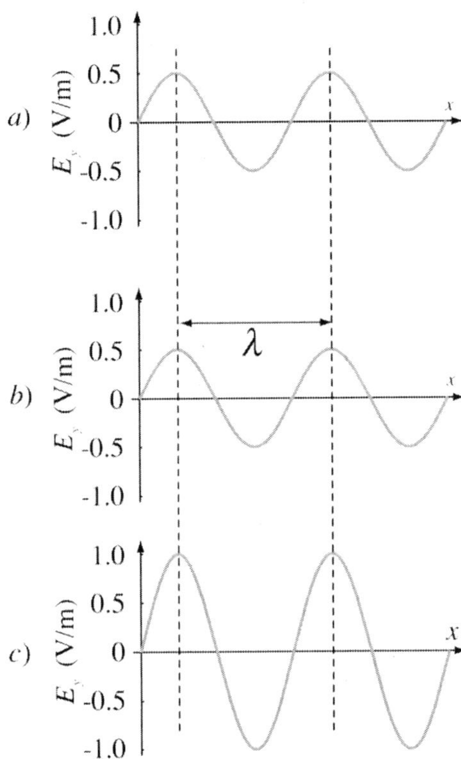

Figure 34.5: *a)* and *b)* light waves in phase with the same amplitude and wavelength λ; *c)* superposition of the two light waves demonstrating constructive interference, producing a wave with twice the amplitude.

In Figure 34.5*a*) and *b*), we plot the electric field component in the y-direction for two electromagnetic waves traveling in the x-direction. Both waves are in phase. The statement that the two waves are in phase is the same as saying that the phase difference between the two waves is zero. A phase difference of 2π radians ($360°$), corresponding to starting with two waves in phase and then displacing one of the waves by one wavelength, will produce two waves that are in phase. If each light wave is traveling from its own point of origin, there will be a phase difference related to the path difference between the two waves even though the waves start in phase. The criterion for constructive interference is characterized by a path difference Δx given by

$$\Delta x = m\lambda \quad (m = 0, m = \pm 1, m = \pm 2, \ldots). \tag{34.12}$$

In Figure 34.5*c*) we show the two waves constructively interfering. The amplitudes of the two waves add and we get a wave with twice the amplitude of the two original waves.

If the two light waves are out of phase, as shown in Figure 34.6*a*) and *b*), the amplitudes of the waves will sum to zero everywhere and the two waves will destructively interfere, as illustrated in Figure 34.6*c*).

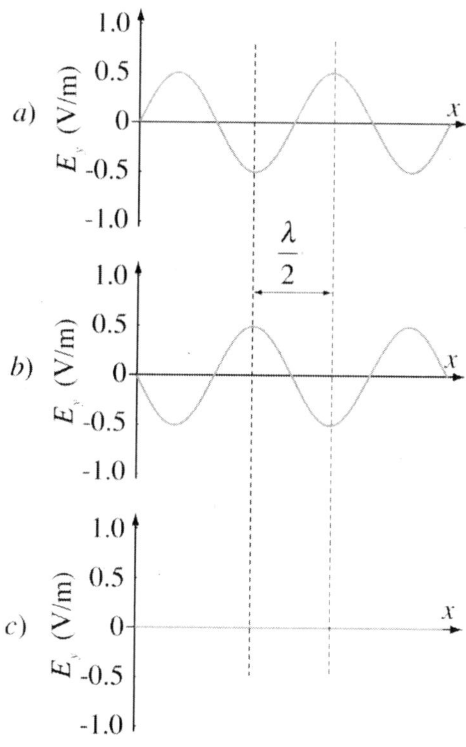

Figure 34.6: *a)* and *b)* light waves out of phase with the same amplitude and wavelength; *c)* superposition of the two light waves demonstrating destructive interference.

Here the phase difference between the two waves is π radians ($180°$). Figure 34.6*a*) and b) show that this situations is equivalent to starting with two waves in phase and then displacing one of the waves by half of one wavelength ($\lambda / 2$). Again, if we think of the two light waves as being emitted from the same source, the phase difference can be related to the path difference. We can see that destructive interference will take place if the path difference is a half wavelength plus an integer times the wavelength

$$\Delta x = \left(m + \frac{1}{2}\right)\lambda \quad \left(m = 0, m = \pm 1, m = \pm 2, \ldots\right). \tag{34.13}$$

In the following sections we will study phenomena that produce interference effects by producing light waves with the same wavelength that are initially in phase but travel different distances or travel with different speeds to reach the same point. At this point, the light waves are superimposed and can interfere.

34.3. Double-Slit Interference

Our first example of the interference of light is Young's double slit experiment, named for English physicist Thomas Young (1773 – 1829) who carried out this experiment in 1801. For this experiment, we assume that we have coherent light (light with the same wavelength and phase) incident on a pair of slits. Such coherent light is inevitably produced by starting with light from a single source. If separate sources of light are used for illuminating the two slits, then the fact that there are random and uncontrollable differences in the light from the two sources means that these two light sources are incoherent. In addition, we use slits that are smaller than the wavelength of light so that single slit diffraction effects are so spread out that the double slit effects are easily discernable. (In section 34.9, we will show the effect of using wide slits in a double slit experiment.)

For each slit we will use a Huygens construction and assume that all the light passing through the slit is due to wavelets emitted from a single point at the center of the slit as shown in Figure 34.7. In this figure, we see that spherical wavelets are emitted from a point in the center of the slit. We assume that the slit is much narrower than the wavelength of light so that we can represent the source of the wavelets with one point.

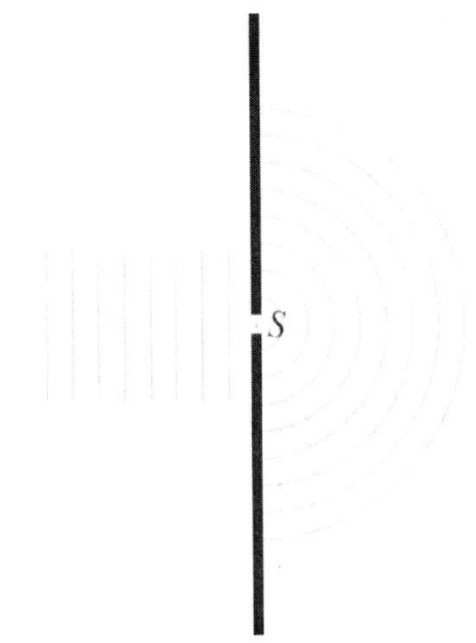

Figure 34.7: Huygens construction for a coherent light wave incident from the left on a single slit.

In Figure 34.8 we show two slits like the one in Figure 34.7. A distance d separates the slits.

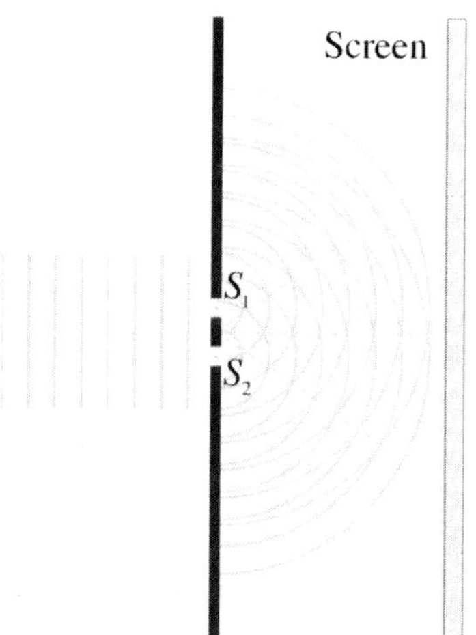

Figure 34.8: Huygens construction for coherent light incident from the left on two slits, S_1 and S_2. The gray dashed lines represent lines of constructive interference.

Again, we have coherent light incident from the left and a source of spherical wavelets at the center of each slit. We see that the gray dashed lines represent lines along which there is constructive interference. If we place a screen to the right of the slits we will observe an alternating pattern of bright lines and dark lines corresponding to constructive and destructive interference between the light waves emitted from the two slits.

To quantify these lines of constructive interference we expand and simplify Figure 34.8 in Figure 34.9.

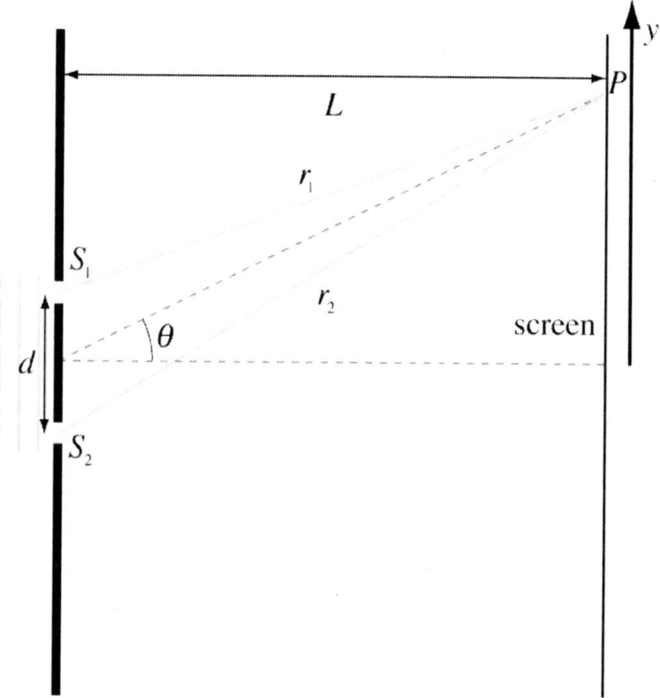

Figure 34.9: Expanded view of coherent light incident on two slits. The green lines to the right of the slits represent the distance light must travel from S_1 and S_2 to the screen.

In this figure, the two lines r_1 and r_2 represent the distance from the centers of slit S_1 and slit S_2 respectively to a point P on a screen that is placed a distance L away from the slits. A line drawn from a point midway between the two slits to point P on the screen makes an angle θ with respect to a line drawn from the slits perpendicular to the screen. The point P on the screen is a distance y above the centerline.

To further quantify the two-slit geometry, we expand and simplify Figure 34.9 in Figure 34.10. In this figure, we assume that we have placed the screen a large distance L away from the slits such that the lines r_1 and r_2 are essentially parallel to each other and to the line drawn from the center of the two slits to point P. We draw a line from S_1 perpendicular to r_1 and r_2 making a triangle with sides d, b, and Δx. The quantity Δx is the path length difference $r_2 - r_1$.

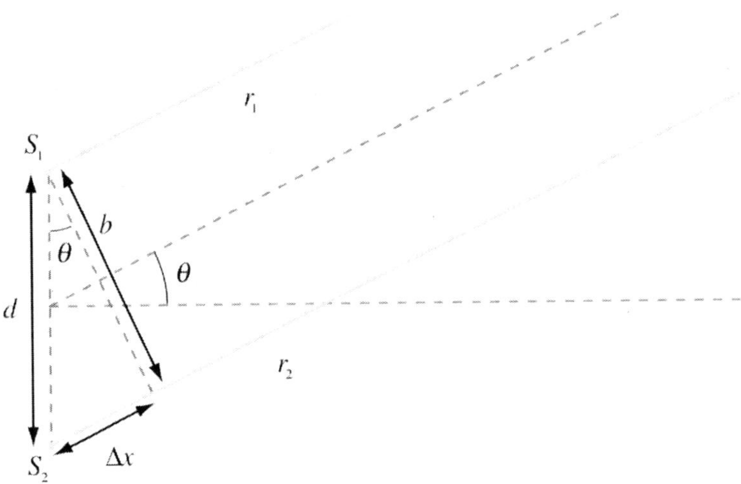

Figure 34.10: Expanded view of two slits where the screen is placed far enough away so that the lines r_1 and r_2 are parallel.

This path length difference $\Delta x = r_2 - r_1$ will produce a phase difference for light originating from the two slits and illuminating the screen at point P. The path length difference can be expressed in terms of the distance between the slits d and the angle θ at which the light is observed

$$\sin\theta = \frac{\Delta x}{d} \tag{34.14}$$

or

$$\Delta x = d\sin\theta . \tag{34.15}$$

For constructive interference, this path length difference must be a multiple of the wavelength of the incident light

$$\Delta x = d\sin\theta = m\lambda \quad (m = 0, m = \pm 1, m = \pm 2, ...) . \tag{34.16}$$

A bright fringe on the screen signals constructive interference.

For destructive interference, the path length difference must be an integer plus a half times the wavelength

$$\Delta x = d\sin\theta = \left(m+\frac{1}{2}\right)\lambda \quad \left(m=0, m=\pm 1, m=\pm 2,...\right). \qquad (34.17)$$

A dark fringe on the screen signals destructive interference.

Note that for constructive interference and $m=0$, we obtain $\theta=0$, which means that $\Delta x=0$ and we have a bright fringe at zero degrees. This bright fringe is called the central maximum. The integer m is called the order of the fringe. The order has a different meaning for bright fringes and for dark fringes. For example, using (34.16) with $m=1$ would give us the angle of the first order bright fringe, $m=2$ would give us the second order fringe, etc. Using (34.17) with $m=0$ would give us the angle of the first order dark fringe, $m=1$ would give us the second order fringe, etc. For both bright and dark fringes, the first order fringe is the one closest to the central maximum.

If the screen is placed a sufficiently large distance from the slits, the angle θ will be small and we can make the approximation $\sin\theta \approx \tan\theta = y/L$. (See Figure 34.9.) Thus, we can express (34.16) as

$$d\sin\theta = d\frac{y}{L} = m\lambda \quad \left(m=0, m=\pm 1, m=\pm 2,...\right) \qquad (34.18)$$

or

$$y = \frac{m\lambda L}{d} \quad \left(m=0, m=\pm 1, m=\pm 2,...\right) \qquad (34.19)$$

which gives the distance of the bright fringes from the central maximum along the screen.

Similarly, we can express the distance of the dark fringes from the central maximum along the screen as

$$y = \frac{\left(m+\frac{1}{2}\right)\lambda L}{d} \quad \left(m=0, m=\pm 1, m=\pm 2,...\right). \qquad (34.20)$$

We have located the positions of the bright and dark fringes. However, we can also calculate the intensity of the light at any point on the screen. We start our calculation by assuming that the light emitted at each slit is in phase. The electric field of the light waves can be described by

$$E = E_{max} \sin \omega t \tag{34.21}$$

where E_{max} is the amplitude of the wave and ω is the angular frequency. (The argument of the sine function could also include a spatial term kx. However, we choose to account for the spatial dependence of the wave using a more physical and intuitive approach rather than in an obscure mathematical manner.) When the light waves arrive at the screen from the two slits, they have traveled different distances, and so can have different phases. Let's express the electric field of the light arriving at a given point on the screen from S_1 as

$$E_1 = E_{max} \sin(\omega t) \tag{34.22}$$

and the electric field of the light arriving at the same point from S_2 as

$$E_2 = E_{max} \sin(\omega t + \phi) \tag{34.23}$$

where ϕ is the phase constant of E_2 with respect to E_1. The two phasors E_1 and E_2 are shown in Figure 34.11*a*).

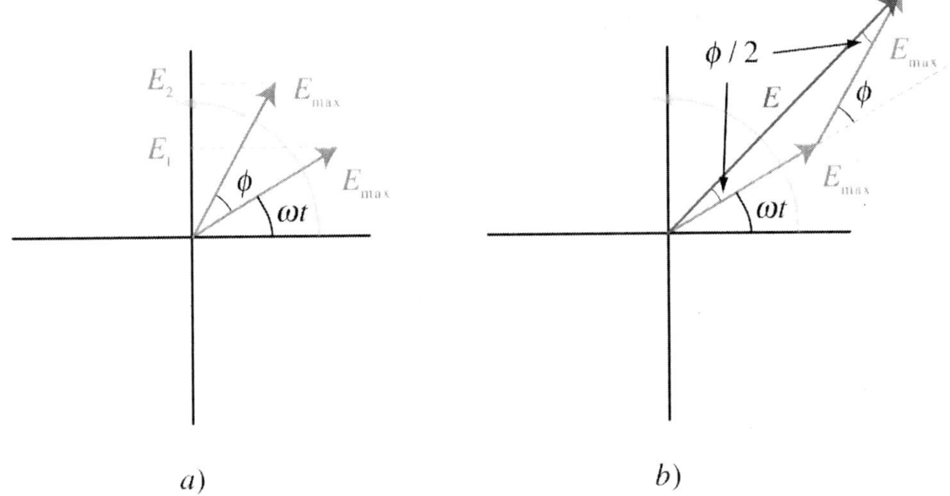

Figure 34.11: *a*) Two phasors E_1 and E_2 separated by a phase ϕ. *b*) Sum of the two phasors E_1 and E_2.

The sum of the two phasors E_1 and E_2 is shown in Figure 34.11*b*). In this figure, we can see that the magnitude E of the sum of the two phasors is

$$E = 2E_{max} \cos(\phi / 2). \tag{34.24}$$

We know that the intensity of an electromagnetic wave is proportional to the square of the electric field so we can write

$$\frac{I}{I_{max}} = \frac{E^2}{E_{max}^2}. \tag{34.25}$$

Using (34.24) we get

$$I = 4I_{max}\cos^2(\phi/2) \tag{34.26}$$

for the intensity of the summed wave as a function of the phase difference between the two light waves. Now we need to relate the phase difference to the path length difference. Looking at Figure 34.10 we can see that the path length difference Δx will cause a phase shift given by

$$\phi = \frac{\Delta x}{\lambda}(2\pi), \tag{34.27}$$

because when $\Delta x = \lambda$, the phase shift $\phi = 2\pi$. Noting that $\Delta x = d\sin\theta$ we can write the phase constant as

$$\phi = \frac{2\pi d}{\lambda}\sin\theta. \tag{34.28}$$

Thus, we can write an equation for the intensity of the light produced by the interference from two slits as

$$I = 4I_{max}\cos^2\left(\frac{\pi d}{\lambda}\sin\theta\right). \tag{34.29}$$

Finally we can obtain an expression for the intensity pattern on a screen resulting from coherent light incident on two narrow widely separated slits using the approximation as before that $\sin\theta \approx \tan\theta = y/L$

$$I = 4I_{max}\cos^2\left(\frac{\pi d y}{\lambda L}\right). \tag{34.30}$$

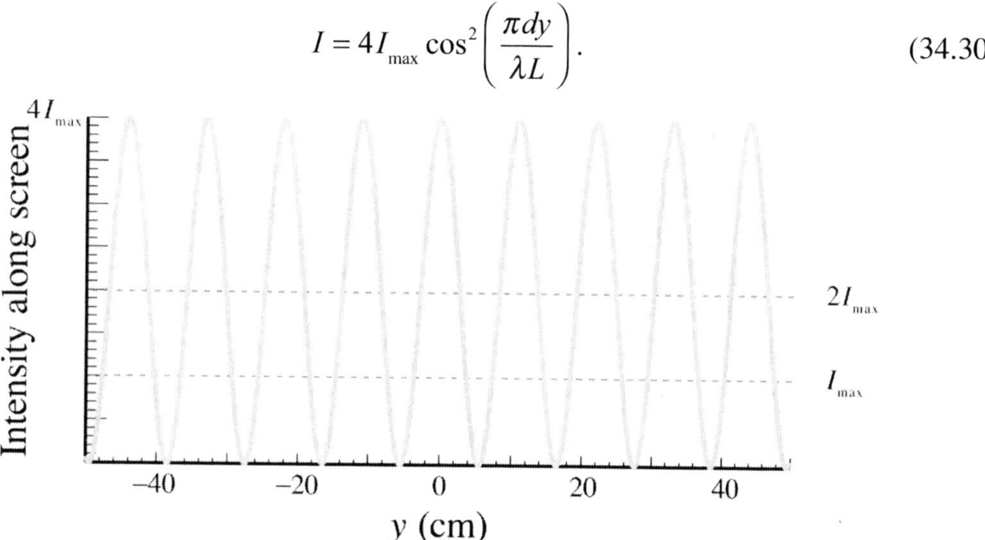

Figure 34.12: Intensity pattern for two slit interference using light with wavelength 550 nm incident on two narrow slits separated by 10^{-5} m at a distance of 2 m from the slits.

If the screen is $L = 2.0\text{ m}$ away from the slits, the slits are separated by $d = 1.0 \cdot 10^{-5}\text{ m}$, and the wavelength of the incident light is $\lambda = 550\text{ nm}$, we get the intensity pattern shown in Figure 34.12. In this figure, we can see that the intensity varies from $4I_{max}$ to zero. If we covered one slit, we would get an intensity of I_{max} at all values of y. If we illuminated both slits with light that has random phases, we would observe an intensity of $2I_{max}$ at all values of y. Only when we illuminate both slits with coherent light do we observe the oscillatory pattern in y that is characteristic of two-slit interference.

In-class exercise: A pair of slits is separated by a distance $d = 1.40\text{ mm}$ and is illuminated with light of wavelength $\lambda = 460.0\text{ nm}$. What is the separation of adjacent interference maxima on a screen a distance $L = 2.90\text{ m}$ away?

a) 0.00332 mm
b) 0.556 mm
c) 0.953 mm
d) 1.45 mm
e) 3.23 mm

34.4. Thin-Film Interference

Another way of producing interference phenomena is by using light that is partially reflected from the front and back layers of thin films. A thin film is an optically clear material with thickness on the order of a few wavelengths of light. Examples of thin films include the walls of soap bubbles and thin layers of oil floating on water. When the light reflected off the front surface constructively interferes with the light reflected off the back surface of the thin film, we see the color corresponding to the wavelength of light traveling in the optical medium that is interfering constructively.

Consider light that is traveling in an optical medium with an index of refraction n_1 that strikes a second optical medium with index of refraction n_2. One possibility is that the light can be transmitted through the boundary. In this case, the phase of the light is not changed. A second process that can occur is that the light can be reflected. In this case, the phase of the light can be changed depending on the index of refraction of the two optical media. If $n_1 < n_2$, the phase of the reflected wave will be changed by 180° (corresponding to half of a wavelength). If $n_1 > n_2$ then there will be no phase change. This reason for this phase change upon reflection follows from the theory of electromagnetic waves and is too complicated for us to cover in this book.

Let's begin our analysis of thin films by studying a thin film with index of refraction n in air as shown in Figure 34.13.

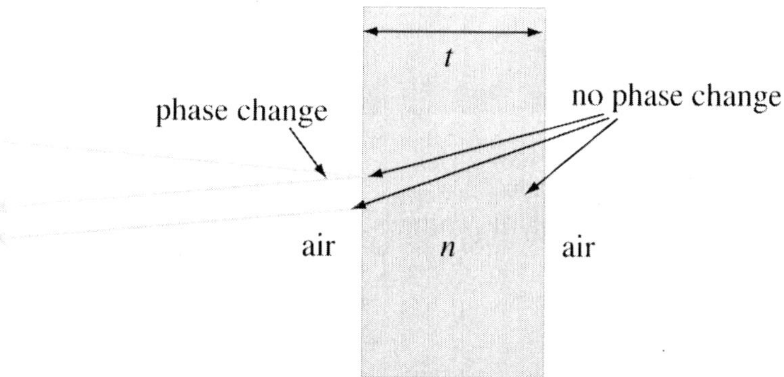

Figure 34.13: Light waves in air incident on a thin film with index of refraction n and thickness t.

We will assume that light is incident perpendicular to the surface of the thin film. An angle of incidence is shown for the light waves in the figure for clarity. When the light wave reaches the boundary between air and the film, part of the wave is reflected and part of the wave is transmitted. The reflected wave undergoes a phase shift of half a wavelength when it is reflected because $n_{air} < n$. The light that is transmitted has no phase shift and continues to the back surface of the film. At the back surface, again part of the wave is transmitted and part of the wave is reflected. The transmitted light passes through the film completely. (We do not show the transmitted wave in Figure 34.13 as this wave does not interest us.) The reflected light has no phase shift because $n > n_{air}$ and travels back to the front surface of the film. At the front surface, some of the light reflected from the back surface is transmitted and some is reflected. The reflected light will not be considered. The transmitted light has no phase shift and emerges from the film and interferes with the light that was reflected when the light first struck the film. The transmitted and then reflected light has traveled a longer distance than the originally reflected light and has a phase shift determined by the path length difference. This difference is twice the thickness t of the film.

The fact that the originally reflected light has undergone a phase shift of half a wavelength and the transmitted and then reflected light has not, means that the criterion for constructive interference is given by

$$\Delta x = \left(m + \frac{1}{2} \right) \lambda = 2t \quad \left(m = 0, m = \pm 1, m = \pm 2, \ldots \right). \qquad (34.31)$$

The wavelength λ refers to the wavelength of the light traveling in the thin film, which has index of refraction n. The wavelength of the light traveling in air is related to the wavelength of the light traveling in the film by

$$\lambda = \frac{\lambda_{air}}{n}. \qquad (34.32)$$

We can then write

$$\left(m+\frac{1}{2}\right)\frac{\lambda_{air}}{n}=2t \quad \left(m=0,m=\pm 1,m=\pm 2,...\right). \tag{34.33}$$

The minimum thickness $t_{\min}$ that will produce constructive interference corresponds to $m=0$

$$t_{\min}=\frac{\lambda_{air}}{4n}. \tag{34.34}$$

An oil slick or a soap bubble will have varying thicknesses and thus will affect different wavelengths differently, sometimes creating a rainbow effect.

Example 34.1: Lens coating

Many high quality lenses are coated to prevent reflections. This coating is designed to set up destructive interference for light that is reflected from the surface of the lens. Assume that the coating is MgF_2, which has $n_{coating}=1.38$, and that the lens is glass with $n_{lens}=1.51$.

Question:

What is the minimum thickness of the coating that will produce destructive interference for light with a wavelength of 550 nm?

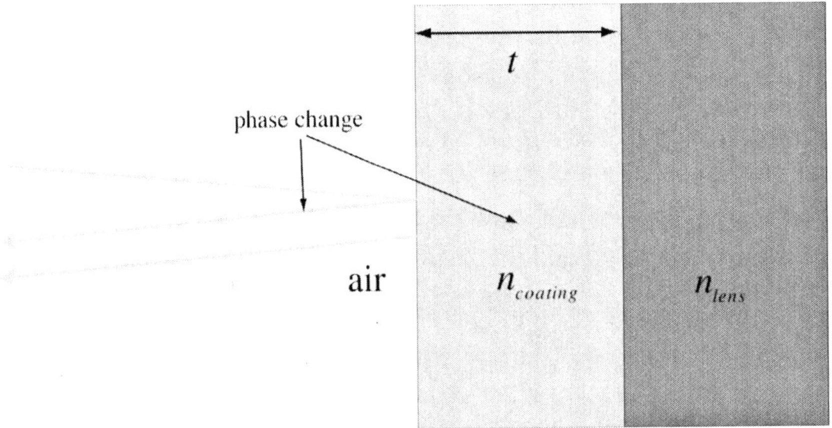

Figure 34.14: Light incident on a coated lens.

Answer:

We assume that the light is incident perpendicularly on the surface of the coated lens as shown in Figure 34.14. Light reflected at the surface of the coating will undergo a phase change of half a wavelength because $n_{air}<n_{coating}$. The light transmitted through the coating has no phase change. Light reflected at the boundary between the coating and the lens will undergo a phase change of half a wavelength because $n_{coating}<n_{lens}$. This

Example

reflected light will travel back through the coating and exit with no phase change. Thus, both the light reflected from the coating and from the lens will have suffered a phase change of half a wavelength. Thus the criterion for destructive interference is

$$\left(m+\frac{1}{2}\right)\frac{\lambda_{air}}{n_{coating}}=2t \quad \left(m=0,m=\pm 1,m=\pm 2,...\right).$$

The minimum thickness for the coating to provide destructive interference corresponds to $m=0$

$$t_{\min}=\frac{\lambda_{air}}{4n}=\frac{550\cdot 10^{-9}\text{ m}}{4\cdot 1.38}=9.96\cdot 10^{-8}\text{ m}=99.6\text{ nm}.$$

In-class exercise: A thin soap film with index of refraction $n=1.35$ hanging in air reflects dominantly red light with $\lambda=682$ nm. What is the minimum thickness of the film?

a) 89.5 nm
b) 126 nm
c) 198 nm
d) 302 nm
e) 432 nm

How CDs, DVDs, and Blu-Ray Work

Previously, in Example 9.1, we calculated the length of a CD track and also showed microscopic images of CD surfaces. Now we want to explore how CD and other disks store digital information, and how computers and consumer electronic devices read it. CDs, DVDs, and Blu-Ray optical disks operate on a similar principle involving destructive interference. A schematic cross section of a CD is shown in Figure 34.15.

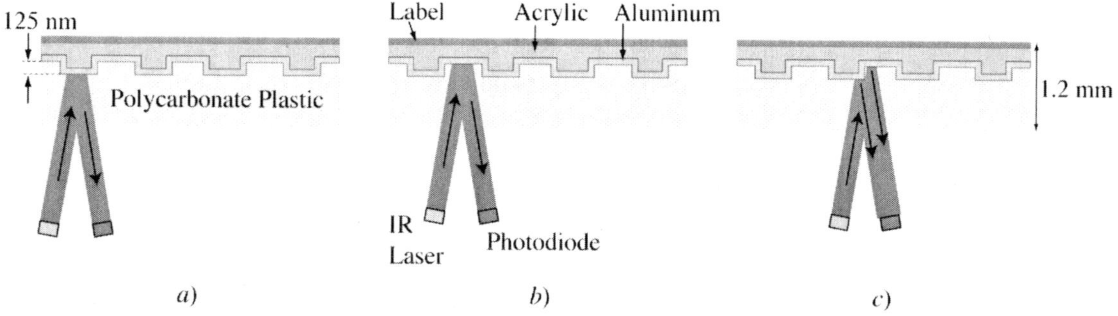

Figure 34.15: A cross section of a CD. *a)* shows the laser shining on a high area of the aluminum layer. *b)* shows the laser shining on a low area of the aluminum layer. *c)* shows the laser shining on the high and low areas of the aluminum layer simultaneously.

A CD stores digital information in terms of one and zeros. These ones and zeros are encoded in the location of the edges of high areas and low areas in the aluminum layer shown in Figure 34.15. The high and low areas rotate with the CD and pass over an infrared solid-state laser that emits light with a wavelength of $\lambda = 780\text{ nm}$. The laser light reflects off the aluminum layer and is detected by a photodiode that produces a voltage proportional to the light it receives.

When the light from the laser is shining completely on a high area as illustrated in Figure 34.15*a*), all of the light is reflected into the photodiode. When the light from the laser is shining completely on a low area, as shown in Figure 34.15*b*), again all the light from the laser is reflected into the photodiode. The light from the laser can also illuminate a high area and a low area at the same time, as depicted in Figure 34.15*c*). In this case, the light that reflects from a low area travels farther than the light reflected from the high area. In both cases the light undergoes a phase change when it is reflected. Thus, we can apply our analysis of destructive interference of a coating on a lens to this case. We assume that the difference in height between the high and low areas is t so that the path length difference for the light from the high and low areas is $2t$. The criterion for destructive interference is

$$\left(m+\frac{1}{2}\right)\frac{\lambda_{air}}{n_{\text{Polycarbonate}}} = 2t \quad \left(m=0, m=\pm1, m=\pm2,...\right) \tag{34.35}$$

where $n_{\text{Polycarbonate}}$ is the index of refraction of polycarbonate in the CD and λ_{air} is the wavelength of the light emitted by the IR laser. For $m = 0$ we have

$$t = \frac{\lambda_{air}}{4n_{\text{Polycarbonate}}}. \tag{34.36}$$

For the CD, $\lambda_{air} = 780\text{ nm}$; therefore the thickness required for destructive interference is

$$t = \frac{\lambda_{air}}{4n_{\text{Polycarbonate}}} = \frac{780\text{ nm}}{4\cdot 1.58} = 123\text{ nm} \tag{34.37}$$

which is very close to the difference of the high and low areas shown in Figure 34.15.

As the CD spins, the high and low areas pass over the laser. When the high or low areas are over the laser, the photodiode produces a constant voltage. When the laser falls on a boundary between the high and low areas, destructive interference occurs and the photodiode signal drops. The electronics of the CD player register this drop. By analyzing the pattern of drops, the electronics can reproduce the digital information encoded in the CD.

A DVD is similar to a CD except the high and low areas are smaller. The distance between tracks on a CD is $1.6\ \mu\text{m}$ while the $0.74\ \mu\text{m}$ separates the tracks on a DVD. In addition, a DVD uses a laser that emits light with a wavelength of 650 nm rather than 780 nm. A CD can hold 650 megabytes of digital information while a DVD can hold 4.7 gigabytes. A Blu-ray disk uses a blue laser with a wavelength of 405 nm and uses a track spacing of 0.30 μm to allow the storage of more data. In addition, the aluminum layer in a Blu-ray disk is closer to the laser than it is in a CD or DVD. A Blu-ray disk can hold 25 gigabytes of digital information.

34.5. Interferometer

An interferometer is a device designed to measure lengths or changes in length using interference of light. An interferometer can measure lengths or changes in lengths to an accuracy of a fraction of the wavelength of the light that it is using. The interferometer works by using interference fringes. Here we will describe an interferometer similar to one constructed by Albert Michelson and Edward Morley at the Case Institute in Cleveland, Ohio in 1887. The interferometer we will describe is simpler than the one used by Michelson and Morley, but is based on the same physical principles.

A photograph and drawing of a commercial interferometer used in physics labs is shown in Figure 34.16.

Figure 34.16: Michelson-type interferometer that is used in an introductory physics laboratory; upper part: photograph; lower part: schematic drawing of the light paths. The laser light is split by the central half-silvered mirror. One part of the light continues in the same direction, is reflected, returns, and is reflected by the half-silvered mirror to the screen. A second part of the light is reflected by the half-silvered mirror, and then reflected back through the half-silvered mirror to the screen.

A more detailed drawing of this same interferometer is shown in Figure 34.17. This particular interferometer consists of a light source in the form of a laser emitting coherent light with wavelength $\lambda = 632.8$ nm. The light passes through a de-focusing lens to spread out the normally very narrowly focused laser beam. The light then passes through a half-silvered mirror m_1. Part of the light is reflected toward the adjustable mirror m_3 and part of the light is transmitted to the movable mirror m_2. The distance between m_1 and m_2 is x_2 and the distance between m_1 and m_3 is x_3. The transmitted light is totally reflected from m_2 back toward m_1. The reflected light is totally reflected from m_3 back toward m_1. Part of the light reflected from m_2 is then reflected by m_1 toward the viewing screen and part of the light is transmitted and not considered. Part of the light from m_3 is transmitted through m_1 and part is reflected and not considered. The actual alignment of the light is such that the two beams that strike the viewing screen are collinear. The separation shown in Figure 34.17 is for clarity.

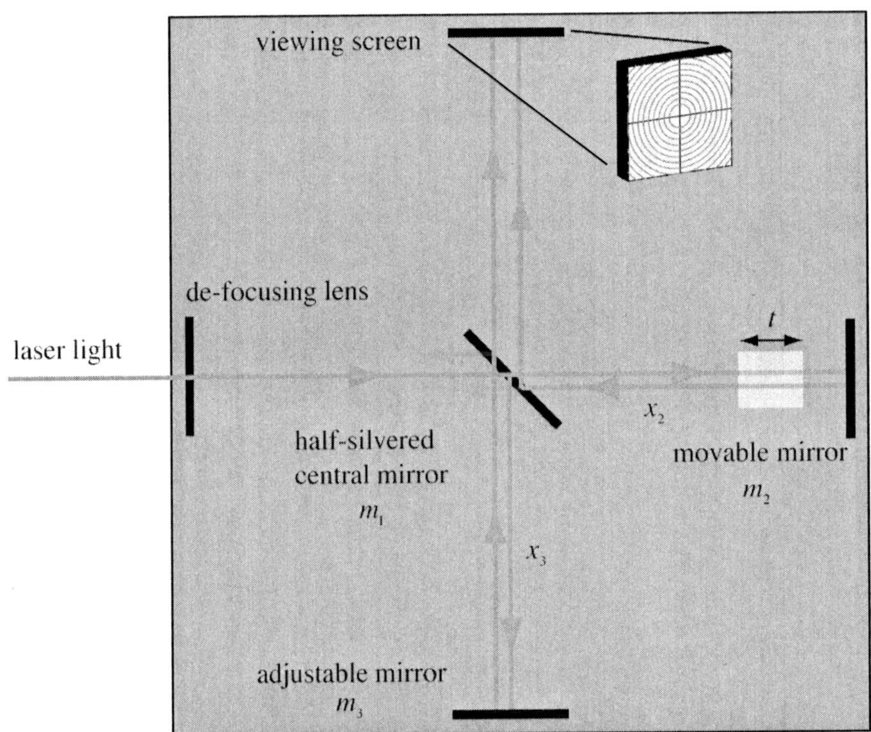

Figure 34.17: Top view of a Michelson-type interferometer showing the detailed light path.

The light from mirrors m_2 and m_3 that strikes the viewing screen will interfere based on their path length difference. Both paths undergo two reflections, each resulting in a phase change of half a wavelength so the condition for constructive interference is

$$\Delta x = m\lambda \quad (m = 0, m = \pm 1, m = \pm 2, \ldots). \tag{34.38}$$

The two different paths will have a path length difference of

$$\Delta x = 2x_2 - 2x_3 = 2(x_2 - x_3). \tag{34.39}$$

The viewing screen will display concentric circles or linear fringes corresponding to constructive and destructive interference depending on the type of de-focusing lens used and the tilt of the mirrors. If the movable mirror m_2 is moved a distance of $\lambda/2$, the fringes will shift by one fringe. Thus, this type of interferometer can be used to measure changes in distance on the order of a fraction of a wavelength of light, depending on how well one can measure the shift of the interference fringes.

Another type of measurement can be made with this interferometer by placing a material with index of refraction n and thickness t in the path of the light traveling to the movable mirror m_2 as depicted in Figure 34.17. The path length difference in terms of the number of wavelengths will change because the wavelength of light in the material λ_n is different from λ. The wavelength in this material is related to the wavelength of light in air by

$$\lambda_n = \frac{\lambda}{n}. \tag{34.40}$$

Thus the number of wavelengths in the material will be

$$N_{material} = \frac{2t}{\lambda_n} = \frac{2tn}{\lambda}. \tag{34.41}$$

The number of wavelength that would have been there if the light traveled through only air is

$$N_{air} = \frac{2t}{\lambda}. \tag{34.42}$$

So the difference in the number of wavelengths is

$$N_{material} - N_{air} = \frac{2tn}{\lambda} - \frac{2t}{\lambda} = \frac{2t}{\lambda}(n-1). \tag{34.43}$$

When the material is placed between m_1 and m_2, an observer will see a shift of one fringe for every wavelength shift in the path length difference. Thus, we can substitute the number of fringes shifted for $N_{material} - N_{air}$ in (34.43) and obtain the thickness of the material knowing the index of refraction. One could also insert material with a well-known thickness and determine the index of refraction.

Self-Test Opportunity: The wavelength of a monochromatic light source is measured using a Michelson interferometer. When the movable mirror is moved a distance $d = 0.250$ mm, $N = 1200$ fringes move by the screen. What is the wavelength of the light?

34.6. Diffraction

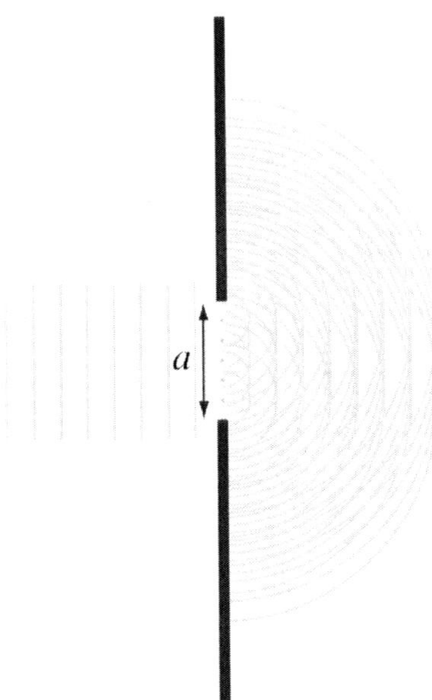

Figure 34.18: Coherent light is incident on an opening with a width comparable to the wavelength of the light. The dots represent sources of spherical wavelets in a Huygens construction.

Any wave passing through an opening will experience diffraction. The diffraction is most noticeable when the opening is about the same size as the wavelength of the wave. The same applies to light waves. Diffraction means that the wave will spread out on the other side of the opening rather than having the opening cast a sharp shadow. In addition, if light passes through a narrow slit, it will produce an interference pattern called a diffraction pattern. Light passing a sharp edge will also exhibit a diffraction pattern.

Figure 34.19: Coherent light is incident on a barrier. The light diffracts around the barrier.

Huygens's principle can describe this spreading out and we can use a Huygens construction to quantify the diffraction phenomenon. For example, in Figure 34.18 we show coherent light incident on an opening, which has dimensions comparable to the wavelength of the light. Rather than casting a sharp shadow, light spreads out on the other side of the opening. We can describe this spreading out by using a Huygens construction and assuming that spherical wavelets are emitted at several points inside the opening. The resulting light waves on the right side of the opening can undergo interference and produce a characteristic diffraction pattern.

Light waves can also encounter barriers such as the one shown in Figure 34.19. In this case, the light far from the edge of the barrier continues to travel like the light waves shown in Figure 34.2. The light near the edge of the barrier seems to bend around the barrier and is described by the sources of wavelets near the edge.

Diffraction phenomena cannot be described by geometric optics. Often diffraction effects rather than geometric effects can limit the resolution of an optical instrument.

34.7. Single-Slit Diffraction

We start our quantitative description of diffraction by studying the diffraction of light through a single slit of width a that is comparable to the wavelength of light that is passing through the slit. We will approach the calculation using a Huygens construction as shown in Figure 34.18.

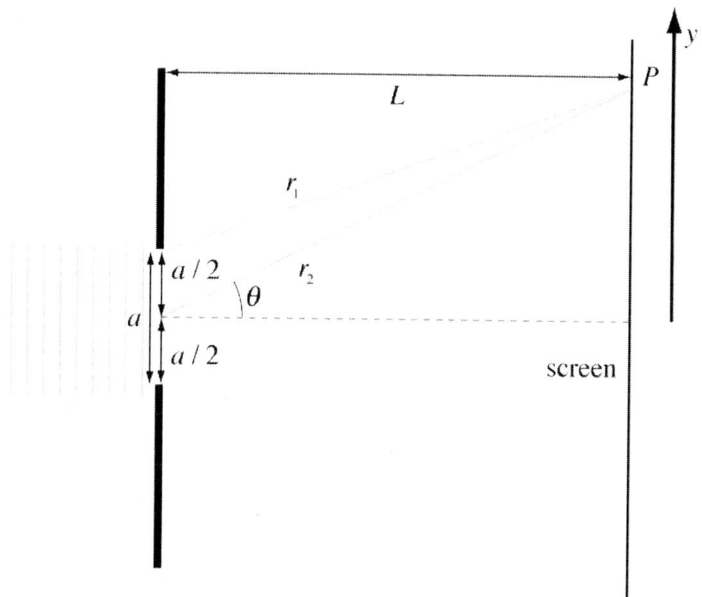

Figure 34.20: Geometry for determining the location of the first dark fringe from a single slit using two rays.

We assume that the light passing through the single slit is described by spherical wavelets emitted from a distribution of points located in the slit. The light emitted from these points will superimpose and interfere based on the path length for each wavelet at each position. At a distant screen, we will observe an intensity pattern characteristic of diffraction. This intensity pattern will consist of bright and dark fringes. For the case of two-slit interference, we were able to work out the equations for the bright fringes based on constructive interference. For diffraction, we will analyze the dark fringes as destructive interference because the constructive interference is beyond the scope of this book.

To study the interference, let's expand and simplify Figure 34.18 as shown in Figure 34.20. We assume that coherent light with wavelength λ is incident on a slit with width a, producing an interference pattern on a screen a distance L away. We employ a simplifying method of analyzing pairs of light waves emitted from points in the slit. We start with light emitted from the top edge of the slit and from the center of the slit as shown in Figure 34.20. To analyze the path difference we show an expanded version of Figure 34.20 in Figure 34.21.

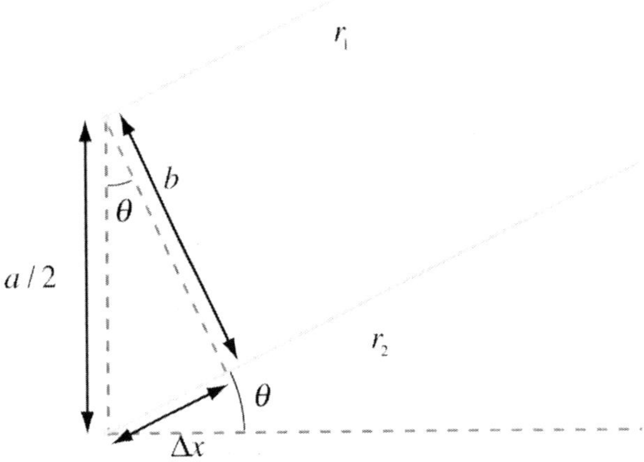

Figure 34.21: Expanded version of geometry for determining the location of the first dark fringe from diffraction from a single slit.

Here we assume that the point P on the screen is far enough away that the rays r_1 and r_2 are parallel and make an angle θ with the central axis. Therefore, the path length difference for these two rays is given by

$$\sin\theta = \frac{\Delta x}{a/2} \tag{34.44}$$

or

$$\Delta x = \frac{a\sin\theta}{2}. \tag{34.45}$$

The criterion for the first dark fringe is

$$\Delta x = \frac{a\sin\theta}{2} = \frac{\lambda}{2}. \tag{34.46}$$

Although we chose one ray originating from the top edge of the slit and one from the middle of the slit to locate the first dark fringe, we could have used any two rays that originated $a/2$ apart inside the slit. All wavelets could be paired up so that the path difference within a pair is $a/2$. (Thus, we have taken into account the entire slit.) Each pair destructively interferes so there remains an overall dark fringe.

Now let's consider four rays instead of two as shown in Figure 34.22.

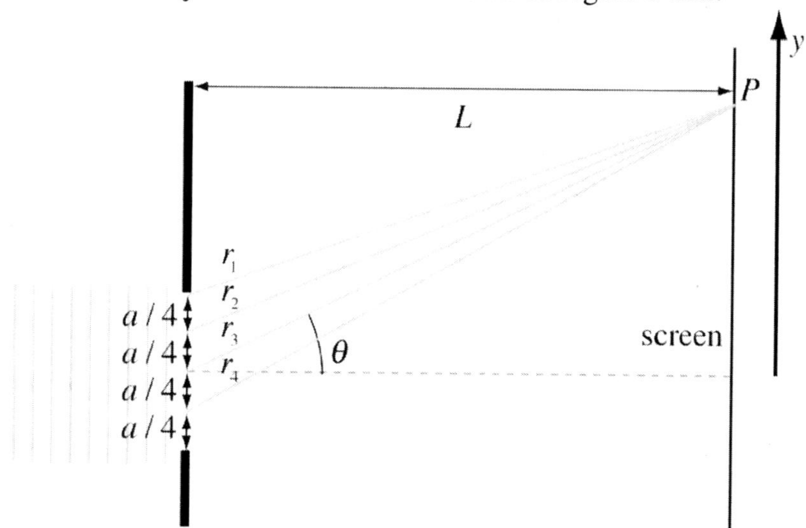

Figure 34.22: Geometry for determining the location of the second dark fringe from a single slit using four rays.

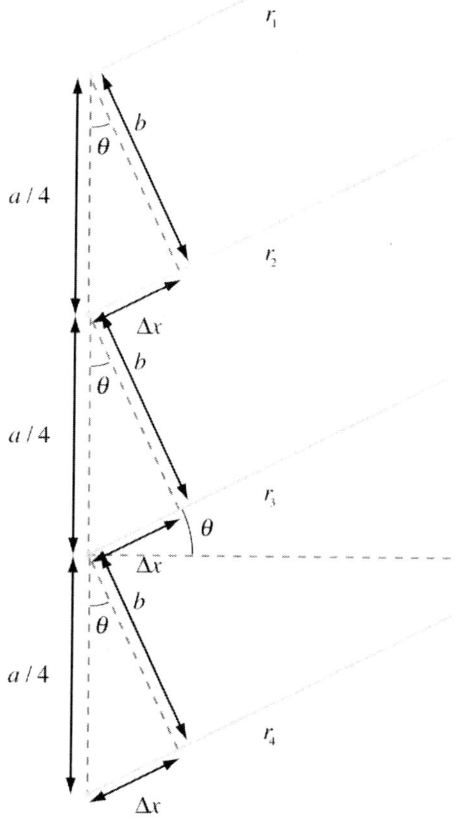

Figure 34.23: Expanded version of geometry for determining the location of the second dark fringe from diffraction from a single slit.

Here we choose a ray from the top edge of the slit and three more rays originating from points spaced $a/4$ apart. We can expand this drawing to represent the case of the screen being far away as shown in Figure 34.23.

Clearly the path length difference between the pairs of rays (r_1,r_2), (r_2,r_3), and (r_3,r_4) is given by

$$\sin\theta = \frac{\Delta x}{a/4} \tag{34.47}$$

or

$$\Delta x = \frac{a\sin\theta}{4}. \tag{34.48}$$

The criterion for a dark fringe is

$$\frac{a\sin\theta}{4} = \frac{\lambda}{2} \tag{34.49}$$

or

$$a\sin\theta = 2\lambda. \tag{34.50}$$

All wavelets could be grouped into four rays similar to those shown in Figure 34.23. Each group destructively interferes so there remains an overall dark fringe. Thus, (34.50) describes the second dark fringe. At this point, we could take six pairs and eight pairs and describe the third and fourth dark fringes, etc. The result is that the dark fringes from single slit diffraction can be described by

$$a\sin\theta = m\lambda \quad (m = 1,2,3,...). \tag{34.51}$$

If the screen is placed a sufficiently large distance from the slits, the angle θ will be small and we can make the approximation $\sin\theta \approx \tan\theta = y/L$. Thus, we can express the position of the dark fringes on the screen as

$$\frac{ay}{L} = m\lambda \quad (m = 1,2,3,...) \tag{34.52}$$

or

$$y = \frac{m\lambda L}{a} \quad (m = 1,2,3,...) \tag{34.53}$$

The intensity of light passing through a single slit can be calculated but we will not present the derivation here. The intensity I relative to I_{max} that we would get if there were no slit is

$$I = I_{max}\left(\frac{\sin\alpha}{\alpha}\right)^2 \tag{34.54}$$

where

$$\alpha = \frac{\pi a}{\lambda}\sin\theta. \tag{34.55}$$

We can see from (34.54) that this expression for the intensity I will be zero for $\sin\alpha = 0$ (unless $\alpha = 0$) which means $\alpha = m\pi$ for $m = 1,2,3,...$ For the special case of $\alpha = 0$ corresponding to $\theta = 0$, we remember that

$$\lim_{\alpha \to 0}\left(\frac{\sin\alpha}{\alpha}\right) = 1. \tag{34.56}$$

We can write

$$m\pi = \frac{\pi a}{\lambda}\sin\theta \quad (m = 1,2,3,...) \tag{34.57}$$

or

$$a\sin\theta = m\lambda \quad (m = 1,2,3,...) \tag{34.58}$$

which gives the same result for the diffraction minima as (34.51).

If the screen is placed a sufficiently large distance from the slits, the angle θ will be small and we can make the approximation $\sin\theta \approx \tan\theta = y / L$. Thus, we can express (34.55) as

$$\alpha = \frac{\pi a y}{\lambda L}. \tag{34.59}$$

If the screen is $L = 2.0$ m away from the slit, the slit has a width of $a = 5.0 \cdot 10^{-6}$ m and the wavelength of the incident light is $\lambda = 550$ nm we get the intensity pattern shown in Figure 34.24.

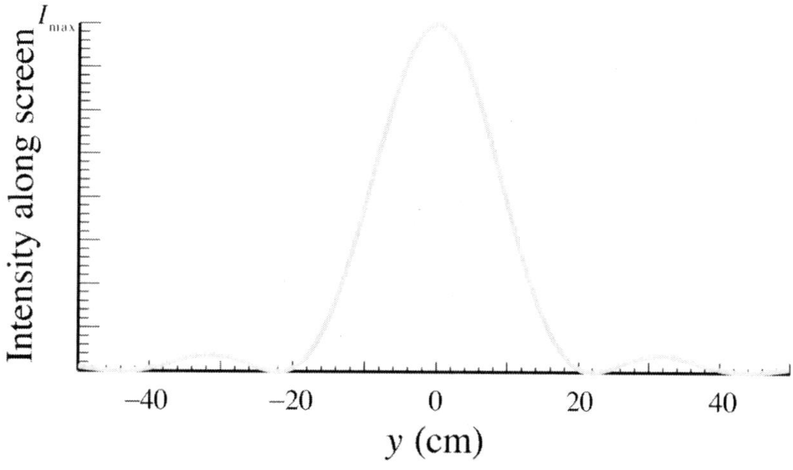

Figure 34.24: Intensity pattern for diffraction through a single slit.

Solved Problem 34.1: Width of central maximum

The single slit diffraction pattern shown in Figure 34.25 was produced with light of wavelength $\lambda = 510.0\ \text{nm}$.

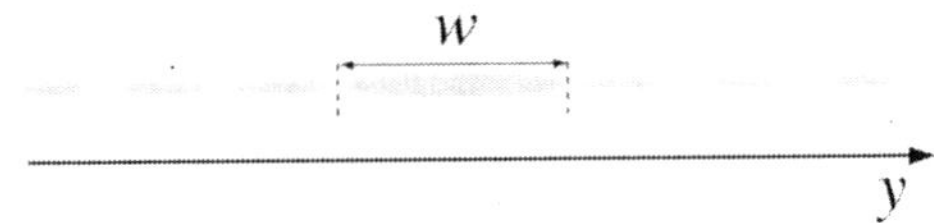

Figure 34.25: Single slit diffraction pattern observed on a screen.

The screen on which the pattern was projected was located a distance $L = 1.40\ \text{m}$ from the slit. The slit had a width of $a = 7.00\ \text{mm}$.

Question:
What is the width w of the central maximum? (The width is equal to the distance between the two first diffraction minima located on either side of the center.)

Answer:

THINK:

The diffraction pattern produced by light incident on a single slit peaks at $y = 0$ and falls to a minimum on both sides of the peak. The first minimum corresponds to $m = 1$. Therefore, the width of the central minimum is equal to twice the y-coordinate of the first minimum.

SKETCH:

A sketch of the single slit diffraction pattern showing the distance from the center of central maximum to the position of the first minimum is shown in Figure 34.26.

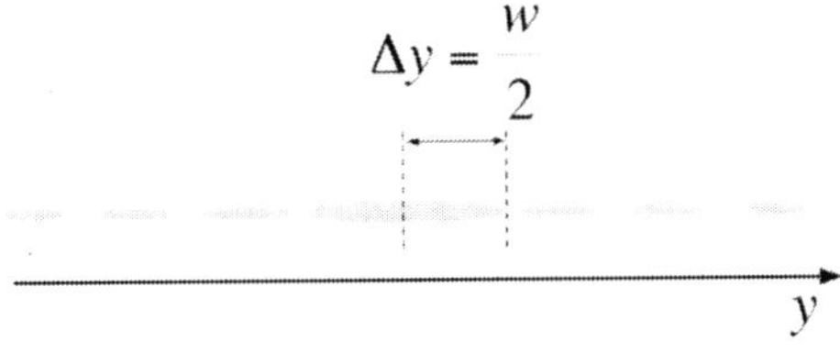

Figure 34.26: Single slit diffraction pattern with the distance from the center of the central maximum to the position of the first diffraction minimum.

RESEARCH:

The location y of the dark fringes along a screen corresponding to diffraction minima are given by

$$y = \frac{m\lambda L}{a} \quad (m = 1,2,3,...) \tag{34.60}$$

where λ is the wavelength of the light incident on the single slit, m is the order of the minimum, L is the distance from the slit to the screen, and a is the width of the screen. For single slit diffraction, the position $y = 0$ corresponds to the position of the central maximum. The first diffraction minimum corresponds to $m=1$. Therefore, the distance Δy from the central minimum to the position of the first minimum is given by

$$\Delta y = \frac{\lambda L}{a}. \tag{34.61}$$

SIMPLIFY:

The width of the central maximum w is then

$$w = 2\Delta y = \frac{2\lambda L}{a}. \tag{34.62}$$

CALCULATE:

Putting in our numerical values gives us

$$w = \frac{2\left(510.0\cdot 10^{-9}\text{ m}\right)\left(1.40\text{ m}\right)}{\left(7.00\cdot 10^{-3}\text{ m}\right)} = 0.000204\text{ m}.$$

ROUND:

We report our result to three significant figures

$$w = 0.000204\text{ m} = 0.204\text{ mm}.$$

DOUBLE-CHECK:

The width of the central maximum projected on the screen is relatively small. A slit that is large compared with the wavelength of light will show little diffraction while a slit that has a width comparable to or smaller than the wavelength of light will a broad diffraction spectrum. The ratio of the wavelength of the light to the slit width is

$$\frac{\lambda}{a} = 510.0\text{ nm} / 7.00\cdot 10^{-3}\text{ m} = 7.23\cdot 10^{-5}.$$

Thus, our answer showing a narrow central maximum seems reasonable.

Solved Problem

34.8. Diffraction by a Circular Opening

We have considered interference through two slits and diffraction through a single slit. Now we consider diffraction of light through a circular opening. Diffraction through a circular opening relates to observing objects with telescopes that have circular mirrors or with cameras that have a circular lens. The resolution of a telescope or camera is limited by diffraction phenomena.

The first diffraction minimum from light with wavelength λ passing through a circular opening with diameter d is given by

$$\sin\theta = 1.22\frac{\lambda}{d} \tag{34.63}$$

where θ is the angle from the central axis through the opening to the first diffraction minimum. This result is similar to the result from a single slit except for the factor of 1.22. We will not derive this expression here.

In Figure 34.27 three different situations are depicted for the observation of two distant point objects using a lens.

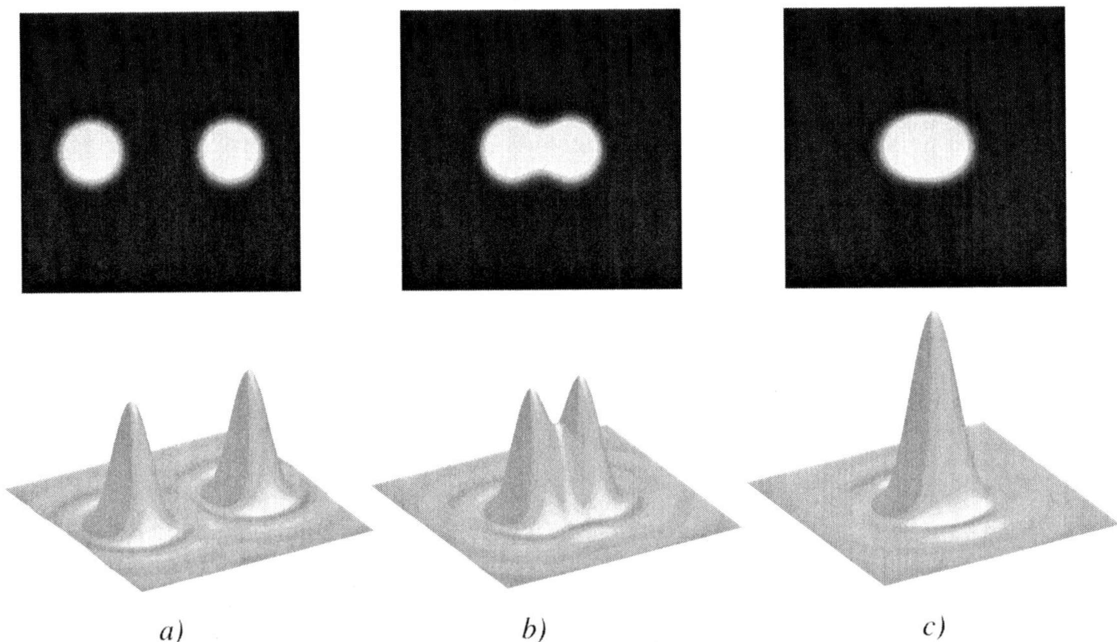

Figure 34.27: Diffraction through a circular opening representing the image one might see with a lens observing two distant point objects: a) the angular separation is large enough to clearly resolve the two object; b) the angular separation is marginally large enough to resolve the two objects; c) the two objects have an angular separation that is too small to allow the objects to be resolved.

In Figure 34.27*a*), the angular separation is clearly large enough to resolve the objects. In Figure 34.27*b*), the angular separation is large enough to just allow one to resolve the objects but not by much. In Figure 34.27*c*), the angular separation is too small to resolve the objects.

If one is using a circular lens to observe two distant point objects, whose angular separation is small (such as two stars), diffraction limits the ability of the lens to distinguish these two objects. The criterion for being able to separate two point objects is based on the idea that if the first image is centered on the first diffraction minimum of the second object, the objects are just resolved. This criterion is called Rayleigh's Criterion and is expressed as

$$\theta_R = \sin^{-1}\left(\frac{1.22\lambda}{d}\right) \tag{34.64}$$

where θ_R is the minimum resolvable angular separation, λ is the wavelength of the light used to observe the objects, and d is the diameter of the lens.

Example 34.2: Rayleigh's criterion for the Hubble Space Telescope

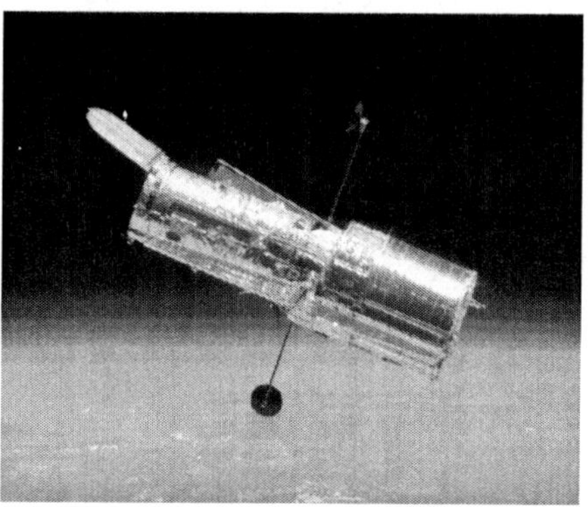

Figure 34.28: The main mirror of the Hubble Space Telescope has a diameter of 2.4 m.

Question:
The diameter of the Hubble Space Telescope (Figure 34.28) is 2.4 m. What is the minimum angular resolution of the Hubble Space Telescope for green light?

Answer:
Using Rayleigh's Criterion with green light of wavelength $\lambda = 550\text{ nm}$ we get

$$\theta_R = 1.22\frac{550\cdot 10^{-9}\text{ m}}{2.4\text{ m}} = 2.8\cdot 10^{-7}$$

which corresponds to the angle subtended by a dime located 64 km away.

When the Hubble Space Telescope was first launched, flaws were discovered in the main mirror that limited its ability to resolve images. A repair mission fixed the mirror so that it now functions at the diffraction limit.

Self-Test Opportunity: Can individual watch towers on the Great Wall of China be seen by astronauts on the Space Shuttle orbiting the Earth at an altitude of 190 km? Assume that the Great Wall is 10.0 m wide.

34.9. Double Slit Diffraction

In section 34.3, we discussed the interference pattern produced by two slits. For that analysis, we assumed that the slits themselves were very narrow compared with the wavelength of light, $a \ll \lambda$. For these narrow slits, the diffraction maximum is very wide and we saw peaks in the intensity that were the same intensity at all angles as depicted in Figure 34.12. There are many sets of double slits for which the condition $a \ll \lambda$ is not met and we observe that not all the interference fringes have the same intensity. With diffraction effects the intensity of the interference pattern from double slits is given by

$$I = I_{max} \cos^2 \beta \left(\frac{\sin \alpha}{\alpha} \right)^2 \tag{34.65}$$

where

$$\alpha = \frac{\pi a}{\lambda} \sin \theta \tag{34.66}$$

and

$$\beta = \frac{\pi d}{\lambda} \sin \theta \tag{34.67}$$

and d is the distance between the slits. If the screen is placed a sufficiently large distance from the slits, the angle θ will be small and we can make the approximation $\sin\theta \approx \tan\theta = y / L$. Thus, we can express (34.66) as

$$\alpha = \frac{\pi a y}{\lambda L} \tag{34.68}$$

and (34.67) as

$$\beta = \frac{\pi d y}{\lambda L}. \tag{34.69}$$

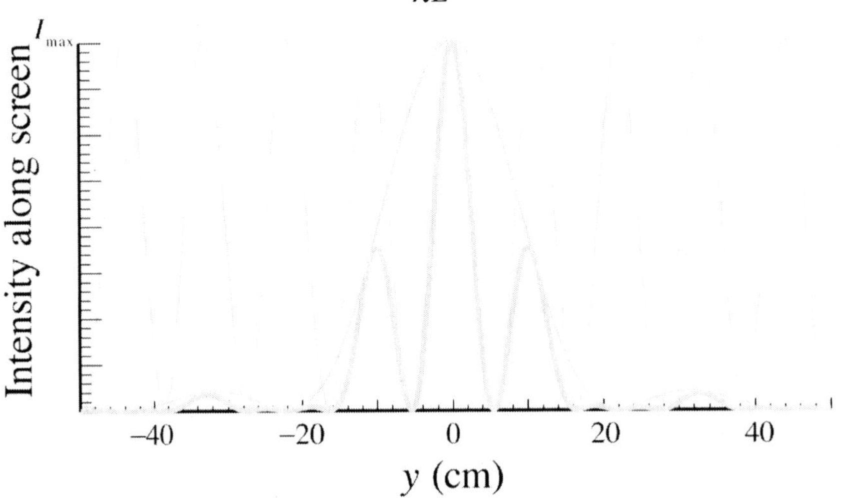

Figure 34.29: Intensity pattern from a double slit. The dark green line is the observed intensity pattern. The faint grey line is the intensity for a single slit with the same width as the two slits. The faint green line is the intensity distribution for two very narrow slits separated by the same distance as the double slit shown in dark green.

If the screen is $L = 2.0$ m away from the slits, each slit has a width of $a = 5.0 \cdot 10^{-6}$ m, the slits are $d = 1.0 \cdot 10^{-5}$ m apart, and the wavelength of the incident light is $\lambda = 550$ nm, we get the intensity pattern shown by the dark green line in Figure 34.29.

In this figure, we see that the positions of the maxima on the screen are not changed from those for the double slit with very narrow slits. However, the maximum intensity is modulated by the diffraction intensity distribution shown in faint grey. The diffraction pattern in Figure 34.29 forms an envelope for the interference intensity distribution. If we covered one of the two slits, we would see only the diffraction pattern. In Figure 34.30, we show a photograph of an interference/diffraction pattern from a double slit projected on a screen using light of wavelength $\lambda = 532$ nm from a green laser.

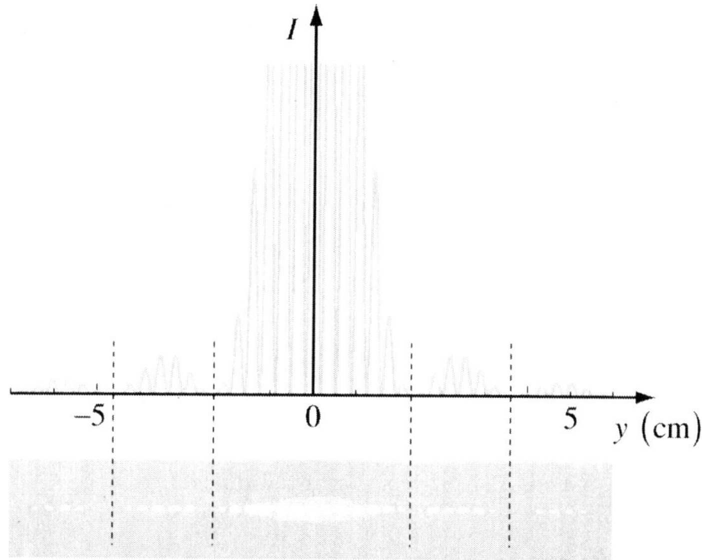

Figure 34.30: Photograph of the intensity pattern produced by a double slit illuminated by green light from a laser. The calculated intensity for the central lines extends above the plotted scale in the vertical direction to allow the lower intensity lines to be visible. The predicted intensity pattern is shown for $a = 0.0452$ mm, $d = 0.300$ mm, and $\lambda = 532$ nm. The dashed lines mark the diffraction minima.

The slits have a width of $a = 4.52 \cdot 10^{-5}$ m and the slits are $d = 3.00 \cdot 10^{-4}$ m apart. The central maxima, which consist of all of the two-slit maxima that reside within the single slit central maximum envelope, are intentionally overexposed in the photograph to allow the secondary maxima to be observed. In Figure 34.30, we also show the predicted intensity pattern at the bottom, effectively overexposed by choosing the maximum value of the plotted intensity to be 38% of the maximum predicted intensity to allow the secondary maxima to be visible. The first two single slit diffraction minima on each side of the central maxima are marked with dashed lines.

34.10. Gratings

We have discussed diffraction and interference for a single slit and for two slits. Now we will discuss the application of diffraction and interference to a system of many slits. Putting many slits together forms a device called a diffraction grating. A diffraction grating has a large number of slits, or rulings, placed very close together. A diffraction grating can also be constructed using an opaque material with grooves rather than actual slits. A diffraction grating produces an intensity pattern that consists of narrow bright fringes separated by wide dark areas. This characteristic pattern results because having many slits means that you can have destructive interference a small distance away from the maxima.

A portion of a diffraction grating is shown in Figure 34.31. In this drawing, we see coherent light with wavelength λ incident on a series of narrow slits each separated by a distance d. A diffraction pattern is produced on a screen a long distance L away.

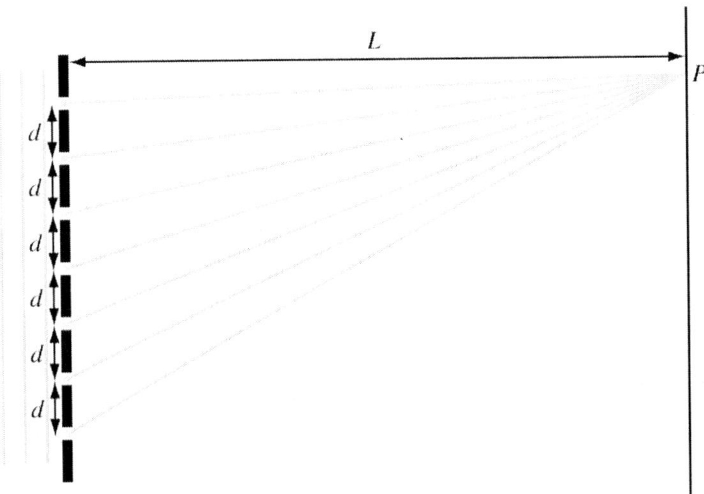

Figure 34.31: A portion of a diffraction grating.

We can expand Figure 34.31 as we did for the single slit and double slit to enable our analysis of the path length difference for the light from each of the slits to the screen as shown in Figure 34.32. We also assume that L is so large that the light rays are approximately parallel to each other.

The distance d is called the grating spacing. If the grating's width is W, the number N of slits or gratings will be

$$N = \frac{W}{d}. \tag{34.70}$$

Diffraction gratings are often specified in terms the number of slits or rulings per unit length n_l. We can obtain d from the specified n_l using

$$d = \frac{1}{n_l}. \tag{34.71}$$

We can calculate the path length differences for the paths shown in Figure 34.32. Using an adjacent pair of rays, the path length difference is

$$\Delta x = d \sin\theta . \tag{34.72}$$

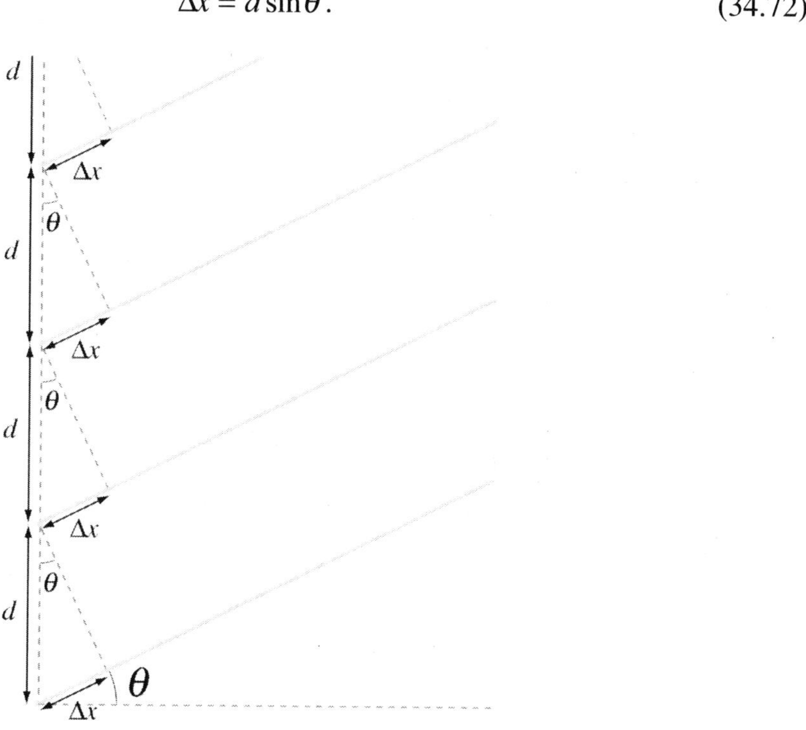

Figure 34.32: Expanded drawing of a diffraction grating assuming that the screen is far away compared to the spacing between the slits of the grating.

To produce bright lines or constructive interference this path length difference must be an integral multiple of the wavelength so

$$d \sin\theta = m\lambda \quad (m = 0,1,2,...). \tag{34.73}$$

The values of m correspond to different bright lines. For $m = 0$ we have the central maximum at $\theta = 0$. For $m = 1$ we have the first order maximum. For $m = 2$ we have the second order maximum, etc. Typically, diffraction gratings are designed to produce large angular separations between the maxima, so we do not make the small angle approximation when discussing diffraction gratings.

Because diffraction gratings produce widely spaced narrow maxima, they can be used to determine the wavelength of monochromatic light by rearranging (34.73)

$$\theta = \sin^{-1}\left(\frac{m\lambda}{d}\right) \quad (m = 0,1,2,...). \tag{34.74}$$

Monochromatic light incident on a diffraction grating will produce lines on a screen at widely separated angles. For example, when a focused laser beam strikes a diffraction grating, a set of widely spaced spots is created.

In addition, diffraction gratings can be used to separate out different wavelengths of light from a spectrum of wavelengths. Sunlight will be dispersed into multiple sets of rainbow-like colors as a function of θ. If the light is composed of several discrete wavelengths, the light will be separated into sets of lines corresponding to each of those wavelengths.

The quality of a diffraction grating can be quantified in terms of its dispersion. The dispersion describes the ability of a diffraction grating to spread apart the various wavelengths in a given order. Dispersion is defined by

$$D = \frac{\Delta\theta}{\Delta\lambda} \qquad (34.75)$$

where $\Delta\theta$ is the angular separation between two lines with wavelength difference $\Delta\lambda$. We can get an expression for the dispersion by differentiating (34.74) with respect to λ

$$\frac{d\theta}{d\lambda} = \frac{d}{d\lambda}\left(\sin^{-1}\left(\frac{m\lambda}{d}\right)\right) = \frac{1}{\sqrt{1-\left(\frac{m\lambda}{d}\right)^2}}\frac{m}{d} = \frac{m}{\sqrt{d^2-(m\lambda)^2}}. \qquad (34.76)$$

We can use (34.73) to get the relation

$$\sin\theta = \frac{m\lambda}{d} \qquad (34.77)$$

which we can substitute back into (34.76) to get

$$\frac{d\theta}{d\lambda} = \frac{1}{\sqrt{1-\sin^2\theta}}\frac{m}{d} = \frac{m}{d\cos\theta} \qquad (34.78)$$

where we have used the identity $\sin^2\theta + \cos^2\theta = 1$. Taking intervals of θ and λ that are not too large, we can write an expression for the dispersion of a diffraction grating

$$D = \frac{\Delta\theta}{\Delta\lambda} = \frac{m}{d\cos\theta} \quad (m = 1,2,3,...). \qquad (34.79)$$

We can see that the dispersion of a diffraction grating increases as the distance d between rulings gets smaller, and as the order m gets higher. Note that the dispersion does not depend on the number of rulings N.

The resolving power R of a diffraction grating describes the ability of the diffraction grating to resolve closely spaced maxima. This ability depends on the width of each maximum. Consider a diffraction grating used to resolve two wavelengths λ_1 and λ_2, with $\lambda_{ave} = (\lambda_1 + \lambda_2)/2$ and $\Delta\lambda = |\lambda_2 - \lambda_1|$. We define the power of the grating as

$$R = \frac{\lambda_{ave}}{\Delta\lambda_{\min}}, \tag{34.80}$$

where $\Delta\lambda_{\min}$ is the minimum value of $\Delta\lambda$ such that the wavelengths are resolved.

In order to discuss the resolving power, we need an expression for the width of each maximum. The width of each maximum is determined by the position of the first minimum on one side of the central maximum. We define the angular half-width θ_{hw} of the maximum as the angle between the maximum and this first minimum as shown in Figure 34.33.

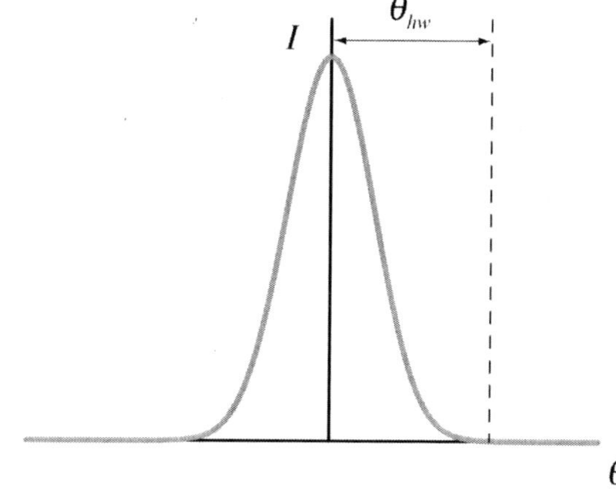

Figure 34.33: The half-width of the central maximum for a diffraction grating.

Equation (34.79) tells us the angular spread for a given $\Delta\lambda$. We can barely resolve the two wavelengths if this spread $\Delta\theta = \theta_{hw}$. To determine the position of the first minimum we do a single slit diffraction analysis using the whole grating as the single slit as shown in Figure 34.34. This approach is justified if the number of slits is large. In any case, it provides a useful and meaningful approximation as opposed to a precise mathematical calculation, which would tend to obfuscate the physics involved.

The angle of the first minimum for single slit diffraction can be obtained from (34.46) where we substitute Nd for the slit width a

$$Nd \sin\theta_{hw} = \lambda . \tag{34.81}$$

Because θ_{hw} is small we can write $\sin\theta_{hw} \approx \theta_{hw}$ or

$$\theta_{hw} = \frac{\lambda}{Nd}. \tag{34.82}$$

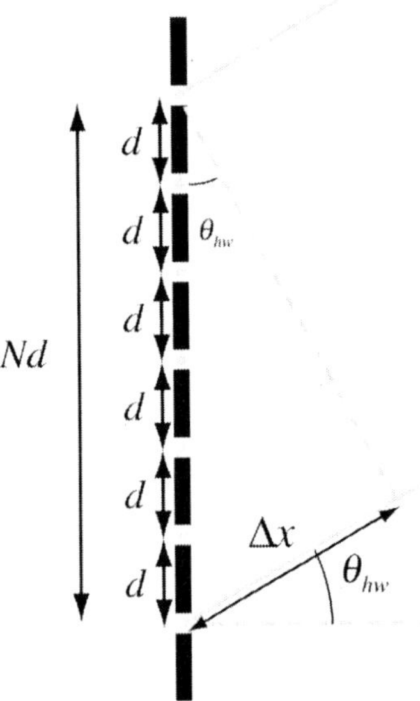

Figure 34.34: Calculation of the half width of the central maximum for a diffraction grating treating the entire grating as a single slit.

One can show that the width of the maxima for other orders can be written as

$$\theta_{hw} = \frac{\lambda}{Nd\cos\theta} \tag{34.83}$$

where θ is the angle corresponding to the maximum intensity for that order. If we substitute θ_{hw} for $\Delta\theta$ in (34.79) we can write

$$\frac{\Delta\theta}{\Delta\lambda} = \frac{\lambda}{Nd\cos\theta\Delta\lambda} = \frac{m}{d\cos\theta} \tag{34.84}$$

or

$$R = \frac{\lambda}{\Delta\lambda} = Nm \tag{34.85}$$

where we have taken $\lambda \approx \left(\lambda + \left(\lambda + \Delta\lambda\right)\right)/2$. Note that the resolving power of a diffraction grating depends on the total number of rulings and the order.

Example 34.3: CD as diffraction grating
A CD can function as a diffraction grating. If we shine a green laser pointer with

wavelength 532 nm perpendicular to the surface a CD, we observe a diffraction pattern in the form of bright spots on a screen located $L = 1.6$ cm away as shown in Figure 34.35 and Figure 34.36. The spacing between the grooves in the CD is $d = 1.60 \cdot 10^{-6}\ \text{m} = 1.6\ \mu\text{m}$.

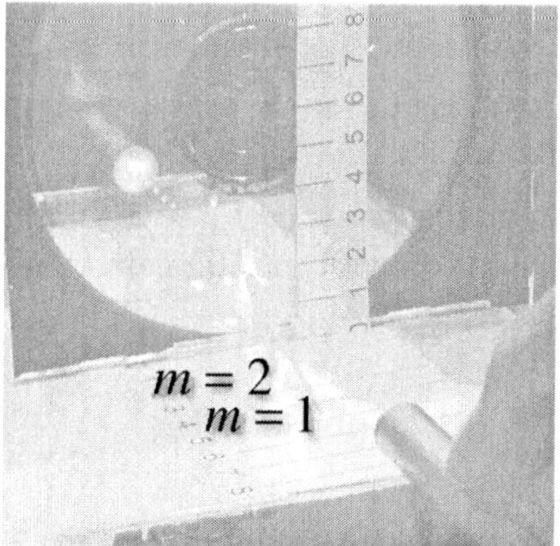

Figure 34.35: Using a CD as a diffraction grating. In the left frame, a photograph is shown of a green laser pointer shining perpendicularly on the bottom surface of a CD. In the right frame, green lines illustrate the light from the laser pointer and the order of each diffraction spots is labeled. The rulers have markings every centimeter.

Example

Question:
What is the distance from the surface of the CD to the spots observed on the screen?

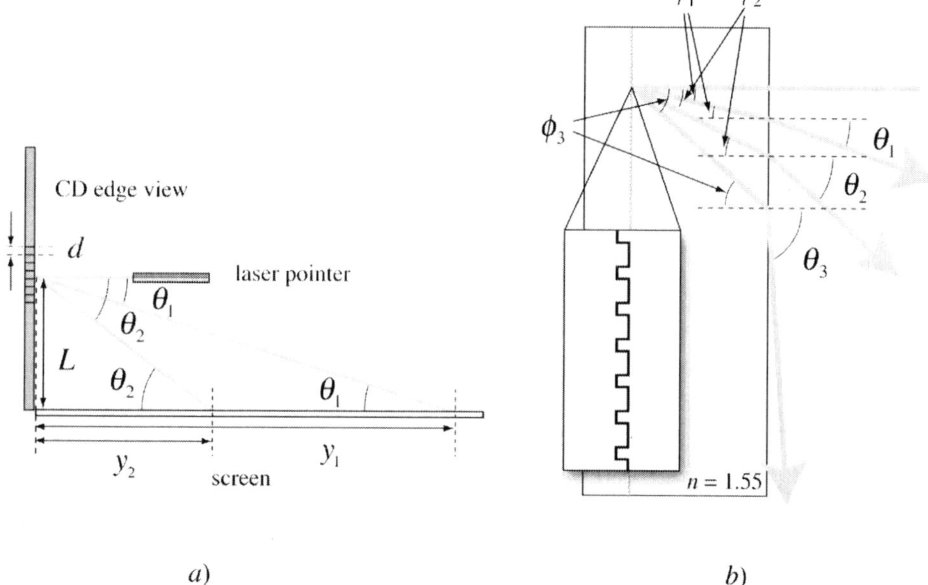

Figure 34.36: Geometry of using a CD as a diffraction grating. In *a)* we illustrate the geometry of the measurement shown in Figure 34.35 in a side-view. A horizontal white screen is used to locate the diffraction maximum. In *b)* we show an expanded drawing of the diffraction grating inside the polycarbonate structure of the CD illustrating the diffraction and refraction that occurs.

Answer:
Diffraction gratings can take the form of a series of narrow slits that light passes through or a series of grooves that reflect light. The resulting diffraction pattern is the same. We

Example

can think of the spiral grooves of a CD as a diffraction grating. We start with our expression for the angle of constructive interference from a diffraction grating

$$d\sin\phi_m = m\lambda \quad (m = 0,1,2,3,...)$$

where d is the distance between adjacent grooves, λ is the wavelength of the light, m is the order, and ϕ_m is the angle of the mth order maximum.

The wavelength that we need for this calculation is the wavelength of light in the polycarbonate plastic that the CD is made from, which has an index of refraction $n = 1.55$

$$\lambda = \frac{\lambda_{air}}{n}.$$

Thus the criteria for diffraction maxima is given by

$$d\sin\phi_m = \frac{m\lambda_{air}}{n}$$

or

$$n\sin\phi_m = \frac{m\lambda_{air}}{d}.$$

This light ray must now pass through the surface of the CD where it will be refracted. Applying Snell's Law at the surface we can get

$$n\sin\phi_m = 1\cdot\sin\theta_m = \sin\theta_m = \frac{m\lambda_{air}}{d}$$

taking $n_{air} = 1$. We can rewrite this equation as

$$d\sin\theta_m = m\lambda_{air},$$

which is exactly what one would have gotten if we had treated the CD as a diffraction grating in air.

Starting with $m = 0$ we find that central maximum produce a spot at $\theta_0 = 0°$ which means that spot will be produced on the front of the laser pointer. One can see this diffraction maximum in the reflection of the laser point from the surface of the CD in Figure 34.36.

Moving to $m = 1$, we find the angle of the first order diffraction maximum, θ_1, using

$$\theta_1 = \sin^{-1}\left(\frac{\lambda_{air}}{d}\right) = \sin^{-1}\left(\frac{532 \cdot 10^{-9}\ \text{m}}{1.60 \cdot 10^{-6}\ \text{m}}\right) = 19.4°.$$

Looking at Figure 34.36*a*), we can see that $\tan\theta_1 = L / y_1$ so we calculate the distance of the first order spot along the screen as

$$y_1 = \frac{1.6\ \text{cm}}{\tan(19.4°)} = 4.54\ \text{cm}.$$

Looking the photograph in Figure 34.35, we can see that this calculation is in good agreement with what we observe for $m = 1$.

The angle of the second order spot is given by

$$\theta_2 = \sin^{-1}\left(\frac{2\lambda_{air}}{d}\right) = \sin^{-1}\left(\frac{2 \cdot 532 \cdot 10^{-9}\ \text{m}}{1.60 \cdot 10^{-6}\ \text{m}}\right) = 41.7°.$$

Thus the position of the second order spot is

$$y_2 = \frac{1.6\ \text{cm}}{\tan(41.7°)} = 1.80\ \text{cm}$$

which is also in good agreement with what we observe for $m = 2$ in Figure 34.35.

The angle of the third order spot is

$$\theta_3 = \sin^{-1}\left(\frac{3\lambda_{air}}{d}\right) = \sin^{-1}\left(\frac{3 \cdot 532 \cdot 10^{-9}\ \text{m}}{1.60 \cdot 10^{-6}\ \text{m}}\right) = 85.9°.$$

The position of the third order spot is

$$y_3 = \frac{1.6\ \text{cm}}{\tan(85.9°)} = 0.11\ \text{cm}.$$

The third order spot is not clearly visible in Figure 34.35 because the third order maximum is dimmer than the first and second maxima and because the angle at which the spot must be observed is very close to $90°$.

What about a fourth order spot? For the angle of the fourth order spot we would have

Example

Example

$$\theta_4 = \sin^{-1}\left(\frac{4\lambda_{air}}{d}\right).$$

However, for the fourth order

$$\frac{4\lambda_{air}}{d} = \frac{4 \cdot 532 \cdot 10^{-9}\ \text{m}}{1.80 \cdot 10^{-6}\ \text{m}} = 1.18$$

which cannot occur because $|\sin\theta| \leq 1$. Therefore, there can be only three spots on the screen, only two of which are easily visible.

If we carried out the same experiment using a common red laser with $\lambda_{air} = 633\ \text{nm}$, we would get only two maxima occurring at $\theta_1 = 23.3°$ and $\theta_2 = 52.3°$.

Self-Test Opportunity: What would happen if we repeated this experiment with a DVD and a green laser pointer?

34.11. X-Ray Diffraction and Structure Experiments

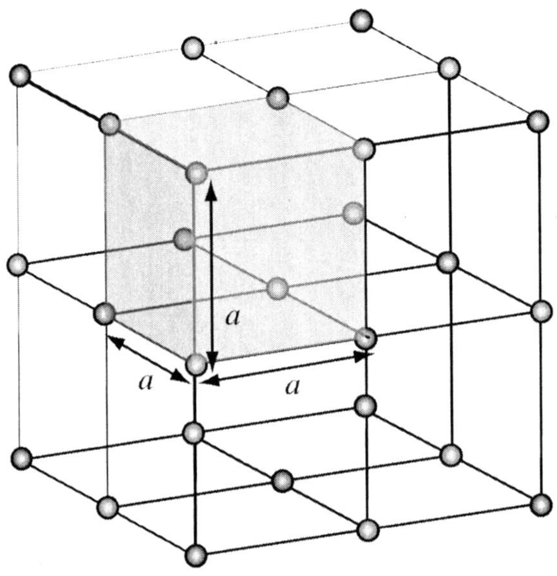

Figure 34.37: A cubic crystal lattice with spacing a.

Wilhelm Röntgen discovered x-rays in the late 1800's. These experiments suggested that x-rays were electromagnetic waves with a wavelength of about $10^{-10}\ \text{m}$. At about the same time, the study of crystalline solids suggested that the atoms of those solids were arranged in a regular repeating pattern with a spacing of about $10^{-10}\ \text{m}$ between the atoms. Putting these two ideas together, Max von Laue proposed in the early 1900's that a crystal could serve as a three dimensional diffraction grating for x-rays. Von Laue and Friederich Knipping did the first x-ray diffraction experiment. It showed diffraction of x-rays by a crystal in 1912. Soon afterwards, Sir William Bragg and his son William Bragg derived Bragg's law and carried out a series of experiments involving x-ray diffraction from crystals.

Let's assume that we have a cubic crystal as shown in Figure 34.37.Each atom in the lattice is a distance a away from its neighboring atom in all three directions. We can imagine various planes of atoms in this crystal. For example, the horizontal planes are composed of atoms spaced a distance a apart with the planes themselves being spaced a distance a from each other. If there are x-rays incident on these planes, we can imagine that the rows of atoms in the crystalline lattice can act like a diffraction grating for the x-rays. The x-rays can be thought of as scattering from the atoms as shown in Figure 34.38.

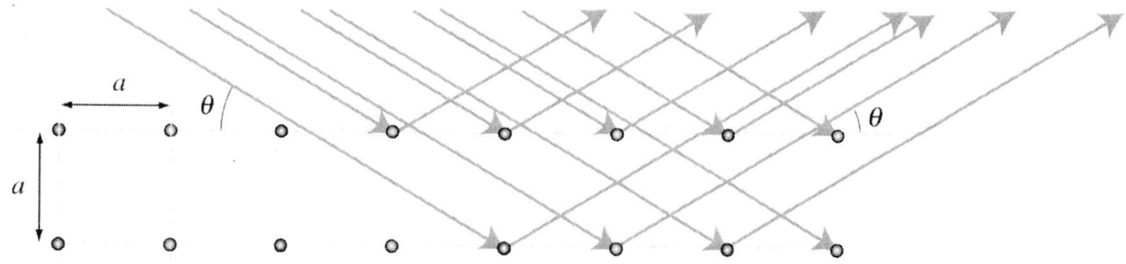

Figure 34.38: Schematic drawing of x-rays scattering off planes of atoms in a crystal.

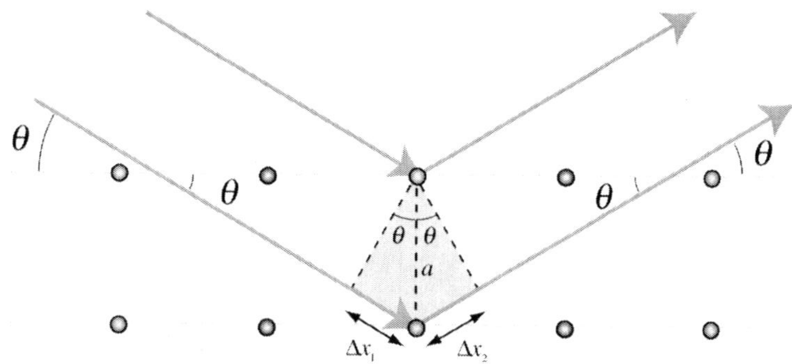

Figure 34.39: Path length difference for x-rays scattered from two adjacent planes.

Interference effects are caused by path length differences. If we look at x-rays scattering off one plane, all the waves remain in phase as long as the incident angle equals the reflected angle. However, if we consider adjacent planes, we can see in Figure 34.39 that the path length difference for the scattered x-rays from the two planes is

$$\Delta x = \Delta x_1 + \Delta x_2 = 2a \sin\theta \qquad (34.86)$$

where θ is the angle between the incoming x-rays and the plane of atoms. Thus, the criterion for constructive interference from Bragg scattering is given by

$$2a\sin\theta = m\lambda \quad (m = 0,1,2,...). \tag{34.87}$$

Of course, when x-rays are incident on a crystal, there can be several different planes that can function as diffraction gratings. Some examples are illustrated in Figure 34.40. These planes will not have the spacing a between the planes.

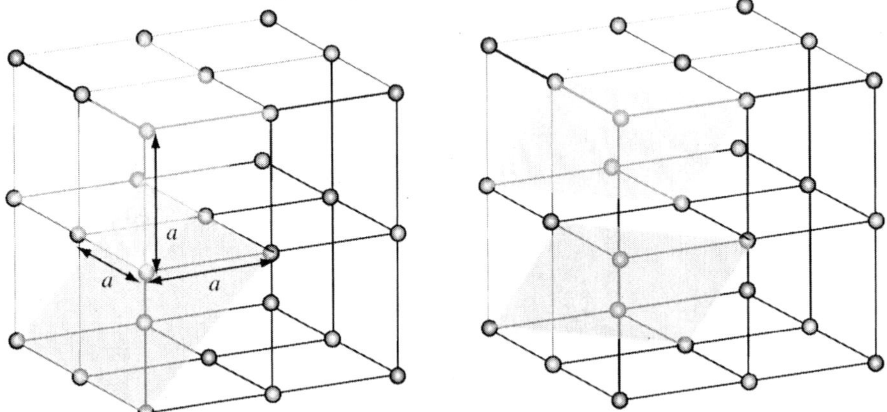

Figure 34.40: Example of planes that could function as diffraction gratings for x-rays in a cubic crystalline lattice.

To study the atomic structure of a substance using x-ray diffraction, one can scatter x-rays that are nearly parallel to the surface of a sample as shown in Figure 34.41*a*). Alternatively, one can transmit the x-rays through the sample and detect the x-rays on the opposite side of the sample as shown in Figure 34.41*b*). For the parallel scattering method, the angle of incidence θ should equal the angle of observation. For the transmission method, the observed angle is twice the Bragg angle θ. By measuring the intensity of the x-rays as a function of θ one can determine details of the structure of the material being studied.

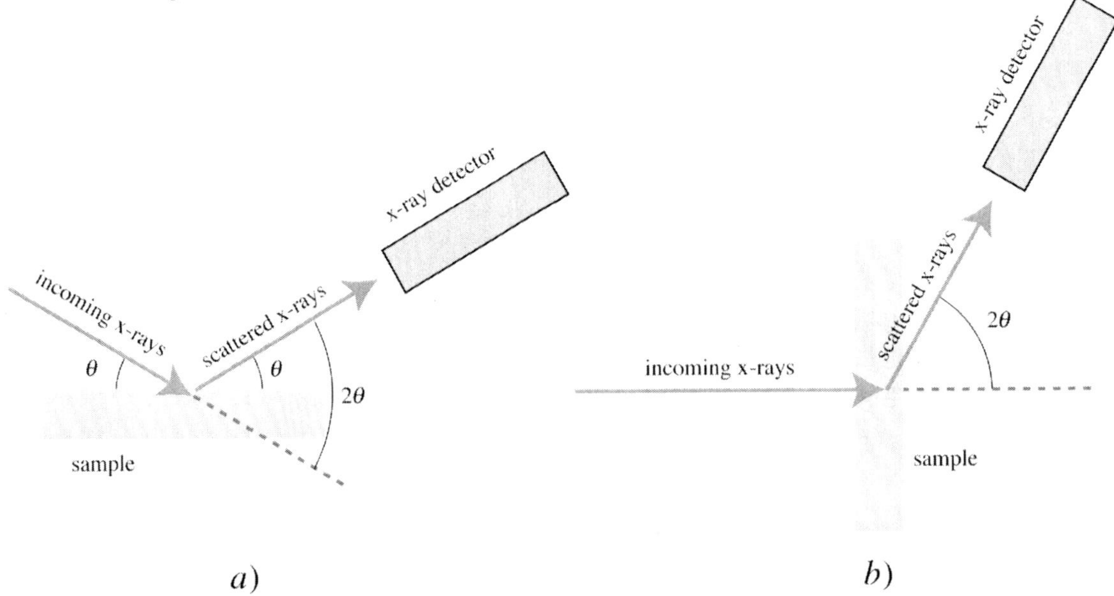

Figure 34.41: Two geometries for studying the atomic structure of a sample using x-ray diffraction. In a) the x-rays are scattered nearly parallel to the surface. In b) the x-rays are transmitted through the sample.

Modern particle accelerators such as the National Synchrotron Light Source at Brookhaven National Laboratory or the Advanced Light Source at Lawrence Berkeley National Laboratory or the Advanced Photon Source at Argonne National Laboratory (see Figure 34.42), and many others around the world, are used to produce high quality, intense beams of x-rays to carry out condensed matter and material science research. In addition, one can gather similar scattering information from bombarding crystalline structures with intense neutron beams. (In order to understand how this works, we have to wait a few more chapters until we examine quantum mechanics). Intense neutron beams for material science research have now become available at the Spallation Neutron Source at Oak Ridge National Laboratory. These huge x-ray and neutron scattering facilities cost hundreds of millions of dollars, but are absolutely essential tools for investigating the nanoscale structure of materials. They are the basic research tools for modern and future nanotechnology advances.

Figure 34.42: Advanced Photon Source (credit: Argonne National Laboratory)

What we have learned/Exam Study Guide:

Most Important Points

- Huygens's principle states that every point on a propagating wave front serves as a source of spherical secondary wavelets. A geometric analysis based on this principle is called a Huygens construction.
- The requirement that two coherent waves with wavelength λ interfere constructively is $\Delta x = m\lambda \; (m = 0, m = \pm 1, m = \pm 2, ...)$ where Δx is the path difference between the two waves.
- The requirement that two coherent waves with wavelength λ interfere destructively is $\Delta x = \left(m + \frac{1}{2}\right)\lambda \quad (m = 0, m = \pm 1, m = \pm 2, ...)$ $\Delta x = m\lambda \; (m = 0, m = \pm 1, m = \pm 2, ...)$ where Δx is the path difference between the two waves.

- The angle of bright fringes from two narrow slits spaced d apart illuminated by coherent light with wavelength λ is given by $d\sin\theta = m\lambda \quad (m=0, m=\pm 1, m=\pm 2,...)$. On a screen a long distance L away, the position y of the bright fringes from the central maximum along the screen is given by $y = \frac{m\lambda L}{d} \quad (m=0, m=\pm 1, m=\pm 2,...)$.
- The angle of dark fringes from two narrow slits spaced d apart illuminated by coherent light with wavelength λ is given by $d\sin\theta = \left(m+\frac{1}{2}\right)\lambda \quad (m=0, m=\pm 1, m=\pm 2,...)$. On a screen a long distance L away, the position y of the dark fringes from the central maximum along the screen is given by $y = \frac{\left(m+\frac{1}{2}\right)\lambda L}{d} \quad (m=0, m=\pm 1, m=\pm 2,...)$.
- The condition for constructive interference for light with wavelength λ_{air} in a thin film of thickness t and index of refraction n in air is $\left(m+\frac{1}{2}\right)\frac{\lambda_{air}}{n} = 2t \quad (m=0, m=\pm 1, m=\pm 2,...)$.
- The angle of dark fringes from a single slit of width a illuminated by light with wavelength λ is given by $a\sin\theta = m\lambda \quad (m=1,2,3,...)$.
- The angle θ of the first minimum from a circular aperture with diameter d illuminated with light of wavelength λ is $\sin\theta = 1.22\frac{\lambda}{d}$. This angle is also called Rayleigh's Criterion expressing the minimum resolvable angle for a telescope or camera lens with diameter d.
- The angle θ of the maxima from a diffraction grating illuminated with light of wavelength λ is given by $\theta = \sin^{-1}\left(\frac{m\lambda}{d}\right) \quad (m=0,1,2,...)$ where d is the distance between the rulings of the grating.
- The dispersion of a diffraction grating is given by $D = \frac{m}{d\cos\theta} \quad (m=1,2,3,...)$ where d is the distance between the rulings of the grating.
- The resolving power of a diffraction grating is given by $R = Nm \quad (m=1,2,3,...)$ where N is the number of rulings in the grating.
- For x-rays scattering off planes of atoms separated by a distance a, the condition for constructive interference is $2a\sin\theta = m\lambda \quad (m=0,1,2,...)$. The angle θ is the angle of incidence and the angle of observation of the x-rays.

New Symbols used in this Chapter

- Δx is the path length difference.
- N is the number of rulings in a diffraction grating.
- n_l is the number of rulings per unit length for a diffraction grating.
- D is the dispersion of a diffraction grating.
- R is the resolving power of a diffraction grating.

Additional Solved Problems

Solved Problem

Solved Problem 34.2: Spy satellite

You have been assigned the job of designing a camera lens for a spy satellite. This satellite will orbit the Earth at an altitude of 201 km. The camera is sensitive to light with a wavelength 607 nm. The camera must be able to resolve objects on the ground that are 0.490 m apart.

Question:
What is the minimum diameter of the lens?

Answer:

THINK:

This camera lens will be diffraction limited. We can apply Rayleigh's criterion to calculate the minimum diameter of the lens given the angle subtended by two objects on the ground as viewed from the spy satellite orbiting above.

SKETCH:

A sketch of the spy satellite observing two objects on the ground is shown in Figure 34.43.

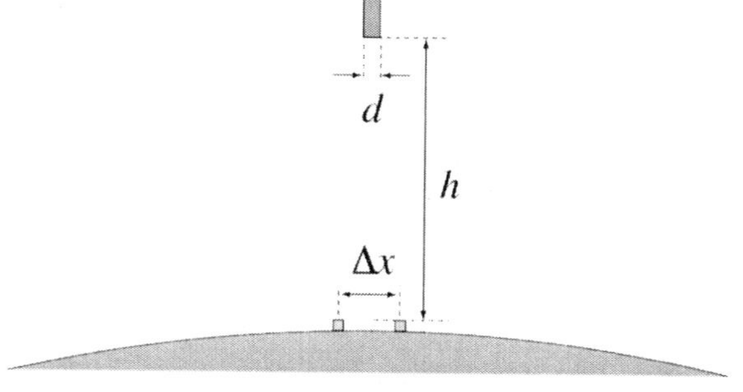

Figure 34.43: A spy satellite observing two objects on the ground.

RESEARCH:

The Rayleigh criterion for resolving two objects separated by an angle θ_R using light with wavelength λ is given by

$$\theta_R = \sin^{-1}\left(\frac{1.22\lambda}{d}\right) \qquad (34.88)$$

where d is the diameter of the circular camera lens in the spy satellite. The angle required for the performance requirement of the spy satellite is given by

$$\theta_s = \tan^{-1}\left(\frac{\Delta x}{h}\right) \tag{34.89}$$

where Δx is the distance between the two objects on the ground and h is the height of the spy satellite above the ground.

SIMPLIFY:

We can equate θ_R and θ_s to get

$$\sin^{-1}\left(\frac{1.22\lambda}{d}\right) = \tan^{-1}\left(\frac{\Delta x}{h}\right). \tag{34.90}$$

Solving for the diameter of the camera lens gives us

$$d = \frac{1.22\lambda}{\sin\left(\tan^{-1}\left(\frac{\Delta x}{h}\right)\right)}. \tag{34.91}$$

CALCULATE:

Putting in our numerical values gives us

$$d = \frac{1.22\left(607 \cdot 10^{-9} \text{ m}\right)}{\sin\left(\tan^{-1}\left(\frac{0.490 \text{ m}}{201 \cdot 10^{3} \text{ m}}\right)\right)} = 0.30377 \text{ m}$$

ROUND:

We report our result to three significant figures

$$d = 0.304 \text{ m}.$$

DOUBLE-CHECK:

To double-check our result, we make the small angle approximation for the Rayleigh criterion and the angle subtended by the two objects. For the case where the wavelength of light is much smaller than the aperture of the camera, we can write

$$\sin\left(\theta_R\right) = \frac{1.22\lambda}{d} \approx \theta_R.$$

For the angle seen by the camera in the spy satellite we can write

Solved Problem

$$\tan(\theta_s) = \frac{\Delta x}{h} \approx \theta_s .$$

Thus we can write

$$\frac{1.22\lambda}{d} = \frac{\Delta x}{h}$$

which we can solve for the minimum diameter of the camera lens

$$d = \frac{1.22\lambda h}{\Delta x} = \frac{1.22\left(607 \cdot 10^{-9} \text{ m}\right)\left(201 \cdot 10^{3} \text{ m}\right)}{0.490 \text{ m}} = 0.304 \text{ m}$$

which agrees with our result within round-off errors. Thus, our result seems reasonable.

Solved Problem 34.3: Air wedge

Light of wavelength $\lambda = 516$ nm is incident perpendicularly on two glass plates. The glass plates are spaced at one end by a thin piece of kapton film. Due to the wedge of air created by this film, 25 bright interference fringes are observed across the top plate with a dark fringe at the end by the film.

Question:

How thick is the film?

Answer:

THINK:

Light passes through the top plate reflects from the bottom plate and then interferes with the reflected incoming light. There is a phase change when the light is reflected from the bottom plate so that the criterion for constructive interference is that the path length is equal to an integer plus one half times the wavelength. The criterion for destructive interference is that the path difference is an integer times the wavelength.

SKETCH:

A sketch showing the two glass plates with a thin piece of film separating the plates at one end is shown in Figure 34.44. Light is incident vertically from the top.

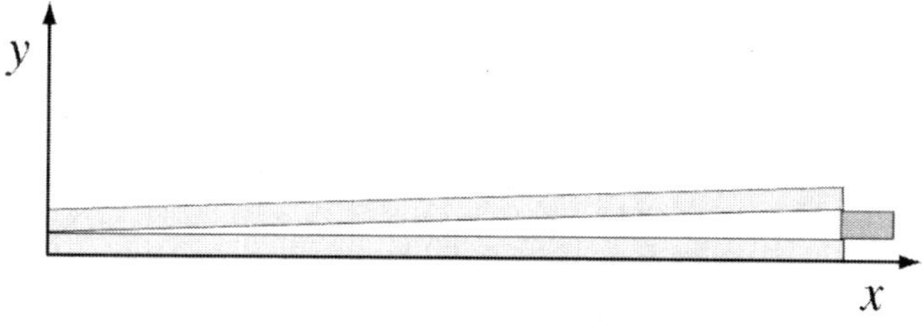

Figure 34.44: Two glass plates with a thin film separating the plates at one end. Light is incident vertically from the top.

Solved Problem

RESEARCH:

At any point along the plates, the criterion for constructive interference is given by

$$2t = \left(m + \tfrac{1}{2}\right)\lambda \tag{34.92}$$

where t is the separation between the plates, m is an integer, and λ is the wavelength of the incident light. There are 25 bright fringes visible. The first bright fringe corresponds to $m = 0$ and the 25th bright fringe corresponds to $m = 24$. Immediately past the 25th is a dark fringe where the piece of film is located. The criterion for destructive interference is $2t = n\lambda$, where n is an integer.

SIMPLIFY:

The dark fringe located at the end of the glass plate where the film is located is given by

$$2t = \left(24 + \frac{1}{2} + \frac{1}{2}\right)\lambda = 25\lambda \tag{34.93}$$

where the factor $\left(24 + \tfrac{1}{2}\right)$ describes the constructive interference and the extra $\tfrac{1}{2}$ produces the dark fringe at the end of the plate with the film. Thus we can solve for the separation of the plates, which corresponds to the thickness of the film

$$t = \frac{25}{2}\lambda. \tag{34.94}$$

CALCULATE:

Putting in our numerical values gives us

$$t = \frac{25}{2}\left(516 \cdot 10^{-9}\text{ m}\right) = 0.00000645\text{ m}$$

ROUND:

We report our result to three significant figures

$$t = 6.45 \cdot 10^{-6}\text{ m}.$$

DOUBLE-CHECK:

The thickness of 6.5 μm is reasonable for thin kapton film. Thus, our answer seems reasonable.

Chapter 35. Relativity

What we will learn:

- Light always moves at the same speed in vacuum, independent of the velocity of the source or the observer.
- The two postulates of special relativity are that the speed of light is an invariant constant and that all physical laws are the same in all inertial reference frames, which are reference frames in which there is no acceleration of an object if there is no net force on it.
- The speed of light is an upper limit for the speed of all moving objects.
- From the postulates of special relativity it follows that time and space measurements are different for different observers who move relative to each other.
- At high speeds, we need to use the Lorentz transformation between reference frames instead of the Galilean transformation.
- Velocities cannot be added linearly. Velocity addition needs to follow the Lorentz transformation and it does conform to the postulate that the speed of light cannot be exceeded.

- Kinetic energy and momentum need to have new definitions and a new relationship with each other.
- All of Newtonian mechanics evolves from relativistic mechanics as a limiting case for speeds small compared to the speed of light.

35.1. Ether

Sound waves and mechanical waves need a medium in which to propagate, as we have seen in chapters 15 and 16 on waves and sound. When we talked about electromagnetic waves (chapter 31), we saw that light is an electromagnetic wave. We also found out that all electromagnetic waves can propagate through a vacuum. However, this knowledge is relatively new in science, only about 100 years old. Up until 1887, scientists believed that light would also need a medium in which to propagate, and they called this medium the ether. Of course, this idea of the ether brought up the question what exactly that medium was. Light from very distant stars and galaxies reaches our eyes and thus is able to propagate outside of the Earth's atmosphere. This observation implies that all of space was filled with this medium. How could one detect it?

If all of space were filled with ether, then Earth would have to move relative to this ether on its path around the sun. When we discussed relative motion in our discussion of kinematics, we found that the motion of the medium makes a clear difference to a trajectory. For example, an airplane moving through wind has a different ground speed when it moves perpendicular to the wind as opposed to when it moves with the wind or against the wind. In addition, we have seen the same basic principle at work with the propagation of sound waves though a medium.

In the 19th century, huge efforts were made to measure the speed of light. From the point of view of science history, this quest is a fascinating story in itself. However, for the present purpose we do not even need the precise number for the speed of light. The only thing that we need to know is that the motion of the Earth relative to the ether would imply different speeds of light measured in the lab, depending on whether the light moved with or against the ether or perpendicular to the ether. This effect is exactly what Albert Michelson and Edward Morley at the Case Institute in Cleveland, Ohio, set out to measure in 1887. They constructed an ingenious device based on interferometry, a topic which we examined in the previous chapter on wave optics, where we also showed a picture of a Michelson-type interferometer.

What they found stunned the world of physics: a null result! Light moves with exactly the same speed in every direction, and no motion relative to the ether could be detected.

People struggled with an explanation for this astounding result, and Lorentz and Fitzgerald came up with the idea that objects moving through the ether become length-contracted when they move through the ether. It took the genius of Albert Einstein, however, to make the conceptual leap required for the new insight and its astounding consequences: the ether does not exist. Thinking through the fact that the speed of light is constant for all observers independent of the observer's motion led Einstein much further to the formulation of the theory of relativity, the topic of this chapter.

35.2. Einstein's Postulates and Reference Frames

Insert: Einstein

It was the year 1905. A 26-year old Swiss patent clerk fresh out of a rather undistinguished university physics career wrote three articles in scientific journals that shook the scientific world. In addition, he did this in his spare time! These three papers were:

1. A paper explaining the so-called *photoelectric effect* as due to the quantum nature of light. This earned him the Nobel Prize in 1922. We will come back to this effect in the next chapter on quantum physics.
2. A paper explaining the effect of Brownian motion, the motion of very small particles in water or other solutions, as due to collisions with molecules and atoms. This result proved that atoms really exist. (This fact was not at all clear before his work.) This work was also worthy of a Nobel Prize.
3. Finally, the most important of all (in the opinion of the authors): the theory of special relativity.

Figure 35.1: Albert Einstein on the cover of Time Magazine.

1905 was called the *annus mirabilis* (miracle year) of physics because of these three papers that were all published in the same volume of the journal Annalen der Physik. Einstein (Figure 35.1) became the symbol for quintessential archetypical scientist, a synonym for genius. Time magazine selected him as the Person of the Twentieth Century.

Einstein was a German and a Jew. As such, he stood at the intersection of the most powerful political movements of the 20th century, the clash between fascism and democracy. The German fascists needed a unifying enemy and made Jews the lightning rod of their aggression. This situation forced Einstein to flee to the U.S. and become an American. In writing his famous letter to President F. D. Roosevelt, he set in motion the largest-ever military-industrial machinery, the Manhattan Project that built the first atomic bomb.

1879 Born in Ulm, Germany (March 14)
1902 Begins work at Swiss patent office
1905 Publishes the three seminal papers on theoretical physics
1916 Proposes general theory of relativity
1919 General relativity is consistent with measurements made during a solar eclipse
1922 Awarded Nobel Prize in Physics
1933 Emigrates to US (Princeton, N.J.)
1939 Urges F. D. Roosevelt to develop atom bomb
1955 Dies in his sleep (April 18)

What exactly did Einstein postulate, from which all of relativity followed? First we will define an inertial reference frame as a reference frame in which an object accelerates only when there is a net external force acting on it. Unless we state otherwise the phrase 'reference frame' in this chapter refers to an inertial reference frame.

Postulate 1:

The laws of physics are the same in every inertial reference frame, independent of the motion of this reference frame.

Postulate 2:

The speed of light c is the same in every inertial reference frame.

The value of the speed of light is:

$$c = 299{,}792{,}458 \text{ m/s} \tag{35.1}$$

As we stated in our first chapter in this book, the value for the speed of light quoted here is the exact value, because it serves as the basis for the definition for the SI unit of the meter. Handy approximate values for the speed of light are $c \approx 186{,}320$ miles/s in British units or the very commonly used $c \approx 3 \cdot 10^8$ m/s.

The first one of the two postulates should not raise any objections. In its motion around the Sun, the Earth moves through space with a speed of more than $29 \text{ km/s} \approx 65{,}000 \text{ mph}$. Because we are moving very nearly in a circle, our velocity vector relative to the Sun continually changes direction. But we still expect that a physics measurement will follow laws of nature that are independent of the season in which the measurement was made (neglecting minor effects due to the small accelerations of the Earth and the Sun relative to the Milky Way)!

The second postulate explains what Michelson and Morley measured. However, this idea is not quite so easy to digest. Let's conduct a thought experiment: You fly in a rocket through space with a speed of $c/2$, directly towards Earth. Now you shine a laser in the forward direction. The light of the laser has a speed c. Naively, and with what we know about velocity addition so far, we would expect that the light of the laser would have a speed of $c + c/2 = 1.5c$ when observed on Earth. This result is what we learned in the section on relative motion in chapter 3.

This velocity addition, however, only works for speeds that are small relative to the speed of light. Einstein's second postulate says that the speed of light as seen on Earth is still c. Later in this chapter, we will actually give a rule for velocity addition that explains the desired result. However, for now we note that this constant c is the maximum possible speed that any object can have in any reference frame. This statement is astounding and leads to all kinds of interesting and borderline unbelievable consequences. All of these consequences have, however, been experimentally verified by now. Therefore, we now know that this theory is almost certainly correct. We may never think of space and time the same way again!

Self-Test Opportunity: A light-year is the distance light travels in a year. Calculate that distance in meters.

Beta and Gamma

Because the speed of light plays such an important role, we will introduce two commonly used dimensionless quantities that depend only on the (constant) speed of light c and the velocity v of an object (which we assume here to be a velocity component which is positive):

$$\beta = \frac{v}{c} \tag{35.2}$$

and

$$\gamma = \frac{1}{\sqrt{1-\beta^2}} = \frac{1}{\sqrt{1-(v/c)^2}}. \tag{35.3}$$

Because we always have the condition $v \le c$ from the second postulate, this definition means that $\beta \le 1$ and $\gamma \ge 1$.

It is instructive to plot γ as a function of β. This plot is shown in Figure 35.2. For speeds that are small compared to the speed of light, β is very small, approximately equal to zero. In that case, γ is very close to the value 1. However as β approaches 1, γ *diverges,* that is to say γ grows larger and larger and eventually becomes infinite when $\beta = 1$.

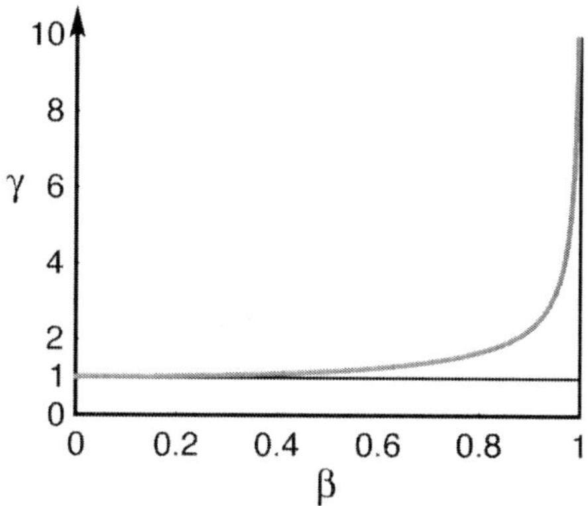

Figure 35.2: Dependence of γ on β.

There is also a useful approximation that is valid for low speeds. In that case, v is small compared to c and therefore β is small compared to 1, and by using the mathematical series expansion $(1-x^2)^{-1/2} = 1 + \frac{1}{2}x^2 + \frac{3}{8}x^4 + ...$ we can approximate γ as:

$$\gamma \approx 1 + \tfrac{1}{2}\beta^2 = 1 + \tfrac{1}{2}\left(\frac{v}{c}\right)^2 \text{ (for } \beta \text{ small compared to 1)} \tag{35.4}$$

Self-Test Opportunity: At what fraction of the speed of light would relativistic effects be a 5% effect? At what fraction of the speed of light would relativistic effects be a 50% effect?

Example

Example 35.1: Apollo spacecraft

On their way to the moon, the Apollo spacecraft reached speeds of 40,000 km/h, almost an order of magnitude (10 times) faster than any airplane.

Question:

What are the values of the relativistic factors β and γ in this case?

Answer:

Let us first convert the speed to SI units:

$$v = 40{,}000 \text{ km/h} = 40{,}000 \text{ km/h} \cdot (1000 \text{ m/km})/(3600 \text{ s/h}) \approx 11{,}000 \text{ m/s}$$

To compute β we simply have to divide the spacecraft's speed by that of the speed of light:

$$\beta = \frac{v}{c} = \frac{1.1 \cdot 10^4 \text{ m/s}}{2.9979 \cdot 10^8 \text{ m/s}} = 3.7 \cdot 10^{-5}$$

Now we simply plug in this result into our formula for γ and obtain:

$$\gamma = \frac{1}{\sqrt{1-\beta^2}} = \frac{1}{\sqrt{1-(3.7 \cdot 10^{-5})^2}} = 1 + 6.8 \cdot 10^{-10} = 1.00000000068$$

From this example you can see that almost all motion of macroscopic objects involves values of β that are very close to zero and values of γ that are very close to one. In all such cases, we will see throughout this chapter that it is safe to neglect the effects of relativity and calculate in the non-relativistic approximation. However, in many interesting cases you need to keep relativity in mind. This difference is the subject of this chapter.

Light Cone

As a corollary of the two Einstein postulates we find that nothing can propagate with a speed greater than the speed of light, because in that object's reference frame light could not be sent into our reference frame, in contradiction to Einstein's second postulate. This also means that there are limits on how events can influence each other. We cannot exchange signals with each other at speeds exceeding the speed of light. Therefore instantaneous effects of events originating from one point in space on another point in space are impossible. It simply takes times for a signal or cause-and-effect to propagate through space.

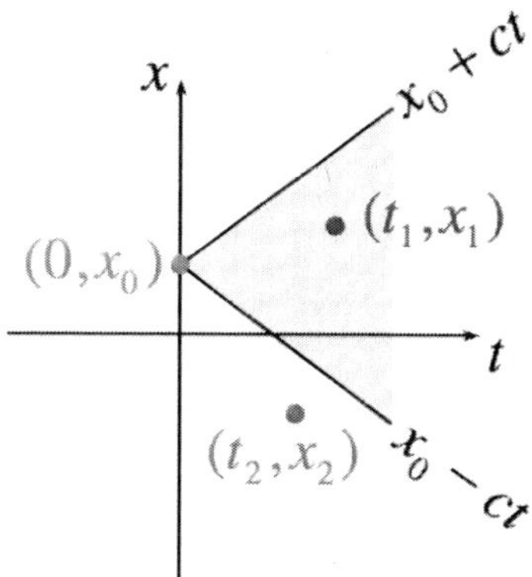

Figure 35.3: Light cone of a point in space.

Let's start our discussion by examining the one-dimensional case shown in Figure 35.3. An event is happening at time 0 at location $x = x_0$ (red dot). The signal that this event occurred at that location in space and instant in time can only propagate with at most the speed of light, i.e. velocity in the interval between $v = -c$ and $v = +c$. We use the tan color triangle to show the region in space in which the event can be noticed as a function of time. This region in Figure 35.3 is called the "positive light cone" of the event $(0, x_0)$. The blue point located at time t_1 and position x_1 is able to receive a signal that the original event has happened, the green point located at time t_2 and position x_2, however, is not. This implies that the event represented by the red dot cannot possibly have caused the event represented by the green dot in Figure 35.3. The two events, red and blue, cannot be causally connected!

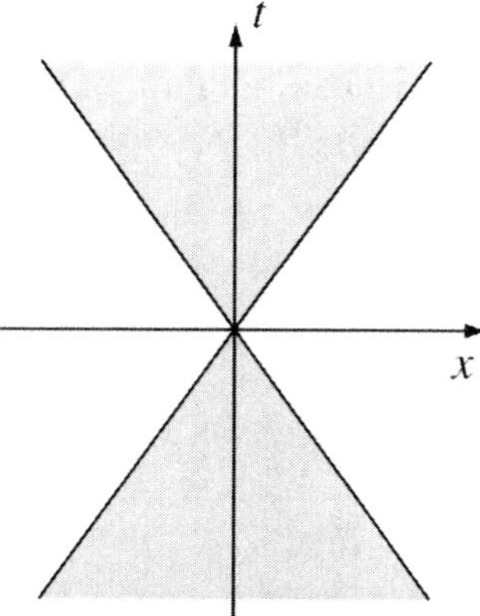

Figure 35.4: Conventional representation of the light cone, with the time axis pointing vertically up.

Conversely, there is also a region in the past that is able to influence the event at $(0, x_0)$. This region is the "negative light cone". In Figure 35.4 we show both light cones in the conventional representation of a vertical time axis. The event, for which the light cone is displayed, is conveniently moved to the origin of the coordinate system.

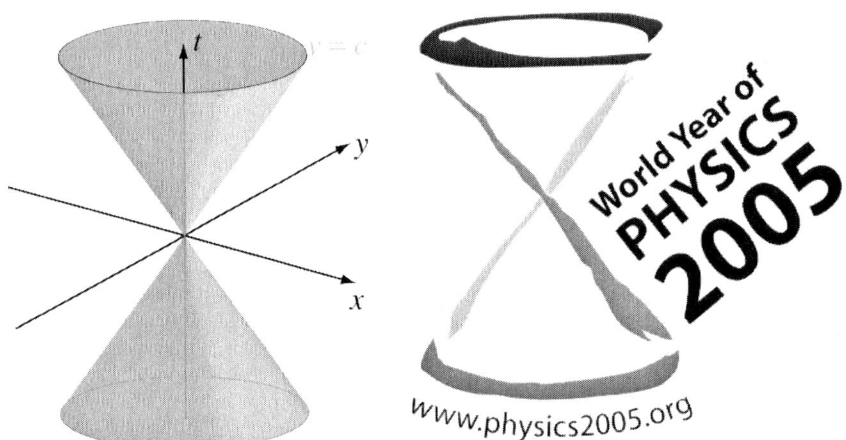

Figure 35.5: Left: light cone in a 2+1-dimensional space;
right: stylized light cone used as the World Year of Physics logo.

Why is the light cone called a cone, and not a triangle? The answer is shown in Figure 35.5, left side. For two space coordinates x and y the condition $v = \sqrt{v_x^2 + v_y^2} = c$ sweeps out a cone in the 2+1 dimensional x, y, t space. Only events inside the negative light cone can influence events at the origin, the tip of the light cone, and conversely only events inside the positive light cone can be influenced by the event located at the origin.

The light cone is one of the iconic symbols of modern theoretical physics. It is a powerful reminder of the limits to causal connections between events at different points in space and time that are imposed by Einstein's postulates and the theory of special relativity. This is the reason that a stylized light cone was chosen as the logo for the World Year of Physics in 2005, commemorating the centennial of Einstein's famous papers on the photoelectric effect (which we will discuss in chapter 36), on Brownian motion (which proved the existence of atoms), and on the theory of special relativity.

Often the axes of light cone diagrams are scaled so that they have the same units. One way to scale the axes is to multiply the time axis by the speed of light so that both axes have the units of length. Another method involves dividing the x-axis by the speed of light so that both axes have the units of time. In this way the speed of light becomes a diagonal line in the light-cone diagram, which is very useful for making quantitative arguments, as we will see in the following.

In a light cone diagram we can draw world lines. A world line is the trajectory of an object in space and time. A typical plot containing world lines is shown in Figure 35.6. In this type of plot, we imagine motion only in one space dimension, x, along with time. Let's imagine we have an object initially located at $x = 0$ and $t = 0$ in this plot. If the object is not moving in the x-direction, the object traces out a vertical line in this plot as shown by vector 1. If the object is moving in the positive x-direction with a constant speed, its trajectory will be represented by a path pointing up and to the right as shown by vector 2. If the object is moving with a constant speed in the negative x-direction, its trajectory will be depicted by a path pointing up and to the left as shown by vector 3. An object traveling with the speed of light in the positive x-direction will be shown as a trajectory with a 45° angle with respect to the vertical axis as shown by vector 4. An object traveling with the speed of light in the negative x-direction will be given by a trajectory with a –45° angle with respect to the vertical axis as shown by vector 5.

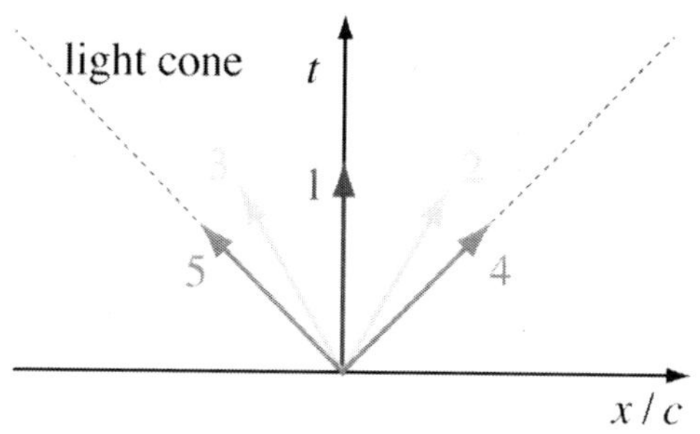

Figure 35.6: A space-time plot showing the positive light cone.

35.3. Time Dilation and Length Contraction

In our everyday experiences, we consider time and space as absolute, without restriction or qualification. However, if one follows Einstein's postulates to their logical conclusion, this absolute reference is not the case any more. This concept of non-absolute time and space leads to conclusions that sound like science fiction, but have been verified experimentally.

Time Dilation

One of the most remarkable consequences of the theory of relativity is that time measurement is not independent of the reference frame. Instead, time in a moving reference frame is dilated (made longer):

$$\Delta t = \gamma \Delta t_0 = \frac{\Delta t_0}{\sqrt{1-(v/c)^2}}. \tag{35.5}$$

This dilation means that if a clock advances Δt_0 while at rest, you observe the clock advancing by $\Delta t > \Delta t_0$ and Δt depends on the speed v with which you are moving relative to the clock! This result is truly revolutionary. However, it has experimentally verifiable consequences - as we will see in Example 35.2.

Derivation 35.1: Time dilation

How can we derive or even just motivate this result? Let us construct a clock as in Figure 35.7 a) that keeps time by bouncing a vertical light beam off a mirror. If we know the distance h between mirror and clock, then the time that it takes for the beam to go up and down is:

$$\Delta t_0 = \frac{2h}{c}$$

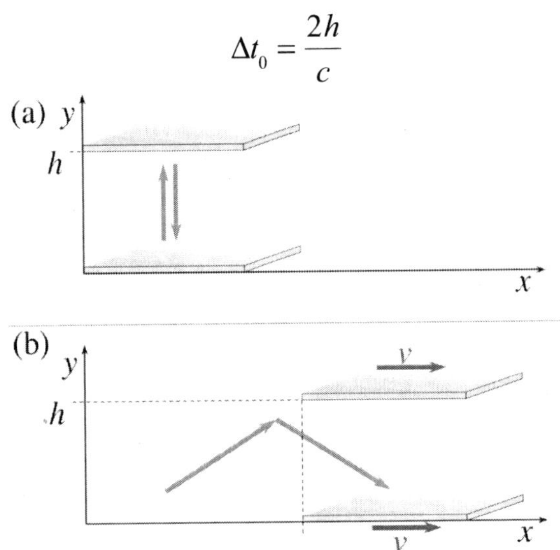

Figure 35.7: Schematic drawing of measuring time in two different reference frames.(a) mirrors are at rest in this reference frame, (b) mirrors are moving with velocity v in this frame.

where the subscript "0" refers to the fact that the observer of this time interval is not moving relative to the measurement apparatus. (It takes the same time to go up as it does to go down.)

Now let's have an observer have a speed of v in a horizontal direction, which we call the $-x$-direction so that this observer sees the clock moving in the $+x$-direction with a speed v as shown in Figure 35.7 b). You can see from the sketch that in this case the observer sees the light beam have a path length of

$$L = 2\sqrt{h^2 + (x/2)^2}\ ,$$

where x is the distance that the clock moves while the light is in the air. This result is simply a consequence of Pythagoras's Theorem. We have tacitly assumed that h is the same for observers at rest in the two reference frames depicted in Figure 35.7. If h were not the same then we could distinguish one reference frame from the other in violation of Einstein's Postulate1.

This observer would say that $x = v\Delta t$, where Δt refers now to the time interval for the light to be emitted and then detected in her system. We can also use the above equation relating h and Δt_0, $h = c\Delta t_0 / 2$ to eliminate h.

At this point the second postulate enters in its essential way. The light beams can only travel with c, the constant speed of light, which is independent of the velocity of the observer! Thus we have the relation

$$L = c\Delta t\ .$$

Derivation

We insert this result into the result of Pythagoras's Theorem above and we get:

$$L = 2\sqrt{h^2 + (x/2)^2} = c\Delta t = 2\sqrt{(c\Delta t_0 / 2)^2 + (v\Delta t / 2)^2} = \sqrt{(c\Delta t_0)^2 + (v\Delta t)^2} .$$

Solving this equation for Δt, we obtain

$$\Delta t = \gamma \Delta t_0 = \frac{\Delta t_0}{\sqrt{1-(v/c)^2}} .$$

In the clock's rest frame - Figure 35.7 a) - there is a time interval Δt_0; this quantity could represent the time between two clicks of the clock. In the frame in which the clock is moving - Figure 35.7 b) – the time interval between these two clicks is $\Delta t = \gamma \Delta t_0 > \Delta t_0$. Thus we say that moving clocks run slow.

Because the velocity of light is independent of the speed of the observer, we had to admit that the time measured by the two observers is different. This step is remarkably bold.

Finally, a remark on notation: Sometimes you will see the time measured in the rest frame of a clock referred to as *proper time*. The proper time interval here is Δt_0.

It is one thing to postulate and then mathematically prove the effect of time dilation. It is, however, altogether different to observe this effect in the laboratory or in nature. Amazingly, this proof can be done.

Example

Example 35.2: Muon decay

A muon is an unstable subatomic particle. It has a mean lifetime τ_0 of only 2.200 μs. This lifetime can be observed easily when muons decay at rest in the lab. However, when muons are produced in flight at very high speeds, then their mean lifetime becomes time dilated. In 1977, such an experiment was carried out at the European CERN particle accelerator, where the muons were produced with a speed of v=0.9994 $c \Rightarrow \beta = 0.9994$. In this case, we have for γ:

$$\gamma = \frac{1}{\sqrt{1-\beta^2}} = \frac{1}{\sqrt{1-0.9994^2}} = 28.87 .$$

Therefore, the mean lifetime, τ, of the muons is expected to be $\gamma = 28.87$ longer at this speed than if they were at rest:

$$\tau = \gamma \tau_0 = 28.87 \cdot 2.200 \ \mu\text{s} = 63.5 \ \mu\text{s} .$$

It is quite straightforward to measure this effect. Without the effect of time dilation,

Example

during its lifetime of 2.200 μs, a muon with this speed could only move a distance of

$$x = v\tau_0 = 0.9994\ c \cdot 2.200\ \mu\text{s}=660\ \text{m}$$

before it decays. However with the effect of time dilation you get a travel distance of

$$x = v\tau = v\gamma\tau_0 = 0.9994\ c \cdot 28.87 \cdot 2.200\ \mu\text{s}=19\ \text{km}.$$

To do this experiment you just need to look how far away from the muon's production site you can detect the decay products. The CERN experiment verified the relativity prediction of time dilation. This measurement shows that time dilation is indeed a real effect. Particles live longer the faster they move. (However they live the usual time according to clocks in their rest frame.) In fact, there are giant accelerators on the drawing board right now that will collide muons. For these accelerators, muons need to be transported over distances of many kilometers. The fact that these muon colliders are possible at all is due to the effect of time dilation.

You may think that these effects relate to subatomic particles only and that the effect of time dilation has no relevance for macroscopic objects. However, this assertion is not true. In 1971, scientists flew four extremely precise atomic clocks around the Earth, once in each direction. They observed that the clocks flying eastward lost 59 ± 10 ns while the clocks flying west gained 275 ± 21 ns compared to a ground based atomic clock. Thus, the effect of time dilation was confirmed by this experiment with macroscopic clocks. Of course, the effect was incredibly small because the speed of an airliner is small compared with the speed of light. The clocks lost 59 ns and gained 275 ns in three days, which corresponds to 259,200 s (a few parts per trillion). However, the basic fact remains that we cannot consider time as an absolute quantity any longer.

In-class exercise: A grandfather clock has a pendulum with a period of 1.00 s. When this grandfather clock is observed moving with a speed of $0.860c$, what is the period of the pendulum?

a) 0.860 s
b) 1.00 s
c) 1.25 s
d) 1.77 s
e) 1.96 s

Length Contraction

Because time is not absolute and indeed is dilated as a function of speed, you may also guess that length is not a constant any more when one considers the implications of relativity. We will see that the length L of a moving object (with speed v) is contracted relative to its length in its own rest frame, its proper length L_0. We will find that

$$L = \frac{L_0}{\gamma} = L_0\sqrt{1-(v/c)^2}\,. \tag{35.6}$$

Derivation 35.2: Length contraction

Derivation

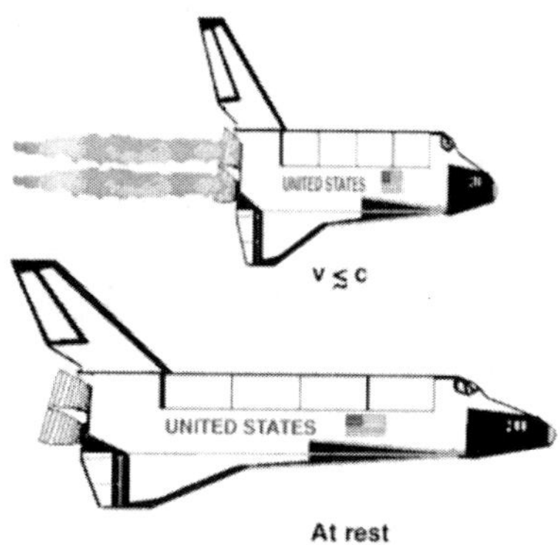

Figure 35.8: Illustration of length contraction (Not to scale!).

Imagine you want to measure the length of this space shuttle (Figure 35.8), which has a speed v and a proper length L_0. The way that you can measure the length without using a meter stick is simple. Using a clock fixed in the laboratory, fire a laser beam (attached to the clock) when the tip of the shuttle passes and fire it again when the end of the shuttle passes. The time between the two firings of the laser is Δt_0, or the proper time and thus $L = v\Delta t_0$.

Inside the shuttle, using a clock fixed to the inside of it, the measured time between laser firings is $\Delta t = \gamma\Delta t_0$ because of time dilation. Thus, an astronaut inside the shuttle observes that a moving clock with speed v emitted light when passing the satellite tip and once again (Δt later) when passing the tail and deduces that $L_0 = v\Delta t = v\gamma\Delta t_0$. Thus we have

$$\frac{L}{L_0} = \frac{v\Delta t_0}{v\gamma\Delta t_0} \text{ or } L = \frac{L_0}{\gamma}.$$

Please note that for this thought experiment it was essential that the length measured is *along the direction of motion.* All lengths perpendicular to the direction of motion remain the same (see the drawing).

As you can see from derivations 35.1 and 35.2, the phenomena of length contraction and time dilation are quite intimately related. Length contraction implies time dilation, and vice versa.

The essential fact that we would like for you to remember from our deliberations on length contraction is that moving objects are shorter. They don't just appear shorter - they are shorter as measured by us! This contraction is another mind-bending consequence of the postulates of special relativity.

Self-Test Opportunity: State whether each of the following statements is true or false.

a) For a moving object, the length along the direction of motion is shorter than when it is at rest.
b) You are stationary. A clock moving past you at a significant fraction of the speed of light seems to run faster than the watch on your wrist.
c) You are moving with a speed that is a significant fraction of the speed of light. You pass by a stationary observer. You observe that your watch seems to be running faster than the watch of the stationary observer.

Twin Paradox

Now that we have seen that the time interval (say between clock ticks) is dependent on the speed of the object (say a clock) in the frame of an observer, $\Delta t = \gamma\ \Delta t_0$, let's perform a little thought experiment:

Astronaut Alice has a twin sister Betty. At the age of 20, Alice boards a space ship that flies to a space station 3.25 light-years away and then returns. The space ship is a good one and can fly with a speed of 65% of the speed of light, resulting in a gamma factor of $\gamma = 1.32$. While the entire trip back and forth takes Alice 7.6 years in Alice's reference frame, time dilation forces $7.6\gamma = 10$ years to pass in Betty's reference frame. Therefore, when Alice steps out of the spaceship after her trip, she will be 27.6 years old, whereas Betty is 30 years old.

Now we can also put ourselves into the reference frame of Alice: In Alice's frame she was at rest and Betty was moving at 65% the speed of light. Therefore, Alice should have aged 1.32 times more than Betty aged. Because Alice knows that she has aged 10 years, she might expect her sister Betty to be only 27.6 years old when they meet again. Both sisters cannot be younger, which is the origin of the twin paradox. Which of these two views is right?

The apparent paradox is resolved when we realize that although Betty remains in an inertial reference frame at rest on the Earth for the duration, Astronaut Alice lives in two different inertial frames during her round trip. During the outbound leg, she is moving away from Earth and toward the distant space station. When she reaches the space station, she turns around, and travels back from the space station at a constant speed to Earth. Thus, the symmetry is broken between the two, once very close, sisters.

We can analyze the path of the two sisters in space-time by using our techniques of light cones and world lines, plotting time in an inertial rest frame versus the position of both sisters in one direction, the x-direction. We will analyze the problem both from the point of view of Betty and the point of view of Alice. We start by analyzing the trip in the rest frame of stay-at-home sister Betty as shown in as shown in Figure 35.9. Here we scale the axes so that the units are in years.

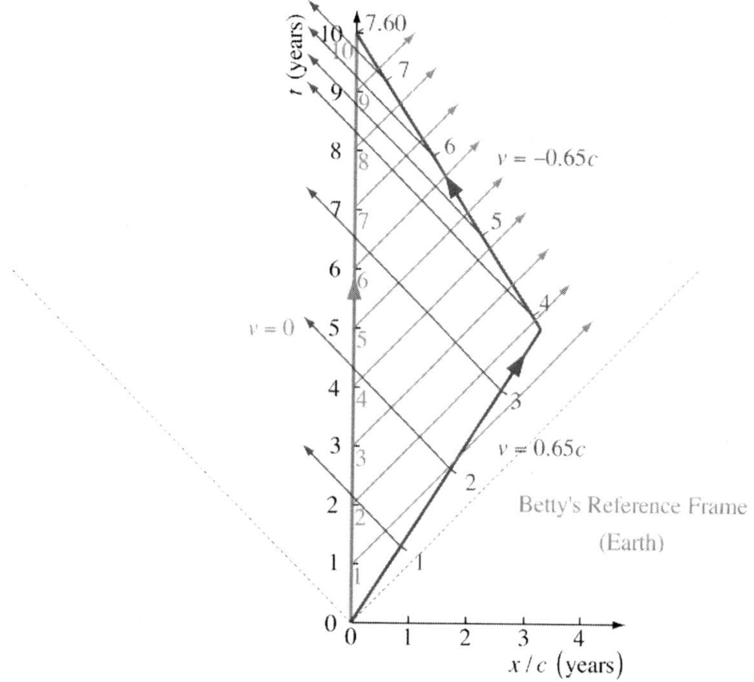

Figure 35.9: Plot showing the velocity of the two sisters in Betty's reference frame, which is at rest on the Earth. The thick, vertical red line represents Betty's trajectory. The two thick blue lines depict Alice's trajectory. Thin red lines labeled by a red number corresponding to the year represent Betty's birthday messages. Thin blue lines labeled by a blue number corresponding to the year depict Alice's birthday messages. The dashed lines show the light cone.

In this figure, Betty's speed is always zero and she remains at $x = 0$. A red, vertical line represents Betty's trajectory. In contrast, Alice is moving with a speed of 65% the speed of light ($v = 0.65c$) away from the Earth. A blue line labeled $v = 0.65c$ depicts Alice's outbound trajectory. We define the positive x-direction as pointing from the Earth to the distant space station. Each sister wants to keep in touch with the other sister. Thus, each sister sends an electronic birthday card to the other sister on her birthday in her reference frame. These messages travel with the speed of light. Betty sends her electronic message directly toward the space station and Alice sends her electronic greeting back directly toward Earth. Betty's messages are shown as red arrows pointing up and to the right. Alice's messages are shown as blue arrows pointing up and to the left. When the message arrows cross the trajectory of each of the sisters, the respective sister receives and enjoys the electronic birthday card.

After 5 years pass in Betty's frame and 3.8 years pass in Alice's frame, Alice reaches the space station and turns for home. Betty is getting a little worried by now because she has received only two birthday cards in five years. Alice is not feeling much better since she has received only one cheery greeting card in 3.8 years. After Alice turns around, she starts to cheer up. She receives eight electronic birthday cards in the next 3.8 years. Betty also feels a little better because she receives five more greetings in the remaining five years. When Alice arrives back home on Earth, she gets a first-hand 30th birthday greeting from Betty, but Alice is not ready to celebrate her 28th birthday yet. Alice's age is 27.6 years. Counting the first hand birthday wish, Alice receives ten birthday greetings while Betty only receives seven.

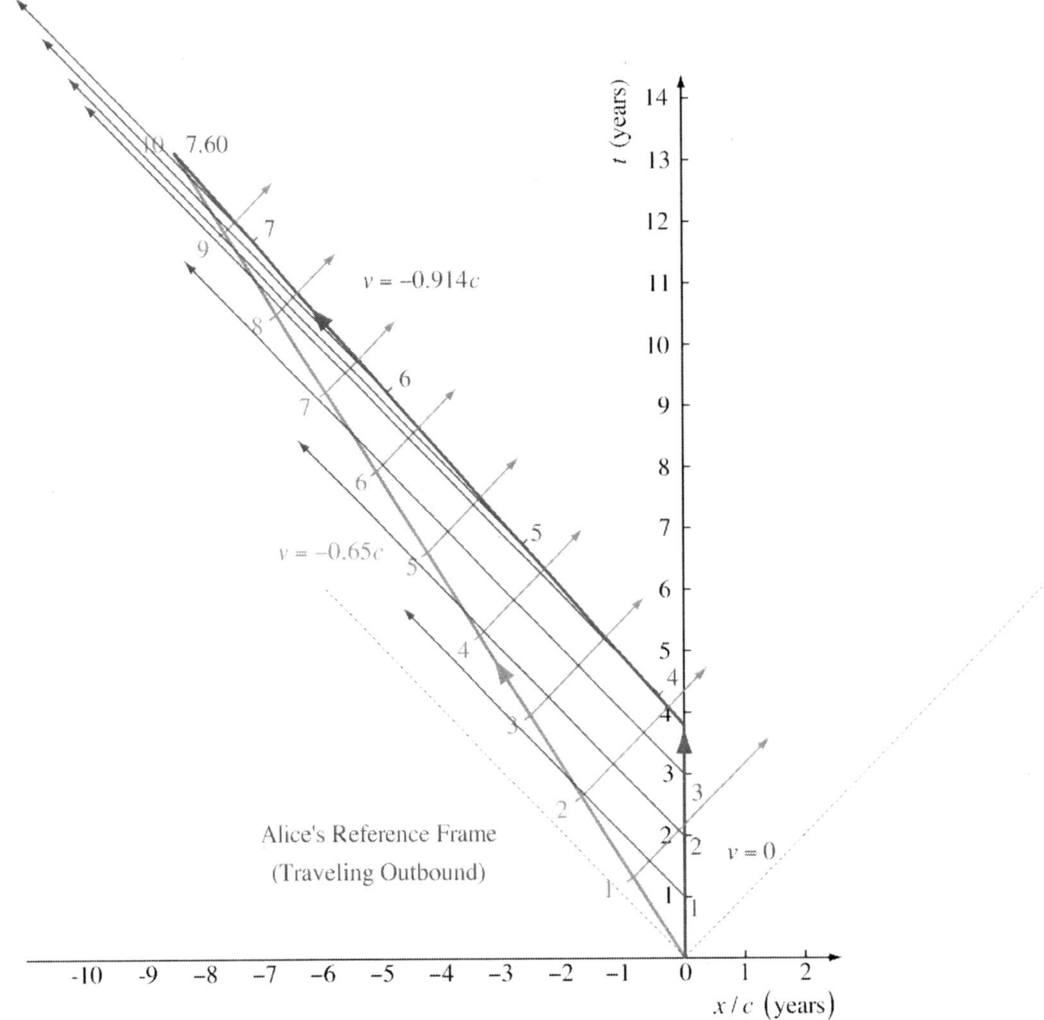

Figure 35.10: Plot showing the velocity of the two sisters in the reference from of Alice's outbound leg. The thick red line represents Betty's trajectory. The two thick blue lines depict Alice's trajectory. Thin red lines labeled by a red number corresponding to the year represent Betty's birthday messages. Thin blue lines labeled by a blue number corresponding to the year depict Alice's birthday messages. The dashed lines represent the light cone.

Now let's analyze the same trip from the inertial rest frame corresponding to Alice's outward-bound leg as shown in Figure 35.10 to show that we can get the same answer from Alice's point of view. In this reference frame, Betty and Earth are both traveling in the negative x-direction with a velocity $v = -0.65c$. During the outbound portion of the trip, Alice's velocity is zero. The space station is traveling toward Betty with a speed of 65% of the speed of light, so the distance of 3.25 light years is covered in 3.8 years. Note that this part of the two diagrams in Figure 35.9 and Figure 35.10 is completely symmetric.

When the space station reaches Betty, the symmetry in the two representations of the above two figures is broken. Betty begins to travel with a speed fast enough to catch up with Earth in the negative x-direction. To establish a relative speed of 65% of the speed of light with respect to Earth, Alice must travel with a speed of 91.4% of the speed of light. This relativistic addition of velocities is discussed in a following section.

Again Betty receives two birthday greetings in the first five years in her reference frame, while Alice again receives one birthday greeting before she starts moving toward Earth. As Alice streaks for Earth at a speed of $0.914c$, she receives eight birthday greetings while Betty again receives five. When the twins are reunited on Earth, Betty is 30 years old and Alice is 27.6 years old. This result using Alice's outbound reference frame is the same as the one we obtained using Betty's reference frame. Thus, the twin paradox is resolved.

Note that the twin paradox was analyzed in terms of special relativity only. One might worry about parts of Alice's journey that involved acceleration. Alice had to accelerate to 65% of the speed of light to begin her journey to the space station. Alice had to slow down, stop, and reaccelerate back up to a speed of 65% back toward Earth. Even at a constant acceleration of three times the acceleration of gravity, it would take less than three months to reach a speed of 65% of the speed of light from rest and the same amount of time to stop starting at a speed of 65% of the speed of light. However, we could postulate various scenarios to remove these objections or at least minimize their importance. For example, we could simply make the trip longer, making the acceleration phase negligible. However, Betty might not be around to greet Alice on her return. Acceleration is necessary to explain the twin paradox because Alice must reverse her course to return to Earth, changing her inertial reference frame. However, the effects of general relativity are not needed to explain the twin paradox.

In-class exercise: The nearest star to us other than the Sun is Proxima Centauri, which is 4.22 light-years away. Suppose we had a spaceship that could travel at a speed of 90.0% of the speed of light. If you were in the spaceship, how long would it take for you to travel from the Sub to Proxima Centauri from your point of view?

a) 2.04 years
b) 2.29 years
c) 3.42 years
d) 3.80 years
e) 4.22 years

35.4. Frequency Shift

If time is not a constant any more, then quantities that are proportional to time, or inversely proportional to it, may also be expected to change as a function of the velocity. The frequency f is just such a quantity.

In chapter 16 on sound waves, we encountered the Doppler effect that describes the frequency change of sound because of the relative motion between observer, source, and medium. We have seen, however, that light does not need a medium in which to propagate. Indeed, the nonexistence of the ether was what got Einstein started in the first place.

Therefore, the relativistic frequency shift is qualitatively new and only remotely connected to the classical Doppler effect. If v is the relative velocity between source and observer, and the relative motion occurs in a radial direction (either directly towards each other or directly away from each other), then the formula for the observed frequency, f, is given by:

$$f = f_0\sqrt{\frac{c-v}{c+v}} \tag{35.7}$$

where $v > 0$ for motion away from each other and $v < 0$ for motion towards each other. (There is also a transverse Doppler shift, purely due to time dilation effects, but we will not concern ourselves with this effect here).

Because we still have the relationship $c = \lambda f$ between speed, wavelength, and frequency, we get for the wavelength:

$$\lambda = \lambda_0\sqrt{\frac{c+v}{c-v}}\,. \tag{35.8}$$

When looking out through our telescopes into the universe, we find that just about all galaxies send light towards us that is red-shifted, meaning $\lambda > \lambda_0$. This means that for all galaxies have $v > 0$, i.e. they are moving away from us. In addition, astoundingly, the further away they are from us the more they are red-shifted. This observation is clear evidence for an ever-expanding universe!

Often one finds a so-called red-shift parameter z quoted. It is defined as the ratio of the wavelength shift of light divided by the wavelength of that light as observed when the source is at rest:

$$z = \frac{\Delta\lambda}{\lambda_0} = \frac{\lambda - \lambda_0}{\lambda_0} = \sqrt{\frac{c+v}{c-v}} - 1\,. \tag{35.9}$$

Solved Problem

Solved Problem 35.1: Galactic red-shift

During a deep space survey, a galaxy was observed with a red-shift of $z = 0.450$.

Question:

With what speed is that galaxy moving away from us?

Answer:

THINK:

The red-shift is a function of the speed v that the galaxy moves away from us. We solve

(35.9) for the speed in terms of the red-shift.

SKETCH:

A sketch showing the galaxy moving away from the Earth is shown in Figure 35.11.

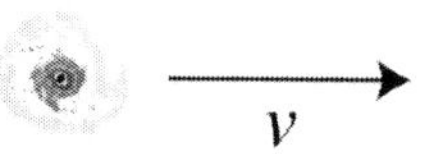

Figure 35.11: A galaxy moves away from the Earth (blue dot).

RESEARCH:

We start with (35.9) relating the red-shift z to the velocity v the galaxy is moving away from us

$$z = \sqrt{\frac{c+v}{c-v}} - 1.$$

We can rearrange this equation to get

$$(z+1)^2 = \frac{c+v}{c-v}.$$

$$c(z+1)^2 - v(z+1)^2 = c + v.$$

Gathering the multiplicative factors of v on one side and factors of c on the other side we get

$$v + v(z+1)^2 = c(z+1)^2 - c.$$

SIMPLIFY:

We can then write an expression for the velocity of the galaxy moving away from us in units of the speed of light

$$\frac{v}{c} = \frac{(z+1)^2 - 1}{(z+1)^2 + 1}. \tag{35.10}$$

CALCULATE:

Putting in our numerical values gives us

$$\frac{v}{c} = \frac{((0.450)+1)^2 - 1}{((0.450)+1)^2 + 1} = 0.355359.$$

ROUND:

We report our result to three significant figures

Solved Problem

$$\frac{v}{c} = 0.355.$$

DOUBLE-CHECK:

A galaxy moving away from us with a velocity of 35.5% of the speed of light seems reasonable in the sense that our answer at least does not exceed the speed of light.

35.5. Lorentz Transformation

In studying time dilation and length contraction, we have seen how we can transform temporal and spatial coordinates from one frame to another. We can combine the transformation of time and space as we go from one reference frame into another that moves with speed v relative to the first one.

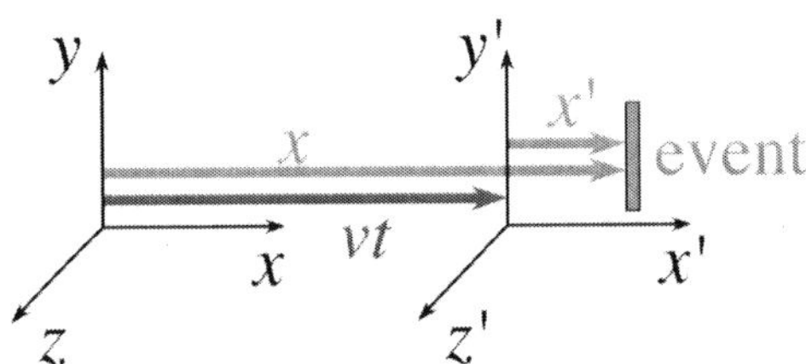

Figure 35.12: Illustration for the Lorentz Transformation.

To be specific, suppose we have the two reference frames F (with coordinate system x, y, z and time t) and F' (with coordinate system x', y', z' and time t') that are at the same point $x = x', y = y', z = z'$ (this arrangement can always be accomplished by a simple shift in the location of the origin of the coordinate systems) at the same time $t = t' = 0$, moving with velocity v relative to each other along the x-axis. Now we want to know how one would describe an event (which is some occurrence like a firecracker explosion) that has coordinates x, y, z and is happening at time t as observed in frame F, using coordinates x', y', z' and time t' (see Figure 35.12).

Classically, this transformation is given by:

$$\begin{aligned} x' &= x - vt \\ y' &= y \\ z' &= z \\ t' &= t \end{aligned} \quad . \tag{35.11}$$

This transformation is known as the Galilean transformation, which we encountered in the chapter on motion in two and three dimensions, chapter 3. It is correct as long as v is small compared to c. Until we had talked about time dilation, the last one of these equations seemed utterly trivial. Now this is not the case any more.

The transformation that is valid for all velocities v is called the Lorentz transformation. It is given by:

$$x' = \gamma(x - vt)$$
$$y' = y$$
$$z' = z \qquad (35.12)$$
$$t' = \gamma(t - vx/c^2)$$

We can, of course, also construct the inverse transformation and get:

$$x = \gamma(x' + vt')$$
$$y = y'$$
$$z = z' \qquad (35.13)$$
$$t = \gamma(t' + vx'/c^2)$$

In the limit of small speeds ($\gamma = 1,\ \beta = v/c = 0$), the Galilean transformation follows from the Lorentz transformation as a special case, as you can easily see. But for speeds that are not small as compared to the speed of light, the Lorentz transformation includes both the effects of time dilation and of length contraction.

35.6. Relativistic Velocity Addition

Let us get back to the problem we touched on earlier, and which got our whole thinking about relativity going:

You fly in a rocket through space with a speed of $c/2$ directly towards Earth. Now you shine a laser in the forward direction. The light of the laser has a speed c in either the Rocket or the Earth reference frame according to Einstein. Naively we would expect that the light of the laser had a speed of $c + c/2 = 1.5c$ when observed on Earth. This observation would follow from the velocity addition formula that we learned in chapter 3, $\vec{v}_{pg} = \vec{v}_{ps} + \vec{v}_{sg}$. Here the subscripts p, g, and s refer to the projectile (light in this case), the ground, and the spaceship.

Because this result contradicts the postulate that no speed is greater than c, we obviously have the need to come up with a new formula to add velocities correctly. We will not derive it here, though it does follow directly from the Lorentz Transformation. We will restrict the use of the relativistic velocity addition formula to one-dimensional projectile motion, so that the projectile travels along the $\pm x$-axis if the spaceship is traveling along the x-axis. This formula is

$$v_{pg} = \frac{v_{ps} + v_{sg}}{1 + \dfrac{v_{ps} v_{sg}}{c^2}} \qquad (35.14)$$

or simply

$$v_{1+2} = \frac{v_1 + v_2}{1 + \frac{v_1 v_2}{c^2}}. \qquad (35.15)$$

We will always choose $v_{sg} = v_2 > 0$ so that the spaceship (or whatever) travels along the axis that we are working with, say the x axis. Now you can see that c "plus" $c/2$ does not yield $1.5c$, but instead:

$$v_{c+c/2} = \frac{c + c/2}{1 + \frac{c \cdot c/2}{c^2}} = c.$$

Therefore this analysis works out just right: the speed of light is the same in every reference frame! For $|v_1| \ll c$ and $v_2 \ll c$, we can neglect the term $(v_1 v_2)/c^2$ in the denominator of (35.15) and obtain the classical approximation $v_{1+2} = v_1 + v_2$ to (35.15). Thus, (35.15) has the proper classical limit and at the same time does not violate the postulates of special relativity.

Solved Problem

Solved Problem 35.2: Shuttlecraft and starship

The shuttlecraft Sacagawea is approaching the starship Voyager. Both of the spacecraft are traveling in the same direction. The speed of Sacagawea is $0.830c$ and the speed of Voyager is $0.750c$, both measured by a stationary observer on Earth.

Question:
What is the speed of Voyager as observed from Sacagawea in units of the speed of light?

Answer:

THINK:

Sacagawea is overtaking Voyager. Therefore, we must find the difference of the velocities of the two spacecraft. We can use (35.14) to calculate the relativistic sum of the velocities.

SKETCH:

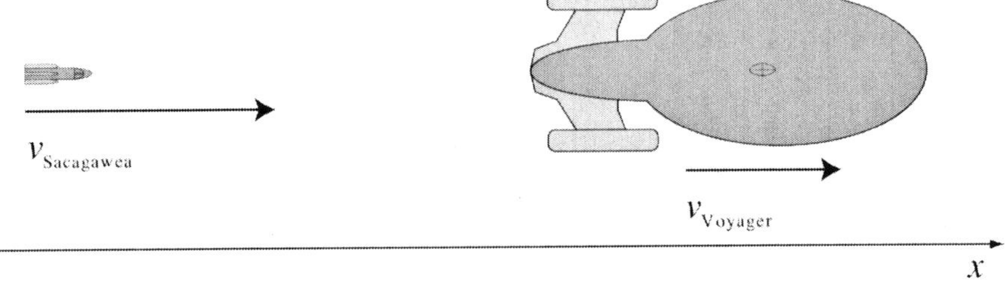

Figure 35.13: Shuttlecraft Sacagawea is overtaking starship Voyager.

Solved Problem

RESEARCH:

This problem involves the relativistic addition of velocities. We can use (35.14) to calculate the relativistic addition of the velocities

$$v_{pg} = \frac{v_{ps} + v_{sg}}{1 + \frac{v_{ps} v_{sg}}{c^2}}.$$

where we think of Sacagawea as the spacecraft with $v_{sg} = v_{\text{Sacagawea}}$ emitting Voyager as a projectile with $v_{pg} = v_{\text{Voyager}}$. The relative velocity of Sacagawea and Voyager is then the relative velocity between the spacecraft and the projectile $v_{ps} = v_{rel}$. Thus we can rewrite the equation for the velocity as

$$v_{\text{Voyager}} = \frac{v_{rel} + v_{\text{Sacagawea}}}{1 + \frac{v_{rel} v_{\text{Sacagawea}}}{c^2}}. \tag{35.16}$$

SIMPLIFY:

We can define the velocity of the shuttlecraft Sacagawea in terms of the speed of light as

$$\beta_{\text{S}} = \frac{v_{\text{Sacagawea}}}{c},$$

the velocity of the starship Voyager as

$$\beta_{\text{V}} = \frac{v_{\text{Voyager}}}{\text{c}},$$

and the relative velocity between Sacagawea and Voyager as

$$\beta_{rel} = \frac{v_{rel}}{c}.$$

We can then rewrite (35.16) as

$$\beta_{\text{V}} = \frac{\beta_{rel} + \beta_{\text{S}}}{1 + \beta_{rel}\beta_{\text{S}}}$$

We can rearrange this to obtain

$$\beta_V\left(1 + \beta_{rel}\beta_{\text{S}}\right) = \beta_{rel} + \beta_{\text{S}} = \beta_V + \beta_V\beta_{rel}\beta_{\text{S}}.$$

$$\beta_V\beta_{rel}\beta_{\text{S}} - \beta_{rel} = \beta_{\text{S}} - \beta_V = \beta_{rel}\left(\beta_V\beta_{\text{S}} - 1\right).$$

$$\beta_{\text{rel}} = \frac{\beta_{\text{S}} - \beta_{\text{V}}}{\beta_{\text{S}}\beta_{\text{V}} - 1}.$$

CALCULATE:

Putting in our numerical values gives us

$$\beta_{rel} = \frac{0.830 - 0.750}{(0.830)(0.750) - 1} = -0.21192.$$

ROUND:

We report our result to three significant figures

$$\beta_{rel} = -0.212.$$

DOUBLE-CHECK:

The negative sign for the relative velocity of Voyager as seen by Sacagawea makes sense because Voyager would be seen to be approaching Sacagawea in the negative x-direction. If we calculate the relative velocity between Sacagawea and Voyager non-relativistically, we obtain

$$v_{rel} = v_{\text{Voyager}} - v_{\text{Sacagawea}} = 0.750c - 0.830c = -0.080c.$$

Looking at our solution above we can see that the non-relativistic velocity difference is modified by a factor of $\left|1/(\beta_S\beta_V - 1)\right|$. As the velocities of Sacagawea and Voyager become a significant fraction of the speed of light, this factor will become larger than one, and the magnitude of the relativistic velocity difference will be larger than magnitude of the non-relativistic difference. Thus, our result seems reasonable.

35.7. Relativistic Momentum and Energy

Length and time are not the only concepts that need revision within the theory of special relativity. Energy and momentum do as well.

Momentum

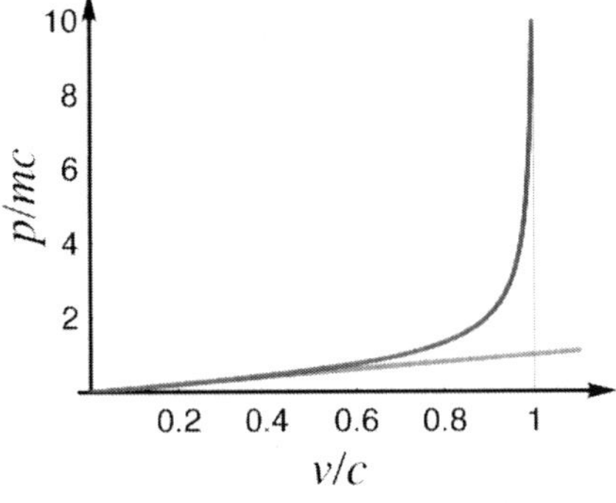

Figure 35.14: Momentum as a function of speed.
Blue line: exact formula, red line non-relativistic approximation.

Classically, the momentum was defined as the product of velocity and mass: $\vec{p} = m\vec{v}$. Because we have now seen that the speed cannot exceed c, this result implies either that the definition of momentum will have to be changed, or that there is a maximum momentum possible for a given particle. It turns out that the first possibility is correct.

The definition of the momentum that is consistent with the theory of special relativity is

$$\vec{p} = \gamma\, m\vec{v} \tag{35.17}$$

where m is the rest mass of the particle (mass as measured in a frame where the particle is at rest). We do not use the concept of "relativistic mass" in this book. When we say mass we always mean rest mass. Equation (35.17) is only valid for particles having mass $m > 0$. We discuss massless particles later in this section.

In Figure 35.14, we compare the two formulas for the momentum. In blue we show the correct formula, and in red the classical approximation. The velocity is shown in units of c, and the momentum in units of mc. You can see that up to speeds of approximately $c/2$, the two formulas give pretty much the same result, but then the correct relativistic momentum goes to infinity as v approaches c.

Newton's Second Law, however, does not have to be modified in the relativistic limit. It remains

$$\vec{F} = \frac{d}{dt}\vec{p} \tag{35.18}$$

where $\vec{p}$ is the relativistic momentum. Note that the simple $F = ma$ does not hold any more in the relativistic limit, at least not in its straightforward interpretation.

Energy

If the momentum needs a change of definition, then we can also expect the energy to be in need of revision.

In our non-relativistic considerations, we had found that the total energy of a particle in the absence of an external potential was just its kinetic energy, $K = \frac{1}{2}mv^2$.

In the relativistic case, we find that we have to consider the contribution of the mass to the energy of a particle. Einstein found that the energy of a particle with mass m at rest is:

$$E_0 = mc^2. \tag{35.19}$$

(Arguably the most famous formula in all of science!)

If the particle is in motion, then the energy increases by the same factor γ that time is dilated for a moving particle. The general case for the energy is then

$$E = \gamma\, E_0 = \gamma\, mc^2 . \tag{35.20}$$

The correct formula for the kinetic energy is obtained by subtracting the "rest energy" from the total energy:

$$K = E - E_0 = (\gamma - 1)E_0 = (\gamma - 1)mc^2 . \tag{35.21}$$

Obviously, the classical formula for the kinetic energy worked for us at speeds small compared to that of the speed of light. So how can we recover the classical approximation $K = \frac{1}{2}mv^2$ from the general relativistic result?

This result is actually quite straightforward, because for small speeds we had already found that $\gamma = 1 + \frac{1}{2}\beta^2 = 1 + \frac{1}{2}v^2/c^2$. We can insert this formula into the kinetic energy formula and get:

$$K_{\text{small } v} = (\gamma - 1)mc^2 \approx (1 + \tfrac{1}{2}v^2/c^2 - 1)mc^2 = \tfrac{1}{2}mv^2 . \tag{35.22}$$

Momentum-Energy Relationship

In the classical limit, we had found that the energy and momentum of an object are related via $E = p^2/2m$. Therefore, it is appropriate to ask what the correct general relationship between energy and momentum is.

With $E = \gamma\, mc^2$ and $\vec{p} = \gamma\, m\vec{v}$ as our starting point, we find:

$$E^2 = p^2c^2 + m^2c^4 . \tag{35.23}$$

Derivation 35.3:
We start with our equations for momentum and energy, and square each of them:

$$\begin{aligned}\vec{p} = \gamma\, m\vec{v} &\Rightarrow p^2 = \gamma^2 m^2 v^2 \\ E = \gamma\, mc^2 &\Rightarrow E^2 = \gamma^2 m^2 c^4\end{aligned} .$$

The square of the relativistic gamma-factor appears in both equations. Expressed in terms of v and c it is:

$$\gamma^2 = \frac{1}{1-\beta^2} = \frac{1}{1 - v^2/c^2} = \frac{c^2}{c^2 - v^2} .$$

Now we can evaluate the expression for the square of the energy and obtain:

Derivation

$$E^2 = \frac{c^2}{c^2 - v^2} m^2 c^4 = \frac{c^2 - v^2 + v^2}{c^2 - v^2} m^2 c^4 = m^2 c^4 + \frac{v^2}{c^2 - v^2} m^2 c^4$$
$$= m^2 c^4 + \frac{c^2}{c^2 - v^2} m^2 v^2 c^2 = m^2 c^4 + \gamma^2 m^2 v^2 c^2$$
$$= m^2 c^4 + p^2 c^2 .$$

In the second step of this computation, we simply added and subtracted v^2 in the numerator, then realized that we could split the numerator in such a way that the factor $c^2 - v^2$ would just cancel the denominator. In the next step, we rearranged the factors in the second term of the sum so that we could factor out γ again, and finally recognized that $\gamma^2 m^2 v^2 = p^2$, which gave us our desired result.

Often you will also encounter the above energy-momentum relationship in the form where one has taken the square root of the above expression,

$$E = \sqrt{p^2 c^2 + m^2 c^4} \tag{35.24}$$

In passing, we note that we have taken the positive root. You may want to ask what happened to the other root, the one that implies negative energy. This root actually leads to an astonishing discovery, that of anti-matter. However, to discuss this result in more detail we have to first get some grounding in quantum physics. Therefore, we will have to postpone the discussion of antimatter until then.

There is a special case that is relevant for particles with zero mass. (Photons, the subatomic particle representation for all radiation and in particular light, are examples of massless particles.) If a particle has $m = 0$, then the energy-momentum relationship simplifies considerably, and the momentum becomes proportional to the energy:

$$E = pc \text{ (for } m = 0\text{)}. \tag{35.25}$$

Speed, Energy and Momentum

If you divide the absolute value of the momentum $p = \gamma\, mv$ by the energy $E = \gamma\, mc^2$, you obtain:

$$\frac{p}{E} = \frac{\gamma\, mv}{\gamma\, mc^2} = \frac{v}{c^2} \Rightarrow v = \frac{pc^2}{E}$$

or, equivalently,

$$\beta = \frac{v}{c} = \frac{pc}{E}. \tag{35.26}$$

This formula is often a very useful relationship to determine the relativistic factor β from the known energy and momentum of particles. However, it also provides another energy-momentum relationship that is useful for the practitioner:

$$\beta = \frac{pc}{E} \Rightarrow p = \frac{\beta E}{c} \text{ or } E = \frac{pc}{\beta}. \quad (35.27)$$

Example

Example 35.3: Energy and momentum of an electron

We have seen that in some applications it is advantageous to use the energy unit electron-Volt (eV), 1 eV = $1.602 \cdot 10^{-19}$ J. The rest energy of an electron is $E_0 = 5.11 \cdot 10^5 \text{ eV} = 0.511 \text{ MeV}$, and its rest mass is $m = 0.511 \text{ MeV}/c^2$.

Question:

If an electron has a speed of 99% of that of light, what is its total energy, what is its kinetic energy, and what is its momentum?

Answer:

Since we have been given the number for the mass of the electron in convenient units, it is simple to calculate the rest energy

$$E_0 = mc^2 = (0.511 \text{ MeV}/c^2)c^2 = 0.511 \text{ MeV}.$$

Next we calculate γ for this case

$$\gamma = \frac{1}{\sqrt{1-\beta^2}} = \frac{1}{\sqrt{1-0.99^2}} = 7.09.$$

The total energy of a particle is given by:

$$E = \gamma\, E_0 = 7.09 \cdot 0.511 \text{ MeV}{=}3.62 \text{ MeV}.$$

The kinetic energy is therefore:

$$K = (\gamma - 1)E_0 = 6.09 \cdot 0.511 \text{ MeV}{=}3.11 \text{ MeV}.$$

The momentum of this electron is then:

$$p = \frac{\beta E}{c} = \frac{0.99 \cdot 3.62 \text{ MeV}}{c} = 3.58 \text{ MeV}/c.$$

Interestingly, one can accelerate electrons to 99% of the speed of light with quite small accelerators, ones that could that fit in labs of a typical physics building. However going above $.99c$ it gets very expensive. To get to 99.9999999% of the speed of light, an electron needs to be accelerated by a giant machine of over 3 km length like SLAC at Stanford.

35.8. General Relativity and Black Holes

So far, we have talked about special relativity. The general theory of relativity encompasses all of special relativity, but in addition provides a theory of gravity. We have seen one theory of gravity that was used rather successfully since the time of Newton. In the Newtonian theory of gravity, the gravitational force acting on a mass m due to another mass M is given as

$$F_g = \frac{GmM}{r^2} = ma\,, \tag{35.28}$$

where we have used Newton's Second Law to relate the force to m and the acceleration a. The mass m appears twice in this equation, but there is one very fine difference. The mass that appears on the right side of these equations is called the "inertial mass." This mass is the mass that undergoes the acceleration. However, the quantity that takes the role of the charge in the force of gravity is also a mass, the "gravitational mass." We find experimentally that inertial mass and the gravitational mass are ***exactly equal.***

The Newtonian theory of gravity served us extremely well. It was in almost complete agreement with all experimental observations. However, there were small problems that occurred in precision observations such as the exact orbit of the planet Mercury, observations that could not be explained with the Newtonian theory of gravity.

Albert Einstein again had the decisive insight in 1907: *"If a person falls freely he will not feel his own weight."* This observation means that you cannot distinguish if you are in an accelerating reference frame or subject to a gravitational force. This idea led to the famous Equivalence Principle:

> ***All local freely falling non-rotating laboratories are equivalent for the performance of all physical experiments.***

From this principle, one can prove that space and time are locally curved due to the presence of masses, and in turn, the *curved spaced-time* affects the motion of masses, telling them how to move. (We have now learned that space and time are intertwined. The term space-time refers to four dimensions, which incorporate both space and time.)

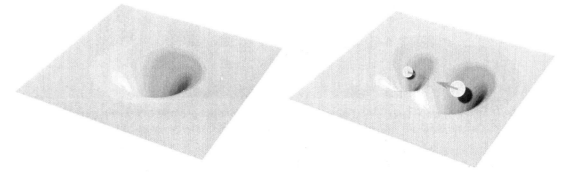

Figure 35.15: 2D-illustration of the deformation of space due to the presence of a massive object. Left: one object deforms space around it; right: two objects attract each other due to the mutual deformation of space.

You may find this concept rather hard to visualize, but a two-dimensional example might help. Consider a flat rubber sheet that symbolizes space in two dimensions. If you put a bowling ball onto this rubber sheet, it will deform the sheet in the way shown in the left panel of Figure 35.15.

Any mass that now comes rolling along the surface of the rubber sheet will experience the curvature of the sheet and thus feel attracted to the bowling ball. The general relativity way of viewing this scenario, however, is a free motion along the shortest path in curved space-time as in the right panel of Figure 35.15. (Of course, the second mass that comes along will also bring with it its own deformation of space, leading to a mutual attraction. But the principle remains the same.)

One of the most striking predictions of general relativity concerns the motion of light. Because light does not have mass, you would expect from the Newtonian formulation of gravity that gravity cannot affect the motion of light. General relativity, however, holds that light moves through curved space-time on the shortest path and thus should be deflected by the presence of large masses.

Observations by British astronomy Arthur Eddington during a solar eclipse in 1919 confirmed this spectacular prediction. Figure 35.16 shows the photograph taken by Eddington's team during the solar eclipse.

Figure 35.16: Photograph taken by Eddington's team of the solar eclipse of 1919 taken May 29, 1919 on the island of Principe, near Africa. The positions of the stars measure are marked by horizontal bars.

To visualize what was happening, we again use our rubber sheet analogy. Light from a distant star that passes near the sun is deflected as in Figure 35.17.

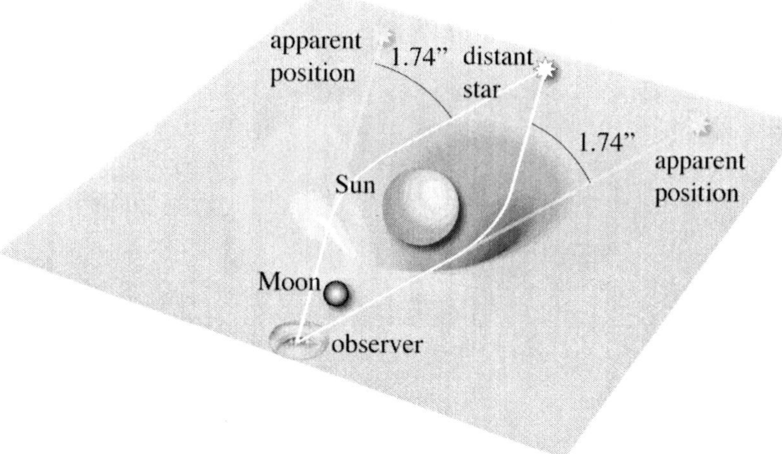

Figure 35.17: Light from a distant star is bent around the Sun. The angle is massively exaggerated for clarity. These stars are visible close to the Sun only during a solar eclipse.

The mass of the sun acts like a lens in a way. Light rays that come close to the sun on either side are deflected as shown in this sketch. The consequence is that an observer will see two stars or even arcs instead of just one star. Eddington measured the undeflected directions of the stars six months later by photographing stars at night when the Sun was not near the path of the light. The observed displacement was about 1/5 the diameter of the image of the distant star. General relativity predicted the angular separation of the observed image and the actual direction of the star to be 1.74", in good agreement with observed angular separation. These measurements could only be carried out during a solar eclipse. Otherwise, the light from the sun would simply overpower the light of stars, and this effect could not be measured in this manner. The systematic accuracy of these results has been criticized, but subsequent measurements in several solar eclipses have verified Eddington's results.

Recent observations with the Hubble Space Telescope have demonstrated gravitation lensing by massive dark objects as shown in Figure 35.18.

In this figure, the top panel shows a sketch of the light from a distant galaxy being bent around an unseen, massive dark object. This effect can produce two images of the distant galaxy as illustrated, or can produce arcs of light originating from the distant galaxy. Several of these arcs resulting from the gravitational lensing of a massive dark object are visible in the bottom panel of Figure 35.18.

When light comes close enough to an object massive enough, it simply cannot escape from the curvature in space-time generated by that object. What we mean by "close enough" is defined by the so-called Schwarzschild radius:

$$R_s = \frac{2GM}{c^2}. \tag{35.29}$$

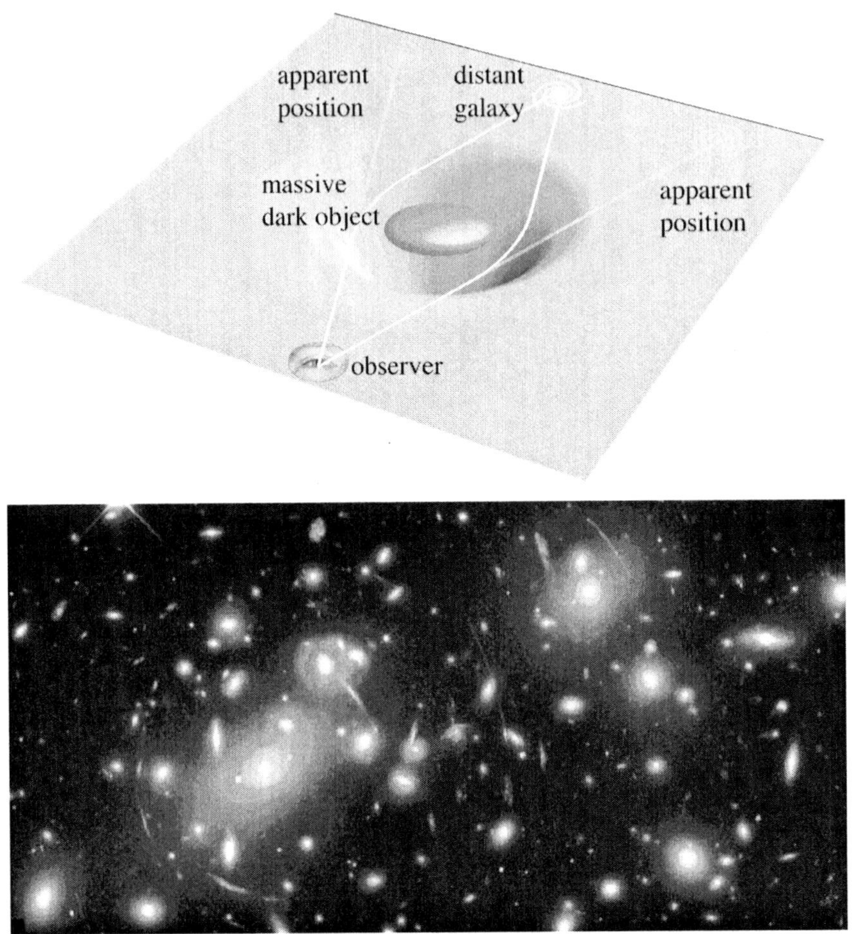

Figure 35.18: Top: Sketch of gravitational lensing of a distance galaxy by a massive dark object; Bottom: arcs due to gravitational lensing around the galaxy cluster Abell 2218 (Andrew Fruchter (STScI) et al., WFPC2, HST, NASA)

Every mass has a Schwarzschild radius that can be easily calculated. However, if this radius lies within the interior of the object, nothing remarkable happens. For example, the Schwarzschild radius of Earth is

$$R_{s,E} = \frac{2GM_E}{c^2} = \frac{2 \cdot (6.67 \cdot 10^{-11}\ \text{Nm}^2/\text{kg}^2) \cdot (6.0 \cdot 10^{24}\text{kg})}{(3.0 \cdot 10^8\ \text{m/s})^2} = 8.9\ \text{mm}.$$

This radius is less than 1/2 of an inch and obviously much less than the radius of Earth.

However, at the end of their lives, stars with masses larger than about 15 solar masses collapse to such high densities that the radius of the resulting object is less than its Schwarzschild radius. No information on this object can then escape from it to the outside. We call such an object a ***Black Hole***. Super-massive black holes of millions of solar masses are at the center of many galaxies, and one such galaxy may be our own.

In-class exercise: What is the Schwarzschild radius of an object with a mass of 14.6 solar masses ($m_{\text{Sun}} = 1.99 \cdot 10^{30}$ kg)?

a) 43.2 cm
b) 55.1 m
c) 1.55 km
d) 43.1 km
e) $4.55 \cdot 10^4$ km

35.9. Relativity in our Daily Lives: GPS

While you may argue that most relativistic effects are only important in outer space, at impossibly large speeds, or at the beginning of our Universe, there is one place where relativity touches all of our lives. This place is the Global Positioning System (GPS). This system consists of 24 satellites that orbit the Earth at an altitude of about 20,000 km above ground, with a period one half of a sidereal day.

The GPS system operates by having clocks on all satellites. The clocks are synchronized to a very high precision. The modern atomic clocks on board of each of these satellites have fractional time stability to typically 1 part in 10^{13}. By sending synchronized timing signals, the satellites enable users with a GPS receiver to determine their own location in space and time. Typically, a receiver can receive signals from at least four satellites simultaneously. For each satellite the receiver's position in space $\vec{r}_r$ and time t_r relative to that of satellite i can be determined from the equation

$$|\vec{r}_r - \vec{r}_i| = c \cdot |t_r - t_i| . \qquad (35.30)$$

Because the positions in time and space of each satellite are known, the above is an equation with 4 unknown quantities, the 3 coordinates and the time on the clock of the receiver. Having 4 satellites gives us 4 equations for 4 unknown quantities. This system of equations can be solved and provides incredible accuracy of about 1 m.

Of course for these equations above to hold, we must rely on the second postulate of special relativity. However, other relativistic effects also need to be included. The satellites move with speeds of approximately 4 km/s relative to earth, and time dilation effects cause frequency shifts in the clocks of 1 part in 10^{10}, about 1,000 times too large to be ignored. In addition, gravitational corrections due to general relativity are at least of the same magnitude. Therefore, a correct use of the theory of relativity is essential for the correct functioning of the Global Positioning Satellite system.

What we have learned/Exam Study Guide:

Most Important Points

- Light always moves at the same speed, independently of the velocity of the source and the observer, $c = 2.9979 \cdot 10^8$ m/s.
- The two postulates of special relativity are:
  i. The laws of physics are the same in each reference frame, independent of the motion of this reference frame.
  ii. The speed of light c is the same in every reference frame.
- The dimensionless quantities $\beta \le 1$ and $\gamma \ge 1$ are define as: $\beta = \dfrac{v}{c}$ and $\gamma = \dfrac{1}{\sqrt{1-\beta^2}} = \dfrac{1}{\sqrt{1-(v/c)^2}}$.
- Time is dilated as a function of the speed of the observer as $\Delta t = \gamma \Delta t_0 = \dfrac{\Delta t_0}{\sqrt{1-(v/c)^2}}$.
- Length is contracted as a function of the speed of the observer according to $L = \dfrac{L_0}{\gamma} = L_0\sqrt{1-(v/c)^2}$.
- The relativistic frequency shift for light from a moving source is $f = f_0\sqrt{\dfrac{c-v}{c+v}}$, and the corresponding wavelength correction is $\lambda = \lambda_0\sqrt{\dfrac{c+v}{c-v}}$. The red-shift is defined as $z = \dfrac{\Delta\lambda}{\lambda} = \sqrt{\dfrac{c+v}{c-v}} - 1$.
- The Lorentz transformation for space and time coordinates is
$$\begin{aligned} x' &= \gamma(x - vt) \\ y' &= y \\ z' &= z \\ t' &= \gamma(t - vx/c^2) \end{aligned}$$
- The correct addition formula compatible with the theory of relativity for two velocities is $v_{1+2} = \dfrac{v_1 + v_2}{1 + \dfrac{v_1 v_2}{c^2}}$.
- The relativistic expression for the momentum is $\vec{p} = \gamma\, m\vec{v}$ and for the energy is $E = \gamma\, E_0 = \gamma\, mc^2$.
- The relationship between energy and momentum is given by $E^2 = p^2c^2 + m^2c^4$.
- The equivalence principle of the theory of general relativity states, "all local freely falling non-rotating laboratories are equivalent for the performance of all physical experiments."

- The Schwarzschild radius of a massive object is given by $R_s = \dfrac{2GM}{c^2}$.

New Symbols used in this Chapter

- β is the speed in units of the speed of light, $\beta = v / c$.
- γ is the relativistic factor, $\gamma = 1 / \sqrt{1-\beta^2}$.

Additional Solved Problem

Solved Problem 35.3: Same velocity

For some purposes, accelerator physicists need to have beams of electrons that have exactly the same velocity as beams of protons. For a proton, $m_pc^2 = 938$ MeV. For an electron, $m_ec^2 = 0.511$ MeV.

Question:

If you have a proton beam with kinetic energy 2.50 GeV, what is the required kinetic energy for the electron beam?

Answer:

THINK:

Particles with the same velocity v have the same γ.

SKETCH:

A sketch of an electron and a proton moving with the same velocity is shown in Figure 35.19.

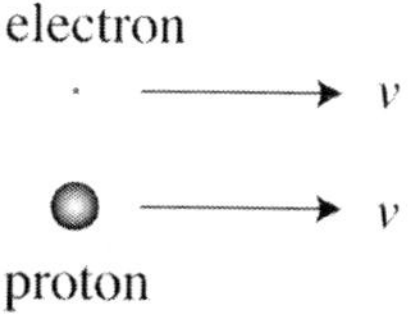

Figure 35.19: An electron and a proton with the same velocity.

RESEARCH:

Particles moving with the same velocity v have the same γ. We can relate the energy E of a particle and γ through

$$E = \gamma mc^2.$$

We can therefore write the energy for an electron as $E_e = \gamma m_e c^2$ and the energy for a proton as $E_p = \gamma m_p c^2$.

We can equate γ for the electron and proton

$$\gamma = \frac{E_e}{m_e c^2} = \frac{E_p}{m_p c^2}.$$

The energy of the electron can be written as the sum of kinetic energy and rest energy, $E_e = K_e + m_e c^2$. In the same way we write for the proton $E_p = K_p + m_p c^2$.

SIMPLIFY:

We can combine the preceding equations to get

$$\frac{K_e + m_e c^2}{m_e c^2} = \frac{K_p + m_p c^2}{m_p c^2}.$$

Solving this for the kinetic energy of the electron we get

$$K_e = \frac{K_e + m_e c^2}{m_e c^2} = m_e c^2 \left(\frac{K_p + m_p c^2}{m_p c^2} \right) - m_e c^2.$$

CALCULATE:

Putting in our numerical values gives us

$$K_e = (0.511 \text{ MeV}) \left(\frac{2500 \text{ MeV} + 938 \text{ MeV}}{938 \text{ MeV}} \right) - (0.511 \text{ MeV}) = 1.36249 \text{ MeV}.$$

ROUND:

We report our result with three significant figures

$$K_e = 1.36 \text{ MeV}.$$

DOUBLE-CHECK:

We will double-check our result by calculating γ for the electron and the proton. For the electron we have

$$\gamma = \frac{E_e}{m_e c^2} = \frac{1.36 \text{ MeV} + 0.511 \text{ MeV}}{0.511 \text{ MeV}} = 3.66.$$

For the proton

$$\gamma = \frac{E_p}{m_p c^2} = \frac{2.50 \text{ GeV} + 938 \text{ MeV}}{938 \text{ MeV}} = 3.67$$

which agrees with our calculated value for the electron. Thus, our result seems reasonable.

Artwork and Photography Credits

All artwork copyright W. Bauer and G.D. Westfall, except as noted below.

Chapter 21
Figure 21.1: R. Morley/PhotoLink/Getty Images; Figure 21.4: left: Kim Steele/Getty Images, right: Geostock/Getty Images; Figure 21.5: Pasco Online Catalog (http://store.pasco.com/pasco/wizards/largerimage.cfm?PN=SF-9069)

Chapter 22
Figure 22.22: Gerd Kortemeyer

Chapter 25
Figure 25.1: Steve Cole/Getty Images; Figure 20.5 (left): Steve Cole/Getty Images

Chapter 26
Figure 26.1: C. Shelburne/Photolink/Getty Iamges

Chapter 27
Figure 27.1: STAR solenoid magnet, http://www.bnl.gov/bnlweb/photos/large/stardetector.jpg; Figure 27.4: (right) Steve Cole/Getty Images; Figure 27.10: National Geophysical Data Center, Based on IGRF 2000, http://www.ngdc.noaa.gov/seg/geomag/icons/Obs1999_lg.gif; Figure 27.12: Event displays generated from data of the STAR collaboration; Figure 27.13: Event displays generated from data of the STAR collaboration; Figure 27.14: Cyclotron drawing by Walter Benenson and MSU Mind Lab; Figure 27.16: http://www.transrapid.de/; Figure 27.23: http://www.maginst.com/probes.html

Chapter 28
Figure 28.1: Royalty-Free/CORBIS; Figure 28.26: High Field Magnet Laboratory, Radboud University Nijmegen, The Netherlands

Chapter 29
Figure 29.1: PhotoLink/Getty Images; Figure 29.10: Picture of the Shuttle and Tether arc from http://liftoff.msfc.nasa.gov/shuttle/sts-75/tss-1r/tss-1r.html, photo of TSS from http://images.jsc.nasa.gov/luceneweb/fullimage.jsp?searchpage=true&selections=STS75&browsepage=Go&hitsperpage=5&pageno=3&photoId=sts075-701-087; Figure 29.14: Ford Motor Company; Figure 29.16: Daisuke Morita/Getty Images

Chapter 30
Figure 30.1: Ryan McVay/Getty Images; Figure 30.26 (left): Edmond Van Hoorick/Getty Images

Chapter 31
Figure 31.1: Kim Steele/Getty Images

Chapter 33
Figure 33.1: StockTrek/Getty Images; Figure 33.2: Burke/Triolo Production/Brand X Pictures/Getty Images; Figure 33.19: Hubble Space Telescope image, NASA, STScI, http://hubblesite.org/newscenter/newsdesk/archive/releases/1994/01/image/a; Figure 28.20: Space Telescope Science Institute

Chapter 34

Figure 34.28: StockTrek/Getty Images; Figure 34.42: Argonne National Laboratory

Chapter 35

Figure 35.16: F. W. Dyson, A. S. Eddington, and C. Davidson, "A Determination of the Deflection of Light by the Sun's Gravitational Field, from Observations Made at the Total Eclipse of May 29, 1919" Philosophical Transactions of the Royal Society of London. Series A, Containing Papers of a Mathematical or Physical Character (1920): 291-333 (public domain); Figure 35.18: Andrew Fruchter (STScI) et al., WFPC2, HST, NASA.